Other Advanced Texts in Econometrics

ARCH: Selected Readings
Edited by Robert F. Engle

Asymptotic Theory for Integrated Processes
By H. Peter Boswijk

Bayesian Inference in Dynamic Econometric Models
By Luc Bauwens, Michel Lubrano, and Jean-François Richard

Co-integration, Error Correction, and the Econometric Analysis of Non-Stationary Data
By Anindya Banerjee, Juan J. Dolado, John W. Galbraith, and David Hendry

Cointegrated VAR Model: Methodology and Applications
By Katarina Juselius

Dynamic Econometrics
By David F. Hendry

Finite Sample Econometrics
By Aman Ullah

Generalized Method of Moments
By Alastair Hall

Likelihood-Based Inference in Cointegrated Vector Autoregressive Models
By Søren Johansen

Long-Run Econometric Relationships: Readings in Cointegration
Edited by R. F. Engle and C. W. J. Granger

Micro-Econometrics for Policy, Program, and Treatment Effect
By Myoung-jae Lee

Modelling Econometric Series: Readings in Econometric Methodology
Edited by C. W. J. Granger

Modelling Non-Linear Economic Relationships
By Clive W. J. Granger and Timo Teräsvirta

Modelling Seasonality
Edited by S. Hylleberg

Non-Stationary Times Series Analysis and Cointegration
Edited by Colin P. Hargeaves

Outlier Robust Analysis of Economic Time Series
By André Lucas, Philip Hans Franses, and Dick van Dijk

Panel Data Econometrics
By Manuel Arellano

Periodicity and Stochastic Trends in Economic Time Series
By Philip Hans Franses

Progressive Modelling: Non-nested Testing and Encompassing
Edited by Massimiliano Marcellino and Grayham E. Mizon

Readings in Unobserved Components
Edited by Andrew Harvey and Tommaso Proietti

Stochastic Limit Theory: An Introduction for Econometricians
By James Davidson

Stochastic Volatility
Edited by Neil Shephard

Testing Exogeneity
Edited by Neil R. Ericsson and John S. Irons

The Econometrics of Macroeconomic Modelling
By Gunnar Bårdsen, Øyvind Eitrheim, Eilev S. Jansen, and Ragnar Nymoen

Time Series with Long Memory
Edited by Peter M. Robinson

Time-Series-Based Econometrics: Unit Roots and Co-integrations
By Michio Hatanaka

Workbook on Cointegration
By Peter Reinhard Hansen and Søren Johansen

The Cointegrated VAR Model: Methodology and Applications

Katarina Juselius

OXFORD
UNIVERSITY PRESS

OXFORD
UNIVERSITY PRESS

Great Clarendon Street, Oxford OX2 6DP

Oxford University Press is a department of the University of Oxford.
It furthers the University's objective of excellence in research, scholarship,
and education by publishing worldwide in

Oxford New York

Auckland Cape Town Dar es Salaam Hong Kong Karachi
Kuala Lumpur Madrid Melbourne Mexico City Nairobi
New Delhi Shanghai Taipei Toronto

With offices in

Argentina Austria Brazil Chile Czech Republic France Greece
Guatemala Hungary Italy Japan Poland Portugal Singapore
South Korea Switzerland Thailand Turkey Ukraine Vietnam

Published in the United States
by Oxford University Press Inc., New York

First published 2006
Reprinted 2007 (with corrections), 2008

British Library Cataloguing in Publication Data
Data available

Library of Congress Cataloging in Publication Data
Data available

Typeset by Newgen Imaging Systems (P) Ltd., Chennai, India
Printed in Great Britain
on acid-free paper by
Biddles Ltd., King's Lynn, Norfolk

ISBN 978–0–19–928566–2
ISBN 978–0–19–928567–9 (Pbk.)

3 5 7 9 10 8 6 4

To Søren

Preface

This book is an attempt to present in a transparent and coherent framework what I see as the main ingredients of the cointegrated VAR methodology. The work started more than ten years ago when I offered a course in likelihood-based cointegration techniques based on Johansen (1996). It soon became obvious that the text was too difficult to stand alone for my economics students and I found myself writing extensive lecture notes to almost every chapter. In the beginning these were fairly simple empirical applications to illustrate the theory. With time, the applications became more comprehensive and the idea to collect them into a book began to take shape. First, I planned to write a companion book to Johansen (1996) stressing applicability rather than mathematical stringency. However, as the writing proceeded I found it increasingly hard to discuss the applications without, at the same time, discussing the underlying theory. Gradually, the companion book was replaced by the present, completely self-contained book, in which the reader is guided step by step through the fairly difficult econometrics of the cointegrated VAR model. At each step the theory is illustrated by the same data set describing monetary policy and inflation. This choice of method turned out to be tremendously challenging. It forced me to understand and explain, econometrically as well as economically, every single estimate and econometric test result, not just in isolation but in the full context of the empirical model. In this sense, the organizing principle of the book comes close to mimicking the organizing principle of a real world empirical analysis. The positive feedback from students and colleagues has convinced me that it was a good choice.

From the outset, the development of the cointegrated VAR model took place in close cooperation between theoretical statisticians and applied econometricians. Needless to say, this has strongly influenced the contents of this book. Almost every empirical problem pointed to a new econometric problem that needed a solution. Most of them were swiftly solved by Søren Johansen, often in cooperation with his PhD students. Thus, most of the theory behind the cointegrated VAR model was developed from a need to solve real life problems. This close interdependence between theory and applications is evident from the Bibliography in which the majority of the references comprise publications by Søren Johansen and myself and by our previous and present PhD students. In this sense, the book is not a balanced view of presently available methods and models in econometrics, but reflects my own personal view on how to apply a cointegrated VAR model and how it was influenced by my close cooperation with Søren Johansen.

The first version of my book, comprising Parts I–IV, discussed the handicraft of a cointegrated VAR analysis. However, as my experience with teaching and supervising students based on the lecture notes increased, I became more and more convinced that this was not enough. What seemed to be needed was a guidance for how to proceed after having learnt how to specify, estimate and interpret a fairly small-dimensional VAR model. This became very obvious when we started to teach Parts I–IV at a summer school in Copenhagen. Almost without any exception, the project papers delivered at the end of the course begged for a continuation. To meet this need, I started working on the second version of the book, expanding the previous version with seven new chapters comprising Parts V and VI. The idea was to take the more experienced user one step further in the empirical analysis by extending the information set to include additional relevant variables, or the same variables from other economies. In the latter case, I believe there is a huge unexploited potential by learning from the experience of other countries in order to better understand the consequences of policy and the role of institutions. My hope is that the new text will inspire the applied economist to address important and policy relevant economic problems in a novel way, thereby adding valuable empirical content to theory.

When the first theoretical results on ML estimation and inference in the cointegrated VAR model became available in the late 1980s they quickly caught the interest of the economics profession. Cointegration was 'in' and many econometrics conferences were over-flooded with cointegration applications. Unfortunately, far from all were empirically convincing. This was partly because the theoretical results were first derived for very basic cointegration models. These 'baby' models were too simple to properly account for many important aspects in our complicated economies. However, when the novelty of cointegration was gone, the modelling philosophy behind the VAR methodology was quickly reduced to 'just applying the Johansen method' often based on these too-simple models. By now we have gained a lot more experience on how to specify and estimate the cointegrated VAR model thereby increasing its realism and usefulness. Many new test procedures have been added to the software packages, and the methodology for how to address important questions about the empirical economy has vastly improved. However, even today many VAR applications are still at the first level of development without coming even close to the ideal that good econometric craftsmanship should take the data, the economics, and the institutions seriously. An important reason for writing this book was to demonstrate that the cointegrated VAR approach has the potential of offering a strong methodology for making such inference.

Many VAR applications in the literature are based on a very small subset of all potentially relevant variables, justified by the *ceteris paribus* assumption in the theory model, without discussing the robustness and the sensitivity of the conclusions to this choice. However, according to our experience, conclusions may, and often do, change when increasing the information set. This is particularly problematic when the omitted *ceteris paribus* variables are non-stationary or highly persistent. In fact, it is quite interesting that many puzzling results in the data seem to be associated with just two or three highly persistent *ceteris paribus* variables. Among the latter, the real exchange rate with its pronounced persistence seemed particularly important followed by the domestic–foreign long-term interest rate spread with a similar persistence. Similarly, the persistent movements in real interest rates, inconsistent with the Fisher parity, are empirically interesting. Since these variables are highly influential for our domestic economies, it goes without saying that estimating models under the *ceteris paribus* assumption 'constant real exchange rate, real interest rate and the spread' is likely to produce empirically fragile conclusions.

For many years I was intrigued by the importance of these three variables in almost every model if allowed enter. The long struggle to understand the effect of these empirical persistencies goes as a red thread through most of my research and has certainly had a strong influence on the content of this book. An important breakthrough came with the recent development of a theory for imperfect knowledge expectations and forecasting in the foreign exchange market (Frydman and Goldberg 2006), which seemed to be able to explain the persistence in real exchange rates and long-term interest rate spreads. This opened up a new understanding of some empirically strong regularities in the data that previously had remained unexplained. The persistence in real interest rates was another empirical puzzle that strongly influenced my own research. After having analysed data from different sectors of the economy over different sample periods and comparing the results for different economies (small, large, open, closed), I began to see a systematic pattern in the results. By now I am convinced that the break-down of the Fisher parity over the last decades is strongly related to the increased globalization and its effect on the determination of nominal product prices and product price inflation.

The long-lasting struggle to understand inflationary mechanisms has not only influenced the empirical discussions in this book, but also shaped the view that empirical modelling should not just be about *testing* pre-specified hypotheses and *estimating* parameters, but also about generating new hypotheses to be subsequently tested on new data. I strongly argue in the book that both deductive and inductive inference should be considered equally important in VAR modelling. Deductive inference because it is needed when testing pre-specified hypotheses derived from relevant theory models; inductive inference because it is needed when generating new hypotheses based on the discovery of new and surprising results. The latter, which are endemic in a modelling approach that attempts to describe all major features of the data, are often suppressed in published papers. Contrary to this, I have generally found the puzzling results to be the most valuable as they signal to the analyst that there are features in the data which are not yet fully understood. By pursuing such a track laid out by the data analysis we might end up in a gold mine, or at least become wiser.

The organization of this book

As a graduate student, I came across Trygve Haavelmo's Nobel Prize winning *Econometrica* monograph (1944) where he discussed how to approach the difficult task of making inference from macroeconomic data based on sound statistical principles. I immediately found great appeal in Haavelmo's discussion of the econometric analysis of data obtained 'by passive observation of reality' as opposed to 'by a designed experiment'. Part I is in many ways influenced by this discussion. Chapter 1 argues that it is often meaningless to test a theory model with 'data by passive observation', whereas specific hypotheses derived from a theory model can often be adequately tested. Chapter 2 discusses a theory model for monetary inflation and specifies a set of specific hypotheses, called a scenario, which should hold in the data for the theory model to have empirical content. Chapter 3 discusses Haavelmo's probability approach to econometrics, how it relates to the VAR model, and under which assumptions the latter can be considered an adequate representation of the data generating process.

Part II focuses on the econometrics of the unrestricted VAR model. Chapter 4 discusses various VAR representations and introduces some frequently used model specification tests. Chapter 5 introduces the concepts of integration, cointegration, and common trends, discusses a classification of the vector process into stationary and non-stationary components, and shows that these statistical concepts can be given an economic interpretation in terms of long-run relations and short-run adjustment versus short-run impulse responses and long-run common trends. Finally, the chapter demonstrates that the specific hypotheses implied by the scenario derived in Chapter 2 can be formulated as testable hypotheses on the pulling and pushing forces of the cointegrated VAR model. Chapter 6 addresses the important issue of how to specify deterministic components (constant, trend, dummy variables) in the cointegrated VAR model and discusses how this can be used to make inference about the effectiveness of policy interventions in the short- and the long-run.

Part III is about the econometrics of estimation and testing in the cointegrated VAR model. Chapter 7 derives the reduced rank maximum likelihood estimator for $\boldsymbol{\alpha}$ and $\boldsymbol{\beta}$ and Chapter 8 the trace test for determining the cointegration rank. It discusses how the asymptotic tables are influenced by the deterministic components in the VAR, and how they are simulated. Chapter 9 introduces a large number of recursive test procedures as a toolbox for detecting possible parameter non-constancy in the model. Chapter 10 introduces three different test procedures to test various hypotheses on the long-run $\boldsymbol{\beta}$ relations and illustrates by testing the derived hypotheses in the scenario of Chapter 2. Chapter 11 discusses two test procedures formulated as hypotheses on the adjustment coefficients $\boldsymbol{\alpha}$ and shows that one can be interpreted as a test of a driving force, and the other of pure adjustment. The link between weak exogeneity and partial models is discussed and illustrated.

Part IV addresses the important issue of identification in the cointegrated VAR framework. Identification has traditionally been discussed for the case when the structure of the model is known and identification is about checking whether the parameters of the model can be uniquely estimated. When the axiom of correct specification is replaced with the assumption of a reasonably well-structured DGP that can be consistent with several theories, the concept of identification has to be widened. In this view, the book makes a distinction between (1) generic identification that relates to a hypothetical model, (2) empirical identification that relates to the estimated parameter values and (3) economic identification, which relates to the economic interpretability of the estimated parameter values. Using this framework, the book discusses the question of just- and overidentification from four angles, namely the identification of the long-run structure in Chapter 12, the short-run adjustment structure in Chapter 13, the common trends structure in Chapter 14, and the impulse response structure in Chapter 15.

Part V discusses different aspects of the $I(2)$ model. The three $I(2)$ chapters contain several new results, all of them implemented in CATS and illustrated with the money market data. As the formal econometrics of the $I(2)$ model is fairly complicated, Chapter 16 introduces the basic intuition for the rich structure of the $I(2)$ model within the framework of the $I(1)$ model now using nominal variables. The chapter demonstrates that one can diagnose symptoms of $I(2)$'ness and tentatively investigates long-run price homogeneity without having to use the whole artillery of the $I(2)$ model. Chapter 17 gives a formal derivation of the $I(2)$ model and shows that the ML estimates can be found by iteratively solving two reduced rank problems. The rich structure of the $I(2)$ model is given an interpretation in terms of static and dynamic long-run relations and second- and first-order stochastic trends. The role of deterministic components is discussed at some length. Chapter 18 discusses a number of test procedures that can be applied in the $I(2)$ model and illustrates with the money market data.

Up to this point, all theoretical results both within the $I(1)$ and the $I(2)$ models have been illustrated with just one data set, the Danish money market data. Part VI addresses the important issue of how to proceed after having analysed a small VAR system, which is statistically, but not necessarily economically, well understood. This is a frequent problem due to the fact that a VAR analysis does not make a prior distinction between 'endogenous' and 'exogenous' variables but treats all of them as stochastic variables to be modelled. However, seen from the economic model only a few of the variables are 'endogenous' whereas the remaining variables are only partially specified. As already touched upon, this is related to the *ceteris paribus* assumption which is legitimate in the economic theory model but not in the statistical model. Chapter 19 discusses some general principles for how to extend the information set, so that puzzling results can be adequately addressed and better understood. Two new (partly overlapping) data sets are introduced describing wage, price, and unemployment dynamics and international parity conditions between Denmark and Germany. Chapter 20 illustrates the specific-to-general principle in the choice of information set with a fairly detailed analysis of the labour market data. Chapter 21 presents a similar analysis of the PPP/UIP conditions between Denmark and Germany. Finally, Chapter 22 combines all three analyses, the money market, the labour market, and the foreign exchange market into one large model, thereby addressing the simultaneous determination of money, prices, wages, productivity, unemployment, interest rates, and exchange rate. The chapter ends with a discussion of the extent to which we have been able to improve our understanding of macroeconomic mechanisms over this period by systematically exploiting the information in the data using the cointegrated VAR approach.

For those who would like to use the cointegrated VAR approach based on another data set, a checklist of the major steps of the analysis is given in Appendix B. In addition, to allow the reader to replicate the empirical results reported in the book, there are links available to the computer output for each chapter. Also a complete set of exercises corresponding to approximately 30 hours in class can be downloaded from the book's homepage http://www.econ.ku.dk/okokj/book.htm

Acknowledgements

Needless to say, the views expressed in this book have been strongly influenced by a number of scholars in the field of theoretical and empirical econometrics as well as economics. As it would lead too far to mention all I shall by necessity only mention those I owe most to.

As long as I have been professionally active, Clive Granger's research in time-series econometrics has been a source of inspiration. However, the importance of Clive's 1981 paper on cointegration and error-correction for this book is hard to overstate. While I was much intrigued by the paper, I also found it hard to grasp. It was difficult to see the intuition of the model in moving average form and how to use it in practise. As I was then organizing an econometrics session at the 9th Nordic Conference on Mathematical Statistics, I decided to invite Søren Johansen to give a prepared discussion of Clive's paper. This turned out to be the beginning of a lifelong project where we have worked closely together developing the cointegrated VAR approach, first as colleagues then as a married couple. Without Søren listening to my, not always very well-formulated, problems, interpreting them in a clear mathematical language, and working out a solution within a day or two, this book would never have been realized in its present form. The number of imprecise formulations he has spotted in the text during all these years hopefully remains a secret between the two of us. No doubt, Søren has taught me to be a much better econometrician. In case the book manages to change some of the empirical practise of today's econometricians, as I hope, it is altogether thanks to Søren's influence. I owe him more thanks than can be expressed.

As a postgraduate student I visited the London School of Economics and came across several papers by David Hendry and co-authors. In them I found many of Haavelmo's ideas being realized and implemented in sophisticated software packages, Give, Rals and Fiml, later to become PcGive. Since then I have followed David's work closely and numerous ideas and results in this book are strongly inspired by his wide-ranging work in theoretical and empirical econometrics. I thank David for being so inspiring and supportive over these years. But, in particular, I owe David a big hug for carefully having read and commented on a first version of the book. It was not without embarrassment I had to face the numerous mistakes and typos David had spotted in the text.

Today's academics living under an increasingly strong pressure 'to publish or perish' can seldom afford to spend time on writing time-consuming computer software. At the same time, econometric results without the necessary computer software are not likely to have much impact on the profession. Over this period, I was very fortunate to have access to the user-friendly menu-driven programs in CATS for RATS, originally developed by Henrik Hansen, and recently completely rewritten and extended by Jonathan Dennis. The possibility to influence the organization and the contents of CATS 2.0 while writing the book has been invaluable. The amount of work invested in CATS is absolutely huge and I owe both Henrik and Jonathan a deep thanks.

Some years ago, my son Mikael Juselius gave me a very pleasant surprise when he decided to do his PhD in econometrics. Even though it can be risky to follow in the footsteps of a parent, it has been a very special and pleasant experience to share my professional interest with Mikael. I have thoroughly enjoyed our many discussions of the contents of this book which often have helped me to sharpen my arguments. I am greatly thankful for his very constructive and substantive criticism.

The methodological approach I advocate for in this book takes a very different route compared to the standard empirical approach favoured by most applied macroeconomists. Claiming that it has been an easy task to convince many of them of the superiority of the cointegrated VAR approach would be an exaggeration. Pretending I did not care would not be according to the truth. Therefore, to experience Dave Colander's open-minded and positive interest in our ideas was heart-warming and I was proud when he considered the cointegrated VAR methodology as a potential building block in a future 'Post-Walrasian macroeconomics' (Colander 2006). I have greatly enjoyed Dave's sharp intellect in our numerous discussions during a three weeks' stay in Copenhagen and I am greatly indebted to Dave for his support and useful comments from the point of view of a non-specialist reader with a strong methodological background.

Kevin Hoover has similarly shown a very positive interest in the methodology developed in this book. During daily brainstorming sessions in front of the computer in connection with two longer visits in Copenhagen, every single stone on the road to a cointegrated US economy was turned several times. In particular, I am grateful to Kevin for his habit to reply to every single explanation with a 'I do not believe this'. It never made our sessions dull and it certainly forced me to sharpen my arguments. I am also greatly indebted to Kevin's detailed and careful comments on most of the chapters which, coming from a methodologist understanding econometrics, were very valuable.

Heino Bohn Nielsen allowed me to use his procedure for simulating the asymptotic tables with mean shifts in the cointegration relations both for the $I(1)$ and the $I(2)$ model as well as his procedure for estimating a structural VAR in Chapter 15. For this and his many useful comments I am greatly thankful.

Michael Goldberg visited Copenhagen for a year and followed my lectures based on this book. His numerous comments and questions not just made the course more lively and enjoyable for me and my students, but also helped to improve the exposition of the book. Also during this year Michael introduced me to the basic ideas underlying the theory of 'imperfect knowledge expectations and forecasting' that he was working on together with Roman Frydman. This meant a huge step forward in my understanding of some of the puzzling features in the data. It also resulted in a joint research project with Michael and Roman which has been highly valuable for the development and refinement of the ideas. I am greatly thankful to Michael and Roman for their continuous support and inspiration.

Massimo Franchi visited Copenhagen first as Marie Curie graduate student later as a postdoc at the Economics Department. He has carefully read and commented on most of the chapters. Also, he has helped me to detect quite a number of typing errors. I am grateful to Massimo for his valuable comments and his active interest in the cointegrated VAR methodology.

In the first version of the book, the money demand data used for the illustrations was based on a sample that ended in 1994:3. As time passed by they began to look somewhat outdated. With butterflies in my stomach I decided to update the data with almost 10 years of quarterly observations. The relief was immense when I realized that all major conclusions remained unchanged and most estimated results were close to the previous ones. Nonetheless, all tables and figures had to be redone and the text had to be revised accordingly. Robert Wagner systematically checked all necessary revisions and changes in Parts I–IV. I am greatly indebted to Robert for his careful and competent work. Niels Framroze Møller similarly checked the empirical results of Chapter 19 for internal consistency. I am grateful to Niels for his careful work and his many detailed and useful comments.

All since the late 1980s, I have been organizing numerous conferences and workshops focusing on topics in cointegration. While in the beginning the participants were mostly from the Nordic countries, as time passed by many European econometricians joined the group. Many of the ideas presented in this book have been influenced by the lively discussions during these meetings. I would like to express my thanks to all participants.

Many colleagues and students have kindly commented on the book in this period. In addition to those already acknowledged, my thanks for useful and constructive comments go to Lars Levent Abat, Christian Groth, Robert Kelm, Daniel le Maire, Anders Rahbek, Bernt Stigum, and Christin Kyrme Tuxen.

Over the last decade, I have used preliminary versions of the book in my regular teaching, as well as in PhD courses and Summer Schools. I would like to thank previous and present MsS and PhD students at the Economics Department, University of Copenhagen, the European University Institute, Scuola Superiore Sant'Anna in Pisa, the CIDE course in Bertinoro, and the Swedish School of Economics in Helsinki for useful comments and suggestions. The teaching of the Copenhagen Summer School in 2003–2006 has been particularly inspiring, partly because it included the supervision of approximately 150 participants applying cointegration analysis in their individual project papers. The experience I gained from closely following the analysis of so many and so diverse empirical problems has been valuable and highly rewarding. I am grateful to all participants for being so enthusiastic and open-minded towards learning the difficult material of this book in only three weeks.

It is a pleasure to thank the Department of Economics, University of Copenhagen, for the continuous support over the long period of writing the book. While my permanent office was in Copenhagen all this period, I spent most of my time at the European University Institute in 1996–2001. I am grateful to the EUI for providing me with research facilities and an inspiring research environment. Also, I would like to express my thanks to the European Central Bank for the support and generosity shown to me during two months at the research department in 2001. The research carried out in this period turned out to be very influential for Chapter 20 of this book.

In all these years, continuous and generous financial support from the Danish Social Sciences Research Council is gratefully acknowledged.

In the last very hectic period of producing a typescript that complied reasonably well with the requirements of the Oxford University Press, I was fortunate to get very competent assistance from Niels Framroze Møller and XuXin Mao. For this I thank both of them.

I would also like to thank Oxford University Press for their encouragement and competent copy editing and, in particular, for putting up with my many delays on the road to the final typescript.

Finally I owe a big, big thanks to a large group of people who put up with me during all these years; my two sons, my Finnish and my Danish family, and all my good friends I hardly had time for.

Katarina Juselius
University of Copenhagen

Contents

IV Identification 205

V The $I(2)$ model 289

Part I

Bridging economics and econometrics

1

Introduction

Economists frequently formulate an *economically* well-specified model as the empirical model and *apply statistical methods* to estimate its parameters. In contrast, statisticians formulate a *statistically* well-specified model for the data and *analyse the statistical model* to answer the economic questions of interest. In the first case, statistics are used passively as a tool to get some desired estimates, and in the second case, the statistical model is taken seriously and used actively as a means of analysing the underlying generating process of the phenomenon in question.

The general principle of analysing statistical models in macro-economics instead of applying statistical methods can be traced back to R. A. Fisher. It was introduced into econometrics by Haavelmo (1944) [hereafter Haavelmo] and operationalized and further developed by Hendry and Richard (1983), Hendry (1987), Johansen (1996) and recent followers. Haavelmo's influence on modern econometrics has been discussed, for example, in Hendry, Spanos and Ericsson (1989) and Anderson (1991).

Few observed macroeconomic variables can be assumed fixed or predetermined *a priori*. Haavelmo's probability approach to econometrics therefore requires a probability formulation of the full process that generated the data. Thus, the statistical model is based on a complete system of equations. The computational complexities involved in the solution of such a system were clearly prohibitive at the time of his monograph when even the estimation of a multiple regression was a non-trivial task. In today's computerized world, it is certainly technically feasible to adopt Haavelmo's guide-lines in empirical econometrics. Although the technical difficulties have been solved long ago, most papers in empirical macroeconomics do not seem to follow the general principles, despite being stated very clearly in his monograph. We shall argue here that the vector autoregressive (hereafter VAR) approach offers a number of advantages as a general framework for addressing empirical questions in (macro)economics at the same time adhering to Haavelmo's general probability principle.

First, we shall discuss a number of important questions raised by Haavelmo and address their relevance for recent developments in the econometric analysis of time series. In so doing, we shall essentially focus on issues in empirical macroeconomic analysis using readily available aggregated data, and only briefly contrast this situation with a hypothetical case in which the data have been collected by controlled experiments.

The last few decades, in particular the 1990s, will probably be remembered as a period when the scientific status of macroeconomics, in particular empirical macroeconomics, was much debated and criticized both by people from outside, but increasingly also from inside the economics profession. See, for example, the discussions in Backhouse and Salanti (2000a, 2000b), Colander (1999, 2000a, 2000b, 2001), Hoover (1988) and Leijonhufvud (2006). Also Summers (1991) discussed 'the scientific illusion in empirical macroeconomics' claiming that applied econometric work has not given much new insight into economic mechanisms and hardly had any influence on the development of economic theory. As an illustration, he discusses two widely different approaches to applied econometric modelling: (1) the representative agent's approach, where the final aim of the empirical analysis is to estimate a few deep parameters characterizing preferences and technology; and (2) the use of sophisticated statistical techniques, exemplified by VAR models, a la Sim's, to 'identify' certain parameters on which inference about the underlying economic mechanisms is based. In neither case does he find that the obtained empirical results can convincingly discriminate between theories nor explain a macroeconomic reality being infinitely more rich and complicated than the highly simplified models. He, therefore, concludes that a less formal examination of empirical observations, the so-called stylized facts (usually given as correlations, mean growth rates, etc.) has generally resulted in more fruitful economic research. This is a very pessimistic view of the usefulness of formal econometric modelling and the aim of this book is to challenge this view. We believe that the reason why empirical results often appear unconvincing is because the principles laid out by Haavelmo have been (and are) frequently neglected.

The formal link between economic theory and empirical modelling lies in the field of statistical inference, and the focus here is on statistical aspects of the proposed VAR methodology, while at the same time stressing applicability in the fields of macroeconomic models. Therefore, all through the text the statistical concepts are interpreted in terms of relevant economic entities. The aim is to define a different class of 'stylized facts' which are statistically well founded and much richer than the conventional graphs, correlations and mean growth rates often referred to in discussions of stylized facts.

In this chapter, which draws on Juselius (1993), we shall revisit Haavelmo's monograph as a background for the discussion of the reasons for the apparent 'scientific illusion in empirical macroeconomics' and ask whether it can be explained by a general failure to follow the principles expressed in his monograph. Section 1.1 discusses the choice of a theoretical model. Sections 1.2–1.4 discuss three issues from Haavelmo that often seem to have been overlooked in empirical macroeconomics: (1) the link between theoretical, true and observed variables; (2) the distinction between testing a hypothesis and testing a theory; and (3) the formulation of an adequate design of experiment in econometrics and its relation to 'a design of experiment by passive observation'. Section 1.5 finally introduces the empirical problem which is to be used as an illustration all through the book, namely the aggregate demand for money and its role for inflation control.

1.1 On the choice of economic models

This section discusses the important link between economic theory and the empirical model. In order to make the discussion more concrete, we shall illustrate the ideas with an example taken from the monetary sector of the economy. In particular, we shall focus on the aggregate demand for money relation, being one of the most analysed relations in empirical macroeconomics. Before selecting a theoretical model describing the demand for money as a function of some hypothetical variables, we shall first discuss the reasons why it is interesting to investigate such a relation.

The empirical interest in money demand relations stems from basic macroeconomic theory postulating that the inflation rate is directly related to the expansion in the (appropriately defined) supply of money at a rate greater than that warranted by the growth of the real productive potential of the economy. The policy implication is that the aggregate supply of money should be controlled in order to control the inflation rate. The optimal control of money, however, requires knowledge of the 'non-inflationary level' of aggregate demand for money at each point of time, defined as the level of money stock, m^*, at which there is no tendency for the inflation rate to increase or decrease. Thus, on a practical level, the reasoning is based on the assumption that there exists a stable aggregate demand-for-money relation, $m^* = f(x)$, that can be estimated. Given this background, what can be learnt from the available economic theories about the form of such a relation, and what are the crucial determinants?

There are three distinct motives for holding money. The transactions motive is related to the need to hold cash for handling everyday transactions. The precautionary motive is related to the need to hold money to be able to meet unforeseen expenditures. Finally, the speculative motive is related to agents' wishes to hold money as part of their portfolio. Since all three motives are likely to affect agents' needs to hold money, let the initial assumption be that $m/p = f(y^r, c)$, saying that real money holdings, m/p, is a function of the level of real income (assumed to determine the volume of transactions and precautionary money) and the cost of holding money, c.

Further assumptions of optimizing behaviour are needed in order to derive a formal model for agents' willingness to hold money balances. Among the available theories, two different approaches can be distinguished: (1) theories treating money as a medium of exchange for transaction purposes, so that minimizing a derived cost function leads to optimizing behaviour; (2) theories treating money as a good producing utility, so that maximizing the utility function leads to optimizing behaviour.

For expository purposes, only the first approach will be discussed here, specifically the theoretical model suggested by Baumol (1952), which is still frequently referred to in this context. The model is strongly influenced by inventory theory, and has the following basic features. Over a certain time period $t_2 - t_1$, the agent will pay out E units of money in a steady stream. Two different costs are involved, the opportunity cost of the foregone investment, measured by the interest rate r, and the so-called 'brokerage' cost b. The latter should be assumed to cover all kinds of costs in connection with a cash withdrawal. It is also assumed that liquid money does not yield interest. The optimal value of cash withdrawn from investment can now be found as:

$$C = \sqrt{2bE/r} \tag{1.1}$$

so that the cost-minimizing agent will demand cash in proportion to the square root of the value of his transactions. The average holding of cash under these assumptions is $C/2$.

Taking the logarithms of (1.1) gives a transactions elasticity of 0.5 and an interest elasticity of -0.5. These have been the prior hypotheses of many empirical investigations based on aggregated data, and estimates supporting this have been found, for instance, in Baba, Hendry and Starr (1992).

If this theoretical model is tested against data, more precise statements of what is meant by the theoretical concepts C, b, E and r need to be made. This is no straightforward task, as expressed by Haavelmo, p. 4:

> When considering a theoretical set-up, involving certain variables and certain mathematical relations, it is common to ask about the actual meaning of this and that variable. But this question has no sense within a theoretical model. And if the question applies to reality it has no precise answer. It is one thing to build a theoretical model, it is another thing to give rules for choosing the facts to which the theoretical model is to be applied. It is one thing to choose the model from the field of mathematics, it is another thing to classify and measure objects of real life.

As a means to clarify this difficult issue, Haavelmo introduces the concepts of true and theoretical variables as opposed to observable variables and proposes that one should try to define how the variables should be measured in an ideal situation. This will be briefly discussed in the next section.

1.2 Theoretical, true and observable variables

In order to operationalize a theoretical concept, one has to make precise statements about how to measure the corresponding theoretical variable, i.e. to give the theoretical variable a precise meaning. This is expressed in Haavelmo, p. 5 as:

> We may express the difference [between the 'true' and the theoretical variables] by saying that the 'true' variables (or time functions) represent our ideal as to accurate measurements of reality 'as it is in fact' while the variables defined in theory are the true measurements that we should make if reality were actually in accordance with our theoretical model.

Say, for example, that a careful analysis of the above example shows that the true measurements are the average holdings of cash and demand deposits by private persons in private banks, postal banks or similar institutions (savings and loans societies, etc.) measured at closing time each trading day of a month. The theoretical variable C as defined by Baumol's model would then correspond to the true measurements given that (1) no interest is paid on this liquid money, (2) transactions are paid out in a steady stream over successive periods, (3) the brokerage cost and interest rate r are unambiguously defined, and (4) no cash and demand deposits are held for speculative or precautionary motives, and so on.

Needless to say, the available measurements from official statistics are very far from the definitions of the true variables. Even if it were possible to obtain measurements satisfying the above definition of the true measurements, it seems obvious that these would not correspond to the theoretical variables.[1]

[1] It should be pointed out that Baumol does not claim any such correspondence. In fact, he gives a long list of reasons why this cannot be the case.

Nevertheless, if the purpose of the empirical investigation is to test a theory, a prerequisite for valid inference about the theoretical model is a close correspondence between the observed variables and the true variables, or in the words of Haavelmo:

> It is then natural to adopt the convention that a theory is called true or false according as the hypotheses implied are true or false, when tested against the data chosen as the 'true' variables. Then we may speak interchangeably about testing hypotheses or testing theories.

For example, the unit-root tests of GDP series to discriminate between different real growth theories are good examples of misleading inference in this respect. Much of the criticism expressed by Summers may well be related to situations in which valid inference would require a much closer correspondence between observed and true variables.

Even if data collected by passive observation do not generally qualify for testing 'deep' theoretical models, most empirical macroeconomic models are nonetheless based on the officially collected data. This is simply because of a genuine interest in the macroeconomic data as such. Since 'data seldom speak by themselves', theoretical arguments are needed to understand the variation in these data in spite of the weak correspondence between the theoretical and observed variables. Nevertheless, the link between the theoretical and the empirical model is rather ambiguous in this case and the interpretation of the empirical results in terms of the theoretical arguments is not straightforward. This leads to the second issue to be discussed here, i.e. the distinction between testing a hypothesis and testing a theory. This monograph will claim that based on macroeconomic data, it is only possible to test theoretical hypotheses but not a theory model as such. The frequent failure to separate between the two might explain a great deal of Summers' critique.

1.3 Testing a theory as opposed to a hypothesis

When the arguments of the theory do not apply directly to the empirical model, one compromise is to be less ambitious about testing theories and instead concentrate on testing specific hypotheses derived from the theoretical model. For example, the hypotheses that the elasticity of the transactions demand for cash $e^c = 0.5$ and of the interest rate $e^r = -0.5$ have frequently been tested within empirical models that do not include all aspects of Baumol's theoretical model. Other popular hypotheses that have been widely tested include long-run price and income homogeneity, the sign of first derivatives, zero restrictions, and the direction of causality. 'Sophisticated statistical techniques' have often been used in this context. Since, according to Summers among others, the outcomes of these exercises have generally not been convincing or interesting enough to change economists' views, there seems to be a need for a critical appraisal of econometric practice in this context. There are several explanations why empirical results are seldom persuasive.

First, not enough care is taken to ensure that the specification of empirical models mimics the general characteristics of the data. If the empirical model is based on a valid probability formulation of the data, then statistical hypothesis testing is straightforward, and valid procedures can be derived by analysing the likelihood function. In this case, inferences about the specified hypotheses are valid, though valid inference about the theory as such depends on the strength of the correspondence between the true and the theoretical variables.

Second, not enough attention is paid to the crucial role of the *ceteris paribus* 'everything else constant' assumption when the necessary information set is specified.

Third, many theories involve agents' expectations rather than observed values, and the validity of implementing such theories depends on how well such expectations are measured. In practice, expectations are not measured but are assumed to be determined by an auxiliary model, which is not directly tested. For example, rational expectations as a behavioural assumption in empirical models has offen been unconvincing as a description of aggregate behavior.

Fourth, the available measurements do not correspond closely enough to the true values of the theoretical variables. For example, in many applications it is assumed that certain (linearly transformed) VAR residuals can be interpreted as structural shocks. This would require the VAR residuals to be invariant to changes in the information set, which is not likely to be the case in practical applications.

These issues will be further discussed in the next chapter and related to some general principles for VAR-modelling with non-stationary data. But, first the concept of 'a design of experiment' in econometrics as discussed by Haavelmo has to be introduced.

1.4 Experimental design in macroeconomics

As discussed above, the link between the true variables suggested by the theory and the actual measurements taken from official statistics is, in most cases, too weak to justify valid inference from the empirical model to the theory. Even in ideal cases, when the official definition of the aggregated variable, say liquid money stock M1, corresponds quite closely to the true measurements, there are usually measurement problems. High-quality, reasonably long aggregated series are difficult to obtain because definitions change, new components have entered the aggregates and new regulations have changed the behaviour. The end result is the best set of measurements in the circumstances, but still quite far from the true measurements of an ideal situation. This problem is discussed in terms of a design of experiment in Haavelmo, p. 14:

> If economists would describe the experiments they have in mind when they construct the theories they would see that the experiments they have in mind may be grouped into two different classes namely, (1) experiments that we should like to make to see if certain real economic phenomena– when artificially isolated from other influences – would verify certain hypothesis and (2) the stream of experiments that nature is steadily turning out from his own enormous laboratory, and which we merely watch as passive observers....
>
> In the first case we can make agreements or disagreements between theory and facts depend on two things: the facts we choose to consider and our theory about them....
>
> In the second case we can only try to adjust our theories to reality as it appears before us. And what is the meaning of a design of experiment in this case. It is this: We try to choose a theory and a design of experiments to go with it, in such a way that the resulting data would be those which we get by passive observation of reality. And to the extent that we succeed in doing so, we become masters of reality – by passive agreement.

Since the primary interest here is design of experiment by passive observation, we shall restrict ourselves to this case. What seems to be needed is a set of assumptions which are general enough to ensure a statistically valid description of typical macroeconomic data, and a common modelling strategy to allow questions of interest to be investigated in a consistent framework. Chapter 3 will discuss under which conditions the VAR model can work as a reasonable formalization of a 'design of experiment' for data by passive observation.

Controlled experiments are not usually possible within a national economy and the only possibility to 'test' hypothetical relationships found in one empirical analysis is to wait for new data which were not used to generate the hypothesis. Another possibility is to rely on the 'experiments' provided by other countries or regions that differ in various aspects with regard to the investigated economic problem. For instance, if the question of interest is whether an expansion of money supply generally tends to increase the inflation rate, it seems advisable to examine this using similar data from countries that differ in terms of the pursued economic policy. But, to learn from such comparative analyses one needs a common modelling strategy.

One important purpose of this book is to discuss the extent to which the VAR approach is the answer to such a strategy. We shall argue that the VAR model, when appropriately allowing for unit roots and, hence, cointegration (to be defined in Chapter 5) offers a potential richness in the specification of economically meaningful short- and long-run structures and components, such as steady-state relations and common trends, interaction and feedback effects. Even more importantly, in the unrestricted general form, the VAR model is essentially only a reformulation of the covariances of the data. Provided that these have remained approximately constant over the sample period, the VAR model can be considered a convenient summary of the 'stylized facts' of the data. To the extent that the 'true' economic model underlying behaviour satisfies a first-order linear approximation (see Hendry and Richard 1983), one can test economic hypotheses expressed by the number of autonomous permanent shocks, steady-state behaviour, feedback and interaction effects, etc. within a statistically valid framework. This is essentially the 'general-to-specific' approach described in Hendry and Mizon (1993), subsequently evaluated in Hoover and Perez (1999) and recently implemented as an automatic selection procedure in PcGets (Hendry and Krolzig 2001). The 'final' empirical model should, in the ideal case, be 'structural' both in the economic and statistical sense of the word.

The VAR procedure is less pretentious about the prior role of a theoretical economic model, but it avoids the lack of empirical relevance the theory-based approach has often been criticized for. Since the starting point is the time-series structure of the chosen data, it is often advantageous to search for structures against the background of not just one but a variety of possibly relevant theories. At the end of the analysis we may have obtained empirical support for a subset of the pre-specified hypotheses as well as a number of new results that can be used to generate new hypotheses to be tested against new data. In this sense the suggested approach is a combination of inductive and deductive inference.

1.5 On the choice of empirical example

Throughout the first 18 chapters of the book, we shall illustrate the econometric and methodological arguments with just one data set describing a money market model for Denmark. Chapters 19–21 introduces two new data sets describing wage, price, and unemployment dynamics in Denmark and the international parity conditions between

Denmark and Germany. The first data set has been extensively analysed by myself and Søren Johansen both as an inspiration for developing new test procedures and as a means to understand the potential use of the cointegrated VAR model. See for example Johansen and Juselius (1990) and Juselius (1993). The analyses of the other two data sets in Chapters 20 and 21 are novel and serve the purpose of illustrating the empirical methodology.

Given the discussion in previous subsections, one should first ask whether there is a close enough correspondence between observed variables and the true versus theoretical variables for example as given by the Baumol model? The answer is clearly no. A detailed examination of the measurements reveal that essentially all the usual problems plague the data. For instance, new components have entered the aggregate, banking technology has changed, the time interval between the measurements is too broad, and so on. Given these observed variables, it would be very hard to justify inference from the empirical analysis to a specific transactions demand-for-money theory.

The main reason why these variables were selected is simply because they were being used by the Central Bank of Denmark as a basis for their policy analysis. In that sense, the data have been collected because of an interest in the variables for their own sake. This choice does not exclude the possibility that these variables are closely related to the theoretical variables, nor that the empirical investigation might suggest other more relevant measurements for policy analysis.

Looking in the rear mirror, after having applied the cointegrated VAR model to many other data sets, it is obvious that we were very fortunate to begin our first cointegration attempts using this data. It is one of the few describing long-run relationships which have remained remarkably stable over the last few decades. However, it should be pointed out that this was true only after having econometrically accounted for a regime shift in 1983 as a consequence of deregulating capital movements in Denmark. In this sense, the Danish data were also able to illustrate a most important finding: the considerable sensitivity of the VAR approach to empirical shifts in growth rates and in equilibrium means.

Many of the theoretical advances were directly influenced by empirical analyses of this data set. In the first applied paper (Johansen and Juselius 1990), a vector of real money, real income, and two interest rates was analysed and only one cointegration relation was found. However, this was based on an implicit assumption of long-run price homogeneity. A need to test this properly resulted in the development of the $I(2)$ analysis (Johansen 1992a, 1996, 1997). The latter approach demonstrated that the original specification in real variables was misspecified by not including the inflation rate. Juselius (1994) tested the long-run price homogeneity assumption in the $I(2)$ model and found that it was accepted.[2] Re-estimating the model with the inflation rate correctly included as a new variable showed that the inflation rate was a crucial determinant in the system, which strongly affected the interpretation of the steady-state relations and the dynamic feedback effects within the system. Including the inflation rate in the vector of variables produced two more cointegration relations (one between the two interest rates and another one between inflation and real income inflation) in addition to the previously found money demand relation.

When the number of potentially interesting variables is large, so is the number of cointegrating relations. In this case, it is often a difficult task to identify them. The

[2] By extending the sample period to 2003 as we do in this book, price homogeneity was lost again as demonstrated in Chapters 16 and 18.

number of possible combinations is simply too large. If, instead, more information is gradually added to the analysis, it is possible to build on previous results and thus not to lose track so easily.

The idea of gradually increasing the data vector of the VAR model, building on previously found results, was also influenced by empirical analyses of the Danish data. Juselius (1993) added the loan rate to the previously used information set and found one additional cointegration relation between the loan rate and the deposit rate. This approach was then further developed in Juselius (1992), where three different sectors of the economy were analysed separately and then combined into one model.

Thus, contrary to the 'general to specific' approach of the statistical modelling process (i.e. of imposing more and more restrictions on the unrestricted VAR), it appeared more advantageous to follow the principle of 'specific to general' in the choice of information set. The principle works in practise because the cointegration property is invariant to extensions of the information set. This is unlike regression analysis where one new variable can alter the existing estimates dramatically.

The representation and statistical analysis of the $I(2)$ model meant a major step forward in the empirical understanding of the mechanisms determining nominal growth rates in Denmark. Juselius (1994) analysed common trends in both the $I(2)$ and $I(1)$ models, and found that the cumulated empirical shocks to nominal interest rates seemed to have generated price inflation. This was clearly against conventional wisdom that predicted the link to be the other way around. Needless to say, such a result could not convince economists as long as it stood alone. Therefore, a similar design was used in a number of other studies (Juselius 1996, 1998a, 2001; Juselius and Toro 2005) based on data from various European countries (with essentially the same conclusions). The experience of looking at various economies characterized by different policies through the same 'spectacles' generated the idea that the VAR approach could possibly be used as a proxy for a 'designed experiment' in a situation where only data by passive observations were available.

2

Models and relations in economics and econometrics

Chapter 1 discussed the difficult link between a theory model and an empirical model based on data collected by passive observation. This chapter discusses the VAR approach as a general framework within which statistical inference on macroeconomic hypotheses can be given a valid formulation. An urge to understand more fully why the VAR approach frequently produced results that seemed to cast doubt on conventional theories and beliefs was the motivation for writing this chapter. It focuses on what could be called the economist's approach, as opposed to the statistician's approach, to macroeconomic modelling, distinguishing between models and relations in economics and econometrics. The aim is to propose a framework for discussing the probability approach to econometrics in contrast to more traditional methods. It draws heavily on Juselius (1999a).

The economic problem is first introduced and important theoretical and empirical concepts are discussed. We then suggest a stochastic formulation of the economic problem which is general enough to encompass all major economic hypotheses while at the same time reflecting the general properties of the data. Based on this we demonstrate that it is possible to translate the major predictions from the theory model into a set of hypotheses formulated on the VAR model, all of which would have to be empirically valid for the theory model to be an acceptable description of reality.

The organization of this chapter is as follows. Section 2.1 discusses in general terms the VAR approach, as contrasted to a theory-based model approach. Section 2.2 briefly considers the treatment of inflation and monetary policy in Romer (1996) with special reference to the equilibrium in the money market. Section 2.3 discusses informally some empirical and theoretical implications of unit roots in the data. Section 2.4 addresses more formally a stochastic formulation based on a decomposition of the data into trends, cycles, and irregular components. Section 2.5 gives an empirical motivation for treating the stochastic trend in nominal prices as $I(2)$, whereas Section 2.6 considers the case when prices are $I(1)$.

2.1 The VAR approach and theory-based models

The vector autoregressive (VAR) process based on Gaussian (normally distributed) errors has frequently been a popular choice as a description of macroeconomic time-series data. There are many reasons for this: the VAR model is flexible, easy to estimate, and it usually gives a good fit to macroeconomic data. However, the possibility of combining long-run and short-run information in the data by exploiting the cointegration property is probably the most important reason why the VAR model continues to receive the interest of both econometricians and applied economists.

Theory-based economic models have traditionally been developed as non-stochastic mathematical entities and often applied to empirical data by adding a stochastic error process to the mathematical model. As an example of this approach we shall use the macroeconomic treatment in 'Inflation and Monetary Policy', Chapter 9 in D. Romer (1996): *Advanced Macroeconomics*.

From an econometric point of view, the two approaches are fundamentally different: one starting from an explicit stochastic formulation of *all* data and then *reducing* the general statistical (dynamic) model by imposing testable restrictions on the parameters, the other starting from a mathematical (static) formulation of a theoretical model and then *expanding* the model by adding stochastic components. For a detailed methodological discussion of the two approaches, see for example Gilbert (1986), Hendry (1995), Juselius (1993), and Pagan (1987).

Unfortunately, the two approaches have been shown to produce very different results even when applied to identical data, and hence lead to different conclusions. From a scientific point of view, this is not satisfactory. Therefore, we shall here attempt to bridge the gap between the two views by starting from some typical questions of theoretical interest and then show how one would answer these questions based on a *statistical* analysis of the VAR model. Because the latter by construction is 'bigger' than the theory model, the empirical analysis not only answers a specific theoretical question, but also gives additional insight into the macroeconomic problem.

A theory model can be simplified by the *ceteris paribus* assumptions 'everything else unchanged', whereas a statistically well-specified empirical model has to address the theoretical problem in the context of 'everything else changing'. By embedding the theory model in a broader empirical framework, the analysis of the statistically based model can provide evidence of possible pitfalls in macroeconomic reasoning. In this sense, the VAR analysis can be useful for generating new hypotheses, or for suggesting modifications of too narrowly specified theoretical models.

Throughout the book, we shall illustrate a variety of econometric problems by addressing questions of empirical relevance based on an analysis of money growth, inflation and the transmission mechanisms of monetary policy. These questions have been motivated by many empirical VAR analyses of money, prices, income and interest rates, and include questions such as:

- How effective is monetary policy when based on changes in money stock or changes in interest rates?
- What is the effect of expanding the money supply on prices in the short run? In the medium run? In the long run?

- Is an empirically stable demand for money relation a prerequisite for monetary policy control to be effective?
- How strong is the direct (indirect) relationship between a monetary policy instrument and price inflation?

Based on the VAR formulation, we shall demonstrate that every empirical statement can, and should, be checked for its consistency with all previous empirical and theoretical statements. This is in contrast to many empirical investigations, where inference relies on many untested assumptions using test procedures that only make sense in isolation, but not in the full context of the empirical model.

2.2 Inflation and money growth

A fundamental proposition in macroeconomic theory is that growth in money supply in excess of real productive growth is the cause of inflation, at least in the long run. Here we shall briefly consider some conventional ideas underlying this belief as described in Chapter 9 by Romer (1996). See also Walsh (1998).

The well-known diagram illustrating the intersection of aggregate demand (AD) and aggregate supply (AS) provides the framework for identifying potential sources of inflation as shocks shifting either aggregate demand upwards or aggregate supply to the left. See the upper panel of Figure 2.1.

As examples of aggregate supply shocks that shift the AS curve to the left, Romer (1996) mentions: negative technology shocks, downward shifts in labour supply, upwardly skewed relative-cost shocks. As examples of aggregate demand shocks that shift the AD curve to the right, he mentions: increases in money stock, downward shifts in money demand, increases in government purchases. Since all these types of shocks, and many others, occur quite frequently, there are many factors that potentially can affect inflation. Some of these shocks may only influence inflation temporarily and are therefore less important than shocks with a permanent effect on inflation. Among the latter, economists usually emphasize changes in money supply as the crucial inflationary source. The economic intuition behind this is that other factors are limited in scope, whereas money in principle is unlimited in supply.

More formally, the reasoning is based on money demand and supply and the condition for equilibrium in the money market:

$$M/P = L(R, Y^r), \quad L_R < 0, \quad L_y > 0 \tag{2.1}$$

where M is the money stock, P is the price level, R the nominal interest rate, Y^r real income, and $L(\cdot)$ the demand for real money balances. Based on the equilibrium condition, i.e. no changes in any of the variables, Romer (1996) concludes that the price level is determined by:

$$P = M/L(R, Y^r). \tag{2.2}$$

The equilibrium condition (2.1) and hence (2.2) is a static concept that can be thought of as a hypothetical relation between money and prices for fixed income and interest rate.

The underlying comparative static analysis investigates the effect on one variable, say price, when changing another variable, say money supply, with the purpose of deriving the new equilibrium position after the change. Thus, the focus is on the hypothetical effect of a change in one variable (M) on another variable (P), when the additional variables (R and Y^r) are exogenously given and everything else is taken account of by the *ceteris paribus* assumption.

However, when time is introduced, the *ceteris paribus* assumption and the assumption of fixed exogenous variables become much more questionable. Neither interest rates nor real income have been fixed or controlled in most periods subject to empirical analysis. Therefore, in empirical macroeconomic analysis *all variables* (inclusive of the *ceteris paribus* ones) are more or less continuously subject to shocks, some of which permanently change the previous equilibrium condition. In this sense an equilibrium position is always related to a specific time point in the empirical modelling. Hence, the static equilibrium point needs to be replaced by a time function, for example $(M/P)_t - L(Y^r, R_t)_t = v_t$, where $(M/P)_t = L(Y^r, R_t)_t$ defines the long-run steady-state relation, or the long-run benchmark value, for money demand. The deviation from the steady-state value (the equilibrium error), v_t, measures the extent of excess money (positive or negative) in the economy at time t relative to its long-run money-demand value. To argue empirically that $(M/P)_t = L(Y^r, R_t)_t$ is a long-run steady-state relation, we need to show that v_t is a stationary process, implying that the economic forces should be activated when $v_t \neq 0$ pulling the process back towards its long-run bench-mark value.

In a typical macroeconomic system, new disturbances push the variables away from steady-state, but the economic adjustment forces pull them back towards a new steady-state position. To illustrate the ideas, one can use an analogy from physics and think of the economy as a system of balls connected by springs. When left alone, the system will be in equilibrium, but pushing a ball will move the system away from equilibrium. Because all balls are connected, the 'shock' will influence the whole system, but after a while the effect will die out and the system move back to equilibrium. In the economy, the balls correspond to the economic variables and the springs to the transmission mechanisms that describe how economic shocks are transmitted through the system. However, economic variables that have been pushed by an exogenous shock, may or may not return to its previous position. In the former case we say that the variable was pushed by a transitory shock, in the latter by a permanent shock. Thus, the above picture should be modified to allow for balls which are moving with some 'controlled' speed. By pushing a ball, the speed will change and influence all the other balls. Left alone, the system will return to the 'controlled' state, i.e. the steady-state.

However, in real applications the adjustment back to steady-state is disturbed by new shocks and the system essentially never comes to rest. Therefore, we shall not be able to observe a steady-state position and the empirical investigation has to account for the stochastic properties of the variables as well as the theoretical equilibrium relationship between them. See the lower panel of Figure 2.1 for an illustration of a stochastic steady-state relation.

In (2.1) the money market equilibrium is an exact mathematical expression and it is straightforward to invert it to determine prices as is done in (2.2). The observations from a typical macroeconomic system are adequately described by a stochastic vector time-series process. But in stochastic systems, inversion of (2.1) is no longer guaranteed (see for instance Hendry and Ericsson 1991a). If the inverted (2.1) is estimated as a

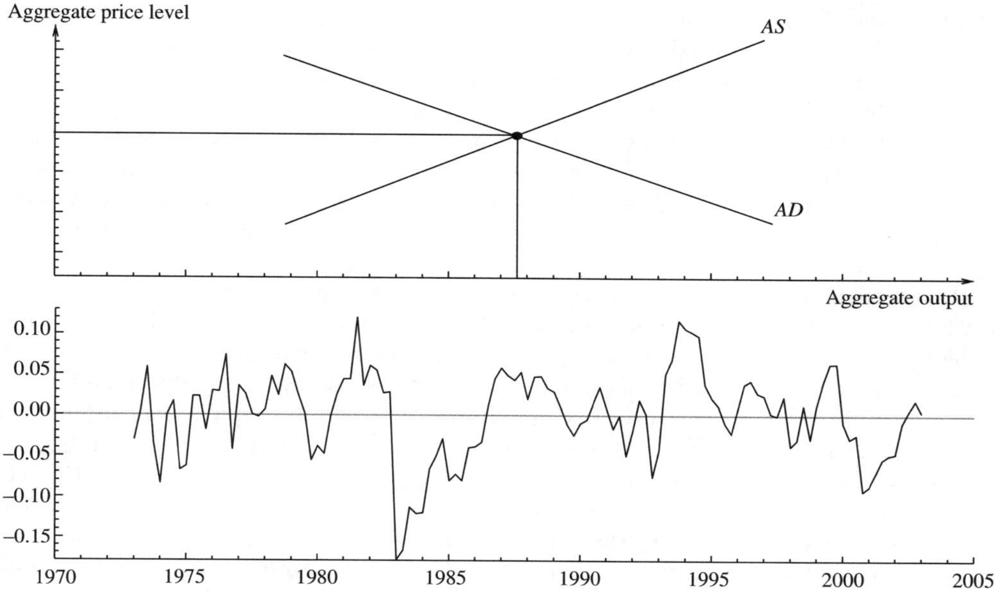

Fig 2.1 An equilibrium position of the AD and AS curve (upper panel) and deviations from an estimated money demand relation for Denmark: $(m - p - y)_t - 13.3(R_m - R_b)$ (lower panel).

regression model, it is likely to result in misleading conclusions. If it is inverted after estimation, then the dependent variable must have been exogenous, invalidating the estimation assumption.

The observed money stock can be demand or supply determined or both, but it is not necessarily a measurement of a long-run steady-state position. This raises the question whether it is possible to empirically identify and estimate the underlying theoretical relations. For instance, if central banks are able to effectively control money stock, then observed money holdings are likely to be supply determined and the demand for money has to adjust to the supplied quantities. This is likely to be the case in trade and capital regulated economies or, possibly, in economies with flexible exchange rates, whereas in open deregulated economies with fixed exchange rates, central banks would not in general be able to control money stock. In the latter case, one would expect observed money stock to be demand determined.

Under the assumption that the money demand relation can be *empirically* identified, the statistical estimation problem has to be addressed. Because macroeconomic variables are generally found to be non-stationary, standard regression methods are no longer feasible from an econometric point of view. Cointegration analysis specifically addresses the non-stationarity problem and is therefore a feasible solution in this respect. The empirical counterpart of (2.1) (with the opportunity cost of holding money, $R = R_b - R_m$) can be written as a cointegrating relation, i.e.:

$$\ln(M/PY^{r})_t - L_R(R_b - R_m)_t = v_t \tag{2.3}$$

where R_b and R_m are the interest rate on government bonds and the own interest on money stock respectively, and v_t is a stationary process measuring the deviation from the steady-state position at time t. The stationarity of v_t implies that whenever the system has been shocked, it will adjust back to equilibrium. This is illustrated in Figure 2.1 (lower panel) by the graph of the deviations from an estimated money demand relation based on Danish data with the opportunity cost of holding money being measured by $R_b - R_m$ (Juselius 1998b). Note the large equilibrium error at about 1983, as a result of removing restrictions on capital movements and the consequent adjustment back to steady-state.

However, empirical investigation of (2.3) based on cointegration analysis poses several additional problems. Although in a theoretical exercise it is straightforward to keep some of the variables fixed (the exogenous variables), in an empirical model none of the variables in (2.1), i.e. money, prices, income or interest rates, can be assumed to be fixed (i.e. controlled). The stochastic feature of all variables implies that the equilibrium adjustment can take place in either money, prices, income or interest rates. Therefore, the equilibrium deviation v_t is not necessarily due to a money supply shock at time t, but can originate from any change in the variables. Hence, one should be cautious to interpret a coefficient in a cointegrating relation as in the conventional regression context, which is based on the assumption of 'fixed' regressors (Johansen 2005a). In multivariate cointegration analysis, all variables are stochastic and a shock to one variable is transmitted to all other variables via the dynamics of the system until the system has found its new equilibrium position.

The empirical investigation of the above questions raises several econometric questions: What is the meaning of a shock and how do we measure it econometrically? How do we distinguish empirically between the long-run, the medium-run and the short-run? Given the measurements, can the parameter estimates be given an economically meaningful interpretation? These questions will be discussed in more detail in the subsequent sections.

2.3 The time dependence of macroeconomic data

As advocated above, the strong time dependence of macroeconomic data suggests a statistical formulation based on stochastic processes. In this context, it is useful to distinguish between:

- stationary variables with a short time dependence; and
- non-stationary variables with a long time dependence.

In practice, it is useful to classify variables exhibiting a high degree of time persistence (insignificant mean reversion) as non-stationary and variables exhibiting a significant tendency to mean reversion as stationary. However, it is important to stress that the stationarity/non-stationarity or, alternatively, the order of integration of a variable, is not in general a *property of an economic variable* but a convenient statistical approximation to distinguish between the short-run, medium-run, and long-run variation in the data. We shall illustrate this with a few examples involving money, prices, income, and interest rates.

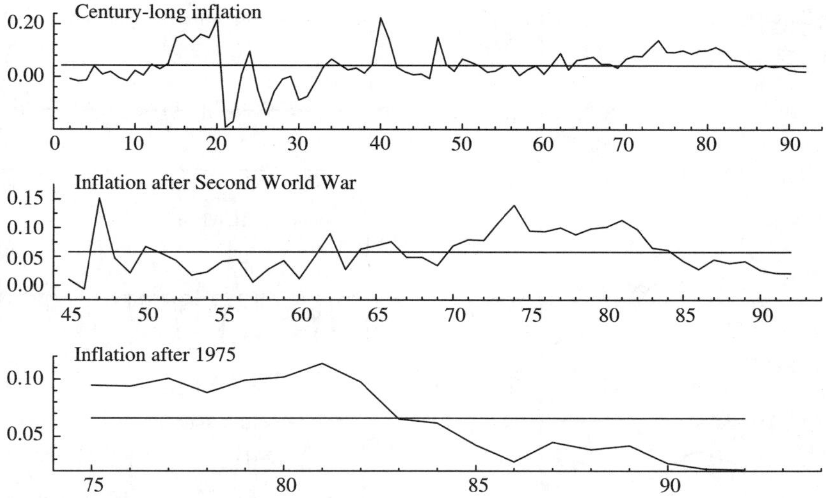

Fig 2.2 Annual Danish inflation 1901–92 (upper panel), 1945–92 (middle panel), and 1975–92 (lower panel) around the sample average.

Most countries have exhibited periods of high and low inflation, lasting sometimes a decade or even more, after which the inflation rate has returned to its mean level. If inflation crosses its mean level, say 10 times, the econometric analysis will find significant mean reversion and hence conclude that the inflation rate is stationary. For this to happen, we might need up to a hundred years of observations. The time path of, for example, quarterly European inflation over the last few decades will cover a high inflation period in the 1970s and beginning of the 1980s and a low inflation period from the mid-1980s until the present date. Crossing the mean level a few times is not enough to obtain statistically significant mean reversion and the econometric analysis will show that inflation should be treated as a non-stationary variable. This is illustrated in Figure 2.2 where annual observations of the Danish inflation rate have been graphed for 1901–1992 (upper panel), for 1945–1992 (middle panel), and for 1975–1992 (lower panel), where the line in each panel is the sample mean for 1901–1992. The first two time series of inflation rates look mean-reverting whereas significant mean-reversion would not be found for the last section of the series.

That inflation is considered stationary in one study and non-stationary in another, where the latter is based, say, on a subsample of the former might seem contradictory. This need not be so, unless a unit root process is given a structural economic interpretation. There are many arguments in favour of considering a unit root (a stochastic trend) as a convenient econometric approximation rather than as a deep structural parameter. For instance, if the time perspective of our study is the macroeconomic behaviour in the medium run, then most macroeconomic variables exhibit considerable inertia, consistent with non-stationary rather than stationary behaviour. Because inflation, for example, would not appear to be statistically different from a non-stationary variable, treating it as a stationary variable is likely to invalidate the statistical analysis and therefore lead to wrong economic conclusions.

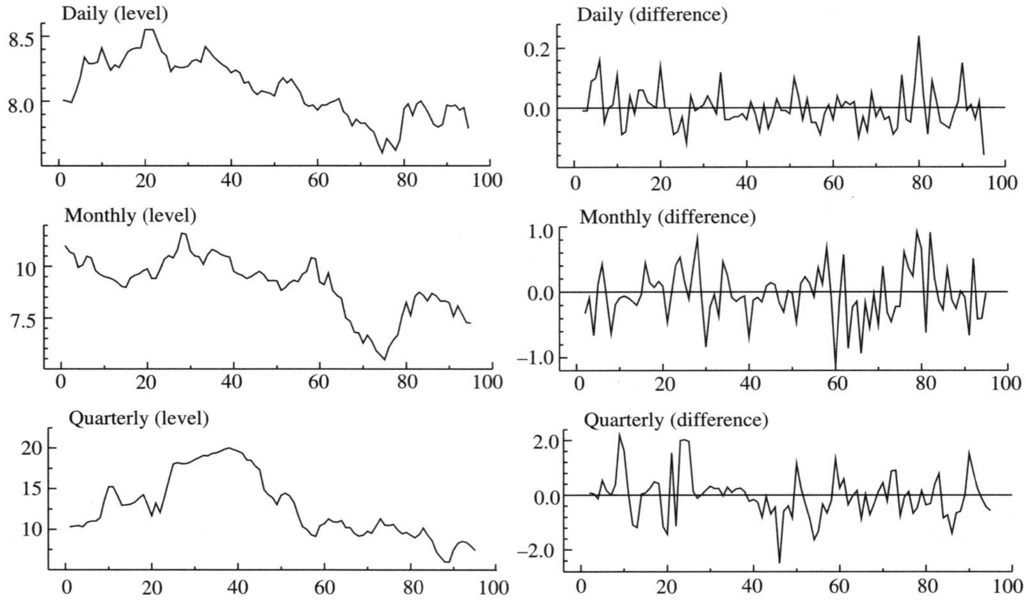

Fig 2.3 Average Danish bond rates, based on daily observations, 1.5.95–25.9.95 (upper panel), monthly observations, Nov. 1987–Sept. 1995 (middle panel), and quarterly observations, 1972:1–1995:3 (lower panel).

Furthermore, treating inflation as a non-stationary variable gives us the opportunity to find out which other variable(s) have exhibited similar persistence by exploiting the cointegration property. This will be discussed at some length in Section 2.5, where we shall demonstrate that the unit root property of economic variables is very useful for the empirical analysis of long- and medium-run macroeconomic relationships.

When the time perspective of our study is the long historical macroeconomic movements, inflation rate is likely to show significant mean reversion and hence can be treated as a stationary variable. This is because even a tiny deviation from unity will be found statistically significant when the sample period is long enough. In such cases it is nevertheless often advantageous to use the unit-root approximation for the purpose of modelling (even though the root is statistically significant from unity) as this allows us to use cointegration techniques to structure the data into persistent and less persistent components. See for example Hendry and Juselius (2000, 2001).

Finally, to illustrate that the same type of stochastic processes are able to adequately describe the data, independently of whether one takes a close-up or a long-distance look, we have graphed the Danish bond rate in levels and differences in Figure 2.3 based on a sample of 95 quarterly observations (1972:1–1995:3), 95 monthly observations (1987:11–1995:9), and 95 daily observations (1.5.95–25.9.95). The daily sample corresponds to the little hump at the end of the monthly time series. It would be considered a small stationary blip from a monthly perspective, whereas from a daily perspective it is non-stationary, showing no significant mean reversion. Altogether, the three time series look very similar from a stochastic point of view.

Thus, econometrically it is convenient to let the definition of long-run or short-run, or alternatively the very long-run, the medium long-run, and the short-run, depend on the time perspective of the study. From an economic point of view, the question remains in what sense a 'unit root' process can be given a 'structural' interpretation.

2.4 A stochastic formulation

To illustrate the above questions we shall consider a conventional decomposition into trend, $\mathcal{T}$, cycle, $\mathcal{C}$, seasonal, $\mathcal{S}$, and irregular component, E of a typical macroeconomic variable.

$$X = \mathcal{T} \times \mathcal{C} \times \mathcal{S} \times E.$$

Instead of treating the trend component as deterministic, as is usually done in conventional analysis, we shall allow the trend to be both deterministic, $\mathcal{T}_d$, and stochastic, $\mathcal{T}_s$, i.e. $\mathcal{T} = \mathcal{T}_s \times \mathcal{T}_d$, and the cyclical component to be of long duration, say 6–10 years, $\mathcal{C}_l$, and of shorter duration, say 3–5 years, $\mathcal{C}_s$, i.e. $\mathcal{C} = \mathcal{C}_l \times \mathcal{C}_s$. The reason for distinguishing between short and long cycles is that a long/short cycle can either be treated as non-stationary or stationary depending on the time perspective of the study. As an illustration of long cycles that have been found non-stationary by the statistical analysis, see the graph of trend-adjusted real income in Figure 2.4, middle panel.

An additive formulation is obtained by taking logarithms:

$$x = (t_s + t_d) + (c_l + c_s) + s + e \tag{2.4}$$

where lower case letters indicate a logarithmic transformation. In the subsequent chapters, the stochastic time dependence of the variables will be of primary interest, but the linear time trend will also be important as a measure of nonzero average linear growth rates usually present in economic data.

To give the economic intuition for the subsequent multivariate cointegration analysis of money demand/money supply relations, we shall illustrate the ideas in Sections 2.5 and 2.6 using the time series vector $\mathbf{x}_t = [m, p, y^r, R_m, R_b]_t$, $t = 1, \ldots, T$, where the variables are defined above. All variables are treated as stochastic and hence from a statistical point of view need to be modelled, independently of whether they are considered endogenous or exogenous in the economic model.

To illustrate the ideas, we shall assume two autonomous shocks u_1 and u_2, where for simplicity u_1 is a nominal shock causing a permanent shift in the AD curve and u_2 is a real shock causing a permanent shift in the AS curve. This would be consistent with the aggregate supply (AS) aggregate demand (AD) diagram in Fig. 2.1.

The concept of a common stochastic trend or a driving force requires a further distinction between:

- an unanticipated shock with a permanent effect (a disturbance to the system with a long-lasting effect);
- an unanticipated shock with a transitory effect (a disturbance to the system with a short duration).

A permanent shock is by definition a shock that has a long-lasting effect on the level of the variable, whereas the effect of a transitory shock disappears either during the next period or over the next few ones. For example, a commodity tax imposed in one period and removed in the next is a transitory price shock. This is because prices increase temporarily but return to their previous level after the tax removal. Therefore, a transitory shock can be described as a shock that occurs a second time in the series but then with opposite sign.

To illustrate the effect of a permanent and a transitory shock on a variable Table 2.1 shows a simple example describing the level of income, y_t, and how it is being influenced by several income changes over seven consecutive periods. The level of income at time t is described by its previous level plus the current change in income:

$$y_t = y_{t-1} + v_t,$$

or equivalently:

$$\Delta y_t = v_t.$$

We shall now assume that the income change can be decomposed into $v_t = v_{p,t} + v_{s,t}$, where $v_{p,t}$ denotes a permanent income change and $v_{s,t}$ a transitory income change.

The table tells the following story: At $t = 0$ income is 100. A permanent wage increase of 4% makes it 104 at $t = 1$. At $t = 2$ the person receives a permanent wage increase of 5% and at the same time a one time child check of 1%, a total increase in income of 6%. Next year the wage increase is 2% but, as there is no child check this year, the level of income only increases with 1%. At $t = 4$ the person gets unemployed and experiences a negative permanent shock of −3%, so that the income level drops to 108. At $t = 5$ the person is still unemployed, but wins a lottery price of 1%. At $t = 6$ he/she gets a new job and experiences a permanent income rise of 3%, but since there is no lottery price this year the level of income increases only by 2%. At $t = 7$ there is another permanent wage increase of 3% and no transitory shock. Altogether the income level has increased over the period from 100 to 114, i.e. an average increase of 2% per year. In such a case it is customary to decompose the income change v_t into the average change b and $\varepsilon_t = v_t - b$. Similarly, we can decompose the total permanent increase, $\Sigma_{i=1}^{t} v_i$ into a total

Table 2.1 Illustrating permanent and transitory income change and shocks.

t	y_t	v_t	$v_{p,t}$	$v_{s,t}$	$\Sigma v_{p,i}$	$\Sigma v_{s,i}$	Σv_i	$v_t - b = \varepsilon_t$	bt	$\Sigma v_i - bt = \Sigma \varepsilon_i$
0	100	–	–	–	–	–	–	–	–	–
1	104	4	4	0	4	0	4	2	2	2
2	110	6	5	1	9	1	10	4	4	6
3	111	1	2	−1	11	0	11	−1	6	5
4	108	−3	−3	0	8	0	8	−5	8	0
5	109	1	0	1	8	1	9	−1	10	−1
6	111	2	3	−1	11	0	11	0	12	−1
7	114	3	3	0	14	0	14	1	14	0

average increase, bt and the deviation from this average trend, $\Sigma_{i=1}^{t}\varepsilon_i = \Sigma_{i=1}^{t}v_i - bt$. This is illustrated in the last three columns for $b = 2\%$.

We can now describe this story with a simple statistical model for y_t:

$$y_t = y_{t-1} + b + \varepsilon_t,$$

or equivalently:

$$\Delta y_t = b + \varepsilon_t$$

where b measures the average growth in income, for example due to the growth in productivity over the period, and ε_t measures a random idiosyncratic shock. Furthermore, the random shocks, $\varepsilon_t = v_t - b$ can be decomposed into $\varepsilon_t = \varepsilon_{p,t} + \varepsilon_{s,t}$, where $\varepsilon_{p,t} = v_{p,t} - b$ denotes a permanent income shock and $\varepsilon_{s,t} = v_{s,t}$ a transitory income shock. Thus, a permanent income change can be decomposed into a permanent fixed effect, b, and a permanent stochastic effect, $\varepsilon_{p,t}$.

We note that:

- $\Sigma_{i=1}^{7}v_i = \Sigma_{i=1}^{7}v_{p,i}$, i.e. the sum of the total income changes is equal to the sum of the permanent changes because the transitory changes disappear in cumulation;
- the cumulated trend-adjusted shocks, $\Sigma_{i=1}^{t}v_i - bt = \Sigma_{i=1}^{t}\varepsilon_i = \Sigma_{i=1}^{t}\varepsilon_{p,i}$, have a sample average of zero and exhibit a high degree of persistence, as the deviations from trend tend to be positive in periods of employment and negative when unemployed.

The time series describing cumulated trend-adjusted shocks is usually called a stochastic trend. It is a cumulation of random shocks with zero mean and constant variance. If the permanent shocks have a mean different from zero we choose to describe this part with a linear deterministic trend component. Thus, the difference between a stochastic and deterministic trend is that the increments of a stochastic trend change randomly, whereas those of a deterministic trend are constant over time.

We shall now use this idea to discuss the meaning of a stochastic trend in the inflation rate, π_t, assuming for simplicity that it follows a random walk:[1]

$$\begin{aligned}\pi_t &= \pi_{t-1} + \varepsilon_t,\\ &= \varepsilon_t(1 + L + L^2 + \cdots + L^t) + \pi_0, \quad t = 1, \ldots, T \qquad (2.5)\end{aligned}$$

where $\varepsilon_t \sim N(0, \sigma^2)$, L is the lag operator such that $L^m x_t = x_{t-m}$, and $\varepsilon_t = \varepsilon_{p,t} + \varepsilon_{s,t}$, consists of a permanent shock, $\varepsilon_{p,t}$, and a transitory shock, $\varepsilon_{s,t}$.[2] By assuming that the inflationary shocks have a zero mean we have from the outset stated that inflation cannot have a deterministic trend.

[1] Later on we will replace the simple random walk model with a more adequate model.

[2] Note that in this case an autoregressive integrated moving average model would give a more appropriate specification provided ε_p and ε_s are white-noise processes.

By cumulating the shocks, starting from an initial value of inflation rate, π_0, we get:

$$\begin{aligned}
\pi_t &= \sum_{i=1}^{t} \varepsilon_i + \pi_0 \\
&= \sum_{i=1}^{t} (\varepsilon_{p,i} + \varepsilon_{s,i}) + \pi_0 \\
&= \varepsilon_{p,t} + \varepsilon_{p,t-1} + \varepsilon_{p,t-2} + \cdots + \varepsilon_{p,1} + \varepsilon_{s,t} + \varepsilon_{s,t-1} + \varepsilon_{s,t-2} + \cdots + \varepsilon_{s,1} + \pi_0 \\
&= \sum_{i=1}^{t} \varepsilon_{p,i} + \sum_{i=1}^{t} \varepsilon_{s,i} + \pi_0 \\
&\approx \sum_{i=1}^{t} \varepsilon_{p,i} + u_{s,t} + \pi_0
\end{aligned}$$

where $u_{s,t}$ is a stationary moving average error process. In the summation of the disturbances ε_i:

$$\pi_t = \sum_{i=1}^{t} \varepsilon_i + \pi_0 \tag{2.6}$$

only the effect of the permanent shocks will remain in the level of π_t as the transitory shocks disappear in cumulation. We say that inflation rate is integrated of first order, or in short hand $\pi_t \sim I(1)$. Under the assumptions given by (2.6) the inflation rate is equal to its stochastic trend apart for the initial value.

A representation of prices instead of inflation is obtained by integrating (2.6) once, i.e.

$$p_t = \sum_{s=1}^{t} \pi_s + p_0 = \sum_{s=1}^{t} \sum_{i=1}^{s} \varepsilon_i + \pi_0 t + p_0. \tag{2.7}$$

It is easy to see that if inflation rate is $I(1)$ with a non-zero mean, then prices will contain a twice cumulated stochastic trend, $\sum_{s=1}^{t} \sum_{i=1}^{s} \varepsilon_i$. We say that trend-adjusted prices are integrated of order two, or in shorthand notation $p_t \sim I(2)$.

Figure 2.4 illustrates different stochastic trends in the Danish quarterly data set. The $I(2)$ trend in the upper panel corresponds to trend-adjusted prices and the $I(1)$ trend in the middle panel corresponds to trend-adjusted real income. The lower panel is a graph of Δp_t and describes the $I(1)$ trend in the inflation rate, which is equivalent to the differenced $I(2)$ trend. Note, however, that inflation has been positive over the full sample, meaning that the price level will contain a linear deterministic trend. Thus, a non-zero sample average of inflation, $\overline{\Delta p} \neq 0$, is consistent with a linear trend in the price levels, p_t.

The question whether inflation rates should be treated as $I(1)$ or $I(0)$ has been subject to much debate. Figure 2.2 illustrated that the Danish inflation rate measured over the last decades was probably best approximated by a non-stationary process, whereas measured over a century by a stationary, though strongly autocorrelated process. For a

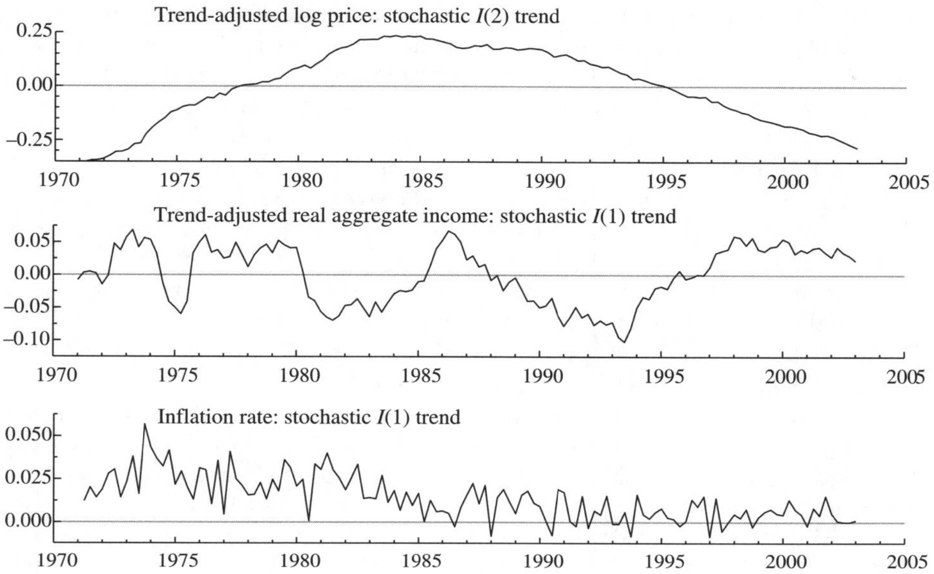

Fig 2.4 Stochastic trends in Danish prices, real income and inflation, based on quarterly data 1971:1–2003:1.

description of the latter case, (2.5) should be replaced by:

$$\begin{aligned}\pi_t &= \rho\pi_{t-1} + \varepsilon_t,\\ &= \varepsilon_t(1 + \rho L + \rho^2 L^2 + \cdots + \rho^{t-1}L^{t-1}) + \rho^t \pi_0, \quad t = 1, \ldots, T\end{aligned} \tag{2.8}$$

which becomes:

$$\pi_t = \sum_{i=1}^{t} \rho^{t-i}\varepsilon_i + \rho^t\pi_0 = \varepsilon_t + \rho\varepsilon_{t-1} + \cdots + \rho^{t-1}\varepsilon_1 + \rho^t\pi_0 \tag{2.9}$$

where the autoregressive parameter ρ is less than but close to one. In this case prices would be represented by:

$$\begin{aligned}p_t &= \sum_{s=1}^{t} \pi_s + p_0 \\ &= \sum_{s=1}^{t}\left(\sum_{i=1}^{s} \rho^{s-i}\varepsilon_i + \rho^s\pi_0\right) + p_0 \\ &= \sum_{s=1}^{t}\sum_{i=1}^{s} \rho^{s-i}\varepsilon_i + \pi_0\sum_{s=1}^{t}\rho^s + p_0\end{aligned} \tag{2.10}$$

i.e. by a strongly autoregressive first-order stochastic trend.

The difference between (2.6) and (2.9) is only a matter of approximation. In the first case, the parameter ρ is approximated with unity, because the sample period is too short for the estimate to be statistically different from one. In the second case, the sample period contains enough turning points for ρ to be significantly different from one. Econometrically, it is more optimal to treat a long business cycle component spanning over, say, 10 years as an $I(1)$ process when the sample period is less than, say, 20 years. In this sense, the difference between the long cyclical component c_l and t_s in (2.4) is that t_s is a true unit root process ($\rho = 1$), whereas c_l is a near unit root process ($\rho \leq 1$) that needs a very long sample to distinguish it from a true unit root process.

We shall argue below that, unless a unit root is given a structural interpretation, the choice of one representation or the other is as such not very important, as long as there is consistency between the economic analysis and the choice. However, from an econometric point of view the choice between the two representations is usually crucial for the whole empirical analysis and should therefore be carefully considered.

Whatever the case, the distinction between a permanent (long-lasting) and a transitory shock is fundamental for the empirical interpretation of integration and cointegration results. The statement that inflation, Δp_t, is $I(1)$ is consistent with inflationary shocks being strongly persistent. Statistically this is expressed in (2.6) as inflation having a first-order stochastic trend defined as the cumulative sum of all previous shocks from the starting date.

Whether inflation should be considered $I(1)$ or $I(0)$ has been much debated, often based on a structural (economic) interpretation of a unit root. We argue here that the order of integration should be based on statistical, rather than economic arguments. If ρ is not significantly different from one (for example because the sample period is short), but we, nevertheless, treat inflation as $I(0)$ then the statistical inference will sooner or later produce logically inconsistent results.

However, the fact that a small value of ρ, say 0.80, is often not significantly different from one in a small sample, whereas a much higher value of ρ, say 0.98, can differ significantly from one in a long sample, is likely to give semantic problems when using 'long-run' and 'short-run' to describe integration and cointegration properties. For example, a price variable could easily be considered $I(2)$ based on a short sample, whereas $I(1)$ based on a longer period. But, as argued above, from an empirical point of view it is often advantageous to approximate a near-unit root with a unit root, even though it is significantly different from one.

Macroeconomic data are generally influenced by regime shifts which may have caused at least some of the VAR parameters to change. Since the inference from the VAR model is only valid provided the parameters are constant, it is frequently the case that one has to split the sample period into subsamples representing constant parameter regimes. In such cases, inference on cointegration and integration will be based on relatively short samples leading to the above interpretational problems.

When interpreting the subsequent results, we shall use the concept of 'long-run relation' to mean a cointegrating relation between $I(1)$ or $I(2)$ variables, as defined above. We shall use the concept of 'short-run adjustment' when a stationary variable is significantly related to a cointegration relation or to another stationary variable. A necessary condition for a 'long-run relation' to be empirically relevant in a model is that at least one of the variables exhibit 'short-run adjustment' to it.[3] Based on this definition, non-cointegrating

[3]When data are $I(2)$, we have integration and cointegration on different levels and the concepts need to be modified accordingly. The need to distinguish between these concepts is moderate here and we refer to Chapters 16–18 for a more formal treatment.

relations incorrectly included in the model will eventually drop out as future observations become available: a stationary variable cannot significantly adjust to a non-stationary variable.

Because a cointegrating relation does not necessarily correspond to an interpretable economic relation, we make a further distinction between the *statistical* concept of a 'cointegration relation' and the *economic* concept of a 'long-run equilibrium relation'.

2.5 Scenario analyses: treating prices as $I(2)$

In this section, we shall assume that the long-run stochastic trend t_s in (2.4) can be described by the twice cumulated nominal (AD) shocks, $\sum\sum u_{1i}$, as in (2.7) and the long cyclical component c_l by the once cumulated nominal (AD) shocks, $\sum u_{1i}$, and the once cumulated real (AS) shocks, $\sum u_{2i}$. This representation gives us the possibility of distinguishing between the long-run stochastic trend in prices, $\sum\sum u_{1i}$, the medium-run stochastic trend in price inflation, $\sum u_{1i}$, and the medium-run stochastic trend in real activity, $\sum u_{2i}$.

As a simple illustration of how the econometric analysis is influenced by the above assumptions we shall consider the following decomposition of the data vector:[4]

$$\begin{bmatrix} m_t \\ p_t \\ y_t^r \\ R_{m,t} \\ R_{b,t} \end{bmatrix} = \begin{bmatrix} c_{11} \\ c_{21} \\ 0 \\ 0 \\ 0 \end{bmatrix} [\sum\sum u_{1i}] + \begin{bmatrix} d_{11} & d_{12} \\ d_{21} & d_{22} \\ d_{31} & d_{32} \\ d_{41} & d_{42} \\ d_{51} & d_{52} \end{bmatrix} \begin{bmatrix} \sum u_{1i} \\ \sum u_{2i} \end{bmatrix} + \begin{bmatrix} g_1 \\ g_2 \\ g_3 \\ 0 \\ 0 \end{bmatrix} [t] + \text{stat. comp.} \tag{2.11}$$

The deterministic trend component, $t_d = t$, accounts for linear growth in nominal money and prices as well as real income. Generally, when $\{g_1 \neq 0, g_2 \neq 0, g_3 \neq 0\}$, then the average growth rate in real income and prices is non-zero consistent with stylized facts in most industrialized countries. If $g_3 = 0$ and $d_{31} = 0$ in (2.11), then $\sum u_{2i}$ is likely to describe a long-run real stochastic trend in the economy, i.e. a 'structural' unit root process as discussed in the many papers on the stochastic versus deterministic real growth models. See, for instance, King, Plosser, Stock, and Watson (1991). If $g_3 \neq 0$, then the linear time trend is likely to capture the long-run growth trend and $\sum u_{2i}$ will describe the medium-run deviations from this trend, i.e. the long business cycles. The trend-adjusted real income variable in the middle panel of Figure 2.4 illustrates such long business cycles. The first case, $g_3 = 0$ explicitly assumes that the average real growth rate is zero whereas $g_3 \neq 0$ implies a non-zero average growth rate. Whether one includes a linear trend or not in (2.11) therefore influences the possibility of interpreting the second stochastic trend, $\sum u_{2i}$, as a long-run structural trend or not. Thus, one might say that the distinction between a long-run and medium-run stochastic trend in this case is between an $I(1)$ stochastic trend with no linear trend and a near $I(1)$ stochastic trend with a linear trend.

[4]Note that this representation of the data is purely conceptual as we have not yet stated any assumptions of the stochastic properties of $u_{1,t}$ and $u_{2,t}$.

The second row describes p_t as a function of the $I(2)$ trend and the two $I(1)$ trends. If $d_{21} = d_{22} = 0$, then the data generating process for p_t corresponds to (2.7). This would imply that the true model for inflation is a random walk, $\Delta p_t = \Delta p_{t-1} + u_{1,t}$, so that in the vector model there would be no other determinants explaining inflation. If, on the other hand, $\Delta p_t = \Delta p_{t-1} + b_1 \Delta x_t + u_{1,t}$, then the data generating process of prices would contain the $I(2)$ trend plus additionally the stochastic trends in x_t.

Conditions for long-run price homogeneity

Let us now take a closer look at the trend components of m_t and p_t in (2.11):

$$\begin{aligned} m_t &= c_{11} \sum\sum u_{1i} + d_{11} \sum u_{1i} + d_{12} \sum u_{2i} + g_1 t + \text{stat. comp.} \\ p_t &= c_{21} \sum\sum u_{1i} + d_{21} \sum u_{1i} + d_{22} \sum u_{2i} + g_2 t + \text{stat. comp.} \end{aligned}$$

If $(c_{11}, c_{21}) \neq 0$, then $\{m_t, p_t\} \sim I(2)$. If, in addition, $c_{11} = c_{21}$ then real money

$$m_t - p_t = (d_{11} - d_{21}) \sum u_{1i} + (d_{12} - d_{22}) \sum u_{2i} + (g_1 - g_2)t + \text{stat. comp.}$$

is at most $I(1)$. If $\{(d_{11} \neq d_{21}), (d_{12} \neq d_{22})\}$, then m_t and p_t are cointegrating from $I(2)$ to $I(1)$, i.e. they are $CI(2,1)$. If, in addition, $(g_1 \neq g_2)$ then real money stock grows around a linear trend.

The case $(m_t - p_t) \sim I(1)$ implies long-run price homogeneity and is a testable hypothesis. Money stock and prices are moving together in the long-run, but not necessarily in the medium-run (over the long business cycle). Long-run and medium-run price homogeneity requires $\{c_{11} = c_{21}$, and $d_{11} = d_{21}\}$, i.e. the nominal (AD) shocks u_{1t} affect nominal money and prices in the same way both in the long-run and in the medium-run. Because the real stochastic trend $\sum u_{2i}$ is likely to enter m_t but not necessarily p_t, testing long- and medium-run price homogeneity jointly is not equivalent to testing $(m_t - p_t) \sim I(0)$. Therefore, the joint hypothesis is not as straightforward to test as long-run price homogeneity alone.

Note that $(m_t - p_t) \sim I(1)$ implies $(\Delta m_t - \Delta p_t) \sim I(0)$, i.e. long-run price homogeneity implies cointegration between price inflation and money growth. If this is the case,[5] then the stochastic trend in inflation can equally well be measured by the stochastic trend in the growth in money stock.

Assuming long-run price homogeneity

In the following we shall assume long-run price homogeneity, i.e. $c_{11} = c_{21}$, and discuss various cases where medium-run price homogeneity is either present or absent. In this case it is convenient to transform the nominal data vector into real money $(m - p)$ and

[5]In periods of financial innovation nominal money and prices need not necessarily be homogeneously related.

inflation rate Δp (or equivalently Δm):[6]

$$\begin{bmatrix} m_t - p_t \\ \Delta p_t \\ y_t^r \\ R_{m,t} \\ R_{b,t} \end{bmatrix} = \begin{bmatrix} d_{11} - d_{21} & d_{12} - d_{22} \\ c_{21} & 0 \\ d_{31} & d_{32} \\ d_{41} & d_{42} \\ d_{51} & d_{52} \end{bmatrix} \begin{bmatrix} \sum u_{1i} \\ \sum u_{2i} \end{bmatrix} + \begin{bmatrix} g_1 - g_2 \\ 0 \\ g_3 \\ 0 \\ 0 \end{bmatrix} [t] + \cdots \tag{2.12}$$

In (2.12) all variables are at most $I(1)$. The inflation rate (measured by Δp_t or Δm_t) is only affected by $\sum u_{1i}$, whereas all the other variables can in principle be affected by both trends, $\sum u_{1i}$ and $\sum u_{2i}$. The simplifying assumption made earlier that $u_{1,t}$ measures a shock to the AD curve appears now too restrictive, as there are no reasons why inflation could not be influenced by shocks to the AS curve. This illustrates that the empirical identification of $u_{1,t}$ and $u_{2,t}$ can be quite complicated, an issue that will be further discussed in Chapters 14 and 15.

The case trend-adjusted $(m_t - p_t) \sim I(0)$ requires that both $d_{11} = d_{21}$ and $d_{12} = d_{22}$, which is not very likely from an economic point of view. *A priori*, one would expect the real stochastic trend $\sum u_{2i}$ to influence money stock (by increasing the transactions, precautionary and speculative demands for money) but not the price level, i.e. that $d_{12} \neq 0$ and $d_{22} = 0$.

The case $(m_t - p_t - y_t^r) \sim I(0)$, i.e. money velocity of circulation is a stationary variable, requires that $d_{11} - d_{21} - d_{31} = 0$, $d_{12} - d_{22} - d_{32} = 0$ and $g_1 - g_2 - g_3 = 0$. If $d_{11} = d_{21}$ (i.e. medium-run price homogeneity), $d_{22} = 0$ (the real stochastic trend does not affect prices), $d_{31} = 0$ (medium-run price growth does not affect the long business cycle in real income), and $d_{12} = d_{32}$, then $m_t - p_t - y_t^r \sim I(0)$. In this case, real money stock and real aggregate income share one common trend, the real stochastic trend $\sum u_{2i}$. The stationarity of money velocity, implying common stochastic movements in money, prices, and income, is then consistent with the conventional monetarist assumption as stated by Friedman (1970) that 'inflation always and everywhere is a monetary problem'. This case, $(m_t - p_t - y_t^r) \sim I(0)$, has generally found little empirical support (see Juselius 1996, 1998b, 2001, and Juselius and Toro 2005). The graph of money velocity in the upper panel of Figure 2.5 illustrates the apparent non-stationarity of this variable.

We shall now turn to the more realistic assumption of money velocity being $I(1)$.

The case $(m_t - p_t - y_t^r) \sim I(1)$ implies that either $\{(d_{11} - d_{21} - d_{31}) \neq 0$ or $(d_{12} - d_{22} - d_{32}) \neq 0\}$. It suggests that the two common stochastic trends affect the level of real money stock and real income differently. A few examples illustrate this:

Example 1: Inflation is cointegrating with velocity, i.e.

$$m_t - p_t - y_t^r + b_1 \Delta p_t \sim I(0), \tag{2.13}$$

or alternatively

$$(m_t - p_t - y_t^r) + b_2 \Delta m_t \sim I(0).$$

[6] Chapters 16, 17, and 18 will discuss this nominal to real transformation in more detail.

Under the previous assumptions that $d_{31}, d_{22} = 0$, and $d_{12} = d_{32}$, the $I(0)$ assumption of (2.13) implies that $d_{11} - d_{21} = -b_1 c_{21}$. If $b_1 > 0$, then (2.13) can be interpreted as a money demand relation, where the opportunity cost of holding money relative to real stock as measured by Δp_t is a determinant of money holdings. On the other hand if $b_1 < 0$, then inflation adjusts to excess money, though if $|\, b_1 \,| < 1$, with some time lag. In this case it is not possible to interpret (2.13) as a money demand relation.

Example 2: The interest rate spread and money velocity are cointegrating, i.e.

$$(m_t - p_t - y_t^r) - b_3(R_m - R_b)_t \sim I(0). \tag{2.14}$$

Because $(R_m - R_b)_t \sim I(1)$, either $(d_{41} - d_{51}) \neq 0$, or $(d_{42} - d_{52}) \neq 0$, or both. In either case, the stochastic trend in the spread has to cointegrate with the stochastic trend in money velocity for (2.14) to hold. If $b_3 > 0$, then (2.14) can be interpreted as a money demand relation in which the opportunity cost of holding money relative to bonds is a determinant of an agent's desired money holdings. On the other hand, if $b_3 < 0$, then the money demand interpretation is no longer possible, and (2.14) could instead be a central bank policy rule. Figure 2.5, middle panel, shows the interest spread between the Danish 10 year bond rate and the deposit rate, and the lower panel shows the linear combination (2.14) with $b_3 = 14$. It is notable how well the non-stationary behaviour of money velocity and the spread cancels in the linear money demand relation.

From the perspective of monetary policy, a non-stationary spread suggests that the short-term central bank interest rate can be used as an instrument to influence money

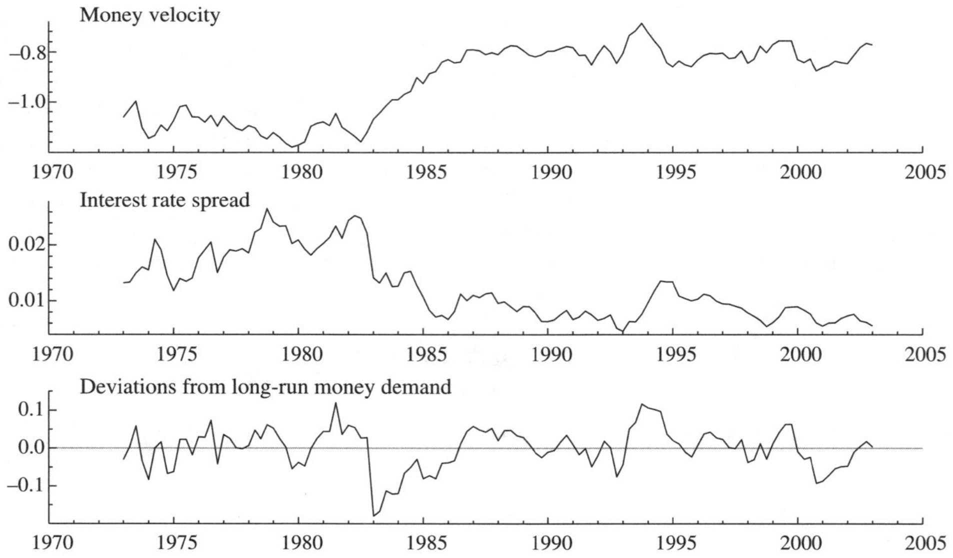

Fig 2.5 The non-stationary money velocity (upper panel). The non-stationary interest rate spread (middle panel). The stationary combination between the money velocity and the interest rate spread (lower panel).

demand. A stationary spread on the other hand signals fast adjustment between the two interest rates, such that changing the short interest rate only changes the spread in the very short run and hence leaves money demand essentially unchanged.

In a model explaining monetary transmission mechanisms, the determination of real interest rates is likely to play an important role. The Fisher parity predicts that real interest rates of maturity m are constant, i.e.

$$R_t = E_t \frac{1}{m}(\Delta_m p_{t+m}) + R_0 = \frac{1}{m} E_t(p_{t+m} - p_t) + R_0 = \frac{1}{m} E_t \sum_{i=1}^{m} \Delta p_{t+i} + R_0 \tag{2.15}$$

where R_0 is a constant real interest rate and $E_t(\Delta_m p_{t+m})/m$ is the expected value formed at time t of inflation at the period of maturity $t+m$.

If $(\Delta_m p_{t+m} - E_t^e \Delta_m p_{t+m}) \sim I(0)$, then the predictions do not deviate from the actual realization with more than a stationary error. If, in addition, $(\Delta p_t - (\Delta_m p_{t+m})/m) \sim I(0)$, then $\Delta p_t - E_t^e \Delta_m p_{t+m}$ is stationary and actual inflation can be used instead of the more correct, but unobserved, expected inflation. From (2.15) it appears that if $(R_m - \Delta p) \sim I(0)$ and $(R_b - \Delta p) \sim I(0)$ then $d_{42} = d_{52} = 0$. Also, if $d_{42} = d_{52} = 0$, then R_m and R_b must be cointegrating, $(R_m - b_4 R_b)_t \sim I(0)$ with $b_4 = 1$ for $d_{41} = d_{51}$. In this sense, stationary real interest rates are both econometrically and economically consistent with the spread and the velocity being stationary. It corresponds to the situation where real income and real money stock share the common real trend, $\sum u_{2i}$, and inflation and the two nominal interest rates share the nominal trend, $\sum u_{1i}$. This case can be formulated as a restricted version of (2.12):

$$\begin{bmatrix} m_t - p_t \\ \Delta p_t \\ y_t^r \\ R_{m,t} \\ R_{b,t} \end{bmatrix} = \begin{bmatrix} 0 & d_{12} \\ c_{21} & 0 \\ 0 & d_{12} \\ c_{21} & 0 \\ c_{21} & 0 \end{bmatrix} \begin{bmatrix} \sum u_{1i} \\ \sum u_{2i} \end{bmatrix} + \cdots \tag{2.16}$$

Though appealing from a theory point of view, (2.16) has not found much empirical support. Instead, real interest rates, interest rate spreads, and money velocity have frequently been found to be non-stationary. This suggests the presence of real and nominal interaction effects, at least over the horizon of a long business cycle.

By modifying some of the assumptions underlying the Fisher parity, the non-stationarity of real interest rates and the interest rate spread can be justified. For example, Frydman and Goldberg (2002) shows that imperfect knowledge expectations (instead of rational expectations) are likely to generate an $I(1)$ trend in the interest rate spread. Also, if agents systematically mispredict the future inflation rate (which would imply irrational agents), we would expect $(\Delta_m p_{t+m} - E_t \Delta_m p_{t+m}) \sim I(1)$ and hence $R_t - \Delta p_t \sim I(1)$. In this case, one would also expect $E_t\{(\Delta_b p_{t+b})/b - (\Delta_m p_{t+m})/m\} \sim I(1)$, and $(R_m - R_b)_t \sim I(1)$ would not be consistent with the predictions from the expectation's hypothesis (or the Fisher parity). Note, however that income from financial assets is generally taxable, whereas income from inflation is generally not so that in practise it might be more relevant to replace $R_t - \Delta p_t$ with $R_t(1 - \text{tax}_t) - \Delta p_t$.

2.6 Scenario analyses: treating prices as $I(1)$

In this case $\rho < 1$ in (2.9) implies that inflation is stationary albeit likely to be strongly autocorrelated. The representation of the vector process becomes:

$$\begin{bmatrix} m_t \\ p_t \\ y_t^r \\ R_{m,t} \\ R_{b,t} \end{bmatrix} = \begin{bmatrix} c_{11} & d_{12} \\ c_{21} & d_{22} \\ 0 & d_{32} \\ 0 & d_{42} \\ 0 & d_{52} \end{bmatrix} \begin{bmatrix} \sum u_{1i} \\ \sum u_{2i} \end{bmatrix} + \begin{bmatrix} g_1 \\ g_2 \\ g_3 \\ 0 \\ 0 \end{bmatrix} [t] + \text{stat. comp.} \tag{2.17}$$

Money and prices are represented by:

$$m_t = c_{11} \sum u_{1i} + d_{12} \sum u_{2i} + g_1 t + \text{stat. comp.}$$
$$p_t = c_{21} \sum u_{1i} + d_{22} \sum u_{2i} + g_2 t + \text{stat. comp.}$$

If $c_{11} = c_{21}$ there is long-run price homogeneity, but $(m_t - p_t) \sim I(1)$ unless $(d_{12} - d_{22}) = 0$. If $d_{12} \neq 0$ and $d_{22} = 0$, then

$$m_t - p_t = d_{12} \sum u_{2i} + (g_1 - g_2)t + \text{stat. comp.}$$

If $d_{12} = d_{32}$ then $(m_t - p_t - y_t^r) \sim I(0)$. From $\{m_t, p_t\} \sim I(1)$ it follows that $\{\Delta p, \Delta m\} \sim I(0)$, and real interest rates cannot be stationary unless $d_{42} = d_{52} = 0$.

Hence, a consequence of treating prices as $I(1)$ is that nominal interest rates should be treated as $I(0)$, unless one is prepared *a priori* to exclude the possibility of stationary real interest rates. The restricted version of (2.17) given below is economically as well as econometrically consistent with these assumptions.

$$\begin{bmatrix} m_t \\ p_t \\ y_t^r \\ R_{m,t} \\ R_{b,t} \end{bmatrix} = \begin{bmatrix} c_{11} & d_{12} \\ c_{21} & 0 \\ 0 & d_{12} \\ 0 & 0 \\ 0 & 0 \end{bmatrix} \begin{bmatrix} \sum u_{1i} \\ \sum u_{2i} \end{bmatrix} + \begin{bmatrix} g_1 \\ g_2 \\ g_3 \\ 0 \\ 0 \end{bmatrix} [t] + \text{stat. comp.} \tag{2.18}$$

However, the assumption that the long-term interest rate is stationary is at odds with arbitrage theory predicting that an asset yield should behave like a martingale difference, i.e. $E_t(\Delta R_{b,t}) = 0$, and, therefore, that the long-term nominal interest rate should be $I(1)$. According to the Fisher parity the inflation rate and the nominal interest rate should be cointegrated to yield a stationary real interest rate, so inflation rate should also be $I(1)$. Therefore, the scenario (2.18) does not seem to be able to provide a representation which satisfies theoretical as well as empirical consistency.

2.7 Concluding remarks

This chapter focused on the link between the theory model and the empirical data collected by passive observation. A general framework for translating major predictions from the theory model into testable hypotheses within the VAR model was suggested. The idea was based on a decomposition of a vector non-stationary time-series process into common stochastic and deterministic trends as well as cycles and other stationary components. This decomposition was used to show that the common trends can be cancelled by taking linear combinations of the variables and that these linear combinations potentially can be interpreted as economic steady-state relations. All this was given in a purely descriptive manner without specifying a statistical model consistent with these features. This is the purpose of the next chapter.

3

The probability approach in econometrics, and the VAR

Chapter 1 discussed Haavelmo's probability approach to empirical macroeconomics and the need to formulate a statistical model describing the data which is general enough to encompass the major features of the economic model. Because most macroeconomic data exhibit strong time dependence, it is natural to formulate the empirical model in terms of time-dependent stochastic processes. The aim of this chapter is to discuss under which simplifying assumptions on the vector time-series process the VAR model can be used as an adequate summary description of the information in the sample data. When these conditions are met we shall argue that the VAR approach can be used as a powerful methodology for inference on macroeconomic questions.

Sections 3.1 and 3.2 discuss the basic characteristics of a single time series and a vector process respectively. Section 3.3 discusses a sequential decomposition of the joint likelihood function, Section 3.4 derives the VAR model under certain simplifying assumptions on the vector process, Section 3.5 gives a general interpretion of the VAR model as a description of the behaviour of rational agents, Section 3.6 discusses the dynamic properties of the VAR model and illustrates with data from the Danish money market, and Section 3.7 concludes.

3.1 A single time-series process

To begin with, we shall look at a single variable observed over consecutive time points and discuss its time-series properties. Let $x_{s,t}$, $s = 1, \ldots, S$, $t = 1, \ldots, T$ describe S realizations of a variable x over T time periods. When $S > 1$ this could, for example describe a variable in a study based on panel data or it could describe a simulation study of a time-series process x_t, in which the number of replications is S. Here we shall focus on the case when $S = 1$, i.e. when there is just one realization $(x_1, \ldots, x_T)$ on the index set T. Since we have just one realization of the random variable x_t, we cannot make inference on the shape of the distribution or its parameter values without making simplifying assumptions. We illustrate the difficulties with two simple examples in Figures 3.1 and 3.2.

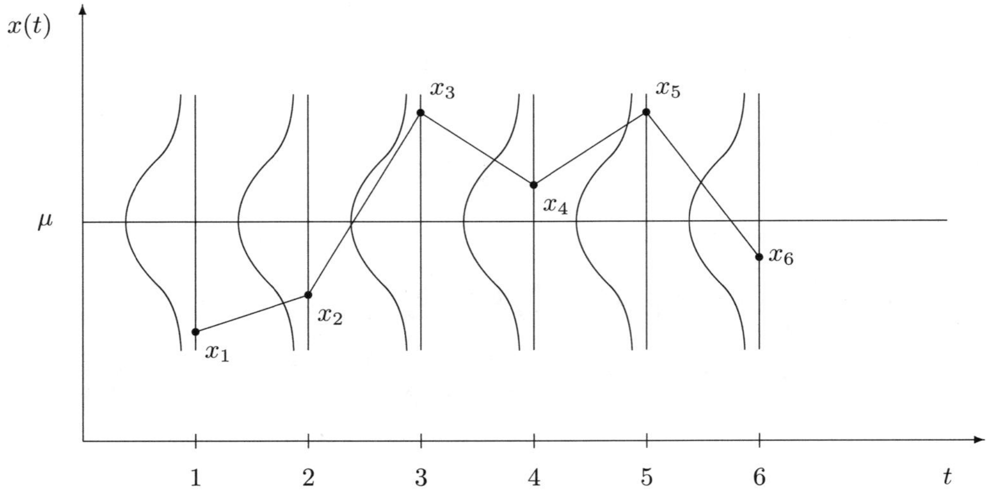

Fig 3.1 $E(x_t) = \mu$, $Var(x_t) = \sigma^2$, $t = 1, \ldots, 6$

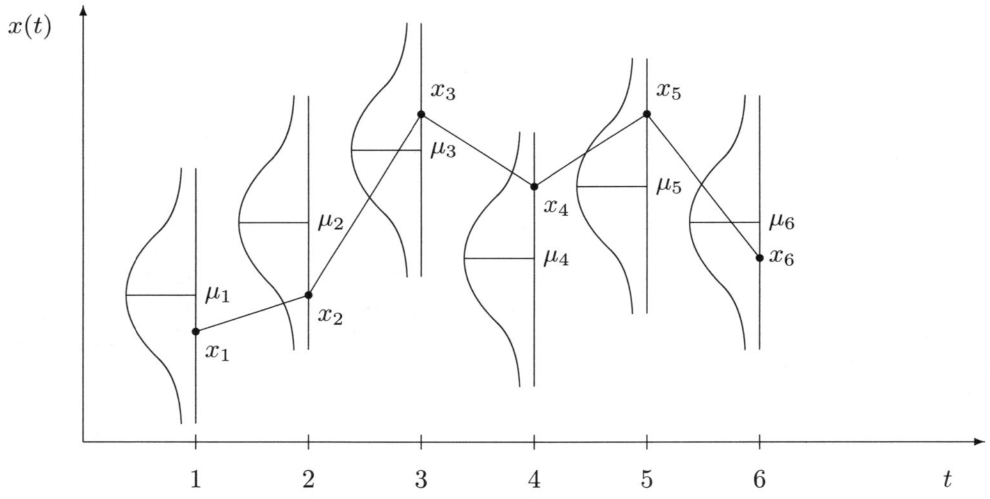

Fig 3.2 $E(x_t) = \mu_t$, $Var(x_t) = \sigma^2$, $t = 1, \ldots, 6$

In the two examples, the line connecting the realizations x_t produces the graph of the time series. For instance, in Figure 3.1 we have assumed that the distribution, the mean value and the variance are the same for each x_t, $t = 1, \ldots, T$. In Figure 3.2, the distribution and the variance are identical, but the mean varies with t. Note that the observed time graph is the same in both cases illustrating the fact, that we often need rather long time series to be able to statistically distinguish between different hypotheses in time-series models.

To be able to make statistical inference we need:

(i) a probability model for x_t, for example the normal distribution;

(ii) a sampling model for x_t, for example independent drawings.

For the normal distribution, the first two moments around the mean are sufficient to describe the variation in the data. Under this assumption, x_t, $t = 1, \ldots, T$ is described by:

$$\begin{aligned} E(x_t) &= \mu_{x,t} \\ \mathrm{Var}(x_t) &= E(x_t - \mu_t)^2 = \sigma^2_{x,t,0} \\ \mathrm{Cov}(x_t, x_{t-h}) &= E[(x_t - \mu_t)(x_{t-h} - \mu_{t-h})] = \sigma_{x,t,h} \quad h = \ldots, -1, 0, 1, \ldots \end{aligned}$$

$$E[\mathbf{x}] = E \begin{bmatrix} x_1 \\ x_2 \\ \vdots \\ x_T \end{bmatrix} = \begin{bmatrix} \mu_1 \\ \mu_2 \\ \vdots \\ \mu_T \end{bmatrix} = \boldsymbol{\mu}_{\mathbf{x}}$$

$$E[\mathbf{x} - \boldsymbol{\mu}_{\mathbf{x}}][\mathbf{x} - \boldsymbol{\mu}_{\mathbf{x}}]' = \begin{bmatrix} \sigma_{1.0} & \sigma_{1.1} & \sigma_{1.2} & \cdots & \sigma_{1.T-1} \\ \sigma_{2.1} & \sigma_{2.0} & \sigma_{2.1} & \cdots & \sigma_{2.T-2} \\ \sigma_{3.2} & \sigma_{3.1} & \sigma_{3.0} & \cdots & \sigma_{3.T-3} \\ \vdots & \vdots & \vdots & \ddots & \vdots \\ \sigma_{T.T-1} & \sigma_{T.T-2} & \sigma_{T.T-3} & \cdots & \sigma_{T.0} \end{bmatrix} = \boldsymbol{\Sigma}_{\mathbf{x}}$$

$$\mathbf{x} = \begin{bmatrix} x_1 \\ x_2 \\ \vdots \\ x_T \end{bmatrix} \sim N(\boldsymbol{\mu}_{\mathbf{x}}, \boldsymbol{\Sigma}_{\mathbf{x}}).$$

Because there is just one realization of the process at each time t, there is not enough information to make statistical inference about the underlying functional form of the distribution of each x_t, $t \in T$ and we have to make simplifying assumptions to secure that the number of parameters describing the process is fewer than the number of observations available. A typical assumption in time-series models is that each x_t has the same distribution and that the functional form is approximately normal. Furthermore, given the normal distribution, it is frequently assumed that the mean is the same, i.e. $E(x_t) = \mu_x$, for $t = 1, \ldots, T$, and that the variance is the same, i.e. $E(x_t - \mu)^2 = \sigma^2_x$, for $t = 1, \ldots, T$.

We use the following notation to describe a normal variable with (i) time varying mean and variance, (ii) time varying mean and constant variance, (iii) constant mean and time varying variance, (iv) constant mean and variance:

$$
\begin{aligned}
&\text{(i)}\ x_t \sim N(\mu_{x,t}, \sigma^2_{x,t}) && t = 1, \ldots, T;\\
&\text{(ii)}\ x_t \sim N(\mu_{x,t}, \sigma^2_{x}) && t = 1, \ldots, T;\\
&\text{(iii)}\ x_t \sim N(\mu_{x}, \sigma^2_{x,t}) && t = 1, \ldots, T;\\
&\text{(iv)}\ x_t \sim N(\mu_{x}, \sigma^2_{x}) && t = 1, \ldots, T.
\end{aligned}
$$

In this book we shall mostly discuss the mean of the process, how to estimate it and how to test hypotheses about it. Even though most economic time-series variables have a non-constant mean, we shall demonstrate that by taking linear transformations of the process we can, nevertheless, achieve a constant mean. For example, the mean of a differenced variable is often constant even though the mean of the variable itself is non-constant, i.e. $E(\Delta x_t) = E(x_t - x_{t-1}) = \mu_{\Delta x}$, even though $Ex_t = \mu_{x,t}$.

For a time-series process, time dependence is an additional problem that has to be addressed. Consecutive realizations of economic time-series process cannot usually be considered as independent drawings from the same underlying stochastic process. For the normal distribution, the time dependence between x_t and x_{t-h}, $h = \ldots, -1, 0, 1, \ldots$ for $t = 1, \ldots, T$ can be described by the covariance function. A simplifying assumption in this context is that the covariance function is a function of h, but not of t, i.e. $\sigma_{t.h} = \sigma_h$, for $t = 1, \ldots, T$. If x_t has constant mean and variance and, in addition, $\sigma_h = 0$ for all $h = 1, \ldots, T$, then $\mathbf{\Sigma}$ is a diagonal matrix and x_t is independent of x_{t-h} for $h = 1, \ldots, t$. In this case we say that:

$$x_t \sim IN(\mu_x, \sigma^2_x),$$

where $\sim$ denotes distributed, I is a shorthand notation for *I*ndependent and N for *N*ormal. Even though economic variables are generally strongly time dependent, it is nevertheless often possible to achieve independence by conditioning on past observations. This will be discussed in Section 3.3.

3.2 A vector process

We shall now move on to the more interesting case where we observe a vector of p variables. In this case, we need additionally to discuss covariances between the variables at time t as well as their covariances between t and $t - h$. The covariances contain information about static and dynamic relationships between the variables which we would like to uncover using econometrics. For notational simplicity, x_t will here be used to denote both a random variable and its realization.

Consider the $p \times 1$ dimensional vector $\mathbf{x}_t$:

$$\mathbf{x}_t = \begin{bmatrix} x_{1,t} \\ x_{2,t} \\ \vdots \\ x_{p,t} \end{bmatrix}, \quad t = 1, \ldots, T.$$

We introduce the following notation for the case when no simplifying assumptions have been made:

$$E[\mathbf{x}_t] = \begin{bmatrix} \mu_{1,t} \\ \mu_{2,t} \\ \vdots \\ \mu_{p,t} \end{bmatrix} = \boldsymbol{\mu}_t, \qquad \mathrm{Cov}[\mathbf{x}_t, \mathbf{x}_{t-h}] = \begin{bmatrix} \sigma_{11.h} & \sigma_{12.h} & \cdots & \sigma_{1p.h} \\ \sigma_{21.h} & \sigma_{22.h} & \cdots & \sigma_{2p.h} \\ \vdots & \vdots & \ddots & \vdots \\ \sigma_{p1.h} & \sigma_{p2.h} & \cdots & \sigma_{pp.h} \end{bmatrix} = \boldsymbol{\Sigma}_{t.h}$$

$$t = 1, \ldots, T, \quad h = 0, 1, 2, \ldots$$

We shall now assume that the same distribution applies for all $\mathbf{x}_t$ and that the distribution is approximately normal so that the first two moments around the mean (central moments) are sufficient to describe the variation in the data. We introduce the notation:

$$\mathbf{Z} = \begin{bmatrix} \mathbf{x}_1 \\ \mathbf{x}_2 \\ \vdots \\ \mathbf{x}_T \end{bmatrix}, \qquad E[\mathbf{Z}] = \begin{bmatrix} \boldsymbol{\mu}_1 \\ \boldsymbol{\mu}_2 \\ \vdots \\ \boldsymbol{\mu}_T \end{bmatrix} = \tilde{\boldsymbol{\mu}} \tag{3.1}$$

where $\mathbf{Z}$ is a $Tp \times 1$ vector. The covariance matrix $\tilde{\boldsymbol{\Sigma}}$ is given by

$$E[(\mathbf{Z} - \tilde{\boldsymbol{\mu}})(\mathbf{Z} - \tilde{\boldsymbol{\mu}})'] = \begin{bmatrix} \boldsymbol{\Sigma}_{1.0} & \boldsymbol{\Sigma}'_{2.1} & \cdots & \boldsymbol{\Sigma}'_{T-1.T-2} & \boldsymbol{\Sigma}'_{T.T-1} \\ \boldsymbol{\Sigma}_{2.1} & \boldsymbol{\Sigma}_{2.0} & & \cdots & \boldsymbol{\Sigma}'_{T.T-2} \\ \vdots & \vdots & \ddots & \vdots & \vdots \\ \boldsymbol{\Sigma}_{T-1.T-2} & \vdots & & \boldsymbol{\Sigma}_{T-1.0} & \boldsymbol{\Sigma}'_{T.1} \\ \boldsymbol{\Sigma}_{T.T-1} & \boldsymbol{\Sigma}_{T.T-2} & \cdots & \boldsymbol{\Sigma}_{T.1} & \boldsymbol{\Sigma}_{T.0} \end{bmatrix} = \underset{(Tp \times Tp)}{\tilde{\boldsymbol{\Sigma}}}$$

where $\Sigma_{t.h} = \mathrm{Cov}(x_t, x_{t-h}) = E(x_t - \mu_t)(x_{t-h} - \mu_{t-h})'$. The above notation provides a completely general description of a multivariate normal vector time-series process. Since there are far more parameters than observations available for estimation, it has no utility from a practical point of view and we need simplifying assumptions to reduce the number of parameters. Empirical models are typically based on the following assumptions:

- $\boldsymbol{\Sigma}_{t.h} = \boldsymbol{\Sigma}_h$, for all $t \in T$, $h = \ldots, -1, 0, 1, \ldots$
- $\boldsymbol{\mu}_t = \boldsymbol{\mu}$ for all $t \in T$.

We can now write the mean and the covariances of the data matrix in the more parsimonious form:

$$\tilde{\boldsymbol{\mu}} = \begin{bmatrix} \boldsymbol{\mu} \\ \boldsymbol{\mu} \\ \vdots \\ \boldsymbol{\mu} \end{bmatrix}, \quad \tilde{\boldsymbol{\Sigma}} = \begin{bmatrix} \boldsymbol{\Sigma}_0 & \boldsymbol{\Sigma}_1' & \Sigma'_2 & \cdots & \boldsymbol{\Sigma}'_{T-1} \\ \boldsymbol{\Sigma}_1 & \boldsymbol{\Sigma}_0 & \boldsymbol{\Sigma}'_1 & \ddots & \vdots \\ \boldsymbol{\Sigma}_2 & \boldsymbol{\Sigma}_1 & \boldsymbol{\Sigma}_0 & \ddots & \boldsymbol{\Sigma}_2' \\ \vdots & \ddots & \ddots & \ddots & \boldsymbol{\Sigma}_1' \\ \boldsymbol{\Sigma}_{T-1} & \cdots & \boldsymbol{\Sigma}_2 & \boldsymbol{\Sigma}_1 & \boldsymbol{\Sigma}_0 \end{bmatrix}.$$

The above two assumptions for infinite T define a weakly stationary process. When these two assumptions are satisfied the VAR model to be defined in Section 3.4 will have constant parameters.

Definition 1 Let $\{\mathbf{x}_t\}$ be a stochastic process (an ordered series of random variables) for $t = \ldots, -1, 0, 1, 2, \ldots$ If

$$\begin{aligned} E[\mathbf{x}_t] &= -\infty < \boldsymbol{\mu} < \infty \;\; \textit{for all } t, \\ E[\mathbf{x}_t - \boldsymbol{\mu}]^2 &= \boldsymbol{\Sigma}_0 < \infty \;\; \textit{for all } t, \\ E[(\mathbf{x}_t - \boldsymbol{\mu})(\mathbf{x}_{t+h} - \boldsymbol{\mu})] &= \boldsymbol{\Sigma}_h < \infty \;\; \textit{for all } t \textit{ and } h = 1, 2, \ldots \end{aligned}$$

then $\{\mathbf{x}_t\}$ is said to be weakly stationary. Strict stationarity requires that the distribution of $(\mathbf{x}_{t_1}, \ldots, \mathbf{x}_{t_k})$ is the same as $(\mathbf{x}_{t_1+h}, \ldots, \mathbf{x}_{t_k+h})$ for $h = \ldots, -1, 0, 1, 2, \ldots$.

3.2.1 An illustration

The data set introduced here will be used throughout the book to illustrate the numerous questions that can be asked within the cointegrated VAR model and how they can be answered. As a matter of fact, the development of many of the subsequent cointegration procedures were more or less forced upon us as a result of the empirical analyses being performed on this data set. The data vector, given by $[m_t^r, y_t^r, \Delta p_t, R_{m,t}, R_{b,t}]$, $t =$ 1973:1,…,2003:1, was already defined in the previous chapter.

Figures 3.3 and 3.4 show the graphs of the data in levels and in first differences. A visual inspection reveals that the assumption of a constant mean does not seem appropriate for the level of the variables, whereas much more so for the differenced data. The assumption of a constant variance is more difficult to assess from the data in levels, but seems approximately satisfied for the differenced data even though there is some evidence of higher variability in the real income, the inflation rate, and the interest rates in the first part of the sample.

Furthermore, if the marginal processes are normal then the observations should lie symmetrically on both sides of the mean. This seems approximately to be the case for real money, but for real income and the two interest rates there are some 'outlier' observations. The question is whether these observations are too far away from the mean to be considered realizations from a normal distribution. At this stage it is a good idea to check the economic calendar to find out whether the outlier observations can be related to some significant economic interventions or reforms.

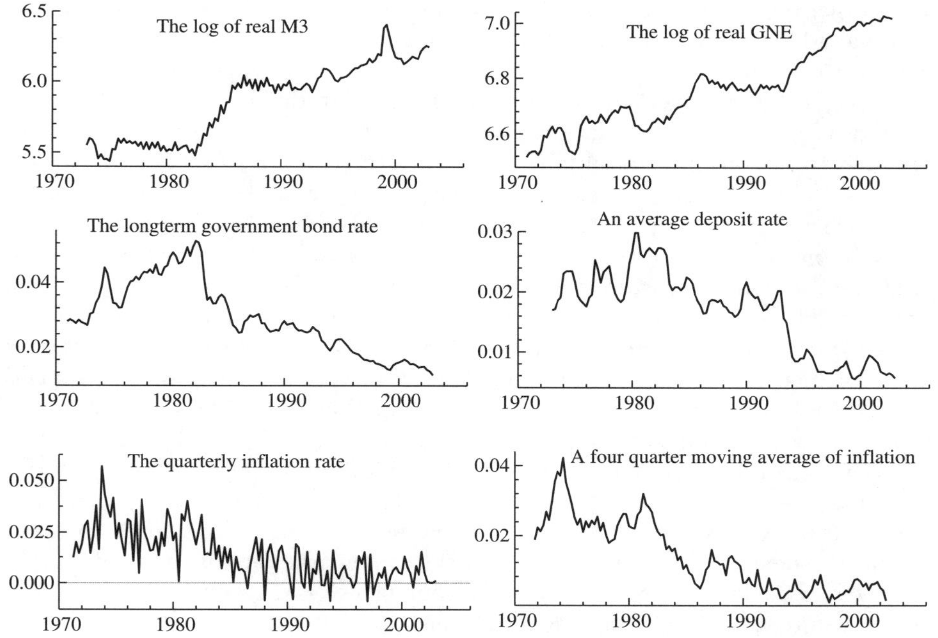

Fig 3.3 The Danish data in levels.

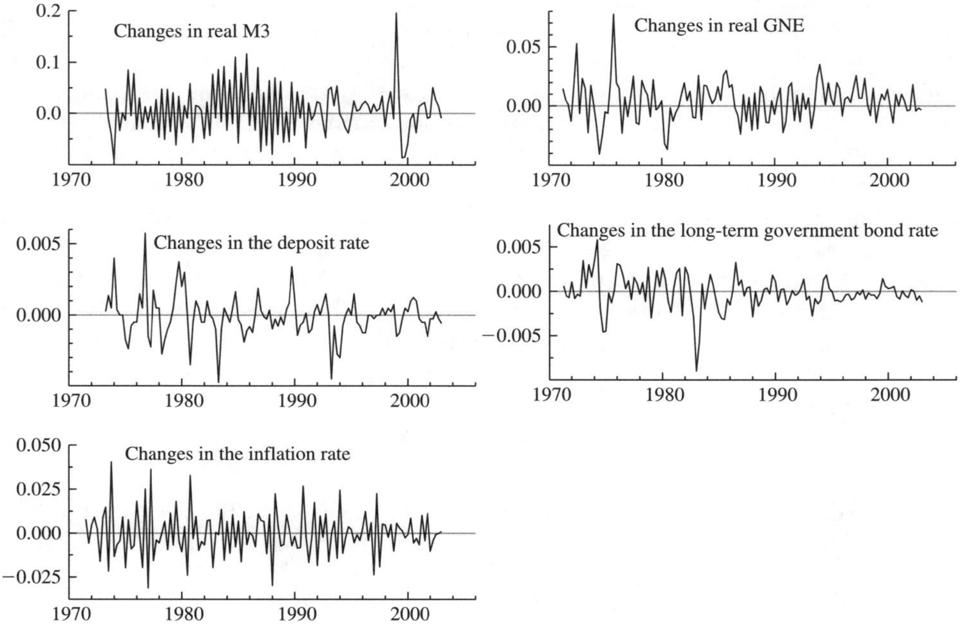

Fig 3.4 The Danish data in first differences.

The outlier observation in real income is likely to be related to a temporary removal of the value added tax rate in 1975:4. Denmark had experienced a stagnating domestic demand in the period after the first oil shock and to boost aggregate activity the government decided to remove VAT for one quarter and gradually put it back again over the next two quarters. The outlier observation in the bond rate is related to the lifting of previous restrictions on capital movements and the start of the 'hard' EMS in 1983, whereas the outliers in the deposit rate are related to Central Bank interventions.

These are realistic examples that point at the need to include additional information on interventions and institutional reforms in the empirical model. This can be done by including new variables measuring the effect of institutional reforms, or if such variables are not available by using dummy variables as a proxy for the change in institutions.

At the start of the empirical analysis, it is not always possible to know whether an intervention was strong enough to produce an 'extraordinary' effect or not. Essentially every single month, quarter, year is subject to some kind of political intervention, but most of them have a minor impact on the data and the model. Thus, if an ordinary intervention does not 'stick out' as an outlier, it will be treated as a random shock for practical reasons. Major interventions, like removing restrictions on capital movements, joining the EMS, etc. are likely to have a much more fundamental impact on economic behaviour and hence need to be included in the systematic part of the model. Ignoring this problem is likely to bias all estimates of our model and result in invalid inference. Chapter 6 will deal with this important problem.

Thus, a visual inspection of the data and their time-series properties is a useful first check of the assumptions of the VAR model. Based on the graphs, we get an impression of whether $x_{i,t}$ looks stationary with constant mean and variance, or alternatively for $\Delta x_{i,t}$. If the data in levels look trending whereas the differenced data are strongly mean reverting, we can solve the problem by respecifying the VAR in equilibrium-correction form. This will be demonstrated in Chapter 4. When the visual inspection indicates that the data, whether in levels or in differences, do not satisfy the constant mean and variance assumption, it is a good idea to consult the economic calendar to find out whether such departures from the assumptions coincide with specific reforms or interventions. The next step is then to include this information in the model and find out whether the intervention or reform have had a permanent or transitory effect and whether it has fundamentally changed the parameters of the model. In the latter case, the intervention is likely to define a regime shift and the model would need to be re-specified allowing for the shift in the model structure. The econometric modelling of intervention effects in the VAR model will be discussed in more detail in Chapter 6.

3.3 Reviewing some useful results

We shall first give a review of the simple multiplicative rule to calculate joint probabilities and illustrate it based on four dependent events, A, B, C and D:

$$\begin{aligned}P(A \cap B \cap C \cap D) &= P(A|B \cap C \cap D)P(B \cap C \cap D)\\ &= P(A|B \cap C \cap D)P(B|C \cap D)P(C \cap D)\\ &= P(A|B \cap C \cap D)P(B|C \cap D)P(C|D)P(D).\end{aligned}$$

Note that the conditional events are now independent, even though the events themselves are strongly dependent. This idea will be used below in the derivation of conditional and marginal distributions and then in the next section to transform highly dependent economic variables to independent conditional variables.

We consider two normally distributed random variables $y_{1,t}$ and $y_{2,t}$ with the joint distribution:

$$\mathbf{Y} \sim N(\mathbf{m}, \mathbf{S})$$

$$\mathbf{Y} = \begin{bmatrix} y_{1,t} \\ y_{2,t} \end{bmatrix}, \quad E[\mathbf{Y}] = \begin{bmatrix} m_1 \\ m_2 \end{bmatrix}, \quad \text{Cov}\begin{bmatrix} y_{1,t} \\ y_{2,t} \end{bmatrix} = \begin{bmatrix} s_{11} & s_{12} \\ s_{21} & s_{22} \end{bmatrix}.$$

The marginal distributions for $y_{1,t}$ and $y_{2,t}$ are given by

$$\begin{aligned} y_{1,t} &\sim N(m_1, s_{11}) \\ y_{2,t} &\sim N(m_2, s_{22}). \end{aligned}$$

The conditional distribution for $y_{1,t}|y_{2,t}$ is given by

$$(y_{1,t}|y_{2,t}) \sim N(m_{1.2}, s_{11.2})$$

where

$$\begin{aligned} m_{1.2} &= m_1 + s_{12}s_{22}^{-1}(y_{2,t} - m_2) \\ &= (m_1 - s_{12}s_{22}^{-1}m_2) + s_{12}s_{22}^{-1}y_{2,t} \\ &= \beta_0 + \beta_1 y_{2,t} \end{aligned} \tag{3.2}$$

and

$$s_{11.2} = s_{11} - s_{12}s_{22}^{-1}s_{21}. \tag{3.3}$$

The joint distribution of $\mathbf{Y}$ can now be expressed as the product of the conditional and the marginal distribution:

$$\underbrace{P(y_{1,t}, y_{2,t}; \boldsymbol{\theta})}_{\text{The joint distribution}} = \underbrace{P(y_{1,t}|y_{2,t}; \boldsymbol{\theta}_1)}_{\text{The conditional distribution}} \times \underbrace{P(y_{2,t}; \boldsymbol{\theta}_2)}_{\text{The marginal distribution}}. \tag{3.4}$$

3.4 Deriving the VAR[1]

The purpose of this section is to demonstrate (i) that the joint likelihood function $P(\mathbf{X}; \boldsymbol{\theta})$ can be sequentially decomposed into T conditional probabilities $P(\mathbf{x}_t \mid \mathbf{x}_{t-1,\dots,}\mathbf{x}_1; \mathbf{X}_0, \boldsymbol{\theta})$, and (ii) that the conditional process $(\mathbf{x}_t \mid \mathbf{x}_{t-1,\dots,}\mathbf{x}_1; \mathbf{X}_0)$ has a parameterization that corresponds to the vector autoregressive model.

[1]This section draws heavily on Hendry and Richard (1983).

The empirical analysis begins with the data matrix $\mathbf{X} = [\mathbf{x}_1, \ldots, \mathbf{x}_T]'$ where $\mathbf{x}_t$ is a $(p \times 1)$ vector of variables. Under the assumption that the observed data $\mathbf{X}$ is a realization of a stochastic process, we can express the joint probability of $\mathbf{X}$ given the initial value $\mathbf{X}_0$ and the parameter value $\boldsymbol{\theta}$ describing the stochastic process:

$$P(\mathbf{X}|\mathbf{X}_0; \boldsymbol{\theta}) = P(\mathbf{x}_1, \mathbf{x}_2, \ldots, \mathbf{x}_T|\mathbf{X}_0; \boldsymbol{\theta}).$$

For a given probability function, maximum likelihood estimates can be found by maximizing the likelihood function. Here we shall restrict the discussion to the multivariate normal distribution. To express the joint probability of $\mathbf{X}|\mathbf{X}_0$, it is convenient to use the stacked process $\mathbf{Z}' = \mathbf{x}_1', \mathbf{x}_2', \mathbf{x}_3', \ldots, \mathbf{x}_T' \sim N_{Tp}(\boldsymbol{\mu}, \boldsymbol{\Sigma})$ defined in (3.1) instead of the $(T \times p)$ data matrix $\mathbf{X}$. Since $\boldsymbol{\mu}$ is $Tp \times 1$ and $\boldsymbol{\Sigma}$ is $Tp \times Tp$, there are many more parameters than observations without simplifying assumptions. But even if we impose simplifying restrictions on the mean and the covariances of the process, they are not directly informative about economic behaviour. Therefore, by decomposing the joint process into a conditional process and a marginal process and then sequentially repeating the decomposition for the marginal process we can obtain a more useful formulation:

$$\begin{aligned} &P(\mathbf{x}_1, \mathbf{x}_2, \mathbf{x}_3, \ldots, \mathbf{x}_T|\mathbf{X}_0; \boldsymbol{\theta}) \\ &\quad = P(\mathbf{x}_T|\mathbf{x}_{T-1}, \ldots, \mathbf{x}_1, \mathbf{X}_0; \boldsymbol{\theta}) P(\mathbf{x}_{T-1}, \mathbf{x}_{T-2}, \ldots, \mathbf{x}_1|\mathbf{X}_0; \boldsymbol{\theta}) \\ &\quad\ \vdots \\ &\quad = \prod_{t=1}^{T} P(\mathbf{x}_t|\mathbf{X}_{t-1}^0; \boldsymbol{\theta}) \end{aligned} \tag{3.5}$$

where

$$\mathbf{X}_{t-1}^0 = [\mathbf{x}_{t-1}, \mathbf{x}_{t-2}, \ldots, \mathbf{x}_1, \mathbf{X}_0].$$

We will now show that the VAR model is approximately the conditional process

$$\{\mathbf{x}_t|\mathbf{X}_{t-1}^0\} \sim N_p(\boldsymbol{\mu}_t, \boldsymbol{\Omega}).$$

By using the rules given in Section 3.3 for calculating the mean and the variance of the conditional distribution (3.2)–(3.3), it is now possible to see how $\boldsymbol{\mu}_t$ and $\boldsymbol{\Omega}$ are related to $\boldsymbol{\mu}$ and $\boldsymbol{\Sigma}$. We first decompose the data into two sets, the vector $\mathbf{x}_t$ and the conditioning set $\mathbf{X}_{t-1}^0$, i.e. $\mathbf{X} = \begin{bmatrix} \mathbf{x}_t \\ \mathbf{X}_{t-1}^0 \end{bmatrix}$. Using the notation of Section 3.3, we write the marginal and the conditional process:

$$\mathbf{y}_{1,t} = \mathbf{x}_t, \qquad \mathbf{m}_1 = E[\mathbf{x}_t],$$

$$\mathbf{y}_{2,t} = \begin{bmatrix} \mathbf{x}_{t-1} \\ \mathbf{x}_{t-2} \\ \vdots \\ \mathbf{x}_1 \end{bmatrix}, \qquad \mathbf{m}_2 = \begin{bmatrix} E[\mathbf{x}_{t-1}] \\ E[\mathbf{x}_{t-2}] \\ \vdots \\ E[\mathbf{x}_1] \end{bmatrix},$$

$$\tilde{\mathbf{\Sigma}} = \left[\begin{array}{c|ccc} \mathbf{\Sigma}_0 & \mathbf{\Sigma}'_1 & \cdots & \mathbf{\Sigma}'_{T-1} \\ \hline \mathbf{\Sigma}_1 & \mathbf{\Sigma}_0 & \mathbf{\Sigma}'_1 & \vdots \\ \vdots & \ddots & \ddots & \mathbf{\Sigma}'_1 \\ \mathbf{\Sigma}_{T-1} & \cdots & \mathbf{\Sigma}_1 & \mathbf{\Sigma}_0 \end{array}\right] = \begin{bmatrix} \mathbf{\Sigma}_{11} & \mathbf{\Sigma}_{12} \\ \mathbf{\Sigma}_{21} & \mathbf{\Sigma}_{22} \end{bmatrix}.$$

We can now derive the parameters of the conditional model:

$$(\mathbf{x}_t | \mathbf{X}^0_{t-1}) \sim N(\boldsymbol{\mu}_t, \mathbf{\Sigma}_{11.2})$$

where

$$\boldsymbol{\mu}_t = \mathbf{m}_1 + \mathbf{\Sigma}_{12}\mathbf{\Sigma}_{22}^{-1}(\mathbf{X}^0_{t-1} - \mathbf{m}_2) \tag{3.6}$$

and

$$\mathbf{\Sigma}_{11.2} = \mathbf{\Sigma}_{11} - \mathbf{\Sigma}_{12}\mathbf{\Sigma}_{22}^{-1}\mathbf{\Sigma}_{21}. \tag{3.7}$$

The difference between the observed value of the process and its conditional mean is denoted $\boldsymbol{\varepsilon}_t$:

$$\mathbf{x}_t - \boldsymbol{\mu}_t = \boldsymbol{\varepsilon}_t.$$

Inserting the expression for the conditional mean gives:

$$\mathbf{x}_t = \mathbf{m}_1 + \mathbf{\Sigma}_{12}\mathbf{\Sigma}_{22}^{-1}(\mathbf{X}^0_{t-1} - \mathbf{m}_2) + \boldsymbol{\varepsilon}_t$$
$$\mathbf{x}_t = \mathbf{m}_1 - \mathbf{\Sigma}_{12}\mathbf{\Sigma}_{22}^{-1}\mathbf{m}_2 + \mathbf{\Sigma}_{12}\mathbf{\Sigma}_{22}^{-1}\mathbf{X}^0_{t-1} + \boldsymbol{\varepsilon}_t.$$

Using the notation: $\boldsymbol{\mu}_0 = \mathbf{m}_1 - \mathbf{\Sigma}_{12}\ \mathbf{\Sigma}_{22}^{-1}\mathbf{m}_2$, $[\mathbf{\Pi}_1, \mathbf{\Pi}_2, \ldots, \mathbf{\Pi}_{T-1}] = \mathbf{\Sigma}_{12}\ \mathbf{\Sigma}_{22}^{-1}$ and assuming that $\mathbf{\Pi}_{k+1}, \mathbf{\Pi}_{k+2}, \ldots, \mathbf{\Pi}_{T-1} = \mathbf{0}$, we arrive at the kth order vector autoregressive model:

$$\mathbf{x}_t = \boldsymbol{\mu}_0 + \mathbf{\Pi}_1\mathbf{x}_{t-1} + \cdots + \mathbf{\Pi}_k\mathbf{x}_{t-k} + \boldsymbol{\varepsilon}_t, \quad t = 1, \ldots, T \tag{3.8}$$

where $\boldsymbol{\varepsilon}_t$ is $NI_p(\mathbf{0}, \mathbf{\Omega})$ and $\mathbf{x}_0, \ldots, \mathbf{x}_{-k+1}$ are assumed fixed.

If the assumption that $\mathbf{X} = [\mathbf{x}_1, \mathbf{x}_2, \ldots, \mathbf{x}_T]$ is multivariate normal $(\tilde{\boldsymbol{\mu}}, \boldsymbol{\Sigma})$ is correct, then it follows that (3.8):

- is linear in the parameters;
- has constant parameters;
- has normally distributed errors ε_t.

Note that the constancy of parameters depends on the constancy of the covariance matrices $\boldsymbol{\Sigma}_{12}$ and $\boldsymbol{\Sigma}_{22}$. If any of them change as a result of a reform or intervention during the sample, both the intercept, $\boldsymbol{\mu}_0$, and the 'slope coefficients' $\boldsymbol{\Pi}_1, \ldots, \boldsymbol{\Pi}_k$ are likely to change. Thus assumptions about parameter constancy clearly depend on the context, and usually require that all major known structural changes are modelled for the relevant time period.

3.5 Interpreting the VAR model

We have shown that the VAR model is essentially a reformulation of the covariances of the data. The question is whether it can be interpreted in terms of rational economic behaviour, and if so, whether it could be used as a 'design of experiment' when data are collected by passive observation. The idea, drawing on Hendry and Richard (1983), is to interpret the conditional mean $\boldsymbol{\mu}_t$ of the VAR model

$$\boldsymbol{\mu}_t = E_{t-1}(\mathbf{x}_t \mid \mathbf{x}_{t-1}, \ldots, \mathbf{x}_{t-k}) = \boldsymbol{\mu}_0 + \boldsymbol{\Pi}_1 \mathbf{x}_{t-1} + \cdots + \boldsymbol{\Pi}_k \mathbf{x}_{t-k}, \tag{3.9}$$

as describing agents' plans at time $t-1$ given the available information $\mathbf{X}^0_{t-1} = [\mathbf{x}_{t-1}, \ldots, \mathbf{x}_{t-k}]$. According to the assumptions of the VAR model, the difference between the mean and the actual realization is a white-noise process

$$\mathbf{x}_t - \boldsymbol{\mu}_t = \boldsymbol{\varepsilon}_t, \quad \boldsymbol{\varepsilon}_t \sim NI_p(\mathbf{0}, \boldsymbol{\Omega}). \tag{3.10}$$

Thus, the $NI_p(\mathbf{0}, \boldsymbol{\Omega})$ assumption in (3.10) is consistent with economic agents who are rational in the sense that they do not make systematic errors when they make plans for time t based on the available information at time $t-1$. For example, a VAR model with autocorrelated and or heteroscedastic residuals would describe agents that do not use all information in the data as efficiently as possible. This is because by including the systematic variation left in the residuals they could improve the accuracy with which they implement their plans. Therefore, checking the assumptions of the model, i.e. checking the white-noise requirement of the residuals, is not only crucial for correct statistical inference, but also for the economic interpretation of the model as a rough description of the behaviour of rational agents.

As an illustration, Figure 3.5 shows the graphs of the standardized residuals from the VAR(2) model based on the Danish data.

The residuals do not look too systematically behaved, though a few outlier observations can be found, approximately corresponding to the interventions and reforms discussed above.

Unfortunately, in many economic applications, the multivariate normality assumption is not satisfied for the VAR in its simplest form (3.8). Since in general, statistical inference

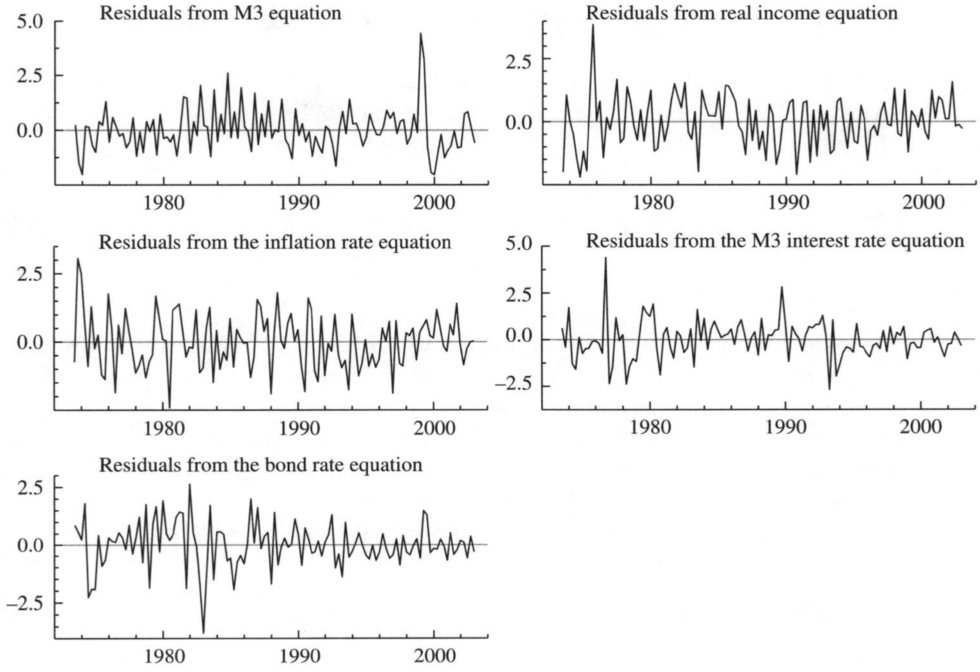

Fig 3.5 The graphs of the residuals from a VAR(2) model of the Danish data.

is valid only to the extent that the assumptions of the underlying model are satisfied, this is potentially a serious problem. Therefore, we have to ask whether it is possible to modify the baseline VAR model (3.8) so that it preserves its attractiveness as a convenient description of the basic properties of the data, while at the same time yielding valid inference.

Simulation studies have shown that valid statistical inference is sensitive to violation of some of the assumptions, such as parameter non-constancy, autocorrelated residuals (the higher, the worse) and skewed residuals, while quite robust to others, such as excess kurtosis and residual heteroscedasticity. This will be discussed in more detail in Chapter 5.

Whatever the case, direct or indirect testing of the assumptions is crucial for the success of the empirical application. As soon as we understand the reasons why the model fails to satisfy the assumptions, it is often possible to modify the model, so that in the end we can have a statistically 'well-behaved' model. Important tools in this context are:

- the use of intervention dummies to account for significant political or institutional events during the sample;
- conditioning on weakly or strongly exogenous variables;
- checking the measurements of the chosen variables;
- changing the sample period to avoid fundamental regime shift or splitting the sample into more homogenous periods.

How to use these tools will be further discussed in the subsequent chapters.

3.6 The dynamic properties of the VAR process

The dynamic properties of the process can be investigated by calculating the roots of the VAR process (3.8). It is convenient to formulate the VAR as a polynomial in the lag operator L, where $L^i\mathbf{x}_t = \mathbf{x}_{t-i}$:

$$\begin{aligned}(\mathbf{I} - \mathbf{\Pi}_1 L - \cdots - \mathbf{\Pi}_k L^k)\mathbf{x}_t &= \mathbf{\Phi}\mathbf{D}_t + \boldsymbol{\varepsilon}_t, \\ \mathbf{\Pi}(L)\mathbf{x}_t &= \mathbf{\Phi}\mathbf{D}_t + \boldsymbol{\varepsilon}_t,\end{aligned} \tag{3.11}$$

and the model has been extended to contain $\mathbf{D}_t$, a vector of deterministic components, such as a constant, seasonal dummies and intervention dummies. The autoregressive formulation is useful for expressing hypotheses on economic behaviour, whereas the moving average representation is useful when examining the properties of the process. When the process is stationary, the latter representation can be found directly by inverting the VAR model so that $\mathbf{x}_t$, $t = 1, \ldots, T$, is expressed as a function of past and present shocks, $\boldsymbol{\varepsilon}_{t-j}$, $j = 0, 1, \ldots$, initial values $\mathbf{X}^0$, and deterministic components $\mathbf{D}_t$:

$$\mathbf{x}_t = \mathbf{\Pi}^{-1}(L)(\mathbf{\Phi}\mathbf{D}_t + \boldsymbol{\varepsilon}_t) + \tilde{\mathbf{X}}^0, \quad t = 1, \ldots, T \tag{3.12}$$

$$= |\mathbf{\Pi}(L)|^{-1}\mathbf{\Pi}^a(L)(\mathbf{\Phi}\mathbf{D}_t + \boldsymbol{\varepsilon}_t) + \tilde{\mathbf{X}}^0, \quad t = 1, \ldots, T \tag{3.13}$$

$$= (\mathbf{I} + \mathbf{C}_1 L + \mathbf{C}_2 L^2 + \cdots)(\mathbf{\Phi}\mathbf{D}_t + \boldsymbol{\varepsilon}_t) + \tilde{\mathbf{X}}^0, \quad t = 1, \ldots, T \tag{3.14}$$

where $\tilde{\mathbf{X}}^0$ summarizes the effect of the initial values of the process and its dynamics, $|\mathbf{\Pi}(L)| = \det(\mathbf{\Pi}(L))$ and $\mathbf{\Pi}^a(L)$ is the adjunct matrix of $\mathbf{\Pi}(L)$. Johansen (1995), Chapter 2 gives a recursive formula for $\mathbf{C}_j = f(\mathbf{\Pi}_1, \ldots, \mathbf{\Pi}_k)$ when the VAR process is stationary. When the VAR process is non-stationary $\mathbf{\Pi}(L)$ is non-invertible and the $\mathbf{C}_j$ matrices have to be derived under the assumption of reduced rank. This case will be discussed in Chapter 5.

3.6.1 The roots of the characteristic function

To calculate the roots of the VAR process, we consider first the characteristic polynomial:

$$\begin{aligned}\mathbf{\Pi}(z) &= \mathbf{I} - \mathbf{\Pi}_1 z - \cdots - \mathbf{\Pi}_k z^k, \\ (\mathbf{\Pi}(z))^{-1} &= |\mathbf{\Pi}(z)|^{-1}\mathbf{\Pi}^a(z).\end{aligned}$$

We shall first illustrate that the roots of $|\mathbf{\Pi}(z)| = 0$ summarize important information about the dynamics and the stability of the process. We assume a stationary two-dimensional VAR(2) model:

$$(\mathbf{I} - \mathbf{\Pi}_1 L - \mathbf{\Pi}_2 L^2)\mathbf{x}_t = \mathbf{\Phi}\mathbf{D}_t + \boldsymbol{\varepsilon}_t.$$

The characteristic function is:

$$
\begin{aligned}
\mathbf{\Pi}(z) &= \mathbf{I} - \begin{bmatrix} \pi_{1.11} & \pi_{1.12} \\ \pi_{1.21} & \pi_{1.22} \end{bmatrix} z - \begin{bmatrix} \pi_{2.11} & \pi_{2.12} \\ \pi_{2.21} & \pi_{2.22} \end{bmatrix} z^2 \\
&= \mathbf{I} - \begin{bmatrix} \pi_{1.11}z & \pi_{1.12}z \\ \pi_{1.21}z & \pi_{1.22}z \end{bmatrix} - \begin{bmatrix} \pi_{2.11}z^2 & \pi_{2.12}z^2 \\ \pi_{2.21}z^2 & \pi_{2.22}z^2 \end{bmatrix} \\
&= \begin{bmatrix} (1 - \pi_{1.11}z - \pi_{2.11}z^2) & (-\pi_{1.12}z - \pi_{2.12}z^2) \\ (-\pi_{1.21}z - \pi_{2.21}z^2) & (1 - \pi_{1.22}z - \pi_{2.22}z^2) \end{bmatrix}
\end{aligned}
$$

and

$$
\begin{aligned}
|\mathbf{\Pi}(z)| &= (1 - \pi_{1.11}z - \pi_{2.11}z^2)(1 - \pi_{1.22}z - \pi_{2.22}z^2) \\
&\quad - (\pi_{1.12}z + \pi_{2.12}z^2)(\pi_{1.21}z + \pi_{2.21}z^2), \\
&= 1 - a_1 z - a_2 z^2 - a_3 z^3 - a_4 z^4, \\
&= (1 - \rho_1 z)(1 - \rho_2 z)(1 - \rho_3 z)(1 - \rho_4 z),
\end{aligned}
$$

i.e. the determinant is a fourth-order polynomial in z which gives us four characteristic roots, $z_1 = 1/\rho_1, \ldots, z_4 = 1/\rho_4$, when solving for $|\mathbf{\Pi}(z)| = \mathbf{0}$. These characteristic roots contain useful information about the dynamic behaviour of the process.

Continuing with the two-dimensional VAR(2) model:

$$
\begin{aligned}
\mathbf{x}_t &= \frac{\mathbf{\Pi}^a(L)(\mathbf{\Phi}\mathbf{D}_t + \boldsymbol{\varepsilon}_t)}{(1-\rho_1 L)(1-\rho_2 L)(1-\rho_3 L)(1-\rho_4 L)} + \tilde{\mathbf{X}}^0, \quad t = 1, \ldots, T, \\
&= \left(\frac{\mathbf{\Pi}_1^a L + \mathbf{\Pi}_2^a L^2}{(1-\rho_2 L)(1-\rho_3 L)(1-\rho_4 L)} \right) \left(\frac{\boldsymbol{\varepsilon}_t + \mathbf{\Phi}\mathbf{D}_t}{(1-\rho_1 L)} \right) + \tilde{\mathbf{X}}^0, \quad t = 1, \ldots, T,
\end{aligned}
$$

for $t = 1, \ldots, T$. As an example of the dynamic behaviour of the process we expand the first root component $(1 - \rho_1 L)^{-1}(\boldsymbol{\varepsilon}_t + \mathbf{\Phi}\mathbf{D}_t) = (1 + \rho_1 L + \rho_1^2 L^2 + \cdots)(\boldsymbol{\varepsilon}_t + \mathbf{\Phi}\mathbf{D}_t)$. Thus, each shock, $\varepsilon_{i,t}$, will *dynamically* affect both present and future values of the variables in $\mathbf{x}_t$. Note that this holds true also for any dummy variable included in $\mathbf{D}_t$. The persistence of the effect depends on the magnitude of $|\rho_1|$, the larger, the stronger the persistence.

It is noteworthy that already the simple two-dimensional VAR(2) model can generate a very rich dynamic pattern in the variables $\mathbf{x}_t$ as a result of the multiplicity of the roots and the additional dynamics given by the $\mathbf{\Pi}^a(L)$ matrix polynomial. A real root $|\rho_j| < 1.0$ will generate exponentially declining behaviour, a complex pair of stable roots $\rho_j = \rho_{\text{real}} \pm i\rho_{\text{complex}}$ exponentially declining cyclical behaviour. If a real root is lying on the unit circle ($\rho = 1$ or $\rho = -1$), it will generate non-stationary behaviour, i.e. a stochastic trend in $\mathbf{x}_t$. If the modulus of a complex root is one, it corresponds to non-stationary seasonal behaviour. An example of the latter is the simple fourth-order difference model for quarterly data:

$$(1-L^4)x_t = (1-L)(1+L)(1+L^2)x_t = \varepsilon_t.$$

We set the characteristic polynomial to zero

$$(1-z)(1+z)(1+z^2) = 0$$

and find the characteristic roots: $z_1 = 1$, $z_2 = -1, z_3 = -i$, $z_4 = i$.

3.6.2 Calculating the eigenvalue roots using the companion matrix

We shall here demonstrate that the roots of the process can be conveniently calculated by first reformulating the VAR(k) model into the 'companion AR(1) form' and then solving an eigenvalue problem. In this case, the eigenvalue solution gives the roots directly as $\rho_1, \ldots, \rho_{p\times k}$ instead of the inverse $\rho_1^{-1}, \ldots, \rho_{p\times k}^{-1}$ obtained by solving the characteristic function. To distinguish between the two cases, we call the former characteristic roots and the latter eigenvalue roots. The latter are calculated by transforming the VAR(k) model into an AR(1) model based on the companion form.

For illustrative simplicity, we assume $k = 2$ and rewrite the VAR(2) model in the AR(1) form:

$$\begin{bmatrix} \mathbf{x}_t \\ \mathbf{x}_{t-1} \end{bmatrix} = \begin{bmatrix} \mathbf{\Pi}_1 & \mathbf{\Pi}_2 \\ \mathbf{I} & \mathbf{0} \end{bmatrix} \begin{bmatrix} \mathbf{x}_{t-1} \\ \mathbf{x}_{t-2} \end{bmatrix} + \begin{bmatrix} \boldsymbol{\varepsilon}_t \\ \mathbf{0} \end{bmatrix},$$

or more compactly:

$$\widetilde{\mathbf{x}}_t = \widetilde{\mathbf{\Pi}}\widetilde{\mathbf{x}}_{t-1} + \widetilde{\boldsymbol{\varepsilon}}_t.$$

The roots of the matrix $\widetilde{\mathbf{\Pi}}$ can be found by solving the eigenvalue problem:

$$\rho\mathbf{V} = \widetilde{\mathbf{\Pi}}\mathbf{V}$$

where $\mathbf{V}$ is a $kp \times 1$ vector.

$$\rho \begin{bmatrix} \mathbf{v}_1 \\ \mathbf{v}_2 \end{bmatrix} = \begin{bmatrix} \mathbf{\Pi}_1 & \mathbf{\Pi}_2 \\ \mathbf{I} & \mathbf{0} \end{bmatrix} \begin{bmatrix} \mathbf{v}_1 \\ \mathbf{v}_2 \end{bmatrix}$$

i.e.

$$\begin{aligned} \rho\mathbf{v}_1 &= \mathbf{\Pi}_1\mathbf{v}_1 + \mathbf{\Pi}_2\mathbf{v}_2 \\ \rho\mathbf{v}_2 &= \mathbf{v}_1. \end{aligned}$$

The solution can be found from:

$$\begin{aligned} \rho\mathbf{v}_1 &= \mathbf{\Pi}_1\mathbf{v}_1 + \mathbf{\Pi}_2(\mathbf{v}_1/\rho) \\ \mathbf{v}_1 &= \mathbf{\Pi}_1(\mathbf{v}_1/\rho) + \mathbf{\Pi}_2(\mathbf{v}_1/\rho^2) \end{aligned}$$

i.e. the eigenvalues of $\tilde{\mathbf{\Pi}}$ are the pk roots of the second-order polynomial:

$$\left|\mathbf{I} - \mathbf{\Pi}_1\rho^{-1} - \mathbf{\Pi}_2\rho^{-2}\right| = \mathbf{0}$$

or

$$\left|\mathbf{I} - \mathbf{\Pi}_1 z - \mathbf{\Pi}_2 z^2\right| = \mathbf{0},$$

where $z = \rho^{-1}$. Note that the roots of the companion matrix ρ_i are the inverses of the roots of the characteristic polynomial. Thus, the solution to

$$\left|\mathbf{I} - z\tilde{\mathbf{\Pi}}\right| = \mathbf{0}$$

gives the stationary roots outside the unit circle, whereas the solution to

$$\left|\rho\mathbf{I} - \tilde{\mathbf{\Pi}}\right| = \mathbf{0}$$

gives the stationary roots inside the unit circle. To summarize:

- if the roots of $|\mathbf{\Pi}(z)|$ are all outside the unit circle (or alternatively if the eigenvalues of the companion matrix are all inside the unit circle) then $\{\mathbf{x}_t\}$ is stationary;
- if the roots are outside or on the unit circle (alternatively if the eigenvalues are inside or on the unit circle) then $\{\mathbf{x}_t\}$ is non-stationary;
- if any of the roots are inside the unit circle (alternatively if the eigenvalues are outside the unit circle) then $\{\mathbf{x}_t\}$ is explosive.

3.6.3 Illustration

Table 3.1 reports the roots of the VAR(2) model for the Danish data and Figure 3.6 shows them in the unit circle. There are altogether six real roots and one is on the unit circle. The remaining roots come in complex pairs. The second largest root has a modulus of 0.86 and one might ask whether it is significantly different from one. This can,

Table 3.1 The roots of the VAR(2) model.

Real	Complex	Modulus
1.00	−0.00	1.00
0.86	0.00	0.86
0.76	0.00	0.76
0.70	0.00	0.70
0.60	0.00	0.60
0.48	−0.00	0.48
−0.31	0.04	0.32
−0.31	−0.04	0.32
0.07	0.15	0.17
0.07	−0.15	0.17

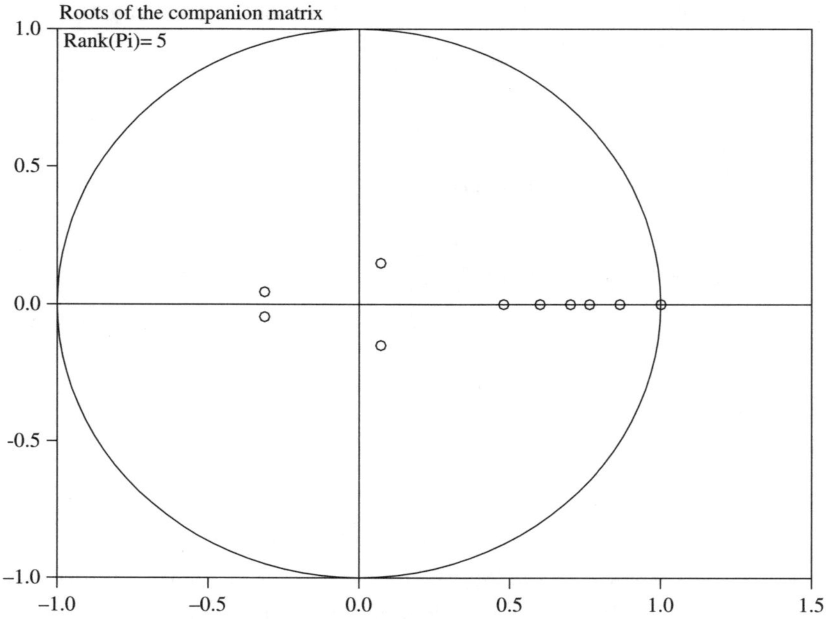

Fig 3.6 The $pk = 10$ roots of the VAR(2) model for the Danish data.

in principle, be tested using the asymptotic variance of the estimated roots in Johansen (2003). But since the derived result is very complicated, we shall here exclusively use the trace test derived in Chapter 8.

3.7 Concluding remarks

The aim of this chapter was to describe a 'design of experiment' for data by passive observation for which the VAR model is an appropriate description. On an aggregate level, economic agents were assumed rational in the sense that they learn by past experience and adjust their behaviour accordingly, so that their plans do not systematically deviate from actual realizations. Thus, the 'design of experiment' consistent with the NI assumption of the residuals relies on the assumption that agents make plans based on conditional expectations using the information set $\{\mathbf{x}_{t-1}, \mathbf{D}_t\}$, so that the residual (the unexpected component given the chosen information set) behaves as a normal innovation process.

In this framework, the success of the empirical analysis relies crucially on the choice of a sufficient and relevant information set of an appropriate sample period and the skilfulness of the investigator to extract economically interesting results from this information.

The purpose of the next chapter is to discuss estimation of the unrestricted VAR and some diagnostic tools which can be used when assessing the appropriateness of the chosen model.

Part II

Specifying the VAR model

4

The unrestricted VAR

The probability approach in econometrics requires an explicit probability formulation of the empirical model so that a fully specified statistical model can be derived and checked against the data. Assume that we have derived an estimator under the assumption of multivariate normality as demonstrated in the previous chapter. We then take the model to the data and obtain model estimates derived under this assumption. If the multivariate normality assumption is correct, the residuals should not deviate significantly from the assumption $\varepsilon_t \sim IN_p(\mathbf{0}, \mathbf{\Omega})$. If they do not pass the tests, for example, because they are autocorrelated or heteroscedastic, or because the distribution is skewed or leptocurtic, then the estimates may no longer have optimal properties and cannot be considered full information maximum likelihood (FIML) estimates. The obtained parameter estimates (based on an incorrectly derived estimator) may not have any meaning, and since we do not know their 'true' properties, inference is likely to be hazardous.

Because some assumptions are more crucial for the properties of the estimates than others we shall discuss robustness properties against modest violations of the assumptions. Nonetheless, if we are going to claim that our conclusions are based on FIML inference, then we also have to demonstrate that our model is capable of mirroring the 'full information' of the data in a satisfactory way.

Before being able to test the assumptions, we need to estimate the model and Section 4.1 derives the ML estimator under the null of correct model specification. Section 4.2 discusses different parametrization of the unrestricted VAR model and illustrates the estimates based on the Danish data. Section 4.3 briefly reports some frequently used misspecification tests.

4.1 Likelihood-based estimation in the unrestricted VAR

Under the assumption that the parameters $\mathbf{\Theta} = \{\boldsymbol{\mu}_0, \mathbf{\Pi}_1, \mathbf{\Pi}_2, \ldots, \mathbf{\Pi}_k, \mathbf{\Omega}\}$ in the VAR model (3.8) of Chapter 3 are unrestricted, it can be shown that the simple OLS estimator is identical to the FIML estimator, conditional on the initial values of the process. See, for example, Hamilton (1994) and Johansen (1996). When the data contain unit roots, we need to derive the likelihood estimator subject to reduced rank restrictions. Chapter 7 will give a detailed discussion of how to solve this problem. To simplify notation we rewrite (3.8) in compact form:

$$\begin{aligned} \mathbf{x}_t &= \mathbf{B}'\mathbf{Z}_t + \boldsymbol{\varepsilon}_t, \quad t = 1, \ldots, T \\ \boldsymbol{\varepsilon}_t &\sim IN_p(\mathbf{0}, \boldsymbol{\Omega}) \end{aligned} \tag{4.1}$$

where $\mathbf{B}' = [\boldsymbol{\mu}_0, \boldsymbol{\Pi}_1, \ \boldsymbol{\Pi}_2, \ldots, \ \boldsymbol{\Pi}_k]$, $\mathbf{Z}_t'= [1, \mathbf{x}_{t-1}', \mathbf{x}_{t-2}', \ldots, \mathbf{x}_{t-k}']$ and the initial values $\mathbf{X}^0 = [\mathbf{x}_0', \mathbf{x}_{-1}', \ldots, \mathbf{x}_{-k+1}']$ are given. For simplicity we assume $\boldsymbol{\Phi}\mathbf{D}_t = \mathbf{0}$. We need to derive the equations for estimating $\mathbf{B}$ and $\boldsymbol{\Omega}$ which can be done by finding the expression for $\mathbf{B}$ and $\boldsymbol{\Omega}$ for which the first order derivatives of the likelihood function are equal to zero.

We consider first the log likelihood function

$$\ln L(\mathbf{B}, \boldsymbol{\Omega}; \mathbf{X}) = -T\frac{p}{2}\ln(2\pi) - T\frac{1}{2}\ln|\boldsymbol{\Omega}| - \frac{1}{2}\sum_{t=1}^{T}(\mathbf{x}_t - \mathbf{B}'\mathbf{Z}_t)'\boldsymbol{\Omega}^{-1}(\mathbf{x}_t - \mathbf{B}'\mathbf{Z}_t),$$

and calculate $\partial \ln L / \partial \mathbf{B} = \mathbf{0}$, which gives

$$\sum_{t=1}^{T} \mathbf{x}_t\mathbf{Z}_t' = \hat{\mathbf{B}}' \sum_{t=1}^{T} \mathbf{Z}_t\mathbf{Z}_t',$$

so that the FIML estimator for $\mathbf{B}$ is:

$$\hat{\mathbf{B}}' = \sum_{t=1}^{T}(\mathbf{x}_t\mathbf{Z}_t')(\sum_{t=1}^{T}\mathbf{Z}_t\mathbf{Z}_t')^{-1} = \mathbf{M}_{xZ}\mathbf{M}_{ZZ}^{-1}. \tag{4.2}$$

Next we calculate $\partial \ln L / \partial \boldsymbol{\Omega} = \mathbf{0}$, which gives the estimator of $\boldsymbol{\Omega}$:

$$\hat{\boldsymbol{\Omega}} = T^{-1}\sum_{t=1}^{T}(\mathbf{x}_t - \hat{\mathbf{B}}'\mathbf{Z}_t)(\mathbf{x}_t - \hat{\mathbf{B}}'\mathbf{Z}_t)' = T^{-1}\sum_{t=1}^{T}\hat{\boldsymbol{\varepsilon}}_t\hat{\boldsymbol{\varepsilon}}_t'. \tag{4.3}$$

The ML estimators (4.2) and (4.3) are identical to the corresponding OLS estimators. We can now find the maximal value of the (log) likelihood function for the ML estimates $\hat{\mathbf{B}}$ and $\hat{\boldsymbol{\Omega}}$:

$$\ln L_{\max} = -\frac{p}{2}T\ln(2\pi) - \frac{1}{2}T\ln\left|\hat{\boldsymbol{\Omega}}\right| - \frac{1}{2}\sum_{t=1}^{T}(\mathbf{x}_t - \hat{\mathbf{B}}'\mathbf{Z}_t)'\hat{\boldsymbol{\Omega}}^{-1}(\mathbf{x}_t - \hat{\mathbf{B}}'\mathbf{Z}_t).$$

We shall now show that $\ln L_{\max} = -\frac{1}{2}T \ln \left|\hat{\mathbf{\Omega}}\right| +$ constant terms. Consider first:

$$\begin{aligned}(\mathbf{x}_t - \hat{\mathbf{B}}'\mathbf{Z}_t)'\hat{\mathbf{\Omega}}^{-1}(\mathbf{x}_t - \hat{\mathbf{B}}'\mathbf{Z}_t) &= \hat{\varepsilon}_t'\hat{\mathbf{\Omega}}^{-1}\hat{\varepsilon}_t \\ &= \sum_{ij} \hat{\varepsilon}_{t,i}(\hat{\mathbf{\Omega}}^{-1})_{ij}\hat{\varepsilon}_{t,j} \\ &= \sum_{ij} (\hat{\mathbf{\Omega}}^{-1})_{ij}\hat{\varepsilon}_{t,j}\hat{\varepsilon}_{t,i} \\ &= \text{trace}\{\hat{\mathbf{\Omega}}^{-1}\hat{\varepsilon}_t\hat{\varepsilon}_t'\}\end{aligned}$$

using the result that $\text{trace}(\mathbf{AB}) = \sum_{ij} \mathbf{A}_{ij}\mathbf{B}_{ji}$.

Summing over T we obtain:

$$\begin{aligned}\sum_{t=1}^{T}(\mathbf{x}_t - \hat{\mathbf{B}}'\mathbf{Z}_t)\hat{\mathbf{\Omega}}^{-1}(\mathbf{x}_t - \hat{\mathbf{B}}'\mathbf{Z}_t)' &= \sum_{t=1}^{T} \text{trace}\{\hat{\mathbf{\Omega}}^{-1}\hat{\varepsilon}_t\hat{\varepsilon}_t'\} \\ &= T\sum_{t=1}^{T} \text{trace}\{\hat{\mathbf{\Omega}}^{-1}\hat{\varepsilon}_t\hat{\varepsilon}_t'/T\} \\ &= T\,\text{trace}\{\hat{\mathbf{\Omega}}^{-1}\hat{\mathbf{\Omega}}\} \\ &= T\,\text{trace}\{\mathbf{I}_p\} = Tp\end{aligned}$$

and

$$\ln L_{\max} = -T\frac{1}{2}\ln\left|\hat{\mathbf{\Omega}}\right| - T\frac{p}{2} - T\frac{p}{2}\ln(2\pi),$$

i.e. apart from constant terms, the maximum of the log likelihood function is proportional to the log determinant of the residual covariance matrix $\hat{\mathbf{\Omega}}$:

$$\ln L_{\max} = -T\frac{1}{2}\ln\left|\hat{\mathbf{\Omega}}\right| + \text{ constant terms.}$$

This result will be used in many of the test procedures discussed below and in the derivation of the maximum likelihood estimator for the cointegrated VAR model in Chapter 7.

To be able to test hypotheses on $\mathbf{B}$, we need the distribution of the estimates $\hat{\mathbf{B}}$. For simplicity we shall here use the simple VAR(2) model to discuss the asymptotic distribution of $\hat{\mathbf{B}}$ under the assumption of stationarity of the process $\mathbf{x}_t$.

Next, consider the estimation error of the VAR(2) coefficients:

$$\hat{\mathbf{B}}' - \mathbf{B}' = \left[\hat{\mathbf{\Pi}}_1, \hat{\mathbf{\Pi}}_2\right] - [\mathbf{\Pi}_1, \mathbf{\Pi}_2]\,. \tag{4.4}$$

The covariance matrix between the 'regressors' $\mathbf{x}_{t-1}$and $\mathbf{x}_{t-2}$ is:

$$\mathbf{\Sigma} = \begin{bmatrix} \mathbf{\Sigma}_{11} & \mathbf{\Sigma}_{12} \\ \mathbf{\Sigma}_{21} & \mathbf{\Sigma}_{22} \end{bmatrix} = \begin{bmatrix} \text{Var}(\mathbf{x}_{t-1}) & \text{Cov}(\mathbf{x}_{t-1}, \mathbf{x}_{t-2}) \\ \text{Cov}(\mathbf{x}_{t-2}, \mathbf{x}_{t-1}) & \text{Var}(\mathbf{x}_{t-2}) \end{bmatrix}.$$

Under the stationarity assumption, the distribution of (4.4) has the following asymptotic property:

$$T^{\frac{1}{2}}(\hat{\mathbf{B}} - \mathbf{B}) \xrightarrow{w} N(\mathbf{0}, \mathbf{\Omega} \otimes \mathbf{\Sigma}^{-1}) \tag{4.5}$$

where

$$\mathbf{\Omega} \otimes \mathbf{\Sigma}^{-1} = \begin{bmatrix} \mathbf{\Omega}\mathbf{\Sigma}^{i}_{11} & \mathbf{\Omega}\mathbf{\Sigma}^{i}_{12} \\ \mathbf{\Omega}\mathbf{\Sigma}^{i}_{21} & \mathbf{\Omega}\mathbf{\Sigma}^{i}_{22} \end{bmatrix}$$

and $\mathbf{\Sigma}^{-1}$ is partitioned into

$$\mathbf{\Sigma}^{-1} = \begin{bmatrix} \mathbf{\Sigma}^{i}_{11} & \mathbf{\Sigma}^{i}_{12} \\ \mathbf{\Sigma}^{i}_{21} & \mathbf{\Sigma}^{i}_{22} \end{bmatrix}.$$

To see how the distribution of the unrestricted VAR estimates relates to the corresponding OLS results for the standard regression model the latter are briefly reviewed below:

$$\begin{aligned} \mathbf{y} &= \mathbf{X}\boldsymbol{\beta} + \boldsymbol{\varepsilon}, \quad \boldsymbol{\varepsilon} \sim NI(\mathbf{0}, \sigma^2_{\varepsilon}\mathbf{I}) \\ \hat{\boldsymbol{\beta}} &= (\mathbf{X}'\mathbf{X})^{-1}\mathbf{X}'\mathbf{y} \\ \hat{\boldsymbol{\beta}} - \boldsymbol{\beta} &= (\mathbf{X}'\mathbf{X})^{-1}\mathbf{X}'\boldsymbol{\varepsilon} \\ \mathrm{Var}(\hat{\boldsymbol{\beta}} - \boldsymbol{\beta}) &= \sigma^2_{\varepsilon}(\mathbf{X}'\mathbf{X})^{-1}. \end{aligned}$$

Thus, the VAR results are similar to the linear regression results, except that the design matrix $\mathbf{X}'\mathbf{X}$ of the regression model is replaced by the $kp \times kp$ covariance matrix $\mathbf{\Sigma}$, where $k = 2$ in the above example. Note that the asymptotic distribution of the regression coefficients are based on the assumption that the design matrix

$$T^{-1}\mathbf{X}'\mathbf{X} \xrightarrow{P} \mathbf{A}$$

where $\mathbf{A}$ is a constant matrix. When the data have unit roots, this assumption no longer holds and the design matrix when normalized differently will instead converge towards a matrix of Brownian motions. This issue will be discussed further in Chapter 8.

Assume now that we would like to test the significance of a single coefficient, for example the first element $\pi_{1,11}$ of $\mathbf{\Pi}_1$. We define two 'design' vectors $\boldsymbol{\xi}' = [1, 0, 0, \ldots, 0]$ and $\boldsymbol{\eta}' = [1, 0, 0, \ldots, 0]$ where $\boldsymbol{\xi}$ is $p \times 1$ and $\boldsymbol{\eta}$ is $2p \times 1$, so that $\boldsymbol{\xi}'\mathbf{B}'\boldsymbol{\eta} = \pi_{1,11}$. Using (4.5), we can find the test statistic for the null hypothesis $\pi_{1,11} = 0$, which has a Normal (0,1) distribution asymptotically. This can be generalized to testing any coefficient in $\mathbf{B}$ by appropriately choosing the vectors $\boldsymbol{\xi}$ and $\boldsymbol{\eta}$:

$$\frac{T^{\frac{1}{2}}\boldsymbol{\xi}'\mathbf{B}'\boldsymbol{\eta}}{(\boldsymbol{\xi}'\mathbf{\Omega}\boldsymbol{\xi}\boldsymbol{\eta}'\mathbf{\Sigma}^{-1}\boldsymbol{\eta})^{\frac{1}{2}}} \xrightarrow{w} N(0, 1). \tag{4.6}$$

4.1.1 The estimates of the unrestricted VAR(2) for the Danish data

The unrestricted VAR(2) model was estimated based on the following assumptions:

$$\begin{aligned} \mathbf{x}_t &= \mathbf{\Pi}_1 \mathbf{x}_{t-1} + \mathbf{\Pi}_2 \mathbf{x}_{t-2} + \mathbf{\Phi} \mathbf{D}_t + \boldsymbol{\varepsilon}_t \\ t &= 1, \ldots, T \quad \boldsymbol{\varepsilon}_t \sim IN_p(\mathbf{0}, \mathbf{\Omega}) \end{aligned} \tag{4.7}$$

where $\mathbf{D}_t = [Dq1_t, Dq2_t, Dq3_t, \mu_0]$ contains three centred seasonal dummies[1] and a constant. The estimates reported in Table 4.1 are calculated in PcGive by running an OLS regression equation by equation. As discussed above, these estimates are ML estimates (conditional on the initial values) as long as no restrictions have been imposed on the VAR model. To increase readability, we have omitted standard errors of estimates and t ratios. Instead, coefficients with a 't'-ratio greater than 1.9 have been given in bold face. Since Chapter 3 found at least one characteristic root very close to the unit circle in the unrestricted VAR, $\mathbf{x}_t$ is not likely to be stationary. As mentioned, this implies that the 'design matrix' normalized differently will no longer converge towards a constant matrix in the limit but, instead, towards a matrix of Brownian motions. In this case, the t-ratios are more likely to be distributed as the Dickey–Fullers' τ and should therefore not be interpreted as Student's t.

An inspection of the estimated coefficients reveals more significant coefficients at lag 1 than lag 2. Most of the coefficients with large t-ratios are on the diagonal, implying that the variables are highly autoregressive. The bond rate seems to be quite important for most of the variables in this system. The residual correlations between equations are generally moderately sized and suggest that the current effects are not likely to be very important in this case. The log likelihood value and $\log\left|\hat{\mathbf{\Omega}}\right|$ are only informative when compared to another model specification. For example, based on the VAR(1) model we obtained $\log\left|\hat{\mathbf{\Omega}}\right| = -51.0 > -51.9$. Even though the $R^2(LR)$ is almost 1.0, it does not imply that we have explained all variation in the data. Instead, R^2 (based on the standard formula) is an incorrect measure when the variables are trending, as they are in the present case. See also the discussion in Section 4.3.2. Section 4.3 will discuss specification tests in more detail.

Finally we report F-tests on the significance of single regressors. The tests are distributed as $F(5, 101)$:

$$\begin{bmatrix} m^r_{t-1} & y^r_{t-1} & \Delta p_{t-1} & R_{m,t-1} & R_{b,t-1} & m^r_{t-2} & y^r_{t-2} & \Delta p_{t-2} & R_{m,t-2} & R_{b,t-2} \\ \mathbf{6.6} & \mathbf{24.4} & 2.22 & \mathbf{30.2} & \mathbf{38.7} & 2.2 & \mathbf{4.7} & 1.5 & 2.1 & \mathbf{5.6} \end{bmatrix}.$$

We note that the second lag of the real money, the inflation rate and the deposit rate could be omitted altogether from the system.

[1] A centred seasonal dummy is defined by $Dq_t = Ds_t - \bar{D}s$, where Ds_t is a standard seasonal dummy $(\ldots 1, 0,0,01, \ldots)$ and $\bar{D}s$ is an average (i.e. 0.25). This means that $Dqi_t = 0.75$ in quarter i, -0.25 in quarter $i+1$, $i+2$, $i+3$. While standard seasonal dummies cumulate to seasonal trends, centred seasonal dummies cumulate to zero, i.e. $\sum_{j=1}^{T} Dqi_j = 0$ in samples covering complete years.

Table 4.1 The estimates of the unrestricted VAR model in levels.

$$\begin{bmatrix} m^r_t \\ y^r_t \\ \Delta p_t \\ R_{m,t} \\ R_{b,t} \end{bmatrix} = \begin{bmatrix} \mathbf{0.55} & 0.12 & \mathbf{-0.93} & 3.97 & \mathbf{-8.05} \\ -0.01 & \mathbf{1.04} & -0.23 & -1.69 & \mathbf{-2.18} \\ -0.01 & -0.11 & 0.02 & \mathbf{-2.46} & \mathbf{1.79} \\ -0.00 & -0.00 & \mathbf{0.03} & \mathbf{1.05} & \mathbf{0.30} \\ \mathbf{-0.01} & \mathbf{0.03} & 0.03 & 0.07 & \mathbf{1.27} \end{bmatrix} \begin{bmatrix} m^r_{t-1} \\ y^r_{t-1} \\ \Delta p_{t-1} \\ R_{m,t-1} \\ R_{b,t-1} \end{bmatrix}$$

$$+ \begin{bmatrix} \mathbf{0.19} & 0.12 & -0.55 & 1.06 & 3.06 \\ 0.03 & -0.16 & -0.10 & -0.43 & \mathbf{2.69} \\ -0.02 & 0.10 & \mathbf{0.21} & \mathbf{1.82} & \mathbf{-1.55} \\ 0.00 & 0.00 & -0.02 & -0.16 & \mathbf{-0.26} \\ 0.01 & \mathbf{-0.04} & 0.00 & -0.06 & \mathbf{-0.37} \end{bmatrix} \begin{bmatrix} m^r_{t-2} \\ y^r_{t-2} \\ \Delta p_{t-2} \\ R_{m,t-2} \\ R_{b,t-2} \end{bmatrix} + \mathbf{\Phi D}_t + \varepsilon_t$$

$$\hat{\mathbf{\Omega}} = \begin{bmatrix} 1.0 & & & & \\ 0.09 & 1.0 & & & \\ -0.34 & -0.12 & 1.0 & & \\ -0.16 & -0.05 & 0.22 & 1.0 & \\ -0.17 & 0.09 & 0.25 & 0.33 & 1.0 \end{bmatrix}, \quad \hat{\boldsymbol{\sigma}}_\varepsilon = \begin{bmatrix} 0.0369 \\ 0.0147 \\ 0.0087 \\ 0.0012 \\ 0.0016 \end{bmatrix}$$

$\text{Log}(L_{\max}) = 2241.28, \log\left|\hat{\mathbf{\Omega}}\right| = -51.9,\ R^2(LR) = 0.99,\ R^2(LM) = 0.68$
F-test on all regressors: $F(50, 463) = 81.1$

4.2 Three different ECM representations

The unrestricted VAR model can be given different parametrizations without imposing any binding restrictions on the model parameters, i.e. without changing the value of the likelihood function. The so-called vector equilibrium correction model (hereafter VECM) gives a convenient reformulation of (4.7) in terms of differences, lagged differences, and levels of the process. There are several advantages of this formulation:

1. The multicollinearity effect which typically is strongly present in time-series data is significantly reduced in the error-correction form. Differences are much more 'orthogonal' than the levels of variables.
2. All information about long-run effects is summarized in the levels matrix (subsequently denoted $\mathbf{\Pi}$) which can, therefore, be given special attention when solving the problem of cointegration.
3. The interpretation of the estimates is more intuitive, as the coefficients can be naturally classified into short-run and long-run effects.
4. The VECM formulation gives a direct answer to the question 'why the inflation rate, say, changed from the previous to the present period as a result of changes in the chosen information set'.

We shall now discuss three different versions of the VAR(k) model formulated in the general VECM form:

$$\Delta \mathbf{x}_t = \mathbf{\Gamma}_1^{(m)} \Delta \mathbf{x}_{t-1} + \mathbf{\Gamma}_2^{(m)} \Delta \mathbf{x}_{t-2} + \cdots + \mathbf{\Gamma}_{k-1}^{(m)} \Delta \mathbf{x}_{t-k+1} + \mathbf{\Pi} \mathbf{x}_{t-m} + \mathbf{\Phi} \mathbf{D}_t + \varepsilon_t \quad (4.8)$$

where m is an integer between 1 and k defining the lag placement of the ECM term. Note that the value of the likelihood function does not change even if we change the value of m. For the Danish data we shall assume the lag length $k = 2$ and report the unrestricted parameter estimates for that choice. Additionally the value of the log likelihood function, some multivariate R^2 measures, and F-tests of the significance of the regressors will be reported. The purpose is to illustrate how widely different the estimates can look although the estimated model is exactly the same in all three cases.

4.2.1 The ECM formulation with $m = 1$

The VAR(2) model is specified as:

$$\Delta \mathbf{x}_t = \mathbf{\Gamma}_1^{(1)} \Delta \mathbf{x}_{t-1} + \mathbf{\Pi} \mathbf{x}_{t-1} + \mathbf{\Phi} \mathbf{D}_t + \varepsilon_t \quad (4.9)$$

where $\mathbf{\Pi} = -(\mathbf{I} - \mathbf{\Pi}_1 - \mathbf{\Pi}_2)$, and $\mathbf{\Gamma}_1^{(1)} = -\ \mathbf{\Pi}_2$. In (4.9) the lagged levels matrix $\mathbf{\Pi}$ has been placed at time $t - 1$.

The estimated coefficients reported in Table 4.2 show that most of the significant coefficients are now in the lagged levels matrix $\mathbf{\Pi}$, whereas only eight out of 25 coefficients in the $\mathbf{\Gamma}_1^{(1)}$ matrix seem significant. Among the former, three are on the diagonal and the remaining two describe the big change in money velocity, as a result of a reallocation of money holdings when restrictions on capital movements were lifted at 1983. This also resulted in a large drop in the long-term bond rate. In Chapter 5, we shall re-estimate the VAR model accounting for this intervention.

We note that estimating the model exclusively in differences, i.e. setting $\mathbf{\Pi} \mathbf{x}_{t-1} = 0$, would not deliver many interesting results. But, including $\mathbf{\Pi} \mathbf{x}_{t-1}$ in the model raises the question of how to handle the non-stationarity problem. Since a stationary process cannot be equal to a non-stationary process, the estimation results can only make sense if $\mathbf{\Pi} \mathbf{x}_{t-1}$ defines stationary linear combinations of the variables. This can be seen by noting that the first row of $\mathbf{\Pi} \mathbf{x}_{t-1}$ can be reformulated as:

$$-0.26(m_{t-1}^r - 0.92 y_{t-1}^r + 5.7 \Delta p_{t-1} - 19.4 R_{m,t-1} + 19.2 R_{b,t-1}).$$

If the linear combination in the parentheses defines a stationary variable, then all components in the first equation would be stationary and the system would, therefore, be balanced with respect to the first equation. This is, in a nutshell, the role of cointegration analysis: it identifies stationary linear combinations between non-stationary variables so that an $I(1)$ model can be reformulated exclusively in stationary variables. Our task is to give the stationary linear combinations an economically meaningful interpretation by imposing relevant identifying or over-identifying restrictions on the coefficients. For example, the above relation can be given an interpretation as deviations of observed money holdings from a steady-state money demand relation, $m^r_{t-1} - m^{r*}_{t-1}$, where

$$m^{r*}_{t-1} = 0.92y^r_{t-1} - 5.7\Delta p_{t-1} + 19.4R_{m,t-1} - 19.2R_{b,t-1}.$$

We might now like to test whether real income has a unit coefficient, whether the coefficient on inflation is zero, and whether the interest rate coefficients are equal with opposite sign. How to do that, will be discussed in Chapter 10.

The trace correlation coefficient will be described in Section 4.3.2. The F-tests on single regressors, distributed as $F(5,101)$ are:

$$\begin{bmatrix} \Delta m^r_{t-1} & \Delta y^r_{t-1} & \Delta p^2_{t-1} & \Delta R_{m,t-1} & \Delta R_{b,t-1} & m^r_{t-1} & y^r_{t-1} & \Delta p_{t-1} & R_{m,t-1} & R_{b,t-1} \\ 2.2 & \mathbf{4.7} & 1.5 & 2.1 & \mathbf{5.6} & \mathbf{5.8} & \mathbf{3.9} & \mathbf{10.3} & \mathbf{4.6} & \mathbf{4.2} \end{bmatrix}.$$

Note that $\mathrm{Log}(L_{\max})$ and $\log\left|\hat{\boldsymbol{\Omega}}\right|$ are exactly the same as for the unrestricted VAR in the previous section, demonstrating that from a likelihood point of view, the models are identical. Because the residuals are identical in all the ECM representations, all residual tests or information criteria are identical, whereas tests of the significance of single variables need not be (and often are not). For example, the F-tests of the lagged variables in differences, distributed as $F(5,101)$, are very different when compared to the two subsequent specifications, whereas the test values for the lagged variables in levels are identical. This illustrates that the $\boldsymbol{\Pi}$ matrix is invariant to linear transformations of the VAR system but not the $\boldsymbol{\Gamma}_1^{(m)}$ matrices, the coefficients of which depend on how we choose m.

Table 4.2 The estimates of the VECM with $m = 1$.

$$\begin{bmatrix} \Delta m^r_t \\ \Delta y^r_t \\ \Delta p^2_t \\ \Delta R_{m,t} \\ \Delta R_{b,t} \end{bmatrix} = \begin{bmatrix} \mathbf{-0.19} & -0.12 & 0.55 & -1.06 & -3.06 \\ -0.03 & 0.16 & 0.10 & 0.43 & \mathbf{-2.69} \\ 0.02 & -0.10 & \mathbf{-0.21} & \mathbf{-1.82} & \mathbf{1.55} \\ -0.00 & -0.00 & 0.02 & 0.16 & \mathbf{0.26} \\ -0.01 & \mathbf{0.04} & -0.00 & 0.06 & \mathbf{0.37} \end{bmatrix} \begin{bmatrix} \Delta m^r_{t-1} \\ \Delta y^r_{t-1} \\ \Delta p^2_{t-1} \\ \Delta R_{m,t-1} \\ \Delta R_{b,t-1} \end{bmatrix}$$

$$+ \begin{bmatrix} \mathbf{-0.26} & \mathbf{0.24} & \mathbf{-1.48} & \mathbf{5.04} & \mathbf{-4.99} \\ 0.02 & \mathbf{-0.12} & -0.33 & \mathbf{-2.11} & 0.51 \\ -0.02 & -0.01 & \mathbf{-0.77} & -0.64 & 0.24 \\ -0.00 & -0.00 & 0.01 & \mathbf{-0.11} & 0.04 \\ -0.00 & -0.00 & 0.03 & 0.01 & -0.09 \end{bmatrix} \begin{bmatrix} m^r_{t-1} \\ y^r_{t-1} \\ \Delta p_{t-1} \\ R_{m,t-1} \\ R_{b,t-1} \end{bmatrix}$$

$$+ \boldsymbol{\Phi}\mathbf{D}_t + \varepsilon_t$$

$\mathrm{Log}(L_{\max}) = 2241.28$, $\log\left|\hat{\boldsymbol{\Omega}}\right| = -51.9$, trace correlation $= 0.40$,
$R^2(LR) = 0.90$, $R^2(LM) = 0.33$, F-test on all regressors: $F(50,463) = 6.2$.

4.2.2 The ECM formulation with $m = 2$

The VAR(2) model is now specified so that $\mathbf{\Pi}$ is placed at $\mathbf{x}_{t-2}$:

$$\Delta \mathbf{x}_t = \mathbf{\Gamma}_1^{(2)} \Delta \mathbf{x}_{t-1} + \mathbf{\Pi}\mathbf{x}_{t-2} + \mathbf{\Phi}\mathbf{D}_t + \varepsilon_t \tag{4.10}$$

with $\mathbf{\Pi} = -(\mathbf{I} - \mathbf{\Pi}_1 - \mathbf{\Pi}_2)$ and $\mathbf{\Gamma}_1^{(2)} = -(\mathbf{I} - \mathbf{\Pi}_1)$. Thus, the $\mathbf{\Pi}$ matrix remains unchanged, but not the $\mathbf{\Gamma}_1^{(2)}$ matrix. The latter measures the cumulative long-run effect, whereas $\mathbf{\Gamma}_1^{(1)}$ in (4.9) describes 'pure' transitory effects measured by the lagged changes of the variables. While the explanatory power is identical for the two model versions, the estimated coefficients and their p-values can vary considerably. This is illustrated in Table 4.3. Usually many more significant coefficients are obtained with the formulation (4.10) than with (4.9). We note that the number of 'significant' coefficients in $\mathbf{\Gamma}_1^{(2)}$ is larger than in $\mathbf{\Gamma}_1^{(1)}$, but that the $\mathbf{\Pi}$ matrix is unchanged. Thus, many significant coefficients does not necessarily imply high explanatory power, but may as well be a consequence of the parametrization of the model. It illustrates that the interpretation of the estimated coefficients in dynamic models is less straightforward than in static regression models.

The F-tests on single regressors, distributed as $F(5, 101)$ are:

$$\begin{bmatrix} \Delta m^r_{t-1} & \Delta y^r_{t-1} & \Delta^2 p_{t-1} & \Delta R_{m,t-1} & \Delta R_{b,t-1} & m^r_{t-2} & y^r_{t-2} & \Delta p_{t-2} & R_{m,t-2} & R_{b,t-2} \\ \mathbf{6.0} & \mathbf{3.7} & \mathbf{30.9} & \mathbf{3.6} & \mathbf{6.9} & \mathbf{5.8} & \mathbf{3.9} & \mathbf{10.3} & \mathbf{4.6} & \mathbf{4.2} \end{bmatrix}.$$

We note that the single F-tests, $F(5, 101)$, on the lagged variables in differences have changed. For example, $\Delta^2 p_{t-1}$ is now highly significant, whereas it was completely insignificant in the case $m = 1$.

Table 4.3 The estimates of the VECM for $m = 2$.

$$\begin{bmatrix} \Delta m^r_t \\ \Delta y^r_t \\ \Delta^2 p_t \\ \Delta R_{m,t} \\ \Delta R_{b,t} \end{bmatrix} = \begin{bmatrix} \mathbf{-0.45} & 0.12 & \mathbf{-0.93} & 3.97 & \mathbf{-8.05} \\ -0.01 & \mathbf{0.04} & -0.23 & -1.69 & \mathbf{-2.18} \\ -0.01 & -0.11 & \mathbf{-0.98} & \mathbf{-2.46} & \mathbf{1.79} \\ -0.00 & -0.00 & \mathbf{0.03} & 0.05 & \mathbf{0.30} \\ \mathbf{-0.01} & \mathbf{0.03} & 0.03 & 0.07 & \mathbf{0.27} \end{bmatrix} \begin{bmatrix} \Delta m^r_{t-1} \\ \Delta y^r_{t-1} \\ \Delta^2 p_{t-1} \\ \Delta R_{m,t-1} \\ \Delta R_{b,t-1} \end{bmatrix}$$

$$+ \begin{bmatrix} \mathbf{-0.26} & \mathbf{0.24} & -1.48 & \mathbf{5.04} & \mathbf{-4.99} \\ 0.02 & \mathbf{-0.12} & -0.33 & \mathbf{-2.11} & 0.51 \\ -0.02 & -0.01 & \mathbf{-0.77} & -0.64 & 0.24 \\ -0.00 & -0.00 & 0.01 & \mathbf{-0.11} & 0.04 \\ -0.00 & -0.00 & 0.03 & 0.01 & -0.09 \end{bmatrix} \begin{bmatrix} m^r_{t-2} \\ y^r_{t-2} \\ \Delta p_{t-2} \\ R_{m,t-2} \\ R_{b,t-2} \end{bmatrix}$$

$$+\mathbf{\Phi}\mathbf{D}_t + \varepsilon_t$$

$\text{Log}(L_{\max}) = 2241.28$, $\log\left|\hat{\mathbf{\Omega}}\right| = -51.9$, $R^2(LR) = 0.90$, $R^2(LM) = 0.33$,
F-test on all regressors: $F(50, 463) = 6.2$.

4.2.3 ECM representation in acceleration rates, changes and levels

Another convenient formulation of the VAR model is in second order differences (acceleration rates), changes, and levels:

$$\Delta^2\mathbf{x}_t = \mathbf{\Gamma}_{1.1}\Delta^2\mathbf{x}_{t-1} + \cdots + \mathbf{\Gamma}_{1.k-2}\Delta^2\mathbf{x}_{t-(k-2)} + \mathbf{\Gamma}\Delta\mathbf{x}_{t-1} + \mathbf{\Pi}\mathbf{x}_{t-2} + \mathbf{\Phi}\mathbf{D}_t + \varepsilon_t \quad (4.11)$$

where $\mathbf{\Gamma} = -\left(\mathbf{I} - \mathbf{\Gamma}_1^{(2)} - \cdots - \mathbf{\Gamma}_{k-1}^{(2)}\right) = -\left(\mathbf{I} + \mathbf{\Pi}_2 + 2\mathbf{\Pi}_3 - \cdots + (k-1)\mathbf{\Pi}_k\right)$, $\mathbf{\Pi} = -(\mathbf{I} - \mathbf{\Pi}_1 - \cdots - \mathbf{\Pi}_k)$ as before, and $\mathbf{\Gamma}_{1.i} = -(\mathbf{\Gamma}_{i+1}^{(2)} + \cdots + \mathbf{\Gamma}_{k-1}^{(2)}) = (\mathbf{\Pi}_{i+2} + 2\mathbf{\Pi}_{i+3} + \cdots + (k-1)\mathbf{\Pi}_k)$. Chapter 17 will show that this formulation is particularly useful when $\mathbf{x}_t$ contains I(2) variables. It is in general a convenient representation when the sample contains periods of rapid change, so that acceleration rates (in addition to growth rates) become relevant determinants of agents' behaviour.

The VAR(2) model for the Danish data now becomes:

$$\Delta^2\mathbf{x}_t = \mathbf{\Gamma}\Delta\mathbf{x}_{t-1} + \mathbf{\Pi}\mathbf{x}_{t-2} + \mathbf{\Phi}\mathbf{D}_t + \varepsilon_t \quad (4.12)$$

where $\mathbf{\Gamma} = -\left(\mathbf{I} - \mathbf{\Gamma}_1^{(1)}\right) = -(\mathbf{I} + \mathbf{\Pi}_2)$, and $\mathbf{\Pi} = -(\mathbf{I} - \mathbf{\Pi}_1 - \mathbf{\Pi}_2)$. At first sight the estimates of the $\mathbf{\Gamma}$ matrix reported in Table 4.4 look very different from the previous case. A second look shows that the coefficients are identical except that a constant factor of -1 has been added to the diagonal elements. Thus, the significance of the diagonal elements are only a consequence of applying the difference operator once more to $\Delta\mathbf{x}_t$. Therefore, it may be more meaningful to test whether the diagonal elements are significantly different from -1 (or from -2 for the inflation rate) than from zero.

Table 4.4 The estimates of the VECM in acceleration rates, changes, and levels.

$$\begin{bmatrix} \Delta^2 m_t^r \\ \Delta^2 y_t^r \\ \Delta\Delta^2 p_t \\ \Delta^2 R_{m,t} \\ \Delta^2 R_{b,t} \end{bmatrix} = \begin{bmatrix} \mathbf{-1.45} & 0.12 & \mathbf{-0.93} & 3.97 & \mathbf{-8.05} \\ -0.01 & \mathbf{-0.96} & -0.23 & -1.69 & \mathbf{-2.18} \\ -0.01 & \mathbf{-0.11} & \mathbf{-1.98} & \mathbf{-2.46} & \mathbf{1.79} \\ -0.00 & -0.00 & \mathbf{0.03} & \mathbf{-0.95} & \mathbf{0.30} \\ -0.01 & \mathbf{0.03} & 0.03 & 0.07 & \mathbf{-0.73} \end{bmatrix} \begin{bmatrix} \Delta m_{t-1}^r \\ \Delta y_{t-1}^r \\ \Delta^2 p_{t-1} \\ \Delta R_{m,t-1} \\ \Delta R_{b,t-1} \end{bmatrix}$$

$$+ \begin{bmatrix} \mathbf{-0.26} & \mathbf{0.24} & \mathbf{-1.48} & \mathbf{5.04} & \mathbf{-4.99} \\ 0.02 & \mathbf{-0.12} & -0.33 & \mathbf{-2.11} & 0.51 \\ -0.02 & -0.01 & \mathbf{-0.77} & -0.64 & 0.24 \\ -0.00 & -0.00 & 0.01 & \mathbf{-0.11} & 0.04 \\ -0.00 & -0.00 & 0.03 & 0.01 & -0.09 \end{bmatrix} \begin{bmatrix} m_{t-2}^r \\ y_{t-2}^r \\ \Delta p_{t-2} \\ R_{m,t-2} \\ R_{b,t-2} \end{bmatrix}$$

$$+ \mathbf{\Phi}\mathbf{D}_t + \varepsilon_t$$

$\text{Log}(L_{\max}) = 2241.28$, $\log\left|\hat{\mathbf{\Omega}}\right| = -51.9$, $R^2(LR) = 0.99$, $R^2(LM) = 0.61$,
F-test on all regressors: $F(50, 463) = 22.0$

The F-tests on single regressors, distributed as $F(5, 101)$ are:

$$\begin{bmatrix} \Delta m^r_{t-1} & \Delta y^r_{t-1} & \Delta^2 p_{t-1} & \Delta R_{m,t-1} & \Delta R_{b,t-1} & m^r_{t-2} & y^r_{t-2} & \Delta p_{t-2} & R_{m,t-2} & R_{b,t-2} \\ \mathbf{48.8} & \mathbf{27.2} & \mathbf{106.9} & \mathbf{23.4} & \mathbf{27.5} & \mathbf{5.8} & \mathbf{3.9} & \mathbf{10.3} & \mathbf{4.6} & \mathbf{4.2} \end{bmatrix}.$$

The F-tests on the significance of the first five regressors have now obtained very large values, which is just an artifact of the Δ^2 transformation, and they do not really say much about how important the lagged $t-1$ variables are for explaining the variation in $\mathbf{x}_t$.

4.2.4 The relationship between the different VAR formulations

We shall now evaluate the above model formulations using the characteristic function based on the slightly more general VAR(3) model:

$$\mathbf{x}_t = \mathbf{\Pi}_1\mathbf{x}_{t-1} + \mathbf{\Pi}_2\mathbf{x}_{t-2} + \mathbf{\Pi}_3\mathbf{x}_{t-3} + \mathbf{\Phi}\mathbf{D}_t + \varepsilon_t \tag{4.13}$$

with the characteristic function:

$$\mathbf{\Pi}(z) = \mathbf{I} - \mathbf{\Pi}_1 z - \mathbf{\Pi}_2 z^2 - \mathbf{\Pi}_3 z^3.$$

The ECM form of (4.13), with $m = 1$, is:

$$\Delta\mathbf{x}_t = \mathbf{\Gamma}_1^{(1)}\Delta\mathbf{x}_{t-1} + \mathbf{\Gamma}_2^{(1)}\Delta\mathbf{x}_{t-2} + \mathbf{\Pi}\mathbf{x}_{t-1} + \mathbf{\Phi}\mathbf{D}_t + \varepsilon_t \tag{4.14}$$

and the characteristic function:

$$\begin{aligned} \mathbf{\Pi}(\mathbf{z}) &= \mathbf{I} - z - \mathbf{\Gamma}_1^{(1)}(1-z)z - \mathbf{\Gamma}_2^{(1)}(1-z)z^2 - \mathbf{\Pi}z, \\ &= \mathbf{I} - (\mathbf{I} + \mathbf{\Gamma}_1^{(1)} + \mathbf{\Pi})z - (\mathbf{\Gamma}_2^{(1)} - \mathbf{\Gamma}_1^{(1)})z^2 + \mathbf{\Gamma}_2^{(1)}z^3. \end{aligned}$$

The relation between the parameters of (4.13) and (4.14) can now be found as:

$$\begin{aligned} \mathbf{\Gamma}_1^{(1)} &= -(\mathbf{\Pi}_2 + \mathbf{\Pi}_3), \\ \mathbf{\Gamma}_2^{(1)} &= -\mathbf{\Pi}_3, \\ \mathbf{\Pi} &= -(\mathbf{I} - \mathbf{\Pi}_1 - \mathbf{\Pi}_2 - \mathbf{\Pi}_3). \end{aligned}$$

The ECM form of (4.13), with $m = 3$, is:

$$\Delta\mathbf{x}_t = \mathbf{\Gamma}_1^{(3)}\Delta\mathbf{x}_{t-1} + \mathbf{\Gamma}_2^{(3)}\Delta\mathbf{x}_{t-2} + \mathbf{\Pi}\mathbf{x}_{t-3} + \mathbf{\Phi}\mathbf{D}_t + \varepsilon_t \tag{4.15}$$

and the characteristic function:

$$\begin{aligned} \mathbf{\Pi}(z) &= \mathbf{I} - z - \mathbf{\Gamma}_1^{(3)}(1-z)z - \mathbf{\Gamma}_2^{(3)}(1-z)z^2 - \mathbf{\Pi}z^3, \\ &= \mathbf{I} - (\mathbf{I} + \mathbf{\Gamma}_1^{(3)})z - (\mathbf{\Gamma}_2^{(3)} - \mathbf{\Gamma}_1^{(3)})z^2 + (\mathbf{\Gamma}_2^{(3)} - \mathbf{\Pi})z^3. \end{aligned}$$

The relationship between (4.13) and (4.15) is:

$$\begin{aligned}\boldsymbol{\Gamma}_1^{(3)} &= -(\mathbf{I} - \boldsymbol{\Pi}_1),\\ \boldsymbol{\Gamma}_2^{(3)} &= -(\mathbf{I} - \boldsymbol{\Pi}_1 - \boldsymbol{\Pi}_2),\\ \boldsymbol{\Pi} &= -(\mathbf{I} - \boldsymbol{\Pi}_1 - \boldsymbol{\Pi}_2 - \boldsymbol{\Pi}_3).\end{aligned}$$

In both cases the $\boldsymbol{\Pi}$ matrix is unchanged, but the $\boldsymbol{\Gamma}_i^{(m)}$ depends on the chosen lag m of $\mathbf{x}_{t-m}$ in the model.

4.3 Misspecification tests

After the model has been estimated, the multivariate normality assumption underlying the VAR model can (and should) be checked against the data using the residuals $\hat{\varepsilon}_t$. In the subsequent sections, we shall briefly discuss some of the test procedures and information criteria contained in CATS in RATS (Dennis, Hansen, Johansen, and Juselius 2006) and in PcGive (Doornik and Hendry 2001b).

4.3.1 Specification checking

It is always useful to begin the specification checking with a graphical analysis. Quite often the graphs reveal specification problems that the tests fail to discover. Figures 4.1–4.5 show the fitted and actual values of $\Delta x_{i,t}$ (panel a), the empirical distribution compared to the normal (panel b), the residuals (panel c), and the autocorrelogram of order 20 (panel d). Figure 4.6 shows all the autocorrelations for the full system. The diagonal autocorrelograms are defined by $\mathrm{Corr}(\varepsilon_{x_{it}}, \varepsilon_{x_{it-h}}), i = 1, \ldots, 5, h = 1, \ldots, 18$, i.e. are the same as in Figures 4.1–4.5, panel *d,* whereas the off-diagonal diagrams define the cross-autocorrelograms $\mathrm{Corr}(\varepsilon_{x_{it}}, \varepsilon_{x_{jt-h}}), i \neq j$.

The graphs help us to spot the big 'value-added' residual in the income equation and the big 'deregulation' residual in the bond rate equation. But even though the graphical analysis is a powerful tool to detect problems in model specification, it cannot replace formal misspecification tests. This section will briefly discuss a variety of information criteria and multivariate and univariate residual tests, all of which are implemented in CATS and PcGive.

4.3.2 Residual correlations and information criteria

The VAR model is often called a 'reduced form' model because it describes the variation in $\mathbf{x}_t$ as a function of lagged values of the process, but not of current values. This means that all information about current effects in the data is contained in the residual covariance matrix $\boldsymbol{\Omega}$. Because correlations (standardized covariances) are easier to interpret, most software programs (including CATS and PcGive) report correlations instead of covariances. The correlation coefficients are calculated as follows:

$$\hat{\rho}_{ij} = \frac{\hat{\sigma}_{ij}}{\sqrt{\hat{\sigma}_{ii}\hat{\sigma}_{jj}}}, \quad i, j = 1, \ldots, p. \tag{4.16}$$

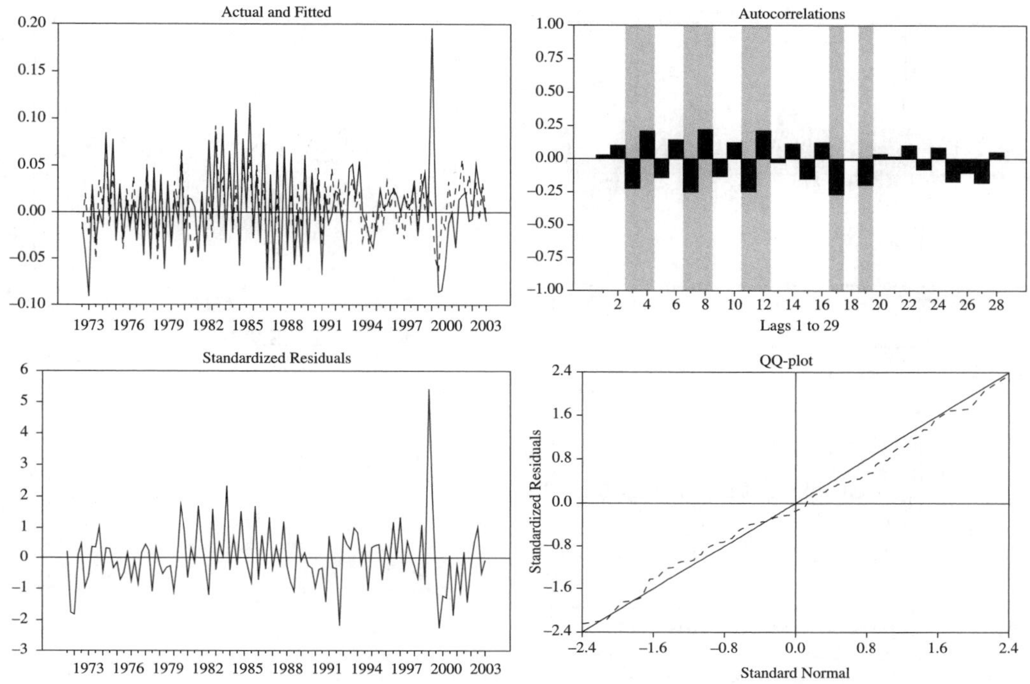

Fig 4.1 Graphs of residuals from the money stock equation.

When the correlation coefficients and the residual variances (or residual standard deviations) are given, it is straightforward to derive the corresponding covariances. The estimated standardized residual covariance matrix for the Danish data is reported in Section 4.1.1. Whether an estimated correlation coefficient is significant or not can be roughly assessed using the result that the standard error of a correlation coefficient is approximately given by $1/\sqrt{T}$.

The residual standard errors, $\hat{\sigma}_i = \sqrt{\hat{\sigma}_{ii}}$, $i = 1, \ldots, p$, are reported below:

Δm^r	Δy^r	$\Delta^2 p$	ΔR_m	ΔR_b
0.0369	0.0147	0.0087	0.0012	0.0016

Note that the residual standard errors, multiplied by 100, can be interpreted as a percentage error for lower case variables because such variables are in logarithmic changes.

When assessing the adequacy of the VAR specification, we frequently make use of the maximal likelihood value given by:

$$-(2/T)\ln L_{\max} = \ln|\hat{\mathbf{\Omega}}| + \text{constant terms}$$

where T is defined as the length of the effective sample, in contrast to the full sample $T + k$. When determining the truncation lag k of the VAR model, one can use the

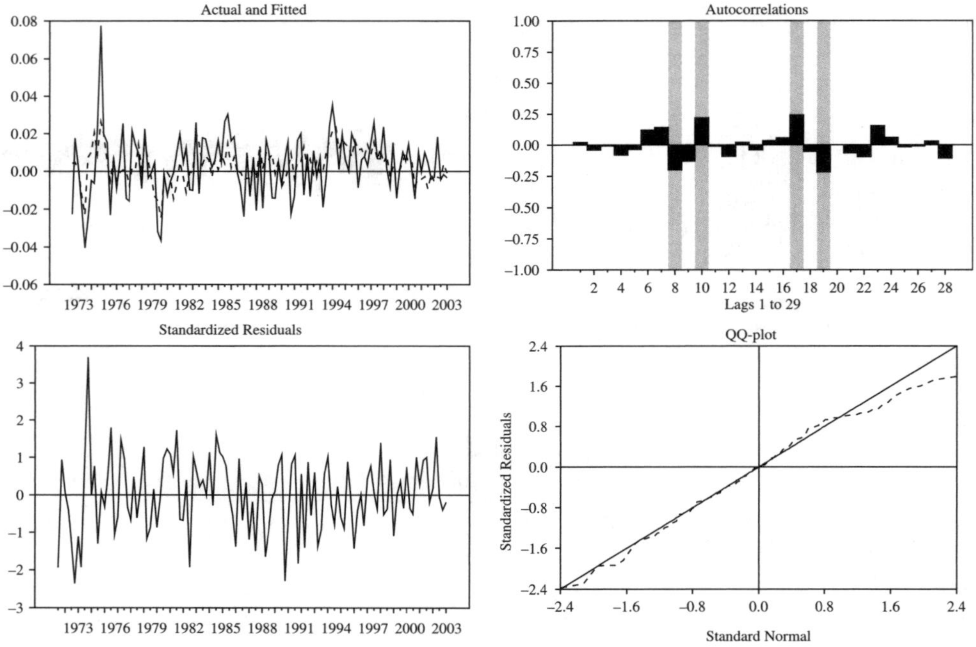

Fig 4.2 Graphs of residuals from the income equation.

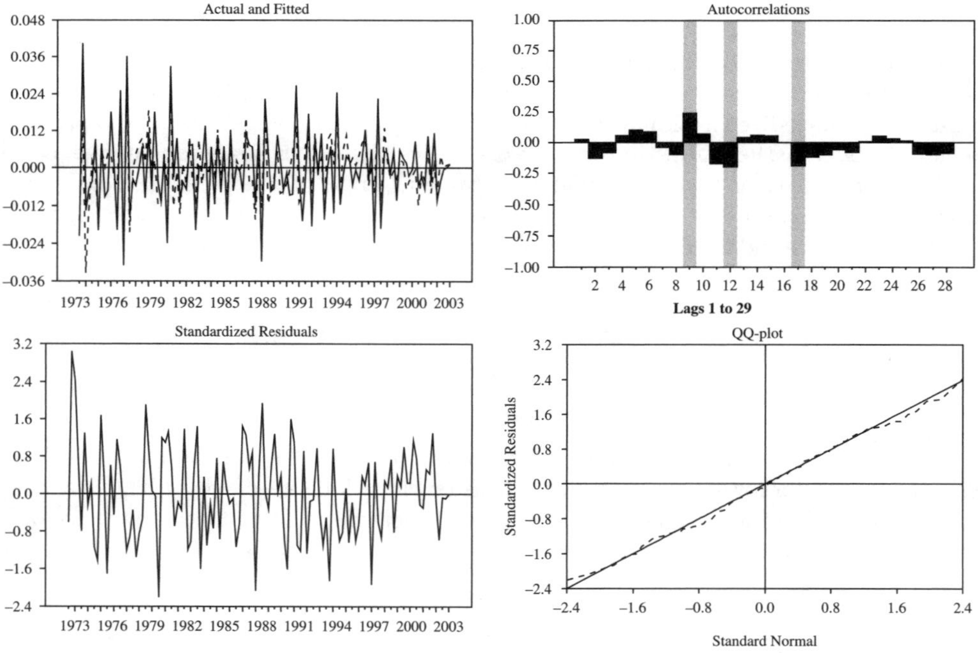

Fig 4.3 Graphs of residuals from the inflation equation.

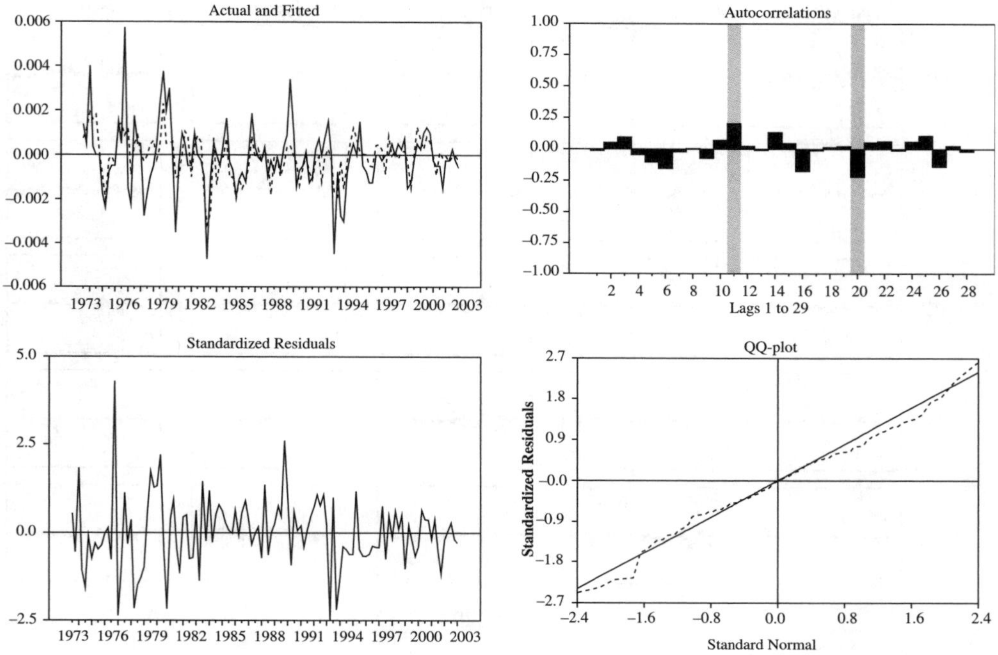

Fig 4.4 Graphs of residuals from the money stock interest rate equation.

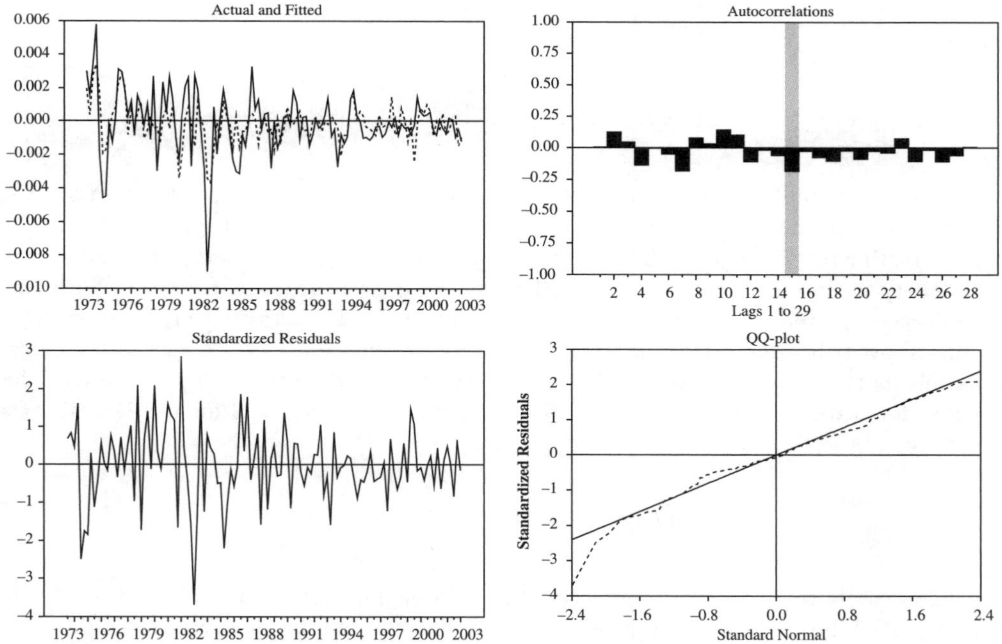

Fig 4.5 Graphs of residuals from the bond rate equation.

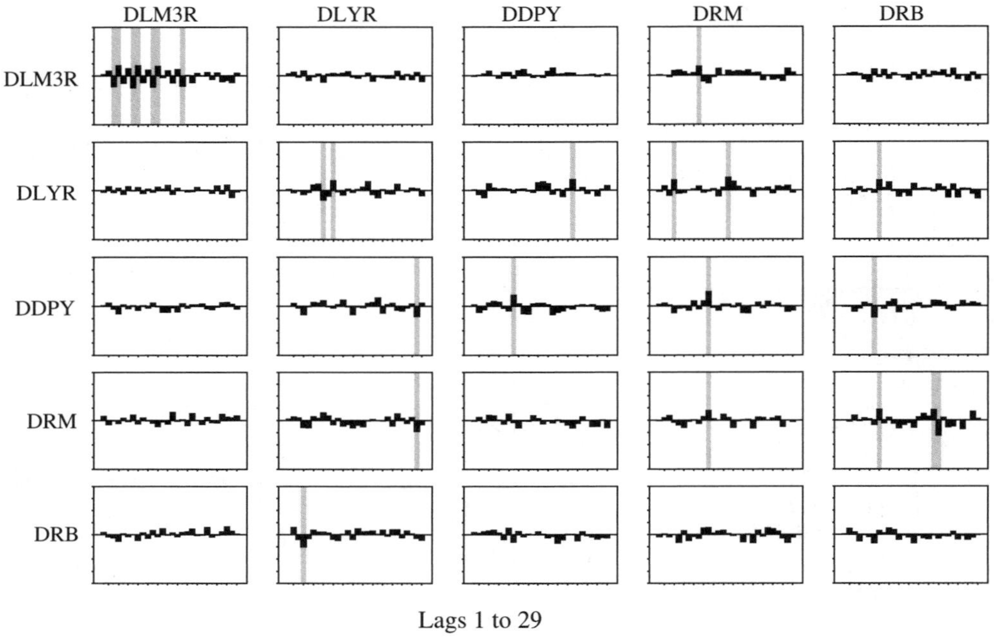

Fig 4.6 Cross- and autocorrelograms of the full system.

likelihood ratio test procedure

$$-2\ln Q(\mathcal{H}_k/\mathcal{H}_{k+1}) = T(\ln|\hat{\mathbf{\Omega}}_k| - \ln|\hat{\mathbf{\Omega}}_{k+1}|)$$

where $\mathcal{H}_k$ is the null hypothesis that the model needs k lags and $\mathcal{H}_{k+1}$ is the alternative hypothesis that the VAR model needs $k+1$ lags. Because the alternative hypothesis entails testing the $p \times p$ coefficients of the matrix Π_{k+1} to be zero, the test statistic $-2\ln Q$ is asymptotically distributed as χ^2 with p^2 degrees of freedom. Note that the effective number of observations has to be identical when testing $\mathcal{H}_k$ against $\mathcal{H}_{k+1}$ in the above LR procedure and in the various information criteria discussed below. This means that the effective number of observations is determined by the longest lag selected for testing. For example the LR test of $k = 1$ versus $k = 2$ for the Danish data becomes:

$$-2\ln Q(\mathcal{H}_1/\mathcal{H}_2) = 119(-51.0 + 51.9) = 107,$$

which is distributed as $\chi^2(25)$ under the null of no significant coefficients at lag 2 in the VAR model. The $\chi^2_{0.95}(25)$ is approximately 35 and the null is therefore rejected.

There are various other test procedures for the determination of the lag length and we shall briefly discuss three of them, the Akaike, the Schwartz and the Hannan–Quinn information criteria. They are defined by:

$$AIC = \ln|\hat{\boldsymbol{\Omega}}| + (p^2k)\frac{2}{T}, \quad (4.17)$$

$$SC = \ln|\hat{\boldsymbol{\Omega}}| + (p^2k)\frac{\ln T}{T} \quad (4.18)$$

$$H\text{-}Q = \ln|\hat{\boldsymbol{\Omega}}| + (p^2k)\frac{2\ln\ln T}{T}. \quad (4.19)$$

All of them are based on the maximal value of the likelihood function with an additional penalizing factor related to the number of estimated parameters. The suggested criteria differ regarding the strength of the penalty associated with the increase in model parameters as a result of adding more lags. The idea is to calculate the test criterion for different values of k and then choose the value of k that corresponds to the smallest value. When using these criteria for the choice of lag length, it is important to remember that they are valid under the assumption of a correctly specified model. If there are other problems with the model, such as regime shifts and non-constant parameters, then these should be accounted for prior to choosing the lag length.

Table 4.5 reports the test results of a batch procedure for lag determination implemented in CATS. The longest lag, $k = 5$, determines the sample length and all tests are based on 1974:02 to 2003:01. This is why the LR test results in the table are not identical to the result reported above.

In the upper part of Table 4.5 the Schwartz criterion suggests $k = 1$ and the H–Q suggests $k = 2$. Because the information criteria are based on different penalties, they

Table 4.5 Lag length determination. Model summary: sample period 1974:2–2003:1.

Model	k	regr	Log-Lik	SC	H–Q	LM(1)	Lm(k)
VAR(5)	5	29	3081.7	−47.19	−49.23	0.662	0.27
VAR(4)	4	24	3056.8	−47.78	−49.48	0.01	0.41
VAR(3)	3	19	3034.7	−48.43	−49.77	0.11	0.07
VAR(2)	2	14	3028.3	−49.17	**−50.16**	0.35	0.02
VAR(1)	1	9	2970.8	**−49.38**	−50.01	0.00	0.00

Lag reduction tests

VAR(4)	>>	VAR(5)	$\chi^2(25)$	=	49.8	[0.002]
VAR(3)	>>	VAR(5)	$\chi^2(50)$	=	93.9	[0.000]
VAR(3)	>>	VAR(4)	$\chi^2(25)$	=	44.1	[0.011]
VAR(2)	>>	VAR(5)	$\chi^2(75)$	=	126.9	[0.000]
VAR(2)	>>	VAR(4)	$\chi^2(50)$	=	77.0	[0.008]
VAR(2)	>>	VAR(3)	$\chi^2(25)$	=	32.9	**[0.133]**
VAR(1)	>>	VAR(5)	$\chi^2(100)$	=	221.7	[0.000]
VAR(1)	>>	VAR(4)	$\chi^2(75)$	=	171.9	[0.000]
VAR(1)	>>	VAR(3)	$\chi^2(50)$	=	127.8	[0.000]
VAR(1)	>>	VAR(2)	$\chi^2(25)$	=	94.8	[0.000]

need not produce the same answer and often do not. Checking the other misspecification tests showed that all of them became much worse for $k = 1$ as compared to $k = 2$ which suggests that *SC* might have penalized too much. The LM tests in the last two columns can be used to check for left-over residual autocorrelation in each VAR(k) model. We note that the tests mostly seem to accept absence of autocorrelation, except for first order autocorrelation in the VAR(4) model, second order in the VAR(2) and first order in the VAR(1).

In contrast, the LR lag reduction tests in the lower part of Table 4.5 seem to suggest that the lag length should be five rather than one or two suggested by the *SC* and *H–Q* criteria. This is because no penalizing factor has been applied to the LR tests. The latter indicate significant autoregressive coefficients at lag 1, 2, 4 and 5, whereas not at lag 3. Significant coefficients at the seasonal lags 4 and 5 are likely to be associated with time-varying seasonality in the data which has not been captured by the fixed seasonal dummies. In Chapter 6 we shall argue that this left-over seasonality is associated with a structural break in the seasonal pattern of M3.

Based on the results of Table 4.5 we could choose $k = 1$ (the *SC* criterion), $k = 2$ (the H–Q criterion) or $k = 5$ (the LR tests). How should we proceed? In Section 3.6.1 we argued that a lag length of two is in most cases sufficient to describe a very rich dynamic structure even in a small-dimensional system. The question is whether it is advisable to increase the lag length at this stage. Since other types of misspecification, such as outlier observations and mean shifts, are likely to generate autocorrelated residuals, the lag tests will often suggest too many lags in a model which suffers from such misspecification. But to be able to diagnose the source of the misspecification we need to determine the lag length, and to determine the lag length we need a well-specified model. Of course, this is a problem with all misspecification tests: each of them are valid given that the others are not violated. Even though it is difficult to give a precise rule for how to proceed, experience suggests that adding too many lags is more harmful for the results than accepting some moderate residual autocorrelation in the model. This is because regime shifts, non-constant parameters, etc. are often difficult to diagnose in a heavily over-parameterized model. Furthermore, experience suggests that residual autocorrelation in a first tentative VAR(2) model is more often associated with structural misspecification, rather than with left-out dynamics.

Even though it is admittedly hard from the outset to know whether significant residual autocorrelation is due to misspecification or too few lags in the model, in practice it is seldom the case that a well-specified model needs more than two lags. Therefore, as a rule of thumb it seems useful to start with a VAR(2) model, search for structural shifts and, if necessary, respecify the model. When the model is well-specified one should test whether the lag length needs to be altered and, in case this is so, one should redo the specification checking in the new model.

Thus, even though the LR tests suggested a lag length of five we continue with the VAR(2) model. As a matter of fact, based on the final respecified VAR model[2] of Chapter 6 the above test procedures suggested unambiguosly a lag length of two. Thus, it is important to keep in mind that the test results remain tentative until the model has been corrected for possible regime shifts and other specification problems.

[2]Corrected for a regime shift in 1983:1, a structural change in the seasonality pattern of M3, and a mistake in the measurements of M3 in 1999.

In the VAR model we can calculate an overall measure of goodness of fit, which is similar to the conventional R^2 in the linear regression model. In CATS this measure is called 'trace correlation'.

$$\text{Trace correlation} = 1 - \text{trace}(\hat{\boldsymbol{\Omega}}\,[\text{Cov}(\Delta\mathbf{x}_t)]^{-1})/p,$$

where $\text{Cov}(\Delta\mathbf{x}_t)$ is the covariance matrix of $\Delta\mathbf{x}_t$. The trace correlation can be roughly interpreted as an average R^2 in the p VAR equations. For the Danish data it is 0.40.

PcGive calculates two alternative measures called $R^2(LR)$ and $R^2(LM)$ in the VAR model which are defined in the PcGive manual, Section 10.8.

Finally, R^2 for each equation is calculated as $R_i^2 = 1 - \hat{\Omega}_{ii}/\text{Var}\Delta \text{x}_{i,t}$, $i = 1, \ldots, p$, where $\hat{\Omega}_{ii}$ is the estimated residual variance of equation i. For the Danish data the estimated R_i^2 for the models in ECM form are:

Δm^r	Δy^r	$\Delta^2 p$	ΔR_m	ΔR_b
0.47	0.30	0.59	0.40	0.38

We recall from Section 4.1.1 that the R^2 values were said to be completely misleading when calculated for the unrestricted VAR(2) in levels, because the dependent variables in this case were non-stationary, trending variables. This is because a conventionally calculated R^2 compares the models ability to explain the variation in the dependent variable as compared to the baseline of a constant mean, i.e. $R^2 = 1 - \Sigma\hat{\varepsilon}_i^2/\Sigma(x_i - \overline{x})^2$. When $x_{i,t}$ is a non-stationary variable, the baseline of a constant mean is no longer appropriate. Essentially any trending variable, however unrelated to $x_{i,t}$, will do better than a constant. Therefore, when the variables are integrated of first order, the R^2 makes sense only when the dependent variable is given as $\Delta x_{i,t}$. In this case R^2 measure the explanatory power of the regressor variables as compared to the random walk model.

4.3.3 Tests of residual autocorrelation

The Ljung–Box test of residual autocorrelation is given by:

$$\text{Ljung–Box} = T(T+2)\sum_{h=1}^{T/4}(T-h)^{-1}\text{trace}(\hat{\boldsymbol{\Omega}}_h'\hat{\boldsymbol{\Omega}}^{-1}\hat{\boldsymbol{\Omega}}_h'\hat{\boldsymbol{\Omega}}^{-1}) \tag{4.20}$$

where $\hat{\boldsymbol{\Omega}}_h = T^{-1}\sum_{t=h}^{T} \hat{\varepsilon}_t\hat{\varepsilon}_{t-h}'$ and the residuals are from the estimated VAR model. The Ljung–Box test is considered to be approximately distributed as χ^2 with $p^2(T/4 - k + 1) - p^2$ degrees of freedom (see Ljung and G. Box (1978); Hosking (1980)). For the Danish data the test becomes $\chi^2(675) = 725.4$ (p-value $= 0.09$).

The LM test of jth order autocorrelation is calculated using an auxiliary regression as proposed in Godfrey (1988). The residuals in the auxiliary model are obtained by regressing the estimated VAR residuals, $\hat{\varepsilon}_t$, on the k lagged variables, $\mathbf{x}_{t-1}, \mathbf{x}_{t-2}, \ldots, \mathbf{x}_{t-k}$, and the jth lagged VAR residual, $\hat{\varepsilon}_{t-j}$, i.e:

$$\hat{\varepsilon}_t = \mathbf{A}_1\mathbf{x}_{t-1} + \mathbf{A}_2\mathbf{x}_{t-2} + \cdots + \mathbf{A}_k\mathbf{x}_{t-k} + \mathbf{A}_\varepsilon\hat{\varepsilon}_{t-j} + \tilde{\varepsilon}_t \tag{4.21}$$

where the first j missing values $\hat{\varepsilon}_{-j}, \cdots, \hat{\varepsilon}_{-1}$ are set to 0. The LM test is calculated as a Wilks' ratio test with a small-sample correction (see Anderson (2003) or Rao (1973)):

$$\text{LM(j)} = -(T - p(k+1) - \tfrac{1}{2}) \ln \left(\frac{|\tilde{\mathbf{\Omega}}(j)|}{|\hat{\mathbf{\Omega}}|} \right). \tag{4.22}$$

The test is approximately distributed as χ^2 with p^2 degrees of freedom. Because the VAR methodology is based on the idea of decomposing the variation in the data into a systematic part describing all the dynamics and an unsystematic random part, this is an important test. If the test suggests that there are significant autocorrelations left in the model, agents plans (based on the conditional expectations of the VAR model) would have deviated systematically from actual realizations. Even more importantly, all χ^2 and F tests derived for the VAR model are based on the assumption of independent errors and if not satisfied the distribution of the tests will deviate from χ^2 and F in unknown ways. Also the properties of the estimators may be sensitive to significant autocorrelations. In particular the OLS estimator is inconsistent when there are residual autocorrelations, the larger the coefficients the worse.

The test statistic for the Danish data became LM(1) : $\chi^2(25) = 23.1$ (p-value $= 0.57$) and LM(4) : $\chi^2(25) = 36.7$ (p-value $= 0.06$). The LM(4) test value suggests that there is some seasonal autocorrelation left in the model after having included quarterly seasonal dummies. A graphical inspection of real money stock shows that the seasonal pattern seems to have changed during the sample, so that the specification of constant seasonal means is not appropriate for the full sample period. This will be further discussed in Chapter 6.

4.3.4 Tests of residual heteroscedasticity

The mth order ARCH test is calculated as $(T + k - m) \times R^2$, where T is the total sample size, k is the lag length of the VAR, and R^2 is from the auxiliary regression,

$$\hat{\varepsilon}^2_{i,t} = \gamma_0 + \sum_{j=1}^{m} \gamma_j \; \hat{\varepsilon}^2_{i,t-j} + \text{error}.$$

The test is approximately distributed as χ^2 with m degrees of freedom. The residuals from each equation of the Danish data were tested individually for ARCH effects with the following result:

Δm^r	Δy^r	$\Delta^2 p$	ΔR_m	ΔR_b
0.9[0.64]	1.4[0.49]	4.8[0.09]	4.8[0.09]	**6.1**[0.05]

Only the residuals from the bond rate equation exhibited borderline significant ARCH effects. However, Rahbek et al. (2002) have shown that the cointegration rank tests are robust against moderate residual ARCH effects.

4.3.5 Normality tests

Most normality tests are based on skewness, i.e. the third moment around the mean, and excess kurtosis, i.e. the forth moment around the mean. Both are asymptotically normal, but unfortunately a fairly large sample is needed before the asymptotics begin to work. Therefore, Shenton–Bowman (1977) suggested a transformation of the two measures and showed that the transformed measures were approximately normal. Both the univariate and the multivariate normality tests discussed here are based on the Shenton–Bowman transformation.

The skewness and kurtosis of the standardized estimated errors $(\hat{\varepsilon}_i/\hat{\sigma}_i)_t$, $i = 1,\ldots,p$, $t = 1,\ldots,T$, are calculated as:

$$\text{skewness}_i = \sqrt{\hat{b}_{1i}} = T^{-1}\sum_{t=1}^{T}(\hat{\varepsilon}_i/\hat{\sigma}_i)_t^3, \tag{4.23}$$

$$\text{kurtosis}_i = \hat{b}_{2i} = T^{-1}\sum_{t=1}^{T}(\hat{\varepsilon}_i/\hat{\sigma}_i)_t^4. \tag{4.24}$$

Under the null of normally distributed errors, the skewness and kurtosis of the residuals $\hat{\varepsilon}_i$ is asymptotically normal with the following mean and variance:

$$\sqrt{T}(\text{skewness}_i - 0) \overset{a}{\sim} N(0,6)$$

and

$$\sqrt{T}(\text{kurtosis}_i - 3) \overset{a}{\sim} N(0,24).$$

Thus, the variance of skewness is smaller than the variance of kurtosis, which means that the normality test is more sensitive to deviations from normality due to skewness (often as a result of outliers) than to excess kurtosis (thick tails or too many small residuals close to the mean). The asymptotic univariate test for normality of a residual $\hat{\varepsilon}_{i,t}$ is based on the sum of the squared standardized skewness and kurtosis, which under the assumption of asymptotic normality and independence is distributed as $\chi^2(2)$. The test statistic is calculated as

$$\eta_i^{as} = T(\text{skewness}_i)^2/6 + T(\text{kurtosis}_i - 3)^2/24 \overset{a}{\sim} \chi^2(2).$$

If the sample is large one can use the asymptotic multivariate test:

$$m\eta_i^{as} = \sum_{i=1}^{p}\eta_i^{as} \overset{a}{\sim} \chi^2(2p).$$

In small samples, skewness and kurtosis are neither asymptotically normal nor independent. The Shenton–Bowman procedure transforms the skewness $\sqrt{b_1}$ to the new variable z_1 based on the formulas:

$$
\begin{aligned}
z_1 &= \delta \log\left\{y + (y^2+1)^{\frac{1}{2}}\right\} \\
y &= \sqrt{b_1}\left\{\frac{\omega^2-1}{2}\frac{(T+1)(T+3)}{6(T-2)}\right\}^{\frac{1}{2}} \\
\delta &= \frac{1}{\left\{\log\sqrt{\omega^2}\right\}^{\frac{1}{2}}} \\
\omega^2 &= -1 + \{2(\beta-1)\}^{\frac{1}{2}} \\
\beta &= \frac{3(T^2+27T-70)(T+1)(T+3)}{(T-2)(T+5)(T+7)(T+9)}.
\end{aligned}
$$

The kurtosis b_2 is transformed to z_2 based on

$$
\begin{aligned}
z_2 &= \left\{(\frac{\chi}{2a})^{\frac{1}{3}} - 1 + \frac{1}{9\alpha}\right\}(9\alpha)^{\frac{1}{2}} \\
\chi &= (b_2 - 1 - b_1)2k \\
\alpha &= a + b_1 c \\
k &= \frac{(T+5)(T+7)(T^3+37T^2+11T-313}{12\delta} \\
c &= \frac{(T-7)(T+5)(T+7)(T^2+2T-5)}{6\delta} \\
a &= \frac{(T-2)(T+5)(T+7)(T^2+27T-70)}{6\delta} \\
\delta &= (T-3)(T+1)(T^2+15T-4).
\end{aligned}
$$

The multivariate test suggested in Hansen and Doornik (1994) uses the Shenton–Bowman transformation to test residual normality in a VAR system. Because the p VAR residuals are generally correlated they first need to be orthogonalized. The orthogonalized residuals are obtained by a principal components decomposition of the original residual correlation matrix, $\boldsymbol{R}$. They are defined by

$$\boldsymbol{r}_t = \mathbf{V}\boldsymbol{\Lambda}^{-\frac{1}{2}}\mathbf{V}'\mathbf{S}\hat{\varepsilon}_t, \tag{4.25}$$

where $\boldsymbol{\Lambda} = \text{diag}(\lambda_1, \ldots, \lambda_p)$ is a diagonal matrix of the eigenvalues and $\mathbf{V}$ are the corresponding eigenvectors, $\mathbf{S} = \text{diag}(\hat{\sigma}_{11}^{-1/2}, \ldots, \hat{\sigma}_{pp}^{-1/2})$ obtained by a principal component decomposition of the residual correlation matrix $\boldsymbol{R}$. The orthogonalized residuals are uncorrelated by construction and independent under the assumption of normality. The multivariate normality test is calculated as the sum of the p univariate Shenton–Bowman (1977) normality tests using the orthogonalized residuals when calculating skewness and kurtosis.

For the Danish data the multivariate Hansen–Doornik test became $\chi^2(10) = 80.9$ (p-value $= 0.00$). Thus, normality is strongly rejected. To find out whether the problem with the lack of normality is associated with some specific variables, it is useful to check the univariate tests. Furthermore, because the VAR estimates are more sensitive to deviations

Table 4.6 Specification tests for the unrestricted VAR(2) model.

Univariate normality tests for:	Δm^r	Δy^r	Δp	ΔR_m	ΔR_b
Norm(2)	**34.7**	3.3	0.8	**20.6**	**9.0**
Skewness	1.33	0.10	0.19	0.48	−0.31
Excess kurtosis	6.26	0.57	−0.17	2.43	1.25

from normality due to skewness than to excess kurtosis, Table 4.6 reports these measures for each variable.

We find that the normality is rejected primarily because of non-normality in real money and the two interest rate equations. This is due to an additive outlier in real money around 1999 (which will be discussed later in Section 6.6) and the big 'deregulation' outlier in 1983 for the bond rate. We see that the outlier in the real money equation gives skewed residuals as well as substantial excess kurtosis. The residuals from the two interest rate equations exhibit excess kurtosis, whereas skewness is less of a problem.

Altogether the formal misspecification tests have confirmed the findings based on the graphical inspection: multivariate normality is rejected due to non-normality in real money and the two interest rates; there is some seasonal autocorrelation left in the residuals; the bond rate exhibits moderate ARCH effects. However, the residual autocorrelation tests and the ARCH tests are derived under the assumption of normally distributed errors and the normality tests are derived under assumption of independent and homoscedastic errors. This means that we do not know whether all the tests which already passed the misspecification checking can be trusted or not and all misspecification tests need to be recalculated after the model has been respecified. As a minimum the respecified model needs to account for the value added reform in 1975, the deregulation in 1983, the outliers in money stock in 1999, and the change in the seasonal pattern. But, even though these problems are satisfactorily solved there is no guarantee that the respecified model will pass the misspecification tests. Solving one problem frequently reveals a new misspecification problem that was previous hidden. This is because misspecification in the model causes the residual variance to become large which will make it more difficult to see other less apparent specification problems.

4.4 Concluding remarks

The VAR(2) model seemed to provide a fairly good description of the information in the data. But the misspecification tests and the graphs suggested, nonetheless, some scope for improvements. In Chapter 6 we shall discuss the important role of deterministic components as a means to improve model specification.

All parameters of the VAR model (4.7)–(4.11) estimated in this chapter were unrestricted and we demonstrated that OLS equation by equation produced ML estimates. In this chapter, the estimates of these models showed that the unrestricted VAR models are heavily over-parametrized. This is consistent with the discussion in Chapter 3 which showed that the VAR model is essentially just a convenient reformulation of the covariances of the data, some of which are very small and statistically insignificant.

The generality of the VAR formulation has a cost: adding one variable to a p-dimensional VAR(k) system introduces $(2p + 1) \times k$ new parameters. When the sample is small, typically 50–100 in quarterly macroeconomic models, adding more variables can easily become prohibitive. However, in some cases there can be a trade-off between the number of variables in the system, p, and the number of lags, k, needed to obtain uncorrelated residuals. Since an extra lag corresponds to $p \times p$ additional parameters one can in some cases reduce the total number of VAR parameters by adding a relevant variable to the model.

By imposing statistically acceptable restrictions on the VAR model such as reduced rank restrictions, zero coefficient restrictions and other linear and nonlinear restrictions, we hope to uncover meaningful and interpretable economic structures. This will be the focus of the remaining chapters of this book.

5

The cointegrated VAR model

The purpose of this chapter is to introduce the non-stationary VAR model and show that the presence of unit roots (i.e. stochastic trends) leads to a reduced rank condition on the long-run matrix $\mathbf{\Pi} = \boldsymbol{\alpha}\boldsymbol{\beta}'$. Section 5.1 defines the concepts of integration and cointegration and Section 5.2 gives an intuitive interpretation of the reduced rank, r, as the number of stationary long-run relations based on the unrestricted VAR estimates of the Danish data. Section 5.3 discusses the interpretation of the number of unit roots, $p - r$, as the number of common driving trends and shows how they can be related to the VAR model by inverting the AR lag polynomial. Based on the simple VAR(1) model, Section 5.4 demonstrates how the parameters of the MA representation are related to the AR parameters. Finally, Section 5.5 concludes the chapter with a discussion of the cointegrated VAR model as a general framework within which one can describe economic behaviour in terms of forces pulling towards equilibrium, generating stationary behaviour, and forces pushing away from equilibrium, generating non-stationary behaviour.

5.1 Defining integration and cointegration

This section demonstrates that the presence of unit roots in the unrestricted VAR model corresponds to non-stationary stochastic behaviour which can be accounted for by a reduced rank ($r < p$) restriction of the long-run levels matrix $\mathbf{\Pi} = \boldsymbol{\alpha}\boldsymbol{\beta}'$. Johansen (1996), Chapter 3, provides a mathematically precise definition of the order of integration and cointegration. Here we only reproduce the basic definitions:

Definition 2 $\mathbf{x}_t$ is integrated of order d if $\mathbf{x}_t$ has the representation $(1 - L)^d\mathbf{x}_t = \mathbf{C}(L)\boldsymbol{\varepsilon}_t$, where $\mathbf{C}(1) \neq \mathbf{0}$, and $\boldsymbol{\varepsilon}_t \sim IN(\mathbf{0}, \mathbf{\Omega})$.

Definition 3 The $I(d)$ process $\mathbf{x}_t$ is called cointegrated *CI*(d,b) with cointegrating vector $\boldsymbol{\beta} \neq \mathbf{0}$ if $\boldsymbol{\beta}'\mathbf{x}_t$ is $I(d\text{-}b)$, $b = 1,\ldots,d$, $d = 1,\ldots$

Cointegration implies that certain linear combinations of the variables of the vector process are integrated of lower order than the process itself. As already discussed informally in Chapter 2, cointegrated variables are driven by the same persistent shocks. Thus, if the non-stationarity of one variable corresponds to the non-stationarity of another variable, then there exists a linear combination between them that becomes stationary. Another way of expressing this is that when two or several variables have common stochastic (and deterministic) trends, they will show a tendency to move together in the long run. Such cointegrated relations, $\boldsymbol{\beta}'\mathbf{x}_t$, can often be interpreted as long-run economic steady-state relations and are therefore of considerable economic interest. In the next section, we shall give an intuitive account of such relations and how one can find them in the long-run matrix $\mathbf{\Pi}$.

5.2 An intuitive interpretation of $\mathbf{\Pi} = \boldsymbol{\alpha\beta}'$

Within the VAR model, the cointegration hypothesis can be formulated as a reduced rank restriction on the $\mathbf{\Pi}$ matrix defined in the previous chapter. Below we reproduce the VAR(2) model in ECM form with $m = 1$:

$$\Delta\mathbf{x}_t = \mathbf{\Gamma}_1\Delta\mathbf{x}_{t-1} + \mathbf{\Pi}\mathbf{x}_{t-1} + \boldsymbol{\mu} + \boldsymbol{\varepsilon}_t \tag{5.1}$$

and give the estimate of the unrestricted $\mathbf{\Pi}$ matrix for the Danish data:[1]

$$\mathbf{\Pi}\mathbf{x}_t = \begin{bmatrix} \mathbf{-0.26} & \mathbf{0.24} & \mathbf{-1.48} & \mathbf{5.04} & \mathbf{-4.99} \\ 0.02 & \mathbf{-0.12} & -0.33 & \mathbf{-2.11} & 0.51 \\ -0.02 & -0.01 & \mathbf{-0.77} & -0.64 & 0.24 \\ -0.00 & -0.00 & 0.01 & \mathbf{-0.11} & 0.04 \\ -0.00 & -0.00 & 0.03 & 0.01 & -0.09 \end{bmatrix} \begin{bmatrix} m^r_{t-1} \\ y^r_{t-1} \\ \Delta p_{t-1} \\ R_{m,t-1} \\ R_{b,t-1} \end{bmatrix}.$$

If $\mathbf{x}_t \sim I(1)$, then $\Delta\mathbf{x}_t \sim I(0)$ implying that $\mathbf{\Pi}$ cannot have full rank as this would lead to a logical inconsistency in (5.1). This can be seen by considering $\mathbf{\Pi} = \mathbf{I}$ as a simple full-rank matrix. In this case each equation would define a stationary variable $\Delta\mathbf{x}_t$ to be equal to a non-stationary variable, $\mathbf{x}_{t-1}$, plus some lagged stationary variables $\mathbf{\Gamma}_1\Delta\mathbf{x}_{t-1}$ and a stationary error term. Because a stationary variable cannot equal a non-stationary variable, either $\mathbf{\Pi} = \mathbf{0}$, or it must have reduced rank:

$$\mathbf{\Pi} = \boldsymbol{\alpha\beta}'$$

where $\boldsymbol{\alpha}$ and $\boldsymbol{\beta}$ are $p \times r$ matrices, $r \leq p$. Thus, under the $I(1)$ hypothesis, the cointegrated VAR model is given by:

$$\Delta\mathbf{x}_t = \mathbf{\Gamma}_1\Delta\mathbf{x}_{t-1} + \cdots + \mathbf{\Gamma}_{k-1}\Delta\mathbf{x}_{t-k+1} + \boldsymbol{\alpha\beta}'\mathbf{x}_{t-1} + \boldsymbol{\mu} + \boldsymbol{\varepsilon}_t \tag{5.2}$$

where $\boldsymbol{\beta}'\mathbf{x}_{t-1}$ is an $r \times 1$ vector of stationary cointegration relations. Under the hypothesis that $\mathbf{x}_t \sim I(1)$, all stochastic components are stationary in model (5.2) and the system is now logically consistent.

[1]Coefficients with a $|t\text{-ratio}| > 2.0$ are given in bold face.

In Chapter 4, Section 4.2.1, we showed that the first row of $\mathbf{\Pi}$ was a linear combination of the five variables which could be given a tentative interpretation as a (stationary) deviation from a long-run money demand relation, i.e. as an equilibrium error. We shall now examine the implications of this for the full VAR model, assuming that $r = 1$, i.e. among the five variables there exists only one stationary relation, the money demand relation. Using (roughly) the estimated coefficients of the Danish data $\alpha_{11} = -0.26$ and $\boldsymbol{\beta}_1' = [1, -0.9, 5.7, -19.3, 19.3]$, we can approximately reproduce the first row of $\mathbf{\Pi}$ as $\alpha_{11}\boldsymbol{\beta}_1'$. If, for simplicity, we assume that $\mathbf{\Gamma}_1 = \mathbf{0}$, the cointegrated VAR model can now be written as:

$$\begin{bmatrix} \Delta m_t^r \\ \Delta y_t^r \\ \Delta^2 p_t \\ \Delta R_{m,t} \\ \Delta R_{b,t} \end{bmatrix} = \begin{bmatrix} -0.26 \\ \alpha_{21} \\ \alpha_{31} \\ \alpha_{41} \\ \alpha_{51} \end{bmatrix} \left[\{m^r - 0.9y^r + 5.7\Delta p - 19.3(R_m - R_b)\}_{t-1} \right]$$
$$+ \begin{bmatrix} \mu_1 \\ \mu_2 \\ \mu_3 \\ \mu_4 \\ \mu_5 \end{bmatrix} + \begin{bmatrix} \varepsilon_{1,t} \\ \varepsilon_{2,t} \\ \varepsilon_{3,t} \\ \varepsilon_{4,t} \\ \varepsilon_{5,t} \end{bmatrix}. \tag{5.3}$$

The question is now how to choose the estimates of $\alpha_{21}, \ldots, \alpha_{51}$ so that the relevant information contained in $\mathbf{\Pi}$ is preserved. An inspection of the unrestricted $\mathbf{\Pi}$ matrix shows that the coefficients to income and the short rate in the second row (the real income equation) are proportional to the corresponding coefficients in the first row. If the remaining coefficients of the second row had also been proportional to the first row, (such as $0.14m^r - 0.12y^r + 0.70\Delta p - 2.11(R_m - R_b)$), then we would have concluded that both real money stock and real aggregate income have adjusted to the same long-run money demand relation with an adjustment coefficient -0.26 and $+0.12$. However, in this case the discrepancy is too large to justify such a choice. Finally, because none of the remaining rows seem to have coefficients even vaguely proportional to $\boldsymbol{\beta}_1'\mathbf{x}_{t-1}$ we conclude that $\alpha_{21} = a_{31} = a_{41} = a_{51} = 0$ seems the only possible choice. Thus, for $r = 1$ the best representation of $\mathbf{\Pi} = \boldsymbol{\alpha\beta}'$ is approximately:

$$\begin{bmatrix} \Delta m_t^r \\ \Delta y_t^r \\ \Delta^2 p_t \\ \Delta R_{m,t} \\ \Delta R_{b,t} \end{bmatrix} = \begin{bmatrix} -0.26 \\ 0.0 \\ 0.0 \\ 0.0 \\ 0.0 \end{bmatrix} \left[\{m^r - 0.9y^r + 5.7\Delta p - 19.3(R_m - R_b)\}_{t-1} \right]$$
$$+ \boldsymbol{\mu} + \boldsymbol{\varepsilon}_t. \tag{5.4}$$

Model (5.4) represents an economy where the deviation between agents' actual money holdings, m_{t-1}^r, and their desired demand for money, $m_{t-1}^{r*} = 0.9y^r - 5.7\Delta p + 19.3(R_m - R_b)\}_{t-1}$, exclusively determines the real money stock. When actual money holdings are above or below the long-run desired level, agents make gradual adjustments of their money holdings until the level of money stock has been brought back to the equilibrium level. 'Excess money' has no short-run or long-run impact on any of the other variables, inclusive inflation rate and the short interest rate. In this simple empirical model it can be shown that the central bank would not be able to exert any long-run influence on the other variables of the system by changing money supply. In the terminology of Chapter 11, shocks to money stock would only have transitory effects on the variables of the system. Thus, the specific values of the coefficients $\boldsymbol{\alpha}$ and $\boldsymbol{\beta}$ can have important implications for whether a chosen policy is likely to be effective or not.

Under the assumption that $\alpha_{21} = a_{31} = a_{41} = a_{51} = 0$, model (5.4) would be equivalent to the single equation equilibrium-correction model. Such models have been widely used to estimate money demand relations based on the assumption that a stable relation is a prerequisite for monetary policy control. Needless to say, the implications of (5.4) as discussed above suggest that the assumption $r = 1$ is too simplistic to be relevant as an analytical tool for monetary policy decisions.[2] We shall argue that one reason why this is necessarily so is that $r = 1$ presumes $p - r = 4$ common stochastic trends. Given the present information set, these seem too many to be consistent with most theoretical assumptions underlying inflation and monetary policy control. However, it is only by formulating a model for the full system that we can examine the implications of this seemingly innocent assumption.

The choice of $r = 1$ forced us to impose many restrictions on $\boldsymbol{\Pi}$, as it implied that the remaining 20 coefficients were all zero, which does not seem to be the case. Thus, the choice of $r = 1$ does not allow for enough flexibility in the description of the feed-back dynamics of the long-run structure. We shall now assume that $r = 2$ and see how this choice can give us more flexibility. The question is how to choose the second relation $\boldsymbol{\beta}_2'\mathbf{x}_{t-1}$ so that the two cointegration relations together approximately describe the structure of the $\boldsymbol{\Pi}$ matrix. Because, the proportionality assumption of the first two rows did not seem consistent with the data, we can instead let the second cointegration relation describe a relation between real income and the short rate with coefficients approximately consistent with the second row of the $\boldsymbol{\Pi}$ matrix. The $r = 2$ system can now be approximately represented as:

$$\begin{bmatrix} \Delta m_t^r \\ \Delta y_t^r \\ \Delta^2 p_t \\ \Delta R_{m,t} \\ \Delta R_{b,t} \end{bmatrix} = \begin{bmatrix} -0.26 & 0 \\ 0 & -0.12 \\ 0 & 0 \\ 0 & 0 \\ 0 & 0 \end{bmatrix} \begin{bmatrix} \{(m^r - 0.9y^r) - 5.7\Delta p - 19.3(R_m - R_b)\}_{t-1} \\ \{y^r + 17.5R_m\}_{t-1} \end{bmatrix} + \boldsymbol{\mu} + \boldsymbol{\varepsilon}_t. \quad (5.5)$$

Although (5.5) can approximately reproduce the relevant information of the first two rows of $\boldsymbol{\Pi}$, it is not be able to reproduce the information in the next two rows related to the inflation rate and the short interest rate. Thus, we might need to increase the rank to three (or even four) to be able to describe all information in the Π matrix.

An inspection of the coefficients in third row shows that only inflation rate seems significant suggesting that inflation rate is a stationary variable by itself. This hypothesis will be formally tested in Chapter 10 and strongly rejected. This illustrates that the 'significance' of the coefficients in the Π matrix is only indicative, partly because the

[2] At this point we will disregard the possibility of extending the information set and how this may change the interpretation of the model.

model is not yet properly specified, partly because the estimated coefficients are not distributed as Student's t when the variables are non-stationary.

For illustrative purposes we shall, nevertheless, choose the third cointegration vector to be the inflation rate and the model for $r = 3$ could, for example, be specified as:

$$\begin{bmatrix} \Delta m_t^r \\ \Delta y_t^r \\ \Delta^2 p_t \\ \Delta R_{m,t} \\ \Delta R_{b,t} \end{bmatrix} = \begin{bmatrix} -0.26 & 0 & -1.5 \\ 0 & -0.12 & 0 \\ 0 & 0 & -0.77 \\ 0 & 0 & 0 \\ 0 & 0 & 0 \end{bmatrix} \begin{bmatrix} \{m^r - 0.9y^r - 19.3(R_m - R_b)\}_{t-1} \\ \{y^r + 17.5R_m\}_{t-1} \\ \Delta p_{t-1} \end{bmatrix} + \boldsymbol{\mu} + \boldsymbol{\varepsilon}_t. \tag{5.6}$$

Note that $\Delta p_t \sim I(0)$ implies that the money demand relation can be specified as the sum of two stationary components:

$$\begin{aligned} & -0.26\{(m^r - 0.9y^r) - 5.7\Delta p - 19.3(R_m - R_b)\}_{t-1} \\ & = -0.26\{(m^r - 0.9y^r) - 19.3(R_m - R_b)\}_{t-1} - 1.5\Delta p_{t-1} \end{aligned}$$

Model (5.6) is now able to roughly reproduce the data information in $\mathbf{\Pi x}_{t-1}$, except that the 'significant' short-term interest rate in the fourth row of $\mathbf{\Pi}$ will not be accounted for.

The above discussion served the purpose of illustrating that the choice of $\boldsymbol{\alpha}$ and $\boldsymbol{\beta}$ has to reproduce the statistical information in the $\mathbf{\Pi}$ matrix. No testing was performed and the proposed decompositions were, therefore, only tentative. Chapters 10 and 11 will discuss likelihood-based test procedures for a wide variety of hypotheses including the above mentioned.

The choice of $\boldsymbol{\alpha}$ and $\boldsymbol{\beta}$, in addition to reproducing the $\mathbf{\Pi}$ matrix, should ideally describe an interpretable economic structure and provide empirical insight on the appropriateness of the underlying economic model. The tentatively proposed cointegration relations given above are quite different from the 'monetary theory' consistent cointegration relations discussed in Chapter 2 and reproduced below. Chapter 2 did not discuss a hypothetical adjustment structure for the cointegration relations and the $\boldsymbol{\alpha}$ coefficients reported below have been chosen to be roughly consistent with plausible predictions from money inflation theory models.

$$\begin{bmatrix} \Delta m_t^r \\ \Delta y_t^r \\ \Delta^2 p_t \\ \Delta R_m \\ \Delta R_{b,t} \end{bmatrix} = \begin{bmatrix} -a_{11} & -a_{12} & -a_{13} \\ 0 & -a_{22} & a_{23} \\ a_{31} & 0 & a_{33} \\ -a_{41} & 0 & 0 \\ 0 & -a_{52} & 0 \end{bmatrix} \begin{bmatrix} (m - p - y^r)_{t-1} \\ (R_b - R_m)_{t-1} \\ (\Delta p - R_m)_{t-1} \end{bmatrix} + \boldsymbol{\mu} + \boldsymbol{\varepsilon}_t. \tag{5.7}$$

We note that $a_{11} = 0.26$ and $a_{12} \approx 5$ would approximately reproduce the money demand relation of (5.6) and that $a_{13} = 1.5$ would be consistent with the estimated inflation cost of holding money in (5.6), except that the latter is now (correctly) measured as the difference between inflation rate and the obtained yield on money. $a_{23} = -a_{22}$ implies that real aggregate income would decrease when the long-term real interest rate increases, i.e. an IS curve effect; $a_{31} > 0$ would imply that excess money leads to higher inflation; $a_{33} > 0$ implies that inflation goes down with an increase in the short-term interest rate, i.e. a monetary policy effect; $a_{41} > 0$ implies that the short-term interest goes down when there are excess liquidity in the economy; $a_{52} > 0$ implies that the long-term interest rate adjusts to the short-term.

The above discussion illustrated that a row in the $\mathbf{\Pi}$ matrix can also be found as a linear combination of several cointegration relations, and that a structure of economically meaningful long-run relations may not be easy to uncover by exclusively inspecting the $\mathbf{\Pi}$ matrix. Therefore, we also need to apply formal test procedures (to be discussed in Chapters 10–13) in the identification of the long-run structure. Nonetheless, a first inspection of the information in the Π matrix is usually indispensable for a successful identification of a long-run structure.

5.3 Common trends and the moving average representation

Chapter 3 showed that the stationary VAR model could be directly inverted into the moving average form. When the VAR model contains unit roots, the autoregressive lag polynomial becomes non-invertible. The purpose of this section is to demonstrate how we can find the moving average representation in this case. For simplicity of notation we focus on the simple VAR(2) model:

$$\mathbf{\Pi}(L)\mathbf{x_t} = (\mathbf{I} - \mathbf{\Pi}_1 L - \mathbf{\Pi}_2 L^2)\mathbf{x}_t = \boldsymbol{\mu} + \boldsymbol{\varepsilon}_t.$$

We assume now that the characteristic polynomial $|\mathbf{\Pi}(z)| = |\mathbf{I} - \mathbf{\Pi}_1 z - \mathbf{\Pi}_2 z^2|$ contains a unit root. In this case the determinant $|\mathbf{\Pi}(1)| = 0$ and $\mathbf{\Pi}(z)$ cannot be inverted for $z = 1$. Therefore, we need to factor out the unit root component of the lag polynomial of the VAR model. First we move the matrix lag polynomial to the right-hand side of the equation for $\mathbf{x}_t$:

$$\begin{aligned}\mathbf{\Pi}(L)\mathbf{x}_t &= \boldsymbol{\mu} + \boldsymbol{\varepsilon}_t \\ \mathbf{x}_t &= \mathbf{\Pi}^{-1}(L)(\boldsymbol{\mu} + \boldsymbol{\varepsilon}_t).\end{aligned} \tag{5.8}$$

Since $\mathbf{\Pi}^{-1}(L) = \mathbf{\Pi}^a(L)/\det(\mathbf{\Pi}(L))$ and $\det(\mathbf{\Pi}(L))$ is a polynomial in z we multiply both sides of (5.8) with the difference operator $(1 - L)$ so that the non-invertible unit root is cancelled out:

$$\begin{aligned}(1 - L)\mathbf{x}_t &= \mathbf{\Pi}^{-1}(L)(1 - L)(\boldsymbol{\varepsilon}_t + \boldsymbol{\mu}) \\ &= \mathbf{C}(L)(\boldsymbol{\varepsilon}_t + \boldsymbol{\mu}) \\ &= (\mathbf{C}_0 + \mathbf{C}_1 L + \mathbf{C}_2 L^2 + \cdots)(\boldsymbol{\varepsilon}_t + \boldsymbol{\mu})\end{aligned}$$

where the lag polynomial $\mathbf{C}(L)$ is now stationary. The characteristic function

$$\mathbf{C}(z) = \mathbf{C}_0 + \mathbf{C}_1 z + \mathbf{C}_2 z^2 + \cdots$$

can be expanded by the Taylor rule and evaluated for $z = 1$. Thus, $\mathbf{C}(L)$ is reformulated as:

$$\mathbf{C}(L) = \mathbf{C}(1) + \mathbf{C}^*(L)(1 - L). \tag{5.9}$$

By inserting (5.9) in (5.8) we get:

$$(1 - L)\mathbf{x}_t = \{\mathbf{C} + \mathbf{C}^*(L)(1 - L)\}(\boldsymbol{\varepsilon}_t + \boldsymbol{\mu})$$

where $\mathbf{C} = \mathbf{C}(1)$. This equation can be written as:

$$\begin{aligned}\mathbf{x}_s &= \mathbf{x}_{s-1} + \mathbf{C}\boldsymbol{\varepsilon}_s + \mathbf{C}\boldsymbol{\mu} + \mathbf{C}^*(L)(\boldsymbol{\varepsilon}_s - \boldsymbol{\varepsilon}_{s-1}),\\ &= \mathbf{x}_{s-1} + \mathbf{C}\boldsymbol{\varepsilon}_s + \mathbf{C}\boldsymbol{\mu} + \mathbf{Y}_s - \mathbf{Y}_{s-1},\end{aligned}$$

where $\mathbf{Y}_s = \mathbf{C}^*(L)\boldsymbol{\varepsilon}_s$ is a shorthand notation for the stationary part of the process, $\mathbf{C}^*(L)\boldsymbol{\varepsilon}_s$. Summing for $s = 1, \ldots, t$ we get:

$$\begin{aligned}\mathbf{x}_t &= \mathbf{C}\sum_{s=1}^{t}\boldsymbol{\varepsilon}_s + \mathbf{C}\boldsymbol{\mu}t + \mathbf{C}^*(L)\boldsymbol{\varepsilon}_t + \mathbf{x}_0 - \mathbf{C}^*(L)\boldsymbol{\varepsilon}_0,\\ &= \mathbf{C}\sum_{s=1}^{t}\boldsymbol{\varepsilon}_s + \mathbf{C}\boldsymbol{\mu}t + \mathbf{C}^*(L)\boldsymbol{\varepsilon}_t + \widetilde{\mathbf{X}}_0,\end{aligned} \tag{5.10}$$

where $\widetilde{\mathbf{X}}_0$ contains both the initial value, $\mathbf{x}_0$, of the process $\mathbf{x}_t$ and the initial value of the short-run dynamics $\mathbf{C}^*(L)\boldsymbol{\varepsilon}_0$. The moving average representation (5.10) shows that $\mathbf{x}_t$ can be described by stochastic trends $\mathbf{C}\sum_{i=1}^{t}\boldsymbol{\varepsilon}_i$, stationary stochastic components $\mathbf{C}^*(L)\boldsymbol{\varepsilon}_t$, and initial values. Thus, the VAR model is consistent with the representation of the vector process into trends, cycles, and irregular components informally discussed in Chapter 2.

5.4 From the AR to the MA representation

We showed above that the $\mathbf{C}_i$ matrices are functions of the $\mathbf{\Pi}_i$ matrices. We shall now use the simple VAR(1) model to illustrate how one can find the $\mathbf{C}$ matrix when $\boldsymbol{\beta}$ and $\boldsymbol{\alpha}$ are known. The discussion here follows the derivation of the so-called Granger representation theorem of Chapter 4 in Johansen (1996) where the interested reader also can find the results for the general VAR(k) model. The general principle behind the representation theorem is much easier to demonstrate using the VAR(1) model as the inclusion of short-run $\mathbf{\Gamma}_i$ effects complicates the derivation significantly.

We consider the VAR(1) model:

$$\Delta\mathbf{x}_t = \boldsymbol{\alpha}\boldsymbol{\beta}'\mathbf{x}_{t-1} + \boldsymbol{\mu} + \boldsymbol{\varepsilon}_t,\ t = 1, \ldots, T, \tag{5.11}$$

with initial value $\mathbf{x}_0$. For given $\boldsymbol{\alpha}$ and $\boldsymbol{\beta}$ we can find the orthogonal complements, $\boldsymbol{\alpha}_\perp$ and $\boldsymbol{\beta}_\perp$ of full rank and of dimension $p \times (p - r)$ so that $\boldsymbol{\beta}'\boldsymbol{\beta}_\perp = \mathbf{0}$, rank $(\boldsymbol{\alpha}, \boldsymbol{\alpha}_\perp) = p$ and $(\boldsymbol{\beta}, \boldsymbol{\beta}_\perp) = p$. Chapter 12 will show that the orthogonal matrices are not uniquely defined without identifying restrictions. However, the results here apply for any admissible choice of $\boldsymbol{\alpha}_\perp$ and $\boldsymbol{\beta}_\perp$.

We shall now make use of the following relationship between $\boldsymbol{\alpha}, \boldsymbol{\beta}, \boldsymbol{\alpha}_\perp$, and $\boldsymbol{\beta}_\perp$:

$$\boldsymbol{\beta}_\perp \left(\boldsymbol{\alpha}'_\perp \boldsymbol{\beta}_\perp\right)^{-1} \boldsymbol{\alpha}'_\perp + \boldsymbol{\alpha} \left(\boldsymbol{\beta}'\boldsymbol{\alpha}\right)^{-1} \boldsymbol{\beta}' = \mathbf{I}. \tag{5.12}$$

Using (5.12) we can decompose any vector $\mathbf{v}$ in R^p into a vector $\mathbf{v}_1 \in sp(\boldsymbol{\beta}_\perp)$ and a vector $\mathbf{v}_2 \in sp(\boldsymbol{\alpha})$, where $sp(\mathbf{z})$ is a shorthand notation for the space spanned by $\mathbf{z}$. We now apply the results to the p-dimensional vector $\mathbf{x}_t$:

$$\begin{aligned} \mathbf{x}_t &= \boldsymbol{\beta}_\perp \left(\boldsymbol{\alpha}'_\perp \boldsymbol{\beta}_\perp\right)^{-1} \boldsymbol{\alpha}'_\perp \mathbf{x}_t + \boldsymbol{\alpha} \left(\boldsymbol{\beta}'\boldsymbol{\alpha}\right)^{-1} \boldsymbol{\beta}'\mathbf{x}_t \\ &= \boldsymbol{\omega}_1 \boldsymbol{\alpha}'_\perp \mathbf{x}_t + \boldsymbol{\omega}_2 \boldsymbol{\beta}'\mathbf{x}_t. \end{aligned} \tag{5.13}$$

Thus, $\mathbf{x}_t$ can be expressed as a linear combination of the common trends, $\boldsymbol{\alpha}'_\perp \boldsymbol{x}_t$, and the cointegration relations, $\boldsymbol{\beta}'\mathbf{x}_t$. The next step is to express them as a function of initial values and the errors $(\boldsymbol{\varepsilon}_t, \boldsymbol{\varepsilon}_{t-1}, \ldots)$.

We first premultiply equation (5.11) with $\boldsymbol{\beta}'$ and then solve for $\boldsymbol{\beta}'\mathbf{x}_t$ to get the equation

$$\boldsymbol{\beta}'\mathbf{x}_t = \left(\mathbf{I} + \boldsymbol{\beta}'\boldsymbol{\alpha}\right) \boldsymbol{\beta}'\mathbf{x}_{t-1} + \boldsymbol{\beta}'\boldsymbol{\mu} + \boldsymbol{\beta}'\boldsymbol{\varepsilon}_t.$$

The eigenvalues of the matrix $\left(\mathbf{I} + \boldsymbol{\beta}'\boldsymbol{\alpha}\right)$ are inside the unit circle when the r-dimensional process $\boldsymbol{\beta}'\mathbf{x}_t$ is stationary, so that $\left(\mathbf{I} + \boldsymbol{\beta}'\boldsymbol{\alpha}\right)^l \to \mathbf{0}$ as $l \to \infty$. It is straightforward to represent $\boldsymbol{\beta}'\mathbf{x}_t$ as a function of $\boldsymbol{\varepsilon}_i$, $i = 1, \ldots, T$ and the constant $\boldsymbol{\mu}$:

$$\boldsymbol{\beta}'\mathbf{x}_t = \sum_{i=0}^{\infty} \left(\mathbf{I} + \boldsymbol{\beta}'\boldsymbol{\alpha}\right)^i \boldsymbol{\beta}' \left(\boldsymbol{\varepsilon}_{t-i} + \boldsymbol{\mu}\right). \tag{5.14}$$

An expression for $\boldsymbol{\alpha}'_\perp \mathbf{x}_t$ as a function of the errors is found by pre-multiplying (5.11) with $\boldsymbol{\alpha}'_\perp$ and get the equation

$$\boldsymbol{\alpha}'_\perp \Delta\mathbf{x}_t = \boldsymbol{\alpha}'_\perp \boldsymbol{\varepsilon}_t + \boldsymbol{\alpha}'_\perp \boldsymbol{\mu},$$

which has the solution:

$$\boldsymbol{\alpha}'_\perp \mathbf{x}_t = \boldsymbol{\alpha}'_\perp \mathbf{x}_0 + \sum_{i=1}^{t} \boldsymbol{\alpha}'_\perp \left(\boldsymbol{\varepsilon}_i + \boldsymbol{\mu}\right). \tag{5.15}$$

Inserting (5.14) and (5.15) into (5.13) we obtain the following result:

$$\begin{aligned} \mathbf{x}_t &= \boldsymbol{\beta}_\perp (\boldsymbol{\alpha}'_\perp \boldsymbol{\beta}_\perp)^{-1} \left[\boldsymbol{\alpha}'_\perp \textstyle\sum_{i=1}^t (\boldsymbol{\varepsilon}_i + \boldsymbol{\mu}) + \boldsymbol{\alpha}'_\perp \mathbf{x}_0\right] \\ &\quad + \boldsymbol{\alpha}(\boldsymbol{\beta}'\boldsymbol{\alpha})^{-1} \textstyle\sum_{i=0}^{\infty} \left(\mathbf{I} + \boldsymbol{\beta}'\boldsymbol{\alpha}\right)^i \boldsymbol{\beta}' \left(\boldsymbol{\varepsilon}_{t-i} + \boldsymbol{\mu}\right) \\ &= \mathbf{C} \textstyle\sum_{i=1}^t \boldsymbol{\varepsilon}_i + \mathbf{C}\boldsymbol{\mu}t + \mathbf{C}\mathbf{x}_0 + \boldsymbol{\alpha} \left(\boldsymbol{\beta}'\boldsymbol{\alpha}\right)^{-1} \textstyle\sum_{i=0}^{\infty} \left(\mathbf{I} + \boldsymbol{\beta}'\boldsymbol{\alpha}\right)^i \boldsymbol{\beta}' \left(\boldsymbol{\varepsilon}_{t-i} + \boldsymbol{\mu}\right). \\ &= \mathbf{C} \textstyle\sum_{i=1}^t \boldsymbol{\varepsilon}_i + \boldsymbol{\tau}_1 t + \boldsymbol{\tau}_0 + \mathbf{Y}_t \end{aligned} \tag{5.16}$$

where $\mathbf{C} = \boldsymbol{\beta}_\perp(\boldsymbol{\alpha}'_\perp\boldsymbol{\beta}_\perp)^{-1}\boldsymbol{\alpha}'_\perp$, $\boldsymbol{\tau}_1 = \mathbf{C}\boldsymbol{\mu}$ measures the slope of a linear trend in $\mathbf{x}_t$, $\boldsymbol{\tau}_0 = \mathbf{C}\mathbf{x}_0$ depends on initial values, and $\mathbf{Y}_t$ is a stationary process.

By expressing the VAR(k) model in the companion form, it is possible to derive the results for the more general case using the same principle as above. This will not be done here but is left for the interested reader to do as an exercise. Here we only reproduce the main result relating the $\mathbf{C}$ matrix to all the parameters of the VAR(k) model:

$$\mathbf{C} = \boldsymbol{\beta}_\perp(\boldsymbol{\alpha}'_\perp\boldsymbol{\Gamma}\boldsymbol{\beta}_\perp)^{-1}\boldsymbol{\alpha}'_\perp, \tag{5.17}$$

where $\boldsymbol{\Gamma} = -(\mathbf{I}-\boldsymbol{\Gamma}_1 - \cdots - \boldsymbol{\Gamma}_{k-1})$; See Johansen (1996), Chapter 4. Thus, (5.16) with $\boldsymbol{\Gamma} = -\mathbf{I}$ is a special case of (5.17).

By expressing (5.17) as:

$$\mathbf{C} = \tilde{\boldsymbol{\beta}}_\perp\boldsymbol{\alpha}'_\perp \tag{5.18}$$

where $\tilde{\boldsymbol{\beta}}_\perp = \boldsymbol{\beta}_\perp\ (\boldsymbol{\alpha}'_\perp\Gamma\boldsymbol{\beta}_\perp)^{-1}$ it is easy to see that the decomposition of the $\mathbf{C}$ matrix is similar to the $\boldsymbol{\Pi}$ matrix, except that in the AR representation $\boldsymbol{\beta}$ determines the common long-run relations and $\boldsymbol{\alpha}$ the loadings, whereas in the moving average representation $\boldsymbol{\alpha}'_\perp$ determines the common stochastic trends and $\tilde{\boldsymbol{\beta}}_\perp$ their loadings. Thus, (5.17) together with (5.16) show that the non-stationarity in the process $\mathbf{x}_t$ originates from the cumulative sum of the $p-r$ combinations $\boldsymbol{\alpha}'_\perp\sum_{i=1}^t\boldsymbol{\varepsilon}_i$, leading to the following definition:

Definition 4 The common driving trends are the variables $\boldsymbol{\alpha}'_\perp\sum_{i=1}^t\boldsymbol{\varepsilon}_i$.

As the remaining chapters will discuss results based on both the AR and the MA representation, it is important to have a good intuition for the meaning of the orthogonal complement matrices $\boldsymbol{\alpha}_\perp$ and $\boldsymbol{\beta}_\perp$. A few simple examples illustrate:

Assume that $r = 1$, so that $p - r = 4$ and $\boldsymbol{\alpha}_\perp$ and $\boldsymbol{\beta}_\perp$ are 5×4 matrices. For $\boldsymbol{\alpha}' = [-0.3, 0.1, 0.0, 0.0, 0.0]$ we find $\boldsymbol{\alpha}'_\perp\sum_{i=1}^t\boldsymbol{\varepsilon}_i$ as:

$$\boldsymbol{\alpha}'_\perp\sum\nolimits_{i=1}^t\boldsymbol{\varepsilon}_i = \begin{bmatrix} 1 & 3 & 0 & 0 & 0 \\ 0 & 0 & 1 & 0 & 0 \\ 0 & 0 & 0 & 1 & 0 \\ 0 & 0 & 0 & 0 & 1 \end{bmatrix} \begin{bmatrix} \sum_{i=1}^t\varepsilon_{1,i} \\ \sum_{i=1}^t\varepsilon_{2,i} \\ \sum_{i=1}^t\varepsilon_{3,i} \\ \sum_{i=1}^t\varepsilon_{4,i} \\ \sum_{i=1}^t\varepsilon_{5,i} \end{bmatrix}. \tag{5.19}$$

It is easy to verify that $\boldsymbol{\alpha}'_\perp\boldsymbol{\alpha} = \mathbf{0}$. We also note that a zero row in $\boldsymbol{\alpha}$ corresponds to a unit vector in $\boldsymbol{\alpha}_\perp$. Chapter 11 will show how to formally test the hypothesis that a variable has a zero row in $\boldsymbol{\alpha}$. As it is the condition for a variable to be weakly exogenous, it is an important hypothesis. Since $\boldsymbol{\alpha}'_\perp\sum_{i=1}^t\boldsymbol{\varepsilon}_i$ provides an estimate of the $p-r$ common stochastic trends, (5.19) says that the first stochastic trend is a weighted sum of the cumulated shocks to real money stock and real income, whereas the next three stochastic trends are equal to the cumulated shocks to inflation, the deposit rate and the bond rate, respectively.

Note that a linear combination of common stochastic trends is also a stochastic trend, so that (5.19) is just one of infinitely many representations. How to impose identifying restrictions on the common trends will be discussed in Chapter 14.

We shall now find $\boldsymbol{\beta}_\perp$ corresponding to $\boldsymbol{\beta}' = [1, -1, 0, 19, -19]$, where for simplicity we have set the coefficient to inflation to zero.

$$\boldsymbol{\beta}_\perp = \begin{bmatrix} 1 & 0 & 0 & 19 \\ 1 & 0 & 0 & 0 \\ 0 & 1 & 0 & 0 \\ 0 & 0 & 1 & 0 \\ 0 & 0 & 1 & 1 \end{bmatrix}. \tag{5.20}$$

Note that the loadings to the common stochastic trends is not $\boldsymbol{\beta}_\perp$ as such but the normalized version $\tilde{\boldsymbol{\beta}}_\perp = \boldsymbol{\beta}_\perp(\boldsymbol{\alpha}'_\perp \boldsymbol{\Gamma} \boldsymbol{\beta}_\perp)^{-1}$ (cf. (5.18)). We leave it to the reader to find the orthogonal complements to $\boldsymbol{\alpha}$ and $\boldsymbol{\beta}$ for (5.5) and (5.6).

5.5 Pulling and pushing forces

The simple equilibrium-correction model (5.11) illustrates how the process is pulled towards steady-state, defined by $\boldsymbol{\beta}'\mathbf{x}_t - \boldsymbol{\beta}_0 = \mathbf{0}$, where $\boldsymbol{\beta}_0 = E(\boldsymbol{\beta}'\mathbf{x}_t)$ with the force $\boldsymbol{\alpha}$ which activates as soon as the process is out of steady-state, defined by $\boldsymbol{\beta}'\mathbf{x}_t - \boldsymbol{\beta}_0 \neq \mathbf{0}$.[3] The common trends representation (5.16) illustrates how the variables move in a non-stationary manner described by the common driving trends $\boldsymbol{\alpha}'_\perp \sum_{i=1}^{t} \boldsymbol{\varepsilon}_i$. In this sense, the AR and the MA representation are two sides of the same coin: the pulling and the pushing forces of the system. Figure 5.1 illustrates these forces for the simple bivariate system with $\mathbf{x}'_t = [m_t^r, y_t^r]$, where m_t^r is real money stock and y_t^r is real income, whereas Figure 5.2 translates the picture to the corresponding geometry of the cointegrated VAR model.

Assume that the steady-state position corresponds to a constant money velocity $m^r - y^r = \beta_0$, so that $\boldsymbol{\beta}' = [1, -1]$ and the attractor set is $\boldsymbol{\beta}_\perp = [1, 1]$. In the picture, this is indicated by the 45° line showing that $m_t^r = y_t^r$ in steady state. If $\boldsymbol{\beta}'\mathbf{x}_t = (m_t^r - y_t^r) - \beta_0 \neq 0$, then the adjustment coefficient, $\boldsymbol{\alpha}$, will force the process back towards the attractor set with a speed of adjustment that depends on the length of $\boldsymbol{\alpha}$ and the size of the equilibrium error $\boldsymbol{\beta}'\mathbf{x}_t - \boldsymbol{\beta}_0$. The (long-run) equilibrium position $\boldsymbol{\beta}'\mathbf{x}_t = \beta_0$ describes a system at rest where there is no economic adjustment force (incentive) to change the system to a new position. But when new (exogenous) shocks hit the system, causing $\boldsymbol{\beta}'\mathbf{x}_t - \beta_0 \neq \mathbf{0}$, the adjustment forces are activated and pull the process back towards the long-run equilibrium point.

The common trend, measured by $\boldsymbol{\alpha}'_\perp \sum_{i=1}^{t} \boldsymbol{\varepsilon}_i$, has pushed money and income along the line defined by $\boldsymbol{\beta}_\perp$, the attractor set. Thus, positive shocks to the system will push the process higher up along $\boldsymbol{\beta}_\perp$, whereas negative shocks will move it down.

The pulling and pushing forces can now be translated into a VAR model and its corresponding VMA representation: First, the pulling forces are described by the equilibrium

[3]This section relies heavily on Johansen (1996), Chapter 3.

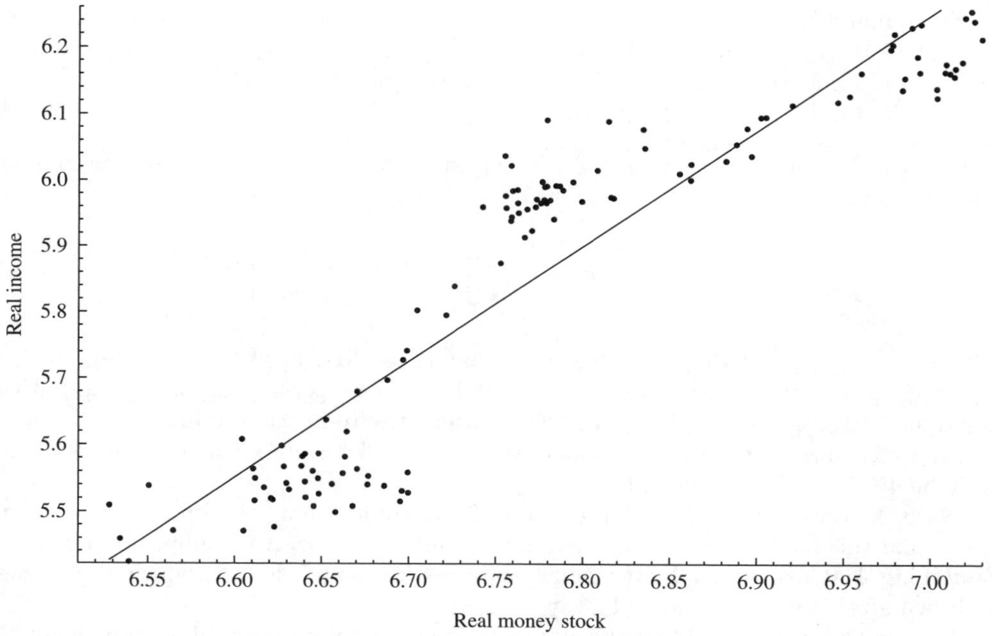

Fig 5.1 A cross-plot of real money stock, m_t^r, and real aggregate income, y_t^r and the regression line.

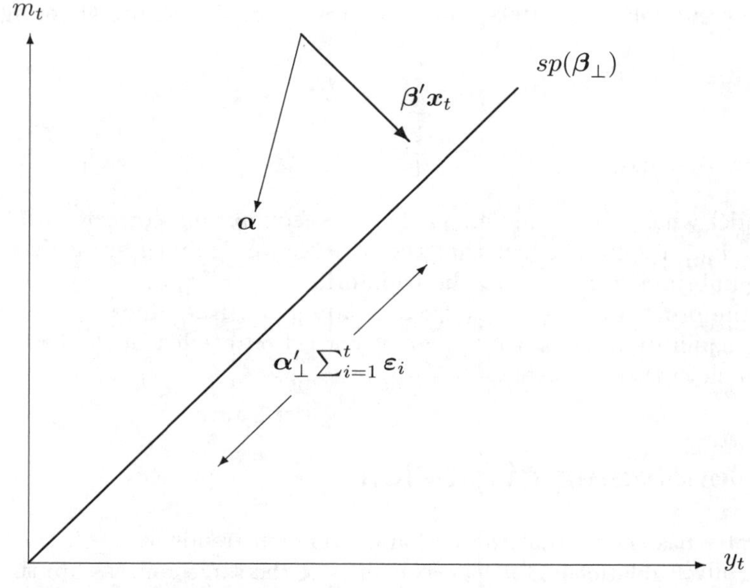

Fig 5.2 The process $\boldsymbol{x}'_t = [m_t^r, y_t^r]$ is pushed along the attractor set by the common trends and pulled towards the attractor set by the adjustment coefficients.

correction model:

$$\begin{bmatrix} \Delta m_t^r \\ \Delta y_t^r \end{bmatrix} = \begin{bmatrix} \alpha_1 \\ \alpha_2 \end{bmatrix} (m_t^r - y_t^r - \beta_0) + \begin{bmatrix} \gamma_1 \\ \gamma_2 \end{bmatrix} + \begin{bmatrix} \varepsilon_{1,t} \\ \varepsilon_{2,t} \end{bmatrix},$$

where $\gamma_1 = E(\Delta m_t^r)$ and $\gamma_2 = E(\Delta y_t^r)$. The pushing forces are described by the common trends model:

$$\begin{bmatrix} m_t^r \\ y_t^r \end{bmatrix} = \begin{bmatrix} 1 \\ 1 \end{bmatrix} \boldsymbol{\alpha}'_\perp \sum_{i=1}^{t} \boldsymbol{\varepsilon}_i + \begin{bmatrix} \gamma_1 \\ \gamma_2 \end{bmatrix} t + \mathbf{C}^*(L) \begin{bmatrix} \varepsilon_{1,t} \\ \varepsilon_{2,t} \end{bmatrix} + \begin{bmatrix} X_{0,1} \\ X_{0,2} \end{bmatrix}$$

with $\boldsymbol{\alpha}'_\perp = \frac{1}{\alpha_1 - \alpha_2}[-\alpha_2, \alpha_1]$. Assume now that $\boldsymbol{\alpha}' = [\alpha_1, 0]$, i.e. only money stock is equilibrium correcting when $m_t^r - y_t^r - \beta_0 \neq 0$. In this case $\boldsymbol{\alpha}'_\perp = [0, 1]$, implying that the common stochastic trend driving this system originates from (real productivity) shocks to aggregate income. The cumulated sum of these shocks determines where on the attractor set (the 45° line) the system is located.

Note, however, that the interpretation of the equilibrium relation, $m_t^r = y_t^r + \beta_0$, is not that this relation will be satisfied in the limit as $t \to \infty$. An equilibrium position is something that exists at all time points as a resting point towards which the process is drawn after it has been pushed away.

It should be emphasized that the picture is strictly speaking only valid for model (5.11) where the short-term dynamics have been left out. When there is short-run adjustment dynamics in the lagged differences of the process, the situation is more complicated and the simple intuition behind the pulling and pushing forces in the above picture can be misleading.

Hansen and Johansen (1998) also discusses a model with overshooting

$$\Delta x_{1,t} = -\frac{1}{2}(x_{1,t-1} - x_{2,t-1}) + \varepsilon_{1,t},$$
$$\Delta x_{2,t} = -\frac{1}{4}(x_{1,t-1} - x_{2,t-1}) + \varepsilon_{2,t},$$

i.e. a model where the variable $x_{2,t}$ does not equilibrium-correct with a coefficient of plausible sign, despite the fact that the variables are cointegrating. In this model, $x_{2,t}$ is not equilibrium-correcting to the equilibrium error $(x_{1,t-1} - x_{2,t-1})$, but instead is pushing the process further away from steady state. But, since $x_{1,t}$ is also reacting on the same equilibrium error with a larger correction coefficient, $|-0.50| > |-0.25|$, the process is, nevertheless, stable.

5.6 Concluding discussion

This chapter has shown that the notion of common trends, $\boldsymbol{\alpha}'_\perp \sum_{i=1}^{t} \boldsymbol{\varepsilon}_i$, and the notion of cointegrating relations, $\boldsymbol{\beta}'\mathbf{x}_t$, are two sides of the same coin, as are the loadings coefficients, $\boldsymbol{\beta}$, and the adjustment coefficients, $\boldsymbol{\alpha}$. Although we can, of course, choose the representation we prefer, there is nonetheless one aspect in which the two concepts differ. A cointegration relation is invariant to changes in the information set, whereas this is not necessarily the case with a common trend. If cointegration holds between a set of variables, then the same cointegration relation will still be found in a larger set of variables. This important property will be exploited in the methodological discussion of Chapter 19. An 'unanticipated disturbance', ε_t, defining the common trend $\boldsymbol{\alpha}'_{\perp}\sum_{i=1}^{t}\varepsilon_i$, is only unanticipated for the chosen information set. Unless the latter is complete in the sense of comprising all relevant variables, the residual, $\hat{\varepsilon}_t$, will necessarily contain the effect of omitted variables. Thus, an unanticipated shock, ε_t, based on a smaller system need no longer be so in a larger system. Generally, both $\boldsymbol{\varepsilon}_t$ and $\boldsymbol{\alpha}_{\perp}$ will change when the information set changes, implying that the definition of a common trend is not invariant to changes in the information set, see Hendry (1995). This will be further discussed in Chapters 13 and 14.

6

Deterministic components in the $I(1)$ model

The purpose of this chapter is to discuss the interpretation of fixed effects, such as constant, deterministic trends, and intervention dummies and show how they affect the mean of the differenced process, $E(\Delta \mathbf{x}_t)$ and the mean of the equilibrium error process, $E(\boldsymbol{\beta}'\mathbf{x}_t)$. Section 6.1 first illustrates the dual role of the constant term and the linear trend in a simple dynamic regression model. Section 6.2 then extends the discussion to the more complicated case of the VAR model. Section 6.3 discusses five cases of different restrictions imposed on the trend and the constant in the VAR model. Section 6.4 derives the MA representation when there is a trend and a constant in the VAR model. Section 6.5 discusses the role of three different types of dummy variables in a simple dynamic regression model and Section 6.6 extends the discussion to the VAR model. Section 6.7 illustrates.

6.1 A trend and a constant in a simple dynamic regression model

When dynamics are introduced in the simple regression model, the meaning of its coefficients changes and it is easy to make interpretational mistakes. We shall use a simple univariate model to demonstrate how the interpretation of a linear time trend and a constant term is crucially related to the dynamics of the model, in particular to whether the dynamics contains a unit root or not.

We consider the following simple regression model for y_t containing a linear trend and a constant:

$$y_t = \gamma t + u_t + \mu, \quad t = 1, \ldots, T \tag{6.1}$$

where the residual u_t is a first order autoregressive process:

$$u_t = \frac{\varepsilon_t}{1 - \rho L} \tag{6.2}$$

and u_0 is assumed fixed. Note that the assumption (6.2) implies that (6.1) is a common factor model. As demonstrated below such a model imposes nonlinear restrictions on the parameters of the AR model and is therefore a special case of the general autoregressive model. Nonetheless, (6.1)–(6.2) serve the purpose of providing a pedagogical illustration of the dual roles of deterministic components in dynamic models.

It is useful to see how the constant μ is related to the initial value of y_t. Using (6.1) we have that $y_0 = \mu + u_0$. Since an economic variable is usually given in logs, y_0 contains information about the unit of measurements (the log of 100.000 euro, say). Therefore, y_0 is usually large compared to the error u_0 so that the value of μ is frequently dominated by y_0. For practical purposes $\mu \simeq y_0$ and in the discussion below we shall set $\mu = y_0$ to emphasize the role of measurements on the constant in a dynamic regression model.

By substituting (6.2) in (6.1) we get:

$$y_t = \gamma t + \frac{\varepsilon_t}{1 - \rho L} + y_0 \tag{6.3}$$

and by multiplying through with $(1 - \rho L)$:

$$(1 - \rho L)y_t = (1 - \rho L)\gamma t + (1 - \rho L)y_0 + \varepsilon_t. \tag{6.4}$$

Rewriting (6.4) using $Lx_t = x_{t-1}$ we get:

$$y_t = \rho y_{t-1} + \gamma(1 - \rho)t + \rho\gamma + (1 - \rho)y_0 + \varepsilon_t. \tag{6.5}$$

It is easy to see that the 'static' regression model (6.1) is equivalent to the following dynamic regression model:

$$y_t = b_1 y_{t-1} + b_2 t + b_0 + \varepsilon_t \tag{6.6}$$

with

$$\begin{aligned} b_1 &= \rho \\ b_2 &= \gamma(1 - \rho) \\ b_0 &= \rho\gamma + (1 - \rho)y_0. \end{aligned} \tag{6.7}$$

We consider the following four cases:

Case 1. $\rho = 1$ and $\gamma \neq 0$. It follows from (6.5) that $\Delta y_t = \gamma + \varepsilon_t$, for $t = 1, \ldots, T$, i.e. 'the random walk with drift' model. Note that $E(\Delta y_t) = \gamma \neq 0$ is equivalent to y_t having a linear trend, γt.

Case 2. $\rho = 1$ and $\gamma = 0$. It follows from (6.5) that $\Delta y_t = \varepsilon_t$, for $t = 1, \ldots, T$, i.e. 'the pure random walk' model. In this case $E(\Delta y_t) = 0$ and y_t contains no linear trend.

Case 3. $|\rho| < 1$ and $\gamma \neq 0$ gives (6.6), i.e. y_t is stationary around its mean, $Ey_t = \gamma t + y_0$ (see 6.1). Note that the coefficients in a dynamic regression model have to be interpreted with caution. For example, b_2 in (6.6) is not an estimate of the trend slope in y_t and b_0 is not an estimate of μ_0.

Case 4. $|\rho| < 1$ and $\gamma = 0$, gives us $y_t = \rho y_{t-1} + (1-\rho)y_0 + \varepsilon_t$, where $Ey_t = y_0$, i.e. 'the stationary autoregressive' model with a constant term.

To summarize:

- in the static regression model (6.1), the constant term is essentially accounting for the unit of measurement of y_t;
- in the dynamic regression model (6.5), the constant term is a weighted average of the growth rate γ and the initial value y_0;
- in the differenced model ($\rho = 1$), the constant term is only measuring the growth rate, γ.

6.2 A trend and a constant in the VAR

The above results were derived for the univariate model. We shall now demonstrate that one can, with some modifications, apply a similar interpretation of the deterministic components in the multivariate model.

A characteristic feature of the equilibrium-correction model given below is the inclusion of both differences and levels in the same model that allows us to investigate short-run as well as long-run effects in the data. When two variables share the same stochastic trend, we showed in the previous chapter that it is possible to find a linear combination that cancels the trend, i.e. a cointegration relation. But many economic variables typically exhibit linear deterministic growth (at least locally over the sample period) in addition to stochastic growth. Statistically it is not always straightforward to distinguish between the two, especially over short sample periods. Sometimes it is preferable to approximate the trend behaviour with a stochastic trend, sometimes it is better to model it with a deterministic trend, and in most cases we need a combination of the two.

We call a variable which contains only a deterministic trend, but no stochastic trend, a trend-stationary variable. In the cointegrated VAR model, the latter case can be modelled by adding a trend to the cointegration space. In other cases, a linear combination between the variables removes the stochastic trend but not the deterministic trend and we need to add a linear trend to the cointegration relation to achieve stationarity. We call it a trend-stationary cointegration relation. See Figure 6.1 below for an illustration.

Because the basic ideas can be illustrated with a simple VAR(1) model containing a constant, $\boldsymbol{\mu}_0$, and a trend, $\boldsymbol{\mu}_1 t$, all short-run dynamic effects, $\boldsymbol{\Gamma}_i$, $i = 1, \ldots, k-1$, have been set to zero and we consider the following model in AR form:

$$\Delta \mathbf{x}_t = \boldsymbol{\alpha}\boldsymbol{\beta}'\mathbf{x}_{t-1} + \boldsymbol{\mu}_0 + \boldsymbol{\mu}_1 t + \boldsymbol{\varepsilon}_t \tag{6.8}$$

and in the MA form:

$$\mathbf{x}_t = \mathbf{C}\sum_{i=1}^{t}(\boldsymbol{\varepsilon}_i + \boldsymbol{\mu}_0 + i\boldsymbol{\mu}_1) + \sum_{i=1}^{\infty}\mathbf{C}_i^*(\boldsymbol{\varepsilon}_{t-i} + \boldsymbol{\mu}_0 + (t-i)\boldsymbol{\mu}_1). \tag{6.9}$$

It is important to notice that the cointegrated VAR model describes p equations, $\Delta\mathbf{x}_t$, and r relations, $\boldsymbol{\beta}'\mathbf{x}$, in just one model. Therefore, the vector of constant terms, $\boldsymbol{\mu}_0$ (and similarly $\boldsymbol{\mu}_1$), can be considered the sum of two vectors, one accounting for the mean value of the equations $\Delta\mathbf{x}_t$ (describing the slope of a linear trend in $\mathbf{x}_t$) and the other for the mean value of the relations, $\boldsymbol{\beta}'\mathbf{x}$ (describing the intercept of a long-run relation). Below, we shall illustrate how one can decompose $\boldsymbol{\mu}_0$ (and $\boldsymbol{\mu}_1$) into the two vectors for the simple model (6.8).

Because $\Delta\mathbf{x}_t$ and $\boldsymbol{\beta}'\mathbf{x}_{t-1}$ are stationary around their mean, we can express (6.8) as:

$$\Delta\mathbf{x}_t - E\Delta\mathbf{x}_t = \boldsymbol{\alpha}(\boldsymbol{\beta}'\mathbf{x}_{t-1} - E(\boldsymbol{\beta}'\mathbf{x}_{t-1})) + \boldsymbol{\varepsilon}_t \tag{6.10}$$

where

$$E\Delta\mathbf{x}_t = \boldsymbol{\alpha}E(\boldsymbol{\beta}'\mathbf{x}_{t-1}) + \boldsymbol{\mu}_0 + \boldsymbol{\mu}_1 t \tag{6.11}$$

and

$$\begin{aligned} E(\boldsymbol{\beta}'\Delta\mathbf{x}_t) &= \boldsymbol{\beta}'\boldsymbol{\alpha}E(\boldsymbol{\beta}'\mathbf{x}_{t-1}) + \boldsymbol{\beta}'\boldsymbol{\mu}_0 + \boldsymbol{\beta}'\boldsymbol{\mu}_1 t \\ E(\boldsymbol{\beta}'\mathbf{x}_t) &= (\mathbf{I} + \boldsymbol{\beta}'\boldsymbol{\alpha})E(\boldsymbol{\beta}'\mathbf{x}_{t-1}) + \boldsymbol{\beta}'\boldsymbol{\mu}_0 + \boldsymbol{\beta}'\boldsymbol{\mu}_1 t. \end{aligned} \tag{6.12}$$

The two $(p \times 1)$ vectors $\boldsymbol{\mu}_0$ and $\boldsymbol{\mu}_1$ can be decomposed into two new vectors in many different ways and we need some principle for doing it. Generally, we would like an equilibrium error to have mean zero so it is natural to decompose $\boldsymbol{\mu}_0 = \boldsymbol{\alpha}\boldsymbol{\beta}_0 + \boldsymbol{\gamma}_0$ and $\boldsymbol{\mu}_1 = \boldsymbol{\alpha}\boldsymbol{\beta}_1 + \boldsymbol{\gamma}_1$ so that $E(\boldsymbol{\beta}'\mathbf{x}_t - \boldsymbol{\beta}_0 - \boldsymbol{\beta}_1 t) = \mathbf{0}$.

To achieve this when $\boldsymbol{\mu}_1 \neq \mathbf{0}$ is quite involved and we shall focus here on the case $(\boldsymbol{\mu}_0 \neq \mathbf{0}, \boldsymbol{\mu}_1 = \mathbf{0})$, i.e. a constant term but no linear trend in the VAR model. In this case, we can use the identity:

$$\boldsymbol{\alpha}(\boldsymbol{\beta}'\boldsymbol{\alpha})^{-1}\boldsymbol{\beta}' + \boldsymbol{\beta}_\perp(\boldsymbol{\alpha}_\perp'\boldsymbol{\beta}_\perp)^{-1}\boldsymbol{\alpha}_\perp' = \mathbf{I} \tag{6.13}$$

to decompose the vector $\boldsymbol{\mu}_0$ into two new vectors:

$$\boldsymbol{\mu}_0 = \boldsymbol{\alpha}(\boldsymbol{\beta}'\boldsymbol{\alpha})^{-1}\boldsymbol{\beta}'\boldsymbol{\mu}_0 + \boldsymbol{\beta}_\perp(\boldsymbol{\alpha}_\perp'\boldsymbol{\beta}_\perp)^{-1}\boldsymbol{\alpha}_\perp'\boldsymbol{\mu}_0, = \boldsymbol{\alpha}\boldsymbol{\beta}_0 + \boldsymbol{\gamma}_0 \tag{6.14}$$

where $\boldsymbol{\beta}_0 = (\boldsymbol{\beta}'\boldsymbol{\alpha})^{-1}\boldsymbol{\beta}'\boldsymbol{\mu}_0$ and $\boldsymbol{\gamma}_0 = \boldsymbol{\beta}_\perp(\boldsymbol{\alpha}_\perp'\boldsymbol{\beta}_\perp)^{-1}\boldsymbol{\alpha}_\perp'\boldsymbol{\mu}_0$. We shall now show that $E(\boldsymbol{\beta}'\mathbf{x}_t + \boldsymbol{\beta}_0) = \mathbf{0}$ and $E\Delta\mathbf{x}_t = \boldsymbol{\gamma}_0$ in (6.8) when $\boldsymbol{\mu}_1 = \mathbf{0}$. In this case (6.9) becomes:

$$\mathbf{x}_t = \mathbf{C}\sum_{i=1}^{\infty}(\boldsymbol{\varepsilon}_i + \boldsymbol{\mu}_0) + \sum_{i=0}^{\infty}\mathbf{C}_i^*(\boldsymbol{\varepsilon}_{t-i} + \boldsymbol{\mu}_0)$$

and

$$\begin{aligned} E\Delta\mathbf{x}_t &= \mathbf{C}\boldsymbol{\mu}_0 \\ E\boldsymbol{\beta}'\mathbf{x}_t &= \boldsymbol{\beta}'\sum_{i=0}^{\infty}\mathbf{C}_i^*\boldsymbol{\mu}_0. \end{aligned} \tag{6.15}$$

Noting that $E(\boldsymbol{\beta}'\Delta\mathbf{x}_t) = \mathbf{0}$ in (6.12) (because $E(\boldsymbol{\beta}'\mathbf{x}_t)$ is constant), we obtain the following expression for $E(\boldsymbol{\beta}'\mathbf{x}_t)$:

$$E(\boldsymbol{\beta}'\mathbf{x}_t) = -(\boldsymbol{\beta}'\boldsymbol{\alpha})^{-1}\boldsymbol{\beta}'\boldsymbol{\mu}_0 = \boldsymbol{\beta}'\sum_{i=0}^{\infty}\mathbf{C}_i^*\boldsymbol{\mu}_0. \tag{6.16}$$

Inserting (6.15) and (6.16) into (6.10) and noting that $\boldsymbol{C} = \boldsymbol{\beta}_\perp(\boldsymbol{\alpha}'_\perp\boldsymbol{\beta}_\perp)^{-1}\boldsymbol{\alpha}'_\perp$ gives:

$$\begin{aligned}\Delta\mathbf{x}_t - \boldsymbol{\beta}_\perp(\boldsymbol{\alpha}'_\perp\boldsymbol{\beta}_\perp)^{-1}\boldsymbol{\alpha}'_\perp\boldsymbol{\mu}_0 &= \boldsymbol{\alpha}\boldsymbol{\beta}'\mathbf{x}_{t-1} + \boldsymbol{\alpha}(\boldsymbol{\beta}'\boldsymbol{\alpha})^{-1}\boldsymbol{\beta}'\boldsymbol{\mu}_0 + \boldsymbol{\varepsilon}_t \\ \Delta\mathbf{x}_t - \boldsymbol{\gamma}_0 &= \boldsymbol{\alpha}(\boldsymbol{\beta}'\mathbf{x}_{t-1} + \boldsymbol{\beta}_0) + \boldsymbol{\varepsilon}_t.\end{aligned} \tag{6.17}$$

Since the left-hand side of (6.17) has a zero mean, as has $\boldsymbol{\varepsilon}_t$, it follows that $E(\boldsymbol{\beta}'\mathbf{x}_{t-1} + \boldsymbol{\beta}_0) = \mathbf{0}$. Thus, we have shown that the decomposition (6.13) satisfies the criterion $E(\boldsymbol{\beta}'\mathbf{x}_t + \boldsymbol{\beta}_0) = \mathbf{0}$.

The motivation for choosing the decomposition (6.13) is that when $\boldsymbol{\Gamma}_1 = \mathbf{0}$ and $\boldsymbol{\mu}_1 = \mathbf{0}$ we have that $E(\Delta\mathbf{x}_t) = \boldsymbol{\gamma}_0$ and hence $E(\boldsymbol{\beta}'\mathbf{x}_t + \boldsymbol{\beta}_0) = \mathbf{0}$. When $\boldsymbol{\Gamma}_1, \ldots, \boldsymbol{\Gamma}_{k-1} \neq \mathbf{0}$ (but $\boldsymbol{\mu}_1 = \mathbf{0}$), we can apply a slightly different decomposition:

$$\boldsymbol{\Gamma}\mathbf{C} + (\mathbf{I} - \boldsymbol{\Gamma}\mathbf{C}) = \boldsymbol{\Gamma}\beta_\perp(\boldsymbol{\alpha}'_\perp\boldsymbol{\Gamma}\boldsymbol{\beta}_\perp)^{-1}\boldsymbol{\alpha}'_\perp + \mathbf{I} - \boldsymbol{\Gamma}\boldsymbol{\beta}_\perp(\boldsymbol{\alpha}'_\perp\boldsymbol{\Gamma}\boldsymbol{\beta}_\perp)^{-1}\boldsymbol{\alpha}'_\perp = \mathbf{I} \tag{6.18}$$

where $\boldsymbol{\Gamma} = \mathbf{I} - \boldsymbol{\Gamma}_1 - \cdots - \boldsymbol{\Gamma}_{k-1}$. However, the derivation of the mean value of $\Delta\mathbf{x}_t$ becomes more complicated in this more general case.

When $\boldsymbol{\mu}_1 \neq \mathbf{0}$ we would need a different, more complicated, decomposition of $\boldsymbol{\mu}_0$ and $\boldsymbol{\mu}_1$ to achieve that the equilibrium error has a zero mean.[1] Nevertheless, a similar logic is used for the decomposition of the constant and the trend into the space spanned by $\boldsymbol{\alpha}$ and $\boldsymbol{\beta}_\perp$:

$$\begin{aligned}\boldsymbol{\mu}_0 &= \boldsymbol{\alpha}\boldsymbol{\beta}_0 + \boldsymbol{\gamma}_0 \\ \boldsymbol{\mu}_1 &= \boldsymbol{\alpha}\boldsymbol{\beta}_1 + \boldsymbol{\gamma}_1.\end{aligned} \tag{6.19}$$

By substituting (6.19) in (6.8) we get:

$$\Delta\mathbf{x}_t = \boldsymbol{\alpha}\boldsymbol{\beta}'\mathbf{x}_{t-1} + \boldsymbol{\alpha}\boldsymbol{\beta}_0 + \boldsymbol{\alpha}\boldsymbol{\beta}_1 t + \boldsymbol{\gamma}_0 + \boldsymbol{\gamma}_1 t + \boldsymbol{\varepsilon}_t, \tag{6.20}$$

and by rearranging (6.20) can be written as:

$$\Delta\mathbf{x}_t = \boldsymbol{\alpha}\left[\boldsymbol{\beta}', \boldsymbol{\beta}_0, \boldsymbol{\beta}_1\right]\begin{bmatrix}\mathbf{x}_{t-1} \\ 1 \\ t\end{bmatrix} + \boldsymbol{\gamma}_0 + \boldsymbol{\gamma}_1 t + \boldsymbol{\varepsilon}_t.$$

Thus, (6.8) can be reformulated as:

$$\Delta\mathbf{x}_t = \boldsymbol{\alpha}\tilde{\boldsymbol{\beta}}'\tilde{\mathbf{x}}_{t-1} + \boldsymbol{\gamma}_0 + \boldsymbol{\gamma}_1 t + \boldsymbol{\varepsilon}_t, \tag{6.21}$$

where $\tilde{\boldsymbol{\beta}}' = [\boldsymbol{\beta}', \boldsymbol{\beta}_0, \boldsymbol{\beta}_1]$ and $\tilde{\mathbf{x}}_{t-1} = (\mathbf{x}_{t-1}, 1, t)'$.

[1]If, nevertheless, (6.13) is used to obtain $(\boldsymbol{\beta}_0, \boldsymbol{\beta}_1, \boldsymbol{\gamma}_0, \boldsymbol{\gamma}_1)$, the consequence is that $E(\boldsymbol{\beta}'\mathbf{x}_{t-1} + \boldsymbol{\beta}_0 + \boldsymbol{\beta}_1 t) \neq \mathbf{0}$. But, in general, the deviation from a zero mean is very small.

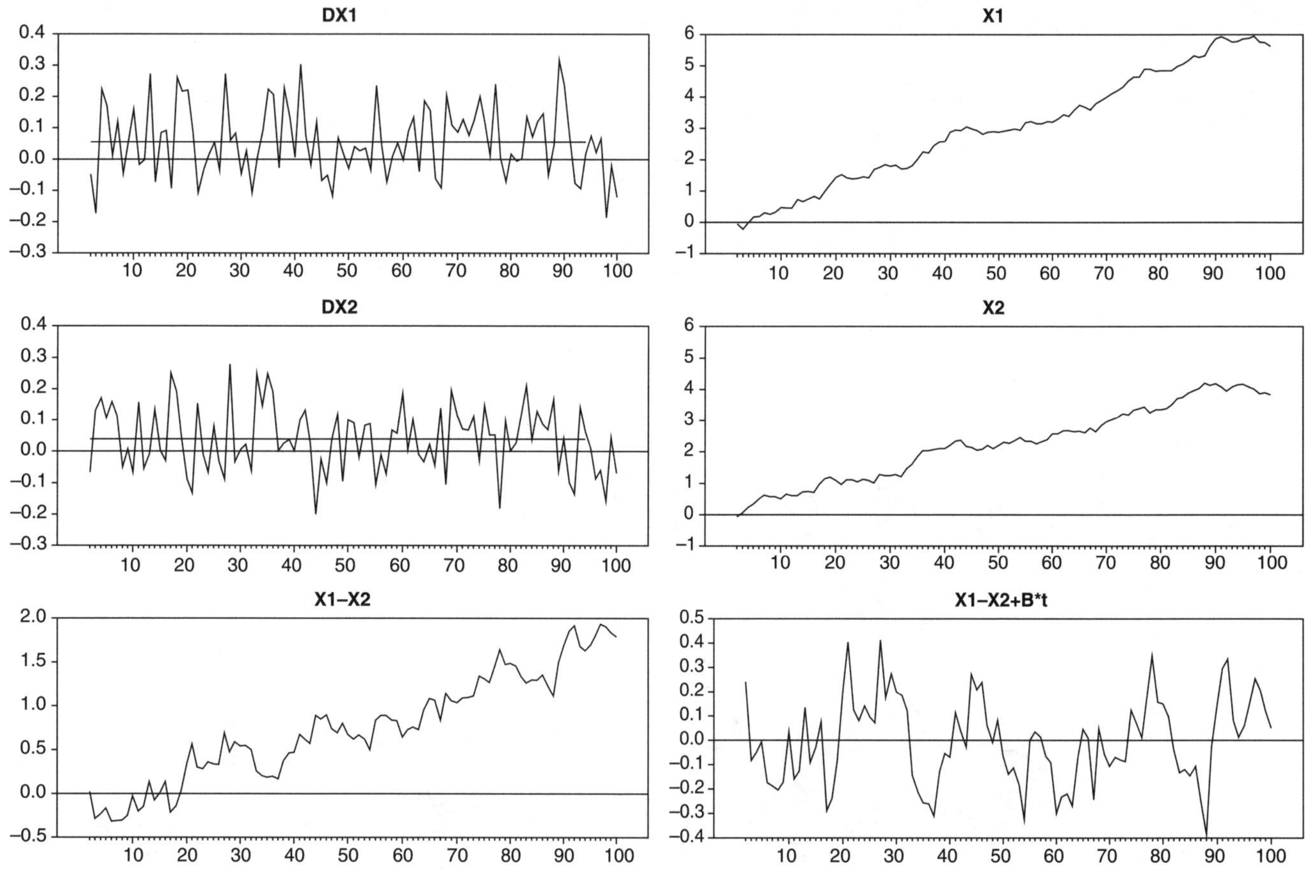

Fig 6.1 The graphs of two trending variables, $x_{1,t}$ and $x_{2,t}$, with different deterministic trends, but the same stochastic trend (upper and middle panels) and of the trend-stationary relation $x_{1,t} - x_{2,t}$ and the stationary relation $x_{1,t} - x_{2,t} - 0.02t$ (lower panels).

The γ components can be interpreted from the equations:

$$E(\Delta \mathbf{x}_t) = \gamma_0 + \gamma_1 t, \tag{6.22}$$

i.e. $\gamma_0 \neq \mathbf{0}$, implies linear growth in at least some of the variables as demonstrated in Case 1 in Section 6.1, and $\gamma_1 \neq \mathbf{0}$ implies quadratic trends in the variables.

Figure 6.1 illustrates the double role of the constant term and the trend in the cointegrated VAR model in the following simple bivariate model

$$\begin{aligned}
\Delta x_{1,t} &= a_{10} - \alpha\{x_{1,t-1} - x_{2,t-1} + (a_{10} - a_{20})t\} + \varepsilon_{1,t} \\
\Delta x_{2,t} &= a_{20} + \varepsilon_{2,t} \quad t = 1, \ldots, 100 \\
a_{10} &= 0.01, \; a_{20} = 0.03, \; \alpha = 0.2, \quad \sigma_1 = \sigma_2 = 0.1.
\end{aligned}$$

The two variables, $x_{1,t}$ and $x_{2,t}$ generated from this model are non-stationary with a common stochastic trend, but with different linear deterministic trends. The two upper panels of Figure 6.1 show $\Delta x_{1,t}$ and $x_{1,t}$ where $\overline{\Delta x_{1,t}} = 0.055$ is an estimate of the slope coefficient of the linear trend in $x_{1,t}$. Thus, the latter has grown approximately $0.055 \times 100 = 5.5\%$ over the period 1,...,100. The middle two panels show the equivalent graphs of $\Delta x_{2,t}$ and $x_{2,t}$ with $\overline{\Delta x_{2,t}} = 0.039$. We note that the estimated mean is higher than the population mean $E\Delta x_{2,t} = 0.030$, which demonstrates that we need a much longer sample before the sample average converges to the true population mean. The left-hand lower panel shows the graph of $x_{1,t} - x_{2,t}$ which is still trending even though the stochastic trend has been eliminated. Thus, $x_{1,t} - x_{2,t}$ is an example of a trend-stationary cointegration relation. Since the deterministic trends have different slope coefficients, the relation $x_{1,t} - x_{2,t}$ needs to be corrected for the difference in trend behaviour to become stationary, and $x_{1,t} - x_{2,t} - 0.02t$ in the lower right-hand side panel is now stationary.

The above discussion served the purpose of pointing out that the constant and the deterministic trend play a double role in the cointegration model and that it is crucial to distinguish between the part (of the constant and the trend) that belongs to the cointegration relations $\boldsymbol{\beta}'\mathbf{x}_t$ and to the equations $\Delta \mathbf{x}_t$.

6.3 Five cases

In empirical work, we generally do not know from the outset whether there are linear trends in some of the variables, or whether they cancel in the cointegrating relations or not. We shall demonstrate in Chapter 9 that such hypotheses can be expressed as testable linear restrictions on the econometric model. The five different models discussed below arise from imposing different restrictions on the deterministic components in (6.8).

Case 1. $\boldsymbol{\mu}_1$, $\boldsymbol{\mu}_0 = \mathbf{0}$. This case corresponds to a model with no deterministic components in the data, i.e. $E(\Delta \mathbf{x}_t) = \mathbf{0}$ and $E(\boldsymbol{\beta}'\mathbf{x}_t) = \mathbf{0}$, implying that the intercept of every cointegrating relation is zero. As demonstrated in the previous section, an intercept is generally needed to account for the initial level of measurements, $\boldsymbol{X}_0$, and only in the exceptional case when the measurements start from zero, or when the measurements cancel in the cointegrating relations can a zero restriction be justified.

Case 2. $\boldsymbol{\mu}_1 = \mathbf{0}, \boldsymbol{\gamma}_0 = \mathbf{0}$ but $\boldsymbol{\beta}_0 \neq \mathbf{0}$, i.e. the constant term is *restricted* to be in the cointegrating relations. In this case, there are no linear trends in the data, consistent with $E(\Delta\mathbf{x}_t) = \mathbf{0}$. The only deterministic component in the model is the intercept of the cointegrating relations, implying that the equilibrium mean is different from zero.

Case 3. $\boldsymbol{\mu}_1 = \mathbf{0}$, i.e. $(\boldsymbol{\beta}_1, \boldsymbol{\gamma}_1) = \mathbf{0}$, and the constant term $\boldsymbol{\mu}_0$ is *unrestricted*, i.e. no linear trends in the VAR model (6.8), but linear trends in the variables (6.9). In this case, there is no trend in the cointegration space, but $E(\Delta\mathbf{x}_t) = \boldsymbol{\gamma}_0 \neq \mathbf{0}$, is consistent with linear trends in the variables but, since $\boldsymbol{\beta}_1 = \mathbf{0}$, these trends cancel in the cointegrating relations. It appears that $\boldsymbol{\mu}_0 \neq \mathbf{0}$ implies both linear trends in the data and a non-zero intercept in the cointegration relations.

Case 4. $\boldsymbol{\gamma}_1 = \mathbf{0}$, but $(\boldsymbol{\gamma}_0, \boldsymbol{\beta}_0, \boldsymbol{\beta}_1) \neq \mathbf{0}$, i.e. the trend is *restricted* only to appear in the cointegrating relations, but the constant is unrestricted in the model. When γ_1 is restricted to zero, we allow linear, but no quadratic trends, in the variables. As illustrated in the previous section, $E(\Delta\mathbf{x}_t) = \boldsymbol{\gamma}_0 \neq \mathbf{0}$, implies a linear trend in the level of $\mathbf{x}_t$. When, in addition, $\boldsymbol{\beta}_1 \neq \mathbf{0}$ the linear trends in the variables do not cancel in the cointegrating relations, i.e. our model contain 'trend-stationary' variables or trend-stationary cointegrating relations. Therefore, the hypothesis that a variable is trend-stationary, for example, that the output gap is stationary, can be tested in this model.

Case 5. No restrictions on $\boldsymbol{\mu}_0$, $\boldsymbol{\mu}_1$, i.e. trend and constant are *unrestricted* in the model. With unrestricted parameters, the model is consistent with linear trends in the differenced variables $\Delta\mathbf{x}_t$ and thus quadratic trends in $\mathbf{x}_t$. Although quadratic trends may sometimes improve the fit within the sample, forecasting outside the sample is likely to produce implausible results. Instead, it seems preferable to find out what has caused this approximate quadratic growth, and if possible include more appropriate information in the model (for example, population growth or the proportion of old/young people in a population).

These are only a few examples showing that the role of the deterministic and stochastic components in the cointegrated VAR is quite complicated. Not only is a correct specification important for the model estimates and their interpretation, but also the asymptotic distribution of the rank test depends on the specification of these components. This aspect will be further discussed in Chapter 8.

6.4 The MA representation with deterministic components

For simplicity, we shall here focus on the derivation of the MA representation when the VAR contains an unrestricted constant and a linear trend. It is straightforward to generalize to other cases.

Chapter 5 showed that the VAR model without short-run dynamics

$$\triangle\mathbf{x}_t = \boldsymbol{\alpha\beta}'\mathbf{x}_{t-1} + \boldsymbol{\mu}_0 + \boldsymbol{\mu}_1 t + \boldsymbol{\varepsilon}_t$$

can be inverted to yield the MA form:

$$\begin{aligned}\triangle \mathbf{x}_t &= \mathbf{C}(L)(\boldsymbol{\varepsilon}_t + \boldsymbol{\mu}_0 + \boldsymbol{\mu}_1 t) \\ &= [\mathbf{C}(1) + \mathbf{C}^*(L)(1-L)](\boldsymbol{\varepsilon}_t + \boldsymbol{\mu}_0 + \boldsymbol{\mu}_1 t)\end{aligned} \tag{6.23}$$

and summed to yield the common-trends representation

$$\mathbf{x}_t = \mathbf{C}(1)\frac{(\boldsymbol{\varepsilon}_t + \boldsymbol{\mu}_0 + \boldsymbol{\mu}_1 t)}{(1-L)} + \mathbf{C}^*(L)(\boldsymbol{\varepsilon}_t + \boldsymbol{\mu}_0 + \boldsymbol{\mu}_1 t) \tag{6.24}$$

$$= \mathbf{C}(1)\sum_{i=1}^{\infty}(\boldsymbol{\varepsilon}_i + \boldsymbol{\mu}_0 + \boldsymbol{\mu}_1 i) + \mathbf{C}^*(L)(\boldsymbol{\varepsilon}_t + \boldsymbol{\mu}_0 + \boldsymbol{\mu}_1 t). \tag{6.25}$$

As before:

$$\mathbf{C}(1) = \mathbf{C} = \boldsymbol{\beta}_\perp(\boldsymbol{\alpha}_\perp'\boldsymbol{\Gamma}\boldsymbol{\beta}_\perp)^{-1}\boldsymbol{\alpha}_\perp'. \tag{6.26}$$

By summing over a finite sample 1 to T and rearranging, (6.25) can be written as:

$$\begin{aligned}\mathbf{x}_t = &\underbrace{\mathbf{C}\boldsymbol{\mu}_0 t + \frac{1}{2}\mathbf{C}\boldsymbol{\mu}_1 t^2 + \frac{1}{2}\mathbf{C}\boldsymbol{\mu}_1 t + \mathbf{C}^*(L)\boldsymbol{\mu}_1 t + \mathbf{C}^*(1)\boldsymbol{\mu}_0}_{\text{determ. comp.}} \\ &+ \underbrace{\mathbf{C}\sum_{i=1}^{t}\boldsymbol{\varepsilon}_i + \mathbf{C}^*(L)\boldsymbol{\varepsilon}_t}_{\text{stoch. comp.}} + \tilde{\mathbf{X}}_0, \quad \text{for } t = 1, \ldots, T\end{aligned} \tag{6.27}$$

where $\tilde{\boldsymbol{X}}_0$ contains the effect of the initial values defined so that $\boldsymbol{\beta}'\tilde{\mathbf{X}}_0 = \mathbf{0}$ and $\mathbf{C}^*(L) = \mathbf{C}_0^* + \mathbf{C}_1^*L + \cdots + \mathbf{C}_t^*L^t$. Substituting (6.26) in (6.27) we get:

$$\begin{aligned}\mathbf{x}_t = &\boldsymbol{\beta}_\perp(\boldsymbol{\alpha}_\perp'\boldsymbol{\Gamma}\boldsymbol{\beta}_\perp)^{-1}\boldsymbol{\alpha}_\perp'\underbrace{\left[\boldsymbol{\mu}_0 t + \frac{1}{2}\boldsymbol{\mu}_1 t + \frac{1}{2}\boldsymbol{\mu}_1 t^2\right]} + \underbrace{[\mathbf{C}^*(L)\boldsymbol{\mu}_1 t]} \\ &+ \mathbf{C}\sum_{i=1}^{t}\boldsymbol{\varepsilon}_i + \mathbf{C}^*(L)\boldsymbol{\varepsilon}_t + \mathbf{C}^*(1)\boldsymbol{\mu}_0 + \tilde{\mathbf{X}}_0.\end{aligned} \tag{6.28}$$

Substituting (6.14) in (6.28) and focusing on the linear and quadratic trend components we get:

$$\boldsymbol{\alpha}_\perp'\boldsymbol{\mu}_0 t = \underbrace{\boldsymbol{\alpha}_\perp'\boldsymbol{\alpha}\boldsymbol{\beta}_0 t}_{0} + \boldsymbol{\alpha}_\perp'\boldsymbol{\gamma}_0 t$$

$$\boldsymbol{\alpha}_\perp'\frac{1}{2}\boldsymbol{\mu}_1 t = \frac{1}{2}(\underbrace{\boldsymbol{\alpha}_\perp'\boldsymbol{\alpha}\boldsymbol{\beta}_1 t}_{0} + \boldsymbol{\alpha}_\perp'\boldsymbol{\gamma}_1 t)$$

and

$$\boldsymbol{\alpha}_\perp'\frac{1}{2}\boldsymbol{\mu}_1 t^2 = \frac{1}{2}(\underbrace{\boldsymbol{\alpha}_\perp'\boldsymbol{\alpha}\boldsymbol{\beta}_1 t^2}_{0} + \boldsymbol{\alpha}_\perp'\boldsymbol{\gamma}_1 t^2),$$

and the MA representation can be written as:

$$\mathbf{x}_t = \boldsymbol{\beta}_\perp(\boldsymbol{\alpha}'_\perp\boldsymbol{\Gamma}\boldsymbol{\beta}_\perp)^{-1}\boldsymbol{\alpha}'_\perp\left\{\gamma_0 t + \frac{1}{2}\gamma_1 t + \frac{1}{2}\gamma_1 t^2\right\} + \mathbf{C}^*(L)\boldsymbol{\mu}_1 t$$
$$+ \mathbf{C}^*(1)\boldsymbol{\mu}_0 + \mathbf{C}\sum_{i=1}^{t}\varepsilon_i + \mathbf{C}^*(L)\varepsilon_t + \tilde{\mathbf{X}}_0. \tag{6.29}$$

Thus, (6.29) shows that linear trends in the variables can originate from three different sources in the VAR model:

1. the $\boldsymbol{\alpha}$ component $(\mathbf{C}^*(L)\boldsymbol{\mu}_1 t)$ of the unrestricted linear trend $\boldsymbol{\mu}_1 t$;
2. the $\boldsymbol{\beta}_\perp$ component $(\gamma_1 t)$ of the unrestricted linear trend $\boldsymbol{\mu}_1 t$;
3. the $\boldsymbol{\beta}_\perp$ component $(\gamma_0 t)$ of unrestricted constant term $\boldsymbol{\mu}_0$.

We write (6.29) in a more compact form:

$$\mathbf{x}_t = \mathbf{C}\{\underbrace{\boldsymbol{\tau}_1 t + \boldsymbol{\tau}_2 t^2\}}_{\text{det . components}} + \underbrace{\mathbf{C}\sum\varepsilon_i + \mathbf{C}^*(L)\varepsilon_t}_{\text{stoch. comp.}} + \tilde{\mathbf{X}}_0, \tag{6.30}$$

where $\boldsymbol{\tau}_1$ and $\boldsymbol{\tau}_2$ can be derived from (6.29).

6.5 Dummy variables in a simple regression model

Similarly as for the trend and the constant, we consider first a simple regression model for y_t containing three different types of dummy variables, $D_{s,t}$, $D_{p,t}$, and $D_{tr,t}$:

$$y_t = \phi_s D_{s,t} + \phi_p D_{p,t} + \phi_{tr} D_{tr,t} + u_t + y_0, \quad t = 1, \ldots, T \tag{6.31}$$

where $D_{s,t}$ is a mean-shift dummy (... 0,0,0,1,1,1,...), $D_{p,t}$ is a permanent intervention dummy (... 0,0,1,0,0,...) and $D_{tr,t}$ is a transitory shock dummy (... 0,0,1,−1,0,0,...), and the residual u_t is a first order autoregressive process:

$$u_t = \frac{\varepsilon_t}{1-\rho L}. \tag{6.32}$$

By substituting (6.32) in (6.31) we get:

$$(1-\rho L)y_t = \phi_s(1-\rho L)D_{s,t} + \phi_p(1-\rho L)D_{p,t}$$
$$+ \phi_{tr}(1-\rho L)D_{tr,t} + (1-\rho L)y_0 + \varepsilon_t, \tag{6.33}$$

$$y_t = \rho y_{t-1} + \phi_s D_{s,t} - \rho\phi_s D_{s,t-1} + \phi_p D_{p,t} - \rho\phi_p D_{p,t-1}$$
$$+ \phi_{tr} D_{tr,t} - \rho\phi_{tr} D_{tr,t-1} + (1-\rho)y_0 + \varepsilon_t,$$
$$= b_1 y_{t-1} + b_2 D_{s,t} + b_3 D_{s,t-1} + b_4 D_{p,t} + b_5 D_{p,t-1}$$
$$+ b_6 D_{tr,t} + b_7 D_{tr,t-1} + b_0 + \varepsilon_t. \tag{6.34}$$

Thus, the ‘static’ regression model (6.31) with autoregressive errors corresponds to a dynamic model with lagged dummy variables. Note that the effects of the dummy variables can equivalently be formulated as:

$$\phi_s D_{s,t} - \rho\phi_s D_{s,t-1} = \phi_s \rho \Delta D_{s,t} + \phi_s(1-\rho)D_{s,t} \tag{6.35}$$
$$\phi_p D_{p,t} - \rho\phi_p D_{p,t-1} = \phi_p \rho \Delta D_{p,t} + \phi_p(1-\rho)D_{p,t} \tag{6.36}$$
$$\phi_{tr} D_{tr,t} - \rho\phi_{tr} D_{tr,t-1} = \phi_{tr} \rho \Delta D_{tr,t} + \phi_{tr}(1-\rho)D_{tr,t} \tag{6.37}$$

where $\Delta D_{s,t}$ now becomes an impulse dummy (... ,0,0,1,0,0,...) describing a permanent intervention, $\Delta D_{p,t}$ becomes a transitory blip dummy (... ,0,0,1,−1,0,0,...), and $\Delta D_{tr,t}$ a double transitory blip dummy (... ,0,0,1,−2,1,0,0,...). Hence, (6.33) can be reformulated as:

$$\begin{aligned}\Delta y_t = {} & -(1-\rho)y_{t-1} + \phi_s(1-\rho)D_{s,t} + [\phi_s\rho + \phi_p(1-\rho)]D_{p,t} \\ & + [\phi_p\rho + \phi_{tr}(1-\rho)]D_{tr,t} + \phi_{tr}\rho\Delta D_{tr,t} + \varepsilon_t\end{aligned} \tag{6.38}$$

When $\rho = 1$ (6.38) becomes:

$$\begin{aligned}\Delta y_t &= \phi_s \Delta D_{s,t} + \phi_p \Delta D_{p,t} + \phi_{tr}\Delta D_{tr,t} + \varepsilon_t, \quad t = 2,\ldots,T, \\ &= \phi_s D_{p,t} + \phi_p D_{tr,t} + \phi_{tr}\Delta D_{tr,t} + \varepsilon_t,\end{aligned}$$

i.e. a shift in the levels of a variable becomes a 'blip' in the differenced variable, a permanent 'blip' in the levels becomes a transitory blip in the differences, and finally a transitory blip in the levels becomes a double transitory blip, $D_{dtr,t}$, in the differences. Table 6.1 illustrates.

It is far from easy to know which type of dummy variables one should choose to account for an outlier observation in the model and how to find them. As it is generally much easier to detect an outlier observation in the differences of a non-stationary variable then in the levels, it is a good idea to start with a graphical inspection of the differences. Figure 6.2 illustrates three different types of outlier effects in the differenced process and their cumulated effect in the levels of the process.

The upper left-hand side panel shows a shift in the mean of $\Delta x_{1,t}$, which becomes a broken linear trend in $x_{1,t}$. Note that $x_{1,t}$ has been generated from a model without

Table 6.1 Various dummy variables in Δx_t and x_t.

Δx_t $D_{s,t}$	x_t $\sum D_{s,t} =$ trend	Δx_t $D_{p,t}$	x_t $\sum D_{p,t} = D_{s,t}$	Δx_t $D_{tr,t}$	x_t $\sum D_{tr,t} = D_{p,t}$	Δx_t $D_{dtr,t}$	x_t $\sum D_{dtr,t} = D_{tr,t}$
⋮	⋮	⋮	⋮	⋮	⋮	⋮	⋮
0	0	0	0	0	0	0	0
0	0	0	0	0	0	0	0
1	1	1	1	1	1	1	1
1	2	0	1	−1	0	−2	−1
1	3	0	1	0	0	1	0
1	4	0	1	0	0	0	0
⋮	⋮	⋮	⋮	⋮	⋮	⋮	⋮

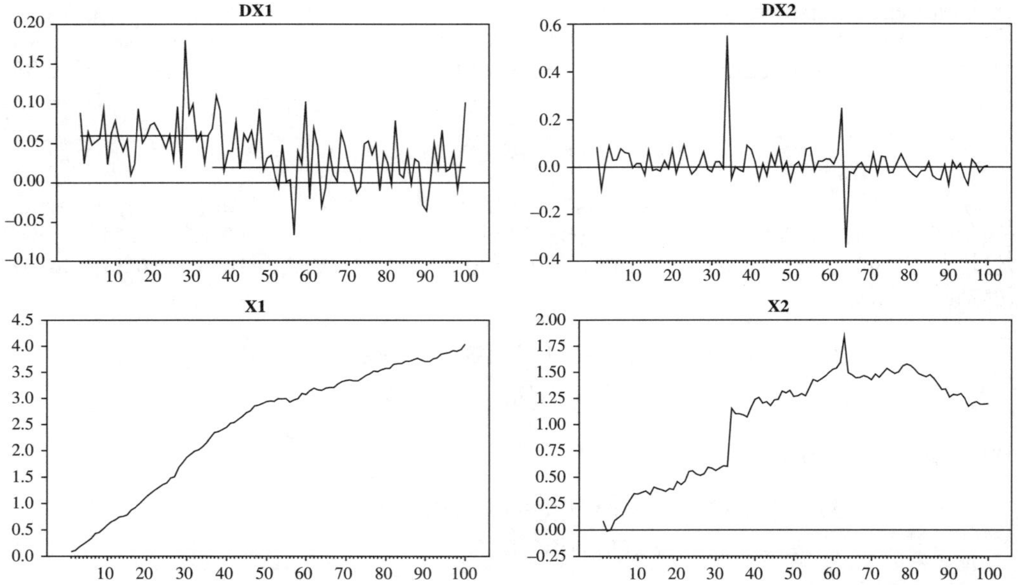

Fig 6.2 Illustrating a mean shift in $\Delta x_{1,t}$ and its effect on $x_{1,t}$ (left-hand side panels) and a permanent and transitory blip in $\Delta x_{2,t}$ and its effect on $x_{2,t}$ (right-hand side panels).

short-run dynamics. When the model contains short-run dynamics, the picture becomes much more blurred and it can be hard to know whether the growth rates have changed deterministically or stochastically. It is, therefore, always advisable to check the economic calendar at the date of the change for a significant intervention and regime change to justify the use of a shift dummy.

The upper right-hand side panel shows a big permanent blip in $\Delta x_{2,t}$ and some periods later a big transitory blip. The former becomes a shift in the level of $x_{2,t}$ and the latter a permanent blip. For the illustrative purpose at hand, these outlier observations have been chosen very big. In empirical work they are usually less striking. Also in this case it is important to understand the underlying reason for the outlier observation to know whether it should be accounted for by a dummy or not. Whatever the case, if a dummy is included in the model, it is absolutely essential that the timing is correct. Missing the right date with just one observation is enough to make the dummy useless and even harmful for the analysis. Choosing a permanent blip dummy instead of a transitory blip dummy can be equally useless or harmful.

6.6 Dummy variables and the VAR

Significant interventions and reforms frequently show up as extraordinary large (non-normal) shocks in the VAR analysis, thus violating the normality assumption. We shall argue below that it would be a mistake to treat them exclusively as a statistical nuisance to be remedied by appropriately correcting the observations. First, we shall illustrate the need for intervention dummies and how to model them based on the analysis of the Danish data, then we shall discuss more formally how they influence the dynamics of the VAR model, and finally discuss their significance for the empirical model estimates.

The question is whether one from the outset should formulate the hypothetical effects of all major interventions and reforms over the sample period and then test whether they are significant or not, or just scrutinize the data and the residuals from the first baseline VAR to diagnose where in the model we need to correct for outlier observations. In practise, it is often hard to know beforehand which interventions and reforms were significant enough to enter the model. Here we shall illustrate the latter approach.

A graphical analysis of the residuals based on the unrestricted VAR(2) model for the Danish data showed that the temporary removal of the VAT in 1975 had a very strong impact on real aggregate expenditure,[2] and that the removal of restrictions on capital movements in 1983 caused the annual long-term bond rate to fall from an internationally high level of ca. 25% to approximately 10%. The huge drop in the bond rate was associated with a similarly large increase in aggregate money stock as a result of the possibility among foreigners to hold Danish assets. The big increase in money stock in 1999:1 was first interpreted as a surprisingly large increase in the liquidity of the private banks at the start of the EMU, but was subsequently found to be an (unexplainable) measurement error affecting the first three quarters of 1999. In this case, the outlier is a so-called additive outlier and should be removed from the data prior to the cointegration analysis. This was done using a program developed by Heino Bohn Nielsen. Among the variables only money stock exhibited seasonal variation. As the seasonal means changed in 1992 (due to new components entering M3) we decided to remove the seasonal mean from M3 using the above program. Thus, the measurements of M3 money stock used in the subsequent analyses have been corrected for the 1999 measurement outlier as well as for seasonal means.

It is often much easier to recognize a possible outlier observation in $\Delta \mathbf{x}_t$ than in the levels $\mathbf{x}_t$. Thus, a first tentative decision to model a political intervention, for example, with a permanent or a transitory blip dummy, can be made by examining the differenced process as illustrated below. The effect on the levels of the process will be discussed subsequently.

The first intervention is transitory in the sense that the VAT was removed for one quarter and gradually restored over two quarters. Nonetheless, it was clearly meant to have a permanent effect on real aggregate income and we might hypothetically expect both a transitory and a permanent effect. The removal of VAT is also likely to influence prices in various ways. For example, if we measure prices by a CPI index, then a change in VAT is likely to be seen as a roughly proportional effect. But it is also possible that some producers, in the expectation of a high demand for their products, will increase prices to some extent. In the present illustration we are using the implicit price deflator of GNE as a measure of prices, so the effect is likely to be much smaller than for the CPI index. The transitory effect of the VAT intervention should be modelled by a transitory blip dummy, for example $D_{tr,t} = [0, 0, 0, \ldots, 0, 1, -0.5, -0.5, 0, 0, \ldots, 0, 0, 0]$, whereas a permanent effect should

[2] The purpose of the intervention was exactly to boost domestic demand to avoid a depression in the aftermath of the first oil shock.

be modelled by a blip dummy, for example $D_{p,t} = [0,0,0,\ldots,0,1,0,0,\ldots,0,0,0]$. The statistical analysis of the VAR model can then be used to find out if the VAT intervention effects were indeed significant, and if this was the case, for which equations.

The second intervention was a result of permanently removing restrictions in the capital market and is therefore first of all likely to have permanent effects on the system. However, markets sometimes overreact and we often see both a permanent effect and a transitory effect as a result of a significant reform or intervention in the market. The latter would show up as a shock in one period, followed shortly afterwards by a similar shock of opposite sign making the variable return to its previous level. Such transitory shocks are quite common, in particular, for high frequency data. Even though they are often of minor significance, and therefore not explicitly modelled, they are likely to produce some negative residual autocorrelation in the VAR model. But, contrary to permanent shocks they will disappear in cumulation and, therefore, will have no effect on the stochastic trends defined as the cumulative sum of all previous shocks (cf. the discussion in Chapter 2).

Using dummies to account for extraordinary mean-shifts, permanent blips, and transitory shocks, the cointegrated VAR model is reformulated as:

$$\begin{aligned}\Delta\mathbf{x}_t &= \boldsymbol{\Gamma}_1\Delta\mathbf{x}_{t-1} + \boldsymbol{\alpha\beta}'\mathbf{x}_{t-1} + \boldsymbol{\Phi}_s\mathbf{D}_{s,t} + \boldsymbol{\Phi}_p\mathbf{D}_{p,t} + \boldsymbol{\Phi}_{tr}\mathbf{D}_{tr,t} + \boldsymbol{\mu}_0 + \boldsymbol{\varepsilon}_t,\\ &\boldsymbol{\varepsilon}_t \sim NI(\mathbf{0},\boldsymbol{\Omega}\ ),\quad t = 1,\ldots,T \end{aligned} \tag{6.39}$$

where $\mathbf{D}_{s,t}$ is a $d_1 \times 1$ vector of mean-shift dummy variables (... ,0,0,0,1,1,1,...), $\mathbf{D}_{p,t}$ is a $d_2 \times 1$ vector of permanent blip dummy variables (... ,0,0,1,0,0,...) and $\mathbf{D}_{tr,t}$ is a $d_3 \times 1$ vector of transitory shock dummy variables (... ,0,0,1,−1,0,0,...).

Because the VAR model contains both differences and levels of the variables, the role of the dummy variables (and other deterministic terms) is more complicated than in the usual regression model (Hendry and Juselius 2001; Johansen, Mosconi, and Nielsen 2000). Figure 6.2 illustrated how an unrestricted mean shift dummy accounts for a mean shift in $\Delta\mathbf{x}_t$ and cumulates to a broken trend in $\mathbf{x}_t$, how an unrestricted permanent blip dummy accounts for a large blip (impulse) in $\Delta\mathbf{x}_t$ and cumulates to a level shift in $\mathbf{x}_t$, and, finally, how an unrestricted transitory blip dummy accounts for two consecutive blips of opposite signs in $\Delta\mathbf{x}_t$ and cumulates to a single blip in $\mathbf{x}_t$.

To understand the role of the dummies in the cointegrated VAR model, it is useful to partition the dummy effects into an $\boldsymbol{\alpha}$ and a $\boldsymbol{\beta}_\perp$ component:

$$\boldsymbol{\Phi}_s = \boldsymbol{\alpha\delta}_0 + \boldsymbol{\delta}_1, \tag{6.40}$$

$$\boldsymbol{\Phi}_p = \boldsymbol{\alpha\varphi}_0 + \boldsymbol{\varphi}_1, \tag{6.41}$$

$$\boldsymbol{\Phi}_{tr} = \boldsymbol{\alpha\psi}_0 + \boldsymbol{\psi}_1. \tag{6.42}$$

Under the simplifying assumption that $\boldsymbol{\Gamma}_1 = 0$ in (6.39) we can use (6.13) to determine the $\boldsymbol{\alpha}$ and $\boldsymbol{\beta}_\perp$ components, so that $\boldsymbol{\delta}_0 = (\boldsymbol{\beta}'\boldsymbol{\alpha})^{-1}\boldsymbol{\beta}'\boldsymbol{\Phi}_s$ and $\boldsymbol{\delta}_1 = \boldsymbol{\beta}_\perp(\boldsymbol{\alpha}'_\perp\boldsymbol{\beta}_\perp)^{-1}\boldsymbol{\alpha}'_\perp\boldsymbol{\Phi}_s$ and $\boldsymbol{\varphi}_0, \boldsymbol{\varphi}_1, \boldsymbol{\psi}_0, \boldsymbol{\psi}_1$ are similarly defined. In this case we can rewrite (6.39) in the following form:

$$\Delta\mathbf{x}_t = \boldsymbol{\alpha}\tilde{\boldsymbol{\beta}}'\tilde{\mathbf{x}}_{t-1} + \boldsymbol{\delta}_1\mathbf{D}_{s,t} + \boldsymbol{\varphi}_1\mathbf{D}_{p,t} + \boldsymbol{\psi}_1\mathbf{D}_{tr,t} + \boldsymbol{\gamma}_0 + \boldsymbol{\varepsilon}_t,$$

where $\tilde{\boldsymbol{\beta}}' = [\boldsymbol{\beta}', \boldsymbol{\beta}_0', \boldsymbol{\delta}_0', \boldsymbol{\varphi}_0', \boldsymbol{\psi}_0']$ and $\tilde{\mathbf{x}}_t' = [\mathbf{x}_t', 1, \mathbf{D}_{s,t}', \mathbf{D}_{p,t}', \mathbf{D}_{tr,t}']$. We can now express the expected value of $\Delta\mathbf{x}_t$ and $\boldsymbol{\beta}'\mathbf{x}_t$ as:

$$\begin{aligned} E\Delta\mathbf{x}_t &= \boldsymbol{\gamma}_0 + \boldsymbol{\delta}_1\mathbf{D}_{s,t} + \boldsymbol{\varphi}_1\mathbf{D}_{p,t} + \boldsymbol{\psi}_1\mathbf{D}_{tr,t} \\ E\boldsymbol{\beta}'\mathbf{x}_t &= \boldsymbol{\beta}_0 + \boldsymbol{\delta}_0\mathbf{D}_{s,t} + \boldsymbol{\varphi}_0\mathbf{D}_{p,t} + \boldsymbol{\psi}_0\mathbf{D}_{tr,t}. \end{aligned} \tag{6.43}$$

Note that when $\boldsymbol{\Gamma}_1 \neq \mathbf{0}$ we need to use a decomposition which is different from (6.13) and the expected value of $\Delta\mathbf{x}_t$ has to be corrected for the short-run dynamics described by $\boldsymbol{\Gamma}_1\Delta\mathbf{x}_{t-1}$.

We shall now investigate the dynamic effects of the dummies in (6.39) on the data using the moving average representation of the model. The latter defines the variables $\mathbf{x}_t$ as a function of $\boldsymbol{\varepsilon}_i$, $i = 1, \ldots, t$, the dummy variables $\mathbf{D}_{s,t}$, $\mathbf{D}_{p,t}$ and $\mathbf{D}_{tr,t}$, and the initial values, $\tilde{\mathbf{X}}_0$:

$$\begin{aligned} \mathbf{x}_t = {} & \mathbf{C}\sum_{i=1}^{t-1}\boldsymbol{\varepsilon}_i + \boldsymbol{C\mu}_0\sum_{i=1}^{t-1}1 + \mathbf{C}\boldsymbol{\Phi}_s\sum_{i=1}^{t-1}\mathbf{D}_{s,i} + \mathbf{C}\boldsymbol{\Phi}_p\sum_{i=1}^{t-1}\mathbf{D}_{p,i} \\ & + \mathbf{C}\boldsymbol{\Phi}_{tr}\sum_{i=1}^{t-1}\mathbf{D}_{tr,i} + \mathbf{C}^*(L)(\boldsymbol{\varepsilon}_t + \boldsymbol{\mu}_0 + \boldsymbol{\Phi}_s\mathbf{D}_{s,t} + \boldsymbol{\Phi}_p\mathbf{D}_{p,t} + \boldsymbol{\Phi}_{tr}\mathbf{D}_{tr,t}) + \tilde{\mathbf{X}}_0 \end{aligned} \tag{6.44}$$

where, as before,

$$\mathbf{C} = \boldsymbol{\beta}_\perp(\boldsymbol{\alpha}_\perp'\boldsymbol{\Gamma}\boldsymbol{\beta}_\perp)^{-1}\boldsymbol{\alpha}_\perp' \tag{6.45}$$

and $\mathbf{C}^*(L)$ is an infinite polynomial in the lag operator L. The first summation in (6.44) produces the common stochastic trends originating from the shocks $\boldsymbol{\varepsilon}_t$, the second summation a linear trend originating from the constant term, the third summation a broken linear trend from the shift dummy, the fourth summation a shift in the level of the variables from the permanent blip dummy, and the fifth summation a blip in the variables from the transitory dummy.

Using (6.45) and (6.40)–(6.42) it is easy to show that the $\boldsymbol{\alpha}$ components will disappear in the summations in (6.44), so that

$$\begin{aligned} \mathbf{C}\boldsymbol{\Phi}_s &= \mathbf{C}\boldsymbol{\delta}_1 \\ \mathbf{C}\boldsymbol{\Phi}_p &= \mathbf{C}\boldsymbol{\varphi}_1 \\ \mathbf{C}\boldsymbol{\Phi}_{tr} &= \mathbf{C}\boldsymbol{\psi}_1. \end{aligned} \tag{6.46}$$

Thus, consistent with $E\Delta\mathbf{x}_t$ in (6.43) only the $\boldsymbol{\beta}_\perp$ component of the dummy variable cumulates in $\mathbf{x}_t$. The implication of this is that dummy variables which are restricted to be only in the cointegration relations do not cumulate in $\mathbf{x}_t$. Using (6.46) we can now reformulate (6.44):

$$\begin{aligned} \mathbf{x}_t = {} & \mathbf{C}\sum_{i=1}^{t-1}\boldsymbol{\varepsilon}_i + \mathbf{C}\boldsymbol{\gamma}_0\sum_{i=1}^{t-1}1 + \mathbf{C}\boldsymbol{\delta}_1\sum_{i=1}^{t-1}\mathbf{D}_{s,i} + \mathbf{C}\boldsymbol{\varphi}_1\sum_{i=1}^{t-1}\mathbf{D}_{p,i} \\ & + \mathbf{C}\boldsymbol{\psi}_1\sum_{i=1}^{t-1}\mathbf{D}_{tr,i} + \mathbf{C}^*(L)(\boldsymbol{\varepsilon}_t + \boldsymbol{\mu}_0 + \boldsymbol{\Phi}_s\mathbf{D}_{s,t} + \boldsymbol{\Phi}_p\mathbf{D}_{p,t} + \boldsymbol{\Phi}_{tr}\mathbf{D}_{tr,t}) + \tilde{\mathbf{X}}_0. \end{aligned} \tag{6.47}$$

It appears from (6.47) that if we want to model a mean shift in the cointegration relations, but at the same time not allow for broken linear trends in the data, $\boldsymbol{\delta}_1 = \mathbf{0}$ has to be imposed from the outset. As $\boldsymbol{\alpha\delta}_0$ in (6.40) is restricted to lie in the cointegration relations, $\boldsymbol{\delta}_0 \neq \mathbf{0}$ describes a mean shift in $\boldsymbol{\beta}'\mathbf{x}_t$ as a result of mean shifts in the variables that do not cancel by cointegration. A mean shift in a variable $x_{j,t}$ implies a permanent blip in $\Delta x_{j,t}$ and hence $\boldsymbol{\delta}_0 \neq \mathbf{0}$ generally implies $\boldsymbol{\Phi}_p \neq \mathbf{0}$.

If $\boldsymbol{\Phi}_s = \mathbf{0}$, then there is no broken trend in the variables nor a mean shift in the cointegration relations, but if $\boldsymbol{\Phi}_p \neq \mathbf{0}$, then $\boldsymbol{\varphi}_1 \neq \mathbf{0}$ describes a level shift in the variables that cancel in $\boldsymbol{\beta}'\mathbf{x}_t$, whereas $\boldsymbol{\varphi}_0 \neq \mathbf{0}$ describes a blip in $\boldsymbol{\beta}'\mathbf{x}_t$. A blip in the variables $\mathbf{x}_t$ implies a transitory shock in $\Delta\mathbf{x}_t$. Thus, $\boldsymbol{\varphi}_0 \neq \mathbf{0}$ is consistent with $\boldsymbol{\Phi}_{tr} \neq \mathbf{0}$, and describes a situation when the blips in the levels of $\mathbf{x}_t$ generated by transitory shocks to $\Delta\mathbf{x}_t$ do not cancel in $\boldsymbol{\beta}'\mathbf{x}_t$. To avoid adding more dummy components, we assume here that $\boldsymbol{\alpha\varphi}_0 = \mathbf{0}$.

Thus, (6.44) shows that a large shock at time t, accounted for by the dummies $\mathbf{D}_{p,t}$ or $\mathbf{D}_{tr,t}$, will influence the variables with the same dynamics as an ordinary shock unless the dummy variable enters the model with lags. Thus, if a dummy variable needs a lag in the model, we shall consider the corresponding 'intervention' shock to be inherently different from the 'ordinary' shocks, whereas if the dummy is needed only once, on the day of the 'news', we shall consider it a big but, nevertheless, ordinary shock.

As briefly discussed above, it is also important to distinguish between additive and innovational outliers (Nielsen 2004a; Franses and Haldrup 1994). The former are extraordinary shocks which are not being influenced by the VAR dynamics (a typical example is a typing error in the data) and the latter are extraordinary shocks which, after they have occurred, have been affected by the VAR dynamics. Since additive outliers are not part of the VAR dynamics, the best procedure is to clean the data for them prior to the econometric analysis. If, instead, we use a dummy variable to correct for an additive outlier, it will additionally create spuriously delayed effects which are likely to bias the estimates. Additive outliers generally appear as transitory shocks (+/− shocks) without any sign of delayed effects in the data.

To summarize: we need to make a distinction between additive and innovational outliers and among the latter between extraordinary intervention shocks with a permanent and a transitory effect. For example, permanent intervention effects are often a result of central bank or government policy interventions, 'temporary' large shocks are often a result of market (over)reaction to various 'news'. Conceptually we can, therefore, distinguish between:

- ordinary (normally distributed) random shocks;
- (extra)ordinary large shocks due to permanent interventions ($|\hat{\varepsilon}_{i,t}| > 3.3\hat{\sigma}_\varepsilon$) with a delayed dynamic effect in the data, to be described by a blip dummy in the model;
- transitory large innovational outliers with a delayed dynamic effect in the data, to be described by a +/− blip dummy in the model;
- additive transitory outliers (typing mistakes, etc.) with no delayed dynamic effect in the data, to be removed prior to modelling.

The occurrence of transitory shocks in the model, whether large or small, will produce some negative (usually small) residual autocorrelations in the model and, hence, violate the independence assumption of the VAR model. Since transitory shocks generally appear in an unsystematic way, this problem is not likely to be solved by increasing the lag length of the VAR or by including a moving average term in the error process. By including transitory intervention dummies to account for the very large transitory shocks and by cleaning the data for additive outliers most of the problem is likely to disappear. However, small transitory shocks will generally not be accounted for by dummies and the empirical model often exhibits small residual autocorrelations.

Similar arguments to the ones we made for the trend and the constant term in the VAR model can be made for intervention dummies. The intervention may have influenced several variables in such a way that the intervention effect is cancelled in a cointegration relation. Alternatively, the intervention may only have affected one of the variables (or several variables but not proportionally with $\boldsymbol{\beta}$), so that the effect does not disappear in a cointegration relation.

6.7 An illustrative example

Consistent with the discussion above, we shall now re-estimate the Danish VAR model with a trend and the 1983 shift dummy restricted to lie in the cointegration space and with the remaining dummies entering the VAR equations unrestrictedly. Note that the 1999 big increase in money stock has now been removed, as has its seasonal means. Figure 6.3 illustrates the effect on money stock.

The dummies are defined as:

- $D_s831_t = 1$ for $t =$ 1983:1,... ,2003:4, 0 otherwise;
- $D_{tr}754_t = 1$ for $t =$ 1975:4, -0.5 for 1976:1 and 1976:2, 0 otherwise;
- $D_p764_t = 1$ for $t =$ 1976:4, 0 otherwise.

Because the shift dummy, D_s831_t, is restricted to lie in the cointegration space, its difference ΔD_s831_t (i.e. D_p831_t) should be included as an unrestricted permanent blip dummy in the VAR equations. In some cases it is not enough to include just the first

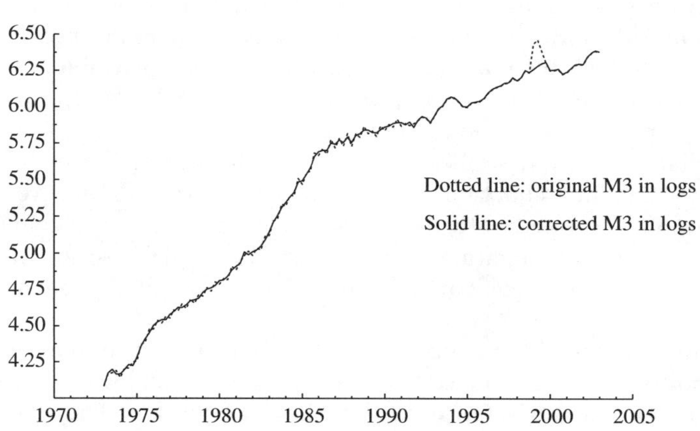

Fig 6.3 The original and corrected M3 in logs.

difference (i.e. $\Delta D_s 831_t$), but also the lagged dummy $\Delta D_s 831_{t-1}$. As a matter of fact, the latter turn out to be significant in the short-term interest rate equation, probably picking up a lagged policy reaction to the large drop in the long-term bond rate.

Finally, because we have corrected M3 for seasonal means we can leave out the seasonal dummies from the model altogether.

The VAR model to be estimated is given by:

$$\begin{aligned}\Delta \mathbf{x}_t &= \mathbf{\Gamma}_1 \Delta \mathbf{x}_{t-1} + \boldsymbol{\alpha}\boldsymbol{\beta}' \mathbf{x}_{t-1} + \boldsymbol{\alpha}\boldsymbol{\beta}_0 + \boldsymbol{\alpha}\boldsymbol{\beta}_1 t + \boldsymbol{\alpha}\boldsymbol{\delta}_0 D_s 831_t \\ &\quad + \mathbf{\Phi}_{p.1} D_p 831_t + \mathbf{\Phi}_{p.2} D_p 831_{t-1} \\ &\quad + \mathbf{\Phi}_{tr} D_{tr} 754_t + \mathbf{\Phi}_{p.3} D_p 764_t + \boldsymbol{\gamma}_0 + \boldsymbol{\varepsilon}_t \\ &= \mathbf{\Gamma}_1 \Delta \mathbf{x}_{t-1} + \boldsymbol{\alpha}\tilde{\boldsymbol{\beta}}' \tilde{\mathbf{x}}_{t-1} + \mathbf{\Phi}_{p.1} D_p 831_t + \mathbf{\Phi}_{p.2} D_p 831_{t-1} \\ &\quad + \mathbf{\Phi}_{tr} D_{tr} 754 tr_t + \mathbf{\Phi}_{p.3} D_p 764_t + \boldsymbol{\gamma}_0 + \boldsymbol{\varepsilon}_t,\end{aligned}$$

where

$$\tilde{\boldsymbol{\beta}} = \begin{bmatrix} \boldsymbol{\beta} \\ \boldsymbol{\beta}_0 \\ \boldsymbol{\beta}_1 \\ \boldsymbol{\delta}_0 \end{bmatrix} \text{ and } \tilde{\mathbf{x}}_{t-1} = \begin{bmatrix} \mathbf{x}_{t-1} \\ 1 \\ t \\ D_s 831_{t-1} \end{bmatrix}.$$

The properties of the residuals from the estimated VAR model with dummies have now improved compared to the unrestricted model of Chapter 4 as can be seen from the misspecification tests reported in Table 6.2. Except for some ARCH effects in the bond rate equation and some evidence of non-normality due to excess kurtosis (which is less serious than skewness for the estimated results) all test statistics are now acceptable. Even though there is still some residual non-normality left in the model, the result is much improved compared to the previous chapter. Note also that the LM_4 test statistic is insignificant, suggesting that there is no seasonal variation left in the data after having corrected M3 for the seasonal means.

The unrestricted estimates of the respecified model are reported in Table 6.3. The estimates of $\mathbf{\Pi}$ and $\mathbf{\Gamma}_1$ have not changed dramatically compared to the no-dummy VAR, but they are more significant now and to some extent more plausible from an economic point of view. All coefficients of the implicit money demand relation in the first row of the $\mathbf{\Pi}$ matrix seem reasonable and are quite significant.

The 1983 shift dummy describes a significant increase in the equilibrium level of money stock in the first equation, a negative effect (though not very significantly so) in the level of the bond rate in the fifth equation, and a significantly positive increase in the short rate equation. The former effect might seem puzzling but can be understood by the subsequent finding in Chapter 11 that the bond rate is weakly exogenous.

The estimated effects of the transitory and permanent blip dummies show that the temporary removal of the value added tax in 1975:4 had a significant positive effect in the income equation and a negative effect in the inflation equation. The short-term interest rate increased in 1976:4 as a result of a central bank intervention to curb inflationary

Table 6.2 Specification tests for the unrestricted VAR(2) model with dummies.

Multivariate tests					
Residual autocorrelations:					
LM_1: $\chi^2(25) =$	30.2		p-val.	0.22	
LM_4: $\chi^2(25) =$	30.4		p-val.	0.21	
Normality:					
LM: $\chi^2(10) =$	21.4		p-val.	0.02	
Univariate tests	Δm^r	Δy^r	Δp	ΔR_m	ΔR_b
ARCH(2)	0.89	0.56	2.36	**7.20**	**15.27**
Normality(2)	4.90	5.78	0.44	5.70	5.16
Skewness	−0.36	−0.25	0.03	0.10	−0.36
Kurtosis	3.76	2.27	3.06	3.85	3.80
Std. deviation	0.023	0.013	0.008	0.001	0.001
R^2	0.34	0.33	0.63	0.56	0.50
Eigenvalue roots of the model (five largest)					
Modulus	0.88	0.88	0.80	0.80	0.45
Real	0.88	0.88	0.79	0.79	0.43
Imaginary	0.06	−0.06	−0.12	0.12	−0.14

expectations. The immediate effect of the capital deregulation in 1983:1 was the dramatic drop in the bond rate followed by a (less dramatic) drop in the deposit rate in the next period. The latter effect was not very significant, so that ΔD_s831_{t-1} can be removed from the model without much influence on the normality test statistics.

Even though the estimates have not changed a lot, there are some notable differences. The income coefficient in the implicit money demand relation (the first row of the $\mathbf{\Pi}$ matrix) is now smaller and the negative inflation effect has become insignificant. This is because in the previous specification with no shift dummy at 1983:1 to account for the large increase in money stock, the latter was econometrically compensated by a larger income effect as well as a large (and positive!) inflation effect.

The residual correlations have increased to some extent, for example the correlation coefficient between the two interest rates has increased quite a lot. Because the inclusion of D_p831 eliminated the big residual in the bond rate equation at 1983:1, and because the short rate did not experience a similar big shock, the *simultaneous* correlation coefficient is likely to become higher when this influential observation is dummied out. The estimated residual standard errors are smaller, partly because the dummy variables enter the model as explanatory variables, partly because the big outlier residuals are likely to have a larger effect on the residual variance than the ordinary residuals. This also holds true for the value of the log likelihood function and other measures of goodness-of-fit. Thus, it would be more appropriate to concentrate out the effect of the dummies before calculating the R^2 values, the trace correlation and the residual standard errors.

Table 6.3 The VAR(2) model with dummies.

$$\begin{bmatrix} \Delta m_t^r \\ \Delta y_t^r \\ \Delta^2 p_t \\ \Delta R_{m,t} \\ \Delta R_{b,t} \end{bmatrix} = \begin{bmatrix} 0.01 & -0.01 & 0.34 & -0.07 & -2.19 \\ 0.01 & \mathbf{0.18} & 0.07 & 0.57 & \mathbf{-2.11} \\ 0.01 & \mathbf{-0.11} & \mathbf{-0.21} & \mathbf{-1.67} & 0.98 \\ \mathbf{-0.01} & 0.00 & 0.01 & 0.11 & \mathbf{0.23} \\ \mathbf{-0.01} & \mathbf{0.03} & -0.01 & -0.02 & \mathbf{0.21} \end{bmatrix} \begin{bmatrix} \Delta m_{t-1}^r \\ \Delta y_{t-1}^r \\ \Delta^2 p_{t-1} \\ \Delta R_{m_{t-1}} \\ \Delta R_{b_{t-1}} \end{bmatrix}$$

$$+ \begin{bmatrix} \mathbf{-0.26} & \mathbf{0.14} & -0.52 & \mathbf{2.74} & \mathbf{-3.29} & \mathbf{0.032} & \mathbf{0.0004} \\ 0.03 & \mathbf{-0.15} & -0.28 & \mathbf{-2.07} & 0.54 & -0.005 & 0.0002 \\ -0.00 & 0.01 & \mathbf{-0.84} & -0.48 & 0.24 & -0.006 & \mathbf{-0.0002} \\ -0.00 & 0.00 & 0.03 & \mathbf{-0.13} & 0.06 & \mathbf{0.002} & -0.0000 \\ 0.00 & 0.00 & 0.01 & 0.07 & \mathbf{-0.10} & -0.001 & -0.0000 \end{bmatrix} \begin{bmatrix} m_{t-1}^r \\ y_{t-1}^r \\ \Delta p_{t-1} \\ R_{m_{t-1}} \\ R_{b,t-1} \\ D_s831_{t-1} \\ t-1 \end{bmatrix}$$

$$+ \begin{bmatrix} 0.01 & -0.02 & 0.03 & -0.02 & 0.64 \\ \mathbf{0.03} & 0.01 & -0.01 & 0.01 & \mathbf{0.88} \\ \mathbf{-0.01} & 0.00 & -0.01 & 0.01 & -0.01 \\ 0.00 & \mathbf{0.01} & 0.00 & \mathbf{-0.00} & -0.01 \\ -0.00 & 0.00 & \mathbf{-0.01} & -0.00 & -0.02 \end{bmatrix} \begin{bmatrix} D_{tr}754_t \\ D_p764_t \\ D_p831_t \\ D_p831_{t-1} \\ 1 \end{bmatrix}$$

The estimated residual covariance matrix (in standardized form) is reported below:

$$\Omega = \begin{bmatrix} 1.0 & & & & \\ 0.13 & 1.0 & & & \\ -0.48 & -0.05 & 1.0 & & \\ -0.23 & -0.00 & 0.28 & 1.0 & \\ -0.08 & 0.12 & 0.16 & 0.39 & 1.0 \end{bmatrix}.$$

6.8 Conclusions

The normality assumption of ε_t is frequently not satisfied in empirical VAR models without accounting for reforms and interventions that have produced extraordinary large residuals. There are several possibilities:

1. The linear relationship of the VAR model does not hold for large shocks: the market reacts differently to ordinary and extraordinary shocks.
2. The linear relationship of the VAR model holds approximately, but the properties of the VAR estimates are sensitive to the presence of extraordinary large shocks. Ordinary and extraordinary shocks are drawn from different distributions.
3. The estimates of the VAR model are generally robust to deviations from normality.

It is almost impossible to know beforehand which of the three cases is closest to the truth in a specific empirical application. It depends very much on such aspects as the length of the sample, how frequently the outliers occur and whether positive and negative outliers occur relatively symmetrically, whether they are additive or innovational to the model. The best advice is to take them seriously. Neglecting the outlier problem is likely to produce unreliable results.

7

Estimation in the $I(1)$ model

We assume here that the empirical VAR model can describe the data and that there are no $I(2)$ components in the model. In the latter case Chapter 17 discusses a formal test for determining whether the data are $I(2)$. This chapter draws heavily on Johansen (1996), Chapter 6.

Section 7.1 demonstrates how the short-run dynamics can be concentrated out from the general VAR model. Section 7.2 derives the ML estimator of $\boldsymbol{\beta}$ and $\boldsymbol{\alpha}$. Section 7.3 shows how to normalize the cointegration vectors. Section 7.4 discusses the uniqueness of the unrestricted estimates and Section 7.5 illustrates the estimation procedure.

7.1 Concentrating the general VAR model

The $I(1)$ condition can be stated as:

$$\boldsymbol{\Pi} = \boldsymbol{\alpha}\boldsymbol{\beta}', \tag{7.1}$$

where $\boldsymbol{\alpha}$ and $\boldsymbol{\beta}$ are $p \times r$ matrices. If $r = p$, then $\mathbf{x}_t$ is stationary and standard inference applies. If $r = 0$, then there are p autonomous trends in $\mathbf{x}_t$, so that each $x_{i,t}$ is non-stationary with its own individual trend. In this case the vector process is driven by p different stochastic trends and it is not possible to obtain stationary cointegration relations between the levels of the variables. We say that the variables have no stochastic trends in common and, hence, do not move together over time. In this case, the VAR model in levels can be reformulated as a VAR model in differences without loss of long-run information. Since $\Delta\mathbf{x}_t \sim I(0)$, standard inference applies in the differenced model. If $p > r > 0$, then $\mathbf{x}_t \sim I(1)$ and there exists r directions into which the process can be made stationary by linear combinations. These are the cointegrating relations. The reason why we are interested in them is that they can often be given an interpretation as deviations from economic steady-state relations.

We consider now a VAR(k) model in ECM form with $\mathbf{\Pi} = \boldsymbol{\alpha\beta}'$:

$$\Delta\mathbf{x}_t = \mathbf{\Gamma}_1\Delta\mathbf{x}_{t-1} + \cdots + \mathbf{\Gamma}_{k-1}\Delta\mathbf{x}_{t-k+1} + \boldsymbol{\alpha\beta}'\tilde{\mathbf{x}}_{t-1} + \mathbf{\Phi}\mathbf{D}_t + \boldsymbol{\varepsilon}_t, \tag{7.2}$$

where $t = 1,\ldots,T$, $\tilde{\mathbf{x}}_{t-1}$ is $p1 \times 1$, $p1 = p + m$, m is the number of deterministic components, such as a constant or a trend, and the initial values $\mathbf{x}_{-1},\ldots,\mathbf{x}_{-k}$ are assumed fixed.

We use the following shorthand notation:

$$\begin{aligned} \mathbf{Z}_{0t} &= \Delta\mathbf{x}_t \\ \mathbf{Z}_{1t} &= \mathbf{x}_{t-1} \\ \mathbf{Z}_{2t} &= [\Delta\mathbf{x}'_{t-1}, \Delta\mathbf{x}'_{t-2}, \ldots, \Delta\mathbf{x}'_{t-k+1}, \mathbf{D}'_t], \end{aligned}$$

and write (7.2) in the more compact form:

$$\mathbf{Z}_{0t} = \boldsymbol{\alpha\beta}'\mathbf{Z}_{1t} + \mathbf{\Psi}\mathbf{Z}_{2t} + \boldsymbol{\varepsilon}_t,$$

where $\mathbf{\Psi} = [\mathbf{\Gamma}_1, \mathbf{\Gamma}_2, \ldots, \mathbf{\Gamma}_{k-1}, \mathbf{\Phi}]$. We shall now concentrate out the short-run 'transitory' effects, $\mathbf{\Psi}\mathbf{Z}_{2t}$, to obtain a 'cleaner' long-run adjustment model. To explain the idea of 'concentration' which is used in many different situations in econometrics, we shall first illustrate its use in a multiple regression model.

Remark 1 The Frisch–Waugh theorem says that the OLS estimate of $\beta_{2.1}$ in the linear regression model, $y_t = \beta_{1.2}x_{1t} + \beta_{2.1}x_{2t} + \varepsilon_t$, can be obtained in two steps

1(a) Regress y_t on x_{1t}, obtaining the residual u_{1t} from $y_t = \hat{b}_1x_{1t} + u_{1t}$.

1(b) Regress x_{2t} on x_{1t}, obtaining the residual u_{2t} from $x_{2t} = \hat{b}_2x_{1t} + u_{2t}$.

2 Regress u_{1t} on u_{2t}, to obtain the estimate of $\beta_{2.1}$, i.e.: $u_{1t} = \beta_{2.1}u_{2t} + \text{error}$.

Hence, we first concentrate out the effect of x_{1t} on y_t and on x_{2t}, and then regress the 'cleaned' y_t, i.e. u_{1t}, on the 'cleaned' x_{2t}, i.e. u_{2t}.

We now use the same idea on the VAR model. First we define the auxiliary regressions:

$$\begin{aligned} \mathbf{Z}_{0t} &= \hat{\mathbf{B}}'_1\mathbf{Z}_{2t} + \mathbf{R}_{0t} \\ \mathbf{Z}_{1t} &= \hat{\mathbf{B}}'_2\mathbf{Z}_{2t} + \mathbf{R}_{1t} \end{aligned} \tag{7.3}$$

where $\hat{\mathbf{B}}'_1 = \mathbf{M}_{02}\mathbf{M}_{22}^{-1}$ and $\hat{\mathbf{B}}'_2 = \mathbf{M}_{12}\mathbf{M}_{22}^{-1}$ are OLS estimates and $\mathbf{M}_{ij} = \mathbf{\Sigma}_t(\mathbf{Z}_{it}\mathbf{Z}'_{jt})/T$. Thus, $\mathbf{M}_{ij} - \bar{\mathbf{Z}}_i\bar{\mathbf{Z}}'_j$ are the empirical counterparts of the covariance matrices $\mathbf{\Sigma}_{ij}$ discussed in Chapter 3. The following scheme shows how these are defined for the VAR(k) model:

	$\Delta\mathbf{x}_t$	$\mathbf{x}_{t-1}$	$\Delta\mathbf{x}_{t-1}$ $\cdots$ $\Delta\mathbf{x}_{t-k+1}$
$\Delta\mathbf{x}_t$	$\mathbf{M}_{00}$	$\mathbf{M}_{01}$	$\mathbf{M}_{02}$
$\mathbf{x}_{t-1}$	$\mathbf{M}_{10}$	$\mathbf{M}_{11}$	$\mathbf{M}_{12}$
$\Delta\mathbf{x}_{t-1}$ $\vdots$ $\Delta\mathbf{x}_{t-k+1}$	$\mathbf{M}_{20}$	$\mathbf{M}_{21}$	$\mathbf{M}_{22}$

The concentrated model

$$\mathbf{R}_{0t} = \boldsymbol{\alpha\beta}'\mathbf{R}_{1t} + \text{error} \tag{7.4}$$

is important for understanding both the statistical and economic properties of the VAR model. By concentration the original 'messy' VAR, containing short-run adjustment and intervention effects, has been transformed into the 'clean' equilibrium adjustment form (7.4), in which the adjustment exclusively takes place towards the long-run equilibrium relations. This means that we not only have transformed the 'dirty' empirical model into a nice statistical model, but also into a more interpretable economic form.

7.2 Derivation of the ML estimator

To simplify the notation we disregard here any deterministic components in the cointegration relations and consider the concentrated model:

$$\mathbf{R}_{0t} = \boldsymbol{\alpha\beta}'\mathbf{R}_{1t} + \boldsymbol{\varepsilon}_t, \quad t = 1, \ldots, T,$$

where

$$\boldsymbol{\varepsilon}_t \sim N_p(\mathbf{0}, \boldsymbol{\Omega}).$$

The ML estimator is derived in two steps: First, we assume that $\boldsymbol{\beta}$ is known and derive an estimator of $\boldsymbol{\alpha}$ under the assumption that $\boldsymbol{\beta}'\mathbf{R}_{1t}$ is a known variable. Then we insert $\boldsymbol{\alpha} = \hat{\boldsymbol{\alpha}}(\boldsymbol{\beta})$ in the expression for the maximum of the likelihood function so that it becomes a function of $\boldsymbol{\beta}$, but not of $\boldsymbol{\alpha}$. We then find the value of $\hat{\boldsymbol{\beta}}$ that maximizes the likelihood function. As soon as we have found the ML estimator of $\boldsymbol{\beta}$, we can calculate $\hat{\boldsymbol{\alpha}} = \boldsymbol{\alpha}(\hat{\boldsymbol{\beta}})$.

Step 1. The ML estimator of $\boldsymbol{\alpha}$ given $\boldsymbol{\beta}$ corresponds to the usual OLS estimator. It can be derived by post-multiplying (7.4) with $\mathbf{R}'_{1t}\boldsymbol{\beta}$ and dropping the error term:

$$\mathbf{R}_{0t}\mathbf{R}'_{1t}\boldsymbol{\beta} = \boldsymbol{\alpha\beta}'\mathbf{R}_{1t}\mathbf{R}'_{1t}\boldsymbol{\beta}.$$

Summing over t, and dividing by T gives:

$$\mathbf{S}_{01}\boldsymbol{\beta} = \boldsymbol{\alpha\beta}'\mathbf{S}_{11}\boldsymbol{\beta}$$

where $\mathbf{S}_{ij} = T^{-1}\Sigma_t\mathbf{R}_{it}\mathbf{R}'_{jt} = \mathbf{M}_{ij} - \mathbf{M}_{i2}\mathbf{M}_{22}^{-1}\mathbf{M}_{2j}$.

It is now easy to derive the least squares estimator of $\boldsymbol{\alpha}$ as a function of $\boldsymbol{\beta}$:

$$\hat{\boldsymbol{\alpha}}(\boldsymbol{\beta}) = \mathbf{S}_{01}\boldsymbol{\beta}(\boldsymbol{\beta}'\mathbf{S}_{11}\boldsymbol{\beta})^{-1}. \tag{7.5}$$

Step 2. Given the assumption of multivariate normality, we have that the maximum of the likelihood function of (7.4) is equal to the determinant of the error covariance matrix as a function of fixed $\boldsymbol{\beta}$ and $\boldsymbol{\alpha}$:

$$L_{\max}^{-2/T}(\boldsymbol{\beta},\boldsymbol{\alpha}) = |\hat{\boldsymbol{\Omega}}(\boldsymbol{\beta},\boldsymbol{\alpha})| \; + \; \text{const. terms} \tag{7.6}$$

where

$$\begin{aligned}\hat{\boldsymbol{\Omega}}(\boldsymbol{\beta},\boldsymbol{\alpha}) &= T^{-1}\sum(\mathbf{R}_{0t}-\boldsymbol{\alpha}\boldsymbol{\beta}'\mathbf{R}_{1t})(\mathbf{R}_{0t}-\boldsymbol{\alpha}\boldsymbol{\beta}'\mathbf{R}_{1t})' \\ &= T^{-1}\left(\sum\mathbf{R}_{0t}\mathbf{R}_{0t}'-\sum\mathbf{R}_{0t}\mathbf{R}_{1t}'\boldsymbol{\beta}\boldsymbol{\alpha}'-\boldsymbol{\alpha}\boldsymbol{\beta}'\sum\mathbf{R}_{1t}\mathbf{R}_{0t}'+\boldsymbol{\alpha}\boldsymbol{\beta}'\sum\mathbf{R}_{1t}\mathbf{R}_{1t}'\boldsymbol{\beta}\boldsymbol{\alpha}'\right) \\ &= \mathbf{S}_{00}-\mathbf{S}_{01}\boldsymbol{\beta}\boldsymbol{\alpha}'-\boldsymbol{\alpha}\boldsymbol{\beta}'\mathbf{S}_{10}+\boldsymbol{\alpha}\boldsymbol{\beta}'\mathbf{S}_{11}\boldsymbol{\beta}\boldsymbol{\alpha}'.\end{aligned} \tag{7.7}$$

By substituting (7.5) in (7.7), we can express the error covariance matrix as a function exclusively of $\boldsymbol{\beta}$:

$$\begin{aligned}\hat{\boldsymbol{\Omega}}(\boldsymbol{\beta}) \;=\; & \mathbf{S}_{00}-\underbrace{\mathbf{S}_{01}\boldsymbol{\beta}(\boldsymbol{\beta}'\mathbf{S}_{11}\boldsymbol{\beta})^{-1}\boldsymbol{\beta}'\mathbf{S}_{10}-\mathbf{S}_{01}\boldsymbol{\beta}(\boldsymbol{\beta}'\mathbf{S}_{11}\boldsymbol{\beta})^{-1}\boldsymbol{\beta}'\mathbf{S}_{10}}_{-2\{\mathbf{S}_{01}\boldsymbol{\beta}(\boldsymbol{\beta}'\mathbf{S}_{11}\boldsymbol{\beta})^{-1}\boldsymbol{\beta}'\mathbf{S}_{10}\}} \\ & \underbrace{+\mathbf{S}_{01}\boldsymbol{\beta}(\boldsymbol{\beta}'\mathbf{S}_{11}\boldsymbol{\beta})^{-1}\underbrace{\boldsymbol{\beta}'\mathbf{S}_{11}\boldsymbol{\beta}(\boldsymbol{\beta}'\mathbf{S}_{11}\boldsymbol{\beta})^{-1}}_{\mathbf{I}}\boldsymbol{\beta}'\mathbf{S}_{10}.}_{\mathbf{S}_{01}\boldsymbol{\beta}(\boldsymbol{\beta}'\mathbf{S}_{11}\boldsymbol{\beta})^{-1}\boldsymbol{\beta}'\mathbf{S}_{10}}\end{aligned}$$

Hence:

$$\hat{\boldsymbol{\Omega}}(\boldsymbol{\beta}) = \mathbf{S}_{00}-\mathbf{S}_{01}\boldsymbol{\beta}(\boldsymbol{\beta}'\mathbf{S}_{11}\boldsymbol{\beta})^{-1}\boldsymbol{\beta}'\mathbf{S}_{10}. \tag{7.8}$$

The ML estimator of $\boldsymbol{\beta}$ is given by the estimate $\hat{\boldsymbol{\beta}}$ that minimizes $|\hat{\boldsymbol{\Omega}}(\hat{\boldsymbol{\beta}})|$. To derive the estimator we use the following result:

$$\begin{vmatrix}\mathbf{A} & \mathbf{B} \\ \mathbf{B}' & \mathbf{C}\end{vmatrix} = |\mathbf{A}|\cdot|\mathbf{C}-\mathbf{B}'\mathbf{A}^{-1}\mathbf{B}| = |\mathbf{C}|\cdot|\mathbf{A}-\mathbf{B}\mathbf{C}^{-1}\mathbf{B}'| \tag{7.9}$$

where $\mathbf{A}$ and $\mathbf{C}$ are non-singular square matrices. Now substitute:

$$\begin{aligned}\mathbf{S}_{00} &= \mathbf{A} \\ \boldsymbol{\beta}'\mathbf{S}_{11}\boldsymbol{\beta} &= \mathbf{C} \\ \mathbf{S}_{01}\boldsymbol{\beta} &= \mathbf{B}\end{aligned}$$

in (7.9), resulting in:

$$|\mathbf{S}_{00}|\cdot|\boldsymbol{\beta}'\mathbf{S}_{11}\boldsymbol{\beta}-\boldsymbol{\beta}'\mathbf{S}_{10}\mathbf{S}_{00}^{-1}\mathbf{S}_{01}\boldsymbol{\beta}| = |\boldsymbol{\beta}'\mathbf{S}_{11}\boldsymbol{\beta}|\cdot\underbrace{|\mathbf{S}_{00}-\mathbf{S}_{01}\boldsymbol{\beta}(\boldsymbol{\beta}'\mathbf{S}_{11}\boldsymbol{\beta})^{-1}\boldsymbol{\beta}'\mathbf{S}_{10}|}_{|\boldsymbol{\Omega}(\boldsymbol{\beta})|}.$$

Hence,

$$\begin{aligned}|\hat{\boldsymbol{\Omega}}(\boldsymbol{\beta})| &= \frac{|\mathbf{S}_{00}|\cdot|\boldsymbol{\beta}'\mathbf{S}_{11}\boldsymbol{\beta}-\boldsymbol{\beta}'\mathbf{S}_{10}\mathbf{S}_{00}^{-1}\mathbf{S}_{01}\boldsymbol{\beta}|}{|\boldsymbol{\beta}'\mathbf{S}_{11}\boldsymbol{\beta}|} \\ &= |\mathbf{S}_{00}|\cdot\frac{|\boldsymbol{\beta}'(\mathbf{S}_{11}-\mathbf{S}_{10}\mathbf{S}_{00}^{-1}\mathbf{S}_{01})\boldsymbol{\beta}|}{|\boldsymbol{\beta}'\mathbf{S}_{11}\boldsymbol{\beta}|}.\end{aligned}$$

Using the result that the function

$$f(x) = \frac{|\mathbf{X}'\mathbf{M}\mathbf{X}|}{|\mathbf{X}'\mathbf{N}\mathbf{X}|}$$

is maximized by solving the eigenvalue problem

$$|\rho\mathbf{N} - \mathbf{M}| = 0, \tag{7.10}$$

we can obtain a solution for $\boldsymbol{\beta}$ that minimizes $|\hat{\boldsymbol{\Omega}}(\boldsymbol{\beta})|$.

We first substitute:

$$\begin{aligned}\mathbf{M} &= \mathbf{S}_{11} - \mathbf{S}_{10}\mathbf{S}_{00}^{-1}\mathbf{S}_{01}\\ \mathbf{N} &= \mathbf{S}_{11}\\ \mathbf{X} &= \boldsymbol{\beta}\end{aligned}$$

in (7.10) to formulate the eigenvalue problem, the solution of which gives the estimates of $\boldsymbol{\beta}$:

$$|\rho\mathbf{S}_{11} - \mathbf{S}_{11} + \mathbf{S}_{10}\mathbf{S}_{00}^{-1}\mathbf{S}_{01}| = 0$$

or equivalently:

$$|\underbrace{(1-\rho)}_{\lambda}\mathbf{S}_{11} - \mathbf{S}_{10}\mathbf{S}_{00}^{-1}\mathbf{S}_{01}| = 0. \tag{7.11}$$

The solution gives p eigenvalues $\lambda_1, \ldots, \lambda_p$ and we can now express the determinant of the residual covariance matrix as:

$$\left|\hat{\boldsymbol{\Omega}}(\hat{\boldsymbol{\beta}})\right| = |\mathbf{S}_{00}| \prod_{i=1}^{p}(1-\lambda_i). \tag{7.12}$$

The corresponding p eigenvectors $\mathbf{v}_1, \ldots, \mathbf{v}_p$ are ordered according to $\hat{\lambda}_1 > \cdots > \hat{\lambda}_p \geq 0$. The magnitude of $\hat{\lambda}_i$ is a measure of the 'stationarity' of the corresponding $\mathbf{v}_i'\mathbf{x}_t$, the larger the $\hat{\lambda}_i$, the 'more' stationary is the relation. These relations are not yet normalized on a variable and in the next section we shall discuss how to choose an appropriate normalization for each vector. The normalized vectors will be called $\boldsymbol{\beta}_i$ to distinguish them from the non-normalized vectors. The next chapter will discuss how to classify the p relations into r stationary relations which correspond to the r largest non-zero eigenvalues and the $p-r$ non-stationary relations which correspond to the $p-r$ zero eigenvalues.

7.3 Normalization

To be able to interpret a cointegration relation as a relation to be primarily associated with a particular economic variable, we need to normalize the former by setting the coefficient of the latter to be unity. This is similar to what we do in a regression model, $x_{1t} = \beta_0 + \beta_1 x_{2t} + \beta_3 x_{3t} + u_t$, when we choose one of the variables, x_{1t}, to be the 'dependent' variable, i.e. to have a unitary coefficient. In a regression model with stochastic variables, it might happen that we choose the 'wrong' variable to be the dependent variable. In such a case it is likely that the regression, $x_{2t} = \widetilde{\beta}_0 + \widetilde{\beta}_1 x_{1t} + \widetilde{\beta}_3 x_{3t} + \widetilde{u}_t$, yields more interpretable coefficient estimates and improved statistical properties.

In an analogous manner, the choice of normalization of a cointegrating relation should make sense economically as well as statistically. For example, normalizing on an insignificant or irrelevant coefficient does not make sense, normalizing on money stock, say, in a relation describing real income seems a bad choice. There is, however, an important difference between a regression model and a cointegration relation. Normalizing on either x_{1t} or x_{2t} in the regression model generally changes the estimates of the regression coefficients, whereas in a cointegration relation, the ratios between coefficients are the same independent on the chosen normalization. In this sense the coefficient estimates in a cointegration relation are more 'canonical'.

7.4 The uniqueness of the unrestricted estimates

For a given choice of the number of stationary cointegrating relations, r, the Johansen procedure gives the maximum likelihood estimates of the unrestricted cointegrating relations $\boldsymbol{\beta}'\mathbf{x}_t$. How to determine r will be discussed in the next chapter. In Chapter 6 we gave these estimates a first tentative interpretation in terms of underlying steady-state relations. In this section, we shall discuss whether such an interpretation is at all meaningful. See also Johansen and Juselius (1994). The unrestricted estimates of $\boldsymbol{\alpha}$ and $\boldsymbol{\beta}$ are calculated given the following conditions:

1. Stationarity, i.e. $\hat{\boldsymbol{\beta}}'\mathbf{x}_t \sim I(0)$.
2. Conditional independence of $\hat{\boldsymbol{\beta}}'_j\mathbf{x}_t$ in the sense of $\hat{\boldsymbol{\beta}}'\mathbf{S}_{11}\hat{\boldsymbol{\beta}} = \mathbf{I}$, where $\mathbf{S}_{11}$ was defined in Section 7.2.
3. The ordering given by the maximal conditional correlation with the stationary process $\Delta\mathbf{x}_t$.

Given the above criteria, the unrestricted cointegration relations are uniquely determined but the question is whether they are meaningful from an economic point of view. As it frequently happens that the unrestricted cointegration relations seem roughly interpretable, it may be of some interest to discuss whether the three conditions (or rather the last two, since stationarity is indisputable) are reasonable from an economic point of view.

The 'conditional' independence, $\hat{\boldsymbol{\beta}}'\mathbf{S}_{11}\hat{\boldsymbol{\beta}} = \mathbf{I}$, is just a convenient normalization of the eigenvalue problem derived from the analysis of the likelihood function. It is a purely statistical condition and is arbitrary in the sense that we could in principle have chosen another normalization. Because this normalization surprisingly often seems to produce economically interpretable relations, it is tempting to look for some regularity in macroeconomic behaviour which could be associated with this purely statistical condition. The following is such an attempt.

If the empirical problem is about macroeconomic behaviour in a market where equilibrating forces are allowed to work without binding regulations, one would generally expect two types of agents with disparate goals interacting in such a way that equilibrium is restored once it has been violated. These can be demanders versus suppliers, producers versus consumers, employers versus employees, etc. Thus, if we choose a sufficiently rich set of variables for the VAR analysis, economic theory would generally suggest at least two (but often more) stationary long-run relationships. The question is whether we should expect them to be 'conditionally' independent.

A somewhat heuristic guess is that the 'conditional' independence may produce empirically interpretable relations when the VAR model contains sufficiently many variables to identify these hypothetical long-run relations. For example, to be able to empirically identify a long-run demand and a supply relation among the unrestricted cointegration relations, there should be at least one variable which is strongly influenced by the demand behaviour but unrelated to the supply behaviour and vice versa. This is, of course, the basic idea behind identification which will be discussed in great detail in Chapter 10, where we discuss how to obtain unique estimates without the need to impose the condition of conditional independence.

The third statistical criterion, the maximal correlation with the stationary part of the process, does not seem easily interpretable as a meaningful economical criterion. Therefore, even if a direct interpretation of the unrestricted cointegration vectors is sometimes possible, the results should be considered indicative rather than conclusive, and cannot replace formal testing of structural hypotheses.

7.5 An illustration

Solving the eigenvalue problem (7.11) for the Danish money market model defined in Section 6.7,[1] produced the five eigenvalues and the corresponding eigenvectors reported in the first part of Table 7.1. The eigenvectors are calculated based on the normalization $\hat{\mathbf{v}}'\mathbf{S}_{11}\hat{\mathbf{v}} = \mathbf{I}$. The ordering is based on the magnitude of $\hat{\lambda}_i$ so that the first relation $\mathbf{v}_1'\mathbf{x}_t$ is most strongly correlated with the stationary part of the process. The squared canonical correlation coefficient $\hat{\lambda}_1 = 0.35$ corresponds to a correlation coefficient $\sqrt{0.35} \approx 0.60$. We note that the last eigenvalue λ_5 is quite close to zero.[2] The question is when the value of λ_i is small enough not to be significantly different from zero. The next chapter will deal with this important and difficult issue.

For each eigenvector $\hat{\mathbf{v}}_i$ there is a corresponding vector of weights (loadings) $\hat{\mathbf{w}}_i = \mathbf{S}_{01}\hat{\mathbf{v}}_i$ satisfying $\sum_{i=1}^{p} \mathbf{w}_i'\hat{\mathbf{v}}_i = \hat{\mathbf{\Pi}}$. The coefficients of the eigenvectors $\hat{\mathbf{v}}_i$ reported in Table 7.1 are generally quite large and the coefficients of the weights $\hat{\mathbf{w}}_i$ correspondingly

[1]The dummy variable $\Delta D_s 83.1_{t-1}$ was only borderline significant and was omitted altogether from the model.

[2]Note that $\lambda_i = 0$ is the equivalent of $\rho = 1$, which implies that the relation $\mathbf{v}_i'\mathbf{x}_t$ is a unit root process.

small. Without an adequate normalization it is hard to see what they mean and the first task is to normalize the eigenvectors by an element $\hat{v}_{ij}$ as follows:

$$\hat{\boldsymbol{\beta}}_{i\cdot} = \hat{\mathbf{v}}_i \hat{v}_{ij}^{-1}, \quad i = 1, \dots, p,$$
$$\hat{\boldsymbol{\alpha}}_{i\cdot} = \hat{\mathbf{w}}_i \hat{v}_{ij}, \quad i = 1, \dots, p.$$

To distinguish between the non-normalized and the normalized vectors we use the notation $\hat{\mathbf{v}}_{i\cdot}$ and $\hat{\mathbf{w}}_{i\cdot}$ for the former and $\hat{\boldsymbol{\beta}}_{i\cdot}$ and $\hat{\boldsymbol{\alpha}}_{i\cdot}$ for the latter. The normalized vectors are reported in the middle part of Table 7.1. The first vector has been normalized on Δp, the second on m^r, the third on R_m, the fourth on y^r, and finally the fifth on R_b. Though the normalization can be done arbitrarily one should always attempt to normalize on a variable that is 'representative' for the relation. For example, normalizing on Δp in the first relation means that the latter should in some sense describe a relation for the inflation rate (with significant equilibrium correction in the inflation rate equation). Note, however, that the initial choice of normalization is tentative by nature and will often change as a result of a more detailed inspection of the results.

The estimated unrestricted cointegration vectors may or may not make economic sense. As already mentioned they are uniquely defined based on (1) the ordering of the $\hat{\lambda}_i$ and (2) the choice of eigenvector normalization $\hat{\boldsymbol{\beta}}'\mathbf{S}_{11}\hat{\boldsymbol{\beta}} = \mathbf{I}$, both of which are statistical criteria without any obvious economic interpretation. Nevertheless, we shall illustrate below that a careful inspection of the unrestricted estimation results can often be helpful as a means to obtain a tentative picture of possible empirical relations in the data.

To be able to roughly discriminate between significant and less significant $\hat{\alpha}_{ij}$ coefficients, we have reported t ratios in brackets (based on OLS standard errors) and indicated the coefficients with a ratio greater than 1.9 in bold face. Note, however, that the 't' values are distributed as Student's t only if the corresponding $\hat{\boldsymbol{\beta}}_i'\mathbf{x}_t$ is stationary. When this is not the case the distribution is probably somewhere between the Student's t and the Dickey–Fullers' τ.

When investigating the $\hat{\boldsymbol{\alpha}}$ coefficients it is often useful to check whether a 'significant' $\hat{\alpha}_{ij}$, $i = 1, \dots, p$ and $j = 1, \dots, r$ corresponds to a $\hat{\beta}_{ij}$ with the opposite sign. When this is the case, i.e. $\hat{\alpha}_{ij} > 0, \hat{\beta}_{ij} < 0$ or vice versa, then the cointegration relation is equilibrium correcting in the equation $\Delta x_{i,t}$. When the $\hat{\alpha}_{ij}$ and the $\hat{\beta}_{ij}$ are of the same sign, it generally means that the cointegration relation describes overshooting behaviour in equation $\Delta x_{i,t}$. With this in mind we note that: (i) the first $\hat{\boldsymbol{\beta}}$ relation is significantly equilibrium correcting in the money stock and the inflation rate equations; (ii) the second $\hat{\boldsymbol{\beta}}$ relation in the money stock equation, but also in the real income, the inflation rate and the short rate equations; (iii) the third $\hat{\boldsymbol{\beta}}$ relation in the real income, the short rate equation and the bond rate equations; (iv) the fourth $\hat{\boldsymbol{\beta}}$ relation only in the real income equation, and (v) the last relation $\hat{\boldsymbol{\beta}}$ in the interest rate equations. Thus, all 'significant' $\hat{\alpha}_{ij}$ coefficients suggest equilibrium correcting behaviour.

The small adjustment coefficients and the rather small t ratios in $\hat{\boldsymbol{\alpha}}_5$ might suggest that the last eigenvector is a non-stationarity relation. Note, however, that the t-ratios as an indicator of stationarity can be misleading, partly because we do not know whether to interpret them as Student's t or Dickey–Fullers' τ, partly because they are sensitive to multicollinearity between the cointegration relations. This is because the condition that

Table 7.1 Estimated eigenvalues, eigenvectors, and adjustment coefficients for the Danish data.

$\hat{\lambda}_i$		m_t^r	y_t^r	Δp_t	$R_{m,t}$	$R_{b,t}$	D_s831_t	Trend
Non-normalized eigenvectors: $\hat{\mathbf{v}}_i'$								
0.35	$\hat{\mathbf{v}}_1'$	12.66	−6.68	193.80	−57.07	110.00	−0.35	0.01
0.23	$\hat{\mathbf{v}}_2'$	−18.44	18.90	−63.59	156.97	−147.57	−4.50	−0.01
0.20	$\hat{\mathbf{v}}_3'$	1.90	−12.48	−8.89	−499.29	310.13	2.84	0.02
0.09	$\hat{\mathbf{v}}_4'$	8.86	14.18	7.50	100.14	211.44	−0.07	−0.03
0.06	$\hat{\mathbf{v}}_5'$	1.07	18.32	−2.54	−148.22	60.12	1.00	−0.10
Normalized eigenvectors: $\hat{\boldsymbol{\beta}}_i'$								
0.35	$\hat{\boldsymbol{\beta}}_1'$	0.07	−0.03	1.00	−0.29	0.57	−0.002	0.000
0.23	$\hat{\boldsymbol{\beta}}_2'$	1.00	−1.02	−3.45	−8.51	8.00	−0.244	−0.001
0.20	$\hat{\boldsymbol{\beta}}_3'$	−0.00	0.03	0.02	1.00	−0.62	−0.006	−0.000
0.09	$\hat{\boldsymbol{\beta}}_4'$	0.62	1.00	0.53	7.06	14.91	−0.005	−0.002
0.06	$\hat{\boldsymbol{\beta}}_5'$	0.02	0.30	−0.04	−2.47	1.00	0.017	−0.002
The weights to the eigenvectors: $\hat{\boldsymbol{\alpha}}_i$								
		$\hat{\boldsymbol{\alpha}}_1$	$\hat{\boldsymbol{\alpha}}_2$	$\hat{\boldsymbol{\alpha}}_3$	$\hat{\boldsymbol{\alpha}}_4$	$\hat{\boldsymbol{\alpha}}_5$		
Δm_t^r		**−1.05** [−2.60]	**−0.15** [−4.01]	1.18 [1.13]	−0.05 [−1.53]	−0.15 [−1.24]		
Δy_t^r		−0.06 [−0.27]	**0.05** [2.16]	**−1.54** [−2.50]	**−0.05** [−2.58]	−0.05 [−0.66]		
$\Delta^2 p_t$		**−0.71** [−5.11]	**0.04** [2.80]	−0.30 [−0.85]	0.01 [0.78]	0.07 [1.54]		
$\Delta R_{m,t}$		0.02 [0.94]	−0.00 [−1.88]	**−0.10** [−2.19]	−0.00 [−0.45]	**0.01** [2.41]		
$\Delta R_{b,t}$		0.02 [0.84]	0.00 [0.92]	**0.16** [2.54]	−0.00 [−1.85]	**0.01** [1.90]		
The combined effects: $\hat{\boldsymbol{\Pi}}$								
Δm_t^r		**−0.26** [−5.13]	**0.13** [1.90]	−0.51 [−1.21]	**2.86** [2.47]	**−3.39** [−3.85]	**0.031** [2.70]	0.0004 [1.73]
Δy_t^r		0.02 [0.73]	**−0.15** [−3.59]	−0.28 [−1.12]	**−2.13** [−3.11]	0.59 [1.13]	−0.004 [−0.56]	0.0002 [1.47]
$\Delta^2 p_t$		−0.00 [−0.12]	0.01 [0.30]	**−0.84** [−5.75]	−0.52 [−1.30]	0.27 [0.88]	−0.005 [−1.28]	**−0.0002** [−2.25]
$\Delta R_{m,t}$		−0.00 [−0.83]	0.00 [1.20]	0.02 [1.33]	**−0.11** [−2.25]	0.05 [1.31]	**0.002** [3.10]	−0.0000 [−1.49]
$\Delta R_{b,t}$		0.00 [0.35]	0.00 [0.52]	0.01 [0.52]	0.08 [1.09]	**−0.10** [−1.98]	−0.001 [−1.77]	−0.0000 [−1.67]

the unrestricted $\hat{\boldsymbol{\beta}}$ vectors are 'conditionally' independent, $\hat{\boldsymbol{\beta}}'\mathbf{S}_{11}\hat{\boldsymbol{\beta}} = \mathbf{I}$, does not imply that $\hat{\boldsymbol{\beta}}'\mathbf{x}_t$ are orthogonal.

The graphs in Figures 7.1–7.5 of $\hat{\boldsymbol{\beta}}_i'\mathbf{x}_t$ and $\hat{\boldsymbol{\beta}}_i'\mathbf{R}_{1t}$, where the latter is derived from the concentrated model (7.4), seem to support the interpretation that the fifth relation is non-stationary. Figures 7.1–7.3 suggest that the first three relations are stationary, whereas the fourth relation in Figure 7.4 is more of a borderline case.

7.6 Interpreting the results

As discussed above, we should not expect the unrestricted $\hat{\boldsymbol{\beta}}$ estimates to be directly interpretable. However, surprisingly often it happens that one can obtain useful information about potentially relevant relations in the data by a first inspection of the $\hat{\boldsymbol{\beta}}$, $\hat{\boldsymbol{\alpha}}$ and the $\hat{\boldsymbol{\Pi}}$. In the ideal case, each unrestricted cointegration relation is primarily significant in just one equation with an α coefficient consistent with equilibrium correction behaviour. It is then often possible to interpret each cointegration relation as a potential candidate for a long-run relation for the variable in question. Unfortunately, the picture is often much more blurred: each cointegration relation appears to be significant in several equations. But even in the latter case, it is often possible to single out one equation in which the cointegration relation is most significantly equilibrium correcting. We shall now make an attempt to tentatively interpret the unrestricted cointegration relations as potential steady-state relations.

The first relation seems roughly to be a relation between inflation and the two interest rates, possibly with some small effects from real money and real income:

$$\Delta p \approx 0.3R_m - 0.6R_b - 0.03(m^r - y^r) - 0.04m^r \cdots . \tag{7.13}$$

It was found to be strongly significant in the inflation rate and in the money stock equations, in both of which the sign of the adjustment coefficient is consistent with equilibrium correction behaviour. Thus, the inflation rate seems to have been positively related to the short-term interest rate, negatively related to the long-term interest rate and, possibly, with the money velocity and real money stock. The equilibrium error $\hat{\boldsymbol{\beta}}_1'\mathbf{x}_t$ graphed in Figure 7.1 seems definitely stationary.

The second relation seems approximately to be a conventional money demand relation where the opportunity cost of holding money is measured by the long-short interest rate spread. However, the sign of the inflation rate is not consistent with a money demand effect.

$$m^r \approx y^r + 3.4\Delta p - 8.2(R_b - R_m) + 0.24D_s831 + \cdots \tag{7.14}$$

Both money stock and inflation rate are significantly adjusting to this relation, both with an α coefficient which is consistent with equilibrium correction behaviour. Also, the short-term interest rate might be affected by this relation but not in an equilibrium correcting way. The equilibrium error, $\hat{\boldsymbol{\beta}}_2'\mathbf{x}_t$, in Figure 7.2 looks very stationary.

The third relation seems to describe an interest rate relation:

$$R_m \approx 0.62R_b + 0.006D_s831 + \cdots \tag{7.15}$$

Real income and the two interest rates are equilibrium correcting to this relation. The graph of $\hat{\boldsymbol{\beta}}_3'\mathbf{x}_t$ in Figure 7.3 suggests a stationary equilibrium error, though with some indication of cyclical swings.

The fourth relation seems to describe an IS type relation with strong negative nominal interest rate effects:

$$y^r \approx -7.1R_m - 14.9R_b + \cdots \tag{7.16}$$

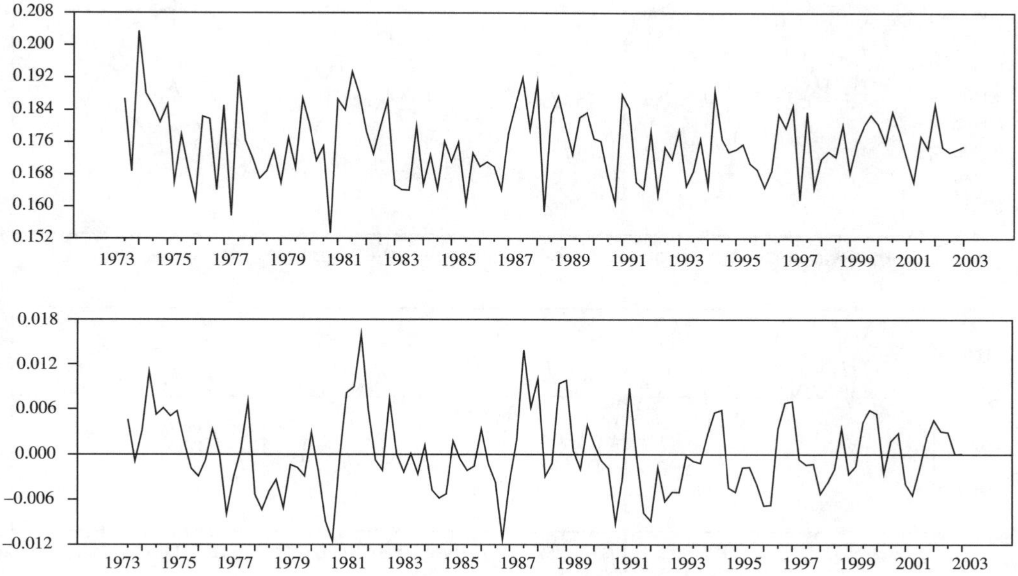

Fig 7.1 The first cointegration relation $\boldsymbol{\beta}_1'\mathbf{x}_t$ (upper panel) and $\boldsymbol{\beta}_1'\mathbf{R}_{1t}$ corrected for short-run effects (lower panel).

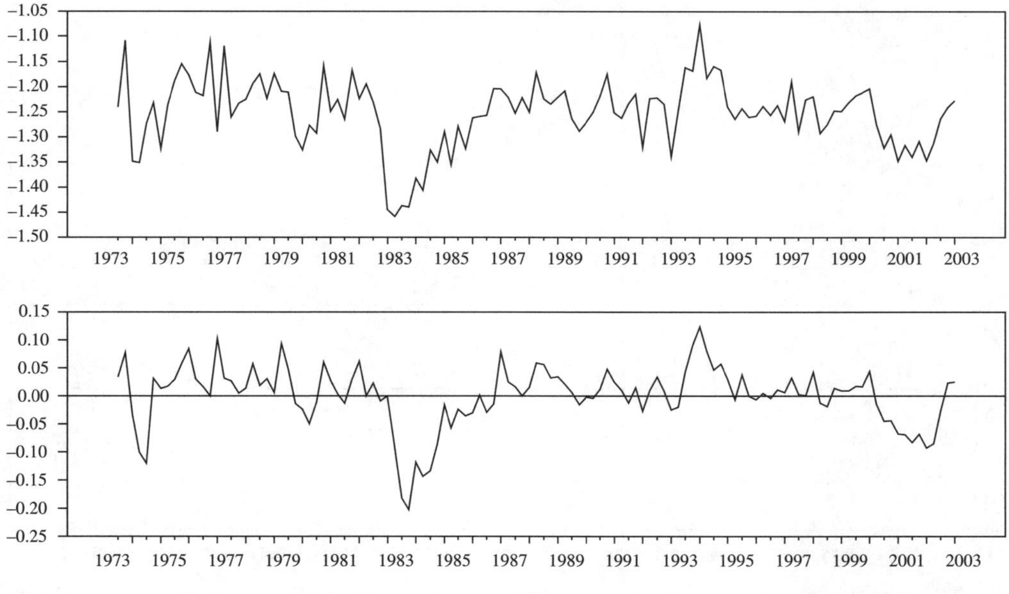

Fig 7.2 The second cointegration relation $\boldsymbol{\beta}_2'\mathbf{x}_t$ (upper panel) and $\boldsymbol{\beta}_2'\mathbf{R}_{1t}$ corrected for short-run effects (lower panel).

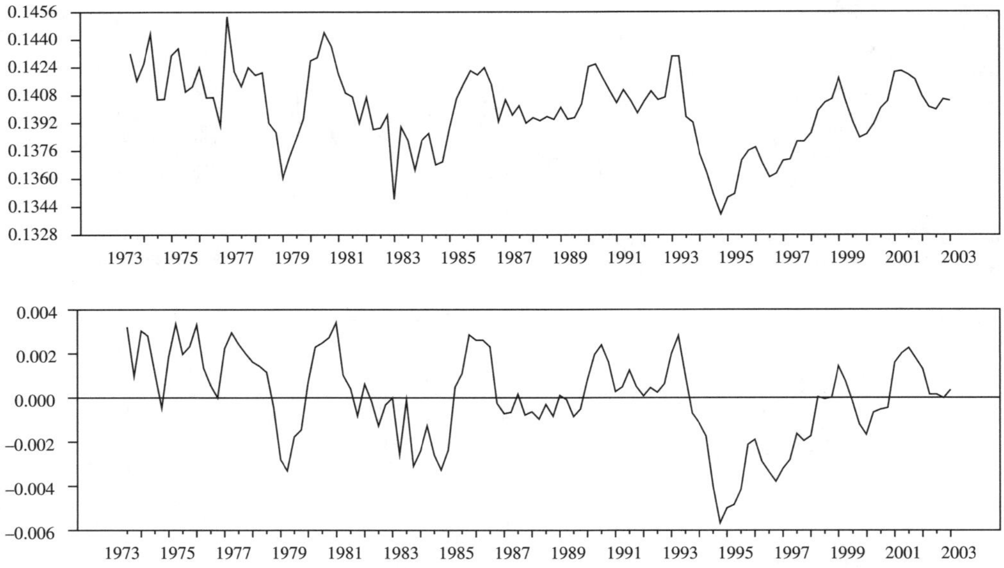

Fig 7.3 The third cointegration relation $\boldsymbol{\beta}_3'\mathbf{x}_t$ (upper panel) and $\boldsymbol{\beta}_3'\mathbf{R}_{1t}$ corrected for short-run effects (lower panel).

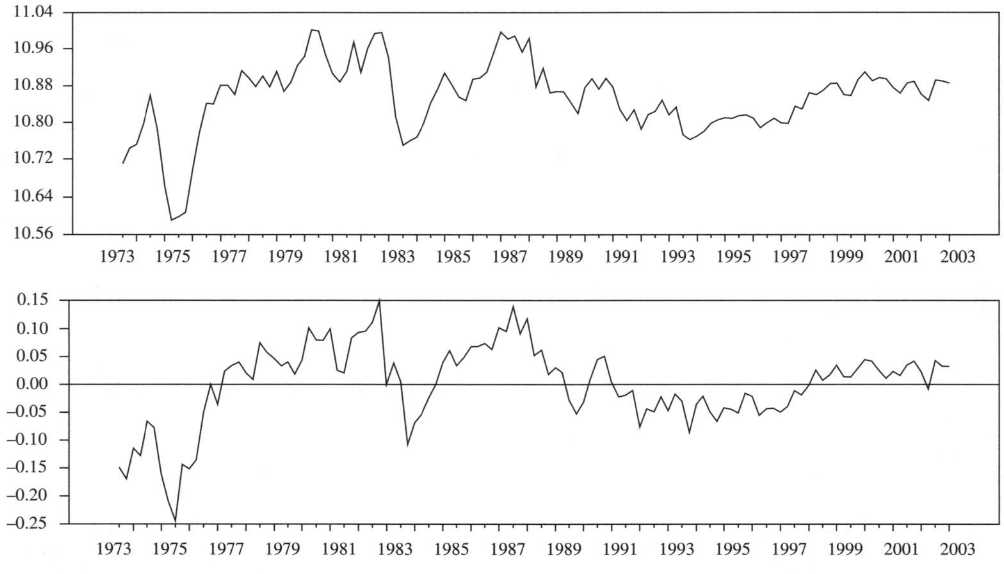

Fig 7.4 The fourth cointegration relation $\boldsymbol{\beta}_4'\mathbf{x}_t$ (upper panel) and $\boldsymbol{\beta}_4'\mathbf{R}_{1t}$ corrected for short-run effects (lower panel).

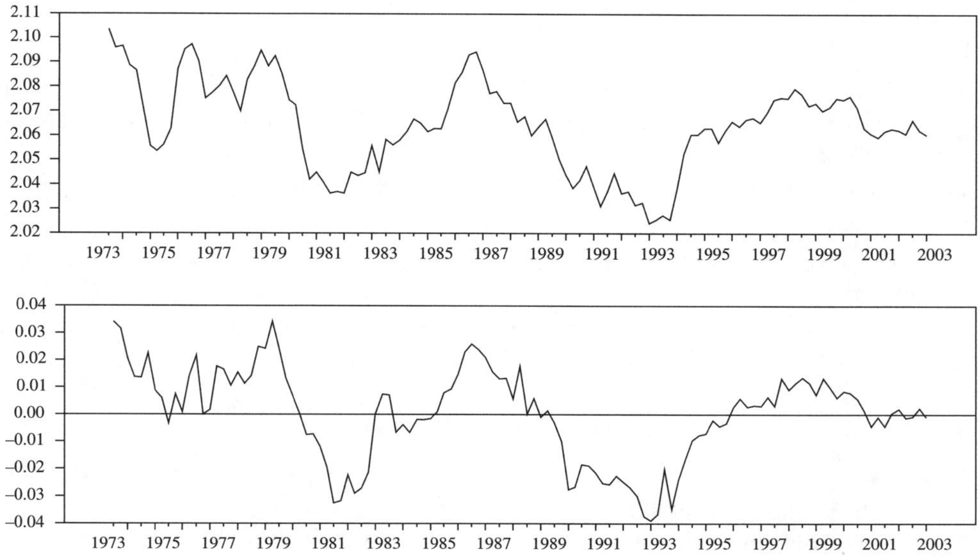

Fig 7.5 The fifth cointegration relation $\boldsymbol{\beta}_5'\mathbf{x}_t$ (upper panel) and $\boldsymbol{\beta}_5'\mathbf{R}_{1t}$ corrected for short-run effects (lower panel).

From a theoretical perspective real, rather than nominal, interest rates should be important for the determination of real aggregate income. But since the inflation rate coefficient was very small (and probably completely insignificant) in $\hat{\boldsymbol{\beta}}_4'\mathbf{x}_t$ it was not included in (7.16). This result can possibly be explained by the fact that inflation rate has varied much less than nominal interest rates in most of the sample period. Thus, fluctuations in the nominal interest rates have probably been relatively more important for aggregate demand than the inflation rate. The graph of $\hat{\boldsymbol{\beta}}_4'\mathbf{x}_t$ in Figure 7.4 exhibits a fair degree of persistence in the equilibrium errors suggesting that $\hat{\boldsymbol{\beta}}_4'\mathbf{x}_t$ may be non-stationary. However, one could equally well argue that it is borderline stationary.

The last relation is essentially relating the short-term interest rate to the bond rate and the real income:

$$R_m \approx 0.4R_b + 0.12y^r + \cdots$$

The graph of $\hat{\boldsymbol{\beta}}_5'\mathbf{x}_t$ in Figure 7.5 exhibits strong persistence which suggests that this relation is likely to be non-stationary.

The last part of Table 7.1 reports the estimates of the unrestricted $\mathbf{\Pi}$ based on full rank. We first note that $\hat{\boldsymbol{\pi}}_{i.}'\mathbf{x}_t$, $i = 1, \ldots, p$, defines a stationary relation only when $\hat{\mathbf{\Pi}} = \hat{\boldsymbol{\alpha}}\hat{\boldsymbol{\beta}}'$ where $\hat{\boldsymbol{\alpha}}$ and $\hat{\boldsymbol{\beta}}$ are reduced rank matrices defining the stationary directions of the process. Because the last relation (possibly the last two relations) define non-stationary relations the t-ratios in the brackets cannot directly be interpreted as Student's t. Nevertheless, the impact of the non-stationary relations on $\mathbf{\Pi}$ should not be very large as the corresponding α coefficients are in general close to zero. An inspection of the $\mathbf{\Pi}$ matrix show that:

- the first row resembles the second beta relation (7.14), but the coefficient of the inflation rate is smaller and the coefficient to the interest rates have increased somewhat;
- the second row resembles an IS relation with a strong negative short-term interest rate effect (7.16);
- the third row suggests that the inflation rate, when corrected for a negatively sloped trend effect, is not strongly related to any of the variables in the system (7.13);
- the fourth row suggests that the short-term interest rate has exhibited an equilibrium mean shift and that it might be related to the bond rate and the inflation rate but not very significantly so;
- the coefficients in the fifth row are all insignificant.

Note that the first row is a linear combination of the first two cointegration relations, $\hat{\boldsymbol{\pi}}_1 \approx \hat{\alpha}_{11}\hat{\boldsymbol{\beta}}_1 + \hat{\alpha}_{12}\hat{\boldsymbol{\beta}}_2$, explaining why the combined results are different from (7.14). A similar explanation is also relevant for the other rows. The finding of essentially no significant coefficients in the fifth row suggests that the bond rate might be weakly exogenous in this model,[3] an issue that will be further discussed in Chapter 11.

Altogether, the inspection of the $\mathbf{\Pi}$ matrix has partly confirmed the tentative interpretation of the $\boldsymbol{\beta}$ relations, partly suggested possible modifications. It seems likely that the first four variables are equilibrium correcting, whereas the bond rate is probably not.

7.7 Concluding remarks

It has been debated whether it is at all meaningful even tentatively to interpret the estimated eigenvectors. In many cases the unrestricted relations are clearly not economically interpretable, and any attempt to do so does not make sense. But, as demonstrated above, the first unrestricted estimates can, nonetheless, give a rough picture of the long-run information in the data. Therefore, a first careful inspection of the unrestricted VAR is likely to facilitate the subsequent identification of an empirically acceptable structure of cointegration relations.

Let us, for example, assume that the cointegration rank is three. In this case the first three eigenvectors (7.14)–(7.15) define stationary relations, provided that the coefficients we tentatively set to zero are in fact zero. This can be formally tested based on a LR test procedure discussed in Chapter 10, and if accepted, we have identified three tentatively interpretable cointegration vectors spanning the cointegration space.

Assume now that the economic model we had in mind contained two steady-state relations: a money demand relation and an aggregate income relation, but due to a *ceteris paribus* assumption, no prior relation for inflation rate and the interest rates. How should we proceed after this first inspection of the results? Already at this stage

[3]Chapter 11 will demonstrate that a zero row of $\boldsymbol{\alpha}$ is a necessary condition for a variable to be weakly exogenenous.

it is useful to adjust our intuition of how the economic and the empirical model work together. One possibility is to go back to the economic model and see whether it is possible to understand the weak exogeneity of the long-term bond rate, and whether it is possible to make inflation and the deposit rate endogenous in the model. In some cases the first inspection may suggest only minor modifications of the economic model, in other cases more fundamental changes. Sometimes, the first inspection will lead to a reconsideration of the choice of variables. For example, in the above example we found that the fourth relation, though borderline non-stationary, resembled an IS type relation. If this relation is important in our economic model then we should extend the data with, for example, the real exchange rate. It seems quite likely that the income relation would then become more stationary and, thus, empirically more relevant.

Thus, a first tentative inspection of the empirical results might at an early stage of the analysis suggest how to modify either our empirical or our economic model. A careful analysis at this stage is likely to save the econometrician from a lot of problems and frustrations in the subsequent empirical analyses.

8

Determination of cointegration rank

The choice of cointegration rank is likely to influence all subsequent inference and is, therefore, a crucial step in the empirical analysis. Unfortunately it is also a difficult decision as the distinction between stationary and non-stationary directions of the vector process is often far from straightforward. The formal test procedure is based on the null of a unit root, which is not always reasonable from an economic point of view. We shall, therefore, argue that the choice of rank preferably should be based on other information as well.

Section 8.1 gives the basic results for the derivation of likelihood ratio tests of the cointegration rank, and discusses whether there is an optimal sequence for these tests. Section 8.2 discusses the derivation of the asymptotic tables, Section 8.3 the role of deterministic components for the asymptotic tables, Section 8.4 how to achieve similarity in the test procedures, and Section 8.5 discusses the difficult choice of the cointegration rank in a practical situation. Section 8.6 provides then an empirical illustration, and Section 8.7 concludes.

8.1 The LR test for cointegration rank

The LR test for the cointegration rank, often called the trace test or the Johansen test, is based on the VAR model in the $\boldsymbol{R}$-form (7.4), where all short-run dynamics, dummies, and other deterministic components have been concentrated out. See Johansen (1996), Chapter 6. Using (7.6) and (7.12) we can write the log likelihood function as:

$$-2\ln L(\boldsymbol{\beta}) = T\ln|\mathbf{S}_{00}| + T\sum_{i=1}^{p}\ln(1-\lambda_i), \tag{8.1}$$

where the eigenvalues, $\lambda_1, \lambda_2, \ldots, \lambda_p$, can be found by solving the eigenvalue problem

$$|\lambda\mathbf{S}_{11} - \mathbf{S}_{01}\mathbf{S}_{00}^{-1}\mathbf{S}_{10}| = 0. \tag{8.2}$$

The eigenvalues λ_i can be interpreted as the squared canonical correlations between a linear combination of the levels, $\boldsymbol{\beta}_i'\mathbf{R}_{1t-1}$, and a linear combination of the differences, $\boldsymbol{\omega}_i'\mathbf{R}_{0t}$. In this sense, the magnitude of λ_i is an indication of how strongly the linear relation $\boldsymbol{\beta}_i'\mathbf{R}_{1t-1}$ is correlated with the stationary part of the process $\mathbf{R}_{0t}$. Another way of expressing this is by noticing that $\text{diag}(\hat{\lambda}_1, \ldots, \hat{\lambda}_r) = \hat{\boldsymbol{\beta}}'\mathbf{S}_{10}\mathbf{S}_{00}^{-1}\mathbf{S}_{01}\hat{\boldsymbol{\beta}} = \hat{\boldsymbol{\alpha}}'\mathbf{S}_{00}^{-1}\hat{\boldsymbol{\alpha}}$, i.e. $\hat{\lambda}_i$ is related to the estimated $\boldsymbol{\alpha}_i$ and $\boldsymbol{\beta}_i$. When $\lambda_i = 0$, the linear combination $\boldsymbol{\beta}_i'\mathbf{x}_t$ is non-stationary and there is no equilibrium correction, i.e. $\boldsymbol{\alpha}_i = \mathbf{0}$.

The statistical problem is to derive a test procedure to discriminate between those λ_i, $i = 1, \ldots, r$ which correspond to stationary relations and those λ_i, $i = r+1, \ldots, p$ which correspond to non-stationary relations. Because $\lambda_i = 0$ does not change the likelihood function, the maximum is exclusively a function of the non-zero eigenvalues:

$$L^{-2/T} = |S_{00}|\,\Pi_{i=1}^{r}(1-\lambda_i). \tag{8.3}$$

Based on (8.3), it is straightforward to derive a likelihood ratio test for the determination of the cointegration rank, r, which involves the following hypotheses:

$\mathcal{H}(p)$: rank $= p$, i.e. no unit roots; $\mathbf{x}_t$ is stationary;
$\mathcal{H}(r)$: rank $= r$, i.e. $p - r$ unit roots, r cointegration relations; $\mathbf{x}_t$ is non-stationary.

The LR test, usually called the trace test, is found as:

$$-2\ln Q(\mathcal{H}_r/\mathcal{H}_p) = T\ln\left\{\frac{|\mathbf{S}_{00}|(1-\hat{\lambda}_1)(1-\hat{\lambda}_2)\cdots(1-\hat{\lambda}_r)}{|\mathbf{S}_{00}|(1-\hat{\lambda}_1)(1-\hat{\lambda}_2)\cdots(1-\hat{\lambda}_r)\cdots(1-\hat{\lambda}_p)}\right\}$$

$$\tau_{p-r} = -T\ln(1-\hat{\lambda}_{r+1})\cdots(1-\hat{\lambda}_p) \tag{8.4}$$

where τ_{p-r} is the LR test statistic for testing the null of $p - r$ unit roots.

As an illustration, consider a VAR with $p = 5$ variables based on which we test the hypothesis $\mathcal{H}_2 : r = 2$, i.e. $p - r = 3$ against the null $\mathcal{H}_5 : r = 5$, i.e. $p - r = 0$. The test value is calculated as:

$$-2\ln Q(\mathcal{H}_2/\mathcal{H}_5) = T\ln\left\{\frac{|\mathbf{S}_{00}|(1-\lambda_1)(1-\lambda_2)}{|\mathbf{S}_{00}|(1-\lambda_1)(1-\lambda_2)(1-\lambda_3)(1-\lambda_4)(1-\lambda_5)}\right\}$$

$$\tau_3 = -T\left\{\ln(1-\lambda_3) + \ln(1-\lambda_4) + \ln(1-\lambda_5)\right\}$$

i.e. the LR test is a test of $\lambda_3 = \lambda_4 = \lambda_5 = 0$, corresponding to three unit roots in the model. When this hypothesis is correct, the test statistic should be 'small' as compared to some critical value derived under the assumption that $\lambda_3 = \lambda_4 = \lambda_5 = 0$. Note, however, that $\mathcal{H}_2$, i.e. $(\lambda_3 = \lambda_4 = \lambda_5 = 0)$ is correctly accepted also when $\lambda_2 = 0$ or $\lambda_2 = \lambda_1 = 0$. Therefore, if $\mathcal{H}_2$ is accepted, we conclude that there are at least three unit roots and hence at most two stationary relations.

Assume now that we have a prior hypothesis of the correct number of common trends $p - r^*$, i.e. r^* cointegrating relations. We could then calculate the test statistic τ_{p-r^*}

using (8.4) and compare it with the appropriate critical value C_{p-r^*} to be discussed in the next section. If $\tau_{p-r^*} > C_{p-r^*}$, we reject the hypothesis of $p-r^*$ unit roots (common trends) in the model, and conclude that there are fewer unit roots than assumed. If $\tau_{p-r^*} < C_{p-r^*}$, we accept the hypothesis of at least $p-r^*$ unit roots in the model, but conclude that there may be more. Hence, the trace test (8.4) does not give us the exact number of unit roots $p-r$ (or cointegration relations r). It only tells us whether $p-r < p-r^*$ $(r \geq r^*)$ when $\tau_{p-r^*} > C_{p-r^*}$, or alternatively $p-r \geq p-r^*$ $(r < r^*)$ when $\tau_{p-r^*} \leq C_{p-r^*}$.

Therefore, to estimate the value of r we have to perform a sequence of tests. The question is whether this sequence should be from top to bottom, i.e. $\{r = 0, p$ unit roots$\}$, $\{r = 1,\ p-1$ unit roots$\}$, ..., $\{r = p,\ 0$ unit roots$\}$ or the other way around.

To answer this, we first note that the asymptotic tables are determined so that when H_r is true, then $P_{p-r}(\tau_{p-r} \leq C_{95\%}(p-r)) = 95\%$, where τ_{p-r} is given by:

$$\tau_{p-r} = -2\ln Q(H_r|H_p) = -T\sum_{i=r+1}^{p} \ln(1-\hat{\lambda}_i). \tag{8.5}$$

Based on the above result we shall now illustrate the 'top → bottom' procedure using a simple case with $p = 3$ and then compare it with the 'bottom → top' procedure.

Applying the 'top→bottom' procedure for the trace test can hypothetically produce four different choices of the cointegration rank $\tilde{r}$ and, hence, the number of unit roots $(p-\tilde{r})$:

$$\begin{array}{ll}
\{p-\tilde{r} = 3,\ \tilde{r} = 0\} & \text{when } \{\tau_3 \leq C_3\} \\
\{p-\tilde{r} = 2,\ \tilde{r} = 1\} & \text{when } \{\tau_3 > C_3, \tau_2 \leq C_2\} \\
\{p-\tilde{r} = 1,\ \tilde{r} = 2\} & \text{when } \{\tau_3 > C_3, \tau_2 > C_2, \tau_1 \leq C_1\} \\
\{p-\tilde{r} = 0,\ \tilde{r} = 3\} & \text{when } \{\tau_3 > C_3, \tau_2 > C_2, \tau_1 > C_1\}.
\end{array}$$

We shall now illustrate the properties of the 'top → bottom' sequence by investigating $P_1\{\tilde{r} = i,\ i = 0,\ldots,3\}$ when the true value of $r = 1$, i.e. $p - r = 2$, and the size of the test is 5%. First,

$$P_1\{\tilde{r} = 0\} = P_1\{\tau_3 \leq C_3\}$$

where

$$\tau_3 = -T\left\{\ln(1-\hat{\lambda}_1) + \ln(1-\hat{\lambda}_2) + \ln(1-\hat{\lambda}_3)\right\}.$$

For $\lambda_1 > 0$, we have that $-T\ln(1-\hat{\lambda}_1) \to \infty$ when $T \to \infty$. Thus, $P_1(\tau_3 \leq C_3) \to 0$ asymptotically. The next value $p - \tilde{r} = 2$ corresponds to $\tilde{r} = 1$, the true cointegration number, and $P_1(\tau_2 \leq C_2) \to 0.95$ in accordance with the way the critical tables have been constructed. Thus, $P_1(p-\tilde{r} = 1) \overset{\text{as.}}{\to} 0.05$ and $P_1(p-\tilde{r} = 0) \overset{\text{as.}}{\to} \leq 5\%$. We summarize:

$$\begin{array}{lll}
P_1(p-\tilde{r} = 3,\ \tilde{r} = 0) = P_1(\tau_3 \leq C_3) & \to & 0 \\
P_1(p-\tilde{r} = 2,\ \tilde{r} = 1) = P_1(\tau_3 > C_3, \tau_2 \leq C_2) & \to & 0.95 \\
P_1(p-\tilde{r} = 1,\ \tilde{r} = 2) = P_1(\tau_3 > C_3, \tau_2 > C_2, \tau_1 \leq C_1) & \to & 0.05 \\
P_1(p-\tilde{r} = 0,\ \tilde{r} = 3) = P_1(\tau_3 > C_3, \tau_2 > C_2, \tau_1 > C_1) & \to & p_0 < 0.05
\end{array}$$

Thus, by applying the 'top $\rightarrow$ bottom' procedure the correct value of r is asymptotically accepted 95% of all cases, which is exactly what a 5% test procedure is supposed to do.

We shall now similarly investigate the 'bottom $\rightarrow$ top' procedure.

For $p = 3$ there are the following four different choices of the cointegration rank:

$$\begin{array}{ll}\{p-\tilde{r}=0,\ \tilde{r}=3\} & \text{when } \{\tau_1 > C_1\} \\ \{p-\tilde{r}=1,\ \tilde{r}=2\} & \text{when } \{\tau_1 \leq C_1, \tau_2 > C_2\} \\ \{p-\tilde{r}=2,\ \tilde{r}=1\} & \text{when } \{\tau_1 \leq C_1, \tau_2 \leq C_2, \tau_3 > C_3\} \\ \{p-\tilde{r}=3,\ \tilde{r}=0\} & \text{when } \{\tau_1 \leq C_1, \tau_2 \leq C_2, \tau_3 \leq C_3\}.\end{array}$$

In this case, we start by testing $p - \tilde{r} = 0$, i.e. stationarity and if rejected continue with $p - \tilde{r} = 1$, and so on until first acceptance.

$$\begin{array}{llll}P_1(p-\tilde{r}=0, \tilde{r}=3) & = P(\tau_1 > C_1) & \rightarrow & p_0 < 0.05 \\ P_1(p-\tilde{r}=1,\ \tilde{r}=2) & = P(\tau_1 \leq C_1, \tau_2 > C_2) & \rightarrow & 0.05 \\ P_1(p-\tilde{r}=2,\ \tilde{r}=1) & = P(\tau_1 \leq C_1, \tau_2 \leq C_2, \tau_3 > C_3) & \rightarrow & \leq 0.95 \\ P_1(p-\tilde{r}=3,\ \tilde{r}=0) & = P(\tau_1 \leq C_1, \tau_2 \leq C_2, \tau_3 \leq C_3) & \rightarrow & 0.\end{array}$$

In this case the probability of wrongly accepting $\tilde{r} = 2$ or $\tilde{r} = 3$ is $0.05 + p_0 \geq 0.05$. Hence, the probability of choosing the correct value $\tilde{r} = 1$ is ≤ 0.95.

The reason why the 'top $\rightarrow$ bottom' procedure is asymptotically more correct is because the probability of incorrectly accepting $\tilde{r} < r^*$ is asymptotically zero, whereas the probability of incorrectly accepting $\tilde{r} > r^*$ in the 'bottom $\rightarrow$ top' procedure is generally greater than the chosen p-value.

8.2 The asymptotic tables with a trend and a constant in the model

The distribution of the likelihood ratio test statistic (8.4) for cointegration rank is non-standard (it does not follow any of the standard distributions χ^2, F, t) and has been determined by simulations. A detailed treatment can be found in Johansen (1996). Here we only give an intuitive account of how to derive the distributions and how they are affected by deterministic components in the VAR model.

The LR test statistic of the hypothesis $\mathcal{H}(r)$ against $\mathcal{H}(p)$ is given by (8.4). Under the null of $p - r$ unit roots, the last $p - r$ relations $\mathbf{v}_i'\mathbf{x}_t$, $i = r+1, \ldots, p$, behave like random walks. Therefore, if the null hypothesis is correct, then the calculated trace test statistic, $-T\sum_{i=r+1}^{p} \ln(1 - \hat{\lambda}_i)$, should not deviate significantly from the simulated test values C^*. Johansen (1996) demonstrated that the asymptotic distribution of $-2\ln LR\{(\mathcal{H}(r)/\mathcal{H}(p)\}$ is the same as $-2\ln LR\{(\mathcal{H}(0)/\mathcal{H}(p-r)\}$. This is because the asymptotic distributions are not affected by the stationary directions of the VAR model. Therefore, the asymptotic tables have been simulated for $(p-r)$-dimensional VAR models where $r = 0$. Under the null hypothesis of $p - r$ unit roots, the following approximation can be used:

$$-T\sum_{i=r+1}^{p}\ln(1-\lambda_i)\approx T\sum_{i=r+1}^{p}\lambda_i.$$

Using (8.2) we note that:

$$\sum_{i=1}^{p}\lambda_i\approx \text{trace}(\mathbf{S}_{11}^{-1}\mathbf{S}_{10}\mathbf{S}_{00}^{-1}\mathbf{S}_{01}). \tag{8.6}$$

When $r=0$, $\sum_{i=r+1}^{p}\lambda_i=\sum_{i=1}^{p}\lambda_i$. Without loss of generality, we let $\mathbf{S}_{00}=\mathbf{I}$ and hence:

$$\sum_{i=1}^{p}\lambda_i\approx \text{trace}(\mathbf{S}_{11}^{-1}\mathbf{S}_{10}\mathbf{S}_{01})=\text{trace}(\mathbf{S}_{01}\mathbf{S}_{11}^{-1}\mathbf{S}_{10}). \tag{8.7}$$

Thus, the idea behind the asymptotic tables is to simulate the distribution of (8.7) by first generating a $(p-r)$-dimensional random walk process of acceptable length and then replicate this process a large number of times.

The asymptotic distributions are strongly dependent on the deterministic terms in the VAR model. In the following, we shall discuss how to simulate the asymptotic tables for the same five assumptions on the deterministic terms in the model as already discussed in Chapter 6. The five cases are all submodels of the following model:

$$\Delta\mathbf{x}_t=\boldsymbol{\alpha}\boldsymbol{\beta}'\mathbf{x}_{t-1}+\boldsymbol{\mu}_0+\boldsymbol{\mu}_1 t+\boldsymbol{\varepsilon}_t \tag{8.8}$$

where

$$\boldsymbol{\mu}_0=\boldsymbol{\alpha}\boldsymbol{\beta}_0+\boldsymbol{\gamma}_0 \tag{8.9}$$

and

$$\boldsymbol{\mu}_1=\boldsymbol{\alpha}\boldsymbol{\beta}_1+\boldsymbol{\gamma}_1. \tag{8.10}$$

Because the asymptotic distributions for the trace test are not affected by the stationary directions of the model the tables are simulated under the assumption that $\boldsymbol{\Gamma}_1=\mathbf{0},\ldots,\boldsymbol{\Gamma}_{k-1}=\mathbf{0}$ and $r=0$. The tables have been simulated for $p-r=1,\ldots,12$ unit roots and for five different assumptions on the deterministic components. Under the assumption that $r=0$ in (8.8), we have that $\boldsymbol{\mu}_0=\boldsymbol{\gamma}_0$, $\boldsymbol{\mu}_1=\boldsymbol{\gamma}_1$ in (8.9) and (8.10). Thus, the process $\mathbf{x}_t$ can be represented as:

$$\mathbf{x}_t=\sum_{i=1}^{t}\boldsymbol{\varepsilon}_i+\boldsymbol{\mu}_0 t+\boldsymbol{\mu}_1\frac{1}{2}t(t+1)+\mathbf{x}_0 \tag{8.11}$$

If $\boldsymbol{\mu}_0$ and $\boldsymbol{\mu}_1$ are unrestricted in (8.8), all non-stationary directions of the process contain stochastic trends as well as linear and quadratic deterministic time trends. If there are linear but no quadratic trends in the data, then $\boldsymbol{\gamma}_1=\mathbf{0}$. If there are no linear trends at all in the data, $\boldsymbol{\mu}_1 = \mathbf{0}$ and $\gamma_0 = \mathbf{0}$. Because the asymptotic distributions change depending on whether $\boldsymbol{\mu}_0$ and $\boldsymbol{\mu}_1$ are restricted or unrestricted in the model, a correct specification of the deterministic components in the VAR model is crucial for correct inference.

The first asymptotic tables reported in Johansen (1996) were derived from 6000 replications of $(p-r)$-dimensional random walk processes, $\Delta\mathbf{x}_t = \boldsymbol{\varepsilon}_t$, $(p-r) = 1, \ldots, 12$ and $\boldsymbol{\varepsilon}_t \sim N_p(\mathbf{0}, \mathbf{I})$, $t = 1, \ldots, 400$. The asymptotic tables used in CATS and reproduced in Appendix A are based on the Gamma approximation in Doornik (1998). The first row gives the asymptotic critical values for the test of a unit root in a one-dimensional VAR model and, thus, corresponds to the critical values for a ML univariate Dickey–Fuller test. As it would be strange to use the critical values for a one-dimensional VAR (variable by variable) when we are estimating a p-dimensional model, there will be no discussion of univariate unit root testing in this book.

The reduced rank regression is based on the covariance matrices $\mathbf{S}_{ij}$, $i, j = 0, 1$ discussed in Chapter 7 and reproduced below:

$$
\begin{aligned}
\mathbf{S}_{11} &= T^{-1}\sum_{t=1}^{T}\mathbf{R}_{1,t}\mathbf{R}_{1,t}' \\
\mathbf{S}_{01} &= T^{-1}\sum_{t=1}^{T}\mathbf{R}_{0,t}\mathbf{R}_{1,t}' \\
\mathbf{S}_{00} &= T^{-1}\sum_{t=1}^{T}\mathbf{R}_{0,t}\mathbf{R}_{0,t}'
\end{aligned}
\tag{8.12}
$$

where $\mathbf{R}_{1,t} = \mathbf{x}_{t-1} - \hat{\mathbf{b}}_{10} - \hat{\mathbf{b}}_{11}t$ and $\mathbf{R}_{0,t} = \Delta\mathbf{x}_t - \hat{\mathbf{b}}_{00} - \hat{\mathbf{b}}_{01}t$ are the residuals in the auxiliary regressions of $\mathbf{x}_{t-1}$ and $\Delta\mathbf{x}_t$ in (8.8). Because the simulated VAR model does not contain any short-run effects, $\mathbf{x}_{t-1}$ and $\Delta\mathbf{x}_t$ will only be corrected in those versions of the model which contain an unrestricted trend and/or a constant.

We shall now show how to simulate the asymptotic tables using an example where $p-r = 3$. The following five VAR models with different assumptions on the deterministic terms have been simulated:

Case 1. $\boldsymbol{\mu}_0, \boldsymbol{\mu}_1 = \mathbf{0}$. This corresponds to the VAR model:

$$\Delta\mathbf{x}_t = \boldsymbol{\alpha}\boldsymbol{\beta}'\mathbf{x}_{t-1} + \boldsymbol{\varepsilon}_t,$$

which under the assumption that $\boldsymbol{\alpha}\boldsymbol{\beta}' = \mathbf{0}$ gives:

$$\mathbf{x}_t = \sum_{i=1}^{t}\boldsymbol{\varepsilon}_i + \mathbf{x}_0.$$

There are no deterministic terms in this model and $\mathbf{R}_{1,t}$ and $\mathbf{R}_{0,t}$ are specified as:

$$\mathbf{R}_{1,t} = \begin{bmatrix} \sum_{i=1}^{t-1}\varepsilon_{1i} \\ \sum_{i=1}^{t-1}\varepsilon_{2i} \\ \sum_{i=1}^{t-1}\varepsilon_{3i} \end{bmatrix} \text{ and } \mathbf{R}_{0,t} = \begin{bmatrix} \varepsilon_{1t} \\ \varepsilon_{2t} \\ \varepsilon_{3t} \end{bmatrix}, \quad t = 1, \ldots, T.$$

Case 2. $\boldsymbol{\mu}_0 \neq \mathbf{0}$*, with* $\boldsymbol{\gamma}_0 = \mathbf{0}$*, and* $\boldsymbol{\beta}_0 \neq \mathbf{0}$*,* $\boldsymbol{\mu}_1 = \mathbf{0}$. This corresponds to the VAR model:

$$\Delta \mathbf{x}_t = \boldsymbol{\alpha} \begin{bmatrix} \boldsymbol{\beta}' & \boldsymbol{\beta}_0 \end{bmatrix} \begin{bmatrix} \mathbf{x}_{t-1} \\ 1 \end{bmatrix} + \boldsymbol{\varepsilon}_t,$$

which under the assumption that $\boldsymbol{\alpha\beta}' = \mathbf{0}$ gives:

$$\mathbf{x}_t = \sum_{i=1}^{t} \boldsymbol{\varepsilon}_i + \mathbf{x}_0.$$

There are no linear trends in the variables, but there is an intercept term, $\boldsymbol{\beta}_0$, in the VAR model so:

$$\mathbf{R}_{1,t} = \begin{bmatrix} \sum_{i=1}^{t-1} \varepsilon_{1i} \\ \sum_{i=1}^{t-1} \varepsilon_{2i} \\ \sum_{i=1}^{t-1} \varepsilon_{3i} \\ 1 \end{bmatrix} \text{ and } \mathbf{R}_{0,t} = \begin{bmatrix} \varepsilon_{1t} \\ \varepsilon_{2t} \\ \varepsilon_{3t} \end{bmatrix}, \quad t = 1, \ldots, T.$$

Case 3. $\boldsymbol{\mu}_1 = \mathbf{0}$*,* $\boldsymbol{\mu}_0$ *is unrestricted.* This corresponds to the VAR model:

$$\Delta \mathbf{x}_t = \boldsymbol{\alpha\beta}' \mathbf{x}_{t-1} + \boldsymbol{\mu}_0 + \boldsymbol{\varepsilon}_t$$

with the vectors of corrected residuals: $\mathbf{R}_{1,t} = \mathbf{x}_{t-1} - \hat{\mathbf{b}}_{10}$ and $\mathbf{R}_{0,t} = \Delta \mathbf{x}_t - \hat{\mathbf{b}}_{00}$. Under the assumption that $\boldsymbol{\alpha\beta}' = \mathbf{0}$ and $\boldsymbol{\mu}_0 \neq \mathbf{0}$ the process $\mathbf{x}_t$ is given by:

$$\mathbf{x}_t = \sum_{i=1}^{t} \boldsymbol{\varepsilon}_i + \boldsymbol{\mu}_0 t + \mathbf{x}_0. \tag{8.13}$$

There are no linear trends in the VAR model but, because of the unrestricted constant $\boldsymbol{\mu}_0$, the data can contain linear trends. In the auxiliary regression of $\mathbf{x}_{t-1}$ on the unrestricted constant in the VAR model, the constant $\mathbf{x}_0$ in (8.13) cancels and $\mathbf{R}_{1,t}$ will contain stochastic trends $\sum_{i=1}^{t-1} \boldsymbol{\varepsilon}_i$ and a linear trend t but no constant. Since a linear deterministic trend asymptotically dominates a stochastic trend, the $(p-r) = 3$ nonstationary directions of the process are decomposed into $(p-r-1) = 2$ directions that contain the corrected stochastic trends and one direction that contains the linear trend. The tables are based on:

$$\mathbf{R}_{1,t} = \begin{bmatrix} (\sum_{i=1}^{t-1} \varepsilon_{1i}) \mid 1 \\ (\sum_{i=1}^{t-1} \varepsilon_{2i}) \mid 1 \\ t \mid 1 \end{bmatrix} \text{ and } \mathbf{R}_{0,t} = \begin{bmatrix} \varepsilon_{1t} \\ \varepsilon_{2t} \\ \varepsilon_{3t} \end{bmatrix}, \quad t = 1, \ldots, T.$$

Case 4. $\boldsymbol{\beta}_1 \neq \mathbf{0}, \boldsymbol{\gamma}_1 = \mathbf{0}$, $\boldsymbol{\mu}_0$ *is unrestricted.* This corresponds to the VAR model:

$$\Delta \mathbf{x}_t = \boldsymbol{\alpha} \begin{bmatrix} \boldsymbol{\beta}' & \boldsymbol{\beta}_1 \end{bmatrix} \begin{bmatrix} \mathbf{x}_{t-1} \\ t \end{bmatrix} + \boldsymbol{\mu}_0 + \boldsymbol{\varepsilon}_t$$

with the vectors of corrected residuals given by: $\mathbf{R}_{1,t} = [\mathbf{x}'_{t-1}, t]' - \hat{\mathbf{b}}_{10}$ and $\mathbf{R}_{0,t} = \Delta \mathbf{x}_t - \hat{\mathbf{b}}_{00}$. Under the assumption that $\boldsymbol{\alpha}\boldsymbol{\beta}' = \mathbf{0}$, the process $\mathbf{x}_t$ becomes:

$$\mathbf{x}_t = \sum_{i=1}^{t} \boldsymbol{\varepsilon}_i + \boldsymbol{\mu}_0 t + \mathbf{x}_0.$$

In this case we have allowed for a linear trend both in the data and in the cointegration relations, but have restricted the quadratic trend to be zero. Because the constant x_0 cancels in the regression of $\mathbf{x}_{t-1}$ on a constant, $\mathbf{R}_{1,t}$ contain three corrected stochastic trends and a linear trend but no constant:

$$\mathbf{R}_{1,t} = \begin{bmatrix} \sum_{i=1}^{t-1} \varepsilon_{1i} \mid 1 \\ \sum_{i=1}^{t-1} \varepsilon_{2i} \mid 1 \\ \sum_{i=1}^{t-1} \varepsilon_{3i} \mid 1 \\ trend \mid 1 \end{bmatrix} \text{ and } \mathbf{R}_{0,t} = \begin{bmatrix} \varepsilon_{1t} \\ \varepsilon_{2t} \\ \varepsilon_{3t} \end{bmatrix}, \quad t = 1, \ldots, T.$$

Case 5. $\boldsymbol{\mu}_1$, $\boldsymbol{\mu}_0$ *are unrestricted.* This corresponds to the VAR model:

$$\Delta \mathbf{x}_t = \boldsymbol{\alpha}\boldsymbol{\beta}' \boldsymbol{x}_{t-1} + \boldsymbol{\mu}_0 + \boldsymbol{\mu}_1 t + \boldsymbol{\varepsilon}_t$$

with the vectors of corrected residuals: $\mathbf{R}_{1,t} = \mathbf{x}_{t-1} - \hat{\mathbf{b}}_{10} - \hat{\mathbf{b}}_{11} t$ and $\mathbf{R}_{0,t} = \Delta \mathbf{x}_t - \hat{\mathbf{b}}_{00} - \hat{\mathbf{b}}_{01} t$. Under the assumption that $\boldsymbol{\alpha}\boldsymbol{\beta}' = \mathbf{0}$ and $\boldsymbol{\mu}_1 \neq \mathbf{0}$, the process $\mathbf{x}_t$ becomes:

$$\mathbf{x}_t = \sum_{i=1}^{t} \boldsymbol{\varepsilon}_i + \boldsymbol{\mu}_0 t + \boldsymbol{\mu}_1 \frac{1}{2} t(t+1) + \mathbf{x}_0. \tag{8.14}$$

This model allows for linear trends and quadratic trends in the data as well as linear trends in the cointegrating relations. Because the constant and the linear trend in (8.14) cancel in the regression of $\mathbf{x}_{t-1}$ on the unrestricted constant and the linear trend, $\mathbf{R}_{1,t}$ only contains the stochastic trends, $\sum_{i=1}^{t-1} \boldsymbol{\varepsilon}_i$, and the quadratic trend, t^2. Furthermore, because a quadratic time trend asymptotically dominates a linear stochastic trend, the $(p-r) = 3$ non-stationary directions of the process are decomposed into $(p-r-1) = 2$ directions which contain the corrected stochastic trends and one direction which contains the quadratic trend.

$$\mathbf{R}_{1,t} = \begin{bmatrix} (\sum_{i=1}^{t-1} \varepsilon_{1i}) \mid 1, t \\ (\sum_{i=1}^{t-1} \varepsilon_{2i}) \mid 1, t \\ t^2 \mid 1, t \end{bmatrix} \text{ and } \mathbf{R}_{0,t} = \begin{bmatrix} \varepsilon_{1t} \\ \varepsilon_{2t} \\ \varepsilon_{3t} \end{bmatrix}, \quad t = 1, \ldots, T.$$

As an example, let us consider a VAR model with an unrestricted constant. In this model, we would like to test the hypothesis of $p-r = 3$ unit roots. This case corresponds to the third row of Table A.3 where the first test value corresponds to the 50% quantile of the test statistics based on the Gamma approximation to the asymptotic tables (see Doornik, 1998). Thus, when there are 3 unit roots in the model, the 50% quantile, 18.65, means that in 50% of all cases we would get a trace test statistic which is smaller or equal to 18.65, and the 95% quantile, 29.38, that in 95% of the cases we would get a test value which is smaller or equal to 29.38.

8.3 The role of dummy variables for the asymptotic tables

We have shown that the asymptotic distributions depend on whether there is a constant and/or a trend in the VAR model and whether they are unrestricted or not. However, other deterministic components, such as intervention dummies, are also likely to influence the shape of the distributions. In particular, care should be taken when a deterministic component generates trending behaviour in the levels of the data. A typical example is an unrestricted shift dummy (...,0,0,0,1,1,1,...) which cumulates to a broken linear trend in the data. A detailed discussion of this case can be found in Johansen, Mosconi, and Nielsen (2000) and Doornik, Hendry, and Nielsen (1998). However, even if the shift dummy is restricted to lie in the cointegration relations, the asymptotic distributions will be affected (Nielsen 2004a). In case 2 and 4 the tables change both as a function of the number of shift dummies, and of their position in the sample period. Thus, whether the equilibrium shift is supposed to take place in the middle or at the end points of the sample matters for the distributions and we need to simulate the distributions for each individual case. In both case the asymptotic tables are shifted to the right for each deterministic component included in the cointegration relations. Case 3 should, if possible, be avoided as the effect of the shift dummies on the distributions is more complicated.

Unrestricted dummy variables which do not cumulate to (broken linear) trends, for example transitory and permanent innovational dummies, are not likely to have an effect on the asymptotic distributions, but can nevertheless influence the finite-sample distributions. Additive outliers should generally be removed prior to the cointegration analysis and in that case will not influence the asymptotic tables.

Note, however, that these are only tentative recommendations. More research needs to be done until we fully understand the important role of dummies in the VAR model.

8.4 Similarity and rank determination

Because the asymptotic distribution for the rank test depends on the deterministic components in the model and whether these are restricted or unrestricted, the rank and the specification of the deterministic components need to be determined jointly. Alternatively, the deterministic components (for example, additive outliers) have to be removed from the model prior to testing. Nielsen and Rahbek (2000) have demonstrated that a test procedure based on a model formulation that allows a deterministic variable $(\text{trend}, \text{constant}, Ds_t)$ to be in the cointegration relations and its difference $(\Delta\text{trend}, \Delta\text{constant}, \Delta\, Ds_t\ =\ \text{constant}, 0, Dp_t)$ to be in the VAR equations yields similarity in the test procedure.

Assume, for example, that the data contain a linear trend t so that $E[\Delta\mathbf{x}_t] = \boldsymbol{\gamma}_0 \neq \mathbf{0}$. In this case, we need to include an unrestricted constant term $\boldsymbol{\mu}_0 = \boldsymbol{\alpha}\boldsymbol{\beta}_0 + \boldsymbol{\gamma}_0$ in the VAR model (cf. the discussion in the previous chapter) to account for the linear growth in the data. However, a linear trend in the variables need not cancel in the cointegrating relations and we should, therefore, allow for the possibility of trend-stationary cointegration relations. This is achieved by allowing the linear trend to enter the cointegrating relations, i.e. $\boldsymbol{\beta}_1 t \neq \mathbf{0}$. Thus, to achieve similarity in the test procedure, the linear trend t needs to be restricted to the cointegration relations and a constant term (i.e. the difference of t) needs to be unrestricted in the equations.

If the differenced data contains an intervention outlier, i.e. $E[\Delta\mathbf{x}_t] = \boldsymbol{\phi}_p\mathbf{Dp}_t \neq \mathbf{0}$, then $E[\mathbf{x}_t] = \boldsymbol{\phi}_p \sum_{i=1}^{t} \mathbf{Dp}_i + \mathbf{x}_0 = \boldsymbol{\phi}_p\mathbf{Ds}_i + \mathbf{x}_0$, then $\mathbf{x}_t$ contains a level shift which may or may not cancel in the cointegration relations. Again, to achieve similarity in the rank test we need to include the shift dummy in the cointegration relations before testing the rank.

To summarize: Given linear trends in the data, case 4 is generally the best specification to start with unless we have strong prior beliefs that the linear trends cancel in the cointegration relations (see also Chapter 6, Section 6.3). This is because case 4 allows for trends both in the stationary and non-stationary directions of the model and hence similarity in the test procedure. When the rank has been determined, it is always possible to test the hypothesis $\boldsymbol{\beta}_1 = \mathbf{0}$ as a linear hypothesis on the cointegrating relations. This will be illustrated in the next chapter. If there are no linear trends in the data, case 2 is the appropriate specification (unless the cointegration relations exceptionally can be assumed to have a zero mean). If the data show evidence of a level shift in $\mathbf{x}_t$, i.e. a blip in $\Delta\mathbf{x}_t$, then we need to include both an unrestricted blip dummy, $\mathbf{Dp}_t$, in the equations and a shift dummy in the cointegration relations. If similar level shifts appear in several variables, it is possible that the shift dummy in the cointegration relations can be set to zero, which again is a testable hypothesis.

8.5 The cointegration rank: a difficult choice

The cointegration rank divides the data into r relations towards which the process is adjusting and $p-r$ relations which are pushing the process. The former are interpreted as equilibrium errors (deviations from steady-state) and the latter as common driving trends in the system. Hence, the choice of r will influence all subsequent econometric analysis and may very well be crucial for whether we accept or reject our prior economic hypotheses.

The previous section showed how the asymptotic distribution depends on the deterministic components in the VAR model. The short-run effects $\boldsymbol{\Gamma}_1\Delta\mathbf{x}_{t-1} + \cdots + \boldsymbol{\Gamma}_{k-1}\Delta\mathbf{x}_{t-k+1}$ were ignored as they do not matter asymptotically. However, these effects are often important in small samples. Johansen (2002b) finds that the closer the model is to the $I(2)$ boundary, the more important are the short-run effects for the trace test. In such cases, the proper solution is probably to simulate tables using bootstrap methods for a model which mimics the short-run dynamics of the empirical model.

When the sample is small, the asymptotic distributions are generally poor approximations to the true distributions. Many simulation studies have demonstrated that using the asymptotic tables in such cases can result in substantial size and power distortions.

To secure a correct test size one can apply the small sample Bartlett corrections developed in Johansen (2002b) and implemented in CATS. For moderately sized samples (50–70) typical of many empirical models in economics, these corrections can be substantial.

Thus, the question of how big the sample should be for the asymptotic tables to hold sufficiently well is clearly important for a VAR modeller. Unfortunately the question has no obvious answer. Whether the sample is 'small' or 'big' is not exclusively a function of the number of observations available in the sample, but also of the amount of information in the data. When the data are very informative about a hypothetical long-run relation, $\boldsymbol{\beta}'\mathbf{x}_t$, we might have good test properties even if the sample period is relatively short. This would be the case when the equilibrium error crosses the mean line several times over the sample period.

The application of a small-sample correction to the trace test statistic leads to a more correct size, but it does not necessarily solve the power problem. In some cases, the size of the test and the power of relevant alternative hypotheses close to the unit circle are almost of the same magnitude. In such cases a 5% test procedure will reject $r = r^*$ incorrectly in 5% of all the cases where r^* is the true value, but it will also incorrectly accept $r = r^*$ in, say, 90% of the cases when the true value of r is greater than r^*. This is particularly worrying when the null of a unit root is not a natural economic hypothesis.

Thus, we may have a problem both with the size and the power when using the trace test to determine the rank. In the ideal case, we would like the probability to reject a correct null hypothesis ($r = r^*$) to be small and the probability to accept a correct alternative hypothesis ($r \neq r^*$) to be high for relevant hypotheses in the 'near unit root' region. This is likely to be the case when the estimated eigenvalues can be classified as either very large or very small.[1] Then the trace test is likely to pick up the correct value of r and also have good power properties for relevant alternative hypotheses.

In other cases, when some of the estimated eigenvalues are in the region where it is hard to discriminate between significant and insignificant eigenvalues, the trace test will usually have low power for stationary near unit root alternatives. For example, if the adjustment back to equilibrium is very slow, then the correct economic hypothesis would be stationarity, albeit with a fairly large root.

As discussed above, the trace test is based on a sequence of tests. In the 'top–bottom' case we test the hypothesis 'p unit roots' and, if rejected, continue until first acceptance of $p - r$ unit roots. Whether we choose the 'top–bottom' or the 'bottom–top', the test procedure is essentially based on the principle of 'no prior economic knowledge' regarding the rank r. This is, in many cases, difficult to justify. For example, in the monetary model of Chapter 2, we demonstrated that the hypothesis ($r = 3$, $p - r = 2$) was *a priori* consistent with two types of autonomous shocks, one shifting the aggregate demand curve and the other the aggregate supply curve. We also discussed that for a more regulated economy, the hypothesis ($r = 2$, $p - r = 3$) might be preferable *a priori* as a result of very slow market adjustment.

An alternative procedure is, therefore, to test a given prior economic hypothesis, say $p - r = 2$, using the trace test and, if accepted, continue with this assumption unless the data strongly suggest the presence of additional unit roots. The latter can be investigated in a number of ways. For example, we can test the significance of the adjustment

[1] Note, however, that a high value of λ_i can also be an indication of a small ratio between the number of estimated parameters and the number of observations.

coefficients $\alpha_{i,r}$, $i = 1, \ldots, p$ of the rth cointegrating vector. If all $\alpha_{i,r}$ coefficients have small t ratios, then including the rth cointegrating relation in the model would not improve the explanatory power of the model but, instead, would invalidate subsequent inference. Also, if the choice of r incorrectly includes a non-stationary relation among the cointegrating relations, then one of the roots of the characteristic polynomial of the model would correspond to a unit root or a near unit root and, thus, be large. If either of these cases occur, then the cointegration rank should be reduced. Note, however, that additional unit roots in the characteristic polynomial can be the result of $I(2)$ components in the data. Reducing the rank in this case will not solve the problem as will be shown in Chapters 16 and 17.

It is also important to note that the cointegration rank is not in general equivalent to the number of theoretical equilibrium relations derived from an economic model. For example, in the monetary model of Chapter 2 there was one equilibrium relation, the money demand relation, whereas Chapter 2, Section 2.4 demonstrated that the monetary model is consistent with $r = 3$ cointegrating relations instead of just one as in Romer's example. The economic prior that $r = 1$ has been incorrectly assumed in many empirical applications of money demand.

Thus, cointegration between variables is a statistical property of the data that only exceptionally can be given a direct interpretation as an economic equilibrium relation. The reason for this is that a theoretically meaningful relation can be (and often is) a linear combination of several 'irreducible' cointegration relations (Davidson 1998). The next chapter will illustrate that these relations contain useful information about common stochastic trends between sets of variables and, therefore, can be used to assess the hypothetical scenario of the economic problem discussed in Chapter 2.

To summarize: When assessing the appropriateness of the asymptotic tables to determine the cointegration rank, we need to consider not only the sample size but also the short-run dynamics. Because the power of the trace test can be very low for relevant alternative hypotheses in the neighbourhood of the unit circle, it is advisable to use as much additional information as possible, such as:

1. The characteristic roots of the model. If the $(r+1)$th cointegration vector is non-stationary and is wrongly included in the model, then the largest characteristic root will be close to the unit circle.
2. The t values of the α-coefficients to the $(r+1)$th cointegration vector. If all of them are small, say less than 2.6, then one would not gain a lot by including the $(r+1)$th vector as a cointegrating relation in the model.
3. The recursive graphs of the trace statistic for $\widetilde{r} = 1, 2, \ldots, p$. Since the variable $-t_1 \ln(1 - \lambda_i)$, $t_1 = T_1, \ldots, T$, grows linearly over time when $\lambda_i \neq 0$, the recursively calculated components of the trace statistic should grow linearly for all $i = 1, \ldots, r$, but stay constant for $i = r + 1, \ldots, p$.
4. The graphs of the cointegrating relations: If the graph of a supposedly stationary cointegration relation reveals distinctly non-stationary behaviour, one should reconsider the choice of r, or find out if the model specification is in fact incorrect. For example, data might be $I(2)$ instead of $I(1)$.
5. The economic interpretability of the results.

The above criteria will now be illustrated based on the Danish data.

8.6 An illustration based on the Danish data

Table 8.1 reports the estimated eigenvalues, λ_i, the trace test, Trace $(i) = -T\sum_{j=1}^{i}\ln(1-\lambda_j)$, the Bartlett corrected trace test, the 95% quantile from the asymptotic tables, $C^*_{.95}$, generated in CATS for case 4,[2] and the asymptotic tables, $C^{D_s}_{.95}$, generated with a trend and a shift dummy in the cointegration relations using the simulation program developed in Nielsen (2004b). Because we have included a shift dummy in the cointegration relations and because this will influence the asymptotic distribution, the C^{D_s} is the correct table to use in this case.

We note that the Bartlett correction has the effect of lowering the calculated trace statistics. Furthermore, including the dummy variable in the cointegration relations has the effect of shifting the asymptotic distribution to the right. Thus, both corrections work in the direction of making it harder to reject the null hypothesis of $p - r$ unit roots. For example, based on a 5% test the Bartlett corrected trace test rejects five unit roots ($119.7 > 100.7$), but the null of four unit roots is borderline accepted ($71.6 < 73.8$), while three unit roots are clearly accepted ($40.7 < 50.9$). Using the tables without a Bartlett correction and ignoring the shift dummy, three unit roots would have been rejected ($44.5 > 42.8$) whereas two unit roots would have been accepted ($18.6 < 25.7$). Based on the 5% Bartlett corrected trace test we would probably choose $r = 2$, but $r = 3$ based on the standard tables. Thus, it does matter whether one uses tables corrected for small sample behaviour and dummies.

Before continuing, it is useful to see how these choices compare with the economic arguments of Chapter 2. We recall that our prior economic hypothesis was $r = 3$ assuming two driving trends; one nominal and one real stochastic trend. However, our present model contains a linear trend which might act as a proxy for a real productivity trend over this period. Thus, $r = 3$ corresponds in fact to $\{p - r = 2$ stochastic trends + 1 deterministic time trend$\}$. If the linear time trend is a proxy for the real productivity trend then our prior hypothesis could as well be $\{p - r = 1$ stochastic trend + 1 deterministic time trend$\}$, which corresponds to $r = 4$, In this case we would expect trend-adjusted real income to be stationary. If, on the other hand, the latter is non-stationary (as a result of very persistent long business cycles) then $r = 3$ would be consistent with our economic prior. Thus, based on economic arguments we might choose between $r = 3$ or $r = 4$, but not consider $r = 2$, unless the additional information in the data based on the other sources discussed in Section 8.3 clearly suggests so. We shall now check the remaining information.

An examination of the *characteristic roots* shows that the largest unrestricted root for $r = 2$ is 0.79, for $r = 3$ it is 0.77 and for $r = 4$ it is 0.82. The difference between the unrestricted roots is small and does not really discriminate between the two alternative choices of rank. Note, however, that the characteristic roots are reported without confidence bands, so the discussion whether a root is big or not is only indicative. This can be a serious problem when the characteristic roots have been determined from a model with too many lags. In this case, the VAR model has been shown to produce numerous large (but insignificant) roots around the unit circle (see Nielsen and Nielsen 2006).

[2]The critical values are not exactly the same as in Table 15.4 in Johansen (1996), because the latter are based on fewer replications.

Table 8.1 The trace test of the cointegration rank and the eigenvalue roots of the model.

r	$p-r$	i	λ_i	$\tau(p-r)$	$\tau^*_{\text{Bart.}}(p-r)$	$C_{.95}$	$C^{D_s}_{.95}$
The trace test							
0	5	1	0.35	126.4	119.7	88.6	100.7
1	4	2	0.23	75.6	71.6	63.7	73.8
2	3	3	0.20	44.5	40.7	42.8	50.9
3	2	4	0.09	18.6	17.0	25.7	31.4
4	1	5	0.06	8.0	7.4	12.5	15.7

Modulus of the five largest roots

$r=5$	$r=4$	$r=3$	$r=2$	$r=1$
0.88 (0.06)	1.0	1.0	1.0	1.0
0.88 (−0.06)	0.82 (0.00)	1.0	1.0	1.0
0.80 (0.12)	0.78 (−0.06)	0.77 (−0.03)	1.0	1.0
0.80 (−0.12)	0.78 (0.06)	0.77 (0.03)	0.79 (−0.00)	1.0
0.45 (0.14)	0.45 (0.11)	0.39 (−0.11)	0.44 (−0.00)	0.47 (0.00)

Note: The imaginary part of the complex roots is in parentheses

Table 7.1 in Chapter 7 reported the $\mathbf{\Pi}$ matrix decomposed into all five $\boldsymbol{\alpha}$ and $\boldsymbol{\beta}$ vectors. An inspection of the *significance of the adjustment coefficients* to the fourth relation shows that the adjustment coefficient $\alpha_{2,4}$, describing equilibrium correction in real income, though borderline significant based on Student's t, would not be so based on the Dickey–Fuller τ. Thus, even though the fourth relation could potentially be a candidate for an IS type of a real aggregate income relation, it does not seem to be convincingly stationary. This is far from surprising since $\boldsymbol{\beta}_4'\mathbf{x}_t$, essentially a relation between real GNE and the domestic interest rates, is only partially specified as a plausible aggregate demand relation for a small open economy. One would, for example, expect real exchange rates and the level of foreign activity, to be relevant omitted variables. The third cointegration relation seems relevant in the real income equation and in the interest rate equations, but not with very significant coefficients.

The *graph of the fourth cointegration relation* in Figure 7.4, Chapter 7 does not strongly suggest stationarity, whereas the *graph of the third cointegration relation* is more satisfactory in this respect.

Finally, *the graphs of the recursively calculated trace tests* in the lower panel of Figure 9.2 in the next chapter exhibit pronounced linear growth in the first three cointegration relations, but much less so in the last two relations. The trace test component of the two smallest eigenvalues are growing so slowly that they are not even close to the 5% critical test value at any time point. Thus, it seems safe to conclude that they correspond to unit roots or near unit roots.

Based on all this, our economic prior of $r = 3$ seems reasonably well supported by the data, whereas this is not the case for $r = 4$. The choice of $r = 2$ would have left out some important information about comovements between the two interest rates. As a matter of fact, Chapter 11 will show that one of the implications of the latter choice is that both interest rates would be weakly exogenous, implying no long-run connection between the two in this model. We do not consider this a plausible scenario.

Finally, it is important to discuss the effect of the sample size on the trace test as illustrated by the recursive graphs in Figure 9.2, lower panel. We first note that the unit root rejection line at 1.0 is based on the asymptotic distribution and needs to be shifted upwards (to approximately 1.25) when accounting for the Bartlett correction and the effect of the shift dummy. In this case we would have accepted five unit roots, i.e. no cointegration, based on the period 1973–1993, and just one cointegration after that. This is a reason for concern considering that Chapters 9 and 12 will demonstrate that the first $\boldsymbol{\beta}$ vector is economically implausible and has been subject to parameter changes over the sample period, whereas the next two $\boldsymbol{\beta}$ vectors describe a plausible money demand relation and an interest rate relation, both of which have been remarkably constant over time. Thus, choosing r based exclusively on the trace test would pick up the relation which is not well-determined based on this data set and leave out the economically 'good' relations.

This is just an illustration of the fact that in small samples we often lack information to make a sharp distinction between unit roots, near unit roots and 'very stationary' roots. In such cases choosing the rank based on a small p-value like 0.05 is likely to exclusively pick up cointegration relations with relatively fast adjustment back to equilibrium. Unfortunately, the probability of excluding stationary relations characterized by slow, but nevertheless significant adjustment, is likely to be high, i.e. the probability of type 2 errors is generally high for such relations. In a world with regulations, strong public governments, labour unions, etc. the latter are the rule rather than the exception. Thus, when the sample size is small it is particularly important to use other sources of information when determining the rank as the power is often low for many economically relevant alternatives.

8.7 Concluding remarks

This chapter has given a detailed account of the LR trace test, explained why its distribution is non-standard, and how one can simulate the latter under different specifications of the VAR model. A good understanding of this material seems crucial for understanding the essence of the cointegrated VAR approach and the important role the choice of rank plays for its empirical success. We have strongly argued that one should not base this choice exclusively on the trace test, because the null of a unit root is not always reasonable from an economic point of view. However, understanding the rational behind the trace test should make it easier for the user to make the choice of r in a manner well adapted to the purpose of the empirical study.

The empirical illustration to the Danish data seemed to suggest a choice of $r = 3$. When this is said we should remember that all the tests performed up to now are valid under the assumption of constant model parameters. Therefore, the choice of $r = 3$ is only tentative until we have been able to demonstrate a reasonable degree of parameter constancy in our model. In the next chapter, we shall discuss some recursive procedures which have been developed to detect possible sources of parameter non-constancy in the VAR model.

Part III

Testing hypotheses on cointegration

9

Recursive tests of constancy

Chapter 4 applied a variety of residual misspecification tests to the VAR model. Even though the empirical model passed these tests sufficiently well to continue the analysis, this does not exclude the possibility that the model suffers from parameter non-constancy. The purpose of this section is to provide a number of diagnostic tests to check for this important feature of the model. The purpose is to find out whether the full sample period, $1, \ldots, T$, defines a constant parameter regime and, when this is not the case, to identify where in the sample period the data strongly suggest a change in the structure. The battery of tests to be introduced here will not be formally derived, instead the interested reader is referred to Hansen and Johansen (1999) where most of the tests are discussed. Here we shall focus on the diagnostic properties of the tests and the interpretation of the results.

Section 9.1 gives a brief introduction to the various tests and their ability to diagnose deviations from parameter constancy in different parts of the model. Section 9.2 discusses a variety of recursively calculated tests of parameter constancy starting from a baseline model estimated for a subsample period, $1, \ldots, T_1$, where $T_1 < T$, and then recursively extending the end point of the recursive sample, t_1, until the full sample is covered, i.e. $t_1 = T_1, T_1 + 1, \ldots, T$. Section 9.3 discusses similar test procedures, but now the recursions are reversed, starting from a subsample period, $T_1, \ldots, T$, and then recursively extending the starting point, t_1, backwards until the full sample period is covered, i.e. $t_1 = T_1, T_1 - 1, \ldots, 1$. Section 9.4 concludes.

9.1 Diagnosing parameter non-constancy

Most of the recursive graphs are based on two versions of the model: the full model version, the **X**-form and the concentrated model version, the **R**-form. In the latter case, the concentrated model, $\mathbf{R}_{0t} = \boldsymbol{\alpha}\boldsymbol{\beta}'\mathbf{R}_{1t} + \boldsymbol{\varepsilon}_t$, discussed in Chapter 7, is estimated once and for all based on the full sample period, i.e. $t = 1, \ldots, T$. After that, the corrected variables, $\tilde{\mathbf{R}}_{0t}$ and $\tilde{\mathbf{R}}_{1t}$, are treated as given and the recursive tests are calculated for the model, $\tilde{\mathbf{R}}_{0t} = \boldsymbol{\alpha}\boldsymbol{\beta}'\tilde{\mathbf{R}}_{1t} + \boldsymbol{\varepsilon}_t$, $t = 1, \ldots, t_1$, $t_1 = T_1, T_1 + 1, \ldots, T$. The question is, in case the two model versions give different test results (they often do), which one to choose and how to interpret the results.

Let us consider a situation where the model suffers from non-constant parameters in the short-run structure, but not in the long-run. Because the effects from the non-constant parameters have been averaged out in the **R**-form, these tests are likely to accept, correctly, parameter constancy of the long-run structure, whereas the **X**-form tests are more likely to be influenced by the instability in the short-run coefficients. Thus, when the recursive tests based on the **R**-form look more 'stable' than the **X**-form over time, as they frequently do, it suggests instability in the short-run coefficients. Another case where the two versions are likely to differ is when the baseline sample is very short. Because the **X**-form version re-estimates all parameters, the degrees of freedom are fewer than for the **R**-form. This can lead to increased volatility in the **X**-form graphs, in particular at the beginning of the recursive sample.

The sheer amount of the tests may easily have an intimidating effect on the reader. How should one make sense of the vast amount of information resulting from running all the recursive tests. It is important from the outset to understand that each test looks at the model from a slightly different angle, so that one test might detect non-constant features not spotted by any of the other tests. It is also important to realize that it is just the question of looking carefully enough to find non-constancies in at least some directions of essentially any empirical model. The important issue is whether the deviation from constancy is serious enough to warrant a re-specification of the model. Unfortunately there is no waterproof rule, but with experience one can usually learn when the tests signal 'major concern' and when it is 'business as usual'.

In the best of all worlds, the recursive tests help to diagnose problems in the model that can be remedied, in other cases the recursive tests continue to signal non-constancies in the model. In the latter case, it might still be useful to continue the empirical analysis, albeit keeping in mind that the estimated parameters measure average effects. In particular, it is important to remember that applied tests might produce unreliable results as the underlying assumptions of the model are not satisfied. One useful way of thinking of the recursive tests is that they can provide a general assessment of the confidence we place on the conclusions from the model.

The recursive tests can be grouped into four broad categories:

1. Recursive tests of the full model, here exemplified by the recursive test of the likelihood function. This is a broad test telling us whether the model is approximately acceptable or not. When the test rejects constancy, the graphs are helpful in approximately localizing the time when the problem begins, but not in suggesting where in the model the problems hide. This test is similar to the recursive Chow tests frequently used in single equation models.
2. Recursive tests based on the eigenvalues, λ_i, as well as transformations of them, exemplified here by the recursively calculated trace tests, the eigenvalues, the log-transformed eigenvalues, and the fluctuations test. These tests provide more detailed information about constancy/non-constancy of the individual cointegration relations. This is because the eigenvalues are a quadratic function of $\boldsymbol{\alpha}$ and $\boldsymbol{\beta}$

as the following equalities show:

$$\hat{\lambda}_i = \hat{\boldsymbol{\alpha}}_i'\mathbf{S}_{00}^{-1}\hat{\boldsymbol{\alpha}}_i$$
$$= \hat{\boldsymbol{\beta}}_i'\mathbf{S}_{10}\mathbf{S}_{00}^{-1}\mathbf{S}_{01}\hat{\boldsymbol{\beta}}_i. \tag{9.1}$$

Thus, if $\boldsymbol{\alpha}_i$ and $\boldsymbol{\beta}_i$ are reasonably constant then λ_i will also be constant.

3. Recursive tests of the constancy of the cointegration space, $\boldsymbol{\beta}'\mathbf{x}_t$, such as the 'max test of a constant $\boldsymbol{\beta}$' and the test of '$\boldsymbol{\beta}_t$ equal to a known $\boldsymbol{\beta}$'. While the previous group of tests did not discriminate between non-constancy associated with $\boldsymbol{\alpha}_i$ or $\boldsymbol{\beta}_i$, the tests in this group focus primarily on spotting any non-constancy in the $\boldsymbol{\beta}$ structure. However, these tests do not discriminate between individual $\boldsymbol{\beta}_i$. A procedure for the latter case will be discussed in Chapter 12 for an identified $\boldsymbol{\beta}$ structure.
4. Recursive tests of predictive failure both for the full system and for the individual series.

9.2 Forward recursive tests

The idea is to choose a baseline sample from the first part of the sample period, estimate a first model, and then recursively test whether the more recent observations have followed the same model. When choosing the baseline sample one has to weight the following two considerations against each other. When the baseline sample is small relative to the number of model parameters, then the latter will be imprecisely estimated and the recursive graphs often exhibit large variability in the beginning of the recursive sample. When the baseline sample is large, a structural break in early part of the model will not be detected.

In the illustrations below, all forward tests are based on a baseline sample of 1973:1–1984:4.

It is also important to remember that after the first rejection of constancy, all subsequent tests may cease to have a meaning. This is because the tests are derived under the null of constant parameters up to time $T_1 + t_1$. If there is a structural break at $T_1 + t_1$, then the remaining tests are derived under an incorrect null hypothesis. In practise, it is not uncommon to see a rejection of constancy, for example in connection with an intervention or a new regime, but after a short period the graphs return back to the acceptance region. This might suggest that economic behaviour was first rather volatile as a result of the intervention, but that after a while things were back to 'business as usual'. In this case, one may not need to be utterly concerned about accounting for such a temporary change of the model parameters.

9.2.1 The recursively calculated log likelihood

The log likelihood test statistic is defined by:

$$Q_T(t_1) = \frac{t_1}{T}\sqrt{\frac{T}{2p}}\left[\frac{1}{t_1}\sum_{i=1}^{t_1} l_i(\hat{\boldsymbol{\theta}}_i) - \frac{1}{T}\sum_{i=1}^{T} l_i(\hat{\boldsymbol{\theta}}_T)\right] = \frac{t_1}{T}\sqrt{\frac{T}{2p}}\left(\log|\hat{\boldsymbol{\Omega}}_{t_1}| - \log|\hat{\boldsymbol{\Omega}}_T|\right),$$

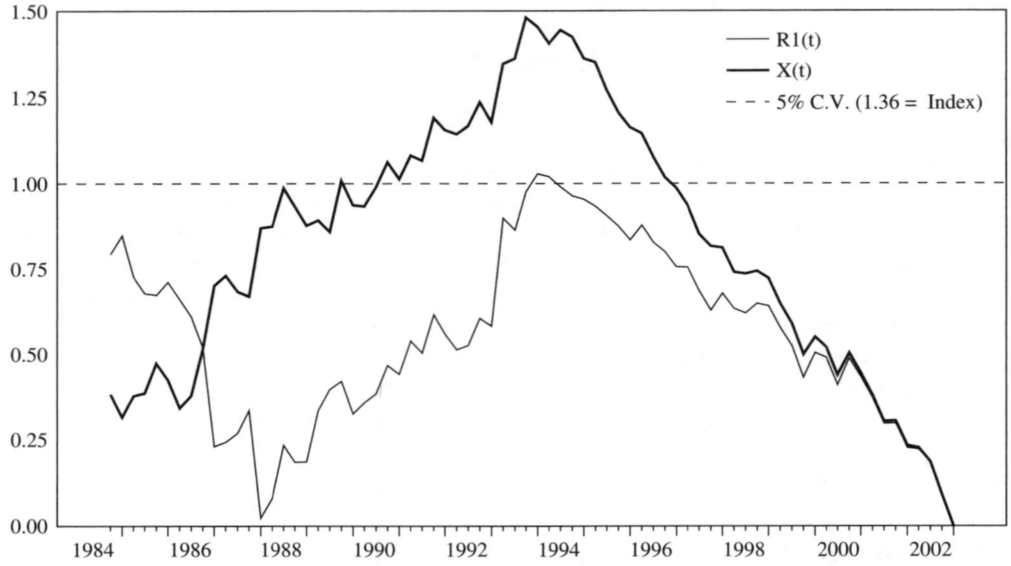

Fig 9.1 The recursive log likelihood function.

where

$$l_i(\boldsymbol{\theta}) = -2\log f_{\boldsymbol{\theta}}(\mathbf{x}_i|\mathbf{x}_{i-1},\ldots,\mathbf{x}_{i-k}) = \log|\boldsymbol{\Omega}| + \boldsymbol{\varepsilon}_i'\boldsymbol{\Omega}^{-1}\boldsymbol{\varepsilon}_i.$$

A bias corrected version of the test is given by:

$$Q_T^{\mathrm{corr}}(t_1) = \frac{t_1}{T}\sqrt{\frac{T}{2p}}\left[(\log|\hat{\boldsymbol{\Omega}}_{t_1}| - \log|\hat{\boldsymbol{\Omega}}_T|) + \frac{1}{T}\left(\frac{1}{2}p(p+1)+r+p(k-1)+1\right)\left(1-\frac{t_1}{T}\right)\right].$$

The bias corrected test has in general slightly better size properties. The limit distribution of $\max_{t_1}|Q_T^{\mathrm{corr}}(t_1)|$ is that of the maximum of a Brownian bridge, which has been determined by simulation. Under the null hypothesis of constant parameters, the 95% quantile of the test is 1.36. In Figure 9.1 the corrected test statistic has been divided by the 95% quantile so that constancy is rejected at the 5% level. We note that model constancy is more or less accepted based on the **R**-form model, though only borderline so around 1994, whereas it is rejected based on the **X**-form model in the first part of the 1990s. This period coincides with the EMS crises, the speculative attack on many European economies, and the breakdown of the previous ERM agreement and comprises a fairly volatile subperiod in the sample. Whether this is enough evidence to conclude that model needs to be respecified is difficult to conclude before we have looked at the evidence from the remaining tests.

9.2.2 Recursively calculated trace test statistics

The recursively calculated trace tests based on (8.1) in Chapter 8 are graphed in Figure 9.2 both for the **X**-form model (upper panel) and the **R**-form model (lower panel). To increase readability, the trace test has been scaled by the 95% quantile of the appropriate asymptotic distribution, which in the present example corresponds to case 4 in Chapter 8. While not a problem here, it sometimes happens that the recursive graphs cross each other as a consequence of the scaling by the critical values. Another point to remember is that the applied 95% quantile is in fact not appropriate when the cointegration relations contain (shift) dummies. Accounting for the dummy variable, $D_s83.1$, would cause the unit line to move upwards. Furthermore, applying a Bartlett correction to the trace test would move the line even higher. In the present case the dummy variable and the Bartlett correction would move the line to approximately 1.25.

The recursive graphs of the trace test divided by the 95% quantile

$$\tau(j) = \left\{ -t_1 \sum_{i=1}^{j} \ln(1 - \hat{\lambda}_i) \right\} / C^*_{.95}(j), \quad j = 1, \ldots, p, \; t_1 = T_1, \ldots, T \tag{9.2}$$

provide a first visual impression of whether the cointegration relations are reasonably constant or not. If $\boldsymbol{\alpha}_i$ and $\boldsymbol{\beta}_i$ are reasonably constant, then λ_i will also be constant and the graph, $-t_1 \ln(1 - \hat{\lambda}_i)$, will grow linearly with the slope coefficient $\ln(1 - \hat{\lambda}_i)$.

The graphs in the upper panel of Figure 9.2 are based on a recursive estimation of the full model, the **X**-form, whereas the ones in the lower panel is based on the **R**-form (see discussion in the introduction). The graphs in the upper panel exhibit slightly more instability than the ones in the lower panel, indicating some instability in the short-run

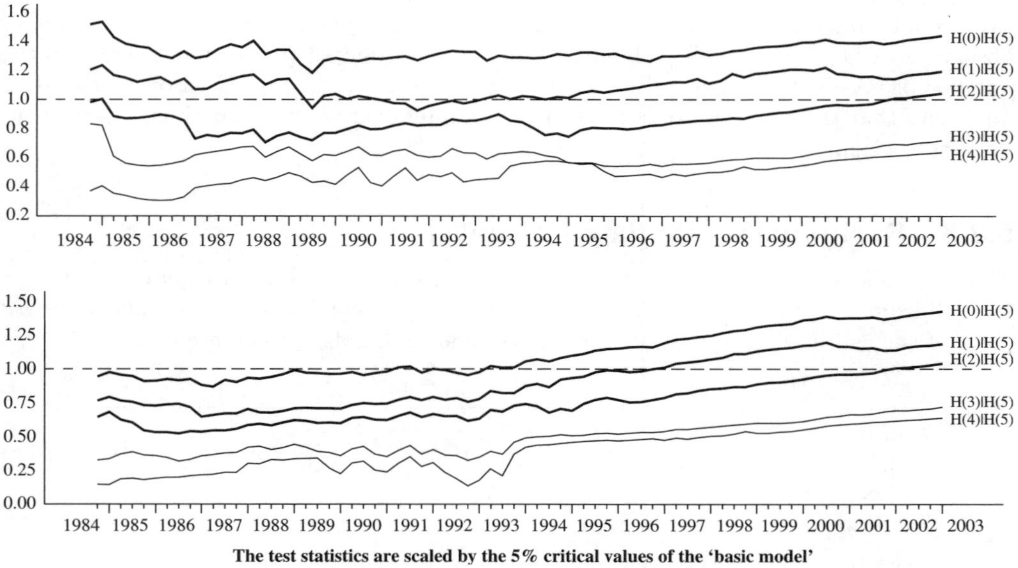

Fig 9.2 The recursive trace test.

coefficients over the sample period. The recursive graphs based on the **R**-form, give the impression that the trace tests for $r = 1, 2, 3$, have grown almost linearly over time, suggesting that the parameters of the first three cointegrating relations have been quite stable for $t_1 = 1984{:}4, \ldots, 2003{:}1$. However, also the two smallest λ values exhibit some linear growth, though the tests do not come even close to acceptance in the recursive sample period. As the model contains a linear trend, this could be an indication that the data are approximately trend-stationary.

The recursive trace tests in Figure 9.2 can be used to illustrate how the power and the size of the trace test depend on the sample size. Based on a 5% test we would have had to wait until the beginning of the 1990s before being able to accept $r = 1$, i.e. that the first relation is stationary (which subsequent tests will show is the most unstable of the first three relations). To accept $r = 2$ we would have had to wait until 1995. Considering that subsequent tests will show that the first relation has non-constant parameters and is difficult to interpret, whereas the second relation has constant parameters and is interpretable as a money-demand relation, such a decision rule does not seem meaningful. As a matter of fact, it is easy to demonstrate that the estimates of the second and the third cointegration relation were almost identical based on the samples 1973 to 1987 and from 1973 to 1993,[1] whereas those of the first relation were not. Thus, focusing exclusively on the size of the trace test would often lead us to reject the stationarity of plausible economic relations. This is, of course, just a consequence of the low power of the trace tests already discussed in Chapter 8. We need a long sample to be able to reject the unit root hypothesis if we choose a small p-value.

Some minor instability can be detected in the last two cointegration relations, but it seems to be of minor importance. Serious instability is likely to show up much more dramatically. The graphs based on the **X**-form seem more diffuse: there is evidence of declining growth in the first part of the recursive sample and then increasing growth. This can often happen when the baseline period is very short, making the effective number of observations $(T_1 - kp)$ small. When the number of estimated parameters is close to the number of observations the estimated λ values tend towards 1.0. This, of course, does not mean that the relations are very stationary, only that we have an almost perfect fit, by construction.

9.2.3 Recursively calculated eigenvalues $\boldsymbol{\lambda}_i$

Figure 9.3 shows the time paths of the recursively calculated r largest eigenvalues λ_i, $i = 1, \ldots, 3$ from the unrestricted VAR model and their 95% confidence bands. The standard error of the estimate $\hat{\lambda}_i(t_1)$ needed for the confidence bands is calculated as:

$$\text{s.e.}(\hat{\lambda}_{i,t_1}) = \sqrt{t_1^{-1} 4(1-\hat{\lambda}_{i,t_1})^2 (\hat{\lambda}_{i,t_1} + \sum_{h=1}^{t_1^{1/3}} \left(1 - \frac{h}{t_1^{1/3}}\right)^2 (r_{i,u}(h)^2 - r_{i,uv}(h)^2))}, \tag{9.3}$$

[1] These were the sample periods many previous papers were based on.

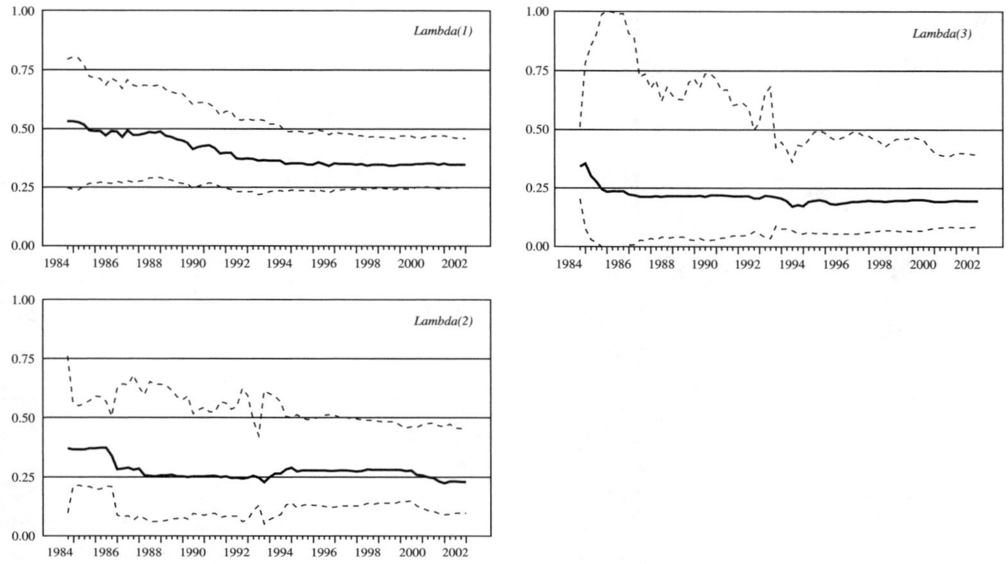

Fig 9.3 Recursively calculated λ_i, $i = 1, 2, 3$, together with 95% confidence bands.

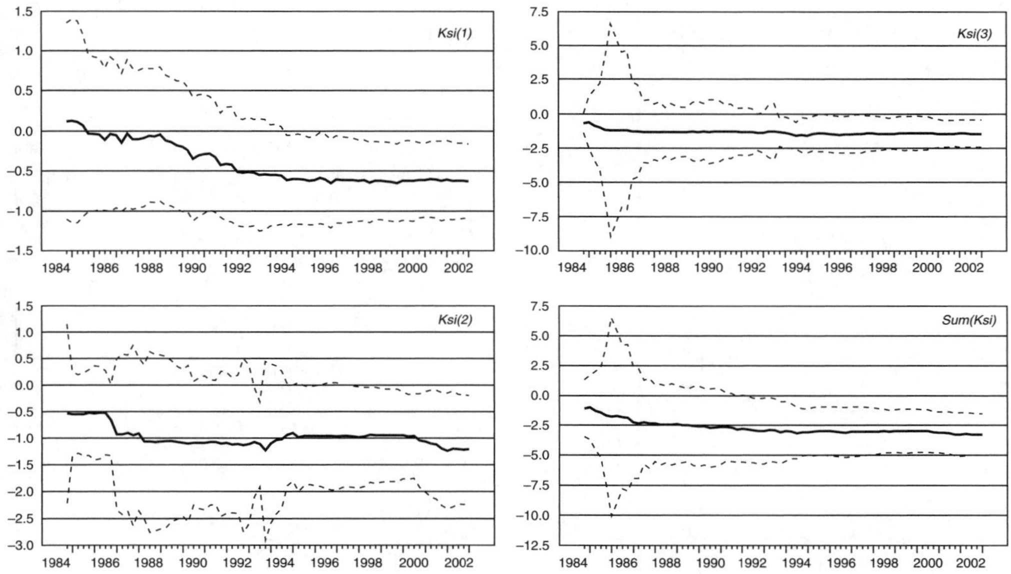

Fig 9.4 Recursively calculated log transformed eigenvalues.

where

$$r_{i,u}(h) = t_1^{-1} \sum_{t=h}^{t_1} \hat{u}_{i,t}\hat{u}_{i,t-h},$$

$$r_{i,uv}(h) = t_1^{-1} \sum_{t=h}^{t_1} \hat{u}_{i,t}\hat{v}_{i,t-h},$$

for

$$\hat{u}_{i,t} = \hat{\lambda}_i^{-\frac{1}{2}} \hat{\boldsymbol{\alpha}}_i' \mathbf{S}_{00}^{-1} \mathbf{R}_{0t},$$

and

$$\hat{v}_{i,t} = (\hat{\lambda}_i(1-\hat{\lambda}_i))^{-\frac{1}{2}} \hat{\boldsymbol{\alpha}}_i' \mathbf{S}_{00}^{-1} (\mathbf{R}_{0t} - \hat{\boldsymbol{\alpha}}\hat{\boldsymbol{\beta}}' \mathbf{R}_{1t}).$$

For further details see Hansen and Johansen (1999). Figure 9.3 shows that the estimated eigenvalues stay within the lowest of the upper bands and the highest of the lower bands for all periods, except for the first few years. We notice that the value of $\hat{\lambda}_1$ is quite large at the beginning of the recursions, and then declines until it reaches a stable value at around 1995. This behaviour can frequently be seen when the baseline period is relatively short so that there are few degrees of freedom (t_1 minus the number of estimated parameters). In the extreme case when the degrees of freedom is close to zero, the estimated $\hat{\lambda}_1$ can be close to 1.0. This, however, is not necessarily an indication that $\boldsymbol{\beta}_1'\mathbf{x}_t$ is very stationary, but that the sample is too short relative to the number of estimated parameters.

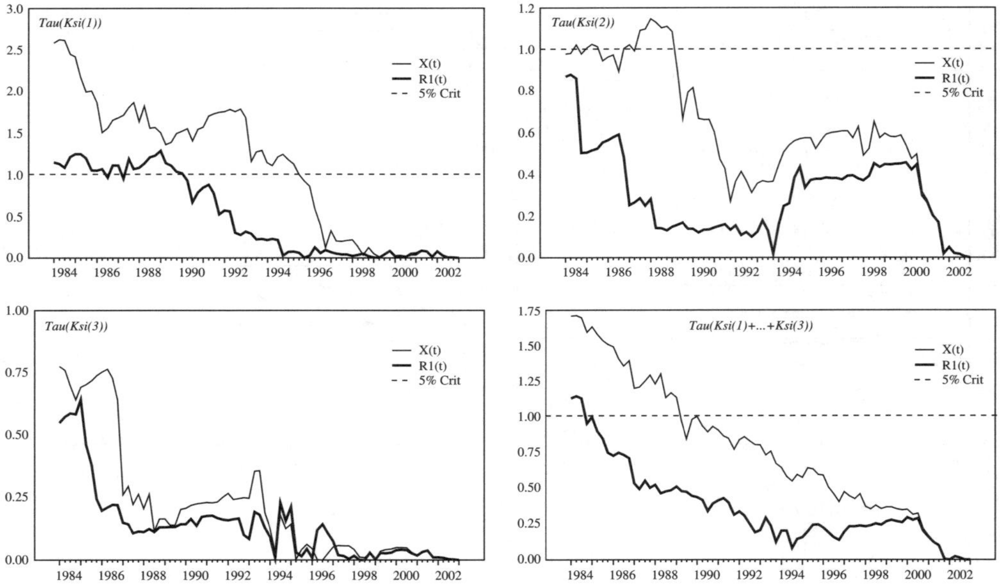

Fig 9.5 Recursively calculated fluctuation tests of constancy.

The wide confidence bands of λ_3 at around 1984–1986 are notable in Figure 9.3, suggesting a lot of variability in the first few years after capital deregulation. The smaller the value of λ_i, the more asymmetrical is its distribution. This effect can easily be seen in the figure, where the distribution of $\hat{\lambda}_1$ is almost symmetric, whereas for $\hat{\lambda}_2$ and $\hat{\lambda}_3$ this is much less so. A symmetrical representation of $\hat{\lambda}_i$ can be achieved by the following log transformation

$$\xi_i = \ln(\lambda_i/(1 - \lambda_i)).$$

The recursive graphs of the log transformed eigenvalues in Figure 9.4 demonstrate that the 95% confidence bands are now symmetrical also for the small eigenvalues. The last graph in the lower right hand side panel of the figure is a weighted sum of all three eigenvalues.

9.2.4 The fluctuations test

The fluctuations test is a recursively calculated constancy test of the individual λ_i, $i = 1, \ldots, r$, as well as a weighted average of them. As (9.1) shows this test can be considered a recursive constancy check of $\boldsymbol{\beta}_i$ and $\boldsymbol{\alpha}_i$, $i = 1, \ldots, r$. The fluctuations test is defined by:

$$\tau_i(t_1) = \frac{t_1}{T}\sqrt{T}\Sigma_{ii}^{-1/2}(\hat{\lambda}_{i,t_1} - \hat{\lambda}_{i,T})$$

where Σ_{ii} is the variance of λ_i defined in Hansen and Johansen (1999). The test is a supremum test and is likely to be rather conservative with respect to the null hypothesis of constancy. Thus, the power of rejecting parameter constancy when there is non-constancy in the model may not be very high. On the other hand, a rejection by this test is often a strong signal of parameter non-constancy. Since the test distinguishes between the constancy of individual λ_i, it is sometimes possible to isolate the sources of non-constancy to a specific cointegration relation.

The graphs of the recursively calculated fluctuation tests in Figure 9.5 show that $\hat{\tau}_1$ is in the rejection region at the beginning of 1984 when the recursions start. The test statistics remain at a fairly high level until approximately 1996, in particular for the **X**-form. The recursive graphs of $\hat{\tau}_2$ suggest that the parameter of the second cointegration relation are reasonably constant over the sample period, and those of $\hat{\tau}_3$ suggest a considerable degree of constancy. The overall test in the lower right-hand side panel picks up the non-constancy at the beginning of the recursions. The fluctuations test is quite useful as it helps us to identify where in the VAR model parameters might be non-constant.

Knowing which cointegration relations have reasonably constant parameters over time and which have not, is clearly valuable from a modelling point of view, but does not necessarily solve the interpretational problem. To be able to identify the underlying source of parameter instability, we also need to understand what they measure so that we can give them a tentative economic interpretation. Even though this is far from always possible, we recall from the discussion in Chapter 7 that the first cointegration relation approximately described an inflation-interest rate relation, the second a money demand relation, and the third a relation between the two interest rates. As the graph of $\hat{\tau}_1$ suggested a regime shift in the mid-1980s we can now formulate the hypothesis

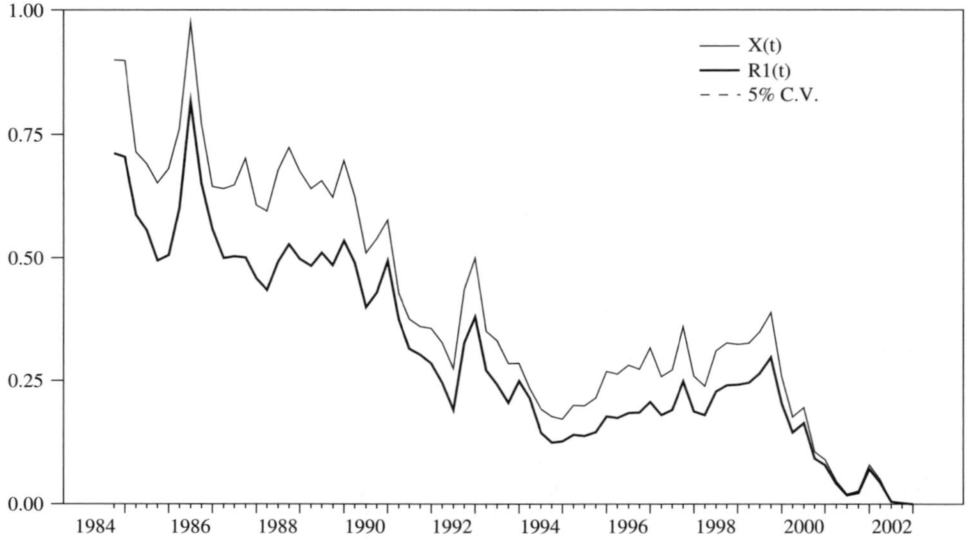

Fig 9.6 The max test of $\boldsymbol{\beta}$-constancy.

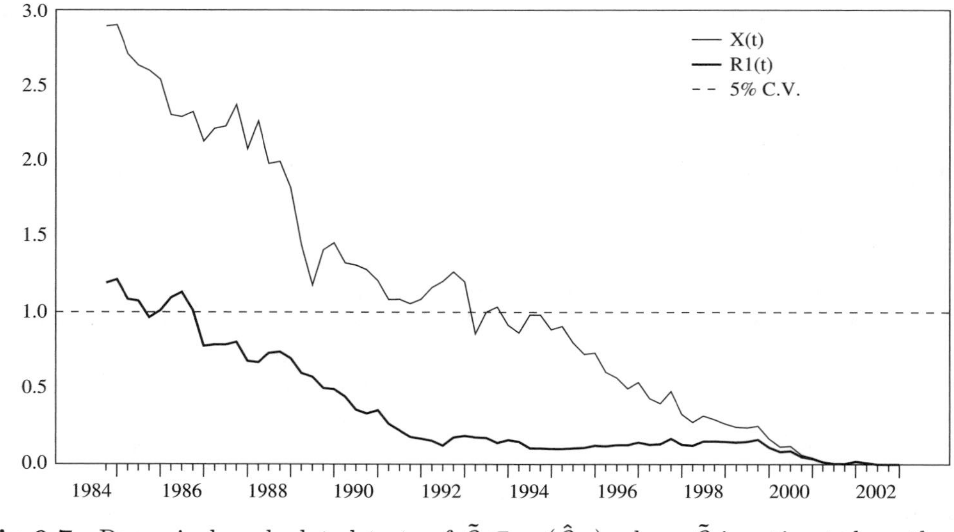

Fig 9.7 Recursively calculated tests of $\tilde{\boldsymbol{\beta}} \subseteq sp(\hat{\boldsymbol{\beta}}_{t_1})$ where $\tilde{\boldsymbol{\beta}}$ is estimated on the full sample 1973:2–2003:1.

that the relationship between inflation and the interest rates changed at the time of the deregulation of capital movements. The recursive graphs of $\hat{\tau}_2$ and $\hat{\tau}_3$ suggest that the money demand relation $\boldsymbol{\beta}_2'\mathbf{x}_t$ and the interest rate relation $\boldsymbol{\beta}_3'\mathbf{x}_t$ have remained reasonably constant over the investigated period.

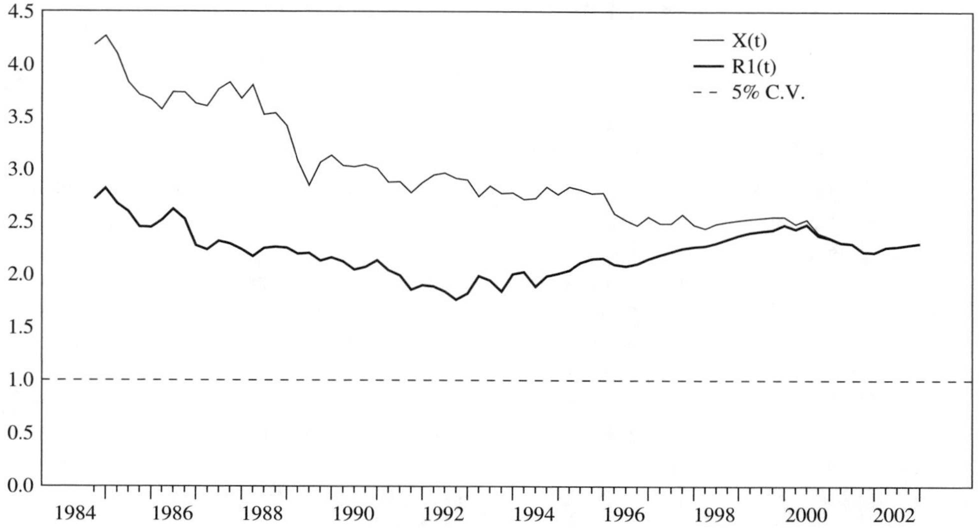

Fig 9.8 Recursively calculated tests of $\tilde{\boldsymbol{\beta}} \subseteq sp(\hat{\boldsymbol{\beta}}_{t_1})$ where $\tilde{\boldsymbol{\beta}}$ is estimated on the subsample 1986:1–2003:1.

Altogether the recursive graphs suggest that some parts of the VAR model might not be very constant, whereas others seem quite satisfactory in this respect. We shall have a further look at this finding after having imposed identifying restrictions on the $\boldsymbol{\beta}$ vectors in Chapter 12.

9.2.5 The max test of constant $\boldsymbol{\beta}$

If the estimated eigenvalues seem to be changing over time based on the above tests, then we might ask whether it is because $\boldsymbol{\beta}$ or $\boldsymbol{\alpha}$ is changing. The test below focuses on testing changes in $\boldsymbol{\beta}$. We normalize $\boldsymbol{\beta}$, so that $\bar{\mathbf{c}}'\boldsymbol{\beta} = \mathbf{I}_r$, where $\mathbf{c}$ is a $r \times r$ normalizing matrix and $\bar{\mathbf{c}} = \mathbf{c}(\mathbf{c}'\mathbf{c})^{-1}$ The test is a sup test following the idea in Nyblom (1989) *inter alia* based upon the score statistic $\mathbf{S}^{(t_1)} = \partial \log L^{(t_1)}/\partial\boldsymbol{\beta} = \boldsymbol{\alpha}'\Omega^{-1}(\mathbf{S}_{01}^{(t_1)} - \boldsymbol{\alpha}\boldsymbol{\beta}'\mathbf{S}_{11}^{(t_1)})\mathbf{c}_\perp$, calculated from the first t_1 observations and the information $\partial^2 \log L^{(T)}/\partial\boldsymbol{\beta}^2 = \mathbf{c}_\perp'\mathbf{S}_{11}^{(T)}\mathbf{c}_\perp \otimes \boldsymbol{\alpha}'\boldsymbol{\Omega}^{-1}\boldsymbol{\alpha}$ based upon all observations. The max test essentially tests the hypothesis:

$$\mathcal{H}_\beta : \hat{\boldsymbol{\beta}}_{t_1} = \boldsymbol{\beta}_0 \text{ for } t_1 = T_1, \ldots, T \tag{9.4}$$

where we use $\boldsymbol{\beta}_0 = \hat{\boldsymbol{\beta}}_T$.

The asymptotic distribution of the test statistic is given as a function of Brownian motions and its distribution has been determined by simulation. This test is rather conservative, implying that there is strong evidence for non-constancy in the model when the test rejects. Figure 9.6 illustrates this feature: the test statistic, which has been divided by the 95% quantile of the distribution under the null of constant parameters, is safely below the rejection line of 1.0 for all t_1 = 1984:4, ..., 2003:1. As the recursive sample approaches the full sample period the test statistic goes to zero and it is not very likely that the test would detect a structural change taking place at the end of the sample period.

9.2.6 Tests of 'β_t equals a known β'

The test of a fixed $\boldsymbol{\beta}$ is based on the following idea. We start with the null hypothesis that the $\boldsymbol{\beta}$ relations are constant over a reference period which, for example, can be the full sample period or a subset of it. If one strongly believes that the full sample period defines a constant parameter regime, then it seems natural to choose the reference period to be the full sample period. The purpose of the recursive testing is then to check whether the constancy hypothesis is in fact acceptable. On the other hand, if one knows from the outset that the full sample period covers several regimes which might have caused the VAR parameters to change, it seems advisable to choose the reference period to be a subset of the sample defining the regime. The recursive testing will then tell us whether the parameters remained constant when extending the sample beyond the reference period.

The first step in the procedure is to obtain an estimate $\tilde{\boldsymbol{\beta}}$ based on the chosen reference period. The second step is to test whether this reference value $\tilde{\boldsymbol{\beta}}$ is in the space spanned by $\hat{\boldsymbol{\beta}}_{T_1}$, where $\hat{\boldsymbol{\beta}}_{T_1}$ is the estimate of $\boldsymbol{\beta}$ based on the sample $1, \ldots, T_1$. The latter defines the shortest sample period we have chosen for comparison with the reference period. The graph of the recursive test is then obtained by recursively adding more observations to T_1. Thus, the recursive test can be described as follows:

$$\mathcal{H}_{\beta_\tau} : \tilde{\boldsymbol{\beta}} \in \text{sp}(\boldsymbol{\beta}_{t_1}), \quad t_1 = T_1, \ldots, T.$$

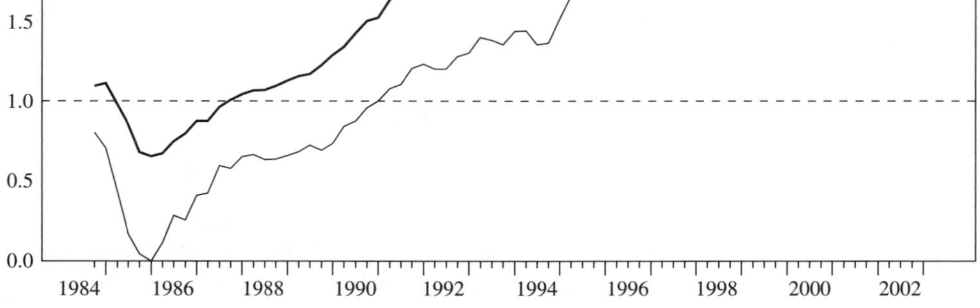

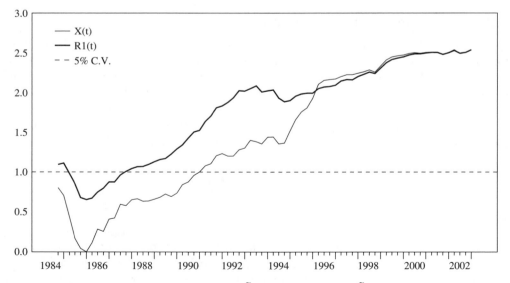

Fig 9.9 Recursively calculated tests of $\tilde{\boldsymbol{\beta}} \subseteq sp(\boldsymbol{\beta}_{t_1})$ where $\tilde{\boldsymbol{\beta}}$ is estimated on the subsample 1973:1–1986:1.

where the estimate $\tilde{\boldsymbol{\beta}}$ is considered a known matrix. The test statistic is given by

$$-2\ln(Q(\mathcal{H}_{\boldsymbol{\beta}_\tau}|\hat{\boldsymbol{\beta}}_{t_1})) = t_1 \sum_{i=1}^{r} \left(\ln(1-\hat{\rho}_{i,t_1}) - \ln(1-\hat{\lambda}_{i,t_1})\right),$$
$$t_1 = T_1, \ldots, T, \tag{9.5}$$

where $\hat{\rho}_{i,t_1}$, $i = 1, \ldots, r$ is the solution of the restricted eigenvalue problem

$$|\rho\tilde{\boldsymbol{\beta}}'\boldsymbol{S}_{11,t_1}\tilde{\boldsymbol{\beta}} - \tilde{\boldsymbol{\beta}}'\boldsymbol{S}_{10,t_1}\mathbf{S}_{00,t_1}^{-1}\mathbf{S}_{01,t_1}\tilde{\boldsymbol{\beta}}| = 0, \quad t_1 = T_1, \ldots, T, \tag{9.6}$$

and $\hat{\lambda}_{i,t_1}$ $i = 1, \ldots, r$ is the solution of the unrestricted eigenvalue problem:

$$|\lambda\mathbf{S}_{11,t_1} - \mathbf{S}_{10,t_1}\mathbf{S}_{00,t_1}^{-1}\mathbf{S}_{01,t_1}| = 0, \quad t_1 = T_1, \ldots, T. \tag{9.7}$$

The test statistic (9.5) is asymptotically distributed as χ^2 with $(p1-r)r$ degrees of freedom (Hansen and Johansen 1999). A detailed discussion of the test procedure will be given in Chapter 12.

Figure 9.7 illustrates the case where $\tilde{\boldsymbol{\beta}}$ is the full sample estimate. To increase readability, the test values have been scaled by the 95% quantile of the χ^2 distribution. A value larger than 1.0 means that the test rejects constancy. The thin line is based on the full model, the thick line based on the **R**-form model. The thick line in the figure shows that the full sample $\hat{\boldsymbol{\beta}}$ would essentially have been accepted in all periods 1973:2–1984:1+j, $j = 1, \ldots, 76$ when the short-run effects had been corrected for,

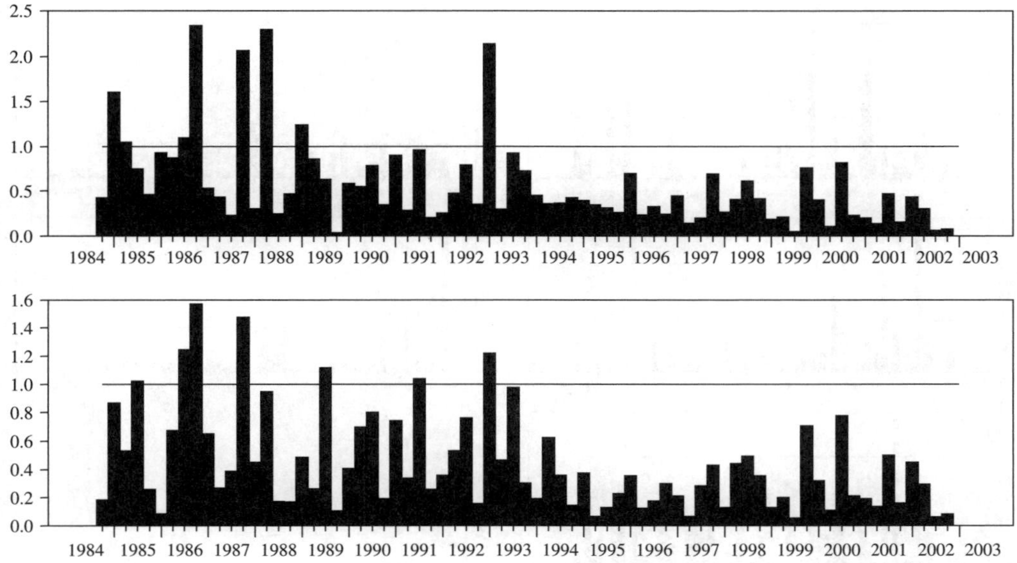

Fig 9.10 Recursively calculated one-step ahead prediction errors of the system scaled by two standard errors. The upper panel is for the full model and the lower panel for the **R**-form.

whereas the dotted line shows that this would not have been the case in the first few years after 1984.

Using the full sample as the reference period might in some cases hide problems of non-constancy. This is because the full sample estimates will describe some sort of average effects over two regimes, so that the parameters of each regime may not differ enough from the average coefficients to yield a significant test value. Therefore, it is a good idea to check parameter constancy also for other reference periods. The graphs in Figure 9.8 are based on a different reference period, 1986:1–2003:1, to find out whether the evidence of non-constancy around the mid-1980s detected in the fluctuations test can be verified in the present test. We note that the previous conclusion is now reversed: Both based on the **R**-form and the **X**-form we would not have accepted that the estimated $\boldsymbol{\beta}$ vectors based on the periods 1973:2–1984:1+j, $j = 1, \ldots, 76$ are empirically the same as the $\boldsymbol{\beta}$ vectors of the reference period 1986:1–2003:1. Thus, the test is now consistent with the fluctuations test, which rejected the constancy of the first cointegration vector. To further investigate this possibility we shall perform a last recursive test in which we choose the reference period to be 1973:2–1986:1 and T_1 to be 1984:1. The graphs in Figure 9.9 confirm the previous finding: the estimated $\boldsymbol{\beta}$ based on the first half of the sample is not likely to remain constant when extending the sample period to the second half of the 1980s and the 1990s. Note also that the recursive estimates contain the reference period, which is why the test is zero in the **X**-form at 1986:1.

The three versions of this recursive constancy test served the purpose of illustrating that one can reach different conclusions depending on how we design the tests. It is, therefore, advisable to perform various versions of the constancy tests to find out how sensitive they are to the choice of reference period and the choice of T_1.

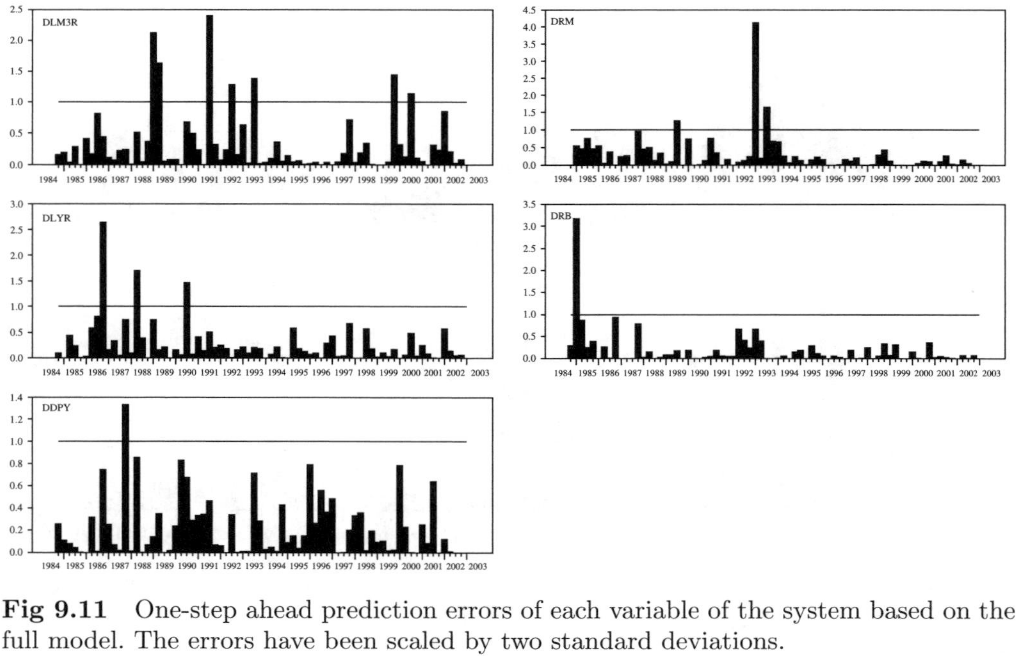

Fig 9.11 One-step ahead prediction errors of each variable of the system based on the full model. The errors have been scaled by two standard deviations.

9.2.7 Recursively calculated prediction tests

The one-step-ahead prediction test is based on the hypothesis that the VAR process that has generated $\Delta\mathbf{x}_1, \ldots, \Delta\mathbf{x}_{t_1-1}$ is identical for $t_1 = T_1, \ldots, T$ (Lütkepohl 2005). The one-step-ahead prediction error for the system is calculated as:

$$\mathbf{f}_{t_1} = \Delta\mathbf{x}_{t_1} - \sum_{j=1}^{k-1} \hat{\mathbf{\Gamma}}_{j,(t_1-1)}\Delta\mathbf{x}_{t_1-j} - \hat{\mathbf{\Pi}}_{(t_1-1)}\mathbf{x}_{t_1-1} - \hat{\boldsymbol{\mu}}_{0,(t_1-1)}$$
$$- \hat{\mathbf{\Phi}}_{(t_1-1)}\mathbf{D}_{t_1}, \quad t_1 = T_1, \ldots, T, \tag{9.8}$$

and the test statistic as:

$$\mathcal{T}(t_1) = \left(\frac{t_1}{d_1 + r} + 1\right) \mathbf{f}'_{(t_1)}\hat{\mathbf{\Omega}}^{-1}_{(t_1-1)}\mathbf{f}_{(t_1)}$$
$$t_1 = T_1 + 1, \ldots, T. \tag{9.9}$$

where $d_1 = k-1+d$ and d is the number of dummy variables in the model. Under the null, $\mathcal{T}(t_1)$ is asymptotically distributed as χ^2 with p degrees of freedom. Figure 9.10 illustrates the $\mathcal{T}(t_1)$ test values scaled by the $\chi^2_{.95}$ critical value. A test value above one implies that the model was not able to predict that observation within the 95% confidence bands. Thus, 5% of the values should lie above the line given the null of constant parameters.

We note that the prediction errors from the full model are generally much larger than from the **R**-form model. This should come as no surprise as the **R**-model is essentially a

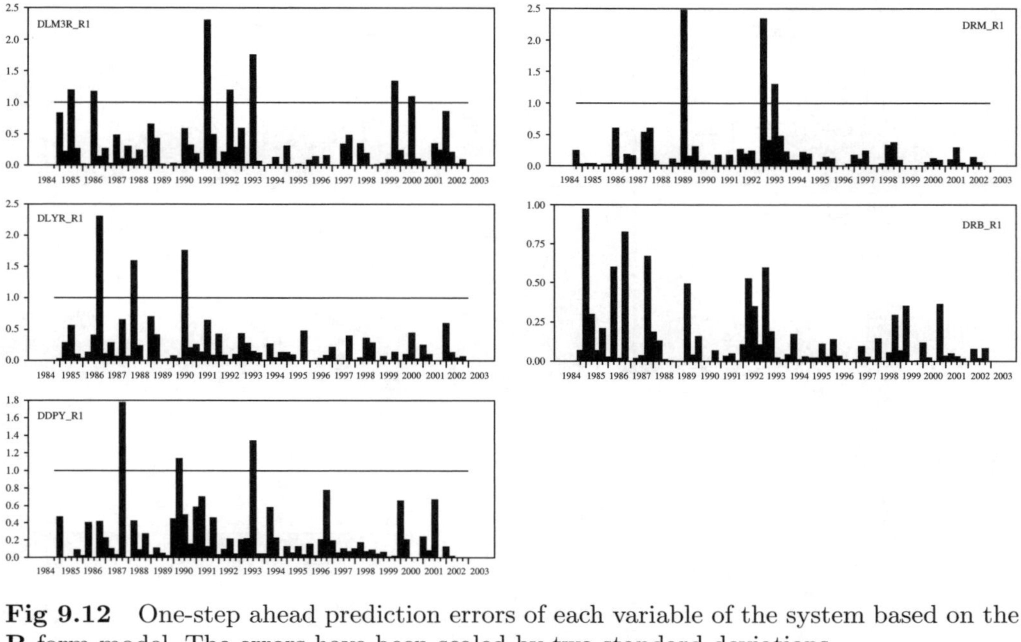

Fig 9.12 One-step ahead prediction errors of each variable of the system based on the **R**-form model. The errors have been scaled by two standard deviations.

test of the model's ability to predict the equilibrium adjustment to the long-run relations when all short-run dynamic effects (inclusive significant interventions effects which have been accounted for by dummy variables) have been averaged out.

The test of one-step-ahead prediction errors for the individual variables x_{i,t_1} is given by:

$$\mathcal{T}_i(t_1) = \left(\frac{t_1}{d_1 + r} + 1\right) f_{i,t_1}^2 / \hat{\Omega}_{ii,(t_1-1)}, \quad t_1 = T_1 + 1, \ldots, T, \tag{9.10}$$

and is asymptotically distributed as $\chi^2(1)$. Also in this case, we can choose between predictions from the full model illustrated in Figure 9.11 and from the **R**-form model illustrated in Figure 9.12.

The above recursive graphs of the one-step-ahead prediction errors exhibit a number of predictive failures, notably every time there is a major shock to the system. This should come as no surprise, as the VAR model need not in general be efficient for predictions (Clements and Hendry 1999a). Even though occasional predictive failures should not be the reason for concern, the prediction tests might be useful as a diagnostic tool for non-constancy in case they show systematic predictive failure over some extended periods of time.

9.3 Backward recursive tests

The previous test procedures were all based on the principle of forward recursive testing, starting from a baseline sample, $1, \ldots, T_1$, and then checking whether the parameters

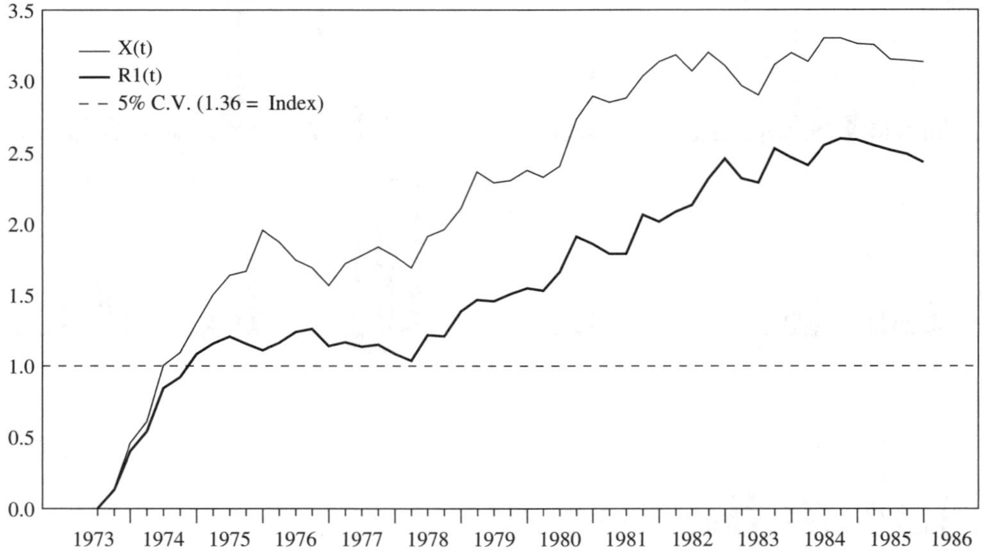

Fig 9.13 The backward recursively calculated log likelihood based on (1986:1–j)–2003:1, $j = 1, \ldots, 51$.

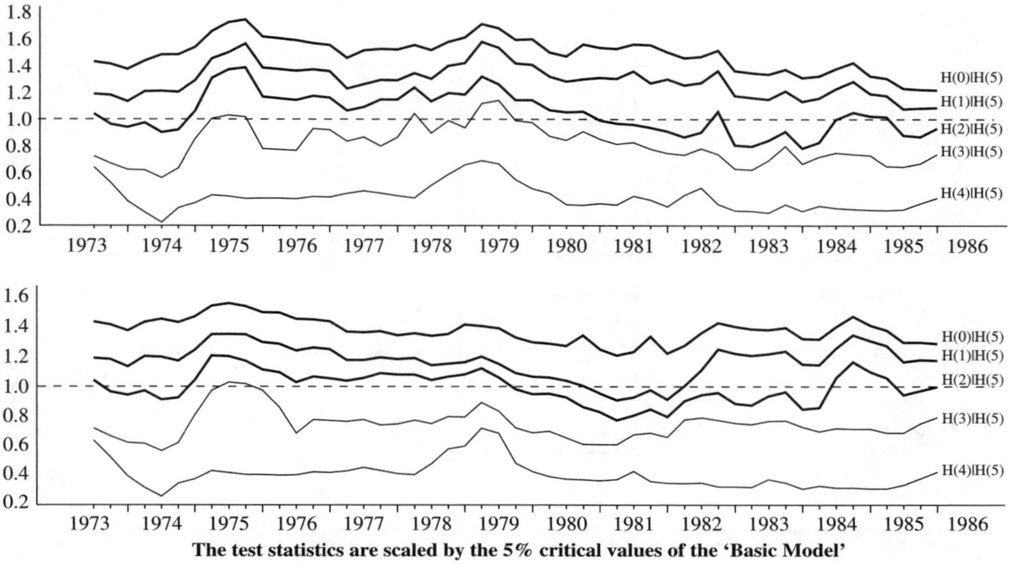

Fig 9.14 The backward recursively calculated trace test statistics for $p - r = p$, $p - 1, \ldots, 1$ scaled by the 95% quantile of the asymptotic distributions. The recursions are for (1986:1–j)–2003:1, $j = 1, \ldots, 51$.

have remained constant when adding more and more observations up to the end point of the full sample. With the forward procedures, we have no possibility of checking whether there was parameter instability in the baseline sample. In many cases, it seems quite likely that the most distant part of the sample represents a different regime, for example because the economy was more regulated. In such a case, it might be preferable to discard some of the first sample observations (or even a big chunk) from the model analysis. Even though we would like our sample to be as long as possible it is, after all, better to have a moderately sized sample with approximately constant parameters than a long sample with non-constant parameters. In the latter case, the results may not have any meaning as the statistical inference is only valid under the assumption of a constant parameter model.

The purpose of the backward recursive tests is to provide information about the possibility of non-constant parameters in the beginning of the sample period. The procedures are the same as in the forward case and will not be defined again, neither will they be given a very detailed interpretation. The main difference to the forward tests is that the baseline period is now defined to be $T_1, \ldots, T$ and the recursions are performed by adding more and more distant observations, i.e. the recursions are defined for the samples $t_1 - T$, $t_1 = T_1, T_1 - 1, T_1 - 2, \ldots, 1$. In the illustrations below, the baseline sample is chosen to be 1986:1–2003:1.

9.3.1 Log likelihood function

Figure 9.13 shows the graph of the backward tests of the log likelihood function. It is notable that the value of the test statistic is outside its 95% confidence bands for almost

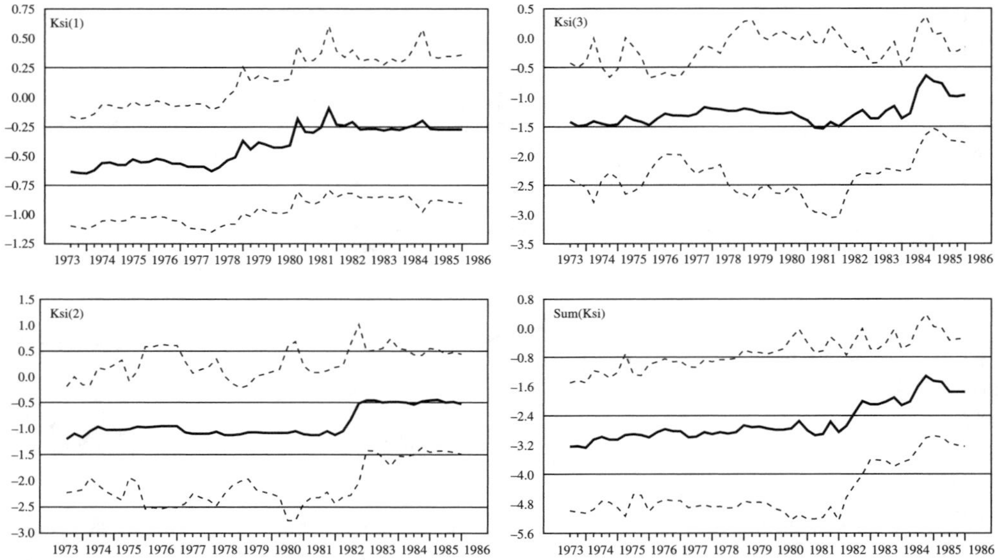

Fig 9.15 Backward recursively calculated log transformed eigenvalues.

all recursions. This is consistent with our previous finding of parameter non-constancy somewhere in the mid-1980s, possibly in just one of the cointegration relations.

9.3.2 The trace test statistics

In the lower panel, we note that the graphs are not growing, possibly even declining, from 1986 to 1981. This might be due to parameter instability or rather few observations per estimated coefficients at the beginning of the recursions. In a constant parameter model the trace test statistics should be slowly growing for all $\lambda_i \neq 0$ from the beginning of the backward recursions at 1986:1 until the full sample is covered at 1973:2. This seems roughly to be the case for the first component, whereas the picture is more blurred for the remaining ones.

9.3.3 The log transformed eigenvalues

All of the log transformed eigenvalues $\xi_i(t_1)$, $i = 1, 2, 3$, in Figure 9.15 seem to have evolved in a fairly stable manner over time, albeit with some indication of parameter instability at around 1983.

9.3.4 Fluctuations tests

The backwards recursive fluctuations tests are reported in Figure 9.16. Even though $\tau_1(t_1)$ starts from a quite high level in 1986:1, the statistic is nevertheless safely below the critical line for all t_1. Both $\tau_2(t_1)$ and $\tau_3(t_1)$ indicate parameter constancy. Thus, it is not possible to detect any deviation from constancy based on the backwards fluctuations test.

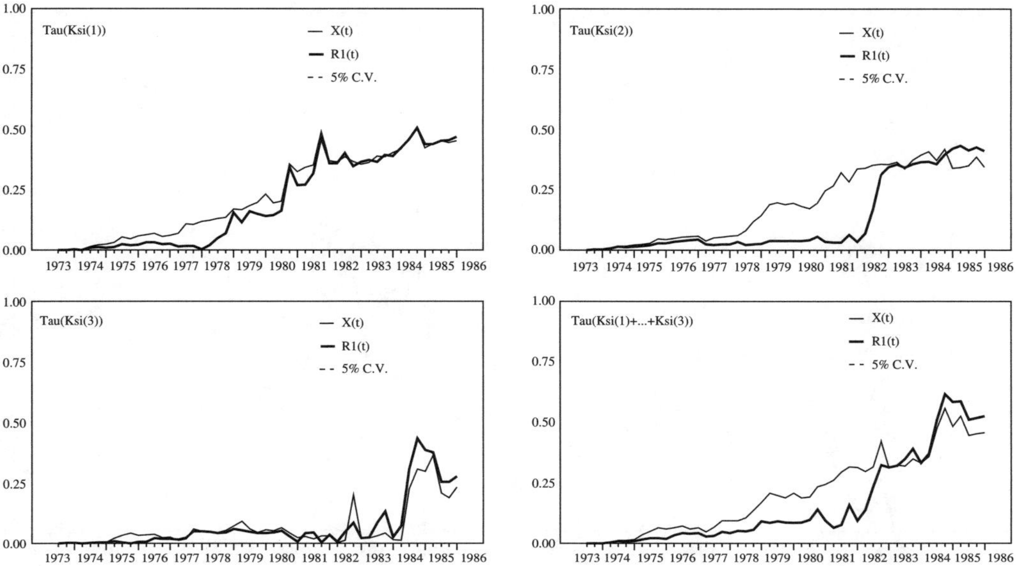

Fig 9.16 Fluctuations test calculated backwards.

9.3.5 Max test of constant $\boldsymbol{\beta}$

The recursively calculated max tests of a constant $\boldsymbol{\beta}$ graphed in Figure 9.17 do not reject constancy for any of the recursive sample periods, even though it is close to the rejection region at around 1985, implying two model regimes, 1973–1985 and 1985–2003. That the max test does not reject parameter constancy even though the log likelihood function strongly suggested non-constant parameters illustrates that the sup tests are generally very conservative.

9.3.6 Test of $\boldsymbol{\beta}_t$ equal to a known $\boldsymbol{\beta}$

As a check for constancy of $\boldsymbol{\beta}$, we have chosen the reference period to be 1983:1–2003:1. The recursions based on the **X**-form model in Figure 9.18 roughly suggest that the VAR model based on the pre-1983 observations differs from the VAR model of the reference period, whereas those based on the **R**-form suggest that the starting date of the reference sample should be chosen later than 1983:1, for example 1985:1.

9.3.7 Backward predictions tests

The one step backward prediction tests for the system in Figure 9.19 generally do not suggest predictive failure, except possibly for the starting years 1973–1974, when the economy was strongly influenced by the first oil crises. A surprising result is that the full model seems to predict better than the **R**-form.

The one step backward prediction tests in Figure 9.20 provide more detailed information on specific variables based on the full model. The prediction failure in 1973–1974 seems to be associated with money stock, inflation and the bond rate. We also note

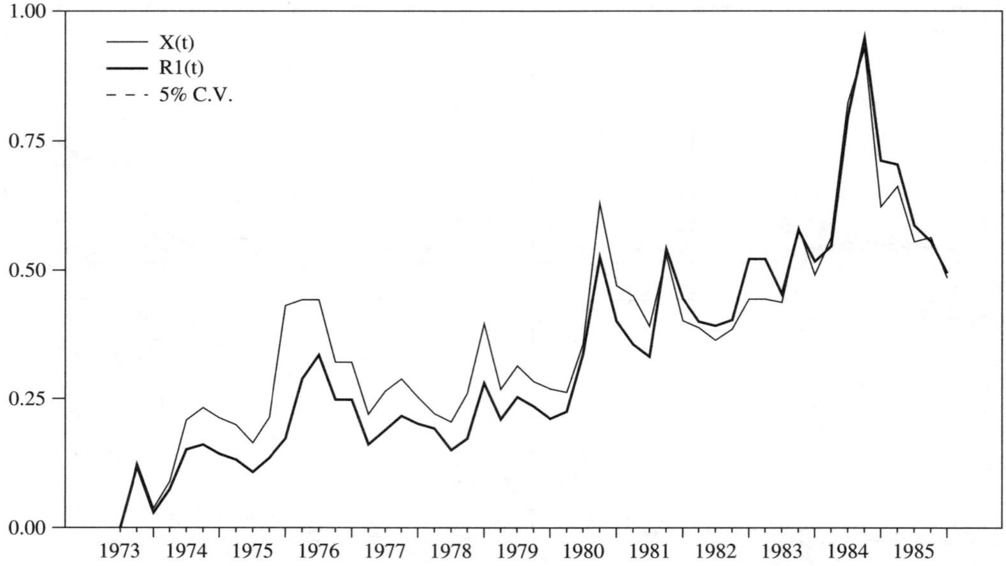

Fig 9.17 The max test of constant $\boldsymbol{\beta}$ calculated backwards.

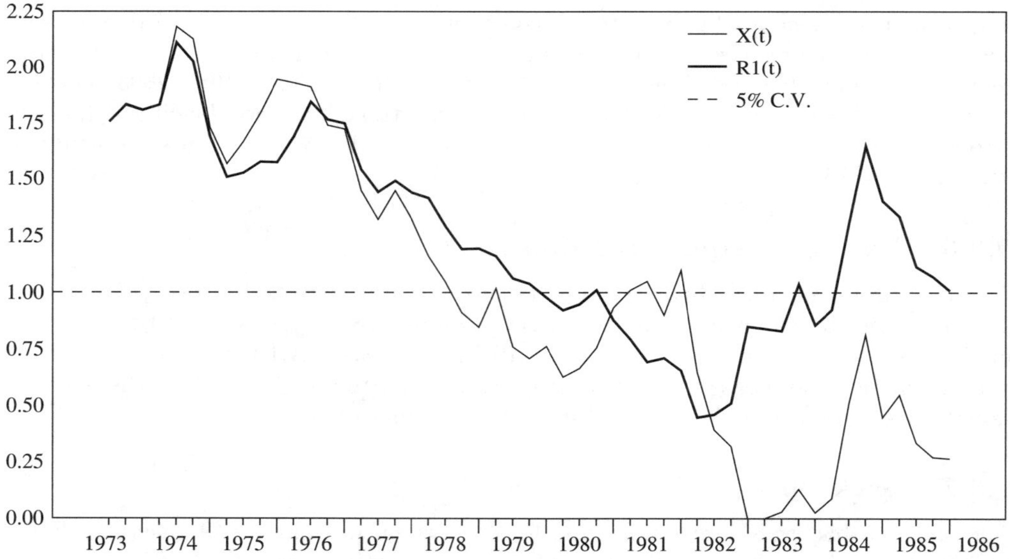

Fig 9.18 Backward recursively calculated tests of $\tilde{\beta} \subseteq sp(\hat{\boldsymbol{\beta}}_{t_1})$ where $\tilde{\beta}$ is estimated on the subsample 1983:1–2003:1.

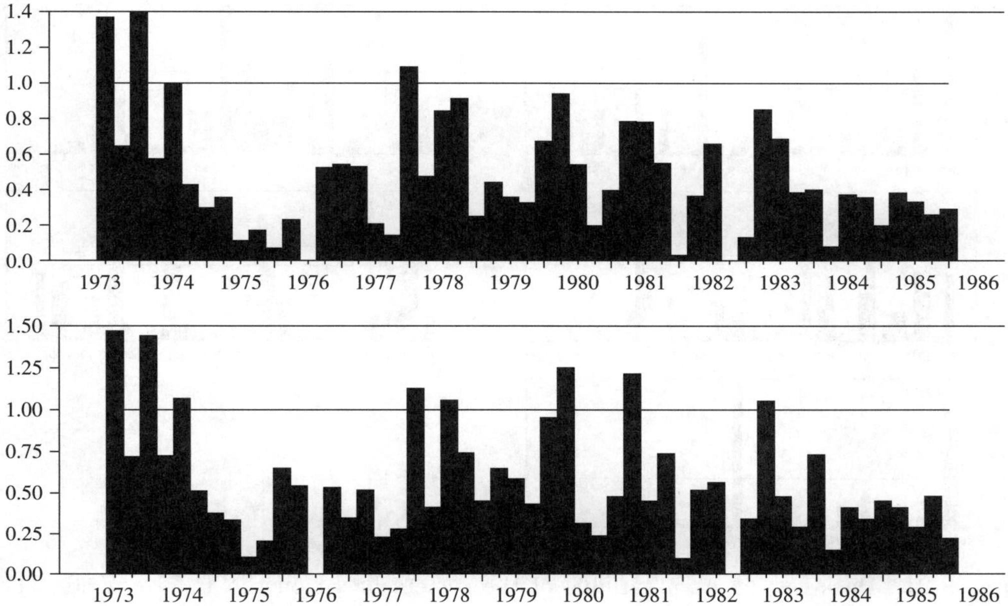

Fig 9.19 Recursively calculated prediction errors scaled by two standard errors when back-casting the system. The upper panel is for the full model and the lower panel for the **R**-form model.

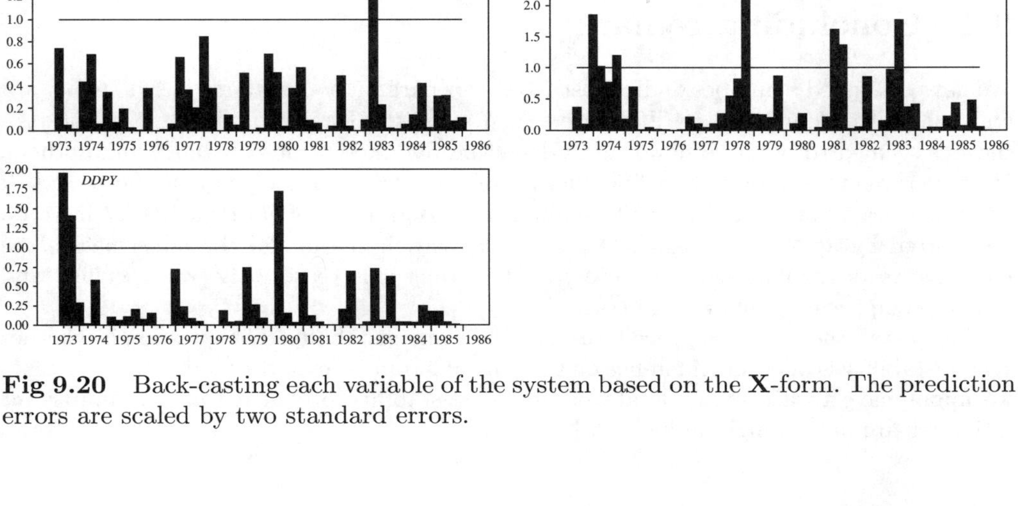

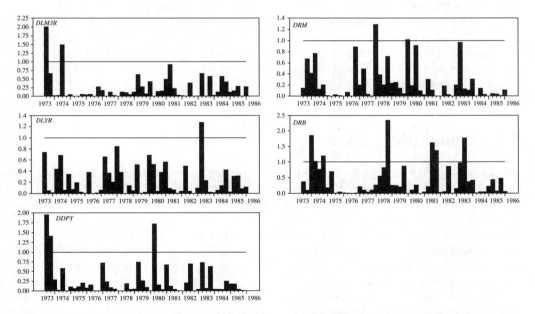

Fig 9.20 Back-casting each variable of the system based on the **X**-form. The prediction errors are scaled by two standard errors.

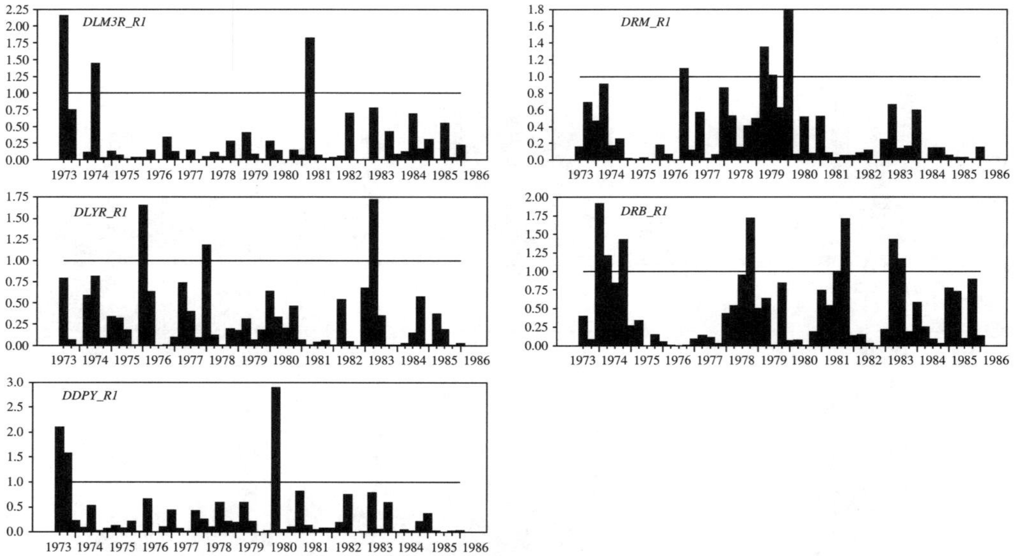

Fig 9.21 Back-casting each variable of the system based on the **R**-form VAR. The predictions errors are scaled by two standard errors.

predictive failure at around 1979–1980, when Denmark joined the EMS, and around 1983, when the restrictions on capital movements were lifted. Since the model is now back-casting the results seem to indicate that agents's forecasting behaviour at the beginning of the new regime was based on imperfect information. If they had fully understood the consequences of the new regime as it turned out to be, we would not have seen the present predictive failures. The backward predictions based on the **R**-form in Figure 9.21 essentially tell a similar story.

9.4 Concluding remarks

We have discussed a number of diagnostic tests for parameter constancy based on forward and backward recursions and illustrated them with the Danish data. Some of the procedures seemed to be more powerful in detecting parameter non-constancy than others. Taken together they provide a first picture of the empirical adequacy of the model. If there is a serious structural break in the sample period it seems quite likely that it would be spotted by at least one of the tests. Conversely, if the model (broadly) passes the recursive tests then we can be quite confident that it is reasonably well-specified and that the empirical results can be trusted.

In general, the recursive procedures will find some instability. The question is whether such instability is affecting inference on the crucial parameters of the model. In some cases we might have to accept moderate parameter instability provided that the important estimates are not strongly influenced by it.

For the Danish data the recursive procedures detected some parameter instability at around the mid-1980s. However, this instability seems to be primarily associated with the first cointegration relation essentially describing an inflation-interest rate relation. Thus, a tentative conclusion is that the determination of inflation rate might have changed after the deregulation of the capital movements in 1983. In Chapter 12 we shall further examine this hypothetical change of the cointegration properties in the inflation rate relation.

10

Testing restrictions on $\boldsymbol{\beta}$

Chapter 7 discussed the eigenvector decomposition of the long-run matrix $\mathbf{\Pi}$ and interpreted the unrestricted estimates as a convenient description of the information given by the covariances of the data. Chapter 8 discussed how to determine the cointegration rank classifying the eigenvectors into r stationary and $p-r$ non-stationary directions. The purpose of this chapter is to discuss a number of test procedures given in Johansen (1996), Chapter 7, which can be used to test various restrictions on the r stationary cointegrating relations. While the final aim is to test and impose over-identifying restrictions on the long-run structure $\boldsymbol{\beta}$, the restrictions discussed here are not identifying by themselves. Nonetheless, they imply binding restrictions on $\mathbf{\Pi} = \boldsymbol{\alpha}\boldsymbol{\beta}'$ and, hence, are testable. By systematic application of these tests one will be able to spot potentially relevant long-run relations. This greatly facilitates the identification of the long-run structure to be discussed in Chapter 12.

The organization of this chapter is as follows: Section 10.1 discusses how to formulate hypotheses as restrictions on the parameter matrices, Section 10.2 how to test the same restriction on all cointegration relations, Section 10.3 how to test the stationarity of a known $\boldsymbol{\beta}$ vector, and Section 10.4 how to test the stationarity of a cointegration relation when some of the coefficients are known and others have to be estimated.

10.1 Formulating hypotheses as restrictions on $\boldsymbol{\beta}$

Hypotheses on the cointegration vectors can be formulated in two alternative ways: either by specifying the s_i free parameters, or alternatively the m_i restrictions of each $\boldsymbol{\beta}_i$ vector. Both cases will be considered here. We first specify the constrained cointegration vector $\boldsymbol{\beta}_i^c$ in terms of the s_i free parameters $\boldsymbol{\varphi}_i$

$$\boldsymbol{\beta}^c = (\boldsymbol{\beta}_1^c, \ldots, \boldsymbol{\beta}_r^c) = (\mathbf{H}_1\boldsymbol{\varphi}_1, \ldots, \mathbf{H}_r\boldsymbol{\varphi}_r), \tag{10.1}$$

where $\boldsymbol{\varphi}_i$ is a $(s_i \times 1)$ coefficient matrix, $\mathbf{H}_i$ is a $(p1 \times s_i)$ design matrix, $p1$ is the dimension of $\tilde{\mathbf{x}}_{t-1}$ in the VAR model, and $i = 1, \ldots, r$. In this case, the design matrices define the s_i free parameters in each cointegration vector.

In the other case, we specify the restriction matrices $\mathbf{R}_i$ $(p1 \times m_i)$ which define the $m_i = p_1 - s_i$ restrictions on $\boldsymbol{\beta}_i$:

$$\mathbf{R}_1'\boldsymbol{\beta}_1 = \mathbf{0}$$
$$\vdots$$
$$\mathbf{R}_r'\boldsymbol{\beta}_r = \mathbf{0}.$$

As an illustration, consider the following specification of $\boldsymbol{\beta}'\tilde{\mathbf{x}}_t$ for the Danish data where for simplicity the trend is excluded as it will be shown to be long-run excludable, i.e. $\tilde{\mathbf{x}}_t' = [m_t^r, y_t^r, \Delta p_t, R_{m,t}, R_{b,t}, D_s831_t]$:

$$\begin{aligned}
\boldsymbol{\beta}_1'\tilde{\mathbf{x}}_t &= m_t^r - y_t^r - b_1(R_{m,t} - R_{b,t}) - b_2 D_s 831_t \\
\boldsymbol{\beta}_2'\tilde{\mathbf{x}}_t &= y_t^r - b_3(\Delta p_t - R_{b,t}) \\
\boldsymbol{\beta}_3'\tilde{\mathbf{x}}_t &= (R_{m,t} - R_{b,t}) + b_4 D_s 831_t.
\end{aligned}$$

The first cointegration relation has three free parameters $(s_1 = 3)$,[1] corresponding to three restrictions $(m_1 = 3)$. The second and the third relation have two free parameters $(s_2 = s_3 = 2)$, corresponding to four restrictions $(m_2 = m_3 = 4)$. The three restricted vectors $\mathbf{H}_i\boldsymbol{\varphi}_i$ take the following form:

$$\boldsymbol{\beta}_1 = \mathbf{H}_1\boldsymbol{\varphi}_1 = \begin{bmatrix} 1 & 0 & 0 \\ -1 & 0 & 0 \\ 0 & 0 & 0 \\ 0 & 1 & 0 \\ 0 & -1 & 0 \\ 0 & 0 & 1 \end{bmatrix} \begin{bmatrix} \varphi_{11} \\ \varphi_{12} \\ \varphi_{13} \end{bmatrix},$$

$$\boldsymbol{\beta}_2 = \mathbf{H}_2\boldsymbol{\varphi}_2 = \begin{bmatrix} 0 & 0 \\ 1 & 0 \\ 0 & 1 \\ 0 & 0 \\ 0 & -1 \\ 0 & 0 \end{bmatrix} \begin{bmatrix} \varphi_{21} \\ \varphi_{22} \end{bmatrix},$$

$$\boldsymbol{\beta}_3 = \mathbf{H}_3\boldsymbol{\varphi}_3 = \begin{bmatrix} 0 & 0 \\ 0 & 0 \\ 0 & 0 \\ 1 & 0 \\ -1 & 0 \\ 0 & 1 \end{bmatrix} \begin{bmatrix} \varphi_{31} \\ \varphi_{32} \end{bmatrix}.$$

[1]Note that the normalization coefficient to $(m_t^r - y_t^r)$ is counted as a free parameter, as it corresponds to an unrestricted α coefficient.

Note that $\varphi_{11} = \beta_{11} = -\beta_{12}$, $\varphi_{12} = \beta_{14} = -\beta_{15}$, $\varphi_{13} = \beta_{16}$. After normalization on real money in the first relation, the normalized coefficients become $b_1 = -\varphi_{12}/\varphi_{11}$, $b_2 = -\varphi_{13}/\varphi_{11}$ and similarly for the remaining relations.

We shall now formulate the above relations as restrictions on the β_{ij} coefficients. They are as follows:

$$\mathbf{R}_1'\boldsymbol{\beta}_1 = \begin{bmatrix} 1 & 1 & 0 & 0 & 0 & 0 \\ 0 & 0 & 1 & 0 & 0 & 0 \\ 0 & 0 & 0 & 1 & 1 & 0 \end{bmatrix} \begin{bmatrix} \beta_{11} \\ \beta_{12} \\ \beta_{13} \\ \beta_{14} \\ \beta_{15} \\ \beta_{16} \end{bmatrix} = \mathbf{0},$$

$$\mathbf{R}_2'\boldsymbol{\beta}_2 = \begin{bmatrix} 1 & 0 & 0 & 0 & 0 & 0 \\ 0 & 0 & 1 & 0 & 1 & 0 \\ 0 & 0 & 0 & 1 & 0 & 0 \\ 0 & 0 & 0 & 0 & 0 & 1 \end{bmatrix} \begin{bmatrix} \beta_{21} \\ \beta_{22} \\ \beta_{23} \\ \beta_{24} \\ \beta_{25} \\ \beta_{26} \end{bmatrix} = \mathbf{0},$$

$$\mathbf{R}_3'\boldsymbol{\beta}_3 = \begin{bmatrix} 1 & 0 & 0 & 0 & 0 & 0 \\ 0 & 1 & 0 & 0 & 0 & 0 \\ 0 & 0 & 1 & 0 & 0 & 0 \\ 0 & 0 & 0 & 1 & 1 & 0 \end{bmatrix} \begin{bmatrix} \beta_{31} \\ \beta_{32} \\ \beta_{33} \\ \beta_{34} \\ \beta_{35} \\ \beta_{36} \end{bmatrix} = \mathbf{0}.$$

Note that $\mathbf{R}_i = \mathbf{H}_{\perp,i}$, i.e. $\mathbf{R}_i'\mathbf{H}_i = \mathbf{0}$.

After the rank has been determined, all tests are about stationarity, i.e. the null hypothesis is now that a restricted linear combination of the vector process $\boldsymbol{\beta}_i^c$ is stationary. This is in contrast to the rank test where the null hypothesis was a unit root. Under the assumption that the rank was correctly chosen, the matrix $\mathbf{\Pi} = \boldsymbol{\alpha}\boldsymbol{\beta}'$, where $\boldsymbol{\alpha}$ and $\boldsymbol{\beta}$ are of dimension r, describes the r stationary directions $\boldsymbol{\beta}$. Hence, testing restrictions on $\boldsymbol{\beta}$ is the same as asking whether a restricted vector $\boldsymbol{\beta}_i^c$ lies in the 'stationarity space' spanned by $\boldsymbol{\beta}$. When a test rejects, it means that the restricted vector points outside the 'stationarity space'.

10.2 Same restriction on all $\boldsymbol{\beta}$

Many empirical models contain linear transformations of economic variables, such as money velocity rather than money and income, profit share rather than output, prices and wages, real interest rate, rather than nominal interest rate and inflation. Such transformations might be relevant for one specific long-run relation, but not necessarily for the full system. Therefore, it is always a good idea first to test such implicit restrictions in a VAR model formulated in the individual variables. If the restrictions are accepted one can reformulate the VAR model in the transformed variables without losing information, otherwise one should impose the restriction on the relevant relation, but not on the system as a whole. The test of the same restriction on all $\boldsymbol{\beta}_i$ is given in Johansen (1996), Section 7.2.1.

One example of this test is the test of long-run exclusion of a variable, i.e. a zero row restriction on $\boldsymbol{\beta}$. If accepted, the variable is not needed in the cointegration space and can be omitted altogether from the long-run relations. Another example is the test of long-run price homogeneity between some (or all) of the variables. For example, we may wish to test whether nominal money and prices are long-run homogeneous in all cointegration relations. If accepted, we can re-specify the long-run relations directly in real money and (as will be shown in Chapter 16) a nominal growth rate.

Although these are testable hypotheses, they are not identifying as will be shown in Chapter 12. This is because they impose identical restrictions on all cointegration relations. All $\mathbf{H}_i$ (or $\mathbf{R}_i$), $i = 1, \ldots, r$, are identical and we can formulate the hypothesis as:

$$\mathbf{H}^c(r) : \boldsymbol{\beta}^c = (\mathbf{H}\boldsymbol{\varphi}_1, \ldots, \mathbf{H}\boldsymbol{\varphi}_r) = \mathbf{H}\boldsymbol{\varphi} \tag{10.2}$$

where $\boldsymbol{\beta}^c$ is $p1 \times r$, $\mathbf{H}$ is $p1 \times s$, $\boldsymbol{\varphi}$ is $s \times r$ and s is the number of unrestricted coefficients in each vector, or alternatively as:

$$\mathbf{H}^c(r) : \mathbf{R}'\boldsymbol{\beta} = \mathbf{0}$$

where $\mathbf{R}$ is $p1 \times m$ and m is the number of restrictions imposed on each vector. The hypothesis $\mathcal{H}^c(r)$ is tested against $\mathcal{H}(r)$: $\boldsymbol{\beta}$ unrestricted, i.e. we test the following restricted model:

$$\Delta \mathbf{x}_t = \boldsymbol{\alpha}\boldsymbol{\varphi}'\mathbf{H}'\tilde{\mathbf{x}}_{t-1} + \sum_{i=1}^{k-1} \boldsymbol{\Gamma}_i \Delta \mathbf{x}_{t-i} + \boldsymbol{\mu}_0 + \boldsymbol{\varepsilon}_t. \tag{10.3}$$

The hypothesis (10.2) implies a transformation of the data vector, $\mathbf{H}'\tilde{\mathbf{x}}_t$, as the following example illustrates. Assume that we wish to test the hypothesis of long-run proportionality between m^r and y^r in all cointegration relations specified by the following design matrix $\mathbf{H}'$:

$$\mathbf{H}' = \begin{bmatrix} 1 & -1 & 0 & 0 & 0 & 0 \\ 0 & 0 & 1 & 0 & 0 & 0 \\ 0 & 0 & 0 & 1 & 0 & 0 \\ 0 & 0 & 0 & 0 & 1 & 0 \\ 0 & 0 & 0 & 0 & 0 & 1 \end{bmatrix}, \quad \boldsymbol{\varphi} = \begin{bmatrix} \varphi_{11} & \varphi_{12} & \varphi_{13} \\ \varphi_{21} & \varphi_{22} & \varphi_{23} \\ \varphi_{31} & \varphi_{32} & \varphi_{33} \\ \varphi_{41} & \varphi_{42} & \varphi_{43} \\ \varphi_{51} & \varphi_{52} & \varphi_{53} \end{bmatrix}.$$

The transformed data vector becomes:

$$\mathbf{H}'\mathbf{x}_t = \begin{bmatrix} (m^r - y^r)_t \\ \Delta p_t \\ R_{m,t} \\ R_{b,t} \\ D_s831_t \end{bmatrix}.$$

If this restriction is accepted, all cointegrating relations can be expressed as a function of the liquidity ratio $(m^r - y^r)_t$. Thus, the coefficient matrix, $\boldsymbol{\varphi}$, is now (5×3) instead of (6×3).

The likelihood ratio test procedure is derived by calculating the ratio between the value of the likelihood function in the restricted and unrestricted model. The maximum likelihood of the unrestricted model is:

$$L_{\max}^{-2/T}(\mathcal{H}(r)) = |\mathbf{S}_{00}| \prod_{i=1}^{r} (1 - \hat{\lambda}_i).$$

From (10.3), we can find the restricted ML estimator in a similar manner as for the unrestricted model, i.e., by solving the reduced-rank regression of $\Delta\mathbf{x}_t$ on $\mathbf{H}'\mathbf{x}_{t-1}$ corrected for the short-run dynamics:

$$\left|\lambda\mathbf{H}'\mathbf{S}_{11}\mathbf{H} - \mathbf{H}'\mathbf{S}_{10}\mathbf{S}_{00}^{-1}\mathbf{S}_{01}\mathbf{H}\right| = 0.$$

This gives $p - m$ eigenvalues $\lambda_1^c, \lambda_2^c, \dots, \lambda_{p-m}^c$ and the eigenvectors $\mathbf{v}_1^c, \mathbf{v}_2^c, \dots, \mathbf{v}_{p-m}^c$.

Note that when we impose m restrictions on the p 'endogenous' variables $\mathbf{x}_t$, the constrained model will have fewer eigenvalues than the unrestricted model. Since $p - m \geq r$, it means that we can only impose a maximum of $p - r$ restrictions on the $\mathbf{x}_t$ variables, whereas there is no such constraint on the deterministic variables. In the money demand example with $r = 3$ and $p - r = 2$, we can, therefore, impose at most two restrictions on the $\mathbf{x}_t$ variables. For example, it would be possible to test whether all long-run relations could be expressed in terms of the liquidity ratio, $(m^r - y^r)$ and the interest rate spread $(R_m - R_b)$. Imposing one more restriction, like the exclusion of Δp, would make the dimension of $p - m = 2$ which would lead to a violation of the condition $p - m \geq r = 3$. However, imposing a zero restriction on the shift dummy, D_s831_t, does not violate the rank condition. For example, the transformed data vector $\mathbf{x}_t'\mathbf{H} = [(m^r - y^r)_t, \Delta p_t, (R_m - R_b)_t]$ would produce $r = 3$ eigenvalues and, therefore, be testable.

The ML estimator of $\boldsymbol{\beta}$ is found by choosing $\hat{\boldsymbol{\varphi}} = [\hat{\boldsymbol{\varphi}}_1, \hat{\boldsymbol{\varphi}}_2, \dots, \hat{\boldsymbol{\varphi}}_r]$ and then transforming the vectors back to $\hat{\boldsymbol{\beta}}^c = \mathbf{H}\hat{\boldsymbol{\varphi}}$. Because these restrictions are not identifying, the estimates of the constrained cointegration relations are based on the normalization condition and the ordering of the eigenvalues as discussed in Section 7.4.

The LR test statistic is calculated as:

$$\Lambda = \left(\frac{L_{\max}\mathcal{H}^c(r)}{L_{\max}\mathcal{H}(r)}\right) = \left(\frac{|\mathbf{S}_{00}| \times (1 - \lambda_1^c)(1 - \hat{\lambda}_2^c)\cdots(1 - \hat{\lambda}_r^c)}{|\mathbf{S}_{00}| \times (1 - \hat{\lambda}_1)(1 - \hat{\lambda}_2)\cdots(1 - \hat{\lambda}_r)}\right)^{-\frac{T}{2}}$$

i.e.

$$-2\ln\Lambda = T\{\ln(1 - \lambda_1^c) - \ln(1 - \hat{\lambda}_1) + \cdots + \ln(1 - \hat{\lambda}_r^c) - \ln(1 - \hat{\lambda}_r)\}.$$

It is asymptotically distributed as $\chi^2(\nu)$ where $\nu = rm$. There are rm degrees of freedom because we have imposed m restrictions on each of the r cointegration vectors.

Chapter 8 gave an interpretation of an eigenvalue λ_i as the squared correlation coefficients between a linear combination of the stationary part of the vector process and a linear combination of the non-stationary part. Thus, if $\hat{\lambda}_i^c$ becomes very small as a result of imposing the restrictions $\mathbf{R}_i$, it is a sign that the restricted cointegration relation has become non-stationary. Another way of expressing this is by recalling that $\text{diag}(\hat{\lambda}_1, \ldots, \hat{\lambda}_r) = \hat{\boldsymbol{\alpha}}'\mathbf{S}_{00}^{-1}\hat{\boldsymbol{\alpha}}$, i.e. $\hat{\lambda}_i$ is related to the estimated $\boldsymbol{\alpha}_i$. Therefore, the rejection of the hypothesis $\boldsymbol{\beta} = \mathbf{H}\boldsymbol{\varphi}$ often implies that at least one of the restricted relations is no longer significantly mean-reverting and the coefficients of the corresponding $\boldsymbol{\alpha}_i$ are likely to be statistically insignificant.

10.2.1 Illustrations

Chapter 6 discussed the role of the deterministic components in the model and showed that if there are linear trends in the data, the most general formulation is to include a linear trend in the cointegration relations and an unrestricted constant in the VAR equations. As discussed in Chapter 8, this formulation delivers 'similar' inference based on the trace test for cointegration rank. After the rank is determined, the first step should be to test whether the linear trend is needed in the cointegration relations, i.e., whether we can impose a zero restriction on the trend coefficient in all cointegrating relations.

Example 1 A test of long-run exclusion of a linear trend in the cointegration relations for $\tilde{\mathbf{x}}_t' = [m_t^r, y_t^r, \Delta p_t, R_{m,t}, R_{b,t}, D_s831_t, t]$.

$$\mathcal{H}_1 : \boldsymbol{\beta}^c = \mathbf{H}\boldsymbol{\varphi} \text{ or } \mathbf{R}'\boldsymbol{\beta} = 0$$

where

$$\mathbf{H} = \begin{bmatrix} 1 & 0 & 0 & 0 & 0 & 0 \\ 0 & 1 & 0 & 0 & 0 & 0 \\ 0 & 0 & 1 & 0 & 0 & 0 \\ 0 & 0 & 0 & 1 & 0 & 0 \\ 0 & 0 & 0 & 0 & 1 & 0 \\ 0 & 0 & 0 & 0 & 0 & 1 \\ 0 & 0 & 0 & 0 & 0 & 0 \end{bmatrix}, \quad \boldsymbol{\varphi} = \begin{bmatrix} \varphi_{11} & \varphi_{12} & \varphi_{13} \\ \varphi_{21} & \varphi_{22} & \varphi_{23} \\ \varphi_{31} & \varphi_{32} & \varphi_{33} \\ \varphi_{41} & \varphi_{42} & \varphi_{43} \\ \varphi_{51} & \varphi_{52} & \varphi_{53} \\ \varphi_{61} & \varphi_{62} & \varphi_{63} \end{bmatrix}$$

and

$$\mathbf{R}' = [0, 0, 0, 0, 0, 0, 1].$$

The design matrix $\mathbf{H}$ is specified to make the last row, corresponding to the trend, equal to zero, whereas the restriction matrix $\mathbf{R}$ is specified to make the last coefficient row of $\boldsymbol{\beta}$ equal to zero. With few restrictions, the $\mathbf{R}$ formulation is more parsimonious than the $\mathbf{H}$ formulation. The restricted estimates $\hat{\boldsymbol{\beta}}^c$ under $\mathcal{H}_1$ reported in Table 10.1 shows that they have hardly changed compared to the unrestricted $\hat{\boldsymbol{\beta}}$ reported at the top of the table. It is, therefore, not surprising that the three zero restrictions on the trend can be accepted with a p-value as high as 0.82. We conclude that the appropriate VAR specification corresponds to case 3 in Section 6.3, i.e., no trend in the cointegration relations and an unrestricted constant in the model.

When testing the hypothesis of long-run exclusion of strongly correlated variables, we sometimes find that long-run exclusion of a variable is accepted even though the variable turns out to be very important in at least one of the long-run relations. Thus, some caution is needed with this test, in particular when the variables are strongly collinear.

Example 2 A test of long-run exclusion of the shift dummy D_s831_t in the cointegration relations $\boldsymbol{\beta}'\tilde{\mathbf{x}}_t$ with $\tilde{\mathbf{x}}_t' = [m_t^r, y_t^r, \Delta p_t, R_{m,t}, R_{b,t}, D_s831_t, t]$. At around this date, the graphs of the variables in levels and differences reported in Section 3.2 showed a major shift in the level of money stock, a less pronounced shift in the level of real aggregate demand, and a big blip in the differences of the bond rate. We shall now test whether the mean shift cancels or not in the cointegration relations. The specification of the **H** and the **R** matrices are similar to those in the test for long-run exclusion of the trend and will not be separately reported. From Table 10.1 we note that the hypothesis of long-run exclusion of the shift dummy D_s831_t was strongly rejected with a p-value of 0.00.

Comparing the $\mathcal{H}_2$ restricted estimates with the unrestricted estimates shows that $\hat{\boldsymbol{\beta}}_1^c$ has hardly changed (implying that the shift dummy was not needed in this relation), whereas this is clearly not the case with $\hat{\boldsymbol{\beta}}_2^c$ and $\hat{\boldsymbol{\beta}}_3^c$. Thus, the estimates of both the money demand relation and the interest rate relation are sensitive to whether we include the shift dummy or not. The income coefficient in $\hat{\boldsymbol{\beta}}_2^c$ is now -1.72 instead of -1.02, the deposit rate coefficient has increased approximately five times, and the bond rate has changed sign. Thus, since the shift to the new (deregulated) equilibrium level of money stock was not accompanied by a corresponding shift in the level of real aggregate income, we need to include the D_s831 dummy in the second cointegration relation. If this is not done, then the statistical analysis will attempt to account for the extraordinary increase in money stock by an (incorrect) increase in the real income and the interest rate coefficients.

The deregulation of capital movements in 1983:1 also affected the Danish interest rates, in particular the long-term bond rate. As a result of the increased foreign demand for Danish bonds, the previously very high yield on bonds dropped dramatically and, after a period of increased volatility, settled down on a much lower level where it has stayed since then. Figure 3.3 in Chapter 3 illustrated this graphically. The effect was a marked decrease in the interest rate spread which gradually stabilized at a much lower level in the new deregulated regime. Figure 2.5 in Chapter 2 illustrates this graphically. Without accounting for this shift in the equilibrium level between the interest rates (in the risk premium), the relationship between the two interest rates becomes negative as $\boldsymbol{\beta}_3^c$ demonstrates.

This serves as an illustration of the importance of appropriately accounting for major reforms and interventions in order not to bias the coefficient estimates of the economic steady-state relations.

Example 3 is a test of long-run homogeneity between m^r and y^r in all cointegrating relations for $\tilde{\mathbf{x}}_t' = [m_t^r, y_t^r, \Delta p_t, R_{m,t}, R_{b,t}, D_s831_t, t]$. Table 10.1 shows that the hypothesis $\mathcal{H}_3$ can be accepted with a p-value of 0.34. The design matrices **H** and **R** have the following form:

$$\mathbf{H} = \begin{bmatrix} 1 & 0 & 0 & 0 & 0 & 0 \\ -1 & 0 & 0 & 0 & 0 & 0 \\ 0 & 1 & 0 & 0 & 0 & 0 \\ 0 & 0 & 1 & 0 & 0 & 0 \\ 0 & 0 & 0 & 1 & 0 & 0 \\ 0 & 0 & 0 & 0 & 1 & 0 \\ 0 & 0 & 0 & 0 & 0 & 1 \end{bmatrix}, \quad \mathbf{R}' = \begin{bmatrix} 1 & 1 & 0 & 0 & 0 & 0 & 0 \end{bmatrix}.$$

The restricted estimates are reported in Table 10.1 under $\mathcal{H}_3$ and show that $\hat{\boldsymbol{\beta}}^c$ does not differ very much from the unrestricted $\hat{\boldsymbol{\beta}}$. However, we note that the change of the real income coefficient from 1.22 to 1.00 has been compensated by a small increase in the coefficient of the linear trend. Thus, there might be a trade-off between homogeneity and a linear trend, contra a zero trend and no homogeneity restriction in the money demand relation. Except for the second cointegration relation, the coefficients to real money and real income are very small, suggesting that the liquidity ratio might be significant just in one of the three cointegration relations. Thus, two of the acceptable long-run homogeneity restrictions seem to be describing a '0, 0' relationship.

Example 4 The test of the interest rate spread in all cointegration relations is similar to the previous example, and the **H** and **R** matrices will not be separately reported. Table 10.1 shows that the hypothesis $\mathcal{H}_4$ was accepted with a p-value of 0.18. Comparing the restricted estimates with the unrestricted estimates reveals that the first and the third restricted cointegration relation have changed to some extent, whereas the second restricted relation is almost identical to the unrestricted. The violation of the spread restriction in the first relation suggests that inflation rate is related not just to the interest rate spread, but also the level of nominal interest rates.

Example 5 is a joint test of $\mathcal{H}_1$ and $\mathcal{H}_3$, both of which were individually accepted. Because the individual tests are not independent, the joint test is not generally the sum of $\mathcal{H}_1$ and $\mathcal{H}_3$. It frequently happens that the joint test rejects, even though the individual tests are accepted. Table 10.1 shows that the hypothesis $\mathcal{H}_5$ was accepted with a p-value of 0.15. The design matrices **H** and **R** are formulated as:

$$\mathbf{H} = \begin{bmatrix} 1 & 0 & 0 & 0 & 0 \\ -1 & 0 & 0 & 0 & 0 \\ 0 & 1 & 0 & 0 & 0 \\ 0 & 0 & 1 & 0 & 0 \\ 0 & 0 & 0 & 1 & 0 \\ 0 & 0 & 0 & 0 & 1 \\ 0 & 0 & 0 & 0 & 0 \end{bmatrix}, \quad \mathbf{R}' = \begin{bmatrix} 1 & 1 & 0 & 0 & 0 & 0 & 0 \\ 0 & 0 & 0 & 0 & 0 & 0 & 1 \end{bmatrix}.$$

Example 6 is a joint test of $\mathcal{H}_1$, $\mathcal{H}_3$, and $\mathcal{H}_4$, all of which were individually accepted. The joint hypothesis was borderline accepted with a p-value of 0.05. Note that the condition for maximum constraints on the variables $\mathbf{x}_t$ has now been reached.

We have given several examples of restrictions which were acceptable and one example, the exclusion of the shift dummy, which was not. In the latter case, it was quite easy to see why the restriction violated the information in the data. This was because the unrestricted cointegration relations were roughly interpretable as plausible steady-state relations. This is far from always the case. When a hypothesis is rejected we often have no clue why this was so. This is a problem, as we need to understand why a restriction rejects to be able to re-specify the hypothesis in a more adequate way.

A comparison of the unrestricted $\hat{\boldsymbol{\Pi}}$ with the restricted $\hat{\boldsymbol{\Pi}}^c$ matrix is often useful for this purpose based on the following logic: If the imposed restrictions are acceptable, then the constrained $\hat{\boldsymbol{\Pi}}^c = \hat{\boldsymbol{\alpha}}^c(\hat{\boldsymbol{\beta}}^c)' \approx \hat{\boldsymbol{\alpha}}\hat{\boldsymbol{\beta}}' = \hat{\boldsymbol{\Pi}}$, i.e. the constrained cointegration relations and the corresponding weights should approximately reproduce the unrestricted $\hat{\boldsymbol{\Pi}}$.

Table 10.1 Tests of same restriction on all cointegration relations.

	m^r	y^r	Δp	R_m	R_b	D_s831	Trend
Unrestricted estimates							
β_1'	0.06	−0.03	1.00	−0.29	0.57	−0.002	0.000
β_2'	1.00	−1.02	−3.45	−8.51	8.00	−0.24	−0.001
β_3'	−0.00	0.02	0.02	1.00	−0.62	−0.01	−0.000
$\mathcal{H}_1 : \boldsymbol{\beta}_{7\cdot} = 0,\ \chi^2(3) = 0.92[0.82]$							
$\beta_1^{c\prime}$	0.07	−0.03	1.00	−0.29	0.59	−0.002	**0.0**
$\beta_2^{c\prime}$	1.00	−1.22	−3.71	−10.39	8.82	−0.25	**0.0**
$\beta_3^{c\prime}$	−0.00	0.02	0.01	1.00	−0.64	−0.00	**0.0**
$\mathcal{H}_2 : \boldsymbol{\beta}_{6\cdot} = 0,\ \chi^2(3) = 19.08[0.00]$							
$\beta_1^{c\prime}$	0.06	−0.03	1.00	−0.32	0.56	**0.0**	0.00
$\beta_2^{c\prime}$	1.00	−1.72	−3.41	−42.2	28.6	**0.0**	−0.00
$\beta_3^{c\prime}$	0.08	0.14	0.09	1.00	2.11	**0.0**	−0.00
$\mathcal{H}_3 : \boldsymbol{\beta}_{1\cdot} = -\boldsymbol{\beta}_{2\cdot},\ \chi^2(3) = 3.36[0.34]$							
$\beta_1^{c\prime}$	**0.06**	**−0.06**	1.00	−0.57	0.59	−0.00	0.000
$\beta_2^{c\prime}$	**1.00**	**−1.00**	−3.46	−8.07	7.82	−0.25	−0.001
$\beta_3^{c\prime}$	**−0.01**	**0.01**	0.03	1.00	−0.76	−0.01	0.000
$\mathcal{H}_4 : \boldsymbol{\beta}_{4\cdot} = -\boldsymbol{\beta}_{5\cdot},\ \chi^2(3) = 4.90[0.18]$							
$\beta_1^{c\prime}$	0.06	−0.05	1.00	**−0.64**	**0.64**	−0.00	0.000
$\beta_2^{c\prime}$	1.00	−1.00	−3.45	**−7.61**	**7.61**	−0.25	−0.001
$\beta_3^{c\prime}$	−0.02	0.02	0.03	**1.00**	**−1.00**	−0.01	0.000
$\mathcal{H}_5 : \boldsymbol{\beta}_{1\cdot} = -\boldsymbol{\beta}_{2\cdot}$ and $\boldsymbol{\beta}_{7\cdot} = 0,\ \chi^2(6) = 9.36[0.15]$							
$\beta_1^{c\prime}$	**0.08**	**−0.08**	1.00	−1.30	0.91	0.001	**0.0**
$\beta_2^{c\prime}$	**1.00**	**−1.00**	−4.56	−1.81	5.21	−0.315	**0.0**
$\beta_3^{c\prime}$	**−0.01**	**0.01**	0.07	1.00	−0.87	−0.004	**0.0**
$\mathcal{H}_6 : \boldsymbol{\beta}_{1\cdot} = -\boldsymbol{\beta}_{2\cdot}, \boldsymbol{\beta}_{4\cdot} = -\boldsymbol{\beta}_{5\cdot}$ and $\boldsymbol{\beta}_{7\cdot} = 0,\ \chi^2(9) = 16.52[0.05]$							
$\beta_1^{c\prime}$	**0.12**	**−0.12**	1.00	**−0.89**	**0.89**	−0.008	**0.0**
$\beta_2^{c\prime}$	**1.00**	**−1.00**	−7.27	**−11.36**	**11.36**	−0.323	**0.0**
$\beta_3^{c\prime}$	**−0.02**	**0.02**	−0.03	**1.00**	**−1.00**	−0.009	**0.0**

If the restrictions are not acceptable, then $\hat{\boldsymbol{\Pi}}^c = \hat{\boldsymbol{\alpha}}^c(\hat{\boldsymbol{\beta}}^c)' \neq \hat{\boldsymbol{\alpha}}\hat{\boldsymbol{\beta}}' = \hat{\boldsymbol{\Pi}}$. In some cases when the imposed restrictions are only borderline acceptable (as was the case with $\mathcal{H}_6$ in Table 10.1), it is often useful to know whether the constrained model suppresses some valuable information in the unconstrained model. Before adopting the constrained model it is, therefore, a good idea to compare the restricted and the unrestricted $\boldsymbol{\Pi}$ matrices. To illustrate this, Table 10.2 reports the restricted $\hat{\boldsymbol{\Pi}}^c$ under $\mathcal{H}_6$ and the unrestricted $\hat{\boldsymbol{\Pi}}$.

Table 10.2 Comparing the combined effects of restricted (R) and unrestricted (UR) cointegration relations for $r = 3$.

	Comparing $\hat{\mathbf{\Pi}}^c = \hat{\boldsymbol{\alpha}}^c \hat{\boldsymbol{\beta}}^{c\prime}$ (R) under $\mathcal{H}_6$ with $\hat{\mathbf{\Pi}} = \hat{\boldsymbol{\alpha}}\hat{\boldsymbol{\beta}}'$ (UR)							
	Eq.\var.	m^r	y^r	Δp	R_m	R_b	D_s831	Trend
R	Δm^r	−0.23 [−4.79]	0.23 [4.79]	−0.33 [−0.87]	2.91 [3.35]	−2.91 [−3.35]	0.03 [2.58]	0 [NA]
UR	Δm^r	−0.23 [−4.78]	0.22 [4.47]	−0.50 [−1.15]	2.80 [2.51]	−2.56 [−3.35]	0.03 [2.91]	0.00 [0.60]
R	Δy^r	0.06 [2.02]	**−0.06** [−2.02]	−0.03 [−0.13]	**−0.89** [−1.68]	**0.89** [1.68]	−0.01 [−1.14]	0 [NA]
UR	Δy^r	0.05 [1.78]	**−0.09** [−2.89]	−0.26 [−1.00]	**−1.93** [−2.90]	**1.31** [2.86]	−0.00 [−0.46]	0.0000 [0.46]
R	$\Delta^2 p$	−0.01 [−0.36]	0.01 [0.36]	−0.66 [−5.04]	−0.20 [−0.66]	0.20 [0.66]	−0.01 [−1.96]	0 [NA]
UR	$\Delta^2 p$	−0.01 [−0.50]	−0.02 [−1.23]	−0.84 [−5.69]	−0.41 [−1.07]	0.08 [0.31]	−0.01 [−1.56]	**−0.0000** [−2.77]
R	ΔR_m	−0.00 [−0.55]	0.00 [0.55]	0.02 [1.26]	−0.03 [−0.78]	0.03 [0.78]	0.00 [2.31]	0 [NA]
UR	ΔR_m	−0.00 [−0.81]	0.00 [0.08]	0.03 [1.35]	−0.08 [−1.58]	0.05 [1.36]	0.00 [2.63]	**0.0000** [2.96]
R	ΔR_b	0.00 [0.19]	−0.00 [−0.19]	0.02 [0.86]	0.12 [2.37]	**−0.12** [−2.37]	−0.00 [−2.11]	0 [NA]
UR	ΔR_b	0.00 [0.99]	0.00 [0.36]	0.02 [0.60]	0.13 [1.98]	**−0.07** [−1.51]	−0.00 [−2.12]	**−0.0000** [−2.05]

To facilitate readability, we have indicated the largest significant changes in coefficient estimates with bold face. It is now easy to see that imposing the three restrictions (the liquidity ratio, the interest rate spread and the long-run exclusion of the trend) on all cointegrating relations leaves the row for real money stock essentially unchanged, and causes some minor changes in the rows of the inflation rate, the deposit rate and the bond rate, whereas it does change the row of the real aggregate income. The consequence of imposing the interest rate spread on the income relation is that the previously significant interest rate effects almost disappear and real income is only borderline significantly equilibrium correcting.

We note that there are some significant trend effects in the inflation rate equation and the interest rate equations of the unrestricted model, probably reflecting the downward trend in nominal growth rates in this period. Since a deterministic trend in inflation and interest rates is economically implausible, the constrained results should, therefore, be considered more appropriate in this case.[2] Altogether it seems as if the constrained structure $\mathcal{H}_6$ preserves most of the relevant information in the data.

In such cases when borderline acceptable restrictions have been imposed on the cointegration relations, the degree of stationarity is likely to worsen, so it is a good idea

[2]Note, however, that a linear trend might sometimes be needed, not to account for a trend in inflation and interest rates, but because the latter are significantly related to, for example, the output gap, $y^r - bt$.

to check the graphs of the constrained relations before finally adopting the constrained structure.

Data transformations, like $\widetilde{\mathbf{x}}_t' = [(m^r - y^r)_t, \Delta p_t, (R_m - R_b)_t]$, are often suggested by the underlying theory models and, therefore, frequently employed in empirical models without first testing for data admissibility. Even though the dimension of the VAR model becomes smaller and the analysis simpler, the cost is that potentially important long-run information based on the original variables has been lost, as well as information on short-run feedback effects within an extended system.

10.3 Some $\boldsymbol{\beta}$ vectors assumed known

This test is useful when we want to test whether a hypothetical known vector is stationary. For example, we might be interested in whether the real interest rate defined as $R-\Delta p$ is stationary, whether Δp is stationary by itself, and whether the income velocity of money, $m^r - y^r$ is stationary.

To formulate this hypothesis, it is convenient to decompose the r cointegrating relations into n_b known vectors $\mathbf{b}$ (in most cases $n_b = 1$) and $r - n_b$ unrestricted vectors $\boldsymbol{\varphi}$ (Johansen 1996), Section 7.2.2:

$$\mathcal{H}^c(r) : \boldsymbol{\beta}^c = (\mathbf{b}, \boldsymbol{\varphi}), \tag{10.4}$$

where $\mathbf{b}$ is a $p1 \times n_b$, and $\boldsymbol{\varphi}$ is a $p1 \times (r - n_b)$ vector. We partition

$$\boldsymbol{\alpha} = (\boldsymbol{\alpha}_1, \boldsymbol{\alpha}_2), \tag{10.5}$$

where $\boldsymbol{\alpha}_1$ are the adjustment coefficients to $\mathbf{b}$, and $\boldsymbol{\alpha}_2$ to $\boldsymbol{\varphi}$. The cointegrated VAR model can now be written as:

$$\Delta\mathbf{x}_t = \boldsymbol{\alpha}_1\mathbf{b}'\mathbf{x}_{t-1} + \boldsymbol{\alpha}_2\boldsymbol{\varphi}'\mathbf{x}_{t-1} + \boldsymbol{\Gamma}_1\Delta\mathbf{x}_{t-1} + \boldsymbol{\Phi}\mathbf{D}_t + \boldsymbol{\varepsilon}_t. \tag{10.6}$$

The unrestricted estimates $\boldsymbol{\alpha}$ and $\boldsymbol{\beta}$ are first obtained from the 'concentrated model':

$$\mathbf{R}_{0,t} = \boldsymbol{\alpha}\boldsymbol{\beta}'\mathbf{R}_{1,t} + \boldsymbol{\varepsilon}_t. \tag{10.7}$$

Inserting (10.4) and (10.5) in (10.7) we get:

$$\mathbf{R}_{0,t} = \boldsymbol{\alpha}_1\mathbf{b}'\mathbf{R}_{1,t} + \boldsymbol{\alpha}_2\boldsymbol{\varphi}'\mathbf{R}_{1,t} + \boldsymbol{\varepsilon}_t. \tag{10.8}$$

Since the variable $\mathbf{b}'R_{1,t}$ is known and stationary under the null, it can be concentrated out from (10.8):

$$\mathbf{R}_{0,t} = \hat{\mathbf{B}}_1\mathbf{b}'\mathbf{R}_{1,t} + \mathbf{R}_{0.\mathbf{b},t}$$

and

$$\mathbf{R}_{1,t} = \hat{\mathbf{B}}_2\mathbf{b}'\mathbf{R}_{1,t} + \mathbf{R}_{1.\mathbf{b},t}$$

The new 'concentrated model' is given by:

$$\mathbf{R}_{0.\mathbf{b},t} = \boldsymbol{\alpha}_2\boldsymbol{\varphi}'\mathbf{R}_{1.\mathbf{b},t} + \varepsilon_t. \tag{10.9}$$

The remaining task is now to derive the ML estimator of $(\boldsymbol{\varphi}, \boldsymbol{\alpha}_1, \boldsymbol{\alpha}_2)$. Two complications have to be solved:

First, if $\boldsymbol{\varphi}$ happens to lie in the space spanned by $\mathbf{b}$, then the model will become singular. Therefore, to avoid this, we can force $\boldsymbol{\varphi}$ to lie in the space spanned by $\mathbf{b}_\perp$. This can be achieved by reformulating model (10.9) for $\boldsymbol{\varphi} = \mathbf{b}_\perp\boldsymbol{\psi}$:

$$\mathbf{R}_{0.\mathbf{b},t} = \boldsymbol{\alpha}_2\boldsymbol{\psi}'\mathbf{b}_\perp'\mathbf{R}_{1.\mathbf{b},t} + \varepsilon_t.$$

Second, because the maximum of the likelihood function is given by:

$$L_{\max}^{-T/2} = |\mathbf{S}_{00.\mathbf{b}}| \prod_{i=1}^{r-n_b} (1 - \hat{\lambda}_i^c)$$

and $|\mathbf{S}_{00.\mathbf{b}}| \neq |\mathbf{S}_{00}|$, the determinants do not cancel in the LR test. This can be circumvented by solving an auxiliary eigenvalue problem:

$$\left|\rho\mathbf{S}_{00} - \mathbf{S}_{01}\mathbf{b}(\mathbf{b}'\mathbf{S}_{11}\mathbf{b})^{-1}\mathbf{b}'\mathbf{S}_{10}\right| = 0$$

from which we get the eigenvalues:

$$\hat{\rho}_1 > \cdots > \hat{\rho}_{n_b} > \hat{\rho}_{n_b+1} = \cdots = \hat{\rho}_p = 0.$$

If $n_b = 1$, as is usually the case in practical applications, only $\hat{\rho}_1 > 0$. It can be shown that

$$|\mathbf{S}_{00.\mathbf{b}}| = |\mathbf{S}_{00}| \prod_{i=1}^{n_b} (1 - \hat{\rho}_i).$$

Therefore,

$$L_{\max}^{-2/T}(\mathcal{H}^c(r)) = |\mathbf{S}_{00}| \prod_{i=1}^{n_b} (1 - \hat{\rho}_i) \prod_{i=1}^{r-n_b} (1 - \hat{\lambda}_i^c)$$

and the LR test procedure

$$\Lambda = \frac{L_{\max}(\mathcal{H}^c(r))}{L_{\max}(\mathcal{H}(r))}$$

gives us the LR test statistic:

$$\begin{aligned} -2\ln\Lambda = T\{&\ln(1 - \hat{\rho}_1) + \cdots + \ln(1 - \hat{\rho}_{n_b}) + \ln(1 - \hat{\lambda}_1^c) + \cdots + \ln(1 - \hat{\lambda}_{r-n_b}^c) \\ &- \ln(1 - \hat{\lambda}_1) - \cdots - \ln(1 - \hat{\lambda}_r)\} \end{aligned}$$

which is asymptotically distributed as χ^2 with $(p1 - r)n_b$ degrees of freedom.

10.3.1 Illustrations

As an illustration of the test procedure, we shall ask whether the inflation rate, nominal and real interest rates, and the interest rate spread are stationary by themselves. Note that the null is stationarity in this case. First, the test that $\Delta p_t \sim I(0)$ is formulated as:

$$\mathcal{H}_6 : \boldsymbol{\beta}^c = (\mathbf{b}, \boldsymbol{\varphi}),$$

where

$$\mathbf{b}' = \begin{bmatrix} 0 & 0 & 1 & 0 & 0 & 0 \end{bmatrix}$$

i.e., $\mathbf{b}$ is a unit vector that picks up the inflation rate. The remaining $r - 1 = 2$ vectors are unrestricted and described by the matrix $\boldsymbol{\varphi}$ of dimension $p1 \times (r-1) = 6 \times 2$. The coefficients φ_{ij} are uniquely determined based on the ordering of eigenvalues and the normalization $\hat{\boldsymbol{\varphi}}'\mathbf{S}_{11.\mathbf{b}}\,\hat{\boldsymbol{\varphi}} = \mathbf{I}$.

In most cases, $\hat{\varphi}_{ij}$ are not of particular interest and Table 10.3 reports only the test results of the stationarity of a specific variable leaving out the estimated coefficients of the unrestricted relations. Each of the hypotheses $\mathcal{H}_7$ to $\mathcal{H}_{12}$ are testing the stationarity of a known vector: $\mathcal{H}_7$ of the inflation rate, $\mathcal{H}_8$ of the nominal and $\mathcal{H}_{10}$ of the real deposit rate, $\mathcal{H}_9$ of the nominal and $\mathcal{H}_{11}$ of the real bond rate, and, finally, $\mathcal{H}_{12}$ of the interest rate spread. Table 10.3 shows that all of them are strongly rejected.

When testing the stationarity of a variable there are two important caveats:

1. The test results are not invariant to the choice of rank r^*. If a conservative value of r is chosen (a small r^*) then stationarity will be more difficult to accept than for a choice of r larger than r^*. Therefore, the test results are crucially dependent on the specific value of cointegration rank being chosen. For a given r^*, we can then ask whether any of the variables is a unit vector in the cointegration space. Thus if, instead, we had chosen $r = 4$, the strong rejection of stationarity of all six hypotheses might have been reversed.
2. If we have included deterministic variables, for example shift dummies, in the cointegration space then a more appropriate hypothesis might be stationarity when allowing for a shift in the mean. Thus, the strong rejection of stationarity might also be related to the shift dummy D_s831_t. For example, if the interest rate spread is stationary around one level before 1983 and another level after that date, then $\mathcal{H}_{12}$ would probably be rejected as a consequence of imposing a zero restriction on D_s831_t. In this case, it would be more relevant to ask whether $(R_m - R_b - b_1 D_s 831)_t \sim I(0)$ rather than $(R_m - R_b)_t \sim I(0)$, where $b_1 D_s 831_t$ is the estimated shift in the level of interest rate spread as a result of deregulation of capital movements.

In the next section, we shall discuss a test procedure for the case where at least one of the coefficients is not known and, therefore, has to be estimated.

10.4 Only some coefficients are restricted

This section is about testing restrictions on one (or a few) of the cointegration vectors assuming that some of the coefficients are known and some have to be estimated. See Johansen (1996), Section 7.2.3. In the general case, we formulate the hypothesis as $\boldsymbol{\beta} = \{\mathbf{H}_1\boldsymbol{\varphi}_1, \mathbf{H}_2\boldsymbol{\varphi}_2, \ldots, \mathbf{H}_r\boldsymbol{\varphi}_r\}$, where $\mathbf{H}_i$ is a $(p1 \times s_i)$ matrix, $i = 1, \ldots, r$. For simplicity, we assume in the following that the r cointegration relations are divided into two groups containing r_1 and r_2 vectors each.

We shall here focus on the special case $\boldsymbol{\beta} = \{\mathbf{H}_1\boldsymbol{\varphi}_1, \boldsymbol{\psi}\}$, where $\mathbf{H}_1$ is $p1 \times s_1$, $\boldsymbol{\varphi}_1$ is $s_1 \times 1$ and $\boldsymbol{\psi}$ is $p1 \times (r-1)$, and leave the more general specification to Chapter 12. It is often useful to know from the outset whether a hypothetical relation is stationary by itself or whether it needs to be further combined with other variables. Since we are specifically interested in the stationarity of a single hypothetical cointegrating relation, the test procedure will focus on this relation while leaving the remaining $r-1$ relations unrestricted.

For example, this type of test would answer the question whether there exists any stationary combination between the nominal deposit rate $R_{m,t}$ and the inflation rate $\triangle p_t$, i.e. whether $(R_{m,t} - \omega\Delta p_t)$ is stationary for some value of ω. The test procedure will find the value ω that produces the 'most stationary' relation and calculate the p-value associated with the null hypothesis:

$$\mathcal{H}_0 : \boldsymbol{\beta}^c = (\boldsymbol{\beta}_1^c, \boldsymbol{\beta}_2) = (\mathbf{H}_1\boldsymbol{\varphi}_1, \boldsymbol{\psi}). \tag{10.10}$$

As before, we partition $\boldsymbol{\alpha}$ so that it corresponds to the partitioning of $\boldsymbol{\beta}^c$:

$$\boldsymbol{\alpha} = (\boldsymbol{\alpha}_1^c, \boldsymbol{\alpha}_2).$$

The concentrated model can be written as:

$$R_{0,t} = \boldsymbol{\alpha}_1\boldsymbol{\varphi}_1'\mathbf{H}_1'R_{1,t} + \boldsymbol{\alpha}_2\boldsymbol{\beta}_2'R_{1,t} + \boldsymbol{\varepsilon}_t.$$

The estimation problem is now more complicated because neither $\boldsymbol{\varphi}_1'\mathbf{H}_1'R_{1,t}$ nor $\boldsymbol{\beta}_2'R_{1,t}$ is known and can be concentrated out. Different algorithms for solving nonlinear estimation problems can be used. CATS uses the switching algorithm described below:

1. Estimate an initial value of $\boldsymbol{\beta}_1^c = \tilde{\boldsymbol{\beta}}_1$.
2. For a fixed value of $\boldsymbol{\beta}_1^c = \tilde{\boldsymbol{\beta}}_1$, estimate $\boldsymbol{\alpha}_2$ and $\boldsymbol{\beta}_2$ by reduced rank regression of $\mathbf{R}_{0.\beta_1,t}$ on $\mathbf{R}_{1.\beta_1,t}$, where $\mathbf{R}_{0.\beta_1,t}$ and $\mathbf{R}_{1.\beta_1,t}$ are corrected for $\tilde{\boldsymbol{\beta}}_1'R_{1,t}$. This defines $\tilde{\boldsymbol{\beta}}_2$ and $L_{\max}(\tilde{\boldsymbol{\beta}}_1)$.
3. For fixed value of $\boldsymbol{\beta}_2 = \tilde{\boldsymbol{\beta}}_2$ estimate $\boldsymbol{\alpha}_1$ and $\boldsymbol{\varphi}_1$ by reduced rank regression of $\mathbf{R}_{0.\beta_2,t}$ on $\mathbf{H}_1'\mathbf{R}_{1.\beta_2,t}$, where $\mathbf{R}_{0.\beta_2,t}$ and $\mathbf{H}_1'\mathbf{R}_{1.\beta_2,t}$ are corrected for $\tilde{\boldsymbol{\beta}}_2'R_{1,t}$. This defines $\tilde{\boldsymbol{\beta}}_1 = \mathbf{H}_1\tilde{\boldsymbol{\varphi}}_1$ and $L_{\max}(\tilde{\boldsymbol{\beta}}_2)$.
4. Repeat the steps, always using the last obtained values of $\tilde{\boldsymbol{\beta}}_i$ until the values of the maximized likelihood function have converged. In CATS the algorithm stops when $|L_{\max}(\tilde{\boldsymbol{\beta}}_1) - L_{\max}(\tilde{\boldsymbol{\beta}}_2)| \leq 0.000\,001$ or after a maximum of 500 iterations has been reached. When needed, these default values can be changed by the user.

The eigenvalue problem for fixed $\boldsymbol{\beta}_1 = \tilde{\boldsymbol{\beta}}_1$ is given by:

$$\left|\rho_1 \mathbf{S}_{11.\boldsymbol{\beta}_1} - \mathbf{S}_{10.\boldsymbol{\beta}_1}(\mathbf{S}_{\mathbf{00}.\boldsymbol{\beta}_1})^{-1}\mathbf{S}_{01.\boldsymbol{\beta}_1}\right| = 0$$

or for fixed $\boldsymbol{\beta}_2 = \tilde{\boldsymbol{\beta}}_2$ by:

$$\left|\rho_2 \mathbf{H}_1' \mathbf{S}_{11.\boldsymbol{\beta}_1}\mathbf{H}_1 - \mathbf{H}_1'\mathbf{S}_{10.\boldsymbol{\beta}_2}(\mathbf{S}_{\mathbf{00}.\boldsymbol{\beta}_2})^{-1}\mathbf{S}_{01.\boldsymbol{\beta}_2}\mathbf{H}_1\right| = 0$$

and the maximum of the likelihood function by:

$$L_{\max}^{-2/T}(\mathbf{H}^c) = |\mathbf{S_{00}}|\,(1-\tilde{\rho}_1)\cdots(1-\tilde{\rho}_r)$$

where $\tilde{\rho}_i$ are the eigenvalues obtained after convergence of the likelihood function.

Using the LR procedure the hypothesis (10.10) can be tested by calculating the test statistic:

$$-2\ln\Lambda = T\{\ln(1-\tilde{\rho}_1) + \cdots + \ln(1-\tilde{\rho}_r) - \ln(1-\hat{\lambda}_1) - \cdots - \ln(1-\hat{\lambda}_r)\}, \qquad (10.11)$$

which is asymptotically χ^2 distributed with the degrees of freedom given by:

$$\nu = (m_1 - r + 1) = (p1 - r) - (s_1 - 1).$$

10.4.1 Illustrations

As an illustration of this procedure, we shall test hypotheses related to (1) the liquidity ratio, $\mathcal{H}_{13}$ to $\mathcal{H}_{16}$, (2) real aggregate income, $\mathcal{H}_{17}$ to $\mathcal{H}_{20}$, (3) inflation rate, real interest rates and the spread, $\mathcal{H}_{21}$ to $\mathcal{H}_{24}$, and (4) combinations of inflation rate and interest rates, $\mathcal{H}_{25}$ to $\mathcal{H}_{29}$.

$\mathcal{H}_{13}$ shows that the liquidity ratio when allowing for a shift in the equilibrium mean can be accepted as a stationary variable with a fairly high p-value. This means that adding a non-stationary variable to this relation does not really make sense as a relation which is already stationary cannot cointegrate with a non-stationary variable. Nevertheless, for the purpose of illustration we shall add the inflation rate, $\mathcal{H}_{14}$, the interest rate spread, $\mathcal{H}_{15}$, and finally both of them, $\mathcal{H}_{16}$, to the liquidity ratio. We notice that the test value is almost unchanged by adding inflation rate, while it drops to a very low value when adding the spread even though the interest rate spread was found to be stationary in $\mathcal{H}_{24}$. The increase in the p-value suggests that the liquidity ratio and the spread share some common autoregressive behaviour, which is annihilated when combining the two so that stationarity is improved. The last relation, $\mathcal{H}_{16}$, is a just identified relation so there are no testable restrictions, i.e. the p-value is 1.00 by construction. We notice that the estimated coefficients are consistent with a plausible money demand relation.

The next group of hypotheses is about stationary relations involving real aggregate income. Real income and inflation appear to be cointegrated in $\mathcal{H}_{17}$ but the coefficient to inflation is very large. Therefore, it might be more reasonable to interpret it as an inflation relation. Note also that the sign of the coefficients suggests that real aggregate income and inflation have been negatively related over the sample period, reflecting the

Table 10.3 Testing the stationarity of single relations.

	m_t^r	y_t^r	Δp_t	$R_{m,t}$	$R_{b,t}$	D_s831_t	$\chi^2(v)$	p-value
Tests of a known β vector								
$\mathcal{H}_7$	0	0	1	0	0	0	20.9 (3)	0.00
$\mathcal{H}_8$	0	0	0	1	0	0	21.1(3)	0.00
$\mathcal{H}_9$	0	0	0	0	1	0	24.2(3)	0.00
$\mathcal{H}_{10}$	0	0	1	−1	0	0	19.4 (3)	0.00
$\mathcal{H}_{11}$	0	0	1	0	−1	0	17.8 (3)	0.00
$\mathcal{H}_{12}$	0	0	0	1	−1	0	24.9 (3)	0.00
Tests of liquidity ratio relations								
$\mathcal{H}_{13}$	1	−1	0	0	0	−0.34	1.5 (2)	**0.47**
$\mathcal{H}_{14}$	1	−1	1.66	0	0	−0.30	1.3 (1)	**0.25**
$\mathcal{H}_{15}$	1	−1	0	−9.02	9.02	−0.21	0.2 (1)	**0.64**
$\mathcal{H}_{16}$	1	−1	1.39	−8.92	8.92	−0.19	–	–
Test of real income relations								
$\mathcal{H}_{17}$	0	1	34.1	0	0	0.43	0.8 (1)	**0.36**
$\mathcal{H}_{18}$	0	1	−54.1	54.1	0	−0.82	8.5 (1)	0.00
$\mathcal{H}_{19}$	0	1	−44.7	0	44.7	0.10	12.7(1)	0.00
$\mathcal{H}_{20}$	0	1	0	−161	161	2.0	3.5 (1)	0.06
Tests of inflation, real interest rates and the spread								
$\mathcal{H}_{21}$	0	0	1	0	0	0.020	9.0 (2)	0.01
$\mathcal{H}_{22}$	0	0	1	−1	0	0.011	10.7 (2)	0.00
$\mathcal{H}_{23}$	0	0	1	0	−1	−0.009	14.3 (2)	0.00
$\mathcal{H}_{24}$	0	0	0	1	−1	−0.014	4.2 (2)	**0.12**
Tests of combinations of interest rates and inflation rates								
$\mathcal{H}_{25}$	0	0	1	−0.44	0	0.015	4.9 (1)	0.03
$\mathcal{H}_{26}$	0	0	1	0	−0.29	0.013	6.7 (1)	0.01
$\mathcal{H}_{27}$	0	0	0	1	−0.81	−0.009	1.7 (1)	**0.19**
Tests of homogeneity between inflation and the interest rates								
$\mathcal{H}_{28}$	0	0	−0.30	1	−0.70	−0.012	0.02 (1)	**0.90**
$\mathcal{H}_{29}$	0	0	0.12	1	−1	−0.012	4.1 (1)	0.04

fact that inflation has been steadily declining whereas real income has been steadily growing (though modestly so) in this period. At the end of this book we shall suggest an explanation to this finding.

The next two hypotheses are asking whether there exists a stationary *IS*-type relationship in this period. Table 10.3 shows that both specifications are rejected. The next hypothesis is whether there is a stationary relationship between real aggregate income and the interest rate spread. It is borderline accepted, but judged by the large coefficients to the spread, the income variable can probably be excluded from the relation. In this case it becomes identical to the spread relation in $\mathcal{H}_{24}$, which indeed is accepted as stationary. Note that the difference between the test values of $\mathcal{H}_{20}$ and $\mathcal{H}_{24}$ is 0.7, which means that real income does not significantly improve stationarity compared to the spread alone.

The tests in the next group, $\mathcal{H}_{21}$ to $\mathcal{H}_{24}$, are similar to those of the first group, except that we now allow for a shift in the equilibrium mean. We notice that although the test values drop quite a lot by including the shift dummy, only the interest rate spread can now be accepted as a stationary variable. Thus, the stationarity of the two real interest rates has been rejected, whether allowing for a mean shift or not.

In the next group, we ask whether nominal interest rates and the inflation rate are cointegrating but now with coefficients which are different from $(1, -1)$. Both $\mathcal{H}_{25}$ and $\mathcal{H}_{26}$ reject stationarity. With the hypotheses $\mathcal{H}_{27}$, we ask whether the stationarity of the spread improves when allowing for an arbitrary coefficient between the two interest rates. Table 10.3 shows that the test statistic does improve to some extent. The next hypothesis $\mathcal{H}_{28}$ tests whether there is a homogeneous relationship between the two interest rates and inflation rate. The design matrices are specified as:

$$\mathbf{H} = \begin{bmatrix} 0 & 0 & 0 \\ 0 & 0 & 0 \\ 1 & 0 & 0 \\ -1 & -1 & 0 \\ 0 & 1 & 0 \\ 0 & 0 & 1 \end{bmatrix}, \quad \mathbf{R}' = \begin{bmatrix} 1 & 0 & 0 & 0 & 0 & 0 \\ 0 & 1 & 0 & 0 & 0 & 0 \\ 0 & 0 & 1 & 1 & 1 & 0 \end{bmatrix}.$$

The hypothesis is accepted with a very high p-value and a test statistic as low as 0.02. Finally, we test the hypothesis, $\mathcal{H}_{29}$, whether the inflation rate is cointegrated with the interest rate spread. Assuming that the interest rate spread reflects inflationary expectations, stationarity could be interpreted as actual and expected inflation sharing a common stochastic trend. The hypothesis is, however, rejected.

Why do we take the trouble of testing all the numerous hypotheses in Table 10.3? The basic reason is that we need to find a set of stationary relations which can potentially qualify as equilibrium relations in the final long-run structure $\boldsymbol{\beta}^{c'}\mathbf{x}_t$. Rejecting the stationarity of a hypothetical relation $\boldsymbol{\varphi}_1'\mathbf{H}_1'\mathbf{x}_t$ implies that it could never be included in an empirically acceptable long-run structure. Therefore, systematically testing the stationarity of all possible relationships helps to spot potentially relevant relations for an identified long-run structure. The test of a set of fully identified cointegration relations will be discussed in more detail in Chapter 12.

We demonstrated above that if a relationship is stationary it does not generally make sense to add more variables. This is closely related to the concept of irreducible sets of cointegrated variables (Davidson 1998). An irreducible cointegration relation is defined as a stationary relation which becomes non-stationary when omitting one of the variables. For example $\mathcal{H}_{13}$ is an irreducible cointegration relation, whereas $\mathcal{H}_{14}$ to $\mathcal{H}_{16}$ are not. Nonetheless, stationarity can be accepted based on a range of p-values[3] and in the lower end of the scale the relationship may not be stationary enough for practical purposes.

[3]Note that a high p-value means that the vector $\boldsymbol{\beta}_i^c$ is almost exactly in the space spanned by the unrestricted $\hat{\boldsymbol{\beta}}$.

In such cases, adding new variables often improves the p-value as well as the empirical robustness of the relation.

An inspection of Table 10.3 shows that we have essentially found three candidates describing irreducible cointegration relations: $\mathcal{H}_{13}, \mathcal{H}_{17}$, and $\mathcal{H}_{24}$. However, $\mathcal{H}_{28}$, which is an extension of $\mathcal{H}_{24}$, represents a significant increase in the p-value and might, therefore, be a preferable choice. These relations will be tested jointly in Chapter 12.

10.5 Revisiting the scenario analysis

The scenario discussed in Chapter 2 was based on the assumption of three cointegration relations consistent with two autonomous common trends. The statement that 'inflation is always and everywhere a monetary phenomenon' was interpreted to mean separation of nominal and real shocks in the sense of nominal shocks exhibiting no real effects (at least in the long-run). Under this assumption, the liquidity ratio, the spread and the real interest rates would be stationary cointegrating relations:

$$\begin{aligned}(m - p - y^r)_t &\sim I(0),\\ (R_b - R_m)_t &\sim I(0),\\ (R_m - \Delta p)_t &\sim I(0),\\ (R_b - \Delta p)_t &\sim I(0).\end{aligned}$$

None of the above relations were found to be stationary as such, but when allowing for an equilibrium mean shift at 1983:1 we found that the liquidity ratio and the interest rate spread could be accepted as stationary. The stationarity of each of the real interest rates was definitely rejected, independently of whether allowing for an equilibrium mean shift or not, or whether relaxing the unitary coefficient or not. Thus, at this stage it seems as if the Fisher parity does not work according to theory, implying that the permanent shocks to the nominal interest rates are different from the permanent shocks to the inflation rate.

The finding that $(m^r - y^r - b_1 D_s 831)_t \sim I(0)$ and $(R_b - R_m - b_2 D_s 831)_t \sim I(0)$ can very well be consistent with a stationary deviation from a money demand relation:

$$(m^r - y^r - b_1 D_s 831)_t - a_1(R_b - R_m - b_2 D_s 831)_t.$$

In this case the coefficient a_1 is not well determined based on the stationarity condition, as any linear combination of two stationary relations would also be stationary. However, if the stationarity of each of the two relations were accepted with a 'not too close to one' p-value, combining the two relations as in $\mathcal{H}_{15}$ can, nevertheless, produce a meaningful estimate of a_1, provided the p-value increases significantly. In most cases the estimate of a_1 would be obtained from combining the two stationary relations with the α_{ij} coefficients in the money stock equation. For example:

$$\Delta m_t^r = \alpha_{11}(m^r - y^r - b_1 D_s 831)_t + \alpha_{12}(R_b - R_m - b_2 D_s 831)_t + \cdots$$

In this case we would find the estimate as $a_1 = \alpha_{12}/\alpha_{11}$.

Thus, it is not sufficient to study the cointegration properties reported in Table 10.3 in order to infer whether the predictions from the monetary model have conformed with the empirical reality. We need to combine the estimated cointegration relations with the appropriately estimated short-run adjustment dynamics. How to identify a structure of cointegration relations will be discussed in Chapter 12 and how to identify the short-run adjustment dynamics for a given long-run structure will be discussed in Chapter 13.

Nevertheless, the cointegration properties are not irrelevant for the effectiveness of monetary policy. As an example, let us consider the simple case when the central bank increases its interest rate in order to curb excess aggregate demand in the economy (and hence inflationary pressure). This is based on the assumption that the interest rate shock will first influence all market interest rates from the short to the long end, then lower the demand for investment, and finally bring inflation down. If $(R_m - R_b) \sim I(0)$, then the shocks will be transmitted one to one and the central bank may very well be successful in its attempts to control inflation. If $(R_m - R_b) \sim I(1)$, then the shocks will not be transmitted one to one and it is less clear what the result will be. For example, it may depend on whether excess aggregate demand is related to the real interest rate, whether the latter is stationary or not, whether excess aggregate demand is related to inflation or not, and so on. In general, whether inflation control is possible or not depends on the cointegration properties of the full system and the dynamics of the system (Johansen and Juselius 2001).

Because the implications of monetary policy are likely to differ depending on the cointegration properties between a policy instrument variable, intermediate targets and a goal variable it is important to have reliable information about these relationships. In periods of deregulation or changes in regimes, the latter are likely to change. Therefore, cointegration properties and changes in them are likely to provide valuable information about the consequences of shifting from one regime to another. See for example Juselius (1998a).

11

Testing restrictions on $\boldsymbol{\alpha}$

Tests on $\boldsymbol{\alpha}$ are closely associated with interesting hypotheses about the common driving forces in the system. The test of a zero row in $\boldsymbol{\alpha}$ is the equivalent of testing whether a variable can be considered weakly exogenous for the long-run parameters $\boldsymbol{\beta}$. When accepted it also defines a common driving trend as the cumulated sum of the empirical shocks to the variable in question. The test of a unit vector in $\boldsymbol{\alpha}$ defines a variable which is exclusively adjusting. Given that the unit vector hypothesis is accepted the corresponding variable has the property that its shocks have no permanent effect on any of the other variables in the system. Thus, the two type of tests can identify (some of) the pushing and pulling forces of the system. The theoretical results of this chapter are based on Johansen (1996), Chapter 8.

Section 11.1 discusses how to test whether a variable is weakly exogenous for the long-run parameters $\boldsymbol{\beta}$ as a row restriction on $\boldsymbol{\alpha}$ and provides an illustration. Section 11.2 discusses weak exogeneity and partial models and Section 11.3 discusses the test of a known vector in $\boldsymbol{\alpha}$ and provides an illustration. Finally, Section 11.4 interprets the obtained test results on $\boldsymbol{\beta}$ and $\boldsymbol{\alpha}$ in terms of the scenario analysis of Chapter 2.

11.1 Long-run weak exogeneity

The hypothesis that a variable has influenced the long-run stochastic path of the other variables of the system, while at the same time has not been influenced by them, is called the hypothesis of 'no levels feedback' or long-run weak exogeneity when the parameters of interest are $\boldsymbol{\beta}$. See Johansen (1996), Section 8.2.1. We test the following hypothesis on $\boldsymbol{\alpha}$:

$$\mathcal{H}^c_{\boldsymbol{\alpha}}(r) : \boldsymbol{\alpha} = \mathbf{H}\boldsymbol{\alpha}_1 \tag{11.1}$$

where $\boldsymbol{\alpha}$ is $p \times r$, $\mathbf{H}$ is a $p \times s$ matrix, $\boldsymbol{\alpha}_1$ is a $s \times r$ matrix of non-zero $\boldsymbol{\alpha}$-coefficients and $s \geq r$. (Compare this formulation with the hypothesis of the same restriction on all $\boldsymbol{\beta}$, i.e. $\boldsymbol{\beta} = \mathbf{H}\boldsymbol{\varphi}$.) As with tests on $\boldsymbol{\beta}$ we can express the restriction (11.1) in the equivalent form:

$$\mathcal{H}^c_{\boldsymbol{\alpha}}(r) : \mathbf{R}'\boldsymbol{\alpha} = \mathbf{0} \tag{11.2}$$

where $\mathbf{R} = \mathbf{H}_{\perp}$.

The condition $s \geq r$ implies that the number of non-zero rows in $\boldsymbol{\alpha}$ must be greater or equal to r. This is because a variable that has a zero row in $\boldsymbol{\alpha}$ does not adjust to the long-run relations and, hence, can be considered a common driving trend in the system. Since there can be at most $(p-r)$ common trends, the number of zero-row restrictions can at most be equal to $(p-r)$.

The hypothesis (11.1) can be expressed as:

$$\mathcal{H}_0 : \boldsymbol{\alpha} = \mathbf{H}\boldsymbol{\alpha}_1 = \begin{pmatrix} \boldsymbol{\alpha}_1 \\ \mathbf{0} \end{pmatrix}.$$

Under $\mathcal{H}^c_{\boldsymbol{\alpha}}(r)$:

$$\Delta \mathbf{x}_t = \boldsymbol{\Gamma}_1 \Delta \mathbf{x}_{t-1} + \mathbf{H}\boldsymbol{\alpha}_1 \boldsymbol{\beta}' \mathbf{x}_{t-1} + \boldsymbol{\mu}_0 + \boldsymbol{\Phi}\mathbf{D}_t + \boldsymbol{\varepsilon}_t. \tag{11.3}$$

We consider first the concentrated model:

$$\mathbf{R}_{0t} = \boldsymbol{\alpha}\boldsymbol{\beta}'\mathbf{R}_{1t} + \boldsymbol{\varepsilon}_t.$$

Under $\mathcal{H}_0$:

$$\mathbf{R}_{0t} = \mathbf{H}\boldsymbol{\alpha}_1\boldsymbol{\beta}'\mathbf{R}_{1t} + \boldsymbol{\varepsilon}_t$$

with $\boldsymbol{\varepsilon}_t \sim IN(\mathbf{0}, \boldsymbol{\Omega})$ and

$$\boldsymbol{\Omega} = \begin{bmatrix} \boldsymbol{\omega}_{11} & \boldsymbol{\omega}_{12} \\ \boldsymbol{\omega}_{21} & \boldsymbol{\omega}_{22} \end{bmatrix}$$

where $\boldsymbol{\omega}_{12}$ is the covariance matrix between the errors from the s 'endogenous' variables $\mathbf{x}_{1,t}$ and the errors from the $p-s$ weakly exogenous variables $\mathbf{x}_{2,t}$. The weak exogeneity hypothesis can be tested with a LR test procedure described in Johansen and Juselius (1990). The idea behind the derivation of the test procedure is to partition the equation system (11.3) into the '$\mathbf{x}_{1,t}$' and the '$\mathbf{x}_{2,t}$' equations. Formally this can be done by multiplying (11.3) with $\mathbf{H}$ and $\mathbf{H}_{\perp}$ respectively. To obtain simpler results, we use the normalized matrix $\overline{\mathbf{H}} = \mathbf{H}(\mathbf{H}'\mathbf{H})^{-1}$ instead of $\mathbf{H}$ (because $\overline{\mathbf{H}}'\mathbf{H} = \mathbf{H}'\overline{\mathbf{H}} = \mathbf{I}$), i.e.

$$\begin{aligned} \overline{\mathbf{H}}'\mathbf{R}_{0t} &= \boldsymbol{\alpha}_1\boldsymbol{\beta}'\mathbf{R}_{1t} + \overline{\mathbf{H}}'\boldsymbol{\varepsilon}_t \\ \mathbf{H}'_{\perp}\mathbf{R}_{0t} &= \mathbf{H}'_{\perp}\boldsymbol{\varepsilon}_t. \end{aligned} \tag{11.4}$$

For the 'baby' equilibrium correction model this would correspond to:

$$\begin{aligned}\Delta \mathbf{x}_{1t} &= \boldsymbol{\alpha}_1 \boldsymbol{\beta}' \mathbf{x}_{t-1} + \boldsymbol{\varepsilon}_{1t} \\ \Delta \mathbf{x}_{2t} &= \boldsymbol{\varepsilon}_{2t}.\end{aligned}$$

The next step is to formulate the joint model (11.4) as a conditional and marginal model using results from multivariate normal distributions:

$$\begin{aligned}\overline{\mathbf{H}}' \mathbf{R}_{0t} &= \boldsymbol{\alpha}_1 \boldsymbol{\beta}' \mathbf{R}_{1t} + \boldsymbol{\rho}_{12} \mathbf{H}'_{\perp} \mathbf{R}_{0t} - \boldsymbol{\rho}_{12} \mathbf{H}'_{\perp} \boldsymbol{\varepsilon}_t + \overline{\mathbf{H}}' \boldsymbol{\varepsilon}_t \\ \mathbf{H}'_{\perp} \mathbf{R}_{0t} &= \mathbf{H}'_{\perp} \boldsymbol{\varepsilon}_t\end{aligned} \tag{11.5}$$

where $\boldsymbol{\rho}_{12} = \boldsymbol{\omega}_{12} \boldsymbol{\omega}_{22}^{-1}$. For the 'baby' model this would correspond to:

$$\begin{aligned}\Delta \mathbf{x}_{1t} &= \boldsymbol{\alpha}_1 \boldsymbol{\beta}' \mathbf{x}_{t-1} + \boldsymbol{\rho}_{12} \Delta \mathbf{x}_{2t} - \boldsymbol{\rho}_{12} \boldsymbol{\varepsilon}_{2t} + \boldsymbol{\varepsilon}_{1t} \\ \Delta \mathbf{x}_{2t} &= \boldsymbol{\varepsilon}_{2t}\end{aligned}$$

i.e.

$$\begin{aligned}\Delta \mathbf{x}_{1t} &= \boldsymbol{\alpha}_1 \boldsymbol{\beta}' \mathbf{x}_{t-1} + \boldsymbol{\rho}_{12} \Delta \mathbf{x}_{2t} + \boldsymbol{\varepsilon}_{1.2t} \\ \Delta \mathbf{x}_{2t} &= \boldsymbol{\varepsilon}_{2t}\end{aligned}$$

where $\boldsymbol{\varepsilon}_{1.2t} = \boldsymbol{\varepsilon}_{1t} - \boldsymbol{\rho}_{12} \boldsymbol{\varepsilon}_{2t}$ and $\text{Cov}(\boldsymbol{\varepsilon}_{1.2t}, \boldsymbol{\varepsilon}_{2t}) = \mathbf{0}$. All relevant information about $\boldsymbol{\alpha}$ and $\boldsymbol{\beta}$ is now in the $\Delta \mathbf{x}_{1t}$ equation, and we can solve the eigenvalue problem entirely based on that equation. Since $\Delta \mathbf{x}_{2t}$ is stationary, we can correct $\mathbf{R}_{0,t}$ ($\Delta \mathbf{x}_{1t}$) and $\mathbf{R}_{1,t}$ ($\mathbf{x}_{t-1}$) for this variable based on the auxiliary regressions:

$$\mathbf{R}_{0t} = \hat{\mathbf{B}}_1 \Delta \mathbf{x}_{2t} + \mathbf{R}_{0.\mathbf{H}_{\perp} t}$$

and

$$\mathbf{R}_{1t} = \hat{\mathbf{B}}_2 \Delta \mathbf{x}_{2t} + \mathbf{R}_{1.\mathbf{H}_{\perp} t}$$

so that:

$$\mathbf{R}_{0.\mathbf{H}_{\perp} t} = \boldsymbol{\alpha}_1 \boldsymbol{\beta}' \mathbf{R}_{1.\mathbf{H}_{\perp} t} + \mathbf{u}_t. \tag{11.6}$$

The 'usual' eigenvalue problem is based on (11.6) and the solution delivers $p - m$ eigenvalues $\hat{\lambda}_i^c$. The r largest are used in the LR test which is given by:

$$-2\ln L(\mathcal{H}_\alpha^c(r)/\mathcal{H}(r)) = -T \sum_{i=1}^{r} \{\ln(1 - \hat{\lambda}_i^c) - \ln(1 - \hat{\lambda}_i)\}.$$

It is asymptotically distributed as $\chi^2(\nu)$ where $\nu = rm$ and m is the number of weakly exogenous variables.

Note that finding weakly exogenous variables is often helpful in the identification of the common driving trends, as will be illustrated in Chapter 15. Thus the hypothesis $\boldsymbol{\alpha}_2 = \mathbf{0}$ is of interest for its own sake as it corresponds to the hypothesis of 'no long-run feedback'.

11.1.1 Empirical illustrations

We shall now test the hypothesis that the bond rate is weakly exogenous for the long-run parameters in the Danish money demand data, i.e. that $\alpha_{51} = \alpha_{52} = \alpha_{53} = 0$. The table below illustrates the restrictions on the parameters of the model for $p = 5$, $r = 3$, $m = 1$, $s = 4$.

$$\begin{bmatrix} \Delta m_t^r \\ \Delta y_t^r \\ \Delta^2 p_t \\ \Delta R_{m,t} \\ \Delta R_{b,t} \end{bmatrix} = \cdots + \begin{bmatrix} \alpha_{11} & \alpha_{12} & \alpha_{13} \\ \vdots & \vdots & \vdots \\ \alpha_{51} & \alpha_{52} & \alpha_{53} \end{bmatrix} \begin{bmatrix} \boldsymbol{\beta}_1'\mathbf{x}_{t-1} \\ \boldsymbol{\beta}_2'\mathbf{x}_{t-1} \\ \boldsymbol{\beta}_3'\mathbf{x}_{t-1} \end{bmatrix}$$

$$= \cdots + \begin{bmatrix} 1 & 0 & 0 & 0 \\ 0 & 1 & 0 & 0 \\ 0 & 0 & 1 & 0 \\ 0 & 0 & 0 & 1 \\ 0 & 0 & 0 & 0 \end{bmatrix} \begin{bmatrix} \alpha_{11}^c & \alpha_{12}^c & \alpha_{13}^c \\ \vdots & \vdots & \vdots \\ \alpha_{41}^c & \alpha_{42}^c & \alpha_{43}^c \end{bmatrix} \begin{bmatrix} \boldsymbol{\beta}_1'\mathbf{x}_{t-1} \\ \boldsymbol{\beta}_2'\mathbf{x}_{t-1} \\ \boldsymbol{\beta}_3'\mathbf{x}_{t-1} \end{bmatrix}$$

$$= \cdots + \begin{bmatrix} \alpha_{11}^c & \alpha_{12}^c & \alpha_{13}^c \\ \vdots & \vdots & \vdots \\ \alpha_{41}^c & \alpha_{42}^c & \alpha_{43}^c \\ 0 & 0 & 0 \end{bmatrix} \begin{bmatrix} \boldsymbol{\beta}_1'\mathbf{x}_{t-1} \\ \boldsymbol{\beta}_2'\mathbf{x}_{t-1} \\ \boldsymbol{\beta}_3'\mathbf{x}_{t-1} \end{bmatrix}$$

The specification of the zero row restriction on the adjustment coefficients of the bond rate is here given by the $\mathbf{R}$ matrix:

$$\mathbf{R}' = [0, 0, 0, 0, 1].$$

The test statistic, distributed as $\chi^2(3)$, is 4.64 and the weak exogeneity of the bond rate is accepted with a p-value of 0.20.

As a sensitivity check of the weak exogeneity test results regarding the choice of cointegration rank, Table 11.1 reports the test statistics with the p-values in the brackets for all variables and for all possible values of r. The row corresponding to our preferred choice $r = 3$ is indicated by two arrows. For example, if we had decided to choose $r = 2$, real income and the two interest rates would have become weakly exogenous, implying that each interest rate would have acted as an independent common driving trend in this system, which *a priori* does not seem very plausible. On the other hand, if we had chosen $r = 4$ none of the variables would have been weakly exogenous. This serves as an illustration of how important the choice of rank is for all subsequent inference.

For the preferred choice, $r = 3$, we were able to accept individual weak exogeneity both for y^r and R_b and it is natural to ask whether they are jointly exogenous. Because in this case $m = 2$ which corresponds to the number of common trends, $p - r$, this is the maximum number of weakly exogenous variables. Since the weak exogeneity tests of a single variable are not independent, the joint hypothesis of two or several variables can be

Table 11.1 Tests of long-run weak exogeneity.

r	v	$\chi^2(v)$	m^r	y^r	Δp	R_m	R_b
1	1	3.84	3.48 [0.06]	0.07 [0.79]	11.49 [0.00]	0.62 [0.43]	0.63 [0.43]
2	2	5.99	8.22 [0.02]	**2.24** [0.33]	16.25 [0.00]	**1.94** [0.38]	**0.78** [0.68]
$\longrightarrow$ 3 $\longleftarrow$	3	7.81	17.56 [0.00]	**6.84** [0.08]	26.65 [0.00]	8.88 [0.03]	**4.64** [0.20]
4	4	9.49	21.14 [0.00]	13.44 [0.01]	27.12 [0.00]	10.92 [0.03]	10.25 [0.04]

(and often is) rejected even though they are individually accepted as weakly exogenous. The design matrix for the joint test is specified as:

$$\mathbf{R}' = \begin{bmatrix} 0 & 0 & 0 & 0 & 1 \\ 0 & 1 & 0 & 0 & 0 \end{bmatrix},$$

and the test statistic, distributed as $\chi^2(6)$, became 15.05 with a p-value of 0.02 and we reject that both variables are jointly weakly exogenous in this system.

11.2 Weak exogeneity and partial models

Assuming that the bond rate is weakly exogenous implies that valid inference on $\boldsymbol{\beta}$ can be obtained from the four-dimensional system describing $m^r, y^r, \Delta p$, and R_m conditional on R_b (Johansen 1992a; Hendry and Richard 1983). The argument is based on a partitioning of the joint density into the conditional and marginal densities:

$$\begin{aligned} D(\Delta\mathbf{x}_t|\Delta\mathbf{x}_{t-1}, \mathbf{x}_{t-1}, D_s831_{t-1}, \mathbf{D}_t; \boldsymbol{\theta}) &= D(\Delta\mathbf{x}_{1,t}|\Delta\mathbf{x}_{2,t}, \Delta\mathbf{x}_{t-1}, \mathbf{x}_{t-1}, D_s831_{t-1}, \mathbf{D}_t; \boldsymbol{\theta}_1) \\ &\quad \times D(\Delta\mathbf{x}_{2,t}|\Delta\mathbf{x}_{t-1}, \mathbf{D}_t; \boldsymbol{\theta}_2) \end{aligned} \tag{11.7}$$

where $\mathbf{x}_t' = [\mathbf{x}_{1,t}', \mathbf{x}_{2,t}']$ and $\mathbf{x}_{1,t}' = [m_t^r, y_t^r, \Delta p_t, R_{m,t}]$, $\mathbf{x}_{2,t}' = [R_{b,t}]$, $\mathbf{D}_t = [Dtr754, Dp764, \Delta D_s831_t]$, $\boldsymbol{\theta}_1, \boldsymbol{\theta}_2$ are variation free and only $\boldsymbol{\theta}_1$ contains the long-run parameters of interest $\boldsymbol{\beta}$.

In this case, the cointegrated VAR(2) model:

$$\Delta\mathbf{x}_t = \boldsymbol{\Gamma}_1\Delta\mathbf{x}_{t-1} + \boldsymbol{\alpha}\boldsymbol{\beta}'\tilde{\mathbf{x}}_{t-1} + \boldsymbol{\Phi}\mathbf{D}_t + \boldsymbol{\varepsilon}_t$$

is equivalent to:

$$\begin{aligned} \Delta\mathbf{x}_{1t} &= \mathbf{a}_1\Delta\mathbf{x}_{2t} + \boldsymbol{\Gamma}_{1.1}\Delta\mathbf{x}_{t-1} + \boldsymbol{\alpha}_1\boldsymbol{\beta}'\tilde{\mathbf{x}}_{t-1} + \boldsymbol{\Phi}_1\mathbf{D}_t + \boldsymbol{\varepsilon}_{1.2,t} \\ \Delta\mathbf{x}_{2t} &= \boldsymbol{\Gamma}_{1.2}\Delta\mathbf{x}_{t-1} + \boldsymbol{\Phi}_2\mathbf{D}_t + \boldsymbol{\varepsilon}_{2,t} \end{aligned}$$

where $\text{Cov}(\boldsymbol{\varepsilon}_{1.2,t}, \boldsymbol{\varepsilon}_{2,t}) = \mathbf{0}$, $\mathbf{a}_1$ is (4×1), $\boldsymbol{\Gamma}_{1.1}$ $(4{\times}5)$, $\boldsymbol{\alpha}_1$ $(4{\times}3)$, $\boldsymbol{\Phi}_1$ (4×3), $\boldsymbol{\Gamma}_{1.2}$ (1×5), and $\boldsymbol{\Phi}_2$ (1×3).

Therefore, when there are $m = p - r$ zero-row restrictions on $\boldsymbol{\alpha}$ (note that, $m \leq p - r$), we can partition the p equations into $(p - m)$ equations which exhibit levels feedback, and m equations with no levels feedback. Because the m weakly exogenous variables do not contain information about the long-run parameters, we can obtain fully efficient estimates of $\boldsymbol{\beta}$ from the $(p-m)$ equations conditional on the marginal models of the m weakly exogenous variables. Thus, weak exogeneity gives the condition for when a partial model can be used to efficiently estimate $\boldsymbol{\beta}$ without loss of information.

More formally: let $\{\mathbf{x}_t\} = \{\mathbf{x}_{1,t}, \mathbf{x}_{2,t}\}$ where $\mathbf{x}_{2,t}$ is weakly exogenous when the parameters of interest are $\boldsymbol{\beta}$. Then a fully efficient estimate of $\boldsymbol{\beta}$ can be obtained from the partial model:

$$\Delta\mathbf{x}_{1,t} = \mathbf{A}_0\Delta\mathbf{x}_{2,t} + \boldsymbol{\Gamma}_{1.1}\Delta\mathbf{x}_{t-1} + \boldsymbol{\alpha}_1\boldsymbol{\beta}'\mathbf{x}_{t-1} + \boldsymbol{\mu}_0 + \boldsymbol{\Phi}_1\mathbf{D}_t + \tilde{\boldsymbol{\varepsilon}}_{1,t}. \tag{11.8}$$

Note, however, that in order to know whether we can estimate $\boldsymbol{\beta}$ from a partial system we need first to estimate the full system and test $\boldsymbol{\alpha}_2 = \mathbf{0}$ in that system. But if we need to estimate the full system, why would we bother to discuss estimation in a partial system? There are two reasons:

1. By conditioning on weakly exogenous variables, one can often achieve a partial system which has more stable parameters than the full system. This is often the case when the marginal model of the weakly exogenous variable has non-constant parameters or exhibit nonlinearities in the parameters.
2. It is sometimes *a priori* very likely that weak exogeneity holds. For example it is almost sure that the US bond rate has an influence on the Danish economy, and it is almost equally sure that the Danish economy is more or less irrelevant for the determination of the US bond rate. Therefore, testing may not always be necessary and we can from the outset estimate a partial system conditional on the US bond rate. In particular when the number of potentially relevant variables to include in the VAR model is large it can be useful to impose weak exogeneity restrictions from the outset.

Note, however, that the tests of cointegration rank will be influenced by the conditioning on weakly exogenous variables and the standard asymptotic tables are no longer valid in this case. However, under the assumption that the variables chosen to be weakly exogenous actually satisfy the conditions for weak exogeneity one can use the results in Harbo, Johansen, Nielsen, and Rahbek (1998) to generate new tables. CATS automatically provides these tables if the VAR model has been specified to contain weakly exogenous variables.

11.2.1 Illustration

Assuming that the bond rate is weakly exogenous for the long-run parameters $\boldsymbol{\beta}$, we shall now estimate a partial model for $\mathbf{x}'_{1,t} = [m^r_t, y^r_t, \Delta p_t, R_{m,t}]$ conditional on $R_{b,t}$. The cointegration rank was already shown to be $r = 3$ based on the full system and need not be re-estimated.

However, in those cases when weak exogeneity is assumed rather than tested and, therefore, imposed from the outset (for example, because the total number of variables is too large for a full system to be feasible) one would need to determine the rank from the partial system. Note that in this case, each weakly exogenous variable is by assumption a common driving trend, i.e. corresponds to a unit root in the full system.

Table 11.2 Tests of cointegration rank with exogenous variables.

$p-r$	r	λ_i	τ_{p-r}	τ^*_{p-r}	Q_{95}	p-val.	p-val.*
4	0	0.34	107.05	103.00	57.27	0.00	0.00
3	1	0.23	57.08	54.98	37.40	0.00	0.00
2	2	0.17	26.43	24.84	21.53	0.01	0.02
1	3	0.04	4.78	4.53	9.34	0.33	0.37

As an illustration of the trace test for cointegration rank in a partial system Table 11.2 reports the trace statistics, τ_{p-r}, the Bartlett corrected ones, τ^*_{p-r}, and the asymptotic tables derived under the assumption of one weakly exogenous variable. These tables are constructed under the assumption that the exogenous variables are random walks. The results show that we would be able to accept one unit root so that the preferred choice would be $r = 3$. In this case the second unit root belongs (by assumption) to the weakly exogenous bond rate.

The estimates of the partial model given below are essentially unchanged compared to the full VAR model, implying that we have neither lost, nor gained much by moving to a partial system.

As already mentioned, when conditioning on a weakly exogenous variable the estimated parameters of the system might become more stable. To check this possibility we

$$
\begin{bmatrix} \Delta m^r_t \\ \Delta y^r_t \\ \Delta^2 p_t \\ \Delta R_{m,t} \end{bmatrix}
=
\begin{bmatrix}
\underbrace{\begin{matrix}
\underset{[-0.24]}{-0.02} & \underset{[0.16]}{0.02} & \underset{[1.27]}{0.35} & \underset{[-0.43]}{-0.86} & \underset{[-1.45]}{-2.22} \\
\underset{[0.51]}{0.03} & \underset{[1.34]}{0.12} & \underset{[0.58]}{0.09} & \underset{[0.39]}{0.46} & \underset{[-3.59]}{\mathbf{-3.25}} \\
\underset{[0.89]}{0.03} & \underset{[-2.66]}{\mathbf{-0.14}} & \underset{[-2.24]}{\mathbf{-0.21}} & \underset{[-2.05]}{\mathbf{-1.38}} & \underset{[1.74]}{0.91} \\
\underset{[-1.20]}{-0.00} & \underset{[-1.29]}{-0.01} & \underset{[1.14]}{0.01} & \underset{[1.29]}{0.10} & \underset{[3.98]}{\mathbf{0.24}}
\end{matrix}}_{\boldsymbol{\Gamma}_{1.1}}
\end{bmatrix}
\begin{bmatrix} \Delta m^r_{t-1} \\ \Delta y^r_{t-1} \\ \Delta^2 p_{t-1} \\ \Delta R_{m,t-1} \\ \Delta R_{b,t-1} \end{bmatrix}
$$

$$
+
\begin{bmatrix}
\underbrace{\begin{matrix}
\underset{[-2.66]}{\mathbf{-1.09}} & \underset{[-3.96]}{\mathbf{-0.15}} & \underset{[0.36]}{0.38} \\
\underset{[-0.41]}{-0.10} & \underset{[2.57]}{\mathbf{0.06}} & \underset{[-2.57]}{\mathbf{-1.60}} \\
\underset{[-5.01]}{\mathbf{-0.70}} & \underset{[2.69]}{\mathbf{0.04}} & \underset{[-0.97]}{-0.35} \\
\underset{[0.95]}{0.02} & \underset{[-1.88]}{\mathbf{-0.00}} & \underset{[-3.88]}{\mathbf{-0.16}}
\end{matrix}}_{\boldsymbol{\alpha}_1}
\end{bmatrix}
\begin{bmatrix}
\underbrace{\begin{matrix}
0.1 & -0.0 & 1.0 & -0.4 & 0.7 & -0.0 \\
1.0 & -1.2 & -3.5 & -13.0 & 10.8 & -0.2 \\
0.0 & 0.0 & 0.0 & 1.0 & -0.5 & -0.0
\end{matrix}}_{\boldsymbol{\beta}'}
\end{bmatrix}
\begin{bmatrix} m^r_{t-1} \\ y^r_{t-1} \\ \Delta p_{t-1} \\ R_{m,t-1} \\ R_{b,t-1} \\ D_s831_{t-1} \end{bmatrix}
$$

$$
+
\begin{bmatrix}
\underbrace{\begin{matrix}
\underset{[-0.67]}{-1.00} \\
\underset{[1.37]}{1.21} \\
\underset{[1.73]}{0.88} \\
\underset{[4.84]}{\mathbf{0.29}}
\end{matrix}}_{\mathbf{a}_1}
\end{bmatrix}
\Delta R_{b,t} +
\begin{bmatrix}
\underbrace{\begin{matrix}
\underset{[0.73]}{0.01} & \underset{[-0.83]}{-0.02} & \underset{[-1.01]}{0.03} \\
\underset{[3.24]}{\mathbf{0.04}} & \underset{[0.29]}{0.00} & \underset{[-0.65]}{-0.01} \\
\underset{[-2.21]}{\mathbf{-0.01}} & \underset{[0.43]}{0.00} & \underset{[-0.32]}{-0.00} \\
\underset{[0.64]}{0.00} & \underset{[5.86]}{\mathbf{0.01}} & \underset{[3.20]}{\mathbf{0.00}}
\end{matrix}}_{\boldsymbol{\Phi}_1}
\underbrace{\begin{matrix}
\underset{[-0.87]}{-0.18} \\
\underset{[3.33]}{\mathbf{0.40}} \\
\underset{[4.45]}{\mathbf{0.31}} \\
\underset{[1.43]}{0.01}
\end{matrix}}_{\boldsymbol{\mu}_0}
\end{bmatrix}
\begin{bmatrix} Dtr75_t \\ Dp764_t \\ Dp831_t \\ 1 \end{bmatrix}
+
\begin{bmatrix} \hat{\varepsilon}_{m^r,t} \\ \hat{\varepsilon}_{y^r,t} \\ \hat{\varepsilon}_{\Delta p,t} \\ \hat{\varepsilon}_{R_m,t} \end{bmatrix}
$$

Table 11.3 Misspecification tests in the partial model.

	ARCH	Normality	R^2
Δm_t^r	0.64	3.14	0.31
Δy_t^r	1.40	3.73	0.31
$\Delta^2 p_t$	2.31	0.11	0.62
$\Delta R_{m,t}$	8.22	6.01	0.61

report the misspecification tests of the partial model in Table 11.3. Compared to the misspecification tests of the full model the test statistics have not changed much.

11.3 Testing a known vector in $\boldsymbol{\alpha}$

We now consider a situation where the restrictions on $\boldsymbol{\alpha}$ are given by

$$\mathcal{H}_0 : \boldsymbol{\alpha} = \{\mathbf{a},\boldsymbol{\tau}\}$$

where $\mathbf{a}$ is a $p \times n_k$ known matrix and $n_k \leq r$ and $\boldsymbol{\tau}$ is a $p \times (r - n_k)$ matrix of unrestricted adjustment coefficients. In most cases $n_k = 1$, so that $\mathbf{a}$ is a vector in $\boldsymbol{\alpha}$. A known vector in $\boldsymbol{\alpha}$ is the equivalent of imposing the same restriction on $\boldsymbol{\alpha}_\perp$, i.e.

$$\boldsymbol{\alpha} = \{\mathbf{a}, \boldsymbol{\tau}\} \Leftrightarrow \boldsymbol{\alpha}_\perp = \mathbf{H}\boldsymbol{\alpha}_\perp^c. \tag{11.9}$$

Thus, imposing a known vector on $\boldsymbol{\alpha}$ is equivalent to imposing the same restriction on each common trend. The hypothesis that $\mathbf{a}' = [\ldots, 0, 0, 1, 0, 0, \ldots]$ is a unit vector is of particular interest, as it corresponds to a situation where the 'shocks' $\mathbf{a}'\boldsymbol{\varepsilon}_t$ to the variable $\mathbf{a}'\mathbf{x}_t$ have transitory but no permanent effects on any of the variables of the system. The case when one vector of $\boldsymbol{\alpha}$ is proportional to a unit vector is illustrated below:

$$\boldsymbol{\alpha}^c = \begin{bmatrix} * & * & * \\ 0 & * & * \\ 0 & * & * \\ 0 & * & * \\ 0 & * & * \end{bmatrix} \rightarrow \boldsymbol{\alpha}_\perp^c = \begin{bmatrix} 0 & 0 \\ * & * \\ * & * \\ * & * \\ * & * \end{bmatrix}.$$

The zero row in $\boldsymbol{\alpha}_\perp^c$ will produce a zero column in the matrix $\mathbf{C} = \tilde{\boldsymbol{\beta}}_\perp \boldsymbol{\alpha}_\perp'$ (see (5.18) in Chapter 5) which means that the shocks to the first variable of the VAR model will have no permanent effects on any of the variables in the system.

As before, we use the decomposition $\boldsymbol{\alpha}'\boldsymbol{\beta} = \{\mathbf{a}\boldsymbol{\beta}_1, \boldsymbol{\tau}\boldsymbol{\beta}_2\}$ and consider only $\boldsymbol{\tau} = \mathbf{a}_\perp \boldsymbol{\psi}$, i.e. the vectors in $\boldsymbol{\tau}$ which are orthogonal to $\mathbf{a}$.

The concentrated model

$$\mathbf{R}_{0,t} = \boldsymbol{\alpha}\boldsymbol{\beta}'\mathbf{R}_{1,t} + \boldsymbol{\varepsilon}_t$$

expressed in terms of (11.9) becomes:

$$\mathbf{R}_{0,t} = \mathbf{a}\boldsymbol{\beta}_1'\mathbf{R}_{1,t} + \mathbf{a}_\perp\boldsymbol{\psi}\boldsymbol{\beta}_2'\mathbf{R}_{1,t} + \boldsymbol{\varepsilon}_t \tag{11.10}$$

with $\boldsymbol{\varepsilon}_t \sim IN(\mathbf{0}, \boldsymbol{\Omega})$ and

$$\boldsymbol{\Omega} = \begin{bmatrix} \boldsymbol{\omega}_{11} & \boldsymbol{\omega}_{12} \\ \boldsymbol{\omega}_{21} & \boldsymbol{\omega}_{22} \end{bmatrix}$$

where $\boldsymbol{\omega}_{12}$ is the covariance matrix between the errors from the variables $\mathbf{a}'\mathbf{x}_t$ and the errors of the other variables $\mathbf{a}_\perp'\mathbf{x}_t$. The remaining covariances are similarly defined. The known $\boldsymbol{\alpha}$ hypothesis can be tested with a LR test procedure described in Johansen (1996), Section 8.2.2. The idea behind the derivation of the test is similar to the weak exogeneity procedure. First we partition the equation system into the $\mathbf{a}'\mathbf{x}_t$ and the $\mathbf{a}_\perp'\mathbf{x}_t$ equations by multiplying (11.10) by $\bar{\mathbf{a}}' = (\mathbf{a}'\mathbf{a})^{-1}\mathbf{a}'$ and by $\bar{\mathbf{a}}_\perp' = (\mathbf{a}_\perp'\mathbf{a}_\perp)^{-1}\,\mathbf{a}_\perp'$, i.e.

$$\begin{aligned} \bar{\mathbf{a}}'\mathbf{R}_{0,t} &= \boldsymbol{\beta}_1'\mathbf{R}_{1,t} + \bar{\mathbf{a}}'\boldsymbol{\varepsilon}_t \\ \bar{\mathbf{a}}_\perp'\mathbf{R}_{0,t} &= \boldsymbol{\psi}\boldsymbol{\beta}_2'\mathbf{R}_{1,t} + \bar{\mathbf{a}}_\perp'\boldsymbol{\varepsilon}_t. \end{aligned} \tag{11.11}$$

For the Danish data, assume that $\mathbf{x}_{1t} = \mathbf{a}'\mathbf{x}_t = m_t^r$ and $\mathbf{x}_{2,t} = \mathbf{a}_\perp'\mathbf{x}_t = [y_t^r, \Delta p_t, R_{m,t}, R_{b,t}]$ and that there are no short-run dynamic effects ($\boldsymbol{\Gamma}_i = \mathbf{0}$). Then the VAR model with a known $\boldsymbol{\alpha}$ vector would correspond to:

$$\begin{aligned} \Delta m_t^r &= \boldsymbol{\beta}_1'\mathbf{x}_{t-1} + \varepsilon_{m^r,t} \\ \Delta\mathbf{x}_{2,t} &= \boldsymbol{\psi}\boldsymbol{\beta}_2'\mathbf{x}_{t-1} + \boldsymbol{\varepsilon}_{2,t} \end{aligned}$$

i.e. the hypothesis of a known $\boldsymbol{\alpha}$ vector is the equivalent of saying that one of the variables is exclusively adjusting to one cointegration relation, whereas the other variables are exclusively adjusting to the remaining $r-1$ cointegration relations.

The next step is to formulate the joint model as a conditional and marginal model using the results from the multivariate normal distributions:

$$\begin{aligned} \bar{\mathbf{a}}'\mathbf{R}_{0,t} &= (\boldsymbol{\beta}_1' - \boldsymbol{\rho}_{12}\boldsymbol{\psi}\boldsymbol{\beta}_2')\boldsymbol{R}_{1,t} + \boldsymbol{\rho}_{12}'\bar{\mathbf{a}}_\perp'\mathbf{R}_{0,t} + \bar{\mathbf{a}}'\boldsymbol{\varepsilon}_t - \boldsymbol{\rho}_{12}'\bar{\mathbf{a}}_\perp'\boldsymbol{\varepsilon}_t \\ \bar{\mathbf{a}}_\perp'\mathbf{R}_{0,t} &= \boldsymbol{\psi}\boldsymbol{\beta}_2'\mathbf{R}_{1,t} + \bar{\mathbf{a}}_\perp'\varepsilon_t \end{aligned} \tag{11.12}$$

where $\boldsymbol{\rho}_{12} = \boldsymbol{\omega}_{12}\boldsymbol{\omega}_{22}^{-1}$. For the above 'baby' model this would correspond to:

$$\begin{aligned} \Delta m_t^r &= (\boldsymbol{\beta}_1' - \boldsymbol{\rho}_{12}\boldsymbol{\psi}\boldsymbol{\beta}_2')\boldsymbol{x}_{t-1} + \boldsymbol{\rho}_{12}'\Delta\mathbf{x}_{2,t} + \underbrace{\varepsilon_{m^r,t} - \boldsymbol{\rho}_{12}'\boldsymbol{\varepsilon}_{2,t}}_{\boldsymbol{\varepsilon}_{1.2,t}} \\ \Delta\mathbf{x}_{2,t} &= \boldsymbol{\psi}\boldsymbol{\beta}_2'\boldsymbol{x}_{t-1} + \varepsilon_{2,t}. \end{aligned}$$

Because $\mathrm{Cov}(\boldsymbol{\varepsilon}_{1.2,t}, \boldsymbol{\varepsilon}_{2,t}) = \mathbf{0}$, the $\Delta\mathbf{x}_{2,t}$ equations contain all relevant information about $\boldsymbol{\psi}$ and $\boldsymbol{\beta}_2$, and we can obtain the ML estimate of $\boldsymbol{\beta}_2$ by solving the usual eigenvalue problem entirely based on the $\Delta \mathbf{x}_{2,t}$ equations, i.e.

$$\left|\lambda \mathbf{S}_{11} - \mathbf{S}_{10}\bar{\mathbf{a}}_{\perp}(\bar{\mathbf{a}}'_{\perp}\mathbf{S}_{00}\bar{\mathbf{a}}_{\perp})^{-1}\bar{\mathbf{a}}'_{\perp}\mathbf{S}_{01}\right| = 0.$$

The estimate of $\boldsymbol{\psi}$ can then be obtained from

$$\hat{\boldsymbol{\psi}}(\boldsymbol{\beta}_2) = \bar{\mathbf{a}}'_{\perp}\mathbf{S}_{01}\boldsymbol{\beta}_2(\boldsymbol{\beta}'_2\mathbf{S}_{11}\boldsymbol{\beta}_2)^{-1}.$$

Finally, (11.12) can be used to get an estimate of $\boldsymbol{\beta}_1$ by regressing $\bar{\mathbf{a}}'\mathbf{R}_{0,t}$ on $\mathbf{R}_{1,t}$ and $\bar{\mathbf{a}}'_{\perp}\mathbf{R}_{0t}$.

The LR test is asymptotically distributed as $\chi^2(\nu)$ where $\nu = m(p-r)$ and m is the number of known α vectors.

11.3.1 Illustration

Under the assumption that $r = 3$, Table 11.4 reports the tests of a known unit vector in $\boldsymbol{\alpha}$, where the unit vector corresponds to each of the variables in turn.

The results show that shocks to the real money stock, to inflation, and to the short-term interest rate have no permanent effects on any of the variables in this system. This is, of course, only the mirror image of the previous result that the bond rate and real aggregate income were individually weakly exogenous. If the joint weak exogeneity test had been accepted, then the cumulated shocks to these variables would have completely defined the autonomous driving trends. In this case, only the shocks to y^r and R_b would have had any permanent effect on the variables of this system. Since the joint weak exogeneity test was rejected, the joint test of the three unit vectors should similarly be rejected. This is also the case: The joint hypothesis was rejected with a p-value of 0.02 based on a test value of 15.05 distributed as $\chi^2(6)$, i.e. exactly the test value of the joint weak exogeneity hypothesis. This is of course no coincidence as it is a mirror image of testing the joint weak exogeneity of the bond rate and real income. Each of the pairwise tests of two unit vectors was borderline accepted with a p-value of 0.05.

The two exogeneity restrictions (if jointly accepted) would have determined the common trends in our empirical model (recalling that $p-r=2$). Consequently, the corresponding two rows of the $\boldsymbol{\Pi}$ matrix would have been zero in this case and the remaining three rows would have been represented as:

$$\boldsymbol{\Pi} = \begin{bmatrix} \alpha_{11} & 0 & 0 \\ 0 & 0 & 0 \\ 0 & \alpha_{32} & 0 \\ 0 & 0 & \alpha_{43} \\ 0 & 0 & 0 \end{bmatrix} \begin{bmatrix} \boldsymbol{\beta}'_1\mathbf{x}_{t-1} \\ \boldsymbol{\beta}'_2\mathbf{x}_{t-1} \\ \boldsymbol{\beta}'_3\mathbf{x}_{t-1} \end{bmatrix}.$$

Thus, when there are exactly $p-r$ weakly exogenous variables each $\boldsymbol{\beta}$ vector can be formulated as a row in the $\boldsymbol{\Pi}$-matrix.

Table 11.4 Tests of known vector in $\boldsymbol{\alpha}$.

r	v	$\chi^2(v)$	m^r	y^r	Δp	R_m	R_b
3	2	5.99	**3.81** [0.15]	10.32 [0.01]	**3.96** [0.14]	**5.09** [0.08]	6.88 [0.03]

11.4 Concluding remarks

The hypothetical scenario in Chapter 2 was based on the assumption of two common trends, $\sum_{i=1}^{t} \mathbf{u}_{1i}$ and $\sum_{i=1}^{t} \mathbf{u}_{2i}$, one describing the effect of cumulated nominal shocks, the other real shocks on the small monetary system. Hypothetically, they were assumed to describe unanticipated monetary shocks and real productivity shocks. Based on the weak exogeneity test results, we have now been able to roughly identify the two pushing forces, one deriving from shocks to the long-term bond rate and the other from shocks to real aggregate income. While the latter at first sight seems to be consistent with the prior assumptions, the former is more difficult to interpret in terms of the scenario. Whether or not we can attach an economic meaning to the estimated residuals will be further discussed in Chapter 14.

Part IV

Identification

12

Identification of the long-run structure

When the empirical model is estimated with data that are non-stationary in levels, we need to discuss two different identification problems: identification of the long-run structure (i.e. of the cointegration relations) and identification of the short-run structure (i.e. of the equations of the system). The former is about imposing long-run economic structure on the unrestricted cointegration relations, the latter is about imposing short-run dynamic adjustment structure on the equations for the differenced process. In this chapter, we shall primarily discuss identification of the long-run relations and leave the short-run adjustment structure to the next chapter.

The organization of this chapter is as follows. Section 12.1 discusses the cointegrated VAR model for first-order integrated data in reduced and structural form. The parameters of the model are partitioned into the short-run and the long-run parameters, and it is shown that the analysis of the long-run structure can be performed in either representation. Section 12.2 discusses the conditions for identification in terms of restrictions on the long-run structure. A general result for formal identification in a statistical model is given, and empirical identification is defined. Section 12.3 discusses how to calculate degrees of freedom when testing over-identifying restrictions. Section 12.4 discusses just-identified restrictions on the long-run structure and provides two illustrations in which economic identification can be addressed. Section 12.5 does the same for an overidentified structure and Section 12.6 for an unidentified structure. Section 12.7 illustrates some recursive procedures to check for parameter constancy and Section 12.8 concludes.

12.1 Identification when data are non-stationary

To illustrate the difference between the two identification problems, it is useful to consider the cointegrated VAR model both in the so-called reduced form and the structural form, and discuss in which aspects they differ. First, consider the usual reduced-form representation:

$$\Delta \mathbf{x}_t = \mathbf{\Gamma}_1 \Delta \mathbf{x}_{t-1} + \boldsymbol{\alpha}\boldsymbol{\beta}'\mathbf{x}_{t-1} + \mathbf{\Phi}\mathbf{D}_t + \boldsymbol{\varepsilon}_t, \quad \boldsymbol{\varepsilon}_t \sim IN(\mathbf{0}, \mathbf{\Omega}) \tag{12.1}$$

and then pre-multiply (12.1) with a non-singular $p \times p$ matrix $\mathbf{A}_0$ to obtain the so-called structural-form representation (12.2):

$$\mathbf{A}_0 \Delta \mathbf{x}_t = \mathbf{A}_1 \Delta \mathbf{x}_{t-1} + \mathbf{a}\boldsymbol{\beta}'\mathbf{x}_{t-1} + \tilde{\mathbf{\Phi}}\mathbf{D}_t + \mathbf{v}_t, \quad \mathbf{v}_t \sim IN(\mathbf{0}, \mathbf{\Sigma}). \tag{12.2}$$

At this stage, we assume that reduced-form parameters $\lambda_{RF} = \{\mathbf{\Gamma}_1, \boldsymbol{\alpha}, \boldsymbol{\beta}, \mathbf{\Phi}, \mathbf{\Omega}\}$ and structural form parameters $\lambda_{SF} = \{\mathbf{A}_0, \mathbf{A}_1, \mathbf{a}, \boldsymbol{\beta}, \tilde{\mathbf{\Phi}}, \mathbf{\Sigma}\}$ are unrestricted. To distinguish between parameters of the long-run and the short-run structure, we partition $\lambda_{RF} = \{\lambda_{RF}^S, \lambda_{RF}^L\}$, where $\lambda_{RF}^S = \{\mathbf{\Gamma}_1, \boldsymbol{\alpha}, \mathbf{\Phi}, \mathbf{\Omega}\}$ and $\lambda_{RF}^L = \{\boldsymbol{\beta}\}$ and $\lambda_{SF} = \{\lambda_{SF}^S, \lambda_{SF}^L\}$, where $\lambda_{SF}^S = \{\mathbf{A}_0, \mathbf{A}_1, \mathbf{a}, \tilde{\mathbf{\Phi}}, \mathbf{\Sigma}\}$ and $\lambda_{SF}^L = \{\boldsymbol{\beta}\}$. The relation between λ_{RF}^S and λ_{SF}^S is given by:

$$\mathbf{\Gamma}_1 = \mathbf{A}_0^{-1}\mathbf{A}_1, \quad \boldsymbol{\alpha} = \mathbf{A}_0^{-1}\mathbf{a}, \quad \boldsymbol{\varepsilon}_t = \mathbf{A}_0^{-1}\mathbf{v}_t, \quad \mathbf{\Phi} = \mathbf{A}_0^{-1}\tilde{\mathbf{\Phi}}, \quad \mathbf{\Omega} = \mathbf{A}_0^{-1}\Sigma\, \mathbf{A}_0'^{-1}.$$

The short-run parameters of the reduced form, λ_{RF}^S, are uniquely defined, whereas those of the structural form, λ_{SF}^S, are not, without imposing $p(p-1)$ just-identifying restrictions. Although the long-run parameters $\boldsymbol{\beta}$ are uniquely defined based on the normalization of the eigenvalue problem, this need not coincide with an economic identification, and in general we need to impose $r(r-1)$ just-identifying restrictions also on $\boldsymbol{\beta}$. Because the long-run parameters remain unaltered under linear transformations of the VAR model, $\boldsymbol{\beta}$ is the same in both forms and identification of the long-run structure can be done in either the reduced form or the structural form.

This gives the rationale for identifying the long-run and the short-run structure as two separate statistical problems, though from an economic point of view they are interrelated. Therefore, we can discuss the statistical problem of how to test structural hypotheses on the long-run structure $\{\boldsymbol{\beta}\}$ before addressing structural hypotheses on the short-run structure $\{\mathbf{A}_0, \mathbf{A}_1, \mathbf{a}, \tilde{\mathbf{\Phi}}, \mathbf{\Sigma}\}$. From a practical point of view this is invaluable, as the joint identification of the long- and short-run structure is likely to be immensely difficult. The identification process starts with the identification of $\boldsymbol{\beta}$ in the reduced form and proceeds to the identification of the short-run structure keeping the identified $\boldsymbol{\beta}$ fixed.

To understand all aspects of identification, Johansen and Juselius (1994) suggest that one should distinguish between identification in three different meanings:

- generic identification, which is related to a statistical model;
- empirical identification, which is related to the significance of actual estimated parameter values; and
- economic identification, which is related to the economic interpretability of the estimated coefficients of a formally and empirically identified model.

For identification to be empirically useful, all three conditions for identification have to be satisfied in the empirical problem, which as a crucial part involves the choice of data.

12.2 Identifying restrictions[1]

In order to identify the long-run structure, we have to impose restrictions on each of the cointegrating relations. As before, $\mathbf{R}_i$ denotes a $p1 \times m_i$ restriction matrix and $\mathbf{H}_i = \mathbf{R}_{i\perp}$ a $p1 \times s_i$ design matrix ($m_i + s_i = p1$) so that $\mathbf{R}_i' \, \mathbf{H}_i = \mathbf{0}$. Thus, there are m_i restrictions and consequently s_i parameters to be estimated in the ith relation. The cointegrating relations are assumed to satisfy the restrictions $\mathbf{R}_i' \boldsymbol{\beta}_i = \mathbf{0}$, or equivalently $\boldsymbol{\beta}_i = \mathbf{H}_i \boldsymbol{\varphi}_i$ for some s_i-vector $\boldsymbol{\varphi}_i$, that is

$$\boldsymbol{\beta} = (\mathbf{H}_1 \boldsymbol{\varphi}_1, \, \ldots \, , \mathbf{H}_r \boldsymbol{\varphi}_r), \tag{12.3}$$

where the matrices $\mathbf{H}_1, \, \ldots \, , \mathbf{H}_r$ express linear hypotheses to be tested against the data. Note that the linear restrictions $\mathbf{H}_i$ do not specify any normalization of the vectors $\boldsymbol{\beta}_i$. In the previous chapter, we gave several examples of design matrices $\mathbf{H}_i$.

The idea here is to discuss some principles for choosing $\mathbf{H}_i$ so that (12.3) identifies the cointegrating relations. The rank condition for identification requires that the first cointegration relation, for example, is identified if

$$\text{rank}(\mathbf{R}_1' \boldsymbol{\beta}_1, \, \ldots \, , \mathbf{R}_1' \boldsymbol{\beta}_r) = \text{rank}(\mathbf{R}_1' \mathbf{H}_1 \boldsymbol{\varphi}_1, \, \ldots \, , \mathbf{R}_1' \mathbf{H}_r \boldsymbol{\varphi}_r) = r - 1. \tag{12.4}$$

This implies that no linear combination of $\boldsymbol{\beta}_2, \, \ldots \, , \boldsymbol{\beta}_r$ can produce a vector that 'looks like' the first relation, i.e. satisfies the restrictions defining the first relation. Note, however, that in order to check the rank condition (12.4) we need to know the coefficients $\boldsymbol{\varphi}_i$, $i = 1, \, \ldots \, , r$, but in order to estimate the coefficients we need to know whether the restrictions are identifying. Most software programs check the rank condition prior to estimation, by first giving the coefficients $\boldsymbol{\varphi}$ some arbitrary numbers. If the rank condition is satisfied, estimation can proceed.

One can, however, avoid the arbitrary coefficients and explicitly check the rank condition based on the known matrices $\mathbf{R}_i$ and $\mathbf{H}_i$. Johansen (1995a) gives the following condition for a set of restrictions to be identifying:

The set of restrictions is formally identifying if for all i and $g = 1, \, \ldots \, , r - 1$ and any set of indices $1 \leq i_1 < \cdots < i_g \leq r$ not containing i, it holds that

$$\text{rank}(\mathbf{R}_i' \mathbf{H}_{i_1}, \, \ldots \, , \mathbf{R}_i' \mathbf{H}_{i_g}) \geq g. \tag{12.5}$$

As an example, we consider $r = 2$, where (12.5) reduces to the condition:

$$r_{i.j} = \text{rank}(\mathbf{R}_i' \mathbf{H}_j) \geq 1, \quad i \neq j.$$

If $r = 3$ the conditions to be satisfied are

$$\begin{aligned} r_{i.j} &= \text{rank}(\mathbf{R}_i' \mathbf{H}_j) \geq 1, \quad i \neq j, \\ r_{i.jm} &= \text{rank}(\mathbf{R}_i' (\mathbf{H}_j, \mathbf{H}_m)) \geq 2, \quad i, j, m \text{ different}. \end{aligned}$$

[1]This section relies strongly on Johansen and Juselius (1994).

The value of $r_{i.jm}$ can be determined by finding the eigenvalues of the symmetric matrix $(\mathbf{H}_j, \mathbf{H}_m)'(\mathbf{I} - \mathbf{H}_i(\mathbf{H}_i'\mathbf{H}_i)^{-1}\mathbf{H}_i')(\mathbf{H}_j, \mathbf{H}_m)$ using the identity:

$$r_{i.jm} = \text{rank}(\mathbf{R}_i'(\mathbf{H}_j, \mathbf{H}_m)) = \text{rank}\left[(\mathbf{H}_j, \mathbf{H}_m)'(\mathbf{I} - \mathbf{H}_i(\mathbf{H}_i'\mathbf{H}_i)^{-1}\mathbf{H}_i')(\mathbf{H}_j, \mathbf{H}_m)\right]. \quad (12.6)$$

Thus, the usual rank condition (12.4) requires the knowledge of the (not yet estimated) parameters, whereas condition (12.5) is a property of the known design matrices. Admittedly, the intuition behind the rank conditions might seem difficult to grasp for an inexperienced reader. However, in connection with the empirical applications below we shall attempt to build up the intuition by demonstrating how the rank conditions (12.6) change when we impose just-, over-, and under-identified restrictions on the $\boldsymbol{\beta}$ structure.

It is useful to distinguish between just-identifying restrictions and over-identifying restrictions. The former can be achieved by linear combinations of the relations (equations) and, hence, do not change the likelihood function, whereas the latter constrain the parameter space and, hence, change the likelihood function. This can be stated as:

For identifying restrictions, the rank condition (12.5) $(\mathbf{R}_i'\mathbf{H}_{i_1}, \ldots, \mathbf{R}_i'\mathbf{H}_{i_g}) \geq g$ holds for all $\mathbf{R}_i$, $i = 1, \ldots, r$. The structure is over-identified if it is identified and inequality ($>$) holds for at least one i. The structure is just-identified if equality holds for all i and the restrictions are zero restrictions. If other than zero restrictions are imposed, such as $(1, -1)$, inequality ($>$) of (12.5) can in some cases be found in a just-identified model. The structure is under-identified if the rank condition (12.5) is violated for at least one i.

It is often useful to start with a just-identified system and then impose further restrictions if the significance of the estimated parameters indicate that a further reduction in the statistical model is possible. For example, one would generally prefer to set insignificant coefficients in the just-identified model to zero. Such restrictions constrain the parameter space and thus are testable. However, they may, but need not, be overidentifying. The reason is that when imposing further restrictions, the rank condition (12.5) might become violated and the more restricted model is no longer identified.

For example, if the rank condition (12.5) is satisfied under the condition that a certain coefficient is non-zero, but the true value is in fact zero, then the rank condition in the 'true' model is not satisfied. Generally the parameter values of the generically identified model are not known but have to be estimated. If the true coefficient is zero, then the estimate will in general not be significantly different from zero and restricting it to zero will in such a case violate the rank condition. Thus, although the original statistical model is generically identified, the economic model is not empirically identified.

This can be formalized as:

An economic model specified by the parameter value ϑ, say, is generically identified if ϑ is contained in the parameter space specified by identifying restrictions. It is empirically identified if ϑ is not contained in any unidentified submodel.

In a generically identified model, the parameters can be estimated subject to the restrictions by the iterative procedure discussed in Chapter 10, Section 10.4. The algorithm can now be generalized to the case where we impose (identifying) restrictions on all cointegrating vectors. We consider the equilibrium error correction term of (12.1) and write it as:

$$\boldsymbol{\alpha\beta}'\mathbf{x}_{t-1} = \boldsymbol{\alpha}_1\boldsymbol{\beta}_1'\mathbf{x}_{t-1} + \cdots + \boldsymbol{\alpha}_r\boldsymbol{\beta}_r'\mathbf{x}_{t-1} = \boldsymbol{\alpha}_1\boldsymbol{\varphi}_1'\mathbf{H}_1'\mathbf{x}_{t-1} + \cdots + \boldsymbol{\alpha}_r\boldsymbol{\varphi}_r'\mathbf{H}_r'\mathbf{x}_{t-1}.$$

The hypothesis on $\boldsymbol{\beta}$ is expressed as:

$$\boldsymbol{\beta} = (\boldsymbol{\beta}_1, \ldots, \boldsymbol{\beta}_r) = (\mathbf{H}_1\boldsymbol{\varphi}_1, \ldots, \mathbf{H}_r\boldsymbol{\varphi}_r) \tag{12.7}$$

where $\mathbf{H}_i$, $i = 1, \ldots, r$, are known design matrices of dimension $p1 \times s_i$, and $\boldsymbol{\varphi}_i$ are $s_i \times 1$ matrices of unrestricted coefficients. Again we partition $\boldsymbol{\alpha}$ so that it corresponds to the partitioning of $\boldsymbol{\beta}$:

$$\boldsymbol{\alpha} = (\boldsymbol{\alpha}_1, \ldots, \boldsymbol{\alpha}_r).$$

The concentrated model can be written as:

$$\mathbf{R}_{0t} = \boldsymbol{\alpha}_1\boldsymbol{\varphi}_1'\mathbf{H}_1'\mathbf{R}_{1t} + \cdots + \boldsymbol{\alpha}_r\boldsymbol{\varphi}_r'\mathbf{H}_r\mathbf{R}_{1t} + \boldsymbol{\varepsilon}_t.$$

The estimation problem can be solved by extending the switching algorithm, introduced in Chapter 10, Section 10.4, as described below:

1. Estimate an initial value of $\left\{\boldsymbol{\beta}_1 = \tilde{\boldsymbol{\beta}}_1, \ldots, \text{ and } \boldsymbol{\beta}_{r-1} = \tilde{\boldsymbol{\beta}}_{r-1}\right\}$.
2. For fixed values of $\left\{\boldsymbol{\beta}_1 = \tilde{\boldsymbol{\beta}}_1, \ldots, \boldsymbol{\beta}_{r-1} = \tilde{\boldsymbol{\beta}}_{r-1}\right\}$ estimate $\boldsymbol{\alpha}_r$ and $\boldsymbol{\varphi}_r$ by reduced rank regression of $\mathbf{R}_{0t}$ on $\mathbf{H}_r'\mathbf{R}_{1t}$ corrected for $\tilde{\boldsymbol{\beta}}_1'\mathbf{R}_{1t}, \ldots, \tilde{\boldsymbol{\beta}}_{r-1}'\mathbf{R}_{1t}$. This defines $\tilde{\boldsymbol{\beta}}_r = \mathbf{H}_r\tilde{\boldsymbol{\varphi}}_r$ and $L_{\max}(\tilde{\boldsymbol{\beta}}_1, \ldots, \tilde{\boldsymbol{\beta}}_{r-1})$.
3. For fixed values of $\left\{\boldsymbol{\beta}_2 = \tilde{\boldsymbol{\beta}}_2, \ldots, \boldsymbol{\beta}_{r-1} = \tilde{\boldsymbol{\beta}}_{r-1}, \boldsymbol{\beta}_r = \tilde{\boldsymbol{\beta}}_r\right\}$ estimate $\boldsymbol{\alpha}_1$ and $\boldsymbol{\varphi}_1$ by reduced rank regression of $\mathbf{R}_{0t}$ on $\mathbf{H}_1'\mathbf{R}_{1t}$ corrected for $\tilde{\boldsymbol{\beta}}_2'\mathbf{R}_{1t}, \ldots, \tilde{\boldsymbol{\beta}}_r'\mathbf{R}_{1t}$. This defines $\tilde{\boldsymbol{\beta}}_1 = \mathbf{H}_1\tilde{\boldsymbol{\varphi}}_1$ and $L_{\max}(\tilde{\boldsymbol{\beta}}_2, \ldots, \tilde{\boldsymbol{\beta}}_r)$.
4. Repeat the steps using the last obtained values of $\tilde{\boldsymbol{\beta}}_i$ until the value of the maximized likelihood function has converged.

The eigenvalue problem for fixed $\tilde{\tilde{\boldsymbol{\beta}}}_1 = \{\boldsymbol{\beta}_1 = \tilde{\boldsymbol{\beta}}_1, \ldots, \boldsymbol{\beta}_{r-1} = \tilde{\boldsymbol{\beta}}_{r-1}\}$ is given by:

$$\left|\rho_r\mathbf{H}_r'\mathbf{S}_{11.\tilde{\tilde{\boldsymbol{\beta}}}_1}\mathbf{H}_r - \mathbf{H}_r'\mathbf{S}_{10.\tilde{\tilde{\boldsymbol{\beta}}}_1}(\mathbf{S}_{00.\tilde{\tilde{\boldsymbol{\beta}}}_1})^{-1}\mathbf{S}_{01.\tilde{\tilde{\boldsymbol{\beta}}}_1}\mathbf{H}_r\right| = 0$$

and for fixed $\tilde{\tilde{\boldsymbol{\beta}}}_2 = \{\boldsymbol{\beta}_2 = \tilde{\boldsymbol{\beta}}_2, \ldots, \boldsymbol{\beta}_r = \tilde{\boldsymbol{\beta}}_r\}$ by:

$$\left|\rho_1\mathbf{H}_1'\mathbf{S}_{11.\tilde{\tilde{\boldsymbol{\beta}}}_1}\mathbf{H}_1 - \mathbf{H}_1'\mathbf{S}_{10.\tilde{\tilde{\boldsymbol{\beta}}}_2}(\mathbf{S}_{00.\tilde{\tilde{\boldsymbol{\beta}}}_2})^{-1}\mathbf{S}_{01.\tilde{\tilde{\boldsymbol{\beta}}}_2}\mathbf{H}_1\right| = 0,$$

and so on. The maximum of the likelihood function is given by:

$$L_{\max}^{-2/T}(\boldsymbol{\beta}^c) = |\mathbf{S}_{00}|\,(1 - \tilde{\rho}_1)\cdots(1 - \tilde{\rho}_r)$$

where $\tilde{\rho}_i$ are the eigenvalues obtained from applying the switching algorithm until convergence of the likelihood function.

Using the LR procedure, the hypothesis (12.7) can be tested by calculating the test statistic:

$$-2\ln\Lambda = T\{\ln(1-\tilde{\rho}_1)+\cdots+\ln(1-\tilde{\rho}_r)-\ln(1-\hat{\lambda}_1)-\cdots-\ln(1-\hat{\lambda}_r)\}, \qquad (12.8)$$

which, under the assumption that all $\mathbf{H}_i$ are identifying, is asymptotically χ^2 distributed with degrees of freedom given by:

$$v = \sum_{i=1}^{r}(m_i - r + 1) = \sum_{i=1}^{r}(p1 - r) - (s_i - 1).$$

How to calculate the degrees of freedom will be given a detailed discussion in the next section.

To summarize: For fixed values of $\boldsymbol{\varphi}_2, \ldots, \boldsymbol{\varphi}_r$, or $\boldsymbol{\beta}_2, \ldots, \boldsymbol{\beta}_r$, we can find the ML estimate of $\boldsymbol{\beta}_1$by performing a reduced rank regression of $\Delta\mathbf{x}_t$ on $\mathbf{H}_1'\mathbf{x}_{t-1}$ corrected for all the stationary and deterministic terms, that is, $\boldsymbol{\beta}_2'\mathbf{x}_{t-1}, \ldots, \boldsymbol{\beta}_r'\mathbf{x}_{t-1}, \Delta\mathbf{x}_{t-1}$ and $\mathbf{D}_t$. This determines the estimate of $\boldsymbol{\varphi}_1$ and hence $\boldsymbol{\beta}_1 = \mathbf{H}_1\boldsymbol{\varphi}_1$. In the next step, we keep the values $\boldsymbol{\beta}_1, \boldsymbol{\beta}_3, \ldots, \boldsymbol{\beta}_r$ fixed and perform a reduced rank regression of $\Delta\mathbf{x}_t$ on $\mathbf{H}_2'\mathbf{x}_{t-1}$ corrected for all stationary and deterministic terms. This determines $\boldsymbol{\beta}_2$. By applying the algorithm until the likelihood function has converged to its maximum, we can find the maximum likelihood estimates of $\boldsymbol{\beta}$ subject to the identifying restrictions.

The speed of convergence of the switching algorithm depends very much on how we choose the initial values of $\boldsymbol{\beta}$. For example, the unrestricted estimates of $\boldsymbol{\beta}$ are not in general the best choice because the unrestricted eigenvectors need not correspond to the ordering given by $\mathbf{H}_1, \ldots, \mathbf{H}_r$ and thus can be very poor initial values. Instead, the linear combination of the unrestricted estimates which is as close as possible to $sp(\mathbf{H}_i)$, $i = 1, \ldots, r$ is clearly preferable as a starting value for $\boldsymbol{\beta}_i$. These can be found by solving the eigenvalue problem:

$$|\rho\hat{\boldsymbol{\beta}}'\hat{\boldsymbol{\beta}} - \hat{\boldsymbol{\beta}}'\mathbf{H}_i(\mathbf{H}_i'\mathbf{H}_i)^{-1}\mathbf{H}_i'\hat{\boldsymbol{\beta}}|$$

for the r eigenvalues $\rho_1 > \cdots > \rho_r$ and $\boldsymbol{v}_1, \ldots, \boldsymbol{v}_r$, and choose as initial value for $\boldsymbol{\beta}_i$ the eigenvector defined by $\mathbf{H}\tilde{\boldsymbol{\beta}}_i = \hat{\boldsymbol{\beta}}\mathbf{v}_i$ This choice of initial values has the extra advantage that for exactly identified equations no iterations are needed.

12.3 Formulation of identifying hypotheses and degrees of freedom

When testing restrictions imposed on the cointegration relations using readily available software packages, the degrees of freedom are usually provided by the program. However, some hypotheses can impose restrictions which are quite complicated and where standard formula for calculating degrees of freedom may no longer be applicable. It is therefore important to understand the logic behind the calculations of the degrees of freedom. Furthermore, even if most software packages check identification using some generic values for the model parameters and inform the user when identification is violated, we need to understand why identification failed in order to re-specify the restrictions.

The following example illustrates how to calculate degrees of freedom when we have imposed over-identifying restrictions on three cointegrating relations in a VAR analysis of the Danish data $(m_t^r, y_t^r, \Delta p_t, R_{m,t}, R_{b,t})$.[2] The first relation expresses that $(m_t^r - y_t^r)$ and $(R_{m,t} - R_{b,t})$ are cointegrated, so are driven by the same stochastic trend;[3] the second relation that $y_t^r, \Delta p_t$ and $R_{b,t}$ are cointegrated, so share two common trends; and the third relation that $R_{m,t}$ and $R_{b,t}$ are cointegrated, so share one common trend.

The first step is to examine whether the restricted structure defined by $\boldsymbol{\beta}^c = \{\mathbf{H}_1\boldsymbol{\varphi}_1, \ldots, \mathbf{H}_r\boldsymbol{\varphi}_r\}$ satisfies the rank and order condition for identification. We shall here illustrate how this can be done analytically using condition (12.5) based on the following example where, for simplicity, we disregard any deterministic components in the cointegration relations.

$$\begin{bmatrix} \beta_{11}^c & -\beta_{11}^c & 0 & \beta_{12}^c & -\beta_{12}^c \\ 0 & \beta_{21}^c & \beta_{22}^c & 0 & \beta_{23}^c \\ 0 & 0 & 0 & \beta_{31}^c & \beta_{32}^c \end{bmatrix} \begin{bmatrix} m_t^r \\ y_t^r \\ \Delta p_t \\ R_{m,t} \\ R_{b,t} \end{bmatrix}. \tag{12.9}$$

The rank conditions (12.5) for the structure (12.9) are given by:

Relation	$r_{i.j}$	Relation	$r_{i.jk}$
1.2	3	1.23	3
1.3	1		
2.1	2	2.13	2
2.3	1		
3.1	1	3.12	3
3.2	2		

The table can be interpreted in the following way: We consider first the identification of $\boldsymbol{\beta}_1$ relative to $\boldsymbol{\beta}_2$ and then $\boldsymbol{\beta}_1$ relative to $\boldsymbol{\beta}_3$. Adding (a fraction of) $\boldsymbol{\beta}_2$ to $\boldsymbol{\beta}_1$ will destroy (1) the homogeneity restriction on money and income, (2) the zero restriction on inflation, and (3) the spread restriction on the two interest rates. Adding $\boldsymbol{\beta}_3$ to $\boldsymbol{\beta}_1$ will only destroy the spread restriction on the interest rates. Thus $R_{1.2} = 3$, and relation $\boldsymbol{\beta}_1$ is overidentified by two restrictions relative to $\boldsymbol{\beta}_2$, whereas $R_{1.3} = 1$, and relation $\boldsymbol{\beta}_1$ is just identified relative to $\boldsymbol{\beta}_3$. An interesting case is $\boldsymbol{\beta}_3$ relative to $\boldsymbol{\beta}_1$. One might think that the rank condition should be two, since adding $\boldsymbol{\beta}_1$ to $\boldsymbol{\beta}_3$ will destroy the zero restrictions on money and income. However, a (0, 0) restriction is also a homogeneity restriction, i.e. $0(\varphi, -\varphi) = (0, 0)$, so adding $\boldsymbol{\beta}_1$ to $\boldsymbol{\beta}_3$ destroys the zero restriction, not the homogeneity restriction. Finally we consider the case $\boldsymbol{\beta}_3$ relative to $\boldsymbol{\beta}_1$ and $\boldsymbol{\beta}_2$. Adding both $\boldsymbol{\beta}_1$ and $\boldsymbol{\beta}_2$ to $\boldsymbol{\beta}_3$ will now destroy all three restrictions in $\boldsymbol{\beta}_3$. Thus, $R_{3.12} = 3$ and $\boldsymbol{\beta}_3$ is overidentified by one restriction relative to $\boldsymbol{\beta}_1$ and $\boldsymbol{\beta}_2$.

[2]For notational simplicity we disregard the shift dummy here.

[3]Note that, this stochastic trend might very well be the sum of two (or several) autonomous trends.

As discussed in Chapter 7, the parameters $(\beta^c_{11}, \beta^c_{12})$, $(\beta^c_{21}, \beta^c_{22}, \beta^c_{23})$ and $(\beta^c_{31}, \beta^c_{32})$ are defined up to a factor of proportionality, and it is always possible to normalize on one element in each vector without changing the likelihood:

$$\begin{bmatrix} 1 & -1 & 0 & \beta^c_{12}/\beta^c_{11} & -\beta^c_{12}/\beta^c_{11} \\ 0 & 1 & \beta^c_{22}/\beta^c_{21} & 0 & \beta^c_{23}/\beta^c_{21} \\ 0 & 0 & 0 & 1 & \beta^c_{32}/\beta^c_{31} \end{bmatrix} \begin{bmatrix} m^r_t \\ y^r_t \\ \Delta p_t \\ R_{m,t} \\ R_{b,t} \end{bmatrix}. \tag{12.10}$$

When normalizing $\boldsymbol{\beta}^c_i$ by diving through with a non-zero element β^c_{ij}, the corresponding $\boldsymbol{\alpha}^c_i$ vector is multiplied by the same element. Thus, normalization does not change $\mathbf{\Pi} = \boldsymbol{\alpha}^c\boldsymbol{\beta}^{c\prime} = \boldsymbol{\alpha}\boldsymbol{\beta}'$ and we can generally choose whether to normalize or not. However, when the long-run structure is identified, normalization becomes more important. This is because it is only possible to get standard errors of $\hat{\beta}_{ij}$ when each cointegration vector is properly normalized. In this case it is convenient to express $\boldsymbol{\beta}^c_i = \mathbf{h}_i + \tilde{\mathbf{H}}_i\tilde{\boldsymbol{\varphi}}_i$ where $\tilde{\boldsymbol{\varphi}}_i$ is now $(s_i - 1) \times 1$, $\mathbf{h}_i$ is a vector in $sp(\mathbf{H}_i)$ defining the chosen normalization, and $sp(\mathbf{h}_i, \tilde{\mathbf{H}}_i) = sp(\mathbf{H}_i)$ (Johansen 1996).

As discussed in Chapter 10.1, hypotheses on the cointegration structure can be formulated either by specifying the number of free parameters $\boldsymbol{\varphi}_i$, i.e. $\boldsymbol{\beta}^c = (\mathbf{H}_1\boldsymbol{\varphi}_1, \ldots, \mathbf{H}_r\boldsymbol{\varphi}_r)$ or the number of restrictions m_i, i.e. $\mathbf{R}'\boldsymbol{\beta} = \mathbf{0}$. When we discuss identification, it is convenient to choose the former formulation, i.e. to express the hypotheses in terms of the number of free parameters. For each cointegration vector $\boldsymbol{\beta}^c_i$, we have to make a distinction between the normalized coefficient and the remaining $s_i - 1$ free coefficients $\tilde{\boldsymbol{\varphi}}_i$. As an illustration, we express the above structure (12.10) using $\boldsymbol{\beta}^c_i = \mathbf{h}_i + \tilde{\mathbf{H}}_i\tilde{\boldsymbol{\varphi}}_i$:

$$\boldsymbol{\beta}^c = \{\mathbf{h}_1 + \tilde{\mathbf{H}}_1\tilde{\boldsymbol{\varphi}}_1,\ \mathbf{h}_2 + \tilde{\mathbf{H}}_2\tilde{\boldsymbol{\varphi}}_2,\ \mathbf{h}_3 + \tilde{\mathbf{H}}_3\tilde{\boldsymbol{\varphi}}_3\}, \tag{12.11}$$

where:

$$\mathbf{h}_1 + \tilde{\mathbf{H}}_1\tilde{\boldsymbol{\varphi}}_1 = \begin{bmatrix} 1 \\ -1 \\ 0 \\ 0 \\ 0 \end{bmatrix} + \begin{bmatrix} 0 \\ 0 \\ 0 \\ 1 \\ -1 \end{bmatrix} [\tilde{\varphi}_{12}],$$

$$\mathbf{h}_2 + \tilde{\mathbf{H}}_2\tilde{\boldsymbol{\varphi}}_2 = \begin{bmatrix} 0 \\ 1 \\ 0 \\ 0 \\ 0 \end{bmatrix} + \begin{bmatrix} 0 & 0 \\ 0 & 0 \\ 1 & 0 \\ 0 & 0 \\ 0 & 1 \end{bmatrix} \begin{bmatrix} \tilde{\varphi}_{22} \\ \tilde{\varphi}_{23} \end{bmatrix},$$

$$\mathbf{h}_3 + \tilde{\mathbf{H}}_3\tilde{\boldsymbol{\varphi}}_3 = \begin{bmatrix} 0 \\ 0 \\ 0 \\ 1 \\ 0 \end{bmatrix} + \begin{bmatrix} 0 \\ 0 \\ 0 \\ 0 \\ 1 \end{bmatrix} [\tilde{\varphi}_{32}].$$

For given estimates of $\boldsymbol{\beta}^c$, the estimates of $\boldsymbol{\alpha}^c$ are given by (7.5) in Chapter 7:

$$\hat{\boldsymbol{\alpha}}^c = \mathbf{S}_{01}\hat{\boldsymbol{\beta}}^c \left(\hat{\boldsymbol{\beta}}^{c\prime}\mathbf{S}_{11}\hat{\boldsymbol{\beta}}^c\right)^{-1}, \tag{12.12}$$

and the standard errors of $\hat{\beta}^c_{ij}$ are calculated as:

$$\hat{\sigma}_{\beta^c_{ij}} = \sqrt{T^{-1}\text{diag}\left\{\tilde{\mathbf{H}}\left[\tilde{\mathbf{H}}'\left(\hat{\boldsymbol{\alpha}}^{c\prime}\hat{\boldsymbol{\Omega}}^{-1}\hat{\boldsymbol{\alpha}}^c \otimes \mathbf{S}_{11}\right)\tilde{\mathbf{H}}\right]^{-1}\tilde{\mathbf{H}}'\right\}_{ij}} \tag{12.13}$$

where diag$[\cdot]_{ij}$ are defined by the ordering $i = 1, \ldots, r$ and $j = 1, \ldots, p1$ and

$$\tilde{\mathbf{H}} = \begin{bmatrix} \tilde{\mathbf{H}}_1 & 0 & \cdots & 0 \\ 0 & \tilde{\mathbf{H}}_2 & 0 & \vdots \\ \vdots & 0 & \ddots & 0 \\ 0 & \cdots & 0 & \tilde{\mathbf{H}}_r \end{bmatrix}$$

The standard errors of the corresponding $\hat{\alpha}^c_{ij}$ coefficients are calculated as:

$$\hat{\sigma}_{\alpha^c_{ij}} = \sqrt{T^{-1}\hat{\boldsymbol{\Omega}}_{ii}\left(\hat{\boldsymbol{\beta}}^{c\prime}\mathbf{S}_{11}\hat{\boldsymbol{\beta}}^c\right)^{-1}_{jj}} \tag{12.14}$$

We shall show below that it is always possible to impose $r(r-1)$ just-identifying restrictions on $\boldsymbol{\beta}$ by linear manipulations of the unrestricted cointegration vectors. Such 'pseudo' restrictions do not change the value of the likelihood function and, thus, no testing is involved in this case. Note that a cointegration structure is just-identified if $r(r-1)$ restrictions have been imposed and the condition (12.5) is satisfied. Additional restrictions on the structure change the value of the likelihood function and, thus, are testable. They are over-identifying if they satisfy rank$(\mathbf{R}_i'\mathbf{H}_{i_1}, \ldots, \mathbf{R}_i'\mathbf{H}_{i_g}) > g$, otherwise they are non-identifying though, nevertheless, testable binding restrictions.

Given that the restrictions satisfy (12.5), the degrees of freedom can be calculated from the formula defined at p. 212:

$$\nu = \sum_{i=1}^{r}(m_i - (r-1)).$$

Consider s_i, the number of free coefficients in $\boldsymbol{\beta}^c_i$, and $m_i = p - s_i$, the total number of restrictions on vector $\boldsymbol{\beta}^c_i$. Then the degrees of freedom in the above example are calculated as follows:

s_i m_i	$s_1 = 2$ $m_1 = 3$	$s_2 = 3$ $m_2 = 2$	$s_3 = 2$ $m_3 = 3$
$r-1$	2	2	2
$m_i - (r-1)$	1	0	1

so the degrees of freedom are $\nu = 2$. Note, however, that some of the restrictions may not be identifying (for example the same restriction on all cointegration relations), but are nevertheless testable restrictions. Whatever the case, an identified structure must, as a minimum, satisfy the condition for just identification.

12.4 Just-identifying restrictions

In general, we can always transform the long-run matrix $\mathbf{\Pi} = \boldsymbol{\alpha}\boldsymbol{\beta}'$ by a non-singular $r \times r$ matrix $\mathbf{Q}$ in the following way: $\mathbf{\Pi} = \boldsymbol{\alpha}\boldsymbol{Q}\boldsymbol{Q}^{-1}\boldsymbol{\beta}' = \tilde{\boldsymbol{\alpha}}\tilde{\boldsymbol{\beta}}'$, where $\tilde{\boldsymbol{\alpha}} = \boldsymbol{\alpha}\boldsymbol{Q}$ and $\tilde{\boldsymbol{\beta}} = \boldsymbol{\beta}\boldsymbol{Q}'^{-1}$. We shall now demonstrate how to choose the matrix $\mathbf{Q}$ so that it imposes $r-1$ just-identifying restrictions on each $\boldsymbol{\beta}_i$. As an example of the latter, we consider the following design matrix $\mathbf{Q} = [\boldsymbol{\beta}_1']$ where $\boldsymbol{\beta}_1'$ is an $(r \times r)$ non-singular matrix defined by $\boldsymbol{\beta}' = [\boldsymbol{\beta}_1', \boldsymbol{\beta}_2']$. In this case $\boldsymbol{\alpha}\boldsymbol{\beta}' = \boldsymbol{\alpha}(\boldsymbol{\beta}_1'\boldsymbol{\beta}_1^{-1\prime}\boldsymbol{\beta}') = \boldsymbol{\alpha}[\mathbf{I}_r, \tilde{\boldsymbol{\beta}}']$ where $\mathbf{I}_r$ is the $(r \times r)$ unit matrix and $\tilde{\boldsymbol{\beta}}' = \boldsymbol{\beta}_1^{-1\prime}\boldsymbol{\beta}_2'$ is a $r \times (p-r)$ matrix of full rank. For example, assume that $\boldsymbol{\beta}$ is (5×3):

$$\boldsymbol{\beta} = \begin{bmatrix} \beta_{11} & \beta_{12} & \beta_{13} \\ \beta_{21} & \beta_{22} & \beta_{23} \\ \beta_{31} & \beta_{32} & \beta_{33} \\ \cdots & \cdots & \cdots \\ \beta_{41} & \beta_{42} & \beta_{43} \\ \beta_{51} & \beta_{52} & \beta_{53} \end{bmatrix} = \begin{bmatrix} \boldsymbol{\beta}_1 \\ \\ \cdots \\ \boldsymbol{\beta}_2 \end{bmatrix}; \begin{bmatrix} \boldsymbol{\beta}_1 \\ \\ \cdots \\ \boldsymbol{\beta}_2 \end{bmatrix} \boldsymbol{\beta}_1^{-1} = \begin{bmatrix} 1 & 0 & 0 \\ 0 & 1 & 0 \\ 0 & 0 & 1 \\ \cdots & \cdots & \cdots \\ \tilde{\beta}_{41} & \tilde{\beta}_{42} & \tilde{\beta}_{43} \\ \tilde{\beta}_{51} & \tilde{\beta}_{52} & \tilde{\beta}_{53} \end{bmatrix}.$$

We notice that the choice of $\mathbf{Q} = \boldsymbol{\beta}_1$ in our example has in fact imposed two zero restrictions and one normalization on each cointegration relation. These just-identifying restrictions have transformed $\boldsymbol{\beta}$ to the long-run 'reduced form'. Thus, the above example for $\mathbf{x}_t = [\mathbf{x}_{1t}', \mathbf{x}_{2t}']'$, where $\mathbf{x}_{1t}' = [x_{1t}, x_{2t}, x_{3t}]$ and $\mathbf{x}_{2t}' = [x_{4t}, x_{5t}]$, would describe an economic application where the three variables in $\mathbf{x}_{1t}$ are 'endogenous' and the two in $\mathbf{x}_{2t}$ are 'exogenous'.

Furthermore, if we decompose $\boldsymbol{\alpha} = \begin{bmatrix} \boldsymbol{\alpha}_1 \\ \boldsymbol{\alpha}_2 \end{bmatrix}$ and $\boldsymbol{\alpha}_2 = \mathbf{0}$, then $\boldsymbol{\beta}'\mathbf{x}_t$ does not appear in the equation for $\Delta\mathbf{x}_{2,t}$ and $\mathbf{x}_{2,t}$ is weakly exogenous for $\boldsymbol{\beta}$. In this case, efficient inference on the long-run relations can be conducted in the conditional model of $\Delta\mathbf{x}_{1,t}$, given $\Delta\mathbf{x}_{2,t}$, as discussed in the previous chapter, see also Johansen (1992a). When 'endogenous' and 'exogenous' are given an economic interpretation this corresponds to the triangular representation suggested by Phillips (2001). Note that the latter requires that $\boldsymbol{\alpha}_2 = \mathbf{0}$, which is a testable hypothesis. Therefore, from an econometric point of view there is no reason to *assume* $\boldsymbol{\alpha}_2 = \mathbf{0}$, instead of first testing whether it is an acceptable description of the data.

Example 1 We consider here a just-identified structure describing the long-run 'reduced form' assuming real money, inflation, and the short-term interest rate to be 'endogenous' and real income and the bond rate to be 'exogenous' corresponding to the following restrictions on $\boldsymbol{\beta}$:

$$\mathcal{H}_{S.1} : \boldsymbol{\beta} = (\mathbf{H}_1\boldsymbol{\varphi}_1, \mathbf{H}_2\boldsymbol{\varphi}_2, \mathbf{H}_3\boldsymbol{\varphi}_3),$$

Table 12.1 Two just-identified long-run structures.

	$\mathcal{H}_{S.1}$			$\mathcal{H}_{S.2}$		
	$\hat{\beta}_1$	$\hat{\beta}_1$	$\hat{\beta}_3$	$\hat{\beta}_1$	$\hat{\beta}_2$	$\hat{\beta}_3$
m^r	**1.0**	0.0	0.0	**1.0**	0.0	0.0
y^r	**−0.94** [−6.55]	**0.04** [3.24]	**0.01** [2.06]	−1.0	**0.03** [3.81]	**0.04** [4.80]
Δp	0.0	**1.0**	0.0	0.0	**1.0**	**1.0**
R_m	0.0	0.0	**1.0**	−4.70 [−1.44]	**−0.54** [−4.53]	**0.32** [2.99]
R_b	3.04 [1.51]	0.20 [1.16]	**−0.63** [−7.03]	**5.99** [2.40]	**0.54** [4.53]	0.0
D_s831	**−0.27** [−8.08]	**0.01** [5.11]	**−0.01** [−5.12]	**−0.24** [−7.46]	**0.02** [6.58]	**0.01** [5.14]
	α_1	α_2	α_3	α_1	α_2	α_3
Δm_t^r	**−0.22** [−4.74]	*	**2.98** [2.64]	**−0.22** [−4.74]	**−2.47** [−2.01]	*
Δy_t^r	0.05 [1.87]	*	**−1.84** [−2.72]	0.05 [1.87]	**1.75** [2.37]	**−2.04** [−2.64]
$\Delta^2 p_t$	*	**−0.82** [−5.49]	*	*	*	**−1.12** [−2.53]
$\Delta R_{m,t}$	*	*	−0.09 [−1.81]	*	**0.12** [2.28]	−0.09 [−1.68]
$\Delta R_{b,t}$	*	*	0.13 [1.86]	*	**−0.15** [−2.08]	**0.17** [2.23]

where

$$\mathbf{H}_1 = \begin{bmatrix} 1 & 0 & 0 & 0 \\ 0 & 1 & 0 & 0 \\ 0 & 0 & 0 & 0 \\ 0 & 0 & 0 & 0 \\ 0 & 0 & 1 & 0 \\ 0 & 0 & 0 & 1 \end{bmatrix}, \quad \mathbf{H}_2 = \begin{bmatrix} 0 & 0 & 0 & 0 \\ 1 & 0 & 0 & 0 \\ 0 & 1 & 0 & 0 \\ 0 & 0 & 0 & 0 \\ 0 & 0 & 1 & 0 \\ 0 & 0 & 0 & 1 \end{bmatrix}, \quad \mathbf{H}_3 = \begin{bmatrix} 0 & 0 & 0 & 0 \\ 1 & 0 & 0 & 0 \\ 0 & 0 & 0 & 0 \\ 0 & 1 & 0 & 0 \\ 0 & 0 & 1 & 0 \\ 0 & 0 & 0 & 1 \end{bmatrix}$$

i.e. $\mathbf{H}_1$ picks up real money, $\mathbf{H}_2$ inflation rate, $\mathbf{H}_3$ the short-term interest rate, and the two weakly exogenous variables and the shift dummy D_s831 enter all three relations. The estimates are reported in Table 12.1. The first relation is similar to $\mathcal{H}_{13}$ in Table 12.2, noticing that the coefficient to bond rate is not significant. The second relation is approximately the inflation–income relation $\mathcal{H}_{17}$, noticing again that the coefficient to bond rate is insignificant. The third relation is similar to the short-term long-term interest rate relation $\mathcal{H}_{27}$, except that real income enters with a tiny coefficient and the coefficient to the bond rate is now smaller. There is no testing involved in this case as the $r - 1 = 2$ restrictions have been achieved by linear combinations of the unrestricted relations, i.e. by rotating the cointegration space.

Only the $\hat{\alpha}$ coefficients with a $|t\text{-value}| > 1.6$ have been reported in the lower part of Table 12.1. Because no binding restrictions have been imposed, the matrix $\hat{\mathbf{\Pi}}^c = \hat{\boldsymbol{\alpha}}^c \hat{\boldsymbol{\beta}}^{c\prime} = \hat{\mathbf{\Pi}} = \hat{\boldsymbol{\alpha}} \hat{\boldsymbol{\beta}}'$, i.e. it is the same as in the unrestricted model. It is now easy to see that the combination $\hat{\boldsymbol{\alpha}}_{11}^{c}\hat{\boldsymbol{\beta}}_{1}^{c\prime}\mathbf{x}_t + \hat{\boldsymbol{\alpha}}_{13}^{c}\hat{\boldsymbol{\beta}}_{3}^{c\prime}\mathbf{x}_t$ will approximately replicate the money demand relation $\mathcal{H}_{15}$ in Table 10.3. Thus, the money demand relation can be considered a linear combination of two stationary relations.

Example 2 Here we give an example of non-zero as well as zero just-identifying restrictions:

$$\mathcal{H}_{S.2} : \boldsymbol{\beta} = (\boldsymbol{H}_1\varphi_1, \mathbf{H}_2\varphi_2, \mathbf{H}_3\varphi_3),$$

where

$$\mathbf{H}_1 = \begin{bmatrix} 1 & 0 & 0 & 0 \\ -1 & 0 & 0 & 0 \\ 0 & 0 & 0 & 0 \\ 0 & 1 & 0 & 0 \\ 0 & 0 & 1 & 0 \\ 0 & 0 & 0 & 1 \end{bmatrix}, \quad \mathbf{H}_2 = \begin{bmatrix} 0 & 0 & 0 & 0 \\ 1 & 0 & 0 & 0 \\ 0 & 1 & 0 & 0 \\ 0 & 0 & 1 & 0 \\ 0 & 0 & -1 & 0 \\ 0 & 0 & 0 & 1 \end{bmatrix}, \quad \mathbf{H}_3 = \begin{bmatrix} 0 & 0 & 0 & 0 \\ 1 & 0 & 0 & 0 \\ 0 & 1 & 0 & 0 \\ 0 & 0 & 1 & 0 \\ 0 & 0 & 0 & 0 \\ 0 & 0 & 0 & 1 \end{bmatrix}.$$

We now check that the restrictions are in fact just-identifying by calculating the rank condition (12.5). We note that just-identification based on zero restrictions corresponds to $\text{rank}(\mathbf{R}_i'\mathbf{H}_j) = 1$ for $i, j = 1, 2, 3$ and $j \neq i$, and $\text{rank}(\mathbf{R}_i'(\mathbf{H}_j, \mathbf{H}_g)) = 2$ for i, j, g different. However, even though $\mathcal{H}_{S.2}$ is just identifying, inequality appears in some cases as shown by the rank indices reported in Table 12.2, column $\mathcal{H}_{S.2}$. The estimates of $\boldsymbol{\alpha}$ and $\boldsymbol{\beta}$ are given in the right-hand side of Table 12.1. The first relation resembles the money demand relation, $\mathcal{H}_{15}$, except that the coefficients to the interest rates are much smaller and not very significant. This is because the stationarity of the liquidity ratio does not improve significantly by adding the non-stationary interest rates. Thus, the money demand relation can only be recovered by the help of the α coefficients, i.e. by $\alpha_{11}\boldsymbol{\beta}_1 + \alpha_{12}\boldsymbol{\beta}_2$.

The two just-identified structures in Table 12.1 illustrate that in general one can find many just-identified structures by rotating the cointegrating space and the question is whether it is at all useful to specify such structures. We shall use the estimated structures $\mathcal{H}_{S.1}$ and $\mathcal{H}_{S.2}$ to illustrate why we believe that the answer is definitely affirmative, in particular as the first step in the identification search. In some cases we are fortunate to know from our prior analysis which variables are primarily adjusting (endogenous) and which are primarily pushing (weakly exogenous). For example based on the weak exogeneity tests in Chapter 11 we know that real aggregate income and the bond rate are mostly pushing, whereas money stock, inflation rate and (probably) the short-term interest are essentially adjusting. The just-identified structure $\mathcal{H}_{S.1}$ exploits this feature by specifying the 'endogenous' variables as a function of the 'exogenous'.

Based on this first identification scheme we have tentatively spotted three irreducible cointegration relations, the first one describing a stationary money velocity with an equilibrium mean shift, the second one a stationary relation between the inflation rate and real aggregate income with a mean shift, and the third a relation between the two interest rates with a mean shift. If we find these 'reduced form' relations to be unsatisfactory we can impose more sophisticated just-identified restrictions as illustrated by $\mathcal{H}_{S.2}$. The first relation in the latter has imposed a homogeneity restriction between m^r and y^r (suggested by $\hat{\boldsymbol{\beta}}_1$ in $\mathcal{H}_{S.1}$) and, thus, needs just one more zero restriction which is imposed on Δp. We have now quite strong evidence of the money demand relation, though the t-values of the interest rates are fairly small due to the fact that money velocity was already found to be stationary. The second relation imposes the interest rate spread restriction and one zero restriction on real money, whereas the third relation is the same as in $\mathcal{H}_{S.1}$.

An important advantage of imposing just-identifying restrictions is that we obtain standard errors on the coefficients and, thus, a first idea of how to simplify the relations. For example, two of the estimated coefficients in the just-identified structures $\mathcal{H}_{S.1}$ and $\mathcal{H}_{S.2}$ are insignificant, suggesting further simplifications of the structures. Another advantage is that we can use this first analysis to infer from the estimated coefficients whether a long-run relation makes economic sense or not. For example $\hat{\boldsymbol{\beta}}_1$ and $\hat{\boldsymbol{\beta}}_2$ in $\mathcal{H}_{S.2}$ seemed to describe a plausible money demand relation and an interest rate inflation rate relation. These results can be exploited in the subsequent search for over-identified and meaningful relations. This will be illustrated in the next section.

12.5 Over-identifying restrictions

We shall now consider two examples of an over-identified long-run structure.

Example 3 We consider the structure:

$$\mathcal{H}_{S.3} : \boldsymbol{\beta} = (\mathbf{H}_1\varphi_1, \mathbf{H}_2\varphi_2, \mathbf{H}_3\varphi_3),$$

where

$$\mathbf{H}_1 = \begin{bmatrix} 1 & 0 \\ -1 & 0 \\ 0 & 0 \\ 0 & 0 \\ 0 & 0 \\ 0 & 1 \end{bmatrix}, \quad \mathbf{H}_2 = \begin{bmatrix} 0 & 0 & 0 \\ 1 & 0 & 0 \\ 0 & 1 & 0 \\ 0 & 0 & 0 \\ 0 & 0 & 0 \\ 0 & 0 & 1 \end{bmatrix}, \quad \mathbf{H}_3 = \begin{bmatrix} 0 & 0 & 0 \\ 0 & 0 & 0 \\ 1 & 0 & 0 \\ -1 & -1 & 0 \\ 0 & 1 & 0 \\ 0 & 0 & 1 \end{bmatrix}.$$

The first two relations, $\mathbf{H}_1\varphi_1$ and $\mathbf{H}_2\varphi_2$, corresponds to $\hat{\boldsymbol{\beta}}_1$ and $\hat{\boldsymbol{\beta}}_2$ in structure $\mathcal{H}_{S.1}$ when the insignificant coefficients have been set to zero. The third relation, $\mathbf{H}_3\varphi_3$, corresponds to the homogeneous inflation–interest rates relation $\mathcal{H}_{28}$ in Table 10.3.

Formal identification requires that $\text{rank}(\mathbf{R}_i'\mathbf{H}_j) \geq 1$ for $i, j = 1, 2, 3$ and $j \neq i$, and that $\text{rank}(\mathbf{R}_i'(\mathbf{H}_j, \mathbf{H}_g)) \geq 2$ for i, j, g different. The rank indices are given in Table 12.2, column $\mathcal{H}_{S.3}$ and $\mathcal{H}_{S.4}$, where the $i.j$ elements should be at least 1 and the $i.jg$ elements at least 2 for generic identification to be satisfied.

The estimates of structure $\mathcal{H}_{S.3}$ are given in the left-hand side of Table 12.3. The degrees of freedom in the test of over-identifying restrictions are given by $\nu = \Sigma_i(m_i - r + 1)$, where m_i is the number of restrictions on $\boldsymbol{\beta}_i$. The degrees of freedom for $\mathcal{H}_{S.3}$

Table 12.2 The rank conditions for identifiction.

$r_{i.j}$	$\mathcal{H}_{S.2}$	$\mathcal{H}_{S.3}$	$\mathcal{H}_{S.4}$	$\mathcal{H}_{S.5}$	$\mathcal{H}_{S.6}$	$r_{i.jg}$	$\mathcal{H}_{S.2}$	$\mathcal{H}_{S.3}$	$\mathcal{H}_{S.4}$	$\mathcal{H}_{S.5}$	$\mathcal{H}_{S.6}$
1.2	2	2	2	2	2	1.23	3	4	3	2	4
1.3	2	2	1	1	4						
2.1	2	1	2	2	1	2.13	3	3	3	2	3
2.3	1	2	2	0	2						
3.1	2	1	1	2	1	3.12	3	3	3	3	1
3.2	1	2	2	1	0						

Table 12.3 Two over-identified long-run structures for the Danish data.

	$\mathcal{H}_{S.3}$			$\mathcal{H}_{S.4}$		
	$\hat{\beta}_1$	$\hat{\beta}_2$	$\hat{\beta}_3$	$\hat{\beta}_1$	$\hat{\beta}_2$	$\hat{\beta}_3$
m^r	**1.0**	0.0	0.0	**1.0**	0.0	0.0
y^r	**−1.0**	**0.03** [3.67]	0.0	**−1.0**	**0.03** [4.07]	0.0
Δp	0.0	**1.0**	**−0.20** [−3.95]	0	**1.0**	0.0
R_m	0.0	0.0	**1.0**	**−13.27** [−5.70]	0.0	**1.0**
R_b	0.0	0.0	**−0.80** [−15.65]	**13.27** [5.70]	0.0	**−0.81** [−10.58]
D_s831	**−0.34** [−13.60]	**0.01** [5.46]	**−0.01** [−10.67]	**−0.15** [−5.19]	**0.01** [5.30]	**−0.01** [−4.77]
	$\hat{\alpha}_1$	$\hat{\alpha}_2$	$\hat{\alpha}_3$	$\hat{\alpha}_1$	$\hat{\alpha}_2$	$\hat{\alpha}_3$
Δm_t^r	**−0.21** [−4.74]	*	**3.38** [3.21]	**−0.23** [−4.89]	*	*
Δy_t^r	**0.06** [2.27]	−0.44 [−1.59]	**−1.40** [−2.21]	0.05 [1.84]	*	*
$\Delta^2 p_t$	*	**−0.84** [−5.33]	*	*	**−0.79** [−5.39]	*
$\Delta R_{m,t}$	*	*	−0.07 [−1.54]	*	0.03 [1.77]	**−0.08** [−2.29]
$\Delta R_{b,t}$	*	0.05 [1.87]	**0.13** [2.04]	*	*	**0.15** [3.04]

are calculated as:

$$\nu = \sum_{i=1}^{r} m_i - (r-1) = (4-2) + (3-2) + (3-2) = 2 + 1 + 1 = 4.$$

The corresponding LR test statistic became $\chi^2(4) = 4.05$ with a p-value of 0.40, so the structure can be accepted.

Example 4 The next structural hypothesis, $\mathcal{H}_{S.4}$, consists of the three stationary relations $\mathcal{H}_{15}$, $\mathcal{H}_{17}$, and $\mathcal{H}_{27}$ from Table 10.3. The rank conditions are given in Table 12.2 and the estimates are reported in Table 12.3. The degrees of freedom are calculated as:

$$\nu = \sum_{i=1}^{r}(m_i - (r-1)) = (3-2) + (3-2) + (3-2) = 3.$$

The test statistic became $\chi^2(3) = 2.84$ with a p-value of 0.42. Thus, both $\mathcal{H}_{S.3}$ and $\mathcal{H}_{S.4}$ are acceptable long-run structures with almost the same p-value. $\mathcal{H}_{S.3}$ has more the character of 'building blocks' (corresponding to the irreducible cointegration vectors in Davidson (1998)) which needs to be weighted by the corresponding α_{ij} to become more interpretable as economic steady-state relations. The relations in $\mathcal{H}_{S.4}$ describe directly interpretable steady-state relations. The difference between the two long-run structures is noticeable when comparing the estimated α coefficients. Most equations have several significant α coefficients in the $\mathcal{H}_{S.3}$ structure, whereas there is just one significant α coefficient per each equation in the $\mathcal{H}_{S.4}$ structure. Thus, the relations in $\mathcal{H}_{S.4}$ can be thought of as linear combinations of the building blocks in $\mathcal{H}_{S.3}$.

Does it matter whether we choose one representation or the other? In the present example, the answer is probably 'not really'. Most economists would probably prefer a structural representation that mimics as closely as possible the hypothetical equilibrium relations. From a statistical point of view, the 'building blocks' representation is preferable for the following reason:

When a steady-state relation is a direct combination of two stationary building blocks, such as $(m^r - y^r) - \omega_1(R_m - R_b) - \omega_2 D_s831$, where $(m^r - y^r - b_1 D_s831) \sim I(0)$ and $(R_m - R_b - b_2 D_s831) \sim I(0)$, then ω_1 is no longer a coefficient between two non-stationary variables, and the super-consistency result for estimated cointegration coefficients no longer holds. In fact, ω_1 has now the meaning of an α coefficient combining two stationary cointegration relations. Nonetheless, $\hat{\omega}_1 = -13.3$ in the money demand relation in $\mathcal{H}_{S.4}$ seems to be a fairly good estimate of the opportunity cost of holding money, even though it is a coefficient combining two stationary relations. This may seem surprising considering that the estimated opportunity cost in $\mathcal{H}_{S.2}$ was not very significant. One explanation is that the liquidity ratio and the spread contain the same small 'left-over' stochastic trend which is cancelled by the combination (1,−13.3). The results in Chapter 10, Table 10.3, which showed that the stationarity of the liquidity ratio was accepted with a p-value of 0.47 and of the spread with a p-value of 0.12, whereas the combined relation with a p-value of 0.67, support this interpretation. Chapter 14 will provide further evidence.

Finally, the identification of a long-run structure of meaningful steady-state relations becomes increasingly difficult when r is large and $p - r$ is small, as a minimum of $r - 1$ restrictions has to be imposed on each relation.

12.6 Lack of identification

Example 5 We consider now the following unidentified structure:

$$\mathcal{H}_{S.5} : \boldsymbol{\beta} = (\mathbf{H}_1\varphi_1, \mathbf{H}_2\varphi_2, \mathbf{H}_3\varphi_3),$$

where

$$\mathbf{H}_1 = \begin{bmatrix} 1 & 0 & 0 & 0 \\ 0 & 1 & 0 & 0 \\ 0 & 0 & 0 & 0 \\ 0 & 0 & 1 & 0 \\ 0 & 0 & -1 & 0 \\ 0 & 0 & 0 & 1 \end{bmatrix}, \quad \mathbf{H}_2 = \begin{bmatrix} 0 & 0 & 0 & 0 \\ 0 & 0 & 0 & 0 \\ 1 & 0 & 0 & 0 \\ 0 & 1 & 0 & 0 \\ 0 & 0 & 1 & 0 \\ 0 & 0 & 0 & 1 \end{bmatrix}, \quad \mathbf{H}_3 = \begin{bmatrix} 0 & 0 & 0 \\ 0 & 0 & 0 \\ 0 & 0 & 0 \\ 1 & 0 & 0 \\ 0 & 1 & 0 \\ 0 & 0 & 1 \end{bmatrix},$$

i.e. a money demand relation without imposing the unitary coefficient on real income, the interest rate spread relation, and an inflation–interest rate relation. The rank conditions of Table 12.2 show that relation 2 is not identified with respect to relation 3. The reason is that the above structure cannot be distinguished from $\{\boldsymbol{\beta}_1, \boldsymbol{\beta}_2 + \omega\boldsymbol{\beta}_3, \boldsymbol{\beta}_3\}$, $\omega \in \mathrm{R}$. In this case $\mathbf{H}_3$ is a subset of $\mathbf{H}_2$. Identification can be recovered, for example, by imposing a homogeneity restriction on $\boldsymbol{\beta}_2$. In this case, adding $\omega\boldsymbol{\beta}_3$ to $\boldsymbol{\beta}_2$ is no longer possible without violating the homogeneity restriction. Thus, identification can be restored either by imposing the homogeneity restriction or by setting one of the coefficients of the two interest rates to zero in $\boldsymbol{\beta}_2$.

Thus, the model specified by the restrictions in $\mathcal{H}_{S.5}$ is not identifying in the sense defined by (12.4), implying that the four parameters φ_{11}, φ_{12}, φ_{13} and φ_{14} cannot be uniquely estimated without further restrictions. Another way of expressing this is that one of the interest rates can be removed from $\hat{\boldsymbol{\beta}}_2$ by adding a linear combination of $\hat{\boldsymbol{\beta}}_3$. For example, $\hat{\boldsymbol{\beta}}_2 + 0.16\hat{\boldsymbol{\beta}}_3$, removes the short rate from $\hat{\boldsymbol{\beta}}_2$. Therefore, in this set-up we can only estimate the impact of a linear combination of the interest rates in the first relation. Nevertheless, even though the restrictions in Table 12.4 are not identifying, they are genuine restrictions on the parameter space and the model can be tested by a likelihood ratio test.

When CATS finds out that the suggested restrictions are not identifying you will be presented with the following options:

1. Let CATS impose identifying restrictions. This is at your own risk! In some cases CATS finds a good solution, but far from always.
2. Edit the restrictions on $\boldsymbol{\beta}$. To do that, you need to understand why identification was violated in the first case.
3. Estimate with non-identifying restrictions. In this case, you need to tell CATS how many degrees of freedom there are in the LR test. Furthermore, CATS will not be able to calculate standard errors for the coefficients of the unidentified relation, as they are not uniquely defined.

The estimates of $\mathcal{H}_{S.5}$ have been calculated under option 3. Note that, the unidentified relation $\hat{\boldsymbol{\beta}}'\mathbf{x}_t$ has no standard errors below the coefficients. The LR test statistic became 7.66. But before calculating the p-value, CATS will suggest one degree of freedom, $\nu = (2-2) + (2-2) + (3-2) = 1$, and then ask whether you agree. In this case the answer is no. The unidentified relation, $\hat{\boldsymbol{\beta}}_2$, contains in fact one more restriction which CATS does not find. This is because we can impose a zero restriction on either the bond rate or the deposit rate by linear combinations of $\boldsymbol{\beta}_2$ and $\boldsymbol{\beta}_3$ without changing the likelihood

Table 12.4 Two unidentified long-run structures for the Danish data.

	$\mathcal{H}_{S.5}$			$\mathcal{H}_{S.6}$		
	$\hat{\beta}_1$	$\hat{\beta}_2$	$\hat{\beta}_3$	$\hat{\beta}_1$	$\hat{\beta}_2$	$\hat{\beta}_3$
m^r	**1.0**	0.0	0.0	**1.0**	0.0	0.0
y^r	**−0.82** [−8.56]	0.0	0.0	**−1.0**	0.0	0.04 [NA]
Δp	0.0	**1.0**	0.0	0.0	0.0	**1.0**
R_m	**−24.40** [−7.74]	1.26 [NA]	**1.0**	0.0	**1.0**	1.59 [NA]
R_b	**24.40** [7.74]	−1.35 [NA]	**−0.81** [−11.83]	0.0	**−0.89** [−13.65]	−1.09 [NA]
D_s831	−0.04 [−0.93]	0.00 [NA]	**−0.01** [−5.11]	**−0.34** [−13.54]	**−0.01** [−6.09]	0.00 [NA]
	$\hat{\alpha}_1$	$\hat{\alpha}_2$	$\hat{\alpha}_3$	$\hat{\alpha}_1$	$\hat{\alpha}_2$	$\hat{\alpha}_3$
Δm_t^r	**−0.24** [−4.95]	*	**−2.47** [−2.11]	**−0.22** [−4.91]	**4.02** [3.47]	*
Δy_t^r	*	*	*	0.05 [1.78]	*	*
$\Delta^2 p_t$	*	**−0.70** [−5.02]	0.77 [1.86]	*	**0.84** [2.09]	**−0.81** [−5.50]
$\Delta R_{m,t}$	*	0.03 [1.83]	**−0.16** [−3.17]	*	*	*
$\Delta R_{b,t}$	*	*	0.12 [1.75]	*	*	*

function. Therefore, $v = 0 + 1 + 1 = 2$, which gives a p-value of 0.02 and the stationarity of the estimated structure cannot be accepted.

Example 6 In some cases, we may choose deliberately to specify and estimate an unidentified model as a step in the search for a good empirical model. Structure $\mathcal{H}_{S.6}$ is an example of this. Assume that we are quite confident that the liquidity ratio, $\hat{\beta}_1$, and the interest rate relation, $\hat{\beta}_2$, should be part of the long-run structure. However, we have no prior hypothesis for the third relation, except that money should be excluded. One exclusion restriction is not enough for identification and we need a good guess for at least another restriction. Instead of randomly choosing the second exclusion restriction we can, instead, estimate the structure even though $\hat{\beta}_3$ is unidentified and hope that the estimates suggest how to impose further restrictions. Since the estimates in Table 12.4 have no standard errors for $\hat{\beta}_3$, it is difficult to decide which coefficients are significant and which are not. We note, however, that $\hat{\beta}_3'\mathbf{x}_t$ is significant only in the inflation equation ($\hat{\alpha}_{33} = -0.81$). This strongly suggests that $\hat{\beta}_3$ should be identified as an inflation relation. Because a negative relationship between inflation and nominal interest rates is not very plausible, one obvious possibility is to impose a zero restriction on the short-term nominal interest rate.

The LR test statistic for $\mathcal{H}_{S.6}$ was 3.22. CATS suggests three degrees of freedom (and asks whether you agree). In this case the answer is yes. This is because we can impose one additional exclusion restriction on $\hat{\beta}_3$ which is just-identified and, therefore, does not change the likelihood function. Thus, $\nu = (4-2)+(3-2)+(2-2) = 3$ and the long-run structure can be accepted with a p-value of 0.36.

The difference between $\mathcal{H}_{S.5}$ and $\mathcal{H}_{S.6}$ is that in both cases we were able to impose one additional restriction without changing the likelihood function, but the restriction was over-identifying in $\mathcal{H}_{S.5}$, whereas just-identifying in $\mathcal{H}_{S.6}$.

12.7 Recursive tests of $\boldsymbol{\alpha}$ and $\boldsymbol{\beta}$

Figure 12.1 shows the recursively calculated LR test for over-identifying restrictions for the structure in $\mathcal{H}_{S.3}$ and Figure 12.2–12.7 the parameters of the identified model, $\hat{\boldsymbol{\beta}}_i^c(t_1)$ and $\hat{\boldsymbol{\alpha}}_i^c(t_1)$ for $t_1 = T_0, \ldots, T$, where the coefficients are only calculated from the **R**-form model because the graphs from the **X**-form model were almost identical. The standard errors are calculated as indicated in (12.13) and (12.14).

We note that the chosen set of over-identifying restrictions would have been accepted in all recursive sample periods since 1985:4. The shift dummy coefficient of the liquidity ratio relation, $\boldsymbol{\beta}_1'\boldsymbol{x}_t$, and the $\boldsymbol{\alpha}_1$ coefficients have been remarkably constant over the whole investigated period. Almost the same can be said about the homogeneous inflation rate–interest rates relation, $\boldsymbol{\beta}_3'\boldsymbol{x}_t$. Even though some fluctuations in the proportions between the inflation rate and the bond rate relative to the short rate were detected, the $\boldsymbol{\alpha}_3$ coefficients have been very stable over time. However, the second relation, $\boldsymbol{\beta}_2'\boldsymbol{x}_t$, exhibits significant changes over time in the cointegration coefficient between inflation rate and real income. Note that the coefficient to the shift dummy varies more or less proportionally with the income coefficient, so that the proportion between the two is almost constant. The non-constancy between inflation and real income is consistent with the previous findings in Chapter 9, which suggested that the relationship between

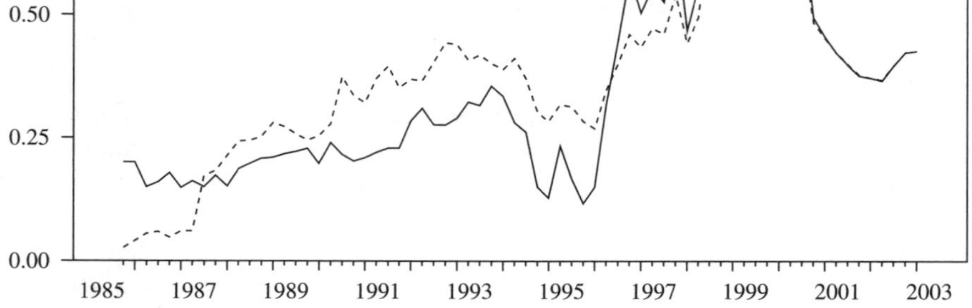

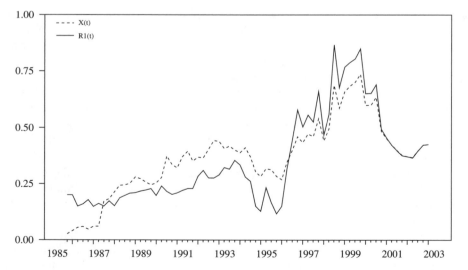

Fig 12.1 The recursively calculated test of over-identifying restrictions for $t_1 =$ 1985.4, ... , 2003.1.

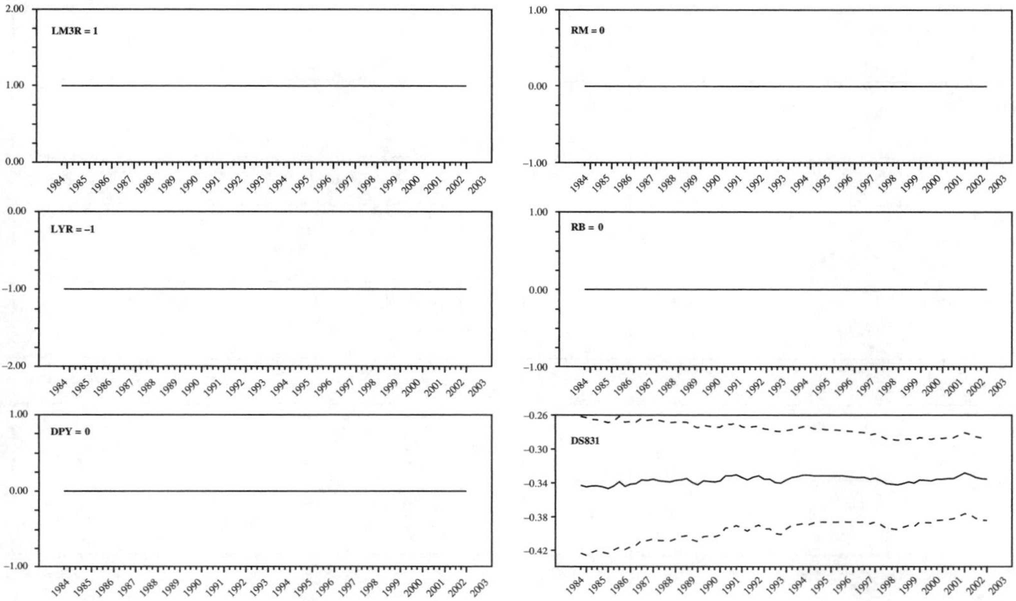

Fig 12.2 The recursively calculated coefficients of $\boldsymbol{\beta}_1(t_1)$ for t_1 =1985:4,... ,2003:1.

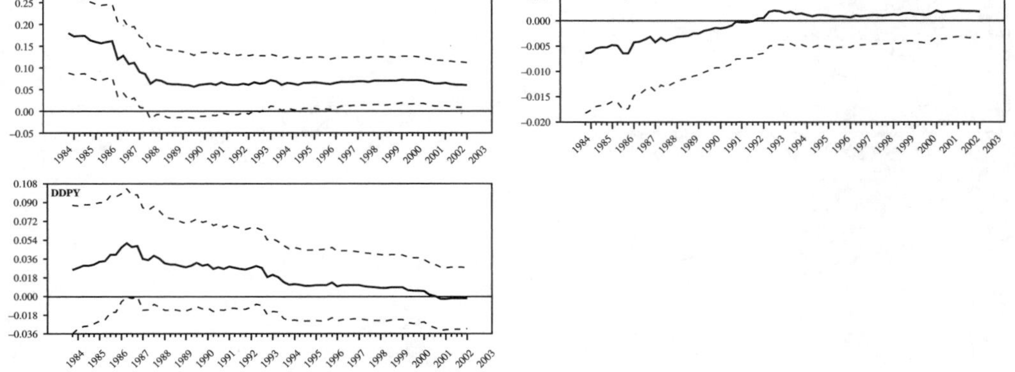

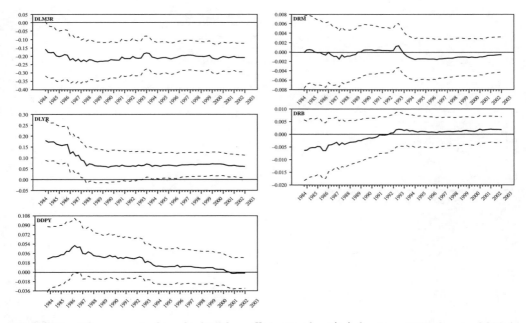

Fig 12.3 The recursively calculated coefficients of $\boldsymbol{\alpha}_1(t_1)$ for t_1 = 1985.4, ... ,2003.1.

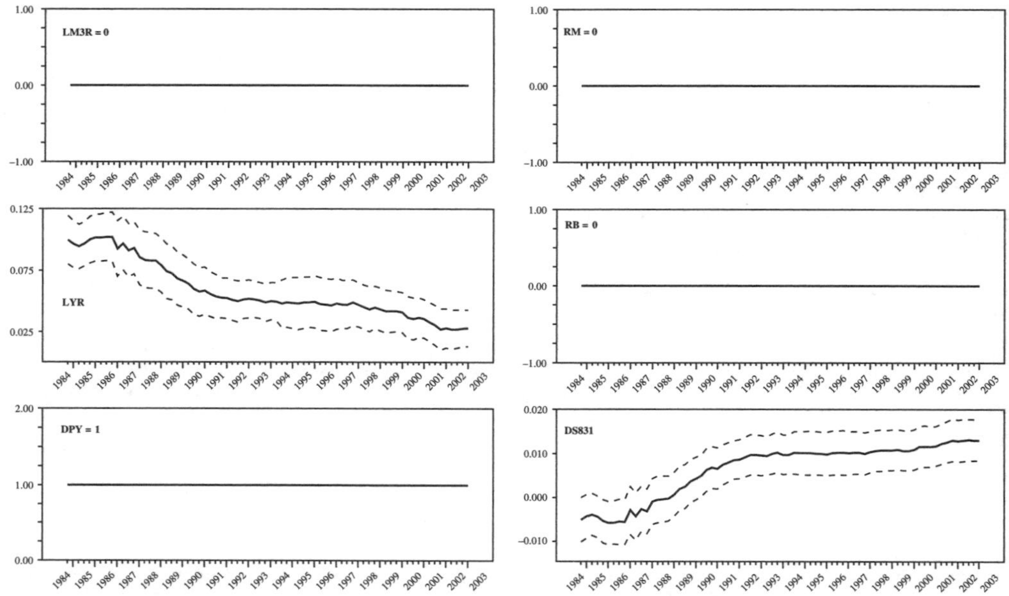

Fig 12.4 The recursively calculated coefficients of $\boldsymbol{\beta}_2(t_1)$ for $t_1 = 1985.4, \ldots, 2003.1$.

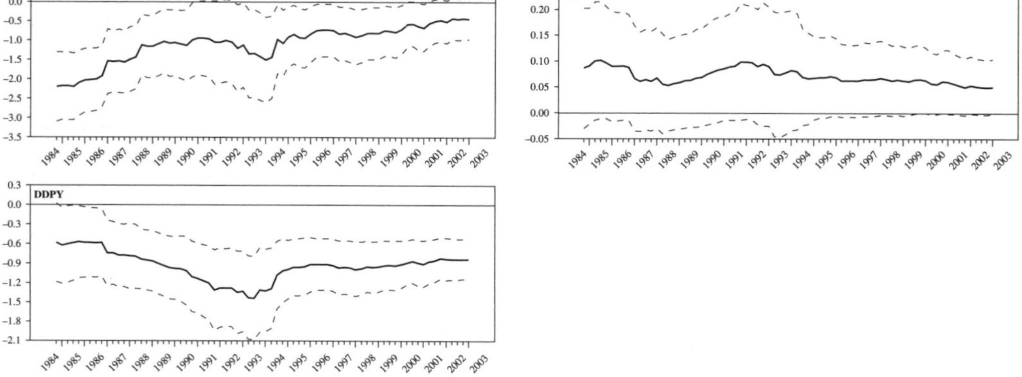

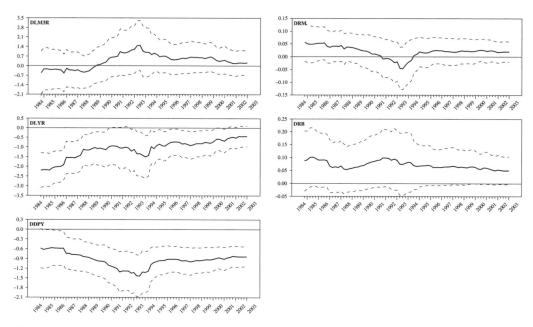

Fig 12.5 The recursively calculated coefficients of $\boldsymbol{\alpha}_2(t_1)$ for $t_1 = 1985.4, \ldots, 2003.1$.

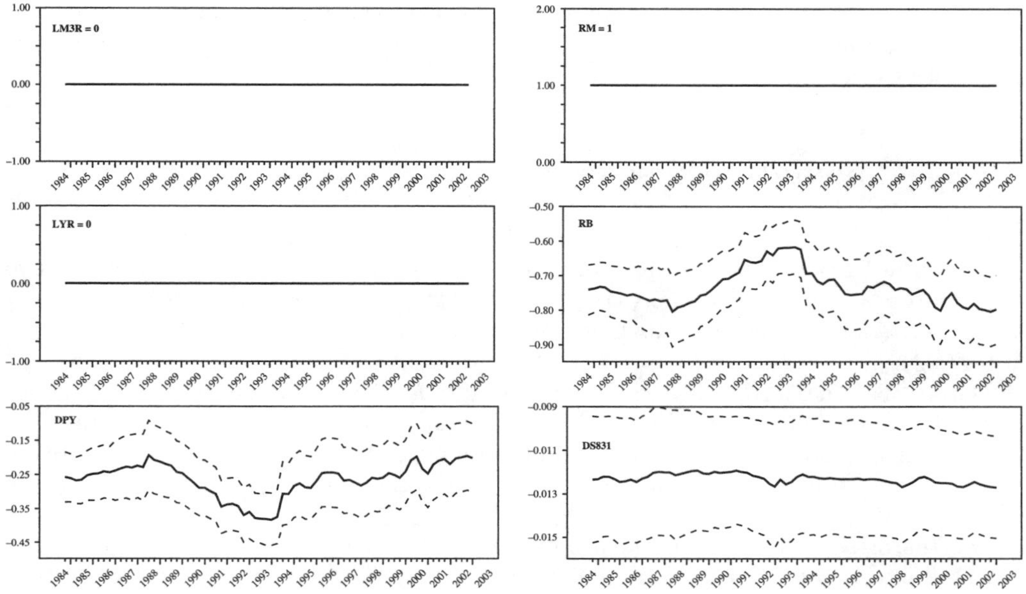

Fig 12.6 The recursively calculated coefficients of $\boldsymbol{\beta}_3(t_1)$ for $t_1 = 1985.4, \ldots, 2003.1$.

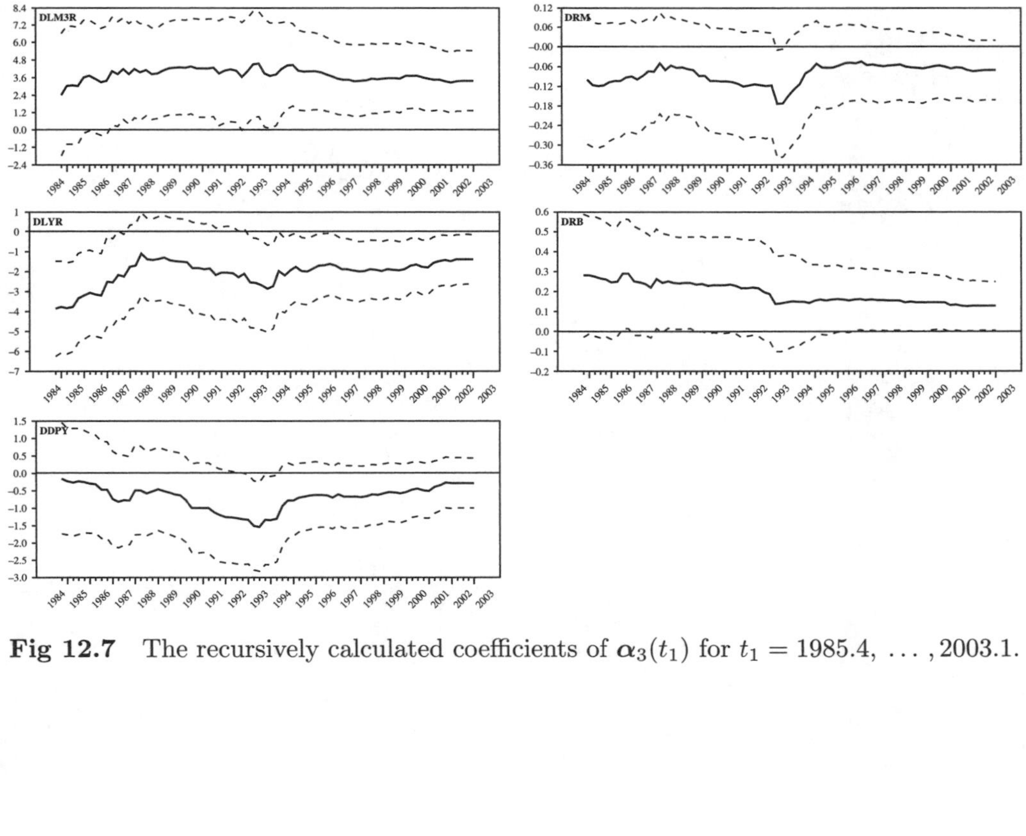

Fig 12.7 The recursively calculated coefficients of $\boldsymbol{\alpha}_3(t_1)$ for $t_1 = 1985.4, \ldots, 2003.1$.

inflation and the other variables in the system seemed to have undergone some significant changes over the present sample period. We shall return to this important finding in the subsequent chapters.

12.8 Concluding discussion

This chapter demonstrated that an empirically stable money demand relation of the type discussed in Romer (1996) can be found as a linear combination (1.0, −13.3) of the two stationary cointegration relations $(m^r - y^r - 0.34D_s831)_t$ and $(R_m - 0.2\Delta p - 0.8R_b - 0.01D_s831)_t$, or, alternatively, as a cointegration relation $(m^r - y^r - 13.3(R_m - R_b) - 0.15D_s831)_t$.

Given that the VAR model is a good description of the information in the data, we not only obtain full information maximum likelihood estimates (which in general have optimal properties) of the money demand parameters but, as discussed in Chapter 5, we also gain information about the number of common stochastic trends driving the system.

Furthermore, by embedding the money demand relation (as well as the other stationary relations) in a dynamic equilibrium correction system, it is possible to gain empirical insight about the dynamics of the short-run adjustment behaviour. This will be the topic of the next chapter.

13

Identification of the short-run structure

In Chapter 12, we gave the arguments for why it is possible to treat identification as two separate, though interdependent, problems. Here we shall show that the conditions for generic identification discussed in Section 12.1 apply for the short-run structure as well. Likewise, a generically identified short-run adjustment structure should also satisfy the conditions for empirical and economic identification. Nevertheless, the identification of the short-run structure differs from the long-run structure in a number of important ways.

The cointegration *relations* are identified as r long-run simultaneous relationships between $p1$ variables which enter the cointegration relations with the same time index, whereas the short-run *equations* consist of p equations between p current variables, $\Delta \mathbf{x}_t$, $p(k-1)$ lagged (predetermined) variables, $\Delta \mathbf{x}_{t-i}, i = 1, \ldots, k-1$, and r lagged (predetermined) equilibrium errors, $(\boldsymbol{\beta}^c)' \mathbf{x}_{t-1}$.

Identification of the r (simultaneous) long-run relations requires at least $r-1$ restrictions on each relation and identification of the simultaneous short-run structure of the p equations requires at least $p-1$ restrictions on each equation. The long-run structure does not necessarily contain any predetermined identification instruments, whereas the short-run structure contains lagged variables ($\Delta \mathbf{x}_{t-i}$ and $\boldsymbol{\beta}^{c\prime} \mathbf{x}_{t-1}$) as identification instruments.

Distinguishing between endogenous and weakly exogenous variables does not change the identification of the long-run structure, as it does not change the number of cointegration relations. Distinguishing between endogenous and exogenous variables may change the identification of the short-run structure as it allows us to condition on p_x exogenous variables in a partial model for $p - p_x$ endogenous variables. In this case, we only need to impose a minimum of $p - p_x - 1$ restrictions with p_x additional instruments.

Identification of the short-run structural equations often requires that the residuals are uncorrelated, or at least not significantly correlated, whereas no such requirement was present for the long-run relations. Thus, the residual covariance matrix plays an important role in the identification of the short-run structure, whereas the long-run covariance matrix of the cointegrating relations is not part of the identification problem. When the residuals of a short-run structural model are approximately uncorrelated, it might be possible to label them as estimated shocks.

The formal conditions for identification of the short-run structure is discussed in Section 13.1 and the conditions under which estimated residuals can be given a structural interpretation is discussed in Section 13.2. Section 13.3 discusses some policy-relevant questions which can be adequately answered by addressing the identification of the short-run structure. Sections 13.4, 13.5 and 13.6 illustrate short-run identification in three different model representations for the Danish data. The first representation is a parsimonious parametrization of the short-run reduced-form model based on two different long-run structures; the next representation is based on a causal chain representation with orthogonal residuals; the third representation discusses three attempts to identify a short-run structure of contemporaneous effects. Section 13.7 illustrates identification of the short-run structure in a partial model and Section 13.8 concludes with a discussion of the economic plausibility of the estimated results based on the identified models for the Danish data.

13.1 Formulating identifying restrictions

As already mentioned in Chapter 12 the identification of the short-run structure is much facilitated by keeping the properly identified cointegrating relations fixed at their estimated values, i.e. by treating $\hat{\boldsymbol{\beta}}'\mathbf{x}_{t-1}$ as predetermined stationary regressors similarly as $\Delta\mathbf{x}_{t-1}$. The statistical justification is that the estimates of the long-run parameters $\hat{\boldsymbol{\beta}}$ are superconsistent, i.e. the speed of convergence toward the true value $\boldsymbol{\beta}$ is proportional to T as $T \to \infty$, whereas the convergence of the estimates of the short-run adjustment parameters is proportional to $\sqrt{T}$.

The VAR model is a reduced-form model in the short-run dynamics in the sense that potentially important current (simultaneous) effects are not explicitly modelled but are left in the residuals. Thus, large off-diagonal elements of the covariance matrix $\boldsymbol{\Omega}$ can be a signal of significant current effects between the system variables. In some cases, the residual covariances are small and of minor importance and can be disregarded altogether. Since the reduced form is always generically identified, additional restrictions on the short-run structure are over-identifying. While a simplification search in the reduced-form VAR model is quite simple, this is generally not the case when the current effects measured by the covariance matrix $\boldsymbol{\Omega}$ are part of the identification process.

When discussing identification of the short-run adjustment parameters, we shall assume that the cointegration relations have been properly identified in the first step of the identification scheme. Thus, the short-run identification problem is about how to impose identifying restrictions on the contemporaneous matrix $\mathbf{A}_0$ given lagged changes of the process, $\Delta\mathbf{x}_{t-1}$, and lagged equilibrium errors, $(\hat{\boldsymbol{\beta}}^c)'\mathbf{x}_{t-1}$, where $\hat{\boldsymbol{\beta}}^c$ is an identified long-run structure. For simplicity, we disregard dummy variables at this stage. Premultiplying the reduced-form model by a non-singular $p \times p$ matrix $\mathbf{A}_0$ gives:

$$\mathbf{A}_0\Delta\mathbf{x}_t = \mathbf{A}_0\boldsymbol{\Gamma}_1\Delta\mathbf{x}_{t-1}+\mathbf{A}_0\boldsymbol{\alpha}(\hat{\boldsymbol{\beta}}^c)'\mathbf{x}_{t-1}+\mathbf{A}_0\boldsymbol{\mu}_0 + \mathbf{A}_0\boldsymbol{\varepsilon}_t, \tag{13.1}$$

$$\boldsymbol{\varepsilon}_t \sim IN_p(\mathbf{0},\boldsymbol{\Omega}) \tag{13.2}$$

or equivalently:

$$\mathbf{A}_0\Delta\mathbf{x}_t = \mathbf{A}_1\Delta\mathbf{x}_{t-1} + \mathbf{a}(\hat{\boldsymbol{\beta}}^c)'\mathbf{x}_{t-1} + \boldsymbol{\mu}_{0,a} + \mathbf{v}_t, \qquad (13.3)$$
$$\mathbf{v}_t \sim IN_p(\mathbf{0}, \boldsymbol{\Sigma})$$

where $\mathbf{A}_1 = \mathbf{A}_0\boldsymbol{\Gamma}_1$, $\mathbf{a} = \mathbf{A}_0\boldsymbol{\alpha}$, $\boldsymbol{\mu}_{0,a} = \mathbf{A}_0\boldsymbol{\mu}_0$ and $\mathbf{v}_t = \mathbf{A}_0\boldsymbol{\varepsilon}_t$.

Multiplying the VAR model by a full matrix $\mathbf{A}_0$ introduces $p\times(p-1)$ new parameters (assuming that the diagonal elements of $\mathbf{A}_0$ have unitary coefficients and that the residual covariance matrix is unrestricted). Thus, we need to impose at least $p \times (p-1)$ just-identifying restrictions on (13.3) to obtain unique parameter estimates.

The structural vector equilibrium-correction model (13.3) can be written in the more compact form:

$$\mathbf{A}'\mathbf{X}_t = \boldsymbol{\mu}_{0,a} + \mathbf{v}_t. \qquad (13.4)$$

where $\mathbf{A}'= (\mathbf{A}_0, -\mathbf{A}_1, -\mathbf{a})$ and $\mathbf{X}_t' = (\Delta\mathbf{x}_t', \Delta\mathbf{x}_{t-1}', \mathbf{x}_{t-1}'\boldsymbol{\beta}^c)$ is a stationary process. It is easy to see that (13.4) resembles the cointegration structure, $\boldsymbol{\beta}'\mathbf{x}_t = \boldsymbol{\beta}_0 + \mathbf{u}_t$. Therefore, when checking for generic identification of the short-run structure (13.4) we can use the same rank conditions defined in Chapter 12 for the long-run structure. Identifying restrictions on the rows of $\mathbf{A}'$ (we assume here that the constant term is not part of the identification process) can, as before, be formulated by the design matrices $\mathbf{H}_i$, $i = 1, \ldots, p$:

$$\mathbf{A} = (\mathbf{H}_1\varphi_1, \ldots, \mathbf{H}_p\varphi_p).$$

Note that when the model contains dummy variables we can, in general, decide whether to include them in the identification process or not. In the latter case, the dummy variables will be unrestricted in all equations, whereas in the former they will be included in the vector $\mathbf{X}_t'$ and, thus, can be used as instruments to achieve identification.

To find out whether the restrictions defining the model are identifying, one can check the rank conditions in (12.4) for some generic parameter values, or calculate the rank indices based on (12.5).

Given that the short-run identification structure is generically identified, estimation can in principle be carried out by the switching algorithm of the eigenvalue routine described in Chapter 10. Since the dimension of the equation system is generally much larger than the dimension of the cointegration space, the switching algorithm can sometimes be a little slow and it is common to apply other maximization algorithms. See, for example, the section on different estimation algorithms in PcGive (Doornik and Hendry 2001a).

13.2 Interpreting shocks

Because different choices of $\mathbf{A}_0$ lead to different estimates of the residuals, the question of how to define an empirical shock is important. The theoretical concept of a shock, and its decomposition into an anticipated and unanticipated part, has a straightforward correspondence in the VAR model as a change of a variable, $\Delta\mathbf{x}_t$, and its decomposition into an explained part, the conditional expectation $E_{t-1}\{\Delta\mathbf{x}_t \mid \mathbf{X}_{t-1}\}$, and an unexplained part, the residual $\boldsymbol{\varepsilon}_t$. The requirement for $\boldsymbol{\varepsilon}_t$ to be a correct measure of an unanticipated (autonomous) shock is that the conditional expectation $E_{t-1}\{\Delta\mathbf{x}_t \mid \mathbf{x}_{t-1}\}$ correctly describes how agents form their expectations. For example, if agents make model-based rational expectations from a model that is different from the VAR model, then the conditional expectation would no longer be an adequate description of the anticipated part of the shock $\Delta\mathbf{x}_t$. However, in this case the VAR model would probably have failed as a good description of the information in the data.

Theories also require shocks to be 'structural', implying that they are, in some sense, objective, meaningful, or absolute. With the reservation that the word structural has been used to cover a wide variety of meanings, we shall here assume that it describes a shock, the effect of which is (a) unanticipated (a surprise), (b) unique (a shock hitting money stock alone), and (c) invariant (no additional explanation by increasing the information set).

The novelty of a shock depends on the credibility of the expectations formation, i.e. whether $\boldsymbol{\varepsilon}_t = \Delta\mathbf{x}_t - E_{t-1}\{\Delta\mathbf{x}_t \mid g(\mathbf{X}_{t-1})\}$ is a correct measure of the unanticipated change in $\mathbf{x}$. The uniqueness can be achieved *econometrically* by choosing $\mathbf{A}_0$ so that the covariance matrix $\boldsymbol{\Sigma}$ becomes diagonal. For example, as will be demonstrated in Section 13.5, by postulating a causal ordering among the variables of the system one can trivially achieve uncorrelated residuals. In general, the VAR residuals can be orthogonalized in many different ways and whether the orthogonalized residuals $\hat{\mathbf{v}}_t$ can be given an *economic* interpretation as a unique structural shock depends crucially on the plausibility of the identifying assumptions. Some of them are just-identifying and cannot be tested against the data. Thus, different schools could claim structural explanations for differently derived estimated shocks based on the same data.

The invariance of a structural shock is probably the most crucial requirement as it implies that an empirically estimated structural shock should not change when increasing the information set. Theory models defining deep structural parameters are always based on many simplifying assumptions inclusive of numerous *ceteris paribus* assumptions. In empirical models the *ceteris paribus* assumptions should preferably be accounted for by conditioning on the *ceteris paribus* variables. Since essentially all macroeconomic systems are stochastic and highly interdependent, the inclusion of additional *ceteris paribus* variables in the model is likely to change the VAR residuals and, hence, the estimated shocks.

Therefore, though derived from sophisticated theoretical models, structural interpretability of estimated shocks seems hard to justify. In the words of Haavelmo there is no close association between the true shocks defined by the theory model and the measured shock based on the estimated VAR residuals. A structural shock seems to be a theoretical concept with little or fragile empirical content in macroeconometric modelling.

In the remaining part of this chapter we shall, therefore, discuss economic identification in the broad sense of answering some questions of economic relevance, and not in the narrow sense of identifying deep structural parameters.

13.3 Which economic questions?

Macroeconomic theory is usually quite informative about prior economic hypotheses relevant for the long-run structure, whereas much less seems to be known about the mechanisms underlying the short-run adjustment dynamics. Thus, the identification of the short-run structure often has the character of data analysis aiming at the 'identification' of a parsimonious parameterization rather than testing well-specified economic hypotheses. Nevertheless, the simplification search should preferably be guided by a set of relevant questions that the empirical analysis should provide an answer to.

From (13.3) we note that the variation in the data can be decomposed into a systematic (anticipated) part and an unsystematic (unanticipated) part. The systematic part explains the change from $t-1$ to t of the system variables as a result of:

1. current (anticipated) changes ($\Delta x_{j,t}$, $j \neq i$) in the system variables, $\Delta x_{i,t}$, $i = 1, \ldots, p$;
2. previous changes of the system variables, $\Delta x_{i,t-m}$, $i = 1, \ldots, p$, $m = 1, \ldots, k-1$;
3. deviations from previous long-run equilibrium states, $\boldsymbol{\beta}_i' \mathbf{x}_{t-1}$, $i = 1, \ldots, r$; and
4. extraordinary events, $\boldsymbol{\Phi}\mathbf{D}_t$, such as reforms and interventions.

Thus, the cointegrated VAR model allows for the *possibility* that the observed change in agents' behaviour from the previous period was a result of (1) an equilibrium correction towards a sustainable long-run equilibrium state, (2) a temporary reaction to previous and current changes in the basic behavioural variables (for example, because of slowly changing habits), and (3) an extraordinary event.

In contrast, most theoretical models make prior *assumptions* on how agents are supposed to react under optimizing behaviour given some *ceteris paribus* assumptions. Based on these assumptions, the model may predict, for example, instantaneous or partial adjustment behaviour towards equilibrium states. In this sense, the specification of an economic model is more precise with respect to the postulated behaviour and its economic consequences. On the other hand, these consequences are only empirically relevant when the postulated behaviour is (at least approximately) correct.

The specification of an empirical model like (13.3) is less precise in terms of an underlying theoretical model, but far more flexible in terms of actual macroeconomic behaviour being influenced by the wider circumstances that generated the data. Thus, the empirical model is in general not constrained by the *ceteris paribus* assumptions of the economic model. In the ideal case, the empirical model should allow for all relevant aspects of (possibly competing) theoretical model(s) as testable hypotheses, but also add to the realism of the empirical model by conditioning on relevant *ceteris paribus* variables. For example, the question of instantaneous or partial adjustment behaviour in the domestic money market can be specified as hypotheses on the adjustment coefficients α_{ij} in the empirical model. A 'surprising' outcome of a test might then be associated with some *ceteris paribus* assumptions of the theoretical model, such as 'constant real exchange rate' or 'no risk aversion in the capital markets' just to mention a few of the probably crucial ones.

We shall illustrate these ideas by recalling that the economic motivation for doing an empirical analysis of the Danish money demand data was the discussion in Chapter 2 of inflation and monetary policy. The latter was influenced by the discussion in Romer (1996), Chapter 9, in which the economic model was based on an assumption about equilibrium behaviour in the money market. The reason why it is relevant to estimate a money demand relation is because if the latter was known and empirically stable, then central banks would be able to supply exactly the amount of money that satisfied agents' demand for money and there would be no excess money in the economy.

Based on the empirical results reported in the preceding chapters, we were able to conclude that the Danish money market behaviour in the post-Bretton–Woods period has been characterized by short-run equilibrium-correction behaviour. By allowing for dynamic adjustment towards long-run steady-states, it is now possible to address a number of additional questions which are directly or indirectly related to the effectiveness of monetary policy. For example:

- Is money stock adjusting to a long-run money demand or supply relation?
- Is an empirically stable demand for money relation a prerequisite for monetary policy to be effective for inflation control?
- Would monetary, interest rate, or inflation targeting have been more effective as a means of controlling inflation?
- How long does it take for a monetary policy shock to affect inflation?

As demonstrated above, the short-run adjustment coefficients are not in general invariant to the choice of $\mathbf{A}_0$, which is why the answers to the above questions are crucially related to the identification issue. In some cases, the empirical answers can be very sensitive to the choice of identification scheme, in other cases results are more robust.

To illustrate how some of the above questions can be investigated in the VAR model, we shall assume that the causal chain model below is an adequately identified representation of the short-run structure of the Danish data. For simplicity of notation, we shall here assume that $\mathbf{A}_1 = \mathbf{0}$, i.e. there is no short-run dynamic adjustment in lagged changes of the process and that the long-run structure can be described by the simple relations discussed in Chapter 2. Generalization to more realistic specifications such as the empirically identified relations of Table 12.3 should be straightforward.

We consider first the following VAR model in reduced form:

$$\begin{bmatrix} 1 & 0 & 0 & 0 & 0 \\ 0 & 1 & 0 & 0 & 0 \\ 0 & 0 & 1 & 0 & 0 \\ 0 & 0 & 0 & 1 & 0 \\ 0 & 0 & 0 & 0 & 1 \end{bmatrix} \begin{bmatrix} \Delta m^r{}_t \\ \Delta^2 p_t \\ \Delta R_{m,t} \\ \Delta y^r_t \\ \Delta R_{b,t} \end{bmatrix}$$

$$= \begin{bmatrix} \mu_{0,1} \\ \mu_{0,2} \\ \mu_{0,3} \\ \mu_{0,4} \\ \mu_{0,5} \end{bmatrix} + \begin{bmatrix} \alpha_{11} & \alpha_{12} & \alpha_{13} \\ \alpha_{21} & \alpha_{22} & \alpha_{23} \\ \alpha_{31} & \alpha_{32} & \alpha_{33} \\ \alpha_{41} & \alpha_{42} & \alpha_{43} \\ \alpha_{51} & \alpha_{52} & \alpha_{53} \end{bmatrix} \begin{bmatrix} (m^r - y^r)_{t-1} \\ (R_b - R_m)_{t-1} \\ (\Delta p - R_m)_{t-1} \end{bmatrix} + \begin{bmatrix} \varepsilon_{m,t} \\ \varepsilon_{\Delta p,t} \\ \varepsilon_{R_{m,t}} \\ \varepsilon_{y^r,t} \\ \varepsilon_{R_{b,t}} \end{bmatrix} \quad (13.5)$$

which is just-identified by the $p(p-1)$ zero restrictions on the current effects matrix. We then consider the following causal chain model assuming that $R_b \rightarrow y^r \rightarrow$

$R_m \rightarrow \Delta p \rightarrow m^r$:

$$\begin{bmatrix} 1 & -a_{12}^0 & -a_{13}^0 & -a_{14}^0 & -a_{15}^0 \\ 0 & 1 & -a_{23}^0 & -a_{24}^0 & -a_{25}^0 \\ 0 & 0 & 1 & -a_{34}^0 & -a_{35}^0 \\ 0 & 0 & 0 & 1 & -a_{45}^0 \\ 0 & 0 & 0 & 0 & 1 \end{bmatrix} \begin{bmatrix} \Delta {m^r}_t \\ \Delta^2 p_t \\ \Delta R_{m,t} \\ \Delta y_t^r \\ \Delta R_{b,t} \end{bmatrix}$$
$$= \begin{bmatrix} \mu_{0,1} \\ \mu_{0,2} \\ \mu_{0,3} \\ \mu_{0,4} \\ \mu_{0,5} \end{bmatrix} + \begin{bmatrix} a_{11} & a_{12} & a_{13} \\ a_{21} & a_{22} & a_{23} \\ a_{31} & a_{32} & a_{33} \\ a_{41} & a_{42} & a_{43} \\ a_{51} & a_{52} & a_{53} \end{bmatrix} \begin{bmatrix} (m^r - y^r)_{t-1} \\ (R_b - R_m)_{t-1} \\ (\Delta p - R_m)_{t-1} \end{bmatrix} + \begin{bmatrix} v_{m,t} \\ v_{\Delta p,t} \\ v_{R_{m,t}} \\ v_{y^r,t} \\ v_{R_{b,t}} \end{bmatrix} \quad (13.6)$$

which is just-identified by the 10 zero restrictions on the current effects and the 10 off-diagonal zero restrictions on the residual covariance matrix.

Based on (13.6) we shall first illustrate how the answers to the economic questions above are crucially related to the identification of the short-run adjustment structure. To simplify the discussion, we shall focus solely on the money and inflation equations, albeit acknowledging that a complete answer should be based on the full system analysis:

$$\begin{aligned} \Delta m_t^r &= a_{12}^0 \Delta^2 p_t + a_{13}^0 \Delta R_{m,t} + a_{14}^0 \Delta y_t^r + a_{15}^0 \Delta R_{b,t} \\ &\quad + a_{11}(m^r - y^r)_{t-1} + a_{12}(R_b - R_m)_{t-1} + a_{13}(\Delta p - R_m)_{t-1} + \mu_{0,1} + v_{m,t} \\ \Delta^2 p_t &= a_{23}^0 \Delta R_{m,t} + a_{24}^0 \Delta y_t^r + a_{25}^0 \Delta R_{b,t} \\ &\quad + a_{21}(m^r - y^r)_{t-1} + a_{22}(R_b - R_m)_{t-1} + a_{23}(\Delta p - R_m)_{t-1} + \mu_{0,2} + v_{\Delta p,t} \\ \Delta y_t^r &= \ldots \\ \Delta R_{m,t} &= \ldots \\ \Delta R_{b,t} &= \ldots \end{aligned}$$

Question 1. Is money stock adjusting to money demand or supply?
If $a_{11} < 0$, $a_{12} < 0$, and $a_{13} < 0$, then the empirical evidence is in favour of money stock adjusting to a long-run money demand relation. The latter can be derived from the money stock equation as follows:

$$\begin{aligned} m^r &= y^r + a_{12}/a_{11}(R_b - R_m) + a_{13}/a_{11}(\Delta p - R_m) \\ &= y^r - \beta_1(R_b - R_m) - \beta_2(\Delta p - R_m). \end{aligned} \quad (13.7)$$

Relation (13.7) corresponds to the aggregate money demand relation discussed in a static equilibrium framework by Romer, with the difference that (13.7) is now embedded in a dynamic adjustment framework. On the other hand, the case $a_{11} < 0$, $a_{12} = 0$, and $a_{13} = 0$, could be consistent with a situation where the central bank has controlled money stock by keeping money velocity stationary around a constant level.

Question 2. Is an empirically stable (constant parameter) money demand relation a prerequisite for central banks to be able to control the inflation rate?

This hypothesis is based on essentially three arguments:

2.1. There exists an empirically stable demand for money relation.

2.2. Central banks can influence the demanded quantity of money.

2.3. Deviations from this relation cause inflation.

The empirical requirement for a stable money demand relation is that $\{a_{11} < 0, a_{12} > 0$, and $a_{13} > 0\}$, and that the estimates are constant over time. In this case money stock is endogenously determined by agents' demand for money and it is not obvious that money stock can be used as a monetary instrument by the central bank. Thus, given the previous result (i.e. $a_{11} < 0$, $a_{12} > 0$, and $a_{13} > 0$), central banks cannot *directly* control money stock. Nevertheless, controlling money stock indirectly might still be possible by changing the short-term interest rate. But $a_{12} > 0$ and $(R_b - R_m) \sim I(0)$ implies that a change in the short-term interest rate will transmit through the system in a way that leaves the spread basically unchanged. Therefore, even if a stable demand for money relation has been found, it may, nevertheless, be difficult to control money stock.

Finally, $\{a_{21} > 0\}$ would be consistent with the situation where deviations from the empirically constant money demand relation influence the inflation rate in the short-run. Under the assumption that agents can obtain their desired level of money (i.e. no credit restrictions), it seems likely that there is 'excess money' in the economy because of 'excess supply' rather than 'excess demand'. Excess money would generally then be the result of central bank printing more money than otherwise demanded by the private sector for a given productivity growth path. For example, by monetizing government debt the central bank might increase money stock above the level demanded by the private sector.

These are simple examples which foremost serve the purpose of illustrating how crucial the adjustment dynamics is for the economic interpretation of the estimated results. In the next chapter we shall further discuss how the dynamics of the process can make the long-run impact of a shock very different from the short-run response.

In the subsequent sections the above questions will be addressed for the Danish data based on the following short-run identification schemes:

1. imposing restrictions on the short-run parameters when $\mathbf{A}_0 = \mathbf{I}$;
2. imposing (just-identifying) zero restrictions on the off-diagonal elements of $\boldsymbol{\Sigma}$;
3. imposing general restrictions on $\mathbf{A}_0$ without imposing restrictions on $\boldsymbol{\Sigma}$;
4. re-specifying the full system model as a partial model based on weak exogeneity test results.

All models in this chapter are estimated with PcGive (Doornik and Hendry 2001a).

13.4 Restrictions on the short-run reduced-form model

The unrestricted short-run reduced-form model is exactly identified by the $p - 1$ zero restrictions on each row of $\mathbf{A}_0 = \mathbf{I}$. Further zero restrictions on $\boldsymbol{\Gamma}_1$, $\boldsymbol{\alpha}$ and $\boldsymbol{\Phi}$ are over-identifying. The estimates of the unrestricted α_{ij} coefficients were given in Table 7.1. and the estimates of the unrestricted $\boldsymbol{\Gamma}_1$ and the dummy variables were given in Chapter 6. We note that (a) the short-run structure is over-parameterized with many insignificant coefficients, (b) the adjustment coefficients α_{ij} seem to comprise most of the significant coefficients (thus, the bulk of explanatory power is associated with equilibrium correction), (c) the signs and the magnitudes of the α_{ij} coefficients seem reasonable, but the coefficients on the lagged changes of the process are more difficult to interpret, and (d) some of the correlations of the standardized residuals are quite large, possibly because of important current effects. Because the short-run reduced-form model does not include any contemporaneous effects, it is exactly identified by the $p-1$ zero restrictions on $\mathbf{A}_0 = \mathbf{I}$, so that additional zero restrictions on $\mathbf{A}_1$, $\mathbf{a}$ and, possibly, $\tilde{\mathbf{\Phi}}$ are over-identifying.

For the Danish data we have no strong prior hypotheses about the short-run structure and imposing over-identifying restrictions has more the character of a simplification search rather than a stringent economic identification. The guiding principle is the plausibility of the results, in particular plausible estimates of the equilibrium-correction coefficients, $\mathbf{a}$.

As discussed above, all the empirical analyses in this chapter are for a given set of identified cointegration relations. The two identified structures, $\mathcal{H}_{S.3}$ and $\mathcal{H}_{S.4}$, in Table 12.3 were accepted with almost identical p-values. The former represents a structure of 'irreducible cointegration relations' whereas the latter is more directly interpretable in terms of economic long-run relations. As it is of some interest for an applied econometrician to see how the interpretation of the model parameters are affected by different parameterizations of the long-run structure, we shall illustrate the simplification search when the cointegration relations have been fixed according to the structures $\mathcal{H}_{S.3}$ and $\mathcal{H}_{S.4}$, respectively. The subsequent short-run analyses will exclusively be based on the long-run structure $\mathcal{H}_{S.4}$.

Many of the short-run adjustment coefficients in the unrestricted reduced-form VAR model discussed in Chapter 4 were statistically insignificant. The aim is, therefore, to test whether they can be jointly set to zero. As a first step, all lagged variables and dummy variables were individually tested whether they were significant or not in the system. The F-tests below are for model version 1 (under structure $\mathcal{H}_{S.3}$):

Variable	Δm^r_{t-1}	$\Delta^2 p_{t-1}$	$\Delta R_{m,t-1}$	Δy^r_{t-1}	$\Delta R_{b,t-1}$	$ecm1_{t-1}$	$ecm2_{t-1}$	$ecm3_{t-1}$	$Dtr754_t$	$Dp764_t$	$Dp831_t$
$F(5,103)$	1.99	1.49	2.01	6.08	6.25	7.12	8.23	5.25	3.00	6.72	7.17
p-value	**0.09**	**0.20**	**0.08**	0.00	0.00	0.00	0.00	0.00	0.01	0.00	0.00

In both model versions, the following lagged variables $\Delta m^r_{t-1}, \Delta^2 p_{t-1}$ and $\Delta R_{m,t-1}$ were found to be insignificant and were removed from the system (altogether 15 coefficients). In this 'trimmed' system, 21 [24][1] additional zero restrictions were accepted based on an LR test of over-identifying restriction, $\chi^2(21) = 22.7$ [$\chi^2(24) = 25.1$] and a p-value of 0.36 [0.40]. The estimates of the retained coefficients are reported in Table 13.1 and Table 13.2. All estimates are roughly significant on the 5% level. In terms of p-values, the two versions are almost identical. The second model version (under structure $\mathcal{H}_{S.4}$) is more parsimonious in the sense of describing the variation in the data with fewer short-run parameters. However, this simplification is somewhat illusory as the long-run structure $\mathcal{H}_{S.4}$ contains one more estimated parameter than $\mathcal{H}_{S.3}$. For example, one of the additional α coefficients under version $\mathcal{H}_{S.3}$ corresponds to a β coefficient in version $\mathcal{H}_{S.4}$. For example, the combination $\alpha^{(a)}_{11} ecm1a + \alpha^{(a)}_{12} ecm3a$ in model version 1

[1]Results in brackets are for model version 2.

reproduces the money demand relation $\alpha_{11}^{(b)} ecm1b$ in model version 2. Thus, the choice between 'building bricks' or 'economic equilibrium relations' is often a choice between fewer $\boldsymbol{\beta}$ coefficients but more $\boldsymbol{\alpha}$ coefficients or the other way around.

However, a more surprising difference appears when comparing the $\boldsymbol{\alpha}$ coefficients of the equations for the supposedly weakly exogenous variables (real income and the bond rate). In model version 2, the estimated $\boldsymbol{\alpha}$ coefficients seem approximately consistent with the weak exogeneity results, whereas in version 1 we find many significant $\boldsymbol{\alpha}$ coefficients in the two equations. This apparently puzzling result need not be inconsistent with the weak exogeneity result as a rotation of the $\boldsymbol{\beta}$ vectors implies a corresponding rotation of the $\boldsymbol{\alpha}$ vectors. To preserve the equality $\boldsymbol{\alpha\beta}' = \boldsymbol{\Pi}$ the $\boldsymbol{\alpha}$ coefficients have to compensate for any changes of the $\boldsymbol{\beta}$ relations. For example the second row of the $\boldsymbol{\Pi}$ matrix can be approximately reproduced either by $\alpha_{21}^{(a)} ecm1a + \alpha_{22}^{(a)} ecm2a + \alpha_{23}^{(a)} ecm3a$ from structure $\mathcal{H}_{S.3}$ or by $\alpha_{21}^{(b)} ecm1b + \alpha_{22}^{(b)} ecm2b + \alpha_{23}^{(b)} ecm3b$ from structure $\mathcal{H}_{S.4}$.

Thus, even though the $\boldsymbol{\alpha}$ coefficients in the income equation are significant under $\mathcal{H}_{S.3}$, the combined effects given by the second row in the $\boldsymbol{\Pi}$ matrix will in general be insignificant, consistent with the weak exogeneity result. This is an illustration of the fact that rotations of $\boldsymbol{\alpha}$ and $\boldsymbol{\beta}$ may very well generate apparently puzzling outcomes but, nevertheless, produce the same $\boldsymbol{\Pi}$ matrix and, hence, correspond to the same value of

Table 13.1 A parsimonious parametrization of the VAR with the *ecms* based on $\mathcal{H}_{S.3}$.

	Δm_t^r	$\Delta^2 p_t$	$\Delta R_{m,t}$	Δy_t^r	$\Delta R_{b,t}$
Δy_{t-1}^r	0	0	0	**0.21** (2.6)	**0.03** (4.7)
$\Delta R_{b,t-1}$	**−3.61** (−2.9)	0.74 (1.8)	**0.34** (6.4)	**−2.93** (−3.8)	**0.33** (4.7)
$ecm1a_{t-1}$	**−0.18** (−5.1)	0	0	**0.06** (2.4)	0
$ecm2a_{t-1}$	0	**−1.04** (−12.2)	**0.06** (5.0)	**−0.47** (−2.5)	**0.07** (3.7)
$ecm3a_{t-1}$	**1.79** (2.4)	0	0	**−1.47** (−2.4)	**0.20** (4.3)
$Dtr754_t$	0	0	0	**0.04** (3.3)	0
$Dp764_t$	0	0	**0.006** (5.7)	0	0
$\Delta Ds831_t$	0	0	0	0	**−0.007** (−5.5)

$\hat{\boldsymbol{\Omega}}$ (standard errors on the diagonal, off-diagonal elements are correlations)

Δm_t^r	0.0243				
$\Delta^2 p_t$	−0.48	0.0088			
$\Delta R_{m,t}$	−0.20	0.22	0.0011		
Δy_t^r	0.14	−0.02	−0.02	0.0144	
$\Delta R_{b,t}$	−0.09	0.18	0.45	0.11	0.0015

$$ecm1a_{t-1} = m_t^r - y_t^r - 0.3355 Ds831_t$$
$$ecm2a_{t-1} = \Delta p_t + 0.0274 y_t^r + 0.013 Ds831_t$$
$$ecm3a_{t-1} = R_{m,t} - 0.2014 \Delta p_t - 0.7986 R_{b,t} - 0.0127 Ds831_t$$

Table 13.2 A parsimonious parametrization of the VAR with the *ecms* based on $\mathcal{H}_{S.4}$.

	Δm_t^r	$\Delta^2 p_t$	$\Delta R_{m,t}$	Δy_t^r	$\Delta R_{b,t}$
Δy_{t-1}^r	0	0	0	**0.24** (2.9)	**0.03** (4.6)
$\Delta R_{b,t-1}$	**−3.62** (−3.0)	**0.82** (1.9)	**0.34** (6.4)	**−3.02** (−3.9)	**0.36** (4.9)
$ecm1b_{t-1}$	**−0.21** (−5.4)	0	0	**0.06** (2.4)	0
$ecm2b_{t-1}$	0	**−1.12** (−13.9)	**0.04** (4.4)	0	0
$ecm3b_{t-1}$	0	0	**−0.07** (−2.0)	0	**0.15** (3.0)
$Dtr754_t$	0	0	0	**0.04** (3.3)	0
$Dp764_t$	0	0	**0.006** (5.8)	0	0
$\Delta Ds831_t$	0	0	0	0	**−0.008** (−5.6)

$\hat{\boldsymbol{\Omega}}$ (standard errors on the diagonal, off-diagonal elements are correlations)

Δm_t^r	0.0240				
$\Delta^2 p_t$	−0.48	0.0088			
$\Delta R_{m,t}$	−0.20	0.20	0.0011		
Δy_t^r	0.13	−0.00	−0.01	0.0146	
$\Delta R_{b,t}$	−0.10	0.18	0.45	0.09	0.0015

$$ecm1b_{t-1} = m_t^r - y_t^r - 13.267(R_{m,t} - R_{b,t}) - 0.1533Ds831_t$$
$$ecm2b_{t-1} = \Delta p_t + 0.0297y_t^r + 0.0124Ds831_t$$
$$ecm3b_{t-1} = R_{m,t} - 0.8087R_{b,t} - 0.009Ds831_t$$

the likelihood function. So the ‘puzzling’ results should be interpreted as a description of the same reality but looked at from different angles.

The original VAR contained 50 autoregressive coefficients, five constant terms, 15 dummy variable coefficients, and 15 parameters in the residual covariance matrix. Of the original (50+15) VAR parameters, only 19 [16] were significant and, therefore, retained in the model. We note that most of the equilibrium-correction coefficients a_{ij} are highly significant, thus demonstrating the major loss of information that would be associated with VAR models specified in differences.

All current effects are accounted for by the residual covariance matrix $\hat{\boldsymbol{\Omega}}$ at the bottom of Tables 13.1 and 13.2. Most of the correlations are relatively small, but the residuals from the money stock and the inflation rate equations are correlated with a coefficient −0.48 and the residuals from the short-term interest rate and the bond rate equations with a coefficient of 0.45. There are at least three explanations for why the residuals from a VAR model are likely to be correlated:

1. Causal chain effects get blurred when the data are temporally aggregated; the more aggregated the data, the higher the correlations. Assume, for example, that the bond rate changes the day after a change in the short-term interest rate (as a result of a central bank intervention, say) and that the central bank changes the

short-term interest rate as a result of a market shock to the long-term bond rate but only after a week. In this case, we would be able to identify correctly the causal links based on daily data. However, when we aggregate the data over time, the information about these links gets mixed up.

2. Expectations are inadequately modelled by the VAR model. Chapter 3 showed that the VAR model is consistent with agents making plans based on the expectation: $E_{t-1}(\Delta\mathbf{x}_t|\Delta\mathbf{x}_{t-1}, \ldots, \Delta\mathbf{x}_{t-k+1}, \boldsymbol{\beta}'\mathbf{x}_{t-1})$. Assume now that agents have forward looking expectations to the variable x_{1t}, so that $E_{t-1}(\Delta x_{1t}) = \Delta x^e_{1t}$, and that they use this value when making plans: $E_{t-1}(\Delta x_{j,t} \mid \Delta x^e_{1t}, \Delta\mathbf{x}_{t-1}, \ldots, \Delta\mathbf{x}_{t-k+1}, \boldsymbol{\beta}'\mathbf{x}_{t-1})$, $j \neq 1$. If $\Delta x^e_{1t} = \Delta x_{1t}$, i.e. the expectation is exactly correct, then the reduced form VAR residuals from equation Δx_{1t} would be correlated with the residuals from the equations in which Δx^e_{1t} was important.
3. Omitted variables effects. In most cases, the VAR model contains only a subset of (the most important) variables needed to explain the economic problem. This is because the VAR model is very powerful for the analysis of small systems, but the identification of cointegration relations becomes increasingly difficult when the dimension of the vector process gets larger. There are two important implications of omitted variables: (a) the estimated short-run adjustment coefficients are likely to change when we increase the number of variables in the model (provided that the new variables are not orthogonal to the old variables), and (b) the residuals generally become smaller when increasing the dimension of the VAR. Thus, the residuals of a 'small' VAR model are likely to contain omitted variables effects and the residuals will be correlated if the left-out variables are important for several of the variables in the 'small' VAR.

The last point makes it very hard to argue that the residuals could possibly be a measure of autonomous errors (structural shocks). Therefore, a large residual correlation coefficient does not necessarily imply a 'structural' simultaneous effect, nor does it imply incorrectly specified expectations. With this in mind, we shall now attempt to 'identify' some of the current effects in the model as if they were a result of either point (a) or (b) above.

13.5 The VAR in triangular form

Assume now that we want to estimate a VAR model with uncorrelated residuals. The most convenient way of achieving this is by choosing $\mathbf{A}_0$ in (13.3) to be an upper triangular matrix $\hat{\boldsymbol{\Omega}}^{-1/2}$, i.e. by premultiplying the VAR model with the inverse of the Choleski decomposition of the covariance matrix $\hat{\boldsymbol{\Omega}} = \hat{\boldsymbol{\Omega}}^{1/2}(\hat{\boldsymbol{\Omega}}^{1/2})'$:

$$\underbrace{\hat{\boldsymbol{\Omega}}^{-1/2}}_{\mathbf{A}_0}\Delta\mathbf{x}_t = \underbrace{\hat{\boldsymbol{\Omega}}^{-1/2}\boldsymbol{\Gamma}_1}_{\mathbf{A}_1}\Delta\mathbf{x}_{t-1} + \underbrace{\hat{\boldsymbol{\Omega}}^{-1/2}\boldsymbol{\alpha}}_{\mathbf{a}}(\boldsymbol{\beta}^c)'\mathbf{x}_{t-1} + \underbrace{\hat{\boldsymbol{\Omega}}^{-1/2}\boldsymbol{\mu}_0}_{\boldsymbol{\mu}_{0,a}} + \underbrace{\hat{\boldsymbol{\Omega}}^{-1/2}\boldsymbol{\varepsilon}_t}_{\mathbf{v}_t}.$$

Because $E(\mathbf{v}_t\mathbf{v}_t') = \hat{\boldsymbol{\Omega}}^{-1/2}\text{Cov}(\boldsymbol{\varepsilon}_t\boldsymbol{\varepsilon}_t')\hat{\boldsymbol{\Omega}}^{-1/2} = \hat{\boldsymbol{\Omega}}^{-1/2}\hat{\boldsymbol{\Omega}}^{1/2}(\hat{\boldsymbol{\Omega}}^{1/2})'(\hat{\boldsymbol{\Omega}}^{-1/2})' = \mathbf{I}$, the triangular form VAR has by construction uncorrelated errors.

The Choleski transformation is equivalent to decomposing the likelihood function into p independent sequential likelihoods (cf. Section 3.3):

$$P(\Delta x_{1,t}, \ldots, \Delta x_{p,t}|\Delta \mathbf{x}_{t-1}, \boldsymbol{\beta}^{c\prime}\mathbf{x}_{t-1}; \boldsymbol{\lambda}^s)$$
$$= \prod_{i=1}^{p} P(\Delta x_{it}|\Delta x_{i+1,t}, \ldots, \Delta x_{p,t}, \Delta \mathbf{x}_{t-1}, \boldsymbol{\beta}^{c\prime}\mathbf{x}_{t-1}; \boldsymbol{\lambda}_i^s)$$

The p sequential conditional expectations are given by:

$$E(\Delta x_{it}|\Delta x_{i+1,t}, \ldots, \Delta x_{p,t}, \Delta \mathbf{x}_{t-1}, \boldsymbol{\beta}^{c\prime}\mathbf{x}_{t-1})$$
$$= \sum_{j=1}^{p-1} a^o_{i,j+1}\Delta x_{j+1,t} + \mathbf{A}_{1,i}\Delta \mathbf{x}_{t-1} + \mathbf{a}_i\boldsymbol{\beta}^{c\prime}\mathbf{x}_{t-1}, \quad i = 1, \ldots, p$$

where $\mathbf{A}_{1,i}$ and $\mathbf{a}_i$ are the ith row vector of $\mathbf{A}_1$, and $\mathbf{a}$ respectively. Because the residuals are uncorrelated in this system, the coefficients can be estimated fully efficiently by OLS equation by equation and the OLS estimates are equivalent to FIML estimates.

The triangular form VAR is exactly identified by the $p(p-1)/2$ zero restrictions on $\mathbf{A}_0$ and $\boldsymbol{\Sigma}$ respectively. However, the triangular system is based on a specific ordering of the p variables and, thus, on an underlying assumption of a causal chain. Since different orderings will, in general, produce different results, and the choice of ordering is subjective, there is an inherent arbitrariness in this model. It is, therefore, important to check the sensitivity of the results to alternative causal chain orderings.

Here we first investigate the consequences of different orderings by performing an OLS regression for each variable as if it had been at the end of the causal chain. The results are reported in Table 13.3 where the coefficients of each column are given by the conditional expectation $E(\Delta \mathbf{x}_{i,t}|\Delta \mathbf{x}_{j,t}(j \neq i), \hat{\boldsymbol{\beta}}^{c\prime}\mathbf{x}_{t-1}, \mathbf{D}_t), i = 1, \ldots, 5$. By this exercise, we can examine how the reduced-form model estimates would have changed for equation $\Delta x_{i,t}$, $i = 1, \ldots, 5$, if we had included current changes of all the other variables in the system as regressors.

The results show significant simultaneous effects between Δm^r_t and $\Delta^2 p_t$ as well as between $\Delta R_{b,t}$ and $\Delta R_{m,t}$, but only moderate effects between Δm^r_t and Δy^r_t. As shown in (13.1), the short-run adjustment parameters are not invariant to transformations by a non-singular matrix $\mathbf{A}_0$, so that previously insignificant adjustment coefficients α_{ij} in the reduced form model might become significant in the transformed model. For example, compared to the reduced-form model in Table 13.2, Table 13.3 shows that $ecm1_{t-1}$ has become significant (but not strongly so) in the real income equation when allowing for current effects and $ecm3_{t-1}$ has become significant in the bond rate equation.

Thus, the hypothesis of a zero row in $\boldsymbol{\alpha}$ as defined in Chapter 11 does not imply a zero row in $\mathbf{a}$, as $\propto$ is not invariant to the inclusion of current effects in the model. For example, by conditioning on the current short-term interest rate in the bond rate

Table 13.3 The fully specified conditional expectations equation by equation.

	Δm_t^r	$\Delta^2 p_t$	$\Delta R_{m,t}$	Δy_t^r	$\Delta R_{b,t}$
Δm_t^r	−1	**−0.16** (5.2)	−0.01 (−1.2)	0.11 (1.6)	0.00 (0.3)
$\Delta^2 p_t$	**−1.24** (−5.2)	−1	0.01 (1.0)	0.06 (0.3)	0.02 (0.9)
$\Delta R_{m,t}$	−2.63 (−1.2)	0.74 (1.0)	−1	−0.43 (−0.3)	**0.60** (4.9)
Δy_t^r	0.22 (1.6)	0.02 (0.3)	−0.00 (−0.3)	−1	0.01 (1.2)
$\Delta R_{b,t}$	0.49 (0.3)	0.51 (0.9)	**0.31** (4.9)	1.29 (1.2)	−1
Δy_{t-1}^r	−0.14 (−1.0)	**−0.10** (−2.0)	−0.01 (−1.0)	**0.18** (1.9)	**0.03** (4.1)
$\Delta R_{b,t-1}$	−0.88 (−0.6)	−0.25 (−0.5)	**0.22** (3.7)	**−3.09** (−3.3)	0.14 (1.6)
$ecm1_{t-1}$	**−0.23** (−5.5)	**−0.04** (−2.3)	−0.00 (−1.4)	**0.08** (2.5)	0.00 (0.7)
$ecm2_{t-1}$	**−1.37** (−3.5)	**−1.18** (−12.7)	**0.06** (3.3)	−0.09 (−0.3)	0.02 (0.7)
$ecm3_{t-1}$	−0.86 (−1.0)	−0.48 (−1.6)	**−0.12** (−3.3)	−0.53 (−0.9)	**0.21** (4.2)
$Dtr754_t$	−0.01 (−0.7)	−0.01 (−1.8)	0.00 (1.1)	**0.04** (3.1)	−0.00 (−1.1)
$Dp764_t$	−0.00 (−0.0)	−0.00 (−0.4)	**0.006** (5.7)	0.01 (0.7)	−0.00 (−1.8)
$Dp831_t$	0.03 (1.1)	−0.00 (−0.3)	**0.003** (3.1)	−0.02 (−0.9)	**−0.007** (−5.2)

ordering should be from the short-term to the long-term interest rate. The effect of $\Delta^2 p_t$ in the Δm_t^r equation is consistent with a money demand effect, whereas the negative effect of Δm_t^r in the $\Delta^2 p_t$ equation is rather implausible. Thus, we would place Δm_t^r prior to $\Delta^2 p$ in the causal chain. Relying on the weak exogeneity results in Chapter 11, we would choose the following ordering for the triangular system:

$$\Delta R_{b,t} \rightarrow \Delta y_t^r \rightarrow \Delta R_{m,t} \rightarrow \Delta^2 p_t \rightarrow \Delta m_t^r. \tag{13.8}$$

The estimates in Table 13.4 are based on this ordering. However, based on the information in Table 13.3 we might as well have chosen the alternative ordering:

$$\Delta R_{m,t} \rightarrow \Delta y_t^r \rightarrow \Delta R_{b,t} \rightarrow \Delta^2 p_t \rightarrow \Delta m_t^r.$$

Note that the upper-triangular representation of the current effects in Table 13.4 corresponds to the Choleski decomposition of the residual covariance matrix when the system variables are ordered as in (13.8).

To increase readability, all coefficients with an absolute t value > 1.9 are in bold face. It appears that the transformation by $\mathbf{A}_0$ does not change the model estimates very much, indicating that the current effects might not be very important for the present model.

Table 13.4 A causal chain representation of the VAR.

	Δm_t^r	$\Delta^2 p_t$	$\Delta R_{m,t}$	Δy_t^r	$\Delta R_{b,t}$
Δm_t^r	−1	0	0	0	0
$\Delta^2 p_t$	**−1.25** (−5.2)	−1	0	0	0
$\Delta R_{m,t}$	−2.63 (−1.2)	1.47 (1.7)	−1	0	0
Δy_t^r	0.22 (1.6)	−0.03 (−0.5)	−0.00 (−0.6)	−1	0
$\Delta R_{b,t}$	0.49 (0.3)	0.54 (0.9)	**0.33** (5.2)	1.06 (1.1)	−1
Δy_{t-1}^r	−0.14 (−1.0)	−0.10 (−1.8)	−0.01 (−1.3)	**0.18** (2.0)	**0.04** (4.2)
$\Delta R_{b,t-1}$	−0.88 (−0.6)	−0.14 (−0.2)	**0.23** (3.9)	**−3.46** (−4.1)	**0.31** (3.9)
$ecm1_{t-1}$	**−0.23** (−5.5)	−0.00 (−0.1)	−0.00 (−0.9)	**0.06** (2.0)	0.00 (0.5)
$ecm2_{t-1}$	**−1.37** (−3.5)	**−1.20** (11.7)	**0.04** (4.0)	−0.19 (−1.1)	**0.03** (1.9)
$ecm3_{t-1}$	−0.86 (−1.0)	−0.43 (−1.3)	**−0.13** (−3.5)	−0.49 (−0.9)	**0.15** (2.8)
$Dtr754_t$	−0.01 (−0.7)	−0.01 (−1.7)	0.00 (0.9)	**0.04** (3.1)	−0.00 (−0.7)
$Dp764_t$	−0.00 (−0.5)	−0.00 (−0.4)	**0.006** (5.8)	0.01 (0.5)	0.00 (0.7)
$Dp831_t$	0.03 (1.1)	−0.01 (−0.9)	**0.003** (2.9)	−0.02 (−0.9)	**−0.007** (−4.7)

13.6 Imposing general restrictions on $\mathbf{A}_0$

We have so far discussed how to impose over-identifying restrictions on a short-run reduced-form model (with the contemporaneous effects in the residual covariance matrix $\mathbf{\Omega}$) and how to impose zero restrictions on the off-diagonal elements of $\mathbf{\Omega}$ by a Choleski transformation of the system. The purpose of this section is to discuss how to impose generically and empirically identifying restrictions on the matrices $\mathbf{A}_0$, $\mathbf{A}_1$, $\mathbf{a}$ and $\mathbf{\Phi}$, so that the generically identified model only contains significant coefficients. For example, many of the estimated coefficients in the triangular system reported in Table 13.4 were insignificant and restricting them to zero seems the obvious thing to do. However, imposing zero restrictions on the triangular model is the same as relaxing the $p-1$ zero restrictions on the residual covariance matrix and OLS estimation equation by equation is no longer equivalent to maximum likelihood estimation. Thus, we need to estimate the system simultaneously subject to the chosen generically identifying restrictions. The discussion of how to impose such identifying restrictions while leaving $\mathbf{\Sigma}$ unrestricted (and, preferably, without any significant residual correlations left) is the purpose of this section.

13.6.1 Is a current effect empirically identifiable?

The general idea of how to account for a residual correlation coefficient as a current effect in matrix $\mathbf{A}_0$ is based on the 'conditioning' rule of Section 3.3. A simple bivariate

VAR(1) model illustrates:

$$\begin{aligned} y_{1,t} &= b_{11}y_{1,t-1} + b_{12}y_{2,t-1} + \varepsilon_{1,t} \\ y_{2,t} &= b_{21}y_{1,t-1} + b_{22}y_{2,t-1} + \varepsilon_{2,t} \end{aligned} \quad (13.9)$$

with $\boldsymbol{\varepsilon}_t \sim NI(\mathbf{0}, \boldsymbol{\Omega})$ and

$$\boldsymbol{\Omega} = \begin{bmatrix} \omega_{11} & \omega_{12} \\ \omega_{21} & \omega_{22} \end{bmatrix}.$$

Section 3.3 demonstrated that the 'reduced form' model (13.9) can alternatively be expressed by the conditional model for $\{y_{1,t} \mid y_{2,t}, y_{1,t-1}, y_{2,t-1}\}$ and the marginal model for $\{y_{2,t} \mid y_{1,t-1}, y_{2,t-1}\}$:

$$\begin{aligned} y_{1,t} &= a_{10}y_{2,t} + a_{11}y_{1,t-1} + a_{12}y_{2,t-1} + u_{1,t} \\ y_{2,t} &= b_{21}y_{1,t-1} + b_{22}y_{2,t-1} + \varepsilon_{2,t} \end{aligned} \quad (13.10)$$

where $a_{10} = \omega_{21}\omega_{22}^{-1}$, $a_{11} = b_{11} - \omega_{21}\omega_{22}^{-1}b_{21}$, $a_{12} = b_{12} - \omega_{21}\omega_{22}^{-1}b_{22}$, $u_{1,t} = \varepsilon_{1,t} - \omega_{21}\omega_{22}^{-1}\varepsilon_{2,t}$, and $E(u_{1,t}\varepsilon_{2,t}) = 0$. The orthogonality of the errors makes (13.10) just-identified.[2] If the orthogonality condition is relaxed, then the model is no longer generically identified. This is because the second equation in this case is a subset of the first equation, so we need to impose another identifying restriction on the first equation, for example $a_{11} = 0$. Such a restriction is just identifying and, hence, can be imposed without changing the likelihood function. However, the residual correlation coefficient between $u_{1,t}$ and $\varepsilon_{2,t}$ will no longer be zero, unless $b_{11} = \omega_{21}\omega_{22}^{-1}b_{21}$.

The latter condition suggests a practical rule for finding out whether a significant residual correlation coefficient can be included as a current effect in an identified equation system and at the same time eliminate (reduce) the residual correlation coefficient. Note, however, that the rule becomes less straightforward in a multiple equation system where the correlation structure is generally more complicated. One way of reducing the complexity is by employing a 'directed graphs' analysis of the covariance structure (Hoover 2005) which aims at uncovering such causal links between the current effects that gives us uncorrelated residuals. This means that the equations are conditionally independent similarly to the triangular model in Table 13.4, even though the causal links may be more complicated.

We use the reduced-form VAR of Table 13.2 to illustrate whether it is possible to include $\Delta^2 p_t$ as an explanatory variable in the equation for Δm_t^r and at the same time get rid of most of the reduced-form residual correlation between $\hat{\varepsilon}_{m^r}$ and $\hat{\varepsilon}_{\Delta p}$ (−0.48).

Step 1. Look for pair(s) of significant regression coefficients with opposite signs (because the residual correlation coefficient is negative) in the equations for $\Delta^2 p_t$ and Δm_t^r. We note that the coefficients to $\Delta R_{b,t-1}$ satisfy this criterion.

Step 2. Check whether the coefficient to $\Delta R_{b,t-1}$ (−3.62) is approximately equal to $(-0.48 \times 0.0240 \times 0.0088 \times 0.0088^{-2}) \times 0.82 = -(0.48 \times 0.0240/0.0088) \times 0.82 = -1.31$.

[2]This is, of course, just a bivariate version of the five-dimensional triangular form model discussed in the previous section.

We note that the two coefficients are not very close to each other, so that adding $\Delta^2 p_t$ to the equation for Δm_t^r and imposing a zero coefficient on $\Delta R_{b,t-1}$ is not likely to solve the problem of residual correlation between $\hat{u}_{m^r}$ and $\hat{\varepsilon}_{\Delta p}$.

Alternatively, we could have chosen to include Δm_t^r in the equation for $\Delta^2 p_t$. However, a negative effect (because the residual correlation coefficient is negative) from a change in Δm_t^r on inflation rate would not be economically plausible, whereas a negative effect from a change in inflation rate on money stock is a plausible money demand reaction. The next question is whether we could include current effects in both equations. The condition for this to work empirically is more complicated and we would now need to check a matrix condition rather than the simple scalar condition in step 2. However, based on the estimates in Table 13.2 it seems highly unlikely that we would be able to identify the joint current effects, as there is just one common pair of significant coefficients between the two equations, which is not sufficient to identify two current effects.

In the following, we shall demonstrate three model structures illustrating different aspects of the identification of the short-run structure. The purpose is to demonstrate some frequently occurring difficulties in the identification of the simultaneous effects matrix $\mathbf{A}_0$ exploiting the information in the residual covariance matrix $\mathbf{\Omega}$. In general, we would like to impose as many zero restrictions as possible on ($\mathbf{A}_0, \mathbf{A}_1, \mathbf{a}$, and $\tilde{\mathbf{\Phi}}$) subject to keeping the residual correlations as small as possible.

13.6.2 Illustration 1: Lack of empirical identification

The short-run structure S1 reported in Table 13.5 is an attempt to account for the residual correlations reported in Tables 13.1 and 13.2 by allowing the model to have simultaneous effects between Δm_t^r and $\Delta^2 p_t$, between Δm_t^r and Δy_t^r and between $\Delta R_{m,t}$ and $\Delta R_{b,t}$ while imposing over-identifying restrictions on the remaining model parameters. The χ^2 test of the 16 over-identifying restrictions has a p-value of 0.26 and the restrictions seem, therefore, acceptable. While generically identified, a closer inspection of the estimated coefficients clearly indicate that the model suffers from near-singularity which usually means a lack of empirical identification. The problem seems particularly serious for the Δm_t^r and Δy_t^r equations. The rank conditions for identification reported in Table 13.8 using (12.5) shows that $r_{1.2}$ and $r_{2.1}$ as well as $r_{4.12}$ exactly satisfies the minimal rank condition. Thus, if just one of the estimated coefficients in the money and inflation equations needed for the identification of the real income equation is not significantly different from zero, empirical identification would be violated.

We also note that violation of empirical identification has very strong effects on the estimated covariance matrix. The correlation coefficient between the inflation residual and the income residual is -0.93 and the residual standard errors of the money and income equations have increased dramatically. This suggests that the condition for a current effect to be empirically identified (see Section 13.6.1) is not met. Thus, violation of empirical identification essentially renders the model estimates useless, prompting for a re-specification of the model.

13.6.3 Illustration 2: The problem of weak instruments

The short-run structure S2 reported in Table 13.6 is an attempt to improve the model specification by refraining from modelling possible simultaneous effects between Δm_t^r

Table 13.5 A generically but not empirically identified short-run structure S1.

	Δm_t^r	$\Delta^2 p_t$	$\Delta R_{m,t}$	Δy_t^r	$\Delta R_{b,t}$
Δm_t^r	-1	-1.05 (-0.68)	0	-1045 (-0.00)	0
$\Delta^2 p_t$	-212 (-0.02)	-1	0	0	0
$\Delta R_{m,t}$	0	0	-1	0	**0.64** (5.0)
Δy_t^r	-65 (-0.02)	0	0	-1	0
$\Delta R_{b,t}$	0	0	0.08 (0.52)	0	-1
Δy_{t-1}^r	0	-0.01 (-0.04)	0	67 (0.00)	**0.04** (4.7)
$\Delta R_{b,t-1}$	0	0	**0.32** (5.33)	-3238 (-0.00)	0.22 (1.8)
$ecm1_{t-1}$	2.49 (0.01)	-0.22 (-0.69)	0	-224 (-0.00)	0
$ecm2_{t-1}$	-249 (-0.02)	$\mathbf{-1.13}$ (-4.73)	**0.05** (4.49)	0	0
$ecm3_{t-1}$	0	0	$\mathbf{-0.08}$ (-2.04)	0	**0.18** (3.82)
$Dtr754_t$	0	0	0	12 (0.00)	0
$Dp764_t$	0	0	**0.006** (5.16)	0	0
$Dp831_t$	0	0	**0.002** (1.20)	0	$\mathbf{-0.008}$ (5.60)

Test of over-identifying restrictions $\chi^2(16) = 19.2[0.26]$

$\hat{\boldsymbol{\Sigma}}$ (standard errors on the diagonal, off-diagonal elements are standardized)

Δm_t^r	2.0811				
$\Delta^2 p_t$	-0.00	0.0222			
$\Delta R_{m,t}$	-0.19	-0.15	0.0010		
Δy_t^r	-0.31	-0.93	-0.21	25.396	
$\Delta R_{b,t}$	-0.08	0.02	-0.13	0.00	0.0014

and Δy_t^r and instead focusing on the simultaneous effects between Δm_t^r and $\Delta^2 p_t$. This was motivated by the moderately sized residual correlation coefficient between the former pair of variables compared to the fairly large (and negative) coefficient between the latter pair of variables. Even though the results in Table 13.6 are now more satisfactory, the simultaneous effects remain poorly determined. To understand why this is the case, we shall take a closer look at the conditions for generic and empirical identification of the equations for Δm_t^r and $\Delta^2 p_t$ and for $\Delta R_{m,t}$ and $\Delta R_{b,t}$, respectively and then discuss whether the condition for economic identification is satisfied.

First, we note that $r_{1.2} = 1$ and $r_{2.1} = 1$ in Table 13.8, so that the first two equations satisfy the minimal rank condition. The zero restriction of $ecm2_{t-1}$ in the equation for Δm_t^r and the corresponding non-zero coefficient in the equation for $\Delta^2 p_t$ are identifying, both generically and empirically (because of the highly significant coefficient of $ecm2_{t-1}$ in the inflation equation). Similarly, the zero restriction of $ecm1_{t-1}$ in the equation for $\Delta^2 p_t$ is identifying (because of the highly significant coefficient of

Table 13.6 The short-run adjustment structure S2.

	Δm_t^r	$\Delta^2 p_t$	$\Delta R_{m,t}$	Δy_t^r	$\Delta R_{b,t}$
Δm_t^r	−1	0.00 (0.1)	0	0	0
$\Delta^2 p_t$	0.11 (0.4)	−1	0	0	0
$\Delta R_{m,t}$	0	0	−1	0	0.30 (1.5)
Δy_t^r	0	0	0	−1	0
$\Delta R_{b,t}$	0	0	−0.12 (1.1)	0	−1
Δy_{t-1}^r	0	0	0	**0.23** (2.9)	**0.03** (4.4)
$\Delta R_{b,t-1}$	**−3.62** (−2.9)	0.80 (1.3)	**0.38** (5.4)	**−3.02** (−3.9)	**0.24** (2.4)
$ecm1_{t-1}$	**−0.21** (−4.7)	0	0	**0.06** (2.4)	0
$ecm2_{t-1}$	0	**−1.09** (−11.8)	**0.05** (4.5)	0	0
$ecm3_{t-1}$	0	0	0	0	**0.20** (4.4)
$Dtr754_t$	0	0	0	**0.04** (3.3)	0
$Dp764_t$	0	0	**0.006** (5.3)	0	0
$Dp831_t$	0	0	0	0	**−0.007** (5.5)

Test of over-identifying restrictions $\chi^2(21) = 25.4[0.23]$

$\hat{\boldsymbol{\Sigma}}$ (standard errors on the diagonal, off-diagonal elements are standardized)

Δm_t^r	0.0244				
$\Delta^2 p_t$	−0.50	0.0088			
$\Delta R_{m,t}$	−0.20	0.22	0.0012		
Δy_t^r	0.13	−0.00	0.02	0.0146	
$\Delta R_{b,t}$	−0.05	0.14	0.37	0.11	0.0014

$ecm1_{t-1}$ in the equation for Δm_t^r). Thus, the first two equations satisfy the conditions for generic and empirical identification.

When, instead, specifying the money equation as $\Delta m_t^r = f(\Delta^2 p_t, ecm1_{t-1}, ecm2_{t-1})$ and the inflation equation as $\Delta^2 p_t = f(\Delta m_t^r, \Delta R_{b,t-1}, ecm2_{t-1})$ (which would be more consistent with the information of Table 13.2), the effect of $\Delta^2 p_t$ in the money equation became borderline significant, while the effect of Δm_t^r in the inflation rate equation remained completely insignificant. However, the residual correlation coefficient between money and inflation increased to −0.67. Consistent with only one pair of common significant coefficients between the money and inflation equations in Table 13.2, we conclude that no more than one contemporaneous effect can be identified by means of zero restrictions on the model parameters[3] and the question is which, if any, should be modelled.

[3]However, by imposing an orthogonality restriction on the residuals from the money and inflation equations it would be possible to estimate the current effect of inflation in the money equation very precisely as Table 13.4 demonstrated.

We first note that our previous conclusion regarding the equilibrium correction of money stock to a long-run money demand relation in principle could be empirically fragile, because of the large residual correlation coefficient between money stock and inflation. This would be the case if by including current changes of money in the inflation equation the recalculated estimates would show a positive effect of money expansion, measured by $ecm1$, on the inflation rate. However, the negatively signed correlation coefficient implies that the effect of a change in money stock would be negative on the inflation rate, as would the effect of excess money. Such a result is economically implausible and would not satisfy economic identification. Therefore, if only one of the current effects can be empirically identified, it should be modelled as a (negative) effect of a change in inflation rate on money stock.

Next, we note that $r_{3.5} = 3$ and $r_{5.3} = 2$ in Table 13.8 so that the two interest rate equations are generically over-identified. Nonetheless, the simultaneous effects between $\Delta R_{m,t}$ and $\Delta R_{b,t}$ are not significant on the 5% level. The short-rate equation contains three identifying zero restrictions (on Δy^r_{t-1}, $ecm3_{t-1}$ and $Dp831_t$) and the long-term bond rate two identifying restrictions (on $ecm2_{t-1}$ and $Dp764_t$). Since the corresponding non-zero coefficients are highly significant, the two interest rate equations are both generically and empirically identified. Note that in this case the strongly significant (and economically interpretable) dummy variables, $Dp764_t$ and $Dp831_t$, have been used as identifying variables and that the zero restrictions on $ecm1_{t-1}$ in the equations for $\Delta R_{m,t}$ and $\Delta R_{b,t}$ are not identifying as they enter similarly in both equations. The negative coefficient of $\Delta R_{b,t}$ in the short-rate equation is, however, not economically plausible. This can be explained by noticing that there are two pairs of common significant coefficients in the interest rate equations of Table 13.2, one with coefficients of the same sign, the other with opposite signs.

Thus, the low t values of the simultaneous effects cannot be explained by the lack of empirical identification. Several new attempts to determine the simultaneous effects more precisely failed. Altogether, the results suggest that the present set of variables does not contain strong identifying information about the simultaneous adjustment structure.

However, it should be mentioned that we would have been able to improve empirical identification by not omitting the lagged short-term interest rate in Section 13.4.[4] But, even though this would have improved empirical identification, the estimates were not easily interpretable so economic identification would not have been satisfied.

Thus, our many attempts to recover a generically identified short-run structure, with empirically significant coefficients and insignificant residual correlations failed on one condition or the other. This is a good illustration of the fragility of identifying contemporaneous effects based on lagged variables, i.e. on weak instruments in the terminology of Sims (1980). The *ecms* would in principle have been strong instruments for the simultaneous effects, but could not be used in this case as they did not enter the short-run reduced VAR equations as pairs of significant coefficients. The latter suggests that the short-run reduced-form model might indeed be the best economic model.

Based on the present information, set we have been able to adequately identify a plausible long-run structure, but not a simultaneous short-run adjustment structure. To obtain a more satisfactory identification of the short-run structure we would need to include stronger instruments. For example, the long-term bond rate is likely to have been

[4]It was only borderline insignificant by the F-test.

Table 13.7 The short-run adjustment structure S3.

	Δm_t^r	$\Delta^2 p_t$	$\Delta R_{m,t}$	Δy_t^r	$\Delta R_{b,t}$
Δm_t^r	**−1**	0	0	0	0
$\Delta^2 p_t$	0	**−1**	0	0	0
$\Delta R_{m,t}$	0	0	**−1**	0	**0.66** (5.2)
Δy_t^r	0	0	0	**−1**	0
$\Delta R_{b,t}$	0	0	0	0	**−1**
Δy_{t-1}^r	0	0	0	**0.24** (2.9)	**0.04** (5.0)
$\Delta R_{b,t-1}$	**−3.69** (−3.0)	0.76 (1.8)	**0.34** (6.4)	**−3.13** (−4.1)	0
$ecm1_{t-1}$	**−0.20** (−5.3)	0	0	**0.06** (2.4)	0
$ecm2_{t-1}$	0	**−1.10** (−13.5)	**0.05** (4.8)	0	0
$ecm3_{t-1}$	0	0	0	0	**0.19** (4.2)
$Dtr754_t$	0	0	0	**0.04** (3.3)	**−0.01** (−5.5)
$Dp764_t$	0	0	**0.006** (5.2)	0	0
$Dp831_t$	0	0		0	0

Test of over-identifying restrictions $\chi^2(25) = 32.9[0.13]$

$\hat{\Sigma}$ (standard errors on the diagonal, off-diagonal elements are standardized)

Δm_t^r	0.0240				
$\Delta^2 p_t$	−0.48	0.0088			
$\Delta R_{m,t}$	−0.19	0.22	0.0011		
Δy_t^r	0.13	−0.00	0.00	0.0146	
$\Delta R_{b,t}$	−0.03	0.07	−0.06	0.11	0.0014

strongly influenced by the German bond rate, but probably not vice versa. Real aggregate income is likely to have been strongly influenced by the real exchange rates, the terms of trade and foreign aggregate demand. The inflation rate may have been influenced by excess wage pressure in the labour market. The last few chapters will extend the information set with the above variables to find out whether the empirical and economic identification of the short-run structure can be improved.

13.6.4 Illustration 3: The preferred structure

The final estimated structure S3 reported in Table 13.7 closely resembles the reduced form model in Table 13.2, except that the bond rate equation contains the current change of the short-term interest rate. We did not include $\Delta^2 p_t$ in the money equation because it increased the residual correlation coefficient and did not improve economic identification.

The 25 zero restrictions imposed on structure S3 were accepted with a p-value of 0.20. The residual correlations reported at the bottom of Table 13.7 are small or

Table 13.8 Checking the rank conditions of short-run structure S1 and S2.

$r_{i.j}$	$S1$	$S2$	$r_{i.jk}$	$S1$	$S2$	$r_{i.jkm}$	$S1$	$S2$	$r_{i.jkmn}$	$S1$	$S2$
			1.23	7	4						
1.2	**1**	**1**	*1.24*	3	4	*1.234*	8	7			
1.3	6	4	*1.25*	6	6	*1.235*	7	7			
1.4	3	3	*1.34*	8	7	*1.245*	7	8	*1.2345*	8	9
1.5	6	5	*1.35*	7	7	*1.345*	8	9			
			1.45	7	7						
			2.13	7	4						
2.1	**1**	**1**	*2.14*	3	4	*2.134*	8	7			
2.3	6	3	*2.15*	6	6	*2.135*	7	7			
2.4	3	4	*2.34*	8	7	*2.145*	7	8	*2.1345*	8	9
2.5	5	5	*2.35*	6	6	*2.345*	8	9			
			2.45	7	8						
			3.12	5	3						
3.1	4	3	*3.14*	6	6	*3.124*	6	6			
3.2	4	2	*3.15*	5	6	*3.125*	5	6			
3.4	5	4	*3.24*	6	6	*3.145*	6	8	*3.1245*	6	8
3.5	**1**	3	*3.25*	4	5	*3.245*	6	8			
			3.45	5	6						
			4.12	**2**	3						
4.1	2	2	*4.13*	7	6	*4.123*	7	6			
4.2	2	3	*4.15*	6	6	*4.125*	6	7			
4.3	6	4	*4.23*	7	6	*4.135*	7	8	*4.1235*	7	8
4.5	4	4	*4.25*	6	7	*4.235*	7	8			
			4.35	6	6						
			5.12	5	4						
5.1	5	3	*5.13*	6	5	*5.123*	6	5			
5.2	4	3	*5.14*	6	5	*5.124*	6	6			
5.3	2	2	*5.23*	5	4	*5.134*	7	7	*5.1234*	7	7
5.4	4	3	*5.24*	6	6	*5.234*	7	7			
			5.34	6	5						

moderate except for between money stock and inflation and the residual standard errors are generally very small. Thus, the empirical model is a fairly precise representation of the information in the data. Based on the estimated results we notice that:

1. Real money stock is exclusively equilibrium correcting to the long-run money demand relation, with a speed of adjustment coefficient suggesting that it takes approximately five quarters for an equilibrium error (excess money demand) to disappear.

Table 13.9 The estimates of a partial system for money, the inflation rate and the deposit rate.

	Δm_t^r	$\Delta^2 p_t$	$\Delta R_{m,t}$	Δy_t^r
Δm_t^r	−1	0	0	0
$\Delta^2 p_t$	0	−1	0	0
$\Delta R_{m,t}$	0	0	−1	0
Δy_t^r	0	0	0	−1
$\Delta R_{b,t}$	0	0	**0.27** (4.9)	0
Δy_{t-1}^r	0	0	0	**0.24** (2.9)
$\Delta R_{b,t-1}$	**−3.63** (3.0)	**0.81** (1.9)	**0.24** (4.7)	**−3.03** (4.0)
$ecm1_{t-1}$	**−0.20** (−5.3)	0	0	**0.06** (2.4)
$ecm2_{t-1}$	0	**−1.10** (−13.4)	**0.05** (4.8)	0
$ecm3_{t-1}$	0	0	**−0.10** (−3.1)	0
$Dtr754$	0	0	0	**0.04** (3.2)
$Dp764$	0	0	**0.006** (6.1)	0
$Dp831$	0	0	**0.003** (3.0)	0

Test of over-identifying restrictions $\chi^2(22) = 25.8[0.26]$

$\hat{\Sigma}$ (standard errors on the diagonal, off-diagonal elements are correlations)

Δm_t^r	0.0240			
$\Delta^2 p_t$	−0.48	0.0088		
$\Delta R_{m,t}$	−0.19	0.18	0.0010	
Δy_t^r	0.13	−0.00	−0.04	0.0146

2. Inflation is exclusively equilibrium correcting to the real income–inflation rate relation.
3. Short-term interest is essentially equilibrium correcting to the real income–inflation rate relation (monetary policy reactions).
4. Real aggregate demand shows a small positive (but only borderline significant) effect from excess money.
5. The bond rate exhibits some equilibrium correction to the homogeneous interest rate–inflation relation.
6. All variables have reacted to the lagged bond rate, signifying the importance of the bond market in Denmark.
7. The simultaneous effects are generally weak or imprecisely determined.

13.7 A partial system

In this section we re-estimate the model as a partial model for real money stock, inflation, the short-run interest rate, and real aggregate demand conditional on the weakly exogenous bond rate. Note, however, that weak exogeneity for the long-run parameters $\boldsymbol{\beta}$ does not imply weak exogeneity for the short-run adjustment parameters ($\boldsymbol{\lambda}_{SF}^{S}$). Therefore, if the parameters of interest are the short-run adjustment coefficients, then $R_{b,t}$ is not weakly exogenous as the estimation results in Table 13.7 demonstrate. But, because the motivation for estimating the cointegrated VAR model is often an interest in the long-run structure, establishing long-run weak exogeneity for a variable is often used as a justification for performing the model analysis conditional on such a variable.

Table 13.9 reports the estimates of the partial model for Δm_t^r, Δp_t^2, $\Delta R_{m,t}$, and Δy_t^r conditional on $\Delta R_{b,t}$. The estimated results are similar, though more significant, to the estimates of the full system reported in Table 13.7. Thus, the empirical conclusions in this case are fairly robust, whether based on the full or the partial system.

13.8 Concluding remarks

In spite of the disappointing results concerning the empirical and economic identification of the simultaneous effects in our model, we shall make an attempt to answer the questions raised in Section 13.2.

Question 1. Is money stock adjusting to money demand or supply?

The result that real money holdings have been exclusively adjusting to a long-run money demand relation seemed relatively robust in all specifications, indicating that the central bank has willingly supplied the demanded money, or that agents have been able to satisfy their desired level of money holdings independently of the central bank. The access to credit outside Denmark as a result of deregulation of capital movements might suggest with the latter.

Question 2. Given the empirically stable money demand relation found in the Danish data, can inflation be effectively controlled by the central bank?

If the level of (the broad measure of) money stock is endogenously determined by agents' demand for money, then the central bank can indirectly influence the level of the demanded quantity by influencing its determinants, i.e. the cost of holding money. According to the estimated money-demand relation this can be achieved by changing the short-term interest rate. But a change in the short-term interest rate is likely to change money demand only to the extent that it changes the spread $(R_m - R_b)$. Even though the stationarity of $(R_m - R_b)$ could be accepted, the next chapter will show that the spread does exhibit a persistent component. Furthermore, an increase in the central bank interest rate is likely to first influence the deposit rate which would increase agents' willingness to hold money. For a formal discussion of the conditions under which a monetary instrument can be used to control inflation see Johansen and Juselius (2001).

Question 3. Does excess money, defined here as the deviation from the long-run money demand relation, cause inflation in the short-run?

For this to be the case, $ecm1$ should have a positive coefficient in the inflation equation. No such evidence is found in any of the short-run structures. If Δm_t^r was included in the inflation equation, the effect of excess money actually became negative. Thus, there is essentially no evidence that inflation has been caused by monetary expansion in this period, at least not in the short-run. The possibility that there is a positive long-run effect on prices of expanding money supply in excess of real productive growth will be analysed in the next two chapters.

To summarize: the empirical and economic identification of the short-run structure was quite disappointing, probably because of weak instruments. Another reason could be that macrodata do not contain very precise information about current effects between variables, for example because of imprecise preliminary measurements and subsequent large revisions or, relatedly, because of adaptive, instead of forward-looking, expectations at the macrolevel of the economy.

14

Identification of common trends

The previous chapter discussed identification of a short-run structure allowing for simultaneous current effects as well as short-run adjustment effects to lagged changes of the variables and to previous equilibrium errors. The model was estimated without imposing identifying restrictions on the residuals, except for trivially in the triangular form model which automatically imposes residual orthogonality. The purpose of this chapter is to discuss how to impose identifying restrictions on the common driving trends, $\boldsymbol{\alpha}'_{\perp}\sum\boldsymbol{\varepsilon}_i$, and their weights, $\tilde{\boldsymbol{\beta}}_{\perp}$ without requiring that the identified permanent shocks satisfy orthogonality. The latter condition will be discussed in connection with the structural MA model in the next chapter, where we also discuss restrictions that aim at identifying r permanent and $p - r$ transitory shocks.

The identification problem for the common trends case is similar to the one of the long-run relations in the sense that one can always choose a normalization and $(p-r-1)$ restrictions without changing the value of the likelihood function, whereas additional restrictions are over-identifying and, hence, testable. The aim of this chapter is primarily to discuss how to impose econometrically reasonable restrictions on the underlying common trends without attaching a structural meaning to the estimated shocks.

The organization of this chapter is as follows: Section 14.1 discusses the common trends decomposition based on the VAR model and some special cases, Section 14.2 illustrates the common trends representation based on unrestricted $\boldsymbol{\alpha}$ and $\boldsymbol{\beta}$ and presents a just-identified structure, Section 14.3 discusses the common trends estimates derived under various restrictions on $\boldsymbol{\alpha}$ and $\boldsymbol{\beta}$. Section 14.4 discusses identification given by economically motivated exclusion restrictions on $\boldsymbol{\beta}_{\perp}$. Section 14.5 assesses the empirical results in terms of the scenario analysis of Chapter 2.

14.1 The common trends representation

Chapters 12 and 13 discussed the fact that the VAR residuals are not in general invariant to linear transformations of the model and, similarly, not to changes in the information set. The question is, therefore, whether the whole exercise of imposing economic structure on the common trends model and then interpreting the estimated results in terms of structural shocks is at all relevant. Many economists would argue that interpretation is only meaningful after one has imposed structural restrictions on the residuals derived from a formal theoretical model. This chapter and the next chapter will argue that such restrictions can only be interpretable and meaningful to the extent that the basic hypotheses derived from the theoretical model are in line with the information in the data.

The discussion here will be based on the VAR model with a linear trend restricted to the cointegration relations but, for simplicity, with no dummy variables:

$$\begin{aligned} \Delta \mathbf{x}_t &= \mathbf{\Gamma}_1 \Delta \mathbf{x}_{t-1} + \boldsymbol{\alpha}\boldsymbol{\beta}'\tilde{\mathbf{x}}_{t-1} + \boldsymbol{\mu}_0 + \boldsymbol{\alpha}\boldsymbol{\beta}_1 t + \boldsymbol{\varepsilon}_t, \\ \boldsymbol{\varepsilon}_t &\sim IN(\mathbf{0}, \mathbf{\Omega}). \end{aligned} \tag{14.1}$$

The corresponding moving-average representation is given by:

$$\mathbf{x}_t = \mathbf{C}\sum_{i=1}^{t} \boldsymbol{\varepsilon}_i + t\boldsymbol{C}\boldsymbol{\mu}_0 + \mathbf{C}^*(L)(\boldsymbol{\varepsilon}_t + \boldsymbol{\mu}_0 + \boldsymbol{\alpha}\boldsymbol{\beta}_1 t) + \tilde{\mathbf{X}}_0, \tag{14.2}$$

where

$$\mathbf{C} = \boldsymbol{\beta}_{\perp}(\boldsymbol{\alpha}'_{\perp}\mathbf{\Gamma}\boldsymbol{\beta}_{\perp})^{-1}\boldsymbol{\alpha}'_{\perp}. \tag{14.3}$$

It is useful to express the $\mathbf{C}$ matrix as a product of two matrices (similarly to $\mathbf{\Pi} = \boldsymbol{\alpha}\boldsymbol{\beta}'$)

$$\mathbf{C} = \widetilde{\boldsymbol{\beta}}_{\perp}\boldsymbol{\alpha}'_{\perp}, \tag{14.4}$$

or, alternatively,

$$\mathbf{C} = \boldsymbol{\beta}_{\perp}\widetilde{\boldsymbol{\alpha}}'_{\perp},$$

where $\widetilde{\boldsymbol{\beta}}_{\perp} = \boldsymbol{\beta}_{\perp}(\boldsymbol{\alpha}'_{\perp}\mathbf{\Gamma}\boldsymbol{\beta}_{\perp})^{-1}$ and $\widetilde{\boldsymbol{\alpha}}'_{\perp} = (\boldsymbol{\alpha}'_{\perp}\mathbf{\Gamma}\boldsymbol{\beta}_{\perp})^{-1}\boldsymbol{\alpha}'_{\perp}$. In the subsequent analyses we shall use the former formulation. Note that the matrices $\boldsymbol{\beta}_{\perp}$ and $\boldsymbol{\alpha}_{\perp}$ can be directly calculated for given estimates of $\boldsymbol{\alpha}, \boldsymbol{\beta}$, and $\mathbf{\Gamma}$ based on (14.3). This means that the common stochastic trends and their weights can be found either based on unrestricted $\hat{\boldsymbol{\alpha}}, \hat{\boldsymbol{\beta}}$, or on restricted estimates, $\hat{\boldsymbol{\alpha}}^c, \hat{\boldsymbol{\beta}}^c$.[1]

Based on (14.4) it appears that the $p \times (p - r)$ matrix $\widetilde{\boldsymbol{\beta}}_{\perp}$ (alternatively $\widetilde{\boldsymbol{\beta}}^c_{\perp}$) can be given an interpretation as the loadings to the $p - r$ common stochastic trends $\boldsymbol{\alpha}'_{\perp}\sum \boldsymbol{\varepsilon}_i$ (alternatively $(\boldsymbol{\alpha}^c_{\perp})'\sum \boldsymbol{\varepsilon}_i$). The formulation (14.2) closely resembles the trend, cycle, and irregular decomposition introduced in Chapter 2 and allows us to assess the empirical content of the theoretical scenario discussed less formally in Chapter 2.

[1]When choosing the moving-average option in CATS the program uses the latest estimates of $\boldsymbol{\alpha}$ and $\boldsymbol{\beta}$ as a basis for the calculations.

The decomposition of $\mathbf{C} = \widetilde{\boldsymbol{\beta}}_{\perp}\boldsymbol{\alpha}'_{\perp}$ resembles the decomposition $\boldsymbol{\Pi} = \boldsymbol{\alpha\beta}'$ but with the important difference that $\widetilde{\boldsymbol{\beta}}_{\perp}$ is a function not only of $\boldsymbol{\beta}_{\perp}$, but also of $\boldsymbol{\alpha}_{\perp}$. Similar to $\boldsymbol{\alpha}$ and $\boldsymbol{\beta}$, one can transform $\widetilde{\boldsymbol{\beta}}_{\perp}$and $\boldsymbol{\alpha}_{\perp}$ by a non-singular $(p-r) \times (p-r)$ matrix $\mathbf{Q}$

$$\mathbf{C} = \widetilde{\boldsymbol{\beta}}_{\perp}\boldsymbol{Q}\boldsymbol{Q}^{-1}\boldsymbol{\alpha}'_{\perp} = \widetilde{\boldsymbol{\beta}}^{c}_{\perp}(\boldsymbol{\alpha}^{c}_{\perp})' \tag{14.5}$$

without changing the value of the likelihood function. Thus, the $\mathbf{Q}$ transformation leads to just-identified common trends for which no testing is involved. Additional restrictions on $\widetilde{\boldsymbol{\beta}}_{\perp}$and $\boldsymbol{\alpha}_{\perp}$ constrain the likelihood function and, hence, are testable. Tests of such over-identifying restrictions on the common trends are in general highly nonlinear and, therefore, difficult to implement.

There are, however, a few special cases of over-identifying restrictions on $\boldsymbol{\alpha}_{\perp}$ and $\boldsymbol{\beta}_{\perp}$ which can be expressed as testable restrictions on $\boldsymbol{\alpha}$ and $\boldsymbol{\beta}$. These are first tested and imposed in the usual way in the VAR model, which is then inverted to give the estimates of the corresponding common trends model. In this case there is no need to derive new test procedures. The following four cases represent restrictions on $\boldsymbol{\beta}$ and $\boldsymbol{\alpha}$ which can be expressed as equivalent linear restrictions on $\boldsymbol{\beta}_{\perp}$ and $\boldsymbol{\alpha}_{\perp}$.

Case 1: Long-run homogeneity:

$$\boldsymbol{\beta} = \begin{bmatrix} a & b & c \\ -\omega_1 a & -\omega_2 b & -\omega_3 c \\ -(1-\omega_1)a & -(1-\omega_2)b & -(1-\omega_3)c \\ * & * & * \\ * & * & * \end{bmatrix} \rightarrow \boldsymbol{\beta}_{\perp} = \begin{bmatrix} 1 & * \\ 1 & * \\ 1 & * \\ 0 & * \\ 0 & * \end{bmatrix},$$

i.e. one of the stochastic trends enters the homogeneously cointegrated variables with equal weights.

Case 2: A stationary variable in $\boldsymbol{\beta}$:

$$\boldsymbol{\beta} = \begin{bmatrix} 0 & * & * \\ 1 & * & * \\ 0 & * & * \\ 0 & * & * \\ 0 & * & * \end{bmatrix} \rightarrow \boldsymbol{\beta}_{\perp} = \begin{bmatrix} * & * \\ 0 & 0 \\ * & * \\ * & * \\ * & * \end{bmatrix},$$

corresponds to a zero row in the $\mathbf{C}$ matrix.

Case 3: A column of $\boldsymbol{\alpha}$ is proportional to a unit vector:

$$\boldsymbol{\alpha} = \begin{bmatrix} * & * & * \\ 0 & * & * \\ 0 & * & * \\ 0 & * & * \\ 0 & * & * \end{bmatrix} \rightarrow \boldsymbol{\alpha}_{\perp} = \begin{bmatrix} 0 & 0 \\ * & * \\ * & * \\ * & * \\ * & * \end{bmatrix},$$

corresponds to a zero column in the $\mathbf{C}$ matrix.

Case 4: A row in $\boldsymbol{\alpha}$ *is equal to zero:*

$$\boldsymbol{\alpha} = \begin{bmatrix} * & * & * \\ * & * & * \\ * & * & * \\ * & * & * \\ 0 & 0 & 0 \end{bmatrix} \rightarrow \boldsymbol{\alpha}_{\perp} = \begin{bmatrix} * & 0 \\ * & 0 \\ * & 0 \\ * & 0 \\ * & 1 \end{bmatrix},$$

i.e. cumulated shocks to the last variable is a common driving trend and the last variable is weakly exogenous for the long-run parameters. If, in addition, the weakly exogenous variable, $x_{i,t}$, exhibits no short-run effects, so that all the coefficients $\Gamma_{ij} = 0$, $j = 1, \ldots, p$ then $x_{i,t}$ will have a unit row vector in the $\mathbf{C}$ matrix.

In the rest of the chapter we shall discuss a variety of decompositions based on various assumptions on just-identifying restrictions on $\boldsymbol{\alpha}_{\perp}$ and $\boldsymbol{\beta}_{\perp}$ as well as over-identifying restrictions based on the above special cases. All decompositions will be illustrated based on the Danish data. Section 14.2 will discuss the unrestricted MA representation for the following two cases:

1. an unrestricted estimate of $\boldsymbol{\alpha}_{\perp}$ and $\tilde{\boldsymbol{\beta}}_{\perp}$ normalized on the largest coefficient;
2. a just-identified estimate of $\boldsymbol{\alpha}_{\perp}$ and $\tilde{\boldsymbol{\beta}}_{\perp}$.

Section 14.3 will discuss the following three restricted versions:

1. an over-identified estimate of $\boldsymbol{\alpha}_{\perp}$ and $\tilde{\boldsymbol{\beta}}_{\perp}$ derived under one weak exogeneity restriction on $\boldsymbol{\alpha}$ (a zero row restriction for the bond rate) and an unrestricted $\boldsymbol{\beta}$;
2. an over-identified estimate of $\boldsymbol{\alpha}_{\perp}$ and $\tilde{\boldsymbol{\beta}}_{\perp}$ derived under the weak exogeneity restriction of the bond rate and $\boldsymbol{\beta}$ restricted to the structure $\mathcal{H}_{S.4}$ of Table 12.3;
3. an over-identified estimate of $\boldsymbol{\alpha}_{\perp}$ and $\tilde{\boldsymbol{\beta}}_{\perp}$derived under two weak exogeneity restrictions on $\boldsymbol{\alpha}$ (a zero row restriction for the real income and the bond rate) and $\boldsymbol{\beta}$ restricted to $\mathcal{H}_{S.4}$.

Section 14.4 will discuss the following two exclusion restrictions on $\tilde{\boldsymbol{\beta}}_{\perp}$ motivated by the assumption that:

1. the real stochastic trend has no long-run impact on the inflation rate;
2. the real stochastic trend has no long-run impact on the inflation rate and the nominal stochastic trend has no long-run impact on the real income.

14.2 The unrestricted MA representation

The moving average representation of the Danish data for $r = 3$ corresponds to $p - r = 2$ common trends. The unrestricted estimates of $\boldsymbol{\alpha}_{\perp}$ and $\widetilde{\boldsymbol{\beta}}_{\perp}$and the deterministic linear trend coefficient $\boldsymbol{\gamma}_0$ reported in the first part of Table 14.1 are determined based on one particular estimate of $\boldsymbol{\alpha}_{\perp}$ and $\boldsymbol{\beta}_{\perp}$. This first set of common trends estimates is not unique in the sense that we can impose $(p - r - 1) = 1$ identifying restriction on each vector without changing the likelihood function. However, the space spanned by $\boldsymbol{\alpha}_{\perp}$ and $\boldsymbol{\beta}_{\perp}$ is uniquely determined, so the estimated $\mathbf{C}$ matrix is unique. This is similar to $\boldsymbol{\alpha}$

and $\boldsymbol{\beta}$ where the $\boldsymbol{\Pi}$ matrix was uniquely estimated, even though the unrestricted $\boldsymbol{\alpha}$ and $\boldsymbol{\beta}$ vectors were not.

The unrestricted estimates of $\boldsymbol{\alpha}_{\perp}$ and $\widetilde{\boldsymbol{\beta}}_{\perp}$ in the upper part of Table 14.1 have been normalized by the largest coefficient in $\boldsymbol{\alpha}_{\perp,i}$. We note that the largest coefficient of $\hat{\boldsymbol{\alpha}}_{\perp,1}$ picks up the weakly exogenous bond rate, whereas the largest coefficient of $\hat{\boldsymbol{\alpha}}_{\perp,2}$ picks up the short-term interest rate rather than the (almost) weakly exogenous real income. But, even though the coefficient to the short-term interest rate is the largest in magnitude, it can be shown to be insignificant. Thus, if we choose this normalization the just-identified estimates would be obtained by dividing through by an insignificant coefficient and the calculated standard errors would essentially not be interpretable.

This serves as an illustration that a large coefficient does not necessarily imply statistical significance and that the magnitude of a coefficient may not be very informative unless the residuals have been standardized. To improve interpretability we have, therefore, reported the residual standard deviations $\hat{\sigma}_{\varepsilon_i}$ in the upper part of Table 14.1. We note that the residual standard error of $\hat{\varepsilon}_{y^r}$ is 14 times as large as the standard error of $\hat{\varepsilon}_{R_m}$, whereas the coefficient of the latter in $\hat{\boldsymbol{\alpha}}_{\perp,2}$ is only five times as large as the coefficient of the former.

Chapter 11 showed that the bond rate was weakly exogenous with a fairly high p-value whereas the real income was borderline so. This suggests that we should impose an identifying (0, 1) restriction on the bond rate/real income residual in one of the common trends and a corresponding (1, 0) restriction in the other. This can be achieved by premultiplying $\hat{\boldsymbol{\alpha}}_{\perp}$ by the transformation matrix $\mathbf{Q}^{-1}$

$$\mathbf{Q}^{-1} = \begin{bmatrix} 0.17 & 1.00 \\ -0.18 & -0.06 \end{bmatrix}^{-1} = \begin{bmatrix} -0.35 & -5.89 \\ 1.06 & 1.00 \end{bmatrix}$$

and by post-multiplying $\hat{\boldsymbol{\beta}}_{\perp}$ by $\mathbf{Q}$. Table 14.1 reports the resulting estimates $\hat{\boldsymbol{\alpha}}_{\perp}^{c}$ and $\hat{\boldsymbol{\beta}}_{\perp}^{c}$. The latter are now uniquely determined which makes it possible to calculate standard error of estimates.[2]

The first stochastic trend seems to describe cumulated effects of empirical shocks to the two interest rates albeit noticing that the coefficient to the short rate is not significant. The second stochastic trend describes cumulative effects of empirical shocks to the real income with some effects from the real money stock and the inflation rate.

The estimates of the $\mathbf{C}$ matrix (similar to the $\boldsymbol{\Pi}$ matrix) contain useful information about the overall effects of the stochastic driving forces in this system. The columns of the $\mathbf{C}$ matrix show how the cumulated residuals from each VAR equation load into each of the variables. For example, a column of insignificant coefficients means that the empirical shocks of the corresponding variable have only exhibited temporary effects on the variables of the system, whereas a column of significant coefficients indicates permanent effects on the system. Row-wise, the $\mathbf{C}$ matrix gives the weights with which each variable in the system has been influenced by any of the cumulated empirical shocks.

[2]This is similar to the $\boldsymbol{\beta}$ relations for which standard errors of the estimates were only available for identified relations.

Table 14.1 The MA representation for unrestricted α and β.

	$\hat{\varepsilon}_{m^r}$	$\hat{\varepsilon}_{y^r}$	$\hat{\varepsilon}_{\Delta p}$	$\hat{\varepsilon}_{R_m}$	$\hat{\varepsilon}_{R_b}$	
σ_{ε_i}	0.0231	0.0138	0.0080	0.0010	0.0014	
The unrestricted estimates						
$\hat{\boldsymbol{\alpha}}'_{\perp,1}$	0.05	0.17	−0.07	0.10	1.00	
$\hat{\boldsymbol{\alpha}}'_{\perp,2}$	0.06	−0.18	0.13	1.00	−0.06	
	m^r	y^r	Δp	R_m	R_b	
$\tilde{\hat{\boldsymbol{\beta}}}'_{\perp,1}$	−4.92	−1.91	−0.13	0.67	1.03	
$\tilde{\hat{\boldsymbol{\beta}}}'_{\perp,2}$	−8.49	−6.72	0.09	0.60	0.81	
A just-identified representation						
$\hat{\boldsymbol{\alpha}}^{c\prime}_{\perp,1}$	0.00 [0.01]	0.00	0.06 [1.08]	1.11 [1.45]	**1.00**	
$\hat{\boldsymbol{\alpha}}^{c\prime}_{\perp,2}$	0.32 [1.63]	**1.00**	−0.78 [−1.49]	−5.94 [−0.84]	0.00	
	m^r	y^r	Δp	R_m	R_b	
$\tilde{\hat{\boldsymbol{\beta}}}^{c\prime}_{\perp,1}$	**−4.46** [−2.06]	−1.56 [−0.79]	−0.13 [−1.75]	**0.64** [4.38]	**0.99** [4.56]	
$\tilde{\hat{\boldsymbol{\beta}}}^{c\prime}_{\perp,2}$	**0.69** [3.62]	**0.83** [4.73]	**−0.04** [−5.69]	0.01 [0.57]	0.03 [1.52]	
The **C** matrix						
	$\hat{\varepsilon}_{m^r}$	$\hat{\varepsilon}_{y^r}$	$\hat{\varepsilon}_{\Delta p}$	$\hat{\varepsilon}_{R_m}$	$\hat{\varepsilon}_{R_b}$	$t \times \gamma_{0,i}$
m^r	0.22 (1.5)	**0.69** (3.6)	**−0.81** (−1.8)	**−9.04** (−1.8)	**−4.46** (−2.1)	0.0038
y^r	**0.26** (1.9)	**0.83** (4.7)	**−0.74** (−1.8)	−6.65 (−1.4)	−1.56 (−0.8)	0.0039
Δp	**−0.01** (−2.3)	**−0.04** (−5.7)	0.02 (1.3)	0.08 (0.4)	**−0.13** (−1.8)	−0.0001
R_m	0.00 (0.2)	0.01 (0.6)	0.03 (1.1)	**0.67** (2.0)	**0.64** (4.4)	−0.0001
R_b	0.01 (0.6)	0.03 (1.5)	0.04 (0.8)	**0.92** (1.8)	**0.99** (4.6)	−0.0001

t ratios in parentheses

A column-wise inspection (focusing on the significant coefficients given in bold face) shows that the cumulated empirical shocks to:

1. the real money stock have had a moderately significant effect on the real income (positive) and on the inflation rate (negative);
2. the real income have had positive (and quite significant) effects on money stock, itself, and negative on the inflation rate (demand-pull effect);
3. the inflation rate have had a negative (but only moderately significant) effect on the real money stock (a money demand effect) and likewise on the real aggregate income;
4. the short-term interest rate have had a moderately significant effect on itself and on the bond rate;

5. the long-term bond rate have had a negative effect on the real money stock and the inflation rate, and a positive effect on itself and the short-term interest rate.

A row-wise inspection shows that:

1. money stock has been permanently influenced by all empirical shocks except by its own shocks, consistent with the previous finding that money stock is exclusively adjusting and not pushing;
2. the real aggregate income has been permanently affected primarily by its own shocks, but also to some extent by empirical shocks to money stock (positively) and to the inflation rate (negatively);
3. the inflation rate has been negatively influenced by empirical shocks to money and the bond rate and positively to the real aggregate income;
4. the two interest rates have not been significantly influenced by any shocks to the macrovariables (not even by shocks to the inflation rate).

Generally, the results are broadly consistent with our previous finding that the empirical shocks to the real income and the bond rate are the most important pushing forces of this system, whereas the pulling forces are primarily given by the equilibrium adjustment mechanisms in the equations for the real money stock, short-term interest rate and the inflation rate.

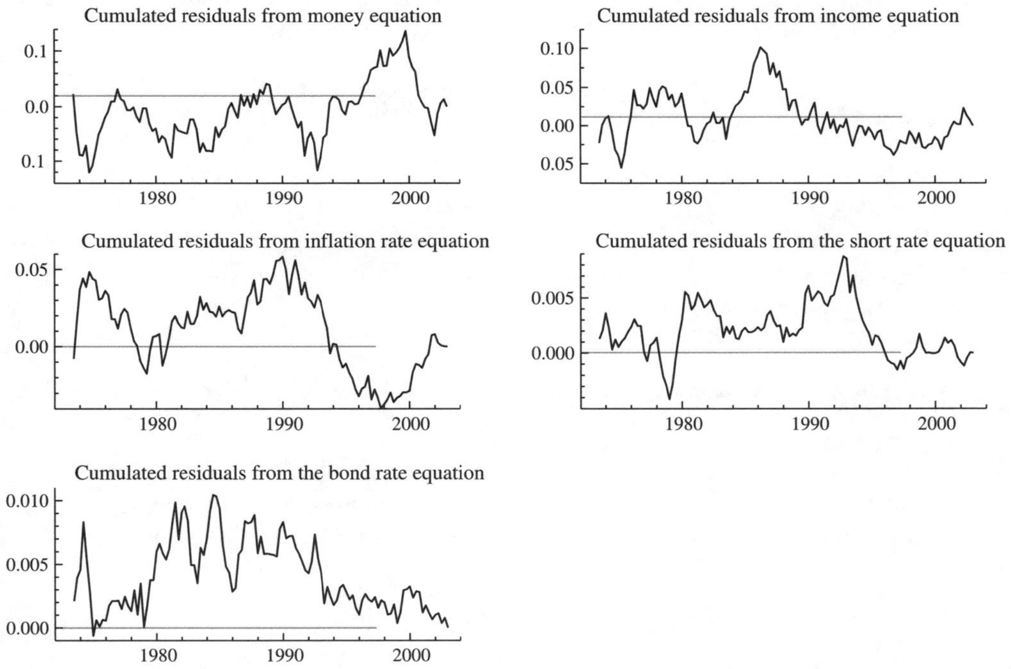

Fig 14.1 Cumulated residuals from each equation of the VAR system.

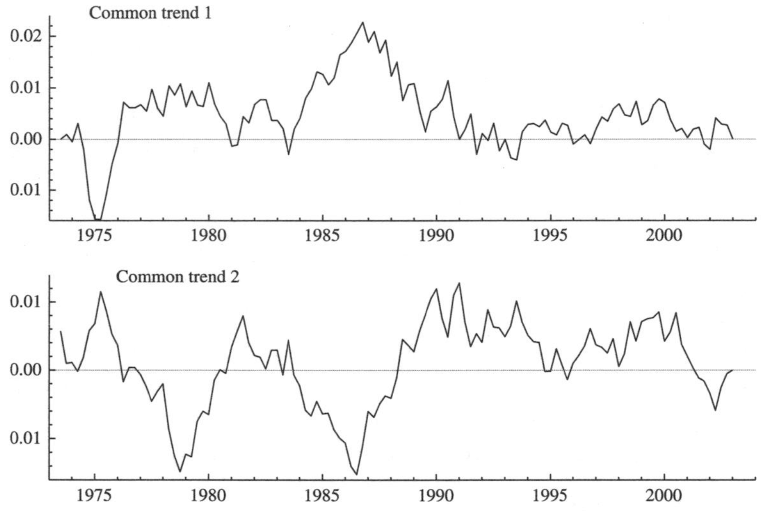

Fig 14.2 The common trends based on the estimates in Table 14.1.

Finally, we note that the slope of the linear trend, $\boldsymbol{\gamma}_0 = \mathbf{C}\boldsymbol{\mu}_0$ (cf. Section 6.2), is almost identical for the real money stock and the real aggregate income and approximately zero for the inflation rate and the two interest rates, consistent with our prior economic hypotheses.

Figure 14.1 shows the graphs of the cumulated VAR residuals equation by equation and Figure 14.2 the two unrestricted common trends defined by:

$$\sum_{i=1}^{t} u_{1,i} = \hat{\boldsymbol{\alpha}}'_{\perp,1} \sum_{i=1}^{t} \hat{\boldsymbol{\varepsilon}}_i,$$
$$\sum_{i=1}^{t} u_{2,i} = \hat{\boldsymbol{\alpha}}'_{\perp,2} \sum_{i=1}^{t} \hat{\boldsymbol{\varepsilon}}_i,$$

where $\hat{\boldsymbol{\alpha}}_{\perp,1}$ and $\hat{\boldsymbol{\alpha}}_{\perp,2}$ are given by the first set of estimates in Table 14.1 and $\hat{\boldsymbol{\varepsilon}}'_i = [\hat{\varepsilon}_{m^r}, \hat{\varepsilon}_{y^r}, \hat{\varepsilon}_{\Delta p}, \hat{\varepsilon}_{Rm}, \hat{\varepsilon}_{Rb}]_i$, $i = 1973{:}3, \ldots, 2003{:}1$.

14.3 The MA representation subject to restrictions on $\boldsymbol{\alpha}$ and $\boldsymbol{\beta}$

In Chapter 11, the bond rate was found to be weakly exogenous for the long-run parameters and the results reported in Table 14.2 are derived under this assumption, i.e. for:

$$\boldsymbol{\alpha}'_{\perp} = \begin{bmatrix} 0 & 0 & 0 & 0 & 1 \\ * & 1 & * & * & 0 \end{bmatrix}.$$

Thus, one of the two common trends is now identified as $\sum_{i=1}^{t} \hat{\varepsilon}_{Rb,i}$. The (0, 1) restriction for $\hat{\varepsilon}_{y^r,i}$ and the (1, 0) restriction for $\hat{\varepsilon}_{R_b,i}$ are just-identifying and the remaining three restrictions are over-identifying. These restrictions correspond to the three degrees of freedom of the weak exogeneity test of the bond rate reported in Table 11.1.

While long-run weak exogeneity of a variable implies that its *cumulated residuals* can be considered a common stochastic trend, it does not necessarily imply that the *variable* itself is a common trend. For this to be the case we need the further condition that the rows of the $\mathbf{\Gamma}_i$ matrices associated with the weakly exogenous variable have to be zero. Given $x_t \sim I(1)$ this is essentially the condition of strong exogeneity, under which the equation for a strongly exogenous variable $x_{j,t}$ becomes $\Delta x_{j,t} = \varepsilon_{j,t}$. In this case, $x_{j,t} = \sum_{i=1}^{t} \varepsilon_{j,i}$, i.e. the common stochastic trend coincides with the variable itself. The various versions of the estimated short-run adjustment structure in Chapter 13 showed that both the bond rate and the real income variable exhibited significant effects from lagged changes of the vector process, so neither of them satisfies the condition for being strongly exogenous. As the subsequent results will show, each of the two variables have indeed been influenced by both of the stochastic trends. Figure 14.3 illustrates the fairly large differences between the bond rate and its cumulated residuals.

Note that the weak exogeneity restrictions on $\boldsymbol{\alpha}_{\perp,1}$ (and the zero restriction on the last element of $\boldsymbol{\alpha}_{\perp,2}$) imply that $\tilde{\boldsymbol{\beta}}_{\perp,1}$ and the last column of the $\mathbf{C}$ matrix are identical in Table 14.2. Compared to the unrestricted estimates in Table 14.1 we note the following:

1. The estimates of $\boldsymbol{\alpha}_{\perp}$ and $\tilde{\boldsymbol{\beta}}_{\perp}$ have now changed quite considerably, due to the rotation of the vector space.
2. The estimated coefficients of the $\mathbf{C}$ matrix have approximately remained the same, except for the columns of $\sum \hat{\varepsilon}_{R_m}$ and $\sum \hat{\varepsilon}_{R_b}$: the coefficients to $\sum \hat{\varepsilon}_{R_b}$ have become more significant and those to $\sum \hat{\varepsilon}_{R_m}$ less significant.

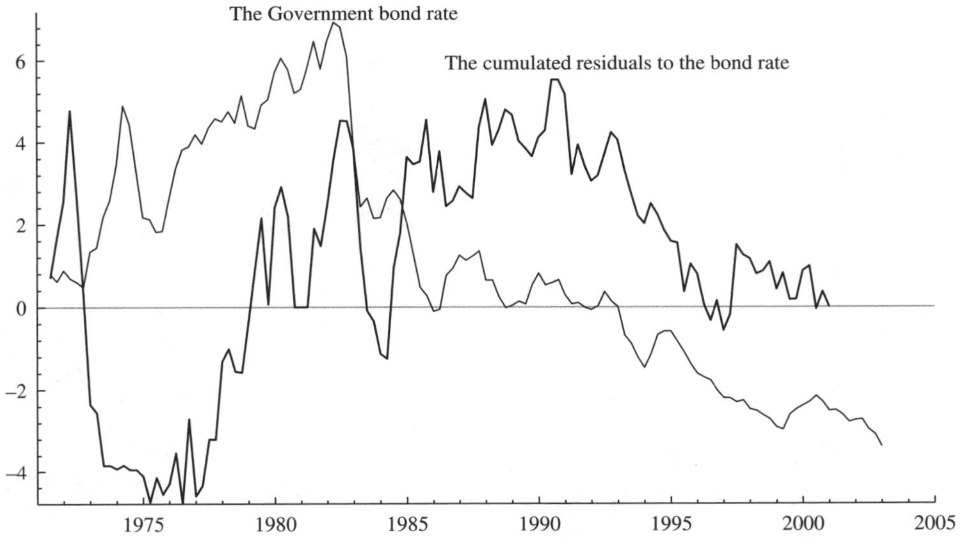

Fig 14.3 The cumulated residuals from the bond rate equation compared to the bond rate.

3. The negative coefficient of $\sum \hat{\varepsilon}_{R_b}$ in real money stock has become much more significant and the previously large negative coefficient to $\sum \hat{\varepsilon}_{R_m}$ has become insignificant.
4. The $\sum \hat{\varepsilon}_{R_b}$ column of the $\mathbf{C}$ matrix is now identical to $\hat{\boldsymbol{\beta}}_{\perp,1}$ and the $\sum \hat{\varepsilon}_{y^r}$ column is approximately equal to $\hat{\boldsymbol{\beta}}_{\perp,2}$.

We recall that the estimated results in Table 14.1 were not very clear regarding the stochastic interest-rate trend: Even though the weak exogeneity test suggested the empirical shocks to the bond rate as the driving force, we could almost equally well have chosen those of the short-term interest rate. By choosing the bond rate to be weakly exogenous, we have been able to remove some of the previous indeterminacy of the long-run impact of shocks to the interest rates. This can explain point 2 above. Even though one can argue that this apparent improvement in precision is based on a rather subjective choice, the strong negative coefficient to the bond rate in the real money stock in Table 14.2 is more plausible than the negative coefficient to the short-term interest rate in Table 14.1. Nevertheless, it seems fair to say that the data do not contain enough information to decisively conclude about the direction of the causal link between the two interest rates.

In Table 14.3 we report the MA representation based on the $\boldsymbol{\beta}$ structure $\mathcal{H}_{S.4}$ together with the previous weak exogeneity restriction on $\boldsymbol{\alpha}$. This means that the estimates are

Table 14.2 The MA representation when the bond rate is assumed weakly exogenous.

	$\hat{\varepsilon}_{m^r}$	$\hat{\varepsilon}_{y^r}$	$\hat{\varepsilon}_{\Delta p}$	$\hat{\varepsilon}_{R_m}$	$\hat{\varepsilon}_{R_b}$
$\hat{\sigma}_{\varepsilon_i}$	0.0231	0.0138	0.0080	0.0010	0.0014
$\hat{\boldsymbol{\alpha}}_{\perp,1}^{c\prime}$	0.00	0.00	0.00	0.00	**1.00**
$\hat{\boldsymbol{\alpha}}_{\perp,2}^{c\prime}$	0.33 [1.61]	**1.00**	−0.82 [−1.61]	−7.32 [−1.28]	0.00
	m^r	y^r	Δp	R_m	R_b
$\tilde{\hat{\boldsymbol{\beta}}}_{\perp,1}^{c\prime}$	**−9.42** [−5.21]	−2.45 [−1.40]	**−0.14** [−2.00]	**0.78** [7.30]	**1.48** [7.30]
$\tilde{\hat{\boldsymbol{\beta}}}_{\perp,2}^{c\prime}$	**0.53** [3.24]	**0.79** [5.00]	**−0.03** [−5.20]	−0.00 [−0.22]	0.03 [1.48]

The $\mathbf{C}$ matrix

	$\hat{\varepsilon}_{m^r}$	$\hat{\varepsilon}_{y^r}$	$\hat{\varepsilon}_{\Delta p}$	$\hat{\varepsilon}_{R_m}$	$\hat{\varepsilon}_{R_b}$	$t \times \gamma_{0,i}$
m^r	0.18 (1.3)	**0.53** (3.2)	−0.43 (−1.1)	−3.88 (−0.7)	**−9.42** (−5.2)	0.0033
y^r	**0.26** (1.9)	**0.79** (5.0)	−0.65 (−1.6)	−5.78 (−1.3)	−2.45 (−1.4)	0.0038
Δp	**−0.01** (−2.0)	**−0.03** (−5.2)	0.03 (1.7)	0.25 (1.4)	**−0.14** (−2.0)	−0.0001
R_m	−0.00 (−0.1)	−0.00 (−0.2)	0.00 (0.1)	0.01 (0.1)	**0.78** (7.3)	−0.0001
R_b	0.00 (0.6)	0.03 (1.5)	−0.02 (−0.5)	−0.20 (−0.4)	1.48 (7.3)	−0.0000

t ratios in parentheses

now subject to six restrictions (three from $\boldsymbol{\beta}$ and three from $\boldsymbol{\alpha}$) which are borderline accepted with a p-value of 0.09. The common trends estimates have not changed much compared to Table 14.2, except that they have become slightly more interpretable as some of the previously borderline significant coefficients have now become clearly insignificant. The significance of the coefficients to $\hat{\varepsilon}_{R_b}$ have decreased to some extent and its negative (previously borderline significant) effect on the inflation rate is now insignificant.

The MA case 4 reported in Table 14.4 differs from case 3 in Table 14.3 by additionally imposing the weak exogeneity restriction on the real income variable. The two zero row restrictions on $\boldsymbol{\alpha}$ correspond to six over-identifying restrictions on the common trends, $\boldsymbol{\alpha}_{\perp}^{c\prime}\sum_{i=1}^{t}\hat{\boldsymbol{\varepsilon}}_i$ with

$$\boldsymbol{\alpha}_{\perp}^{c\prime} = \begin{bmatrix} 0 & 1 & 0 & 0 & 0 \\ 0 & 0 & 0 & 0 & 1 \end{bmatrix},$$

i.e. $\hat{u}_{1,t} = \sum_{i=1}^{t}\hat{\varepsilon}_{y^r,i}$ and $\hat{u}_{2,t} = \sum_{i=1}^{t}\hat{\varepsilon}_{R_b,i}$.

In addition to the weak exogeneity restrictions on $\boldsymbol{\alpha}$, the MA case 4 has imposed the structure $\mathcal{H}_{S.4}$ on $\boldsymbol{\beta}$. Note that the two non-zero columns of the $\mathbf{C}$ matrix are equivalent to $\hat{\boldsymbol{\beta}}_{\perp,1}^{c}$ and $\hat{\boldsymbol{\beta}}_{\perp,2}^{c}$.

Table 14.3 The MA representation when $\boldsymbol{\beta}$ is restricted to $\mathcal{H}_{S.4}$ and the bond rate is assumed weakly exogenous.

	$\hat{\varepsilon}_{m^r}$	$\hat{\varepsilon}_{y^r}$	$\hat{\varepsilon}_{\Delta p}$	$\hat{\varepsilon}_{R_m}$	$\hat{\varepsilon}_{R_b}$	
σ_{ε_i}	0.0231	0.0138	0.0080	0.0010	0.0014	
$\hat{\boldsymbol{\alpha}}_{\perp,1}^{c\prime}$	0.00	0.00	0.00	0.00	**1.00**	
$\hat{\boldsymbol{\alpha}}_{\perp,2}^{c\prime}$	0.26	**1.00**	−0.46	−1.94	0.00	
	[1.64]		[−1.20]	[−0.45]		
	m^r	y^r	Δp	R_m	R_b	
$\tilde{\hat{\boldsymbol{\beta}}}_{\perp,2}^{c\prime}$	**−8.29**	−3.29	0.10	**1.02**	**1.42**	
	[−3.11]	[−1.38]	[1.38]	[4.84]	[4.84]	
$\tilde{\hat{\boldsymbol{\beta}}}_{\perp,1}^{c\prime}$	**0.82**	**0.92**	**−0.03**	0.02	0.03	
	[4.26]	[5.32]	[−5.32]	[1.27]	[1.27]	
The $\mathbf{C}$ matrix						
	$\hat{\varepsilon}_{m^r}$	$\hat{\varepsilon}_{y^r}$	$\hat{\varepsilon}_{\Delta p}$	$\hat{\varepsilon}_{R_m}$	$\hat{\varepsilon}_{R_b}$	$t \times \gamma_{0.i}$
m^r	0.21	**0.82**	−0.38	−1.60	**−8.29**	0.0038
	[1.55]	[4.26]	[−0.89]	[−0.34]	[−3.11]	
y^r	**0.23**	**0.92**	−0.42	−1.78	**−3.29**	0.0037
	[1.93]	[5.32]	[−1.11]	[−0.42]	[−1.38]	
Δp	**−0.01**	**−0.03**	0.01	0.05	0.10	−0.0001
	[−1.93]	[−5.32]	[1.11]	[0.42]	[1.38]	
R_m	0.00	0.02	−0.01	−0.04	**1.02**	−0.0000
	[0.46]	[1.27]	[−0.27]	[−0.10]	[4.84]	
R_b	0.01	0.03	−0.01	−0.05	**1.42**	−0.0000
	[0.46]	[1.27]	[−0.27]	[−0.10]	[4.84]	

t ratios in parentheses

Table 14.4 The MA representation when $\boldsymbol{\beta}$ is restricted to $\mathcal{H}_{S.4}$ and both the bond and the real income are assumed weakly exogenous.

	$\hat{\varepsilon}_{m^r}$	$\hat{\varepsilon}_{y^r}$	$\hat{\varepsilon}_{\Delta p}$	$\hat{\varepsilon}_{R_m}$	$\hat{\varepsilon}_{R_b}$	
$\hat{\boldsymbol{\alpha}}_{\perp,1}$	0	0	0	0	**1**	
$\hat{\boldsymbol{\alpha}}_{\perp,2}$	0	**1**	0	0	0	
The **C** matrix						
	$\hat{\varepsilon}_{m^r}$	$\hat{\varepsilon}_{y^r}$ $(\tilde{\hat{\boldsymbol{\beta}}}_{\perp,2})$	$\hat{\varepsilon}_{\Delta p}$	$\hat{\varepsilon}_{R_m}$	$\hat{\varepsilon}_{R_b}$ $(\tilde{\hat{\boldsymbol{\beta}}}_{\perp,1})$	$t \times \gamma_{0,i}$
m^r	0	1.02 [4.17]	0	0	−10.12 [−3.65]	0.0031
y^r	0	1.14 [5.24]	0	0	−5.42 [−2.20]	0.0029
Δp	0	−0.03 [−5.24]	0	0	0.16 [2.20]	−0.0001
R_m	0	0.02 [1.32]	0	0	1.00 [4.72]	−0.0000
R_b	0	0.03 [1.32]	0	0	1.35 [4.72]	−0.0001

A comparison of the columns for $\hat{\varepsilon}_{y^r}$ and $\hat{\varepsilon}_{R_b}$ in Tables 14.2–14.4 reveals that the conclusions remain relatively robust whether we have imposed the various restrictions on $\boldsymbol{\alpha}$ and $\boldsymbol{\beta}$ or not. The only exception is the coefficient to the inflation rate in the column for $\hat{\varepsilon}_{R_b}$, which becomes positive instead of negative when imposing the structure $\mathcal{H}_{S.4}$ on $\boldsymbol{\beta}$. It is, however, not unusual that the estimates of the **C** matrix change quite considerably when imposing restrictions on $\boldsymbol{\alpha}$ and $\boldsymbol{\beta}$ and a sensitivity check of major conclusions is generally advisable.

14.4 Imposing exclusion restrictions on $\boldsymbol{\beta}_\perp$

Up to this point we have essentially discussed identifying and over-identifying restrictions on $\boldsymbol{\alpha}_\perp$. Most common trends models are, however, identified based on exclusion restrictions on $\boldsymbol{\beta}_\perp$ together with orthogonality restrictions on $\boldsymbol{\alpha}_\perp$. The latter restriction will be discussed in the next chapter. Two of the most popular exclusion restrictions on $\boldsymbol{\beta}_\perp$ are motivated by economic theory saying that (1) a nominal shock should have no long-run effect on real income and (2) a real shock should have no long-run effect on the inflation rate. The latter is the equivalent of the exclusion restriction motivated by the $I(2)$ assumption of the nominal variables. We recall from Chapter 2 that under the assumption of just one $I(2)$ trend influencing the nominal variables in levels (which is usually the case in practice), the inflation rate should only be affected by the nominal stochastic trend.

However, Table 14.4 shows that inflation rate is affected by both trends (though the bond rate trend is only borderline significant), violating the econometric specification of Chapter 2. Furthermore, the effect from the real trend on inflation is highly significant and negative. The latter seems counterintuitive, at least in terms of a conventional Phillips curve relationship. The finding of two stochastic trends in inflation rate could in principle be consistent with prices containing two, rather than one, stochastic $I(2)$ trends. This possibility is however ruled out as the $I(2)$ tests in Chapter 17 unambiguously suggested no more than one $I(2)$ trend. At this stage the common trends results regarding the inflation rate seems puzzling. Fortunately, the common trends result for the $I(2)$ model in Chapter 17 will provide a plausible explanation.

Even though the exclusion restriction on the real stochastic trend in the inflation rate is not likely to work well empirically we shall demonstrate below how to impose it. The constrained estimates serve as an illustration of how uninterpretable the results can become when theoretically motivated restrictions are imposed on data for which the theory model is an inadequate description.

Assuming that the nominal stochastic trend derives from shocks to the nominal bond rate we can achieve the exclusion restriction by redefining the common nominal trend as a linear combination of the shocks to the real income and to the nominal bond rate. By transforming $\tilde{\tilde{\boldsymbol{\beta}}}_\perp = \tilde{\boldsymbol{\beta}}_\perp \boldsymbol{Q}$ using the transformation matrix

$$\mathbf{Q} = \begin{bmatrix} 1.0 & 0.03/0.16 \\ 0.0 & 1.0 \end{bmatrix}$$

where 0.03/0.16 is from Table 14.4, we obtain the following common trends representation

$$\begin{bmatrix} m^r \\ y^r \\ \Delta p \\ R_m \\ R_b \end{bmatrix} = \begin{bmatrix} -0.87 & -10.1 \\ 0.12 & -5.42 \\ \mathbf{0.00} & \mathbf{0.16} \\ 0.21 & 1.00 \\ 0.28 & 1.35 \end{bmatrix} \begin{bmatrix} \sum u_{1i} \\ \sum u_{2i} \end{bmatrix} + \begin{matrix} \text{stationary and} \\ \text{deterministic} \\ \text{components} \end{matrix} \tag{14.6}$$

where $u_{2,t} = \boldsymbol{\varepsilon}_{Rb,t}$ as before, $u_{1,t} = \varepsilon_{y^r,t} - 0.1875\boldsymbol{\varepsilon}_{Rb,t}$, and inflation is exclusively affected by empirical shocks to the bond rate. But by imposing the above zero restriction on $\tilde{\boldsymbol{\beta}}_{\perp.1}$ we have changed the definition of the autonomous shocks and, therefore, the correlation coefficient between them. Because $u_{1,t} = \hat{\varepsilon}_{y^r,t}$ and $u_{2,t} = \hat{\boldsymbol{\varepsilon}}_{Rb,t}$ were approximately uncorrelated in the unrestricted VAR with a residual correlation coefficient of only 0.07 (see Table 13.1), the new empirical shocks in (14.6) are no longer uncorrelated. We note that the condition that the real money stock and the real aggregate demand should be affected similarly by the real stochastic trend (which was almost satisfied in the previous cases) is now completely lost, as has the interpretation of $u_{1,t}$ as a real shock to the system.[3]

Another possibility is to transform $\tilde{\boldsymbol{\beta}}_\perp$ based on the transformation matrix

$$\mathbf{Q} = \begin{bmatrix} 1.0 & (0.16/0.03) \\ 0.0 & 1.0 \end{bmatrix},$$

[3]In the next chapter, we will illustrate how to impose both an exclusion restriction on one of the stochastic trends in the inflation rate and at the same time preserve orthogonality between $u_{1,t}$ and $u_{2,t}$.

which makes the inflation rate exclusively a function of empirical shocks to the real income, i.e. $u_{1,t} = \varepsilon_{y^r,t}$ and $u_{2,t} = \varepsilon_{Rb,t} - 5.3\varepsilon_{y^r,t}$. The common trends representation becomes:

$$\begin{bmatrix} m^r \\ y^r \\ \Delta p \\ R_m \\ R_b \end{bmatrix} = \begin{bmatrix} \mathbf{1.02} & \mathbf{-4.7} \\ \mathbf{1.14} & \mathbf{0.67} \\ \mathbf{-0.03} & 0.0 \\ 0.02 & \mathbf{1.11} \\ 0.03 & \mathbf{1.51} \end{bmatrix} \begin{bmatrix} \sum u_{1i} \\ \sum u_{2i} \end{bmatrix} + \begin{array}{l} \text{stationary and} \\ \text{deterministic} \\ \text{components.} \end{array} \qquad (14.7)$$

Compared to (14.6) the above results look much more plausible, but inflation rate is now exclusively affected by the *real* stochastic trend, $u_{1,t}$ and $u_{2,t}$ are no longer uncorrelated and the interpretation of $u_{2,t}$ as an empirical shock to the bond rate has been lost.

We shall finally illustrate how to impose one just-identifying restriction on both $\tilde{\boldsymbol{\beta}}_{\perp,1}$ and $\tilde{\boldsymbol{\beta}}_{\perp,2}$ by assuming that a nominal shock has no long-run effect on real growth and a real shock has no long-run effect on inflation rate. This can be achieved by the following transformation matrix:

$$\mathbf{Q} = \begin{bmatrix} 1.0 & 5.42/1.14 \\ 0.1875 & 1.0 \end{bmatrix}$$

which yields the estimated common trends representation:

$$\begin{bmatrix} m^r \\ y^r \\ \Delta p \\ R_m \\ R_b \end{bmatrix} = \begin{bmatrix} \mathbf{-0.87} & \mathbf{-5.30} \\ \mathbf{0.12} & \mathbf{0.00} \\ \mathbf{0.00} & \mathbf{0.02} \\ \mathbf{0.21} & \mathbf{1.09} \\ \mathbf{0.28} & \mathbf{1.49} \end{bmatrix} \begin{bmatrix} \sum u_{1i} \\ \sum u_{2i} \end{bmatrix} + \begin{array}{l} \text{stationary and} \\ \text{deterministic} \\ \text{components.} \end{array} \qquad (14.8)$$

In (14.8) $u_{1,t} = \varepsilon_{y^r,t} \cdot - 0.1875\varepsilon_{Rb,t}$ and $u_{2,t} = \varepsilon_{Rb,t} - 4.75\varepsilon_{y^r,t}$, so the common shocks are now correlated and, therefore, difficult to interpret. With two zero restrictions on $\tilde{\boldsymbol{\beta}}_{\perp}$, it is no longer possible, in addition, to impose orthogonality between $u_{1,t}$ and $u_{2,t}$ without changing the likelihood function. The tests of such over-identifying restrictions are outside the scope of this book.

14.5 Assessing the economic model scenario

We shall now evaluate the empirical content of the real money scenario discussed in Chapter 2 using the estimated common trends representation of Table 14.4. The theoretical model predicted that the nominal stochastic trend should be associated with money expansion in excess of real productive growth in the economy and the real stochastic trend with productivity shocks to the economy, i.e. $u_{1t} = \varepsilon_{m^r,t}$ and $u_{2t} = \varepsilon_{y^r,t}$ or in vector notation $u_{1t} = \boldsymbol{\alpha}'_{\perp,1}\varepsilon_t$ and $u_{2t} = \boldsymbol{\alpha}'_{\perp,2}\varepsilon_t$ with $\boldsymbol{\alpha}'_{\perp,1} = [*, 0, 0, 0, 0]$ and

$\alpha'_{\perp,2} = [0, *, 0, 0, 0]$. The loadings of the stochastic trends were supposed to enter the variables in the following way:

$$\begin{bmatrix} m_t^r \\ y_t^r \\ \Delta p_t \\ R_{m,t} \\ R_{b,t} \end{bmatrix} = \begin{bmatrix} 0 & d_{12} \\ 0 & d_{12} \\ c_{21} & 0 \\ c_{21} & 0 \\ c_{21} & 0 \end{bmatrix} \begin{bmatrix} \sum u_{1i} \\ \sum u_{2i} \end{bmatrix} + \begin{array}{l} \text{stationary and} \\ \text{deterministic} \\ \text{components.} \end{array} \tag{14.9}$$

The empirical model was consistent with two autonomous disturbances, one of which (the real disturbance) seemed consistent with the prior assumption, $u_{2t} = \varepsilon_{y^r,t}$, whereas the other seemed not. The finding that $u_{1t} = \hat{\varepsilon}_{R_b,t}$ suggests that financial behaviour in the long-term government bond market, rather than excess monetary expansion in the domestic market, has generated the other stochastic trend.

The cointegration implications of the theory model (14.9) are that money velocity, $(m^r - y^r)$, the interest rate spread, $(R_m - R_b)$, and the real interest rates, $(R_m - \Delta p)$, and $(R_b - \Delta p)$ should all be stationary. Chapter 10 demonstrated that money velocity and the interest rate spread were roughly stationary when allowing for an equilibrium mean shift at 1983, whereas the real interest rates were clearly non-stationary. To get some empirical insight into why this was the case, we shall exploit the duality between the pulling forces of the cointegration relations and the pushing forces of the common trends discussed in Chapter 5.

To facilitate the comparison between the theoretical model (14.9) and the empirical results, we reproduce the estimates of the MA case 4 in Table 14.4 with $u_{1,t} = \alpha'_{\perp,1}\hat{\varepsilon}_t = \hat{\varepsilon}_{Rb,t}$ and $u_{2,t} = \alpha'_{\perp,2}\hat{\varepsilon}_t = \hat{\varepsilon}_{y,t}$:[4]

$$\begin{bmatrix} m_t^r \\ y_t^r \\ \Delta p_t \\ R_{m,t} \\ R_{b,t} \end{bmatrix} = \underbrace{\begin{bmatrix} \underset{[4.2]}{\mathbf{1.02}} & \underset{[-3.7]}{\mathbf{-10.1}} \\ \underset{[5.2]}{\mathbf{1.14}} & \underset{[-2.2]}{\mathbf{-5.4}} \\ \underset{[-5.2]}{\mathbf{-0.03}} & \underset{[2.2]}{\mathbf{0.16}} \\ \underset{[1.3]}{0.02} & \underset{[4.7]}{\mathbf{1.00}} \\ \underset{[1.3]}{0.03} & \underset{[4.7]}{\mathbf{1.35}} \end{bmatrix}}_{\tilde{\beta}_\perp} \underbrace{\begin{bmatrix} \sum_{i=1}^t \varepsilon_{y,i} \\ \sum_{i=1}^t \varepsilon_{Rb,i} \end{bmatrix}}_{\alpha'_\perp \sum \hat{\varepsilon}_i} + \begin{bmatrix} 0.0031 \\ 0.0029 \\ 0.0001 \\ 0.0000 \\ 0.0001 \end{bmatrix} t + \cdots \tag{14.10}$$

According to (14.9) the real stochastic trend should influence real money stock and real income with the same coefficients. The estimated coefficients in (14.10) are 1.02 to money stock and 1.14 to real income. Both are positive and not significantly different from the prior hypothesis of a unitary coefficient. However, the prior assumption that the nominal stochastic trend should not influence real money stock nor real aggregate income is clearly violated, in the sense that the nominal trend (defined here as the cumulated empirical shocks to the long-term bond rate) has significantly affected both

[4] Even though the joint weak exogeneity of the bond rate and real aggregate income was only borderline acceptable, the subsequent conclusions are robust to whether weak exogeneity is imposed or not.

the real money stock and the real income negatively, but the former much more so.[5] Note, however, that the interpretation of the empirical results based on the priors in (14.9) is no longer straightforward, as one of the basic hypotheses that the nominal stochastic trend derives from empirical shocks to excess money was already rejected.

Altogether, some of the empirical results were consistent with the hypothetical structure (14.9), others were not. To gain some insight into the empirical mechanisms and how they have departed from the theoretical assumptions we shall take a closer look at the estimated cointegration structure given by $\mathcal{H}_{S.4}$ in Table 12.3 using the common trends representation (14.10).[6] The liquidity ratio is described by

$$\begin{aligned} m^r - y^r &= (1.02 - 1.14)\sum \varepsilon_y - (10.1 - 5.4)\sum \varepsilon_{Rb} + \cdots \\ &= -0.12\sum \varepsilon_y - 6.3\sum \varepsilon_{Rb} + \cdots \end{aligned}$$

and the interest rate spread by

$$\begin{aligned} R_m - R_b &= (0.02 - 0.03)\sum \varepsilon_y + (1.00 - 1.35)\sum \varepsilon_{Rb} \\ &\approx -0.01\sum \varepsilon_y - 0.35\sum \varepsilon_{Rb}. \end{aligned}$$

The latter can be compared with the interest rate relation in Table 12.3 which is described by:

$$\begin{aligned} R_m - 0.81R_b &= (0.02 - 0.03 * 0.81)\sum \varepsilon_y - (1.00 - 0.81 * 1.35)\sum \varepsilon_{Rb} \\ &\approx 0.09\sum \varepsilon_{Rb}. \end{aligned}$$

It appears that the interest rate spread is 'more' non-stationary than the interest rate relation, which explains why the money demand relation in $\mathcal{H}_{S.4}$ needs the former to cancel the two small stochastic trend components in the liquidity ratio:

$$\begin{aligned} m^r - y^r - 13.3(R_m - R_b) &= -(0.012 - 0.013)\sum \varepsilon_y - (6.3 - 4.7)\sum \varepsilon_{Rb} \\ &\approx 1.6\sum \varepsilon_{Rb}. \end{aligned}$$

From (22.3) we note that the inflation rate has been significantly (and negatively) influenced by $\sum \varepsilon_y$ but positively by $\sum \varepsilon_{Rb}$, whereas the opposite is true for the real income.

[5]This is a tentative finding, suggesting that money demand is more interest-rate elastic than investment demand.

[6]Note that the cointegration structure $\mathcal{H}_{S.4}$ was estimated without imposing the two weak exogeneity restrictions on $\boldsymbol{\alpha}$, whereas the common trends representation is based on a restricted $\boldsymbol{\beta}$ and $\boldsymbol{\alpha}$. This is the reason why the stochastic trends do not cancel exactly in the cointegration relations.

This explains the negative relationship between the inflation rate and the real income in $\mathcal{H}_{S.4}$:

$$\begin{aligned}\Delta p + 0.03y^r &= -(0.03 - 0.03)\sum \varepsilon_y + (0.16 - 0.16)\sum \varepsilon_{Rb} \\ &= 0.0\sum \varepsilon + 0.0\sum \varepsilon_{Rb}\end{aligned}$$

The economic interpretation of this result is, however, not straightforward and in Chapter 19 we shall demonstrate that we have to extend the information set before a more satisfactory explanation can be given.

Based on (14.10) it is now easy to see that the stationarity of the real interest rates was rejected because the inflation rate is primarily affected by $\sum \varepsilon_y$, whereas the interest rates primarily by $\sum \varepsilon_{Rb}$. The short-term interest rate was described by:

$$\begin{aligned}R_m - \Delta p &= (0.02 + 0.03)\sum \varepsilon_y + (1.00 - 0.16)\sum \varepsilon_{Rb} \\ &= 0.05\sum \varepsilon_y + 0.84\sum \varepsilon_{Rb},\end{aligned}$$

and the long-term bond rate by:

$$\begin{aligned}R_b - \Delta p &= (0.03 + 0.03)\sum \varepsilon_y + (1.35 - 0.16)\sum \varepsilon_{Rb} \\ &= 0.06\sum \varepsilon_y + 1.19\sum \varepsilon_{Rb}.\end{aligned}$$

Thus, the violation of the Fisher parity is because the two stochastic trends have a different impact on the inflation rate than on the interest rates. Even though the two interest rates exhibit some minor effects from the real stochastic trend, these effects are of opposite sign as compared to the effect on the inflation rate. Therefore, cointegration between the inflation rate and any one of the two interest rates is not possible, whereas a combination between all three can yield stationarity as demonstrated in Chapter 10.

The non-stationarity of the short-term and the long-term real interest rate appears to differ in the sense that the real short-term interest rate is 'less' non-stationary than the real long-term rate. This is because the real bond rate has been more strongly affected by the two stochastic trends than the real short-term interest rate. Furthermore, it is interesting to notice that the first stochastic trend, describing shocks to real income, has had a positive impact on both interest rates but a negative on the inflation rate, whereas the second trend describing shocks to the bond rate has had a positive impact on the inflation rate and the two interest rates. In the last part of the book, we shall argue that the non-stationarity of the real interest rates in this period is associated with the changes in the determination of the inflation rate as a result of the increased globalization.

Thus, the empirical analysis of our small monetary model has pointed out a number of 'surprises' which ideally should be used to generate new hypotheses.

1. The finding that the empirical shocks to excess money, to inflation and to the short-term interest rate have been transitory is a strong indication that monetary policy has been adjusting to, but not pushing, the money market.

2. The finding that shocks to the long-term bond rate, instead of the money stock, were an important driving force, suggests that financial markets and the increased globalization may have played a more crucial role for nominal growth in the domestic economy than the actions of the central bank.
3. The finding that the Fisher hypothesis has not been empirically valid in this period suggests that the determination of inflation as well as the relationship between expected inflation and nominal interest rates has to be reconsidered.

Taken together, the empirical evidence based on the present sample does not seem to provide much support for the Danish inflation rate to have been a monetary problem in this period. Thus, we need to expand the number of hypotheses and models that are potentially relevant for the mechanisms behind price determination in a period of increasing global competition. This is the purpose of the last part of the book, in which we shall suggest an empirically more satisfactory explanation of the determination of the Danish prices in the post-Bretton–Woods period.

14.6 Concluding remarks

In this chapter, we have illustrated different ways of imposing structure on the common trends without forcing the empirical shocks to be orthogonal. One could say that we have illustrated how to structure the long-run information about driving forces in the data using the econometric results on the $\boldsymbol{\alpha}$ and $\boldsymbol{\beta}$ structures obtained in the previous chapters. A major advantage is that the results of this chapter can be used to assess the credibility of the labels attached to the structural MA results of the next chapter.

We first demonstrated how to impose just-identifying restrictions on $\boldsymbol{\alpha}_{\perp}$, then how to derive constrained estimates of $\boldsymbol{\alpha}_{\perp}$ and $\widetilde{\boldsymbol{\beta}}_{\perp}$ consistent with various restrictions on $\boldsymbol{\alpha}$ and $\boldsymbol{\beta}$ and, finally, how to impose exclusion restrictions on $\widetilde{\boldsymbol{\beta}}_{\perp}$. Recalling the discussion in Chapter 13 about interpreting shocks we showed that the estimated empirical shocks, $\hat{u}_{1t}$ and $\hat{u}_{2t}$, based on the common trends model formulation in Tables 14.1–14.4 may satisfy the requirement of uniqueness and, possibly novelty, but failed to satisfy the economic (and econometric) condition that a real shock should not have a long-run impact on the inflation rate. The common trends representation based on exclusion restrictions on $\widetilde{\boldsymbol{\beta}}_{\perp}$ satisfied the economic conditions that a real shock should have no long-run impact on the inflation rate and a nominal shock no long-run impact on the real income, but failed on the uniqueness condition and on the economic plausibility of the estimated coefficients.

The unsatisfactory results are likely to be associated with the finding showing that (1) the nominal stochastic trend did not seem to arise from shocks to money stock nor to the short-term interest rate, (2) the inflation rate seemed to be negatively related to the real money and to the real income, (3) the Fisher parity did not hold, and (4) the expectations hypothesis was not very strong in the data. As all this is evidence against some of the basic assumptions in the monetary model it may not be so surprising that theoretically motivated restrictions produce completely uninterpretable results. It has, however, served the purpose of illustrating how a structural interpretation of VAR residuals based on a theoretical model not being well supported by the data can be (and often is) very fragile.

Even though the empirical shocks to the (almost) weakly exogenous bond rate and the real income happened to be (almost) orthogonal, we did not explicitly introduce orthogonality of the estimated shocks as an identification condition in this chapter. The next chapter will discuss identification by explicitly separating between permanent and transitory shocks and by requiring that all empirical shocks are orthogonal.

15

Identification of a structural MA model

Chapter 13 discussed the case in which the orthogonality of the residuals was trivially achieved by assuming a causal chain structure. This chapter will discuss the case where the orthogonality condition is imposed on the residuals, while at the same time separating between transitory and permanent shock and imposing exclusion restrictions on the parameters of the model. Chapter 14 discussed the identification of the permanent 'shocks' by imposing just-identifying restrictions on $\boldsymbol{\alpha}_{\perp}$ or $\tilde{\boldsymbol{\beta}}_{\perp}$. Transitory 'shocks' were not discussed except for in the special case of $p-r$ weakly exogenous variables and r purely adjusting variables. In this case the transitory 'shocks' were uniquely identified as the residuals to the r adjusting equations, whereas the permanent 'shocks' as the residuals in the equations of the weakly exogenous variables. No attempt was made to distinguish between transitory and permanent shocks and how to measure them empirically in a more general setting. In particular, no attempt was made to make a distinction between orthogonalized permanent and transitory shocks and how to interpret the results empirically. This is the purpose of the present chapter.

Section 15.1 introduces the structural VAR model, Section 15.2 discusses how to separate between transitory and permanent shocks in the VAR model, and Section 15.3 how to formulate and interpret some conditions conventionally assumed to define a structural shock. Section 15.4 illustrates a structural common trends model based on the Danish data and Section 15.5 concludes with a discussion of the structural labelling of empirical shocks.

15.1 Reparametrization of the VAR model

We consider the usual VAR(2) model with no linear trends in the data and the model

$$\Delta\mathbf{x}_t = \boldsymbol{\Gamma}_1\Delta\mathbf{x}_{t-1} + \boldsymbol{\alpha}\tilde{\boldsymbol{\beta}}'\tilde{\mathbf{x}}_{t-1} + \boldsymbol{\varepsilon}_t, \qquad (15.1)$$

where $\tilde{\boldsymbol{\beta}}' = [\boldsymbol{\beta}', \boldsymbol{\beta}_0']$, $\tilde{\mathbf{x}}_t = [\mathbf{x}_t', 1]$, and $\boldsymbol{\varepsilon}_t \sim N_p(\mathbf{0}, \boldsymbol{\Omega})$.

The MA representation of the VAR model (15.1) is given by:

$$\mathbf{x}_t = \mathbf{C}\sum_{i=1}^{t}\boldsymbol{\varepsilon}_i + \mathbf{C}^*(L)\boldsymbol{\varepsilon}_t + \tilde{\mathbf{X}}_0, \tag{15.2}$$

where

$$\mathbf{C} = \boldsymbol{\beta}_\perp(\boldsymbol{\alpha}_\perp'\boldsymbol{\Gamma}\boldsymbol{\beta}_\perp)^{-1}\boldsymbol{\alpha}_\perp' \tag{15.3}$$
$$= \tilde{\boldsymbol{\beta}}_\perp\boldsymbol{\alpha}_\perp'. \tag{15.4}$$

By premultiplying (15.1) with a non-singular $p\times p$ matrix $\mathbf{A}_0$ (diag $\mathbf{A}_0 = 1.0$) we obtain the VAR model with simultaneous effects:

$$\mathbf{A}_0\Delta\mathbf{x}_t = \mathbf{A}_1\Delta\mathbf{x}_{t-1} + \boldsymbol{a}\tilde{\boldsymbol{\beta}}'\tilde{\mathbf{x}}_{t-1} + \mathbf{u}_t, \tag{15.5}$$
$$\mathbf{u}_t \sim IN(\mathbf{0}, \boldsymbol{\Sigma})$$

where $\mathbf{A}_1 = \mathbf{A}_0\boldsymbol{\Gamma}_1$, $\mathbf{a} = \mathbf{A}_0\boldsymbol{\alpha}$, $\mathbf{u}_t = \mathbf{A}_0\boldsymbol{\varepsilon}_t$, and $\boldsymbol{\Sigma} = \mathbf{A}_0\boldsymbol{\Omega}\mathbf{A}_0'$. As long as the parameters $\{\mathbf{A}_0, \mathbf{A}_1, \mathbf{a}, \boldsymbol{\Sigma}\}$ are unrestricted, the system (15.5) is unidentified and we need to impose at least $p \times (p-1)$ restrictions to achieve identification. For example, in the causal chain model of Chapter 13, the $5 \times 4 = 20$ just-identifying restrictions were achieved by imposing the off-diagonal elements of the covariance matrix to be zero (10 restrictions) and the lower triangular elements of $\mathbf{A}_0$ to be zero (10 restrictions). Because the choice of causal ordering is generally arbitrary, we shall here discuss other identification schemes, albeit often equally arbitrary.

The MA representation of (15.5) can be formulated by substituting $\boldsymbol{\varepsilon}_t = \mathbf{A}_0^{-1}\,\mathbf{u}_t$ in (15.2):

$$\mathbf{x}_t = \tilde{\boldsymbol{\beta}}_\perp\boldsymbol{\alpha}_\perp'\mathbf{A}_0^{-1}\sum_{i=1}^{t}\mathbf{u}_i + \mathbf{C}^*(L)\mathbf{A}_0^{-1}\mathbf{u}_t + \tilde{\mathbf{X}}_0. \tag{15.6}$$

Thus, by including current effects in the VAR model we have changed the definition of an empirical shock and, therefore, the $\mathbf{C}$ matrix, which is now defined by $\tilde{\mathbf{C}} = \mathbf{C}\mathbf{A}_0^{-1} = \tilde{\boldsymbol{\beta}}_\perp\boldsymbol{\alpha}_\perp'\mathbf{A}_0^{-1}$, and the impulse response functions $\mathbf{C}^*(L)$, which are now defined by $\tilde{\mathbf{C}}^*(L) = \mathbf{C}^*(L)\mathbf{A}_0^{-1}$.

Furthermore, we know from Chapter 14 that the decomposition of the $\mathbf{C}$ matrix into $\tilde{\boldsymbol{\beta}}_\perp$ and $\boldsymbol{\alpha}_\perp$ is arbitrary in the sense that we can always post-multiply $\tilde{\boldsymbol{\beta}}_\perp$ by a non-singular $(p-r)\times(p-r)$ matrix $\tilde{\mathbf{Q}}$ and $\boldsymbol{\alpha}_\perp$ by its inverse without changing the likelihood function, i.e.:

$$\mathbf{x}_t = \tilde{\boldsymbol{\beta}}_\perp\tilde{\mathbf{Q}}\tilde{\mathbf{Q}}^{-1}\boldsymbol{\alpha}_\perp'\mathbf{A}_0^{-1}\sum_{i=1}^{t}\mathbf{u}_i + \mathbf{C}^*(L)\mathbf{A}_0^{-1}\mathbf{u}_t + \tilde{\mathbf{X}}_0. \tag{15.7}$$

Thus, how to impose just-identifying restrictions in the MA representation is essentially about how to choose $\tilde{\mathbf{Q}}$ and how to choose $\mathbf{A}_0^{-1}$ so that the empirical shocks satisfy some desired properties. In this chapter we shall focus on the case where $\mathbf{u}_t' = [\mathbf{u}_{s,t}'\mathbf{u}_{l,t}'] \sim IN(\mathbf{0}, \mathbf{I})$.

In many ways, the econometrics of the just-identified MA model is similar to just-identification in the VAR model, where we also had to choose a $\mathbf{Q}$ matrix to uniquely identify $\boldsymbol{\beta}$, and a current effects matrix $\mathbf{A_0}$ to uniquely identify the equations. Also, the identification of $\tilde{\boldsymbol{\beta}}_{\perp}$ is not affected by the identification of $\mathbf{u}_t$, just as the identification of $\boldsymbol{\beta}$ was not affected by the identification of the short-run dynamics.

15.2 Separation between transitory and permanent shocks

Before discussing the 'new' identification conditions it is useful to see how they differ from the MA results in Chapter 14. We recollect that Section 14.2 discussed how to impose just-identifying restrictions on $\boldsymbol{\alpha}_{\perp}$, Section 14.3 how to impose over-identifying restrictions on $\boldsymbol{\alpha}_{\perp}$ and $\boldsymbol{\beta}_{\perp}$ which corresponded to (previously tested) restrictions on $\boldsymbol{\alpha}$ and $\boldsymbol{\beta}$, and Section 14.4 how to impose exclusion restrictions on $\tilde{\boldsymbol{\beta}}_{\perp}$ as a means to achieve identification. Each of these 'identification schemes' was shown to change the definition of the two permanent 'empirical shocks' and, hence, the correlation between the common stochastic trends. By and large, the identification in Chapter 14 was an attempt to translate previously identified structures for $\boldsymbol{\alpha}$ and $\boldsymbol{\beta}$ into the moving average form. At no stage was identification discussed in terms of orthogonal errors, even though by coincidence the residuals to the two (almost) weakly exogenous variables happened to be (almost) uncorrelated. Furthermore, Chapter 14 exclusively discussed the $p-r$ long-term (permanent) 'shocks', but not the r short-term (transitory) shocks.

Contrary to the above identification schemes, the empirical shocks of the structural MA model are defined by the following basic assumptions:

1. the p VAR residuals are assumed to be related to p underlying 'structural' shocks which are linearly independent;
2. the p 'structural shocks' can be divided into $(p-r)$ permanent and r transitory shocks;
3. a transitory shock is defined as a zero column in the $\tilde{\mathbf{C}}$ matrix, so that a transitory shock has by construction no long-run impact on the variables of the system;
4. a permanent shock is defined as a non-zero column in the $\tilde{\mathbf{C}}$ matrix, so that a permanent shock must have a significant long-run impact on at least one of the variables of the system.

Based on these conditions we shall discuss a 'structural' representation defined by the matrix $\mathbf{B}$, which is similar to the matrix $\mathbf{A}_0$ in (15.5) except that the diagonal elements of $\mathbf{B}$ are no longer assumed to be normalized to have unitary coefficients. The $\mathbf{B}$ matrix defines how the 'structural' shocks $\mathbf{u}_t$ are associated with the VAR residuals:

$$\mathbf{u}_t = \mathbf{B}\varepsilon_t \tag{15.8}$$

where $\mathbf{u}_t \sim IN(\mathbf{0}, \mathbf{I})$, i.e. the structural shocks are assumed to be uncorrelated, standardized normal variables with mean zero. Thus, the standardization of the structural shocks has replaced the previous normalization of equations given by $\text{diag}(\mathbf{A}_0) = 1$. The reason for this choice is that the impulse response functions are generally defined for a unitary shock of one standard deviation.

Alternatively, $\mathbf{B}^{-1}$ defines how the VAR residuals are associated with the underlying structural shocks:

$$\boldsymbol{\varepsilon}_t = \mathbf{B}^{-1}\mathbf{u}_t. \tag{15.9}$$

We can now reformulate (15.2) using (15.9):

$$\mathbf{x}_t = \underbrace{\tilde{\boldsymbol{\beta}}_\perp \boldsymbol{\alpha}'_\perp \mathbf{B}^{-1}}_{\tilde{\mathbf{C}}} \sum \mathbf{u}_i + \mathbf{C}^*(L)\mathbf{B}^{-1}\mathbf{u}_t + \tilde{\mathbf{X}}_0, \tag{15.10}$$

which corresponds to the simultaneous VAR model:

$$\mathbf{B}\Delta\mathbf{x}_t = \mathbf{B}_1\Delta\mathbf{x}_{t-1} + \boldsymbol{b}\tilde{\boldsymbol{\beta}}'\tilde{\mathbf{x}}_{t-1} + \mathbf{u}_t \tag{15.11}$$

where $\mathbf{B}_1 = \mathbf{B}\boldsymbol{\Gamma}_1$ and $\boldsymbol{b}=\mathbf{B}\boldsymbol{\alpha}$. The idea is to choose $\mathbf{B}$ so that the 'usual' assumptions underlying a structural interpretation are satisfied:

1. A distinction between r transitory and $p-r$ permanent shocks is made, i.e. $\mathbf{u}_t = [\mathbf{u}_s, \mathbf{u}_l] = [u_{s,1}, \ldots, u_{s,r}, u_{l,1}, \ldots, u_{l,p-r}]$.
2. The transitory shocks have no long-run impact on the variables of the system whereas the permanent shocks have such effects on at least one variable in the system.
3. $E(\mathbf{u}_t\mathbf{u}'_t) = \mathbf{I}_p$, i.e. all 'structural' shocks are linearly independent or, alternatively
4. $E(\mathbf{u}_{s,t}\mathbf{u}'_{s,t}) = \mathbf{I}_r$ and $E(\mathbf{u}_{l,t}\mathbf{u}'_{l,t}) = \mathbf{I}_{p-r}$, but $E(\mathbf{u}_{s,t}\mathbf{u}'_{l,t}) \neq 0$.

Empirical applications based on these conditions can be found for example in Mellander, Vredin, and Warne (1992), Hansen and Warne (2001), and Coenen and Vega (1999). Obviously these conditions will change the interpretation of an empirical shock. Whether the resulting estimate $\hat{\mathbf{u}}_t$ can be given an *economic* interpretation as a unique structural shock, depends on the plausibility of the identifying assumptions. But, as we shall argue below, even in the case when the identifying assumptions are plausible the labelling of empirical shocks can be (and often is) hazardous.

It is customary to distinguish between the following two cases:

Case 1. $\mathbf{B}$ *is defined by conditions 1, 2, and 3* In this case orthogonality of the transitory shocks, $\mathbf{u}_{s,t}$ and the permanent shocks $\mathbf{u}_{l,t}$ can be achieved by choosing:

$$\begin{aligned}\mathbf{u}_{s,t} &= \boldsymbol{\alpha}'\boldsymbol{\Omega}^{-1}\boldsymbol{\varepsilon}_t\\ \mathbf{u}_{l,t} &= \boldsymbol{\alpha}'_\perp\boldsymbol{\varepsilon}_t\end{aligned}$$

and orthogonality within the two groups can be achieved by choosing:

$$\mathbf{B} = \begin{bmatrix} (\boldsymbol{\alpha}'\boldsymbol{\Omega}^{-1}\boldsymbol{\alpha})^{-1/2}\boldsymbol{\alpha}'\boldsymbol{\Omega}^{-1} \\ (\boldsymbol{\alpha}'_\perp\boldsymbol{\Omega}\boldsymbol{\alpha}_\perp)^{-1/2}\boldsymbol{\alpha}'_\perp \end{bmatrix}. \tag{15.12}$$

which defines:

$$\mathbf{B}^{-1} = \begin{bmatrix} \boldsymbol{\alpha}(\boldsymbol{\alpha}'\boldsymbol{\Omega}^{-1}\boldsymbol{\alpha})^{-1/2}, & \boldsymbol{\Omega}\alpha_\perp(\boldsymbol{\alpha}'_\perp\boldsymbol{\Omega}\boldsymbol{\alpha}_\perp)^{-1/2} \end{bmatrix}.$$

Case 2. $\mathbf{B}$ *is defined by conditions 1, 2, and 4* The assumption that permanent and transitory shocks are uncorrelated is now relaxed, while the orthogonality assumption within the groups is maintained. Thus, we still need to distinguish between permanent and transitory shocks, but transitory shocks, say, can be correlated with permanent shocks: This can be achieved by the following choice:

$$\mathbf{B} = \begin{bmatrix} \overline{\boldsymbol{\alpha}}' \\ \boldsymbol{\alpha}'_{\perp} \end{bmatrix}$$

and

$$\mathbf{B}^{-1} = [\ \boldsymbol{\alpha}, \quad \overline{\boldsymbol{\alpha}}_{\perp}\ ]$$

where $\overline{\boldsymbol{\alpha}} = \boldsymbol{\alpha}(\boldsymbol{\alpha}'\boldsymbol{\alpha})^{-1}$ and $\overline{\boldsymbol{\alpha}}_{\perp} = \boldsymbol{\alpha}_{\perp}(\boldsymbol{\alpha}'_{\perp}\boldsymbol{\alpha}_{\perp})^{-1}$, so that $\overline{\boldsymbol{\alpha}}'\boldsymbol{\varepsilon}_t$ defines the transitory shocks, and $\boldsymbol{\alpha}'_{\perp}\boldsymbol{\varepsilon}_t$ defines the permanent shocks.

Orthogonality of the transitory shocks requires that $E\{(\overline{\boldsymbol{\alpha}}'\boldsymbol{\varepsilon}_t)(\boldsymbol{\varepsilon}'_t\overline{\boldsymbol{\alpha}})\} = \overline{\boldsymbol{\alpha}}'\Omega\overline{\boldsymbol{\alpha}} = \mathbf{I}$, which can be achieved by:

$$\mathbf{u}_{s,t} = (\overline{\boldsymbol{\alpha}}'\boldsymbol{\Omega}\overline{\boldsymbol{\alpha}})^{-1/2}\overline{\boldsymbol{\alpha}}'\boldsymbol{\varepsilon}_t,$$

whereas orthogonality of the permanent shocks requires that $E\{(\boldsymbol{\alpha}'_{\perp}\boldsymbol{\varepsilon}_t)(\boldsymbol{\varepsilon}'_t\boldsymbol{\alpha}_{\perp})\} = \boldsymbol{\alpha}'_{\perp}\Omega\boldsymbol{\alpha}_{\perp} = \mathbf{I}$, which can be achieved by:

$$\mathbf{u}_{l,t} = (\boldsymbol{\alpha}'_{\perp}\boldsymbol{\Omega}\boldsymbol{\alpha}_{\perp})^{-1/2}\boldsymbol{\alpha}'_{\perp}\boldsymbol{\varepsilon}_t.$$

15.3 How to formulate and interpret structural shocks

VAR residuals are usually correlated (sometimes strongly so) and the residual covariance matrix, $\boldsymbol{\Omega}$, is seldom a diagonal matrix. Chapter 13 already discussed this issue and gave many reasons for why this is the case. In particular, it was pointed out that omitted relevant variables are likely to generate correlated residuals in VAR models. However, this is not a feature assumed to be present in the structural VAR model, where the orthogonality of SVAR errors is based on an assumption that our model is complete and, thus, contains all relevant variables. In the SVAR model, the residual correlations of the VAR model are assumed to be a reduced-form phenomenon which is not present in the structural form. At the end of this chapter we shall argue that this assumption is seldom valid in empirical models and that this is the main reason why the labelling of empirical residuals as structural shocks can be (and often is) misleading.

A consequence of defining the structural errors by (15.8) is that we have added $p \times p$ additional parameters to the unrestricted VAR model so we need to impose exactly the same number of restrictions on the parameters of the model to achieve just identification. In the Danish money demand VAR model, $p = 5$ and the $\mathbf{B}$ matrix introduces 25 additional coefficients. The assumption that $\mathbf{u}_t \sim IN(\mathbf{0}, \mathbf{I})$ implies $\{p \times (p+1)\}/2 = 15$ restrictions on $\mathbf{B}$ (10 zero restrictions on the off-diagonal elements and five unit coefficients on the diagonal elements). By this we achieve that the errors $\mathbf{u}_t$ are (0, 1) independent variables.

The second condition, the separation between permanent and transitory shocks, introduces $(p-r) \times r = 6$ additional restrictions to be explained below. Together, these two conditions give us 21 restrictions and we need to impose four additional restrictions to achieve a just-identified 'structural' MA model. The latter four restrictions are needed because there are two possible orderings of the permanent shocks and four different orderings of the transitory shocks, all of which correspond to identical values of the likelihood function. A unique specification can be achieved by imposing one exclusion restriction on the common trends and three exclusion restrictions on the (time t) transitory impulse responses.

To illustrate the ideas behind the structural VAR model (15.11), we shall discuss a typical identification scheme based on the Danish monetary VAR model. For illustrative purposes, the ordering of the variables has been changed so that the adjusting variables (the endogenous variables) real money, inflation and the short rate come first and the (almost) weakly exogenous bond rate and real income are at the end of the variable vector. The structural VAR defined by (15.11) can now be formulated as:

$$\underbrace{\begin{bmatrix} (\boldsymbol{\alpha}'\boldsymbol{\Omega}^{-1}\boldsymbol{\alpha})^{-1/2}\boldsymbol{\alpha}'\boldsymbol{\Omega}^{-1} \\ \\ (\boldsymbol{\alpha}'_{\perp}\boldsymbol{\Omega}\boldsymbol{\alpha}_{\perp})^{-1/2}\boldsymbol{\alpha}'_{\perp} \end{bmatrix}}_{\mathbf{B}} \begin{bmatrix} \Delta m_t^r \\ \Delta^2 p_t \\ \Delta R_{m,t} \\ \Delta y_t^r \\ \Delta R_{b,t} \end{bmatrix} = \underbrace{\begin{bmatrix} 1 & 0 & 0 \\ 0 & 1 & 0 \\ 0 & 0 & 1 \\ 0 & 0 & 0 \\ 0 & 0 & 0 \end{bmatrix}}_{\mathbf{b}} \begin{bmatrix} \boldsymbol{\beta}'_1\mathbf{x}_{t-1} \\ \boldsymbol{\beta}'_2\mathbf{x}_{t-1} \\ \boldsymbol{\beta}'_2\mathbf{x}_{t-1} \end{bmatrix} + \begin{bmatrix} u_{s1,t} \\ u_{s2,t} \\ u_{s3,t} \\ u_{l1,t} \\ u_{l2,t} \end{bmatrix} \tag{15.13}$$

where for simplicity the short-run effects, $\mathbf{B}_1\Delta\mathbf{x}_{t-1}$, have been left out. We note that the first three equations describe combinations of the variables which are subject to unanticipated transitory shocks, whereas the last two combinations of variables are subject to unanticipated permanent shocks.

Since an intuitive understanding of the current effects matrix $\mathbf{B}$ is not straightforward, we shall first discuss how it can be interpreted in the special case of $p-r$ weakly exogenous variables plus some simplifying assumptions about the covariance matrix $\boldsymbol{\Omega}$. We recall from Chapter 11 that the joint hypothesis of a weakly exogenous bond rate and real income was equivalent to the following hypothesis on $\boldsymbol{\alpha}_{\perp}$:

$$\boldsymbol{\alpha}'_{\perp} = \begin{bmatrix} 0 & 0 & 0 & 1 & 0 \\ 0 & 0 & 0 & 0 & 1 \end{bmatrix}. \tag{15.14}$$

If, in addition the VAR residuals are uncorrelated

$$\boldsymbol{\Omega} = \begin{bmatrix} \omega_{11} & 0 & 0 & 0 & 0 \\ 0 & \omega_{22} & 0 & 0 & 0 \\ 0 & 0 & \omega_{33} & 0 & 0 \\ 0 & 0 & 0 & \omega_{44} & 0 \\ 0 & 0 & 0 & 0 & \omega_{55} \end{bmatrix},$$

then standardized permanent shocks are defined by $u_{l1,t} = \varepsilon_{y,t}/\sigma_{\varepsilon_y}$ and $u_{l2,t} = \varepsilon_{Rb,t}/\sigma_{\varepsilon_{Rb}}$, and

$$(\boldsymbol{\alpha}'_{\perp}\boldsymbol{\Omega}\boldsymbol{\alpha}_{\perp})^{-1/2}\boldsymbol{\alpha}'_{\perp} = \begin{bmatrix} 0 & 0 & 0 & \omega_{44}^{-1/2} & 0 \\ 0 & 0 & 0 & 0 & \omega_{55}^{-1/2} \end{bmatrix}.$$

We recall from Chapter 11 that the hypothesis of $p - r$ weakly exogenous variables is equivalent to the hypothesis of r unit vectors in $\boldsymbol{\alpha}$. Under this hypothesis and in the special case of $\boldsymbol{\Omega}$ being a diagonal matrix (i.e. all VAR residuals are uncorrelated) we have that:

$$(\boldsymbol{\alpha}'\boldsymbol{\Omega}^{-1}\boldsymbol{\alpha})^{-1/2}\boldsymbol{\alpha}'\boldsymbol{\Omega}^{-1} = \begin{bmatrix} \omega_{11}^{-1/2} & 0 & 0 & 0 & 0 \\ 0 & \omega_{22}^{-1/2} & 0 & 0 & 0 \\ 0 & 0 & \omega_{33}^{-1/2} & 0 & 0 \end{bmatrix},$$

i.e. under the assumption of $p - r$ weakly exogenous variables and uncorrelated residuals, the structural VAR model is equivalent to the reduced-form VAR model with standardized residuals and the matrix $\mathbf{B}$ would be the diag $(\omega_{ii}^{-1/2})$ matrix.

If the VAR residuals are not uncorrelated, then $\mathbf{u}_{l,t} = (\boldsymbol{\alpha}'_{\perp}\boldsymbol{\Omega}\boldsymbol{\alpha}_{\perp})^{-1/2}\boldsymbol{\alpha}'_{\perp}\boldsymbol{\varepsilon}_t$ will transform the correlated residuals to uncorrelated residuals. Thus, linear combinations of the VAR residuals, rather than the residuals themselves, would now be orthogonal. Thus, the choice of $\mathbf{B}$ according to (15.12) imposes orthogonality of $\mathbf{u}'_t = [\mathbf{u}'_{s,t}, \mathbf{u}'_{l,t}]$ (15 restrictions) as well as separates between transitory and permanent empirical shocks (six restrictions). The latter correspond to the six zero restrictions in the last two rows of $\mathbf{b}$ in (15.13) or, equivalently, the six over-identifying restrictions in (15.14).

Based on these 21 restrictions we can formulate the orthogonal permanent shocks as:

$$\begin{aligned} u_{l,1} &= (\boldsymbol{\alpha}'_{\perp,1}\boldsymbol{\Omega}\boldsymbol{\alpha}_{\perp,1})^{-1/2}\boldsymbol{\alpha}'_{\perp,1}\boldsymbol{\varepsilon}_t \\ u_{l,2} &= (\boldsymbol{\alpha}'_{\perp,2}\boldsymbol{\Omega}\boldsymbol{\alpha}_{\perp,2})^{-1/2}\boldsymbol{\alpha}'_{\perp,2}\boldsymbol{\varepsilon}_t \mid (\boldsymbol{\alpha}'_{\perp,1}\boldsymbol{\Omega}\boldsymbol{\alpha}_{\perp,1})^{-1/2}\boldsymbol{\alpha}'_{\perp,1}\boldsymbol{\varepsilon}_t \end{aligned} \tag{15.15}$$

and the orthogonal transitory shocks as:

$$\begin{aligned} u_{s,1} &= (\boldsymbol{\alpha}'_1\boldsymbol{\Omega}^{-1}\boldsymbol{\alpha}_1)^{-1/2}\boldsymbol{\alpha}'_1\boldsymbol{\varepsilon}_t. \\ u_{s,2} &= (\boldsymbol{\alpha}'_2\boldsymbol{\Omega}^{-1}\boldsymbol{\alpha}_2)^{-1/2}\boldsymbol{\alpha}'_2\boldsymbol{\varepsilon}_t \mid (\boldsymbol{\alpha}'_1\boldsymbol{\Omega}^{-1}\boldsymbol{\alpha}_1)^{-1/2}\boldsymbol{\alpha}'_1\boldsymbol{\varepsilon}_t, \\ u_{s,3} &= (\boldsymbol{\alpha}'_3\boldsymbol{\Omega}^{-1}\boldsymbol{\alpha}_3)^{-1/2}\boldsymbol{\alpha}'_3\boldsymbol{\varepsilon}_t \mid (\boldsymbol{\alpha}'_1\boldsymbol{\Omega}^{-1}\boldsymbol{\alpha}_1)^{-1/2}\boldsymbol{\alpha}'_1\boldsymbol{\varepsilon}_t, (\boldsymbol{\alpha}'_2\boldsymbol{\Omega}^{-1}\boldsymbol{\alpha}_2)^{-1/2}\boldsymbol{\alpha}'_2\boldsymbol{\varepsilon}_t, \end{aligned} \tag{15.16}$$

The purpose of the remaining four restrictions is to uniquely define the 'causal' ordering of the permanent and the transitory shocks. One restriction is needed to uniquely define the 'causal' ordering of the two common trends. In practice, this is done by specifying an exclusion restriction on $\tilde{\boldsymbol{\beta}}_{\perp}$. The three restrictions needed to uniquely identify the transitory shocks are usually specified as exclusion restrictions on the current effects matrix $\tilde{\mathbf{C}}_0$.

The next section provides an illustration of how to choose these exclusion restrictions and how the choice can be used to attach labels on the empirical shocks.

15.4 An illustration

The estimates of the common trends model for the Danish data are derived under the above assumption of orthogonality of the standardized errors (15 restrictions), separation of transitory and permanent shocks (six restrictions), and four exclusion restrictions. The latter are of particular interest as they allow us to put labels on the empirical shocks as illustrated below.

To impose an identifying restriction on $\tilde{\boldsymbol{\beta}}_{\perp}$, we first use the conventional assumption that a nominal shock cannot have a long-run impact on real income. This implies that u_{l1} is allowed to have a long-run impact on all system variables, and u_{l2} on all variables except for real income. Thus, the real permanent shock can now be uniquely defined as $u_{l1,t} = \tilde{\mathbf{C}}'_{y^r}\varepsilon_t$, where $\tilde{\mathbf{C}}'_{y^r}$ is the real income row in the $\tilde{\mathbf{C}}$ matrix. It satisfies the requirement that in the long-run the real income is exclusively affected by this shock. The nominal permanent shock is then uniquely defined by the condition that it has to be orthogonal to the real permanent shock.

The three exclusion restrictions on the transitory shocks are defined by assuming that

1. the short-term interest rate reacts immediately to a 'monetary policy' shock, but only with a lag to the other transitory shocks;
2. the inflation rate reacts immediately to a 'monetary policy' shock and to a shock to 'inflationary expectations' but only with a lag to the third transitory shock;
3. a 'money demand' shock is allowed to have an immediate effect on all variables except for short-term interest rate and inflation rate.

This defines u_{s1} to be a 'monetary policy' shock, u_{s2} to be a shock to 'inflationary expectations', and u_{s3} to be 'money demand' shock.

In the representation below, the 10 separation and exclusion restrictions are given in bold face.

$$
\begin{bmatrix} m_t^r \\ \Delta p_t \\ R_{m,t} \\ y_t^r \\ R_{b,t} \end{bmatrix} = \underbrace{\begin{bmatrix} \mathbf{0} & \mathbf{0} & \mathbf{0} & * & * \\ \mathbf{0} & \mathbf{0} & \mathbf{0} & * & * \\ 0 & 0 & 0 & * & * \\ 0 & 0 & 0 & * & \mathbf{0} \\ 0 & 0 & 0 & * & * \end{bmatrix}}_{\mathbf{CB}^{-1}} \begin{bmatrix} \sum_{i=t}^{t} u_{s1,i} \\ \sum_{i=t}^{t} u_{s2,i} \\ \sum_{i=t}^{t} u_{s3,i} \\ \sum_{i=t}^{t} u_{l1,i} \\ \sum_{i=t}^{t} u_{l2,i} \end{bmatrix}
$$

$$
+ \underbrace{\begin{bmatrix} * & * & * & * & * \\ * & * & \mathbf{0} & * & * \\ * & \mathbf{0} & \mathbf{0} & * & * \\ * & * & * & * & * \\ * & * & * & * & * \end{bmatrix}}_{\mathbf{C}_0\mathbf{B}^{-1}} \begin{bmatrix} u_{s1,t} \\ u_{s2,t} \\ u_{s3,t} \\ u_{l1,t} \\ u_{l2,t} \end{bmatrix}
$$

$$
+ \mathbf{C}_1\mathbf{B}^{-1} \begin{bmatrix} u_{s1,t-1} \\ u_{s2,t-1} \\ u_{s3,t-1} \\ u_{l1,t-1} \\ u_{l2,t-1} \end{bmatrix} + \cdots
$$

Based on this identification scheme the estimates of $\tilde{\boldsymbol{\beta}}_{\perp}$ become:

$$\begin{bmatrix} m^r \\ \Delta p \\ R_m \\ y^r \\ R_b \end{bmatrix} = \begin{bmatrix} \mathbf{1.04} & \mathbf{-3.04} \\ \mathbf{-0.03} & \mathbf{-0.20} \\ \mathbf{-0.03} & \mathbf{0.63} \\ \mathbf{1.00} & \mathbf{0.00} \\ \mathbf{-0.03} & \mathbf{1.00} \end{bmatrix} \begin{bmatrix} \sum u_{l,1i} \\ \sum u_{l,2i} \end{bmatrix} + \begin{array}{l} \text{stationary and} \\ \text{deterministic} \\ \text{components.} \end{array} \tag{15.17}$$

It is interesting to notice that the coefficients of $\tilde{\boldsymbol{\beta}}_{\perp,1}$ approximately satisfy the homogeneity restrictions for m^r and y^r, as well as for $\Delta p, R_m$, and R_b, whereas this is not the case for $\tilde{\boldsymbol{\beta}}_{\perp,2}$. According to the identification scheme, $u_{l,1t}$ is labelled a real shock and $u_{l,2t}$ a nominal shock. Thus, $\tilde{\boldsymbol{\beta}}_{\perp,1}$ would closely correspond to the hypothetical scenario (2.16) in Chapter 2, provided the coefficients to $\Delta p, R_m$, and R_b were zero. Though small, they cannot be set zero. Thus we have obtained some results tentatively showing that real permanent shocks are also influencing the nominal variables in a homogeneous way. However, the coefficients in $\tilde{\boldsymbol{\beta}}_{\perp,2}$ do not correspond at all to the hypothetical scenario (2.16) for the nominal shocks. The coefficient to m^r is large and negative instead of zero, and the coefficients to $\Delta p, R_m$, and R_b are far from identical. An interesting result is the negative coefficient to Δp, suggesting that the nominal shock $u_{l,2t}$ has *lowered* inflation.

The estimated matrix $\mathbf{B}$ (normalized at the largest coefficient in each row) defines how the orthogonalized permanent and transitory shocks are associated with the estimated VAR residuals through the equation $\mathbf{u}_t = \mathbf{B}\varepsilon_t$,

$$\mathbf{B} = \begin{bmatrix} 0.00 & -0.04 & \mathbf{1.00} & 0.01 & -0.54 \\ 0.03 & 0.37 & -0.03 & 0.10 & \mathbf{-1.00} \\ 0.54 & 0.68 & \mathbf{1.00} & -0.45 & 0.17 \\ 0.04 & -0.11 & \mathbf{-1.00} & 0.12 & -0.24 \\ -0.02 & -0.01 & -0.75 & -0.06 & \mathbf{-1.00} \end{bmatrix}. \tag{15.18}$$

From (15.12) it appears that

$$\mathbf{B} = \begin{bmatrix} (\boldsymbol{\alpha}'\boldsymbol{\Omega}^{-1}\boldsymbol{\alpha})^{-1/2}\boldsymbol{\alpha}'\boldsymbol{\Omega}^{-1} \\ (\boldsymbol{\alpha}'_{\perp}\boldsymbol{\Omega}\boldsymbol{\alpha}_{\perp})^{-1/2}\boldsymbol{\alpha}'_{\perp} \end{bmatrix} = \begin{bmatrix} \mathbf{B}'_s \\ \mathbf{B}'_l \end{bmatrix}$$

where $\mathbf{B}'_s$ is $r \times p$ and $\mathbf{B}'_l$ is $(p-r) \times p$. Thus, the last two rows of the $\mathbf{B}$ matrix define the permanent shocks:

$$\begin{aligned} u_{l,1t} &= \mathbf{B}'_{l,1}\hat{\varepsilon}_t = 0.04\varepsilon_{m^r,t} - 0.11\varepsilon_{\Delta p,t} - \varepsilon_{R_m,t} + 0.12\varepsilon_{y^r,t} - 0.24\varepsilon_{R_b,t} \\ u_{l,2t} &= \mathbf{B}'_{l,2}\hat{\varepsilon}_t = -0.02\varepsilon_{m^r,t} - 0.01\varepsilon_{\Delta p,t} - 0.75\varepsilon_{R_m,t} - 0.06\varepsilon_{y^r,t} - \varepsilon_{R_b,t}. \end{aligned}$$

The estimated weights, $\mathbf{B}'_l$, have a similar interpretation as the estimated $\boldsymbol{\alpha}_{\perp}$ of the unrestricted VAR model reported in the upper part of Table 14.1, Chapter 14.[1]

[1]Note, however, that the ordering of the variables has changed.

The first three rows of the **B** matrix define the transitory shocks:

$$\hat{u}_{s,1} = \mathbf{B}'_{s,1}\hat{\varepsilon}_t \simeq \hat{\varepsilon}_{Rm} - 0.54\hat{\varepsilon}_{Rb}$$
$$\hat{u}_{s,2} = \mathbf{B}'_{s,2}\hat{\varepsilon}_t \simeq 0.37\hat{\varepsilon}_{\Delta p} + 0.10\hat{\varepsilon}_{y^r} - \hat{\varepsilon}_{Rb}$$
$$\hat{u}_{s,3} = \mathbf{B}'_{s,3}\hat{\varepsilon}_t \simeq 0.54\hat{\varepsilon}_{m^r} + 0.68\hat{\varepsilon}_{\Delta p} + \hat{\varepsilon}_{Rm} - 0.45\hat{\varepsilon}_{y^r} + 0.17\hat{\varepsilon}_{Rm}$$

which are derived based on the three identifying restrictions on the matrix $\tilde{\mathbf{C}}_0 = \mathbf{B}^{-1}\mathbf{C}_0$. The estimates of the latter define the immediate (time t) effect of the structural shocks on the variables. The assumed exclusion restrictions are in bold face:

$$\tilde{\mathbf{C}}_0 = \begin{bmatrix} 0.25 & -0.28 & 1.71 & 1.48 & -0.30 \\ -0.20 & 0.59 & \mathbf{0.00} & -0.49 & -0.10 \\ 0.06 & \mathbf{0.00} & \mathbf{0.00} & -0.06 & -0.06 \\ 0.12 & 0.55 & -0.54 & 0.91 & -0.70 \\ -0.05 & -0.04 & -0.00 & -0.04 & -0.12 \end{bmatrix}. \tag{15.19}$$

The first three columns describe the time t effect of the transitory shocks on the variables of the system, whereas the last two columns describe the immediate effect of the permanent shocks. The m-period effects can be read from Figure 15.1 describing the dynamic impulse response functions for each of the system variables as a result of a one standard deviation shock to the $u_{i,t},\ i = 1, \ldots, p$. The above estimates of $\tilde{\mathbf{C}}_0$ can be found as the first value of the 25 impulse response functions. We note that all transitory shocks have a zero long-run impact on the five variables, whereas all permanent shocks have a non-zero long-run impact (even though some of them might be insignificant), except for the identifying zero impact of $\sum u_{l,2i}$ on real income.

Finally, we note from (15.13) that the matrix **B** can also be interpreted in terms of the current effects in a system of equations having orthogonalized errors and being ordered such that the first three equations describe purely adjusting behaviour, whereas the last two equations describe pushing behaviour.

The purely adjusting equations in the structural VAR formulation differs from the purely adjusting equations in the VAR model (the equations with a unit vector in $\boldsymbol{\alpha}$ discussed in Chapter 11) by defining the equations as a linear combination of the time t variables and by requiring that the 'transitory' residuals are orthogonal. Because the equations for $\Delta m^r_t, \Delta^2 p_t$, and $\Delta R_{m,t}$ were (almost) found to be purely adjusting, it is of some interest to compare the results of the SVAR model and the VAR model. We note that in both models each equation is adjusting to just one cointegration relation. They differ in the sense that the SVAR allows for simultaneity effects in the equations, but no residual correlation, whereas the VAR allows for residual correlation, but no simultaneity effects.

The purely adjusting equations of the SVAR are given by:

$$\Delta(R_{m,t} - 0.5R_{b,t}) = + \cdots + \tilde{\boldsymbol{\beta}}'_1\mathbf{x}_{t-1} + u_{s1,t}$$
$$\Delta(\Delta p_t - 2.2R_{b,t} + 0.22y^r_t) = + \cdots + \tilde{\boldsymbol{\beta}}'_2\mathbf{x}_{t-1} + u_{s2,t}$$
$$\Delta(m^r_t - 0.9y^r_t + 1.2\Delta p_t + 0.3R_{b,t}) = + \cdots + \tilde{\boldsymbol{\beta}}'_3\mathbf{x}_{t-1} + u_{s3,t}.$$

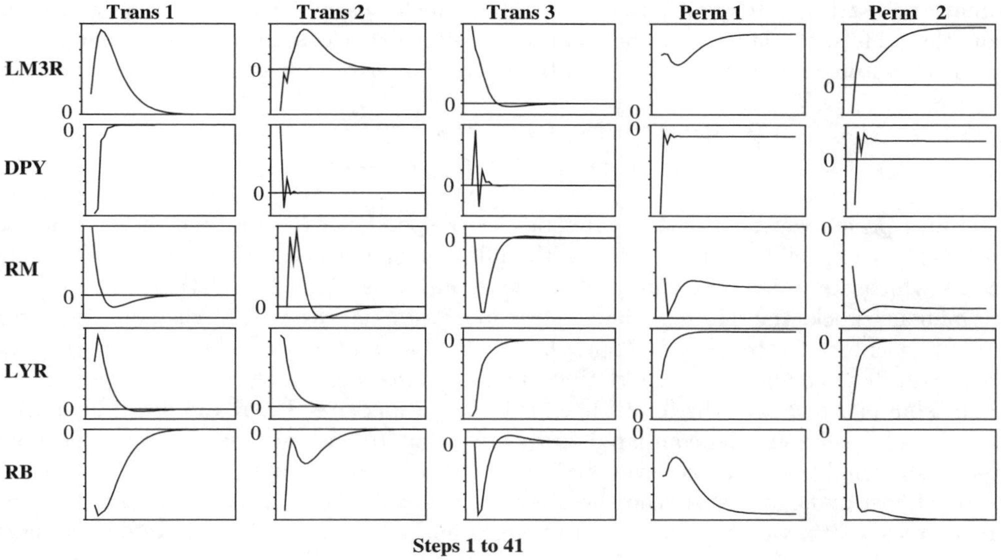

Fig 15.1 The impulse response functions for the three transitory shocks and the two permanent shocks.

The purely adjusting equations of the 'unit vectors in $\boldsymbol{\alpha}$' of the VAR model were given by:

$$\begin{aligned}\Delta R_{m,t} &= + \cdots + \boldsymbol{\beta}_1' \mathbf{x}_{t-1} + \varepsilon_{R_m,t} \\ \Delta^2 p_t &= + \cdots + \boldsymbol{\beta}_2' \mathbf{x}_{t-1} + \varepsilon_{\Delta p,t} \\ \Delta m_t^r &= + \cdots + \boldsymbol{\beta}_3' \mathbf{x}_{t-1} + \varepsilon_{m^r,t}.\end{aligned}$$

The six restrictions separating transitory from permanent shocks in the SVAR are the equivalent of the six restrictions associated with the three unit vectors in $\boldsymbol{\alpha}$. The latter constrained the likelihood function and were, therefore, testable, whereas the SVAR restrictions are just-identifying and, therefore, not testable.

Based on the above estimates it is now possible to ask whether the labels attached to the transitory shocks (motivated by the three exclusion restrictions) are plausible given the above estimates. The first transitory shock, $u_{s,1}$, was supposed to measure a 'monetary policy' shock. *A priori* we would expect such a shock to be relevant in an equation containing at least the short-term interest rate. Based on the above estimates we find that the 'monetary policy' shock is the residual to an equation for $\Delta(R_m - 0.5R_b)$, which makes the label 'monetary policy' look quite plausible. The next shock was supposed to measure a shock to inflationary expectations. We note that it is estimated as the residual to an equation for $\Delta(\Delta p_t - 2.2R_{b,t} + 0.22y_t^r)$, i.e. an equation in which the inflation rate enters together with real income and the long-term interest rate. The coefficient to real income does not seem very plausible, but is probably a reflection of the negative correlation between inflation and real income previously discussed. Thus, the label 'shock to inflationary expectations' can be defendable. The third shock was supposed to be a 'money demand' shock. We find that it is estimated as an unanticipated shock to the equation for $\Delta(m_t^r - 0.9y_t^r + 1.2\Delta p_t + 0.3R_{b,t})$, which closely resembles a money demand equation. Thus, the labels attached to the transitory shocks seem quite reasonable.

The two pushing equations defined by orthogonal errors are approximately given by:

$$\begin{aligned}\Delta(y_t^r - \Delta p_t - 8.5R_{m,t} - 2R_{b,t}) &= + \cdots + u_{l1,t},\\ \Delta(R_{b,t} - 0.75R_{m,t}) &= + \cdots + u_{l2,t}.\end{aligned}$$

The first permanent shock, the real shock, corresponds to the residual in an equation for Δy_t^r, as expected, but together with inflation and interest rates that have coefficients which are difficult to interpret (at least in terms of an IS relation). The second permanent shock, the nominal shock, corresponds to the residual in the equation for a 'modified' interest rate spread. Thus, the labels 'real' and 'nominal' seem more difficult to defend. The coefficients suggest that the label 'financial' might be more appropriate than 'nominal' and that the 'real' shock is in fact a mixture of real and nominal shocks. The above results can be compared to the residuals to the (almost) weakly exogenous real income and bond rate equations of the VAR model in Chapter 14, which were found to be almost orthogonal between themselves but not to the other VAR residuals. Thus, the orthogonality condition between transitory and permanent shocks have on one hand made the 'labelling' more difficult, on the other hand produced estimates of $\tilde{\boldsymbol{\beta}}_\perp$ that seemed interpretable and interesting.

Finally, the relationship between the VAR residuals and the 'structural shocks' is given by $\boldsymbol{\varepsilon}_t = \mathbf{B}^{-1}\mathbf{u}_t$, with

$$\mathbf{B}^{-1} = \begin{bmatrix} 0.15 & -0.16 & \mathbf{1.00} & 0.87 & -0.18 \\ -0.33 & \mathbf{1.00} & -0.00 & -0.83 & -0.17 \\ \mathbf{1.00} & 0.00 & -0.00 & -0.94 & -1.02 \\ 0.13 & 0.60 & -0.59 & \mathbf{1.00} & -0.77 \\ 0.45 & 0.30 & 0.00 & 0.30 & \mathbf{1.00} \end{bmatrix}. \tag{15.20}$$

For example, the third row shows that $\hat{\varepsilon}_{R_m} \simeq u_{s1} - u_{l2} - 0.9u_{l1}$.

15.5 Are the labels credible?

The above application to the Danish data illustrated how the exclusion restrictions allow us to put 'economic labels' on the empirical shocks. Whether these labels are credible or not depends on the plausibility of the underlying economic model inclusive the plausibility of the orthogonalization of the shocks. No testing was involved, as the derived restrictions were just-identifying. In this sense, the above definition of shocks (and, hence, the labels) was arbitrary. Therefore, it might be interesting to ask whether a different choice of identifying assumptions may lead to completely different results and different conclusions even though based on the same data and the same underlying VAR model.

We shall illustrate this question by comparing the common trends result from two different identification schemes with the results from the standard moving average model in Chapter 14. Because shocks with a long-run impact are generally more important than shocks with a transitory impact, we shall primarily focus on the labelling of the permanent shocks. Thus, the exclusion restrictions of the transitory shocks will be identical to the restrictions in (15.19), while the permanent shocks will be identified using two different assumptions:

1. A nominal shock has no long-run impact on real income (SVAR 1).
2. A real shock has no long-run impact on inflation (SVAR 2).

The estimated results from SVAR 1 and SVAR 2 will then be compared to the results of the just-identified MA model in Table 14.1 to find out (a) whether the 'structural' identification scheme improves our understanding by adding features not present in the reduced-form VAR model, (b) whether it significantly changes our previous conclusions, and (c) whether the two identification schemes tell a similar story.

The results are reported in Table 15.1. We note that the estimated shocks in all three models are (surprisingly) similar, even though there are some differences. The first common trend corresponds to $\boldsymbol{\alpha}'_{\perp,1}\sum\boldsymbol{\varepsilon}_i$ from the VAR model where the permanent shock, u_{l1}, was estimated as the weighted average of the residuals to the two interest rates. However, the weight to the short-term interest rate was not very significant. The two SVAR estimates of $\mathbf{B}_{l,1}$ were very similar, but the labels were not. While the first

Table 15.1 Comparing the common trends representation of the VAR model with two SVAR representations.

The estimated common trends							
		$\hat{\varepsilon}_{m^r}$	$\hat{\varepsilon}_{\Delta p}$	$\hat{\varepsilon}_{R_m}$	$\hat{\varepsilon}_{y^r}$	$\hat{\varepsilon}_{R_b}$	
Common trend 1:							Label:
VAR (*Table* 14.1)	$\hat{\boldsymbol{\alpha}}'_{\perp,1}$	0.00 [0.01]	0.06 [1.08]	1.11 [1.45]	0.00	**1.00**	Interest rate trend
SVAR 1 (*Eq.* 15.18)	$\mathbf{B}_{l,2}$	0.02	0.01	0.75	0.06	1.00	Nominal trend
SVAR 2		0.01	0.06	1.09	0.00	1.00	Real trend
Common trend 2:							Label:
VAR (*Table* 14.1)	$\hat{\boldsymbol{\alpha}}'_{\perp,2}$	0.32 [1.63]	−0.78 [−1.49]	−5.94 [−0.84]	**1.00**	0.00	Income trend
SVAR 1 (*Eq.* 15.18)	$\mathbf{B}_{l,1}$	0.33	−0.92	−8.33	1.00	−2.00	Real trend
SVAR 2		0.32	−0.57	−2.05	1.00	3.49	Nominal trend
The loadings to:							
		m^r	Δp	R_m	y^r	R_b	
Common trend 1:							
VAR		**−4.46** [−2.06]	−0.13 [−1.75]	**0.64** [4.38]	−1.56 [−0.79]	**0.99** [4.56]	Interest rate tr.
SVAR 1		−3.04	−0.20	0.63	**0.00**	**1.00**	Nominal trend
SVAR 2		−7.77	**0.00**	0.69	−5.04	**1.00**	Real trend
Common trend 2:							
VAR		**0.69** [3.62]	**−0.04** [−5.69]	0.01 [0.57]	**0.83** [4.73]	0.03 [1.52]	Real income tr.
SVAR 1		1.04	−0.03	−0.03	**1.00**	−0.03	Real
SVAR 2		0.84	−0.05	0.01	**1.00**	0.03	Nominal

common stochastic shock in the VAR model was identified as a shock to the bond rate (or to both interest rates), the SVAR 1 would label it 'a real permanent shock' and the SVAR 2 label it 'a nominal permanent shock'. The estimates of the second stochastic shock u_{l2} are also quite similar in all three models, but the interpretation is less straightforward. Based on the t values it seems reasonable to interpret it as a real shock. This was also the label attached to it in the VAR and the SVAR 2 model, but not in the SVAR 1 model, where it was defined as a nominal shock.

This serves as an illustration of how hazardous it can be to (blindly) associate theoretically motivated labels with empirically defined shocks. This is particularly the case when some of the underlying theoretical assumptions are not valid in the data. The results of the two SVAR analyses confirm what we have already learned in the previous chapters. Shocks to the level of the interest rates and shocks to real income (corrected for interest rate effects) seem to be the main driving forces of this system. Furthermore, the mechanisms behind the inflation rate do not follow any conventional economic model in this period.

To conclude, whether one can attach a meaningful economic interpretation to the orthogonalized shocks seems questionable, except possibly in the very special case when $\boldsymbol{\alpha}$ and $\boldsymbol{\alpha}_{\perp}$ define specific equations and variables. Whether the orthogonalization of the errors facilitates the economic interpretation or makes it more blurred remains an open question.

Part V

The $I(2)$ model

16

Analysing $I(2)$ data with the $I(1)$ model

Empirical evidence of $I(2)$ is often found in models containing nominal variables in levels, whereas such evidence is rarely reported in models based on real transformations. Hence, from a logical point of view, the statistical analysis of the nominal variables (m, p, y^r, R_m, R_b) should precede the $I(1)$ analysis of the real variables $(m - p, y^r, \Delta p, R_m, R_b)$. This was indeed the order of the scenario analysis of the monetary transmission mechanism in Chapter 2. It was first done for nominal money stock and prices, assumed to be $I(2)$, and then for real money stock and inflation, assumed to be $I(1)$ under the assumption of long-run price homogeneity.

Up to this point, we have exclusively analysed the real money model, so it is now time to focus on the nominal $I(2)$ model. Since the adequacy of the real transformation relies on long-run price homogeneity, which can only be tested in the nominal model, a more logical sequence would have been to start with the nominal $I(2)$ model. But, because the latter is much more complex than the $I(1)$ model, starting with the $I(2)$ model would not have been defensible from a pedagogical point of view, albeit empirically more appropriate to commence from a general model. Due to the complexity of the $I(2)$ model, this chapter will offer a soft introduction to the basic ideas before moving to a full-fledged $I(2)$ analysis in the next chapter. Because most econometric software packages contain a procedure for cointegration analysis in the $I(1)$ model, but not many include tests and estimation procedures for the $I(2)$ model, this chapter will point out typical 'symptoms' in the $I(1)$ model signalling $I(2)$ problems.

One might ask if it is meaningful to analyse $I(2)$ data with the $I(1)$ model. Section 16.1 discusses in what sense it makes sense and offers an intuitive explanation using the so-called $\boldsymbol{R}$ model already discussed in Chapter 7. Section 16.2 discusses the role of deterministic and stochastic components in models with nominal variables and suggests how to re-specify the deterministic components of the Danish nominal money model, and Section 16.3 discusses a few typical symptoms in the $I(1)$ model signalling $I(2)$ problems. Section 16.4 discusses the conditions under which the data can be transformed to $I(1)$ variables without loss of information, whether the nominal-to-real transformation of the Danish real money data was appropriate, and how to investigate the consequences of using the nominal-to-real transformation when the conditions are not satisfied. Section 16.5 concludes.

16.1 Linking the $I(1)$ and the $I(2)$ model

It sometimes happens that we analyse $I(2)$ data as if they were $I(1)$ because we never checked for other possibilities. One might ask whether the findings from such analyses are totally useless, misleading, or can be trusted to some extent. Before answering these questions, it is useful to examine the so-called **R**-model already discussed in Section 7.1 We consider the simple VAR(2) model:

$$\begin{aligned}\Delta\mathbf{x}_t &= \mathbf{\Gamma}_1\Delta\mathbf{x}_{t-1} + \boldsymbol{\alpha}\boldsymbol{\beta}'\mathbf{x}_{t-1} + \boldsymbol{\mu}_0 + \boldsymbol{\varepsilon}_t \\ \boldsymbol{\varepsilon}_t &\sim N_p(\mathbf{0}, \mathbf{\Omega}\ ), \quad t = 1, \ldots, T\end{aligned} \tag{16.1}$$

and the corresponding **R**-model:

$$\mathbf{R}_{0t} = \boldsymbol{\alpha}\boldsymbol{\beta}'\mathbf{R}_{1t} + \boldsymbol{\varepsilon}_t \tag{16.2}$$

where $\mathbf{R}_{0t}$ and $\mathbf{R}_{1t}$ are found by concentrating out the lagged short-run effects, $\Delta\mathbf{x}_{t-1}$:

$$\Delta\mathbf{x}_t = \hat{\mathbf{B}}_1\Delta\mathbf{x}_{t-1} + \hat{\boldsymbol{\mu}}_0 + \mathbf{R}_{0t} \tag{16.3}$$

and

$$\mathbf{x}_{t-1} = \hat{\mathbf{B}}_2\Delta\mathbf{x}_{t-1} + \hat{\boldsymbol{\mu}}_0 + \mathbf{R}_{1t}. \tag{16.4}$$

When $\mathbf{x}_t \sim I(2)$, both $\Delta\mathbf{x}_t$ and $\Delta\mathbf{x}_{t-1}$ contain a common $I(1)$ trend which, therefore, cancels in the regression of one on the other as in (16.3). Thus, $\mathbf{R}_{0t} \sim I(0)$ even if $\Delta\mathbf{x}_t \sim I(1)$. On the other hand, an $I(2)$ trend cannot be cancelled by regressing on an $I(1)$ trend. Therefore, regressing $\mathbf{x}_{t-1}$ on $\Delta\mathbf{x}_{t-1}$ as in (16.4) does not cancel the $I(2)$ trend and $\mathbf{R}_{1t} \sim I(2)$.

Because $\mathbf{R}_{0t} \sim I(0)$ and $\boldsymbol{\varepsilon}_t \sim I(0)$, the equation (16.2) can only hold if $\boldsymbol{\beta} = \mathbf{0}$, or alternatively if $\boldsymbol{\beta}'\mathbf{R}_{1t} \sim I(0)$. Therefore, unless the rank is zero, the linear combination $\boldsymbol{\beta}'\mathbf{R}_{1t}$ transforms the process from $I(2)$ to $I(0)$.

The connection between $\boldsymbol{\beta}'\mathbf{x}_{t-1}$ and $\boldsymbol{\beta}'\mathbf{R}_{1t}$ can be seen by inserting (16.4) into (16.2):

$$\begin{aligned}\underbrace{\mathbf{R}_{0t}}_{I(0)} &= \boldsymbol{\alpha}\boldsymbol{\beta}'(\underbrace{\mathbf{x}_{t-1}}_{I(2)} - \mathbf{B}_2\underbrace{\Delta\mathbf{x}_{t-1}}_{I(1)} - \hat{\boldsymbol{\mu}}_0) + \boldsymbol{\varepsilon}_t \\ &= \boldsymbol{\alpha}(\underbrace{\boldsymbol{\beta}'\mathbf{x}_{t-1}}_{I(1)} - \underbrace{\boldsymbol{\beta}'\mathbf{B}_2\Delta\mathbf{x}_{t-1}}_{I(1)} - \hat{\boldsymbol{\mu}}_0) + \boldsymbol{\varepsilon}_t \\ &= \boldsymbol{\alpha}(\underbrace{\boldsymbol{\beta}'\mathbf{x}_{t-1} - \boldsymbol{\omega}'\Delta\mathbf{x}_{t-1}}_{I(0)} - \hat{\boldsymbol{\mu}}_0) + \boldsymbol{\varepsilon}_t\end{aligned} \tag{16.5}$$

where $\boldsymbol{\omega} = \boldsymbol{\beta}'\mathbf{B}_2$. Thus, the stationary relations $\boldsymbol{\beta}'\mathbf{R}_{1t}$ consist of two components $\boldsymbol{\beta}'\mathbf{x}_{t-1}$ and $\boldsymbol{\omega}'\Delta\mathbf{x}_{t-1}$. For the cointegration relations $\boldsymbol{\beta}_i'\mathbf{R}_{1t}$, $i = 1, \ldots, r$ to be stationary there are two possibilities: (1) either $\boldsymbol{\omega}_i = \mathbf{0}$ and $\boldsymbol{\beta}_i'\mathbf{x}_{t-1} \sim I(0)$, or (2) $\boldsymbol{\beta}_i'\mathbf{x}_t \sim I(1)$ cointegrates with $\boldsymbol{\omega}_i'\Delta\mathbf{x}_{t-1} \sim I(1)$ to produce the stationary relation $\boldsymbol{\beta}'\mathbf{R}_{1t} \sim I(0)$. In the first case, we talk about directly stationary relations, in the second case about polynomially cointegrated relations. Here we shall consider $\boldsymbol{\beta}'\mathbf{x}_t \sim I(1)$ without separating between the two cases, albeit recognizing that some of the cointegration relations $\boldsymbol{\beta}_i'\mathbf{x}_t$ may be stationary by themselves. The next chapter will discuss more formally how to distinguish between the two cases.

We have demonstrated above that $\mathbf{R}_{0t} \sim I(0)$ and $\boldsymbol{\beta}'\mathbf{R}_{1t} \sim I(0)$ in (16.2) which is the model based on which all $I(1)$ estimation and test procedures are derived. In this sense, the procedures are equally valid in the case of $I(2)$ data, albeit noticing the following:

1. The $I(1)$ rank test cannot say anything about the reduced rank of the $\boldsymbol{\Gamma}$ matrix, i.e. about the number of $I(2)$ trends. Also, the determination of the reduced rank of the $\boldsymbol{\Pi}$ matrix, though asymptotically unbiased, might have poor small sample properties (Nielsen and Rahbek 2004).
2. The $\hat{\boldsymbol{\beta}}$ coefficients relating $I(2)$ variables are T^2 consistent and, thus, very precisely estimated. We say that the estimate $\hat{\boldsymbol{\beta}}$ is super-super consistent.
3. The tests of hypotheses on $\boldsymbol{\beta}$ are not tests of cointegration from $I(1)$ to $I(0)$, but instead from $I(2)$ to $I(1)$, as evident from (16.5) and a cointegration relation should in general be considered $I(1)$, albeit recalling that a cointegration relation $\boldsymbol{\beta}_i'\mathbf{x}_t$ can be $CI(2{,}2)$, i.e. be cointegrating from $I(2)$ to $I(0)$,

Thus, one can test a number of hypotheses based on the $I(1)$ procedure even if $\mathbf{x}_t$ is $I(2)$, but the interpretation of the results has to be modified to some extent as compared to the $I(1)$ case.

16.2 Stochastic and deterministic trends in the nominal variables

Chapter 9 found that the inflation rate was empirically $I(1)$, even when allowing for a shift in the mean at 1983, based on the data vector $x_t' = [m^r, y^r, \Delta p, R_m, R_b]$, where $m^r = m - p$. This suggests that prices are $I(2)$ and, therefore, that the nominal money stock is likely to be $I(2)$ as well. Because deterministic trends in m_t and p_t might very well cancel in $(m - p)_t$, one should generally expect the deterministic components to be different in the nominal model as compared to the real model.

A priori, we would expect a linear trend to be present in nominal prices reflecting the fact that average inflation rates have, in general, been non-zero in our economies. The question is whether we should allow for more elaborate specifications like broken linear trends or not. Because the typical smooth behaviour of a stochastic $I(2)$ trend can often be approximated with an $I(1)$ stochastic trend around a broken linear deterministic trend, one can in some cases avoid the $I(2)$ analysis altogether by allowing for sufficiently many breaks in the linear trend.[1] Whether one specification is preferable to the other is difficult to decide prior to the empirical analysis, but we need to pay sufficient attention to this question, as this choice is likely to significantly influence the empirical results.

Thus, prior to the model analysis we need to consider which deterministic components to include in the model and whether they should be restricted to the cointegration relations or not.

As a first step in the analysis one should always take a look at the graphs of the data in levels and differences. Because an $I(2)$ variable typically exhibits smooth behaviour, which can be difficult to distinguish from an $I(1)$ variable with a linear trend, the graphs of the differenced data are often more informative about potential $I(2)$ behaviour than the graphs of the data in levels. Since the slope coefficient of a linear trend in $\mathbf{x}_t$ corresponds to an average growth rate of $\Delta\mathbf{x}_t$, inspecting the graph of the latter gives a first hint of whether the average growth rate has been approximately zero or not, whether the growth rates have been changing over the sample period, and whether there is significant mean reversion in the differences. Quarterly differences can be quite noisy and it is often useful to apply a moving average filter to the original data to be able to distinguish the long-run movements from the transitory noise. For example, the trending behaviour in nominal money growth and inflation becomes more pronounced in Figure 16.1 when filtered through a four-quarter moving average.

The graphs of nominal money stock and prices in the left-hand side panels of Figure 16.1 exhibit smooth trending behaviour over the whole sample period but, seemingly,

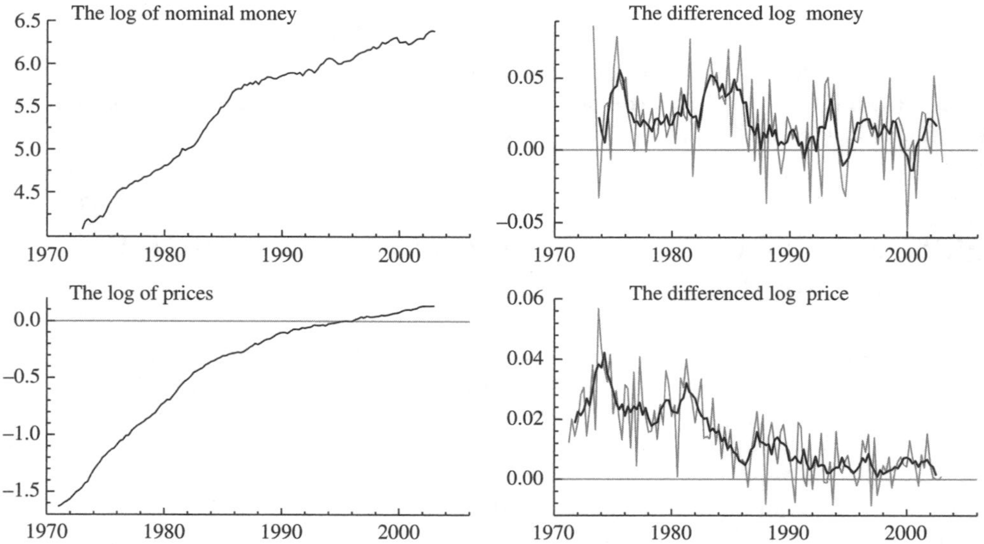

Fig 16.1 Nominal money stock and prices in levels and differences with a four-quarter moving average in bold.

[1] As a matter of fact, it may even be possible to avoid the $I(2)$ analysis altogether by fitting sufficiently many deterministic (linear, broken linear, quadratic) trends to the data. This, of course, is just another way of modelling second order non-stationary data.

with a change in the slope at around 1982–1983. Consistent with this, the growth rates in the right-hand side of Figure 16.1 seem to fluctuate around a higher mean value up to 1983 and a lower value thereafter.

To avoid the $I(2)$ problem it might be tempting to model such shifts in nominal growth rates deterministically rather than stochastically. Obviously, trend-adjusted nominal money and prices will be found empirically $I(1)$ if one allows for sufficiently many inflation rate regimes with different average growth rates. The question is whether the choice between a deterministic or stochastic specification matters or not. As a matter of fact, there are arguments, economic as well as econometric, in favour and against either choice.

If the change in the growth rates at the regime shift was fully anticipated, it seems reasonable to model the shift deterministically. But one can also argue that if economic agents correctly anticipated the change in behaviour, then a model derived under the assumption of such forward looking behaviour should be able to account for these large changes in the data. For example, if agents' forecasting behaviour is adequately described by model based rational expectations, then the linear VAR model is misspecified (which is testable) and we should be able to do better by moving to a nonlinear rational expectations model (testable by encompassing tests).

If the effects of the new regime were unanticipated, it might be more reasonable to model the change stochastically rather than deterministically. But, if the behaviour of economic agents changed significantly in the new regime, for example causing the growth rates to become *systematically* smaller, then we should probably model the shift deterministically.

For example, in the Danish data, we detected an extraordinary large shock in the bond rate and real money stock at 1983:1 which approximately coincided with a change in inflationary regimes. From an econometric point of view, this shock violated the normality assumption of the VAR model and, hence, was accounted for by a blip dummy. The previous $I(1)$ analysis showed that the blip dummy in the differenced process cumulates to a level shift in the variables (significant for the bond rate and the real money stock). In this case when $(m - p)$ and Δp are being replaced by m and p, an unrestricted step dummy in $\Delta^2 p$ ($\Delta^2 m$) corresponds to a level shift in Δp (Δm) and a broken linear trend in p (m). Thus, accounting for the extraordinary large shock at 1983:1 with a blip dummy in $\Delta^2 p$ or $\Delta^2 m$ and a shift dummy in Δp is econometrically consistent with broken linear trends in the data. If the blip dummy was only needed for the interest rates, say, and the shift dummy was only needed to account for a level shift in $m - p$, then we may not need a broken linear trend in p and m.

In some cases one might argue that a shift dummy/linear broken trend is a proxy for an omitted variable which, if included, would have made the trend/dummy variable superfluous in the model. Thus, the question of how to specify and interpret the deterministic components in the VAR model has no straightforward or easy answer.

The graphs in Figure 16.2 illustrate the above discussion. The large increase in money stock after the deregulation of capital movements in 1983 is strongly visible in the upper panel showing the comovement between nominal money stock and prices. This suggests that we probably need to account for a level shift in nominal money holdings (even though some of the shift might be due to the dramatic drop in the cost of holding money) by including a shift dummy in the cointegration relations. The persistent deviations from the linear trend in the cross-plot between nominal money and prices in the lower panel

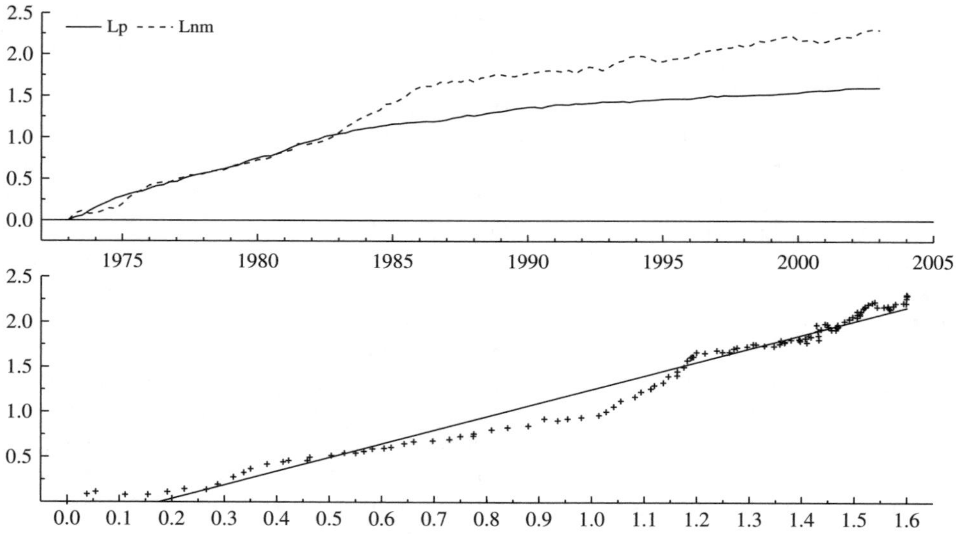

Fig 16.2 The comovements of nominal money and prices over the sample period (upper panel) and a cross-plot between the two (lower panel).

demonstrate that the two nominal variables have not followed each other very closely in this period. This is also evident from the graphs of the nominal growth rates in Figure 16.1, which exhibit quite different growth paths.

Thus there seem to be several possibilities regarding the specification of the deterministic components:

1. m and p are $I(2)$ with linear, but no broken trends, i.e. $(m - b_0 D_s 83 - b_1 t) \sim I(2)$ and $(p - b_2 t) \sim I(2)$, and, provided that m and p share the same stochastic $I(2)$ trend, $\{m - p - b_0 D_s 83 - (b_1 - b_2)t\} \sim I(1)$, i.e. real money adjusted for a linear deterministic trend is $I(1)$. If, in addition, the linear trend in real money is the same as the linear trend in real income then $\{m - p - y^r - b_0 D_s 83\} \sim I(1)$, or possibly even $I(0)$. This corresponds more or less to what we found in Chapter 10.
2. m and p are $I(2)$ with broken linear trends, i.e. $(m - b_0 D_s 83 - b_{11} t - b_{12} t_{83}) \sim I(2)$ and $(p - b_{21} t - b_{22} t_{83}) \sim I(2)$, and, provided that m and p share the same stochastic $I(2)$ trend, $\{m - p - b_0 D_s 83 - (b_{11} - b_{21})t - (b_{12} - b_{22})t_{83}\} \sim I(1)$, i.e. real money adjusted for a broken linear trend is $I(1)$. If, in addition, real income contains the same broken linear trend as real money then $\{m - p - y^r - b_0 D_s 83\} \sim I(1)$, or possibly even $I(0)$. In the special case when $b_{12} = b_{22}$ real money corrected for a linear trend is $I(1)$ and we are back in case 1. Thus, our finding in Chapter 10, that real money corrected for a linear trend and a shift dummy is $I(1)$, can also be consistent with the case of broken linear trends in the nominal variables provided they cancel in $m - p$.
3. m and p are $I(2)$ with linear, or broken linear trends but they do not cancel in $m - p$ or in $m - p - y^r$. In this case we shall have an inconsistency in the nominal results as compared to the real analysis and we can use the $I(2)$ analysis to find out

whether the previous conclusions derived from the real money model are robust to this misspecification of the deterministic components.

To illustrate this question, we shall discuss two alternative model specifications, one based on the assumption that the regime shift in 1983 resulted in a broken linear trend which does not cancel in the cointegration relations, the other that a broken linear trend present in the data cancels in the cointegration relations.

16.3 $I(2)$ symptoms in $I(1)$ models

The empirical analyses of Chapter 10 suggested that the real money stock and the real income variable contained a linear trend and a level shift around 1983, but no broken linear trend. The question is whether we need to reconsider the possibility of a broken linear trend when analysing the nominal variables. As already mentioned, nominal money and prices might very well contain a broken linear trend even though $(m-p)$ showed no such evidence. Thus, based on the principle of general-to-specific modelling, we should allow for the possibility of broken linear trends in the data and then test whether they cancel in $m-p$. This means that *a priori* we do not exclude the possibility that the shift in nominal growth rates around 1983 was a deterministic phenomenon and that it may not cancel in the cointegration relations.

To illustrate this possibility we re-specify the VAR model so that it is consistent with broken linear trends both in the data and in the cointegration relations:

$$\begin{aligned} &\Delta \mathbf{x}_t = \mathbf{\Gamma}_1 \Delta \mathbf{x}_{t-1} + \boldsymbol{\alpha}\tilde{\boldsymbol{\beta}}' \tilde{\mathbf{x}}_{t-1} + \mathbf{\Phi}\mathbf{D}_{pt} + \boldsymbol{\mu}_{01} + \boldsymbol{\mu}_{02}\mathbf{D}_{st} + \boldsymbol{\varepsilon}_t \\ &\boldsymbol{\varepsilon}_t \sim N_p(\mathbf{0}, \mathbf{\Omega}), \quad t = 1, \ldots, T \end{aligned} \tag{16.6}$$

where $\tilde{\boldsymbol{\beta}}' = [\boldsymbol{\beta}', \boldsymbol{\beta}_{11}, \boldsymbol{\beta}_{12}]$ and $\tilde{\mathbf{x}}_t' = [\mathbf{x}_t, t, t\mathbf{Ds}_t]$, $\mathbf{\Phi}$, $\boldsymbol{\mu}_{01}$, and $\boldsymbol{\mu}_{02}$ are unrestricted and the broken linear trend is restricted to lie in the cointegration relations to avoid quadratic trends in the data. Note that the real money model we have analysed so far was based on the assumption that $\boldsymbol{\beta}_{11} = \mathbf{0}$ and $\boldsymbol{\beta}_{12} = \mathbf{0}$. Therefore, if there are broken linear trends in the data we would prefer them to cancel in the cointegration relations.

The first step in the analysis is to find out whether the data are $I(2)$ or not. The $I(1)$ trace test is designed to determine the number of unit roots associated with the levels matrix, $\mathbf{\Pi}$, but not with the differences matrix $\mathbf{\Gamma}$. Thus, it cannot be used to find out whether there are double unit roots in the data or not. The next chapter will introduce the $I(2)$ trace test procedure as a joint test of the reduced rank of the $\mathbf{\Gamma}$ matrix, appropriately transformed by $\boldsymbol{\beta}_\perp$ and $\boldsymbol{\alpha}_\perp$, and the reduced rank of the $\mathbf{\Pi}$ matrix. If the $\mathbf{\Gamma}$ matrix is found to have reduced rank, then some of the unit roots in the model belong to the differenced process, $\Delta \mathbf{x}_t$, which, therefore, is non-stationary.

Many empirical applications use univariate Dickey–Fuller type tests as a basis for deciding whether any of the variables might contain a double unit root or not. Because univariate tests of individual variables cannot (and should not) replace the multivariate $I(1)$ or $I(2)$ test procedures, there will be no discussion of the univariate tests in this book. Instead, we shall here stick to $r = 3$ as our maintained hypothesis but use a number of diagnostic checks to find out whether the results of the nominal model are in accordance with this choice. We note that if the nominal-to-real transformation behind the real money model was correct in the sense defined below, then the rank in the nominal $I(2)$ model should be the same as in the real $I(1)$ model.

More specifically, we shall demonstrate that the characteristic roots of the model and the graphs of the cointegrating relations exhibit certain typical features when the data are $I(2)$ which are not present in $I(1)$ data. This gives us a powerful tool for detecting symptoms signalling that the data are $I(2)$.

16.3.1 The characteristic roots of the model

When $\mathbf{x}_t \sim I(2)$ and, hence $\Delta\mathbf{x}_t \sim I(1)$, it is not sufficient to impose the reduced rank restriction on the matrix $\mathbf{\Pi}$ to get rid of all (near) unit roots in the model. This is because $\Delta\mathbf{x}_t$ is also a unit root process. Therefore, even if the rank of $\mathbf{\Pi} = \boldsymbol{\alpha}\boldsymbol{\beta}'$ has been correctly determined there will remain additional unit roots among the characteristic roots of the VAR model. Thus, a straightforward way of finding out whether this is the case is to check the characteristic roots of the vector process (as described in Chapter 3) after a given rank r has been imposed. If one or several large roots remain in the model for any reasonable choice of r, then it is a sign of $I(2)$ behaviour in at least one of the variables. Because the extra unit root(s) belong to the difference matrix $\mathbf{\Gamma} = -(\mathbf{I} - \mathbf{\Gamma}_1)$, lowering the value of r does not remove these unit roots. Note, however, that this diagnostic check is only reliable in a VAR model with a correct lag length. A VAR model with too many lags will often generate complex pairs of large (albeit insignificant) roots in the characteristic polynomial (Nielsen and Nielsen 2006).

In the Danish nominal money model, there are altogether $p \times k = 5 \times 2 = 10$ roots in the characteristic polynomial. Since the specification of the deterministic components is likely to influence the inference on the $I(2)$ components in the VAR model we shall estimate the following two versions of the Danish nominal money model:

1. with a broken linear trend (t_{83}) restricted to be in the cointegration relations and an unrestricted constant, a shift dummy (D_s831), and a blip dummy (D_p83);
2. with a linear trend restricted to be in the cointegration relations and an unrestricted constant, a shift dummy (D_s831), and a blip dummy (D_p83).

The modulus of the characteristic roots for the first model version are:

VAR(p)	**0.90**	**0.87**	**0.87**	0.74	0.74	0.32	0.35	0.35	0.23	0.05
$r=4$	**1.0**	**0.90**	0.74	0.74	0.71	0.71	0.36	0.36	0.24	0.10
$r=3$	**1.0**	**1.0**	**0.90**	0.73	0.73	0.48	0.29	0.29	0.21	0.06
$r=2$	**1.0**	**1.0**	**1.0**	**0.83**	0.63	0.63	0.22	0.21	0.06	0.06

There appear to be three large roots in the unrestricted model which could suggest $r = 2$. When imposing this rank restriction, the model contains three unit roots plus an additional fairly large root (0.83). If the rank is three as argued in Chapter 8 and we impose two unit roots, then the largest unrestricted root is 0.90. This seems to suggest that there is still an $I(2)$ unit root in the data even though we have allowed for a broken linear trend.

The modulus of the characteristic roots for the second model version are:

VAR(p)	**0.99**	**0.84**	**0.84**	0.67	0.67	0.53	0.33	0.33	0.07	0.07
$r = 4$	**1.0**	**0.95**	0.74	0.74	0.62	0.62	0.34	0.34	0.10	0.10
$r = 3$	**1.0**	**1.0**	**0.88**	0.63	0.63	0.55	0.31	0.31	0.09	0.06
$r = 2$	**1.0**	**1.0**	**1.0**	**0.81**	0.45	0.45	0.43	0.23	0.23	0.10

Compared to the model with broken linear trends the results are not too different. However, if instead we had excluded broken linear trends both in the data and the cointegration relations by restricting the shift dummy to be in the cointegration relations, the largest unrestricted root for $r = 3$ had been very close to 1.0. We conclude that there is probably a double unit root in the nominal model but that it becomes less pronounced when allowing for a broken linear trend.

16.3.2 The graphs of the cointegration relations

When $\mathbf{x}_t \sim I(2)$, (16.5) showed that $\boldsymbol{\beta}_i'\mathbf{x}_t \sim I(1)$ but $\boldsymbol{\beta}_i'\mathbf{R}_{1t} \sim I(0)$ for $i = 1, \ldots, r$. This gives us another diagnostic tool for checking $I(2)$ behaviour in the model. However, in the next chapter, we shall show that when the number of cointegration relations, r, is greater than the number of $I(2)$ trends, s_2, then it is possible to make $(r - s_2)$ of the $\boldsymbol{\beta}$ relations stationary by linear combinations. Therefore, when the graph of at least one of the cointegration relations, $\boldsymbol{\beta}_i'\mathbf{x}_t$, looks non-stationary but the corresponding $\boldsymbol{\beta}_i'\mathbf{R}_{1t}$ stationary, one should consider the possibility of double unit roots in the data.

Because the typical $I(2)$ symptoms are more visible in the model with no broken trend in the cointegration relations, the graphs in Figures 16.3–16.7 are based on this

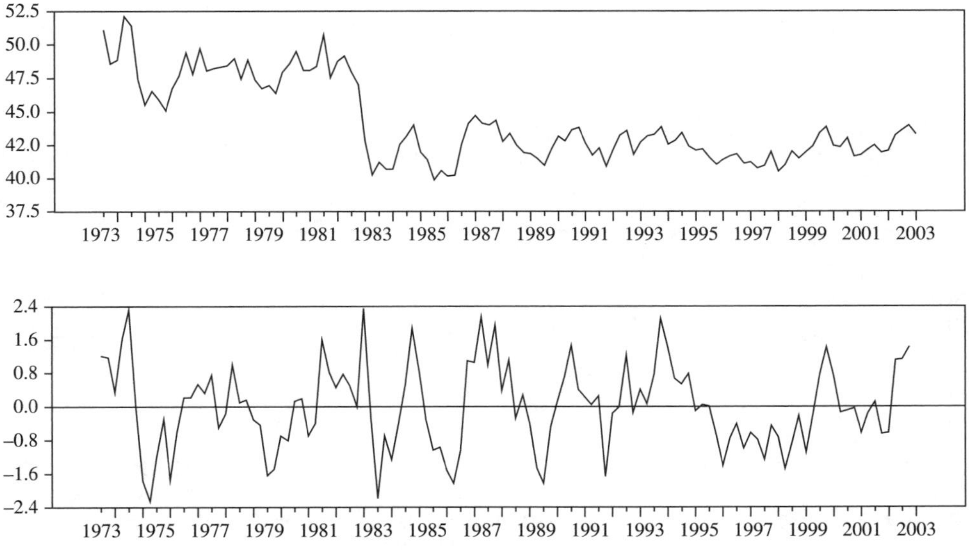

Fig 16.3 The graphs of $\boldsymbol{\beta}_1'\mathbf{x}_t$ (upper panel) and $\boldsymbol{\beta}_1'\mathbf{R}_{1t}$ (lower panel) from model with no broken trends.

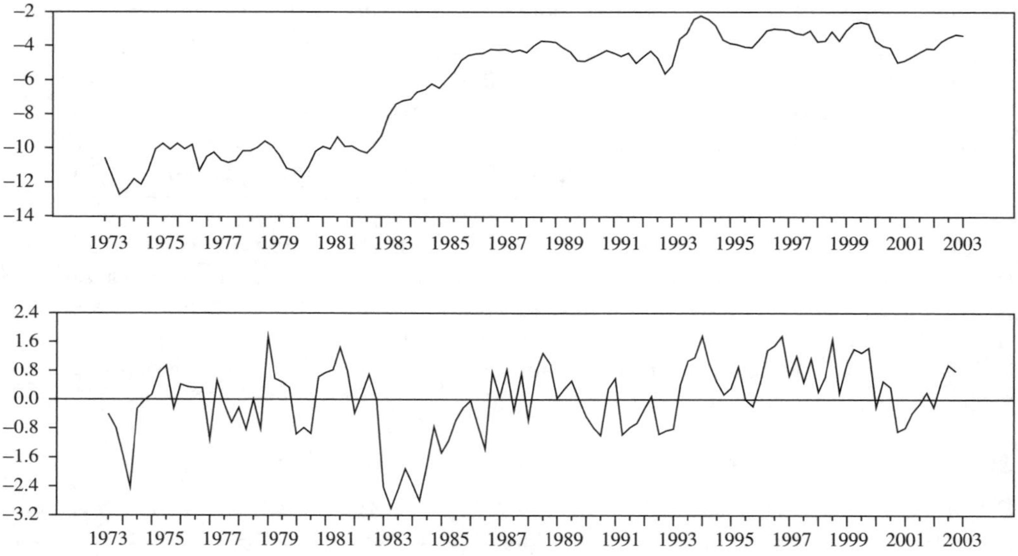

Fig 16.4 The graphs of $\boldsymbol{\beta}_2'\mathbf{x}_t$ (upper panel) and $\boldsymbol{\beta}_2'\mathbf{R}_{1t}$ (lower panel).

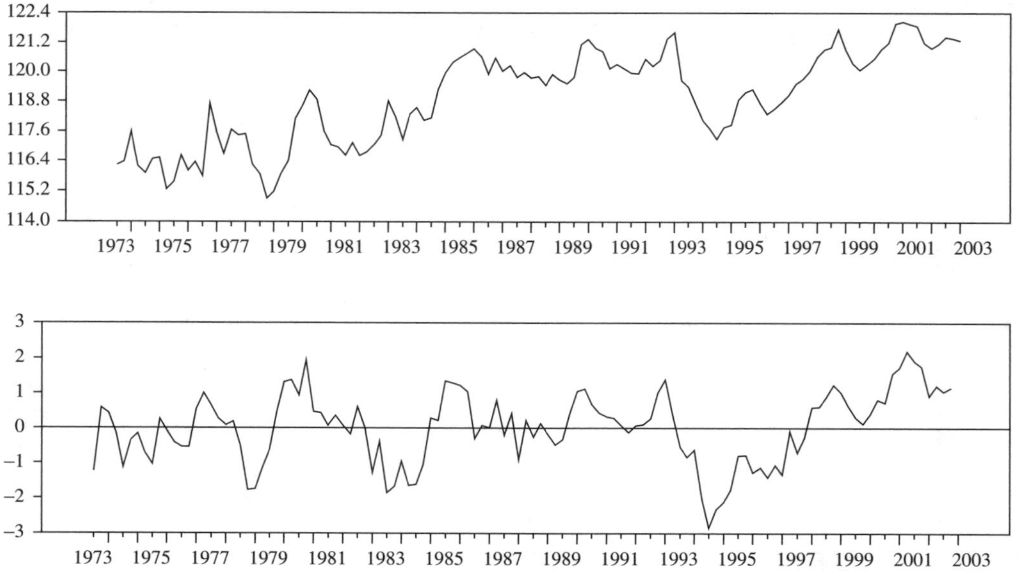

Fig 16.5 The graphs of $\boldsymbol{\beta}_3'\mathbf{x}_t$ (upper panel) and $\boldsymbol{\beta}_3'\mathbf{R}_{1t}$ (lower panel).

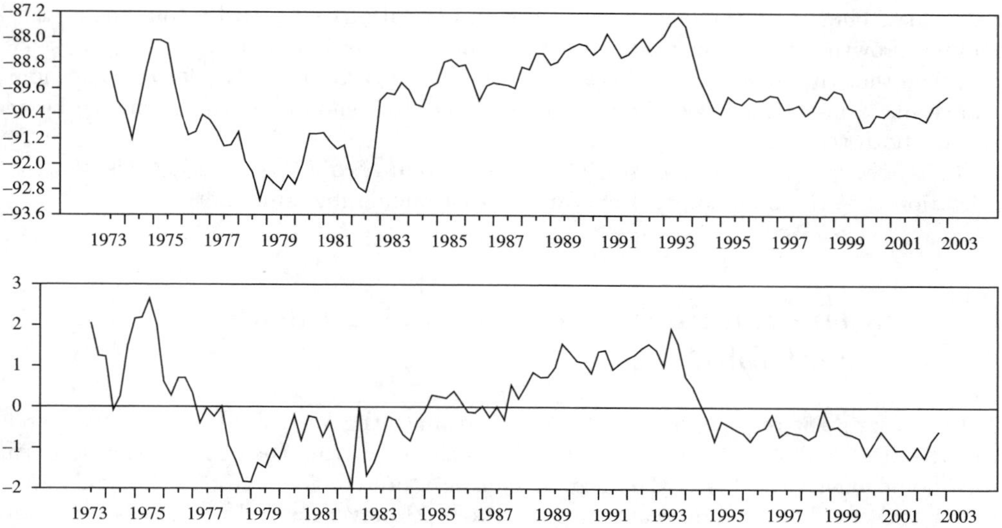

Fig 16.6 The graphs of $\boldsymbol{\beta}_4'\mathbf{x}_t$ (upper panel) and $\boldsymbol{\beta}_4'\mathbf{R}_{1t}$ (lower panel).

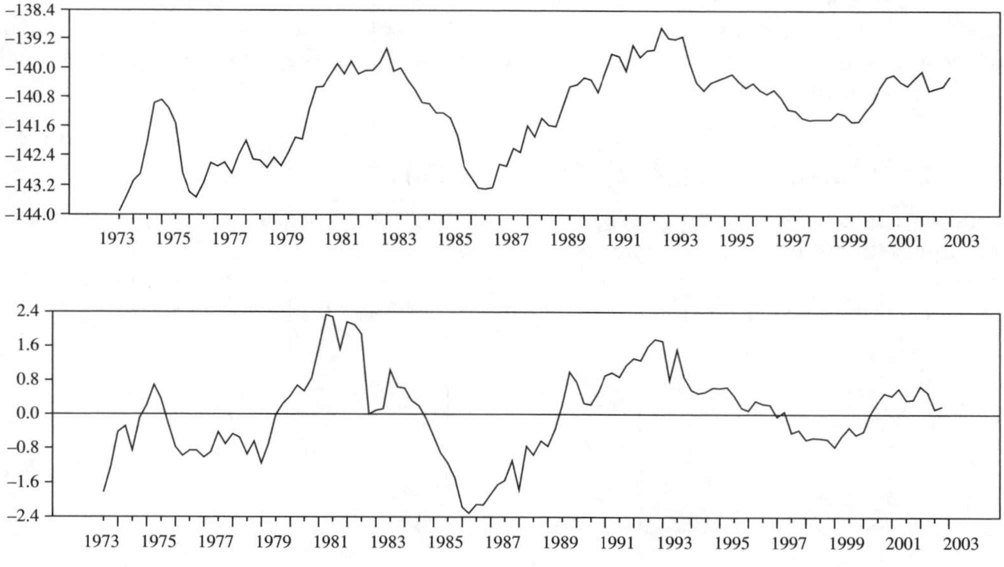

Fig 16.7 The graphs of $\boldsymbol{\beta}_5'\mathbf{x}_t$ (upper panel) and $\boldsymbol{\beta}_5'\mathbf{R}_{1t}$ (lower panel).

model. The upper panels show the relations, $\boldsymbol{\beta}_i'\mathbf{x}_t,\ i = 1, \ldots, 5$, and the lower panels the same relations corrected for short-run dynamics, $\boldsymbol{\beta}_i'\mathbf{R}_{1t}$.

The graphs of the first three cointegration relations in Figures 16.3–16.5 show that $\boldsymbol{\beta}_i'\mathbf{x}_t$ is drifting off in a typical non-stationary manner, whereas $\boldsymbol{\beta}_i'\mathbf{R}_{1,t}$ seems definitely stationary. Thus, to become stationary the $\boldsymbol{\beta}_i'\mathbf{x}_t$ relations need to be combined with a nominal growth rate (either price inflation or money inflation or both).

Given that the choice of $r = 3$ is correct, then both $\boldsymbol{\beta}_i'\mathbf{x}_t$ and $\boldsymbol{\beta}_i'\mathbf{R}_{1t}$ for $i = 4, 5$ should behave like non-stationary variables. Figures 16.6–16.7 show that this seems to be the case for both relations.

Thus, the pronounced non-stationary behaviour of $\boldsymbol{\beta}_i'\mathbf{x}_t$, $i = 1, 2, 3$, is a strong indication that the nominal data contain at least one double unit root.

16.4 Is the nominal-to-real transformation acceptable?

The most frequent reason why we choose to estimate the VAR model for $I(2)$ variables with the $I(1)$ model is because we would like to check whether the data satisfies long-run price homogeneity. If this is the case we can be more confident about the conclusions from a VAR model based on real transformations. However, as will be discussed in more detail in the next chapter, long-run price homogeneity in $\boldsymbol{\beta}$ is a necessary but not sufficient condition for the validity of the nominal-to-real transformation. Even so it seems, nevertheless, useful to test for long-run price homogeneity in $\boldsymbol{\beta}$ as a first indication of whether the nominal-to-real transformation is empirically applicable. If the test rejects we know that the transformation is not valid, if the test accepts we know that, although long-run homogeneity may fail on the sufficient condition, the results are probably not too far away from acceptance.

16.4.1 Transforming $I(2)$ data to $I(1)$

Chapter 2 demonstrated that $(m-p) \sim I(1)$ when both nominal money and prices contain the same $I(2)$ trend with the same coefficients. If $(m_t, p_t) \sim I(2)$, $(y_t^r, R_{m,t}, R_{b,t}) \sim I(1)$, and $m_t - p_t$ is $CI(2,1)$, then the data satisfy long-run price homogeneity and the $I(2)$ model can be transformed to an $I(1)$ model without loss of information:

$$\begin{bmatrix} m_t \\ p_t \\ y_t^r \\ R_{m,t} \\ R_{b,t} \end{bmatrix} \sim I(2) \rightarrow \begin{bmatrix} (m-p)_t \\ \Delta p_t \\ y_t^r \\ R_{m,t} \\ R_{b,t} \end{bmatrix} \sim I(1).$$

Given long-run price homogeneity, the VAR analyses based on either of the two data vectors are essentially identical in terms of likelihood except that a VAR(k) model based on the real vector has one more lag in prices (p_{t-k-1}) compared to a VAR(k) in nominal variables. As most macroeconomic models contain real rather than nominal magnitudes the above result has the following important implication for empirical macromodels:

1. If long-run price homogeneity is violated in the data, so that $(m_t - ap_t) \sim I(1)$, but the real transformation is used nonetheless, then $(m_t - p_t) =$

$\{(m_t - p_t) - (1-a)p_t\} \sim I(2)$, and the real variable will contain a small $I(2)$ component. If the coefficient $(1-a)$ is small (as is usually the case), available test procedures are likely to have low power in detecting the $I(2)$ component, but the latter may influence the analysis in unexplainable ways (Kongsted and Nielsen 2004).

2. Models containing real $I(1)$ variables would generally need a measure of a nominal growth rate to be properly specified. This implies that non-stationary real variables are econometrically and empirically consistent with dynamic steady-state relations, so that macroeconomic models without this feature will, in general, not be able to satisfactorily describe macrodata.

16.4.2 Testing long-run price homogeneity

Because the finding of long-run price homogeneity is likely to be strongly dependent on the specification of the deterministic trends in the model we shall report the estimates and the tests for the above two alternative model specifications, one with a broken linear trend in the cointegration relations, the other with a linear trend in the cointegration relations and an unrestricted shift dummy in the model. The latter corresponds to our previously analysed real money model, the former includes features which we previously assumed to be absent in the model and the data. By comparing the estimated results we shall be able to investigate the empirical implications of either choice. The estimates of the first model version are reported in Tables 16.1, 16.2 and 16.3, those of the second version in Table 16.4.

The first step in the analysis is to test whether the broken linear trend can be excluded from the $\boldsymbol{\beta}$ relations. The joint test of $\boldsymbol{\beta}_{11} = \mathbf{0}$ and $\boldsymbol{\beta}_{12} = \mathbf{0}$ was strongly rejected based on the following test value $\chi^2(6) = 69.85[0.00]$. Thus, the results suggest (broken) linear trends in the data and, moreover, they do not seem to cancel in the cointegration relations. This implies that the specification of the real money model of the previous chapters is not fully consistent with the properties of the nominal data.

Even though the joint test was rejected it is still possible that some of the exclusion hypotheses can be accepted when tested separately. We first test $\boldsymbol{\beta}_{12} = \mathbf{0}$, implying that a linear but not a broken linear trend is needed in the cointegration relations. It was rejected based on $\chi^2(3) = 33.13[0.00]$. We then test $\boldsymbol{\beta}_{11} = \mathbf{0}$, implying that a linear trend is only needed in the more recent regime. It was rejected based on $\chi^2(3) = 29.15, 3[0.00]$. Finally we test $\boldsymbol{\beta}_{11} - \boldsymbol{\beta}_{12} = \mathbf{0}$, implying that a linear trend is only needed in the first regime. It was rejected based on $\chi^2(3) = 24.64, 3[0.00]$. We conclude that broken linear trends seem to be present both in the cointegration relations and in the data.

The relationship between nominal money and prices based on the unrestricted VAR reported in the left-hand side of Table 16.1 seem at first sight to be far from homogeneous. However, using appropriately selected weights we can always find a new cointegration vector $\tilde{\boldsymbol{\beta}}_i = \alpha_{1i}\hat{\boldsymbol{\beta}}_1 + \alpha_{2i}\hat{\boldsymbol{\beta}}_2 + \alpha_{3i}\hat{\boldsymbol{\beta}}_3$ which is homogeneous even though the individual $\boldsymbol{\beta}$ vectors are distinctly non-homogeneous. This is because one can always impose $r-1$ restrictions on a $\boldsymbol{\beta}$ vector without changing the value of the likelihood function. For example, the linear combination $\tilde{\boldsymbol{\beta}}_1 = -0.14\hat{\boldsymbol{\beta}}_1 - 0.01\hat{\boldsymbol{\beta}}_2 + 0.27\hat{\boldsymbol{\beta}}_3$, where $\hat{\boldsymbol{\beta}}_i$ are given by the unrestricted estimates in the left-hand side of Table 16.1 and the weights by the α coefficients in the money equation, gives us a homogeneous relation between money and

Table 16.1 Two unconstrained long-run structures allowing for broken linear trends.

	Unrestricted *VAR*			Homogeneity on $\hat{\beta}_1, \hat{\beta}_2$		
	$\hat{\beta}_1$	$\hat{\beta}_2$	$\hat{\beta}_3$	$\hat{\beta}_1$	$\hat{\beta}_2$	$\hat{\beta}_3$
m	**1.00**	**−0.26**	**−0.66**	**1.0**	**1.0**	**−0.15**
p	**−0.08**	**1.00**	**1.18**	**−1.0**	**−1.0**	**1.0**
y^r	0.33	0.54	1.00	−0.41	−0.04	0.58
R_m	−1.60	−0.01	8.75	−3.64	2.43	−0.10
R_b	40.82	−4.75	−3.26	30.20	42.77	0.03
Trend83	0.04	0.01	0.01	0.02	0.03	0.01
Trend	−0.04	−0.02	−0.01	−0.01	−0.02	−0.02
	$\hat{\alpha}_1$	$\hat{\alpha}_2$	$\hat{\alpha}_3$	$\hat{\alpha}_1$	$\hat{\alpha}_2$	$\hat{\alpha}_3$
Δm	**−0.14** [−5.32]	−0.01 [−0.16]	**0.27** [4.86]	**−0.55** [−5.78]	**0.24** [3.76]	0.00 [0.01]
Δp	−0.01 [−1.42]	**−0.21** [−6.07]	−0.00 [−0.02]	0.00 [0.12]	0.01 [0.29]	**−0.20** [−5.76]
Δy^r	**−0.07** [−3.80]	−0.03 [−0.43]	**−0.16** [−4.12]	**0.22** [3.32]	**−0.20** [−4.71]	**−0.19** [−3.10]
ΔR_m	**−0.00** [−2.69]	**0.01** [2.35]	−0.00 [−0.86]	0.00 [0.16]	−0.00 [−1.56]	0.00 [0.89]
ΔR_b	**−0.01** [−5.20]	0.00 [0.72]	**−0.01** [−1.95]	0.01 [0.85]	**−0.01** [−2.95]	−0.01 [−1.72]

prices. Thus, it can be (and often is) misleading to interpret unrestricted estimates, such as the present ones, as strong evidence against long-run homogeneity.

In the right-hand side of Table 16.1 we report the estimates of $\boldsymbol{\beta}$ and $\boldsymbol{\alpha}$ where two of the $\boldsymbol{\beta}$ vectors satisfy long-run price homogeneity whereas the third vector is unrestricted. Because the two homogeneity restrictions can be imposed by linear combinations of the unrestricted $\boldsymbol{\beta}$ vectors, the likelihood function is unchanged and there is no test involved. In the case when long-run price homogeneity is rejected (as it will be here) this is often a useful way of isolating the non-homogeneous effect to one relation in the system and, thereby, possibly learning why it was rejected. We note that the third unrestricted relation is very far from being homogeneous in money and prices. Moreover, inflation is exclusively adjusting to this non-homogeneous relation, whereas money is exclusively adjusting to the first two homogeneous relations. Hence, money must adjust homogeneously to prices whereas prices cannot adjust homogeneously to money. Thus, $\tilde{\beta}_1 = -0.55\hat{\boldsymbol{\beta}}_1 + 0.24\hat{\boldsymbol{\beta}}_2 + 0.00\hat{\boldsymbol{\beta}}_3$, where $\hat{\boldsymbol{\beta}}_i$ are given by the unrestricted estimates in the right-hand side of Table 16.1 and the weights by the α coefficients in the money equation, gives us a homogeneous relation between money and prices, which is identical to the one discussed above.

Since the weights have been chosen so that they correspond to the α coefficients in the money equation, it is easy to verify the homogeneity results by inspecting the first row of $\hat{\mathbf{\Pi}} = \hat{\boldsymbol{\alpha}}\hat{\boldsymbol{\beta}}'$ in Table 16.2. We note that:

1. Homogeneity seems approximately satisfied in the money equation, but not in the price and real income equations.

2. The first row corresponds almost exactly to the long-run money demand relation estimated in previous chapters and shows that nominal money has followed prices and that no deterministic trends are needed to obtain stationarity.
3. The second row shows that prices have not moved proportionally to money (1 to 0.2), that they have been negatively related to real income and that they exhibited an additional 'autonomous' annual growth of approximately 1.6% in the first regime but no longer in the recent regime.
4. The third row shows that nominal income ($y^r + p = y^n$) has been negatively related to nominal interest rates (evidence of IS type effects) and has exhibited an autonomous annual growth of approximately 2.4% in the first regime, but only 0.4% in the more recent regime.
5. The linear growth in money, prices, and income has primarily been a dominant feature of the first regime, but not of the more recent regime.

These are interesting results showing that our empirical results regarding the long-run money demand relation can be verified in the nominal model. Even more interesting, the result that prices are causing money one to one, but not the other way around, is a strong result supporting the previous conclusion that money is purely adjusting and not pushing. Thus the 'new' results from the nominal analysis seems to be related to the determination of prices and real income, on which our real money model had little to say.

The test of long-run price homogeneity in all three cointegrating relations with a broken linear trend in the data and in the cointegration relations was rejected based on a test value $\chi^2(3) = 26.0[0.00]$.[2] Because long-run price homogeneity is a crucial property economically as well as econometrically, we need to understand why long-run price homogeneity is rejected, and how it may have affected the empirical results of the previous chapters. Based on the above unconstrained results we already found that the lack of homogeneity was primarily related to the determination of prices and income, but not money.

Table 16.2 The unrestricted estimates of $\mathbf{\Pi}$ for $r = 3$.

	m^n	p	y^r	R_m	R_b	$trend83$	$trend$
Δm^n	**−0.31**	**0.31**	**0.22**	**2.57**	**−6.47**	−0.00	0.00
	[−6.16]	[2.80]	[2.90]	[5.30]	[−5.57]	[−1.78]	[0.97]
Δp	**0.04**	**−0.21**	**−0.12**	0.02	0.42	**−0.003**	**0.004**
	[2.12]	[−4.92]	[−4.17]	[0.12]	[0.95]	[−4.51]	[5.22]
Δy^r	0.04	**−0.21**	**−0.19**	**−1.27**	**−2.16**	**−0.005**	**0.006**
	[1.21]	[−2.68]	[−3.79]	[−3.78]	[−2.69]	[−4.64]	[4.08]
ΔR_m	−0.00	0.01	0.00	−0.02	**−0.19**	−0.00	0.00
	[−1.86]	[1.46]	[0.60]	[−0.63]	[−3.20]	[−0.88]	[0.09]
ΔR_b	−0.01	−0.00	−0.01	−0.05	**−0.36**	**−0.0004**	**0.0004**
	[−1.61]	[−0.45]	[−1.57]	[−1.50]	[−4.73]	[−4.04]	[3.09]

[2] In a previous paper (Juselius 1994) long-run price homogeneity was similarly tested based on the sample 1974:2–1983:3 and was accepted. This could imply that the violation of price homogeneity is primarily associated with the more recent period, or that the precision of the results due to the longer sample has now improved sufficiently to make the deviation from homogeneity statistically visible.

Table 16.3 Two constrained long-run structures with a broken linear trend.

	Long-run price homogeneity $\chi^2(3) = 26.0[0.00]$			Restrictions on $\hat{\beta}_1, \hat{\beta}_2$ $\chi^2(6) = 31.3[0.00]$		
	$\hat{\beta}_1$	$\hat{\beta}_2$	$\hat{\beta}_3$	$\hat{\beta}_1$	$\hat{\beta}_2$	$\hat{\beta}_3$
m	**1.0**	**1.0**	**−0.06**	1.0	0.0	**−1.02** [−370.58]
p	**−1.0**	**−1.0**	**0.06**	−1.0	0.0	**1.00** [0.00]
y^r	−0.27	−1.19	1.00	−1.0	0.0	**0.99** [233.77]
R_m	−1.45	−16.37	31.69	4.78 [60.46]	1.0	0.0
R_b	32.91	0.31	−19.97	−4.78 [−60.46]	−0.83 [−46.16]	0.0
trend83	0.02	−0.01	−0.00	0.0	0.0	−0.001 [−9.04]
trend	−0.01	0.01	0.00	0.0	0.0	0.001 [8.08]
	$\hat{\alpha}_1$	$\hat{\alpha}_2$	$\hat{\alpha}_3$	$\hat{\alpha}_1$	$\hat{\alpha}_2$	$\hat{\alpha}_3$
Δm	**−0.19** [5.46]	**−0.12** [−4.71]	0.00 [0.09]	**4.91** [3.62]	**−20.92** [−3.10]	**5.10** [3.78]
Δp	0.00 [−0.22]	**−0.02** [−2.36]	**−0.03** [−2.31]	0.45 [0.76]	−2.11 [−0.72]	0.47 [0.80]
Δy^r	**−0.08** [3.27]	**0.06** [3.29]	**−0.05** [−2.81]	**4.54** [4.84]	**−23.43** [−5.02]	**4.46** [4.77]
ΔR_m	**−0.01** [3.16]	0.00 [1.62]	−0.00 [−1.19]	**0.23** [3.36]	**−1.21** [−3.60]	**0.23** [3.35]
ΔR_b	**−0.01** [4.97]	**0.00** [1.98]	**0.00** [2.02]	**0.46** [5.35]	**−2.17** [−5.03]	**0.46** [5.34]

In the left-hand side of Table 16.3, we report the cointegration results subject to long-run price homogeneity. Albeit empirically rejected, they are of interest because the real money model was estimated subject to this restriction. We note that $\hat{\beta}_1 + \hat{\beta}_2$ approximately reproduce the money demand relation, that $\hat{\beta}_3$ closely resembles the interest rate relation of the real money model, but that the 'real income–inflation' relation cannot as easily be reproduced.

So far, we have allowed the broken linear trend to enter all cointegration relations, a feature not present in the real money model. To isolate the joint effect of the broken linear trend and the violation of price homogeneity we finally estimate an over-identified β structure in which the first two β vectors represent the money demand and the interest rate relations of $\mathcal{H}_{S.4}$ whereas the third vector imposes a zero restriction on the two interest rates and leaves all other coefficients unrestricted. We note that the first two relations are characterized by long-run homogeneity as well as absence of long-run deterministic trend effects. The right-hand side of Table 16.3 reports the estimates. Even though the six over-identifying restrictions are strongly rejected, the estimated results resemble the previously estimated structural relations (though the opportunity cost of holding money relative to bonds is now smaller than the previously estimated coefficient, 13.3). The third relation, which is just-identified, reports a small but significant non-homogeneous

Table 16.4 Estimated long-run structures allowing for a linear trend.

	Unrestricted *VAR*			Price homogeneity on $\hat{\beta}_1, \hat{\beta}_2$		
	$\hat{\beta}_1$	$\hat{\beta}_2$	$\hat{\beta}_3$	$\hat{\beta}_1$	$\hat{\beta}_2$	$\hat{\beta}_3$
m	1.0	1.0	0.02	**1.0**	0.42	1.00
p	−1.80	−0.53	−0.02	**−1.0**	−0.42	−0.72
y^r	−0.83	−0.84	1.00	−1.24	1.00	−0.38
R_m	−1.89	−15.66	29.55	−22.26	35.12	−0.13
R_b	24.60	2.43	−13.24	15.98	−13.39	−0.32
trend	0.01	−0.01	−0.00	0.00	−0.00	−0.00

	Price homogeneity on all β $\chi^2(3) = 43.0[0.00]$			Restrictions on $\hat{\beta}_1, \hat{\beta}_2$ $\chi^2(4) = 7.99[0.09]$		
	$\hat{\beta}_1$	$\hat{\beta}_2$	$\hat{\beta}_3$	$\hat{\beta}_1$	$\hat{\beta}_2$	$\hat{\beta}_3$
m	1.0	0.02	−0.22	1.0	0.0	1.0
p	−1.0	−0.02	0.22	−1.0	0.0	−0.96 [−253.27]
y^r	−0.82	1.00	1.00	−1.0	0.0	−1.01 [−156.56]
R_m	−10.22	29.55	−9.44	−3.91 [−36.07]	1.0	0.0
R_b	10.90	−13.24	13.98	3.91 [36.07]	−0.74 [−30.14]	0.0
trend	0.00	−0.00	−0.00	0.0	0.0	−0.00 [−7.79]

effect between money and prices as well as significant trend effects. The estimates are approximately consistent with money velocity around a broken linear trend and suggest that 'money velocity' grew with a linear trend up to 1983, after which excess money growth stopped. The effect on inflation is, however, insignificant.

We shall now briefly discuss the results of the second model remembering that the previous results already demonstrated that it is in fact inconsistent with some of the features in the data. The four structures reported in Table 16.4 correspond to the ones in Table 16.1 and 16.3 except that the broken linear trend has now been restricted to zero in the cointegration relations, while it is still allowed to be the data. To economize on space we have not reported the α estimates for this model. The upper left-hand side of Table 16.4 gives the unrestricted estimates which, similar to the previous case, seem to suggest (though incorrectly) that long-run price homogeneity is far from present in the data. The upper right-hand side reports the estimates when price homogeneity has been imposed on two of the β vectors, while leaving the third unrestricted. We note that the third relation is not even close to being homogeneous in prices. The lower left-hand side of Table 16.4 reports the estimates subject to price homogeneity on all β. The homogeneity hypothesis is strongly rejected. We note that the first relation closely reproduces our previous money demand relation, the second is quite close to our previous interest rate relation, and the third resembles the real income relation but without the inflation rate.

Finally the lower right-hand side reports the estimates an over-identified structure consisting of the money demand relation and the interest rate relation of structure $\mathcal{H}_{S.4}$, as well as the just-identified relation between money, prices, real income and the trend. It is accepted with a p-value of 0.09, demonstrating that the model with a linear trend is closer to our previously estimated real money model. We note that the non-homogeneous effect between money and prices in the third $\boldsymbol{\beta}$ vector is slightly more pronounced as compared to the broken linear trend case.

Even though long-run price homogeneity was rejected in both models the estimates suggested that the deviation was indeed very small and the test results might seem surprising. We believe that they can be explained partly by the very high precision in these models (the $\boldsymbol{\beta}$ estimates are super-superconsistent) and by the fact that the test statistics have been calculated without applying a small sample Bartlett correction. The latter is likely to have reduced the test statistics quite substantially. It is even possible that in the latter case the p-value might have increased enough to accept price homogeneity. Whatever the case, the results seem to indicate that we need to include additional nominal variables to fully understand the determination of nominal growth in this period.

16.5 Concluding remarks

This chapter has given an intuitive account of the basic differences between the $I(1)$ and the $I(2)$ model and demonstrated at least three straightforward ways of checking the possibility of double unit roots in the data:

1. the graphs of the data in levels and differences;
2. the graphs of the cointegration relations $\boldsymbol{\beta}'\mathbf{x}_t$ compared to $\boldsymbol{\beta}'\mathbf{R}_{1,t}$;
3. the characteristic roots of the model for reasonable choices of cointegration rank.

When nominal variables are found to be $I(2)$, we showed that the model can be transformed into an $I(1)$ model without loss of information provided long-run price homogeneity is found to be acceptable. However, when long-run price homogeneity is not present and we use the nominal-to-real transformation of the data nonetheless, there will be some loss of information and possibly some violation of the $I(1)$ properties in the transformed model. When this is the case we need to find out whether our conclusions are robust to this misspecification.

For the Danish data we gained some useful insight from performing the nominal VAR analysis. We found that:

1. The broken linear trend effect seems to be strongly present in the data and in the cointegration relations, contrary to the assumptions made in the real money model.
2. Long-run price homogeneity was rejected, violating the nominal-to-real transformation of the data.
3. All the main results of the real money model seemed to be robust to these new findings, whereas the puzzling 'real income–inflation rate' relation was not.

4. The linear growth in money, prices and income was in fact quite dominant in the first regime whereas much less so in the second, explaining why a constant linear trend was long-run excludable in the real model.
5. The problems with non-homogeneity and the possibility of different growth rates between the pre-EMS period in the 1970s and the beginning of the 1980s and the subsequent EMS period seemed primarily to be associated with the (non-constant) relationship between real income and inflation (prices) already detected in Chapters 9 and 12.

Thus, we have been able to recover most of the results of the previous real analyses, but at the same time gained some further understanding for the nominal mechanisms in this system. In the last part of the book we shall try to improve our understanding of these mechanisms by increasing the information set.

17

The $I(2)$ model: Specification and estimation

Even though the statistical theory of the $I(2)$ model has been available since the beginning of the 1990s, only few applications can be found in the literature. There seem to be several reasons for this. One frequent argument is that $I(2)$ prices would lead to economically implausible conclusions if the model is taken to infinity and, hence, that the $I(2)$'ness can be disregarded from the outset. As already argued in Chapter 2, this argument is flawed because it confuses a statistical approximation with a structural economic parameter. Another argument is that $I(2)$ trends can only be found over very long time periods and, hence is of no concern in the analysis based on 10–30 years of data. This again is completely at odds with the fact that significant mean reversion in nominal growth rates is more likely to be found in large than in small samples. Even in moderately sized samples is it often hard to reject the hypothesis of a double unit root when the adjustment behaviour is sluggish. Thus, the interpretation of a double unit root to mean the existence of a 'very' long-run relationship in the data is generally not granted. The third and probably most important reason is that the $I(2)$ model structure is quite complicated so that understanding its many components requires a fair amount of time and effort.

Therefore, an important aim of this chapter is to discuss the components of the $I(2)$ model in a more intuitive language, to avoid lengthy technical derivations, but nevertheless providing the necessary theoretical basis for understanding the essential features of the model and how it can be used. This will be done based on two parametrizations; one relevant for the so-called two-step estimation procedure, the other for the full maximum likelihood procedure. The first one is useful because it is a more straightforward extension of the $I(1)$ model and, hence, a good start for building up the intuition for the components of the $I(2)$ model. The second one is useful because it is the formulation that allows us to formulate relevant hypotheses in a ML framework.

Section 17.1 introduces the $I(2)$ model as a parameter restriction on the unrestricted VAR model and discusses the role of deterministic components. Section 17.2 discusses the two-step and the ML trace test procedure for the determination of the number of stationary cointegration relations and the number of $I(2)$ trends in the model. Section 17.3

discusses the difference between long-run relations in the $I(1)$ and the $I(2)$ model and gives an interpretation of the various components in the $I(2)$ model. Finally, Section 17.4 defines long-run price homogeneity based on the $I(2)$ model and shows how the test it.

17.1 Structuring the $I(2)$ model

For simplicity, the discussion of the various components in the $I(2)$ model will be based on the VAR(3) model formulated in differences and levels:

$$\begin{aligned}\Delta\mathbf{x}_t &= \boldsymbol{\Gamma}_1\Delta\mathbf{x}_{t-1} + \boldsymbol{\Gamma}_2\Delta\mathbf{x}_{t-2} + \boldsymbol{\Pi}\mathbf{x}_{t-1} \\ &\quad + \boldsymbol{\Phi}_s\mathbf{D}_{s,t} + \boldsymbol{\Phi}_p\mathbf{D}_{p,t} + \boldsymbol{\Phi}_{tr}\mathbf{D}_{tr,t} + \boldsymbol{\mu}_0 + \boldsymbol{\mu}_1 t + \boldsymbol{\varepsilon}_t, \\ \boldsymbol{\varepsilon}_t &\sim N_p(\mathbf{0}, \boldsymbol{\Omega}\ ), \quad t = 1, \ldots, T\end{aligned}$$

or, equivalently, in acceleration rates, changes and levels:

$$\begin{aligned}\Delta^2\mathbf{x}_t &= -\boldsymbol{\Gamma}_2\Delta^2\mathbf{x}_{t-1} + \boldsymbol{\Gamma}\Delta\mathbf{x}_{t-1} + \boldsymbol{\Pi}\mathbf{x}_{t-1} \\ &\quad + \boldsymbol{\Phi}_s\mathbf{D}_{s,t} + \boldsymbol{\Phi}_p\mathbf{D}_{p,t} + \boldsymbol{\Phi}_{tr}\mathbf{D}_{tr,t} + \boldsymbol{\mu}_0 + \boldsymbol{\mu}_1 t + \boldsymbol{\varepsilon}_t,\end{aligned} \tag{17.1}$$

where $\boldsymbol{\Gamma} = -(\mathbf{I} - \boldsymbol{\Gamma}_1 - \boldsymbol{\Gamma}_2)$ and all parameters are unrestricted. Similar to the $I(1)$ model, we need to define the concentrated $I(2)$ model:

$$\mathbf{R}_{0,t} = \boldsymbol{\Gamma}\mathbf{R}_{1,t} + \boldsymbol{\Pi}\mathbf{R}_{2,t} + \boldsymbol{\Phi}_s\mathbf{D}_{s,t} + \boldsymbol{\Phi}_p\mathbf{D}_{p,t} + \boldsymbol{\mu}_0 + \boldsymbol{\mu}_1 t + \boldsymbol{\varepsilon}_t \tag{17.2}$$

where $\mathbf{R}_{0,t}$, $\mathbf{R}_{1,t}$, and $\mathbf{R}_{2,t}$ are defined by:

$$\Delta^2\mathbf{x}_t = \hat{\mathbf{B}}_1\Delta^2\mathbf{x}_{t-1} + \hat{\mathbf{B}}_2\mathbf{D}_{tr,t} + \mathbf{R}_{0,t}, \tag{17.3}$$

$$\Delta\tilde{\mathbf{x}}_{t-1} = \hat{\mathbf{B}}_3\Delta^2\mathbf{x}_{t-1} + \hat{\mathbf{B}}_4\mathbf{D}_{tr,t} + \mathbf{R}_{1,t}, \tag{17.4}$$

and

$$\tilde{\mathbf{x}}_{t-1} = \hat{\mathbf{B}}_5\Delta^2\mathbf{x}_{t-1} + \hat{\mathbf{B}}_6\mathbf{D}_{tr,t} + \mathbf{R}_{2,t} \tag{17.5}$$

where $\tilde{\mathbf{x}}_t$ indicates that $\mathbf{x}_t$ has been augmented with some deterministic components such as trend, constant, and shift dummy variables. Note that we need to define three types of 'residuals' in the $I(2)$ model rather than two in the $I(1)$ model. Similar to the $I(1)$ model all estimation and test procedures are based on (17.2). Note also that only the transitory blip dummies have been concentrated out in (17.3)–(17.5). This is because in general only the transitory blip dummies should be unrestricted in the $I(2)$ model whereas the other deterministic components should be restricted to the cointegration relations. Section 17.2 will discuss this in more detail.

Chapter 5 formulated the hypothesis that $\mathbf{x}_t$ is $I(1)$ as a reduced rank hypothesis

$$\boldsymbol{\Pi} = \boldsymbol{\alpha}\boldsymbol{\beta}', \quad \text{where } \boldsymbol{\alpha}, \boldsymbol{\beta} \text{ are } p \times r \tag{17.6}$$

implicitly assuming that $\boldsymbol{\Gamma}$ was unrestricted, i.e. full rank. Johansen (1992c) formulated the hypothesis that $\mathbf{x}_t$ is $I(2)$ as an additional reduced rank hypotheses

$$\boldsymbol{\alpha}_\perp'\boldsymbol{\Gamma}\boldsymbol{\beta}_\perp = \boldsymbol{\xi}\boldsymbol{\eta}', \quad \text{where } \boldsymbol{\xi}, \boldsymbol{\eta} \text{ are } (p-r) \times s_1. \tag{17.7}$$

Thus, the $\boldsymbol{\Gamma}$ matrix is no longer unrestricted in the $I(2)$ model. The first reduced rank condition (17.6) is associated with the variables in levels and the second (17.7) with the variables in differences. The intuition is that the differenced process also contains unit roots when data are $I(2)$.

There is, however, an important difference between the first and the second condition. The former is formulated as a reduced rank condition directly on $\boldsymbol{\Pi}$, whereas the latter is on a transformed $\boldsymbol{\Gamma}$. Below we shall show that this is the basic reason why the ML estimation procedure needs a different parametrization than the one in (17.1).

The intuition behind (17.7) can be seen by premultiplying (17.1) with $\boldsymbol{\alpha}_\perp'$. This makes the levels component $\boldsymbol{\alpha}\boldsymbol{\beta}'\mathbf{x}_{t-2}$ disappear and reduces the model to a $(p-r)$-dimensional system of equations in first and second order differences. In this system the hypothesis of reduced rank of the matrix $\boldsymbol{\alpha}_\perp'\boldsymbol{\Gamma}\boldsymbol{\beta}_\perp$ is tested in the usual way. Thus, the second condition is similar to the first except that the second reduced rank regression is performed on the $p-r$ common driving trends, rather than on the p variables.

Using (17.7) it is possible to decompose $\boldsymbol{\alpha}_\perp$ and $\boldsymbol{\beta}_\perp$ into the $I(1)$ and $I(2)$ directions $\boldsymbol{\alpha}_\perp = [\boldsymbol{\alpha}_{\perp 1}, \boldsymbol{\alpha}_{\perp 2}]$ and $\boldsymbol{\beta}_\perp = [\boldsymbol{\beta}_{\perp 1}, \boldsymbol{\beta}_{\perp 2}]$. The matrices $\boldsymbol{\alpha}_{\perp 1}$ and $\boldsymbol{\beta}_{\perp 1}$ of dimension $p \times s_1$, and $\boldsymbol{\alpha}_{\perp 2}$ and $\boldsymbol{\beta}_{\perp 2}$ of $p \times s_2$ are defined by $\boldsymbol{\alpha}_{\perp 1} = \overline{\boldsymbol{\alpha}}_\perp\boldsymbol{\xi}$, $\boldsymbol{\beta}_{\perp,1} = \overline{\boldsymbol{\beta}}_\perp\boldsymbol{\eta}$, $\boldsymbol{\alpha}_{\perp 2} = \boldsymbol{\alpha}_\perp\boldsymbol{\xi}_\perp$ and $\boldsymbol{\beta}_{\perp 2} = \boldsymbol{\beta}_\perp\boldsymbol{\eta}_\perp$, where $\boldsymbol{\xi}_\perp, \boldsymbol{\eta}_\perp$ are the orthogonal complements of $\boldsymbol{\xi}$ and $\boldsymbol{\eta}$, respectively,[1] and $\overline{\boldsymbol{\alpha}} = \boldsymbol{\alpha}_\perp(\boldsymbol{\alpha}_\perp'\boldsymbol{\alpha}_\perp)^{-1}$ denotes a shorthand notation used all through the chapter.

The moving average representation of the $I(2)$ model was derived in Johansen (1992c, 1996, 1997). The baseline VAR model (17.1) contains a constant, a trend and several dummy variables that will have to be restricted in certain ways to avoid undesirable effects. Without such restrictions the MA model can be given in its completely unrestricted form:

$$\begin{aligned}\mathbf{x}_t = {} & \mathbf{C}_2\sum_{j=1}^{t}\sum_{i=1}^{j}(\boldsymbol{\varepsilon}_i + \boldsymbol{\mu}_0 + \boldsymbol{\mu}_1 i + \boldsymbol{\Phi}_s\mathbf{D}_{s,i} + \boldsymbol{\Phi}_p\mathbf{D}_{p,i} + \boldsymbol{\Phi}_{tr}\mathbf{D}_{tr,i}) \\ & + \mathbf{C}_1\sum_{j=1}^{t}(\boldsymbol{\varepsilon}_j + \boldsymbol{\mu}_0 + \boldsymbol{\mu}_1 j + \boldsymbol{\Phi}_s\mathbf{D}_{s,j} + \boldsymbol{\Phi}_p\mathbf{D}_{p,j} + \boldsymbol{\Phi}_{tr}\mathbf{D}_{tr,j}) \\ & + \mathbf{C}^*(L)(\boldsymbol{\varepsilon}_t + \boldsymbol{\mu}_0 + \boldsymbol{\mu}_1 t + \boldsymbol{\Phi}_s\mathbf{D}_{s,t} + \boldsymbol{\Phi}_p\mathbf{D}_{p,t} + \boldsymbol{\Phi}_{tr}\mathbf{D}_{tr,t}) + \mathbf{A} + \mathbf{B}t\end{aligned} \tag{17.8}$$

[1]Note that the matrices $\boldsymbol{\alpha}_{\perp 1}, \boldsymbol{\alpha}_{\perp 2}, \boldsymbol{\beta}_{\perp 1}$, and $\boldsymbol{\beta}_{\perp 2}$ are called $\boldsymbol{\alpha}_1, \boldsymbol{\alpha}_2, \boldsymbol{\beta}_1$ and $\boldsymbol{\beta}_2$ in the many papers on $I(2)$ by Johansen and coauthors. The reason why we deviate here from the simpler notation is that we need to distinguish between different $\boldsymbol{\beta}$ and $\boldsymbol{\alpha}$ vectors in the empirical analysis and, hence, use the latter notation for this purpose.

where $\mathbf{A}$ and $\mathbf{B}$ are functions of the initial values $\mathbf{x}_0, \mathbf{x}_{-1}, \ldots, \mathbf{x}_{-k+1}$, and the coefficient matrices satisfy:

$$\mathbf{C}_2 = \boldsymbol{\beta}_{\perp 2}(\boldsymbol{\alpha}'_{\perp 2}\Psi\boldsymbol{\beta}_{\perp 2})^{-1}\boldsymbol{\alpha}'_{\perp 2},$$

$$\begin{aligned} \boldsymbol{\beta}'\mathbf{C}_1 &= -\overline{\boldsymbol{\alpha}}'\boldsymbol{\Gamma}\mathbf{C}_2, \quad \boldsymbol{\beta}'_{\perp 1}\mathbf{C}_1 = -\overline{\boldsymbol{\alpha}}'_{\perp 1}(\mathbf{I} - \boldsymbol{\Psi}\mathbf{C}_2), \\ \boldsymbol{\Psi} &= \boldsymbol{\Gamma}\overline{\boldsymbol{\beta}}\overline{\boldsymbol{\alpha}}'\boldsymbol{\Gamma} + \mathbf{I} - \boldsymbol{\Gamma}_1. \end{aligned} \tag{17.9}$$

To facilitate the interpretation of the $I(2)$ trends and how they load into the variables we denote $\tilde{\boldsymbol{\beta}}_{\perp 2} = \boldsymbol{\beta}_{\perp 2}(\boldsymbol{\alpha}'_{\perp 2}\boldsymbol{\Psi}\boldsymbol{\beta}_{\perp 2})^{-1}$, so that

$$\mathbf{C}_2 = \tilde{\boldsymbol{\beta}}_{\perp 2}\boldsymbol{\alpha}'_{\perp 2}. \tag{17.10}$$

Alternatively we can denote $\tilde{\boldsymbol{\alpha}}'_{\perp 2} = (\boldsymbol{\alpha}'_{\perp 2}\Psi\boldsymbol{\beta}_{\perp 2})^{-1}\boldsymbol{\alpha}'_{\perp 2}$, so that

$$\mathbf{C}_2 = \boldsymbol{\beta}_{\perp 2}\tilde{\boldsymbol{\alpha}}'_{\perp 2}.$$

The alternative (17.10) will be used here. It is now easy to see that the $\mathbf{C}_2$ matrix has a similar reduced rank representation as $\mathbf{C}_1$ in the $I(1)$ model, so that it is straightforward to interpret $\boldsymbol{\alpha}'_{\perp 2}\sum\sum\boldsymbol{\varepsilon}_i$ as a measure of the s_2 second order stochastic trends which load into the variables $\mathbf{x}_t$ with the weights $\tilde{\boldsymbol{\beta}}_{\perp 2}$.

From (17.9) we note that the $\mathbf{C}_1$ matrix in the $I(2)$ model cannot be given a simple decomposition as it depends on both the $\mathbf{C}_2$ matrix and the other model parameters in a complex way. Johansen (2005) derived an analytical expression for $\mathbf{C}_1$, essentially showing that:

$$\mathbf{C}_1 = \boldsymbol{\omega}_0\boldsymbol{\alpha}' + \boldsymbol{\omega}_1\boldsymbol{\alpha}'_{\perp 1} + \boldsymbol{\omega}_2\boldsymbol{\alpha}'_{\perp 2} \tag{17.11}$$

where $\boldsymbol{\omega}_i$ are complicated functions of the parameters of the model (not to be reproduced here).

17.2 Deterministic components in the $I(2)$ model

The MA representation (17.8) showed that unrestricted deterministic components cumulate both once and twice in the $I(2)$ model, so that an unrestricted constant cumulates once to a linear trend and twice to a quadratic trend, and an unrestricted trend cumulates once to a quadratic trend and twice to a cubic trend in $\mathbf{x}_t$. As we would generally like to avoid quadratic and cubic trends in the variables, the deterministic components need to be appropriately restricted. As an illustration of deterministic components likely to be relevant for $I(2)$ data we use the specification of the nominal money model in Chapter 16. This includes a broken linear trend, a constant, a shift dummy, and permanent and transitory blip dummies. A correct specification of these components is even more important in the $I(2)$ model than in the $I(1)$ model.

17.2.1 Restricting the constant term and the trend

To demonstrate how to restrict the deterministic components we shall use a similar decomposition of $\boldsymbol{\mu}_0$ and $\boldsymbol{\mu}_1$ as in Chapter 6, except that we now have to separate between the components that belong to the $\boldsymbol{\alpha}$, $\boldsymbol{\alpha}_{1\perp}$, and $\boldsymbol{\alpha}_{2\perp}$ space. We first consider a decomposition of the constant term:

$$\boldsymbol{\mu}_0 = \boldsymbol{\alpha}\boldsymbol{\gamma}_0 + \boldsymbol{\alpha}_{1\perp}\boldsymbol{\gamma}_1 + \boldsymbol{\alpha}_{2\perp}\boldsymbol{\gamma}_2,$$

and use (17.8) together with (17.10) and (17.11) to investigate the effect of an unrestricted constant term on $\mathbf{x}_t$. The effect of cumulating the constant term twice is given by:

$$\begin{aligned}\mathbf{C}_2\sum_{j=1}^{t}\sum_{i=1}^{j}\boldsymbol{\mu}_0 &= \sum_{j=1}^{t}\sum_{i=1}^{j}\tilde{\boldsymbol{\beta}}_{\perp 2}\boldsymbol{\alpha}'_{\perp 2}(\boldsymbol{\alpha}\boldsymbol{\gamma}_0 + \boldsymbol{\alpha}_{1\perp}\boldsymbol{\gamma}_1 + \boldsymbol{\alpha}_{2\perp}\boldsymbol{\gamma}_2)\\ &= \tilde{\boldsymbol{\beta}}_{\perp 2}\boldsymbol{\alpha}'_{\perp 2}\boldsymbol{\alpha}_{2\perp}\boldsymbol{\gamma}_2(t(t-1)/2) \end{aligned} \tag{17.12}$$

as $\boldsymbol{\alpha}'_{\perp 2}\boldsymbol{\alpha} = \mathbf{0}$ and $\boldsymbol{\alpha}'_{\perp 2}\boldsymbol{\alpha}_{1\perp} = \mathbf{0}$. Thus, an *unrestricted constant* term in the VAR model will allow for a quadratic trend in $\mathbf{x}_t$ so we need to restrict the $\boldsymbol{\alpha}_{2\perp}$ component of $\boldsymbol{\mu}_0$ to avoid this. However, the $\boldsymbol{\alpha}_{2\perp}$ component of $\boldsymbol{\mu}_0$ will not be restricted to zero but to be equal with opposite sign to the quadratic trend component arising from $\boldsymbol{\alpha}\boldsymbol{\rho}_0 t \neq \mathbf{0}$. This will be discussed in more detail below.

The effect of cumulating the constant term once is given by:

$$\begin{aligned}\mathbf{C}_1\sum_{j=1}^{t}\boldsymbol{\mu}_0 &= (\boldsymbol{\omega}_0\boldsymbol{\alpha}' + \boldsymbol{\omega}_1\boldsymbol{\alpha}'_{\perp 1} + \boldsymbol{\omega}_2\boldsymbol{\alpha}'_{\perp 2})\sum_{j=1}^{t}(\boldsymbol{\alpha}\boldsymbol{\gamma}_0 + \boldsymbol{\alpha}_{1\perp}\boldsymbol{\gamma}_1 + \boldsymbol{\alpha}_{2\perp}\boldsymbol{\gamma}_2)\\ &= [(\boldsymbol{\omega}_0\underbrace{\boldsymbol{\alpha}'\boldsymbol{\alpha}\boldsymbol{\gamma}_0}_{\widetilde{\gamma_0}} + \boldsymbol{\omega}_1\underbrace{\boldsymbol{\alpha}'_{\perp 1}\boldsymbol{\alpha}_{1\perp}\boldsymbol{\gamma}_1}_{\widetilde{\gamma_1}} + \boldsymbol{\omega}_2\underbrace{\boldsymbol{\alpha}'_{\perp 2}\boldsymbol{\alpha}_{2\perp}\boldsymbol{\gamma}_2}_{\widetilde{\gamma_2}})]t \end{aligned} \tag{17.13}$$

as $\boldsymbol{\alpha}'\boldsymbol{\alpha}_{\perp 1} = \mathbf{0}$, $\boldsymbol{\alpha}'\boldsymbol{\alpha}_{\perp 2} = \mathbf{0}$ and $\boldsymbol{\alpha}'_{\perp 1}\boldsymbol{\alpha}_{2\perp} = \mathbf{0}$. Thus, there will be three different linear trends arising from the $\mathbf{C}_1$ components of the constant term. Section 17.3.2 will discuss in more detail how these trends are related to the rich structure of the $I(2)$ model.

Most applications of the $I(2)$ model are for nominal variables implying that linear trends in the data is a natural starting hypothesis (because average nominal growth rates are generally non-zero). To achieve similarity in the rank test procedure we need to allow for linear trends in all directions of the $I(2)$ model. In particular, this means that we need to allow for trend-stationary relations as a starting hypothesis (Rahbek, Kongsted, and Jørgensen 1999). In such a case $\boldsymbol{\mu}_1 t \neq \mathbf{0}$ so the vector $\boldsymbol{\mu}_1$ needs to be decomposed similarly as the constant term:

$$\boldsymbol{\mu}_1 = \boldsymbol{\alpha}\boldsymbol{\rho}_0 + \boldsymbol{\alpha}_{1\perp}\boldsymbol{\rho}_1 + \boldsymbol{\alpha}_{2\perp}\boldsymbol{\rho}_2.$$

The effect of cumulating the linear trend term twice is given by:

$$\begin{aligned}\mathbf{C}_2\sum_{j=1}^{t}\sum_{i=1}^{j}\boldsymbol{\mu}_1 i &= \sum_{j=1}^{t}\sum_{i=1}^{j}\tilde{\boldsymbol{\beta}}_{\perp 2}\boldsymbol{\alpha}'_{\perp 2}(\boldsymbol{\alpha}\boldsymbol{\rho}_0+\boldsymbol{\alpha}_{1\perp}\boldsymbol{\rho}_1+\boldsymbol{\alpha}_{2\perp}\boldsymbol{\rho}_2)i\\ &= \sum_{j=1}^{t}\sum_{i=1}^{j}\tilde{\boldsymbol{\beta}}_{\perp 2}\boldsymbol{\alpha}'_{\perp 2}\underbrace{\boldsymbol{\alpha}_{2\perp}\boldsymbol{\rho}_2}_{=0}i. \end{aligned} \tag{17.14}$$

Thus, unless we restrict $\boldsymbol{\alpha}_{2\perp}\boldsymbol{\rho}_2 = \mathbf{0}$ we shall have cubic trends in the data. The $I(2)$ procedure in CATS imposes this restriction. The effect of cumulating the linear trend term once is given by:

$$\begin{aligned}\mathbf{C}_1\sum_{j=1}^{t}\boldsymbol{\mu}_1 j &= \sum_{j=1}^{t}(\boldsymbol{\omega}_0\boldsymbol{\alpha}'+\boldsymbol{\omega}_1\boldsymbol{\alpha}'_{\perp 1}+\boldsymbol{\omega}_2\boldsymbol{\alpha}'_{\perp 2})(\boldsymbol{\alpha}\boldsymbol{\rho}_0+\boldsymbol{\alpha}_{1\perp}\boldsymbol{\rho}_1+\boldsymbol{\alpha}_{2\perp}\boldsymbol{\rho}_2)j\\ &= \sum_{j=1}^{t}(\boldsymbol{\omega}_0\boldsymbol{\alpha}'\underbrace{\boldsymbol{\alpha}\boldsymbol{\rho}_0}_{\neq 0}+\boldsymbol{\omega}_1\boldsymbol{\alpha}'_{\perp 1}\underbrace{\boldsymbol{\alpha}_{1\perp}\boldsymbol{\rho}_1}_{=0}+\boldsymbol{\omega}_2\boldsymbol{\alpha}'_{\perp 2}\underbrace{\boldsymbol{\alpha}_{2\perp}\boldsymbol{\rho}_2}_{=0})j. \end{aligned} \tag{17.15}$$

We note that all three $\mathbf{C}_1$ components of the linear trend will generate quadratic trends in the data. Based on (17.14) we already know that $\boldsymbol{\alpha}_{2\perp}\boldsymbol{\rho}_2 = \mathbf{0}$. Unless we are willing to accept linear trends in $\boldsymbol{\alpha}'_{\perp 1}\Delta\mathbf{x}_t$,[2] we should also restrict $\boldsymbol{\alpha}_{1\perp}\boldsymbol{\rho}_1 = \mathbf{0}$. This leaves us with the $\boldsymbol{\alpha}$ component of $\mathbf{C}_1$ which cannot be set to zero, because $\boldsymbol{\alpha}\boldsymbol{\rho}_0 \neq \mathbf{0}$ is needed to allow for a linear trend in $\boldsymbol{\beta}'\mathbf{x}_t$. The problem is that a linear trend in a polynomially cointegrating relation, unless restricted in some way, generates the quadratic trend in $\mathbf{x}_t$ we wanted to avoid from the outset. However, this can be solved by noticing that $\boldsymbol{\alpha}_{2\perp}\boldsymbol{\gamma}_2 \neq \mathbf{0}$ in (17.12) also generates a quadratic trend in $\mathbf{x}_t$, so that by restricting $\boldsymbol{\omega}_0\boldsymbol{\alpha}'\boldsymbol{\alpha}\boldsymbol{\rho}_0 = -\tilde{\boldsymbol{\beta}}_{\perp 2}\boldsymbol{\alpha}'_{\perp 2}\boldsymbol{\alpha}_{2\perp}\boldsymbol{\gamma}_2$ the two trend components cancel and there will be no quadratic trends in the data. The trend-stationary (multi)cointegration relations in Rahbek, Kongsted, and Jørgensen (1999) was estimated subject to this constraint. In Section 17.3.2 we shall demonstrate another solution to this problem based on the ML formulation.

To summarize: To avoid quadratic and cubic trends in the $I(2)$ model we need to impose altogether three restrictions: two zero restrictions, $\boldsymbol{\alpha}_{2\perp}\boldsymbol{\rho}_2 = \mathbf{0}$ and $\boldsymbol{\alpha}_{1\perp}\boldsymbol{\rho}_1 = \mathbf{0}$ and the restriction $\boldsymbol{\omega}_0\boldsymbol{\alpha}'\boldsymbol{\alpha}\boldsymbol{\rho}_0 = -\tilde{\boldsymbol{\beta}}_{\perp 2}\boldsymbol{\alpha}'_{\perp 2}\boldsymbol{\alpha}_{2\perp}\boldsymbol{\gamma}_2$.

17.2.2 Restricting a broken trend and the dummy variables

The effect of a shift dummy and a broken linear trend on the data generating process is similar to the constant and the trend, except that a differenced shift dummy becomes a blip dummy, whereas a differenced constant is zero. Thus, an unrestricted permanent blip dummy, such as $\mathbf{D}_p83.1_t = \Delta\mathbf{D}_s83.1_t$, in (17.1) is consistent with a blip in the

[2] A linear trend in $\boldsymbol{\alpha}'_{\perp 1}\Delta\mathbf{x}_t$ would imply that inflation rate, say, is allowed to grow with a linear trend and, thus, prices with a quadratic trend. It would be hard to argue for such a specification except, possibly, as a local approximation.

acceleration rates, $\Delta^2\mathbf{x}_t$, a level shift in the differences, $\Delta\mathbf{x}_t$, and a broken linear trend in the variables, $\mathbf{x}_t$. As we do not know *a priori* whether the level shift in the differences will cancel in $\boldsymbol{\tau}'\Delta\mathbf{x}_t$ and/or in $\boldsymbol{\delta}'\Delta\mathbf{x}_t$ (see Section 17.3.2), or whether the broken linear trend cancels in $\boldsymbol{\beta}'\mathbf{x}_t$, we need from the outset to include a shift dummy and a broken linear trend in (17.1). However, to avoid undesirable effects, the coefficients to the shift dummy and the broken linear trend need to be appropriately restricted.

The effect of including an unrestricted shift dummy in (17.1), such as $\boldsymbol{\Phi}_s\mathbf{D}_s83.1_t$, is similar to an unrestricted constant and can be decomposed into:

$$\boldsymbol{\Phi}_s = \boldsymbol{\alpha}\boldsymbol{\gamma}_{01} + \boldsymbol{\alpha}_{1\perp}\boldsymbol{\gamma}_{11} + \boldsymbol{\alpha}_{2\perp}\boldsymbol{\gamma}_{21}.$$

Based on the same arguments as for the constant term, $\boldsymbol{\alpha}_{2\perp}\boldsymbol{\gamma}_{21} \neq \mathbf{0}$ will allow for a broken quadratic trend in the variables unless appropriately restricted as discussed below. Furthermore, $\boldsymbol{\alpha}_{1\perp}\boldsymbol{\gamma}_{11} \neq \mathbf{0}$ implies a mean shift in $\Delta\mathbf{x}_t$ which corresponds to a broken linear trend in $\mathbf{x}_t$. In this case, (17.1) also needs a broken linear trend, such as $\boldsymbol{\mu}_{11}t83$, where $t83 = (t-(t_1-1)) \times \mathbf{D}_s83.1_t$, where t_1 is the number of observations up to 1983:1. The broken linear trend coefficient can be decomposed into:

$$\boldsymbol{\mu}_{11} = \boldsymbol{\alpha}\boldsymbol{\rho}_{01} + \boldsymbol{\alpha}_{1\perp}\boldsymbol{\rho}_{11} + \boldsymbol{\alpha}_{2\perp}\boldsymbol{\rho}_{21}, \tag{17.16}$$

where $\boldsymbol{\alpha}_{1\perp}\boldsymbol{\rho}_{11} = \mathbf{0}$ and $\boldsymbol{\alpha}_{2\perp}\boldsymbol{\rho}_{21} = \mathbf{0}$ prevents cubic and quadratic broken linear trends in the variables, whereas $\boldsymbol{\alpha}\boldsymbol{\rho}_{01} \neq \mathbf{0}$ is needed to allow for a cointegration relation to be stationary around a broken linear trend. To avoid quadratic broken linear trends in the variables, the once cumulated part of the $\boldsymbol{\alpha}$ component of $\boldsymbol{\mu}_{11}$, $\boldsymbol{\omega}_0\boldsymbol{\alpha}'\boldsymbol{\alpha}\boldsymbol{\rho}_{01}$ is needed to cancel the twice cumulated part of the $\boldsymbol{\alpha}_{\perp 2}$ component of $\boldsymbol{\Phi}_s$.

Finally, an unrestricted transitory dummy in (17.1) will cumulate once to a blip in the differences and twice to a level shift in the variables. These effects are not as serious as those of an unrestricted blip dummy and an unrestricted shift dummy and we leave it to the interested reader to do the derivations.

The moving average representation of (17.1) describes the variables as a function of stochastic and deterministic trends, stationary components, initial values and deterministic dummy variables. The representation given below is derived under the assumption that $\boldsymbol{\rho}_1 = \boldsymbol{\rho}_2 = \mathbf{0}$ and $\boldsymbol{\omega}_0\boldsymbol{\alpha}'\boldsymbol{\alpha}\boldsymbol{\rho}_0 = -\tilde{\boldsymbol{\beta}}_{\perp 2}\boldsymbol{\alpha}'_{\perp 2}\boldsymbol{\alpha}_{2\perp}\boldsymbol{\gamma}_2$ as well as $\boldsymbol{\rho}_{11} = \boldsymbol{\rho}_{21} = \mathbf{0}$ and $\boldsymbol{\omega}_0\boldsymbol{\alpha}'\boldsymbol{\alpha}\boldsymbol{\rho}_{01} = -\tilde{\boldsymbol{\beta}}_{\perp 2}\boldsymbol{\alpha}'_{\perp 2}\boldsymbol{\alpha}_{2\perp}\boldsymbol{\gamma}_{21}$:

$$\begin{aligned}
\mathbf{x}_t = {} & \mathbf{C}_2\sum_{j=1}^{t}\sum_{i=1}^{j}\boldsymbol{\varepsilon}_i + \mathbf{C}_1\sum_{j=1}^{t}\boldsymbol{\varepsilon}_j + \mathbf{Y}_t + \mathbf{C}_1\boldsymbol{\gamma}_0 t + \boldsymbol{\rho}_0 t + \mathbf{A} + \mathbf{B}t \\
& + \mathbf{C}_2\boldsymbol{\alpha}_{2\perp}\boldsymbol{\gamma}_{21}\sum_{j=1}^{t}\sum_{i=1}^{j}\mathbf{D}_{s,i} + \mathbf{C}_1\boldsymbol{\Phi}_s\sum_{j=1}^{t}\mathbf{D}_{s,j} \\
& + \mathbf{C}_2\boldsymbol{\Phi}_p\sum_{j=1}^{t}\sum_{i=1}^{j}\mathbf{D}_{p,i} + \mathbf{C}_1\boldsymbol{\Phi}_p\sum_{j=1}^{t}\mathbf{D}_{p,j} \\
& + \mathbf{C}_2\boldsymbol{\Phi}_{tr}\sum_{j=1}^{t}\sum_{i=1}^{j}\mathbf{D}_{tr,i} + \mathbf{C}_1\boldsymbol{\Phi}_{tr}\sum_{j=1}^{t}\mathbf{D}_{tr,j}, \quad t = 1, \ldots, T.
\end{aligned} \tag{17.17}$$

As the above discussion demonstrated, the specification of dummies is very complicated in the $I(2)$ model. A correct specification is, however, important as the dummies are likely to strongly affect the model estimates as well as the asymptotic distribution of the rank test.

17.3 ML estimation and some useful parametrizations

Johansen (1997) provided the solution to the full ML estimation problem approximately five years after the two-step estimation procedure. Nielsen and Rahbek (2006) derived the asymptotic distribution of the LR test for cointegration rank and showed that the small sample properties of the LR test is superior to the two-step test. Therefore, subsequent estimates results are based on the ML procedure. Here we shall discuss both procedures; the two-step procedure because it helps to build up the intuition for the complicated $I(2)$ structure, the ML procedure because it seems to be the best available choice.

17.3.1 The two-step procedure

Originally, the $I(2)$ model was estimated based on the two-step procedure discussed in Johansen (1992c). It applies the standard eigenvalue procedure derived for the $I(1)$ model twice, first to estimate the reduced rank of $\mathbf{\Pi}$ ignoring the reduced rank restriction on $\mathbf{\Gamma}$ and then, for given estimates of $\boldsymbol{\alpha}$ and $\boldsymbol{\beta}$, to estimate the reduced rank of $\hat{\boldsymbol{\alpha}}'_{\perp}\mathbf{\Gamma}\hat{\boldsymbol{\beta}}_{\perp}$. In the first step, the reduced rank, $r = \bar{r}$, of $\mathbf{\Pi} = \boldsymbol{\alpha}\boldsymbol{\beta}'$ was determined based on the standard $I(1)$ trace test. In the second step $s_1 = \bar{s}_1$ is determined by solving the reduced rank problem for the matrix, $\hat{\boldsymbol{\alpha}}'_{\perp}\mathbf{\Gamma}\hat{\beta}_{\perp} = \boldsymbol{\xi}\boldsymbol{\eta}'$. Thus, the first step decomposes the vector process into r cointegrating relations and $p - r$ common stochastic trends and the second step decomposes the latter into first order stochastic trends (s_1) and second order stochastic trends ($p - r - s_1 = s_2$). The intuition of this procedure was already demonstrated in Chapter 16. It showed that the implications of $\mathbf{x}_t \sim I(2)$ for the concentrated model, $\mathbf{R}_{0t} = \boldsymbol{\alpha}\boldsymbol{\beta}'\mathbf{R}_{1t} + \boldsymbol{\varepsilon}_t$, is that $\mathbf{R}_{0t} \sim I(0)$ and $\mathbf{R}_{1t} \sim I(2)$, but $\boldsymbol{\beta}'\mathbf{R}_{1t} \sim I(0)$. Hence, the estimate of $\boldsymbol{\beta}$ is super-superconsistent because the linear combination $\boldsymbol{\beta}'\mathbf{R}_{1t}$ transforms the process from $I(2)$ all the way down to $I(0)$. Therefore, $\boldsymbol{\beta}$ and $\boldsymbol{\alpha}$ are likely to be quite precisely estimated in the first step, at least for reasonably large T providing a justification for considering the estimates $\hat{\boldsymbol{\beta}}$ and $\hat{\boldsymbol{\alpha}}$ as fixed matrices in the second step. But, because the first step estimation procedure ignores the restriction(s) on the $\mathbf{\Gamma}$ matrix given by (17.7), the estimates of $\boldsymbol{\alpha}$ and $\boldsymbol{\beta}$ in the first step are not full ML estimates.

17.3.2 The ML procedure

The full ML procedure derived in Johansen (1997) exploits the fact that the $I(2)$ model contains $p - s_2$ cointegration relations of which the r relations, $\boldsymbol{\beta}'\mathbf{x}_t \sim I(1)$, can become stationary by polynomial cointegration, $\boldsymbol{\beta}'\mathbf{x}_t + \boldsymbol{\psi}'\Delta\mathbf{x}_t \sim I(0)$, and the s_1 relations, $\boldsymbol{\beta}'_{\perp 1}\mathbf{x}_t \sim I(1)$, can become stationary by differencing, $\boldsymbol{\beta}'_{\perp 1}\Delta\mathbf{x}_t \sim I(0)$. Thus, $\boldsymbol{\tau} = (\boldsymbol{\beta}, \boldsymbol{\beta}_{\perp 1})$ define $r + s_1 = p - s_2$ directions in which the process is cointegrated from $I(2)$ to $I(1)$. This means that the space spanned by $\boldsymbol{\tau} = (\boldsymbol{\beta}, \boldsymbol{\beta}_{\perp 1})$ can be determined by solving just one reduced rank regression, after which the vector space can be separated into $\boldsymbol{\beta}$ and $\boldsymbol{\beta}_{\perp 1}$. However, this necessitates a reparametrization of the $I(2)$ model. The following parametrization (here extended with the deterministic components discussed above) was suggested by Johansen (1997):

$$\underbrace{\Delta^2\mathbf{x}_t}_{I(0)} = \boldsymbol{\alpha}\underbrace{(\boldsymbol{\rho}'\underbrace{\tilde{\boldsymbol{\tau}}'\tilde{\mathbf{x}}_{t-1}}_{I(1)} + \underbrace{\tilde{\boldsymbol{\psi}}'\Delta\tilde{\mathbf{x}}_{t-1}}_{I(1)})}_{I(0)} + \boldsymbol{\omega}'\underbrace{\tilde{\boldsymbol{\tau}}'\Delta\tilde{\mathbf{x}}_{t-1}}_{I(0)} + \boldsymbol{\Phi}_p\mathbf{D}_{p,t} + \boldsymbol{\Phi}_{tr}\mathbf{D}_{tr,t} + \boldsymbol{\varepsilon}_t,$$

$$\boldsymbol{\varepsilon}_t \sim N_p(\mathbf{0}, \boldsymbol{\Omega}\ ), \quad t = 1, \ldots, T \qquad (17.18)$$

where $\boldsymbol{\rho} = (\mathbf{I}, \mathbf{0})$ is a $(r + s_1) \times r$ selection matrix designed to pick out the r cointegration vectors $\boldsymbol{\beta}'\mathbf{x}_t$ (so that $\boldsymbol{\rho}'\boldsymbol{\tau}' = \boldsymbol{\beta}'$), $\boldsymbol{\psi}' = -(\boldsymbol{\alpha}'\boldsymbol{\Omega}^{-1}\boldsymbol{\alpha}\ )^{-1}\boldsymbol{\alpha}'\boldsymbol{\Omega}^{-1}\boldsymbol{\Gamma}$, $\boldsymbol{\omega}' = -\boldsymbol{\Omega}\boldsymbol{\alpha}_\perp(\boldsymbol{\alpha}'_\perp\boldsymbol{\Omega}\boldsymbol{\alpha}_\perp)^{-1}(\boldsymbol{\alpha}'_\perp\boldsymbol{\Gamma}\bar{\boldsymbol{\beta}}, \boldsymbol{\xi})$, $\boldsymbol{\rho}'\tilde{\boldsymbol{\tau}}' = [\boldsymbol{\beta}', \boldsymbol{\rho}_0, \boldsymbol{\rho}_{01}]$, $\tilde{\boldsymbol{\psi}}' = [\boldsymbol{\psi}', \boldsymbol{\gamma}_0, \boldsymbol{\gamma}_{01}]$, $\tilde{\mathbf{x}}'_t = [\mathbf{x}'_t, t, t83]$ and $\Delta\tilde{\mathbf{x}}'_t = [\Delta\mathbf{x}'_t, 1, Ds831]$.

The relations $\tilde{\boldsymbol{\tau}}'\Delta\tilde{\mathbf{x}}_t$ define the $p - s_2$ stationary relations between the growth rates, of which r correspond $\boldsymbol{\beta}'\Delta\mathbf{x}_t + \boldsymbol{\rho}_0 + \boldsymbol{\rho}_{01}Ds831$ and s_1 to $\boldsymbol{\beta}'_{\perp 1}\Delta\mathbf{x}_t + \tilde{\boldsymbol{\gamma}}_0 + \tilde{\boldsymbol{\gamma}}_{01}Ds831$. In some cases they might be given an interpretation as medium run steady-state relations. Based on an iterative estimation algorithm, $\boldsymbol{\alpha}$ and $\boldsymbol{\beta}$ are estimated subject to the reduced rank restriction(s) (17.7) on the $\boldsymbol{\Gamma}$ matrix. This is the reason why the estimates of $\boldsymbol{\alpha}$ and $\boldsymbol{\beta}$ based on the ML procedure can differ to some degree from the estimates based on the $I(1)$ model.

The FIML estimates of $\boldsymbol{\tau} = (\boldsymbol{\beta}, \boldsymbol{\beta}_{\perp 1})$ are obtained using an iterative procedure which at each step delivers the solution of just one reduced rank problem. In this case the eigenvectors are the estimates of the $CI(2, 1)$ relations, $\boldsymbol{\tau}'\mathbf{x}_t$, among the variables $\mathbf{x}_t$, i.e. they give a decomposition of the vector $\mathbf{x}_t$ into the $p - s_2$ directions $\boldsymbol{\tau} = (\boldsymbol{\beta}, \boldsymbol{\beta}_{\perp 1})$ in which the process is $I(1)$ and the s_2 directions $\boldsymbol{\tau}_\perp = \boldsymbol{\beta}_{\perp 2}$ in which it is $I(2)$.

The matrix $\boldsymbol{\psi}$ in (17.18) does not make a distinction between stationary and non-stationary components in $\Delta\mathbf{x}_t$. For example, when $\mathbf{x}_t$ contains variables which are $I(2)$ (such as nominal money and prices in the Danish data) as well as $I(1)$ (such as nominal interest rates) then some of the differenced variables picked up by $\boldsymbol{\psi}$ will be $I(0)$. As the latter do not contain any stochastic $I(1)$ trends, they are by definition excludable from the polynomially cointegrated relations. The idea behind the parametrization in Paruolo and Rahbek (1999) was to express the polynomially cointegrated relations exclusively in terms of the $I(1)$ differenced variables by noticing that

$$\boldsymbol{\psi}'\Delta\mathbf{x}_{t-1} = \boldsymbol{\psi}'(\bar{\boldsymbol{\tau}}\boldsymbol{\tau}' + \bar{\boldsymbol{\tau}}_\perp\boldsymbol{\tau}'_\perp)\Delta\mathbf{x}_{t-1}$$

so that (17.18) can be reformulated as:

$$\underbrace{\Delta^2 \mathbf{x}_t}_{I(0)} = \boldsymbol{\alpha}\underbrace{\underbrace{\{[\boldsymbol{\beta}', \boldsymbol{\rho}_0, \boldsymbol{\rho}_{01}]\}\begin{bmatrix} \mathbf{x}_{t-1} \\ t \\ t83 \end{bmatrix}}_{I(1)} + \underbrace{[\boldsymbol{\delta}', \gamma_0, \gamma_{01}]\begin{bmatrix} \Delta\mathbf{x}_{t-1} \\ c \\ D_s831_{t-1} \end{bmatrix}}_{I(1)}}_{I(0)}$$

$$+ \boldsymbol{\zeta}\underbrace{\begin{bmatrix} \boldsymbol{\beta}', \boldsymbol{\rho}_0, \boldsymbol{\rho}_{01} \\ \boldsymbol{\beta}'_{\perp 1}, \tilde{\gamma}_0, \tilde{\gamma}_{01} \end{bmatrix}\begin{bmatrix} \Delta\mathbf{x}_{t-1} \\ c \\ D_s831_{t-1} \end{bmatrix}}_{I(0)} \tag{17.19}$$

$$+ \boldsymbol{\Phi}_p \mathbf{D}_{p,t} + \boldsymbol{\Phi}_{tr}\mathbf{D}_{tr,t} + \boldsymbol{\varepsilon}_t,$$
$$\boldsymbol{\varepsilon}_t \sim N_p(\mathbf{0}, \boldsymbol{\Omega}\ ), \quad t = 1, \ \dots\ , T$$

where $\boldsymbol{\delta}' = \boldsymbol{\psi}'\bar{\boldsymbol{\tau}}_{\perp}\boldsymbol{\tau}'_{\perp}$ and $\boldsymbol{\zeta}' = \boldsymbol{\omega}' + \boldsymbol{\psi}'\bar{\boldsymbol{\tau}}$. Note that the parametrization in (17.18) and (17.19) defines the $I(2)$ model directly in terms of stationary components contrary to the two-stage parametrization (17.1) where $\boldsymbol{\Gamma}\Delta\mathbf{x}_t$ is non-stationary and cannot easily be reformulated into a stationary expression. Note also that the ML parametrization avoids the problem of quadratic trends by restricting the constant term and linear trend to the various cointegration relations.

It can finally be noted that the crucial estimates are $\boldsymbol{\tau} = (\boldsymbol{\beta}, \boldsymbol{\beta}_{\perp 1})$ independently of whether we use the ML or the two-step procedure. This is because for given values of these it is possible to derive the remaining estimates of $(\boldsymbol{\alpha}, \boldsymbol{\alpha}_{\perp 1}, \boldsymbol{\alpha}_{\perp 2}, \boldsymbol{\beta}_{\perp 2})$. Furthermore, when $r > s_2$, it is possible to further decompose $\boldsymbol{\beta}$ and $\boldsymbol{\alpha}$ into $\boldsymbol{\beta} = \{\boldsymbol{\beta}_0, \boldsymbol{\beta}_1\}$ and $\boldsymbol{\alpha} = \{\boldsymbol{\alpha}_0, \boldsymbol{\alpha}_1\}$ where $\boldsymbol{\beta}'_0\mathbf{x}_t$ defines $r_0 = r - s_2$ directly stationary $CI(2,2)$ relations (cointegrating from $I(2)$ to $I(0)$) and $\boldsymbol{\beta}'_1\mathbf{x}_t$ defines s_2 polynomially cointegrating relations, i.e. cointegration relations that can only become stationary with the help of the differenced process.

17.3.3 Decomposing the Γ and the Π matrix

It is useful to see how the formulation (17.19) relates to the usual VAR formulation (17.1). Relying on results in Johansen (1997) the levels and difference components of model (17.1) can be decomposed as:

$$\begin{aligned} \boldsymbol{\Gamma}\Delta\mathbf{x}_{t-1} + \boldsymbol{\Pi}\mathbf{x}_{t-1} = {} & (\boldsymbol{\Gamma}\overline{\boldsymbol{\beta}})\underbrace{\boldsymbol{\beta}'\Delta\mathbf{x}_{t-1}}_{I(0)} \\ & + (\boldsymbol{\alpha}\overline{\boldsymbol{\alpha}}'\boldsymbol{\Gamma}\overline{\boldsymbol{\beta}}_{\perp 1} + \boldsymbol{\alpha}_{\perp 1})\underbrace{\boldsymbol{\beta}'_{\perp 1}\Delta\mathbf{x}_{t-1}}_{I(0)} \\ & + (\boldsymbol{\alpha}\overline{\boldsymbol{\alpha}}'\boldsymbol{\Gamma}\overline{\boldsymbol{\beta}}_{\perp 2})\underbrace{\boldsymbol{\beta}'_{\perp 2}\Delta\mathbf{x}_{t-1}}_{I(1)} \\ & + \boldsymbol{\alpha}\underbrace{\boldsymbol{\beta}'\mathbf{x}_{t-1}}_{I(1)} \end{aligned} \tag{17.20}$$

where $\overline{\boldsymbol{\beta}} = \boldsymbol{\beta}(\boldsymbol{\beta}'\boldsymbol{\beta})^{-1}$ and $\overline{\boldsymbol{\alpha}}$ is similarly defined.

As shown in Johansen (1997), the $\boldsymbol{\Gamma}$ matrix can be decomposed into three parts

$$\boldsymbol{\Gamma} = (\boldsymbol{\Gamma}\overline{\boldsymbol{\beta}})\boldsymbol{\beta}' + (\boldsymbol{\alpha}\overline{\boldsymbol{\alpha}}'\boldsymbol{\Gamma}\overline{\boldsymbol{\beta}}_{\perp 1} + \boldsymbol{\alpha}_{\perp 1})\,\boldsymbol{\beta}'_{\perp 1} + (\boldsymbol{\alpha}\overline{\boldsymbol{\alpha}}'\boldsymbol{\Gamma}\overline{\boldsymbol{\beta}}_{\perp 2})\,\boldsymbol{\beta}'_{\perp 2}$$

describing three types of linear relations between growth rates, $\boldsymbol{\beta}'\Delta\mathbf{x}_{t-1}$, $\boldsymbol{\beta}'_{\perp 1}\Delta\boldsymbol{x}_{t-1}$ and $\boldsymbol{\beta}'_{\perp 2}\Delta\mathbf{x}_{t-1}$, with the corresponding adjustment coefficients given in soft brackets.

1. The first two components in (17.20), $(\boldsymbol{\Gamma}\overline{\boldsymbol{\beta}})\boldsymbol{\beta}'\Delta\mathbf{x}_{t-1}$ and $(\boldsymbol{\alpha}\overline{\boldsymbol{\alpha}}'\boldsymbol{\Gamma}\overline{\boldsymbol{\beta}}_{\perp 1} + \boldsymbol{\alpha}_{\perp 1})\,\boldsymbol{\beta}'_{\perp 1}\boldsymbol{\Delta}\boldsymbol{x}_{t-1}$, describe stationary medium-run relations between the growth rates.
2. The third component, $(\boldsymbol{\alpha}\overline{\boldsymbol{\alpha}}'\boldsymbol{\Gamma}\overline{\boldsymbol{\beta}}_{\perp 2})\ \boldsymbol{\beta}'_{\perp 2}\boldsymbol{\Delta}\boldsymbol{x}_{t-1}$, is $I(1)$ and has to be combined with $\boldsymbol{\beta}'\mathbf{x}_{t-1}$ to yield a stationary polynomially cointegrated relation, $\boldsymbol{\alpha}(\boldsymbol{\beta}'\mathbf{x}_{t-1} + (\overline{\boldsymbol{\alpha}}'\boldsymbol{\Gamma}\overline{\boldsymbol{\beta}}_{\perp 2})\,\boldsymbol{\beta}'_{\perp 2}\Delta\mathbf{x}_{t-1}) \sim I(0)$.

It is now easy to see how the parametrization in (17.1) relates to the one in (17.18):

$$\boldsymbol{\alpha}(\boldsymbol{\beta}'\mathbf{x}_{t-1} + (\overline{\boldsymbol{\alpha}}'\boldsymbol{\Gamma}\overline{\boldsymbol{\beta}}_{\perp 2})\,\boldsymbol{\beta}'_{\perp 2}\Delta\mathbf{x}_{t-1}) = \boldsymbol{\alpha}(\boldsymbol{\beta}'\mathbf{x}_{t-1} + \boldsymbol{\delta}'\Delta\mathbf{x}_{t-1}) \tag{17.21}$$

and

$$(\boldsymbol{\Gamma}\overline{\boldsymbol{\beta}})\boldsymbol{\beta}'\Delta\mathbf{x}_{t-1} + (\boldsymbol{\alpha}\overline{\boldsymbol{\alpha}}'\boldsymbol{\Gamma}\overline{\boldsymbol{\beta}}_{\perp 1} + \boldsymbol{\alpha}_{\perp 1})\,\boldsymbol{\beta}'_{\perp 1}\boldsymbol{\Delta}\mathbf{x}_{t-1} = \boldsymbol{\zeta}'\boldsymbol{\tau}'\Delta\mathbf{x}_{t-1}. \tag{17.22}$$

We note that the $I(2)$ model allows the VAR variables to adjust to a medium-run equilibrium error, $\boldsymbol{\beta}'_{\perp 1}\Delta\mathbf{x}_{t-1}$, to a change in the long-run 'static equilibrium' error, $\boldsymbol{\beta}'\Delta\mathbf{x}_{t-1}$, and to the long-run 'dynamic equilibrium' error, $\boldsymbol{\beta}'\mathbf{x}_{t-1} + \boldsymbol{\delta}\Delta x_{t-1}$. In this sense, the $I(2)$ model offers a much richer dynamic adjustment structure than the $I(1)$ model.

Finally we note that when $r > s_2$ the long-run matrix $\boldsymbol{\Pi}$ can be expressed as the sum of the two levels components measured by:

$$\boldsymbol{\Pi} = \boldsymbol{\alpha}_0\boldsymbol{\beta}'_0 + \boldsymbol{\alpha}_1\boldsymbol{\beta}'_1$$

where $\boldsymbol{\beta}'_0\mathbf{x}_{t-1}$ define $r - s_2$ directly stationary $CI(2,2)$ relations, whereas $\boldsymbol{\beta}'_1\mathbf{x}_{t-1}$ define s_2 non-stationary $CI(2,1)$ cointegrating relations which needs to be combined with the differenced process to become stationary through polynomial cointegration.

Thus, the $I(2)$ model can distinguish between the $CI(2,1)$ relations between levels $\{\boldsymbol{\beta}'\mathbf{x}_t, \boldsymbol{\beta}'_{\perp 1}\mathbf{x}_t\}$, the $CI(1,1)$ relations between levels and differences $\{\boldsymbol{\beta}'\mathbf{x}_t + \boldsymbol{\delta}'\Delta\mathbf{x}_t\}$, and finally the $CI(1,1)$ relations between differences $\{\boldsymbol{\tau}'\Delta\mathbf{x}_t\}$. As a consequence, when discussing the economic interpretation of these components, we need to modify the generic concept of 'long-run' steady-state relations accordingly. We shall here interpret

- $\boldsymbol{\beta}'\mathbf{x}_t + \boldsymbol{\delta}'\Delta\mathbf{x}_t$ as r *dynamic long-run equilibrium relations*, or alternatively when $r > s_2$
  - $\boldsymbol{\beta}'_0\mathbf{x}_t$ as $r - s_2$ *static long-run equilibrium relations*, and
  - $\boldsymbol{\beta}'_1\mathbf{x}_t + \boldsymbol{\delta}'_1\Delta\mathbf{x}_t$ as s_1 *dynamic long-run equilibrium relations*;
- $\boldsymbol{\tau}'\Delta\mathbf{x}_t$ as *medium-run equilibrium relations.*

17.4 Estimating the $I(2)$ model

As already discussed, a correct specification of the deterministic components is necessary to get reliable estimates in the $I(2)$ model. Unfortunately, in many cases there is no clear answer to the question whether one should model a change in the trend, say, deterministically or stochastically. The two alternative specifications of the deterministic components in Chapter 16 essentially differed with respect to the trend component. The first one allowed a broken linear trend to be in the cointegration relations, $\boldsymbol{\beta}'\mathbf{x}_t$, whereas the second one assumed that the broken linear trend cancelled in $\boldsymbol{\beta}'\mathbf{x}_t$. Because the model version with a broken linear trend in $\boldsymbol{\beta}'\mathbf{x}_t$ is more general and was a more adequate description of the data we shall exclusively use it to illustrate the various features of the $I(2)$ model. This means that our model will be specified according to (17.19), with $\mathbf{D}_{p,t} = [D_p 831]$ and $\mathbf{D}_{tr,t} = [D_{tr}764_t]$ where $D_{tr}764_t$ corresponds to the permanent dummy D_p764_t in the $I(1)$ model. The transitory value added tax dummy, $D_{tr}754_t$, was not very significant in the $I(2)$ model and was left out altogether.

To summarize: Provided that we are willing to consider broken linear trends in the variables, but no quadratic or cubic trends, then we need to restrict the trend, t, and the broken linear trend, t_{83}, to exclusively enter the $\boldsymbol{\beta}'\mathbf{x}_{t-1}$ relations, and the constant and the shift dummy D_s831_t to exclusively enter the $\boldsymbol{\delta}'\Delta\mathbf{x}_{t-1}$ and $\boldsymbol{\tau}'\Delta\mathbf{x}_{t-1}$ relations, whereas the permanent blip dummy, D_p831_t, and transitory blip dummy, $D_{tr}764_t$, can enter the VAR model unrestrictedly.

17.4.1 Determining the two reduced rank indices

As already mentioned, the number of stationary multicointegrating relations, r, and the number of $I(1)$ trends, s_1, among the common stochastic trends, $p-r$, can be determined by the ML procedure in (Nielsen and Rahbek 2006), where the trace test is calculated for all possible combinations of r and s_1 so that the joint hypothesis (r, s_1) can be tested as explained below.

Table 17.1 reports the ML tests of the joint hypothesis (r, s_1). Because our model has a broken linear trend restricted to be in the cointegration relations (and, therefore, a shift dummy restricted to the differences) the asymptotic trace test distribution provided by CATS is no longer correct. The 95% critical values given in the brackets below the test values have been simulated for a model with a linear broken trend restricted to be in the cointegration relations, $\boldsymbol{\beta}'\mathbf{x}_t$, and a shift dummy restricted to be in $\boldsymbol{\delta}'\Delta\mathbf{x}_t$ using a program developed by Nielsen (2004a).[3] This asymptotic distribution depends on the occurrence of the break, T_{break} in the sample period and the critical test values need to be simulated for a given value of T_{break}/T. In the Danish data the break at 1983 corresponds approximately to $40/120 = 0.33$.

To illustrate the effect of a broken linear trend as opposed to no such break on the asymptotic tables, Table 17.2 reports the 95% quantile of the simulated asymptotic distribution for a model with a linear trend and compares it with the more appropriate table simulated for a broken linear trend. In both cases the trend (broken trend) is restricted to lie in the cointegration relations and a constant (shift dummy) is restricted

[3]Because the effect of the transitory impulse dummy on the asymptotic tables is not likely to be very substantial, the simulated tables have disregarded this feature of the model.

Table 17.1 The trace tests for the model with broken linear trends.

$p-r$	r	The joint ML test of $(r=\bar{r}, s_1=\bar{s}_1)$					
5	0	611.30 [240]	514.39 [207]	378.98 [177]	296.45 [152]	234.00 [130]	185.51 [112]
4	1		355.11 [170]	267.28 [142]	197.50 [119]	145.33 [99]	116.27 [83]
3	2			173.91 [112]	117.13 [90]	86.57 [72]	68.65 [58]
2	3				70.09 [65]	**45.11** [49]	**29.61** [36]
1	4					**20.70** [29]	**9.43** [18]
	s_2	5	4	3	2	1	0

Table 17.2 Approximate tables for the 95% test.

$p-r$	r \ s_1	5	4	3	2	1	0
A linear trend in $\boldsymbol{\beta}'\mathbf{x}_t$							
5	0	206.06	174.29	146.64	123.11	103.75	88.55
4	1		141.53	115.82	94.24	76.84	63.66
3	2			89.02	69.38	53.92	42.77
2	3				48.52	34.98	25.73
1	4					20.02	12.45
A change in the slope of the linear trend in $\beta'\mathbf{x}_t$ at $0.33T$							
5	0	240.4	206.7	177.3	152.1	130.0	112.5
4	1		170.1	142.3	118.8	99.0	83.4
3	2			111.6	89.8	72.0	58.2
2	3				64.6	48.5	36.5
1	4					28.7	18.5

to lie in $\boldsymbol{\delta}'\Delta\mathbf{x}_t$. Comparing the two asymptotic tables shows that the inclusion of a broken linear trend in the cointegration relations has the effect of shifting the tables to the right. The correct table deviates quite significantly from the standard table, implying that the test will be undersized if one ignores the effect of the broken trend.

The test procedure starts with the most restricted model $(r=0, s_1=0, s_2=5)$ in the upper left-hand corner, continues to the end of the first row $(r=0, s_1=5, s_2=0)$, and proceeds similarly row-wise from left to right until the first acceptance. Based on the simulated table the first (borderline) acceptance is at $(r=3, s_1=1, s_2=1)$ which is consistent with the choice we made previously in the $I(1)$ analysis. Because the test statistics in Table 17.2 have not been Bartlett corrected, the p-value for accepting two common stochastic trends is likely to be undersized.

In the present case, the trace test supported our previously preferred choice of $r=3$, consistent with our economic prior. The choice of r is often less straightforward and the arguments in Section 8.5 (for checking all relevant information before making the choice of rank in the $I(1)$ model) are equally relevant in the $I(2)$ model. Similar to the $I(1)$ model, the above sequence of $I(2)$ trace tests is based on the assumption of 'no prior economic hypothesis regarding the rank'. This may not be reasonable considering that a scenario analysis (cf. Chapter 2) suggested one economically plausible hypothesis.

Two independent stochastic trends implies two types of 'permanent' disturbances u_{1t} and u_{2t}, measured for instance by $u_{1t} = \boldsymbol{\alpha}'_{\perp 1}\boldsymbol{\varepsilon}_t$ and $u_{2t} = \boldsymbol{\alpha}'_{\perp 2}\boldsymbol{\varepsilon}_t$ where $\boldsymbol{\varepsilon}_t$ is the vector of residuals from the VAR. As discussed in Chapter 1, u_{1t} and u_{2t} could conceptually be considered a nominal and a real disturbance, respectively. For the $I(2)$ model the number of unit roots for $\{r = 3,\ s_1 = 1 \text{ and } s_2 = 1\}$ is $s_1 + 2s_2 = 3$, i.e. the $I(2)$ trend produces an additional unit root in the model as compared to the $I(1)$ case. Chapter 17 demonstrated the usefulness of this information for the choice of cointegration rank.

Similar to the $I(1)$ analysis it is often a good idea to inspect the graphs of the polynomially cointegrated relations, the number of (near) unit roots in the characteristic polynomial of the VAR, and the t values of $\boldsymbol{\alpha}_i$ before the final choice of r and s_1. Figures 17.1–17.3 show the graphs of $\boldsymbol{\beta}'\mathbf{x}_{t-1} + \boldsymbol{\delta}'\Delta\mathbf{x}_{t-1}$ (upper panel) and $\boldsymbol{\beta}'\mathbf{R}_{2,t} + \boldsymbol{\delta}'\mathbf{R}_{1t}$ (lower panel) where $\mathbf{R}_{2,t}$ and $\mathbf{R}_{1t}$ are given by (17.5) and (17.4). We note that all three polynomially cointegrating relations look very stationary and that the $\mathbf{x}$ and the $\mathbf{R}$ graphs are very similar. The latter can be explained by the fact that our estimates are based on a VAR(2) model. This means that $\boldsymbol{\Gamma}_2 = \mathbf{0}$ in (17.1) and there are no lagged acceleration rate effects to be concentrated out. The coefficients to $\boldsymbol{\alpha}_i$ reported in Table 17.4 indicate significant equilibrium correction in all three polynomially cointegrating relations. The

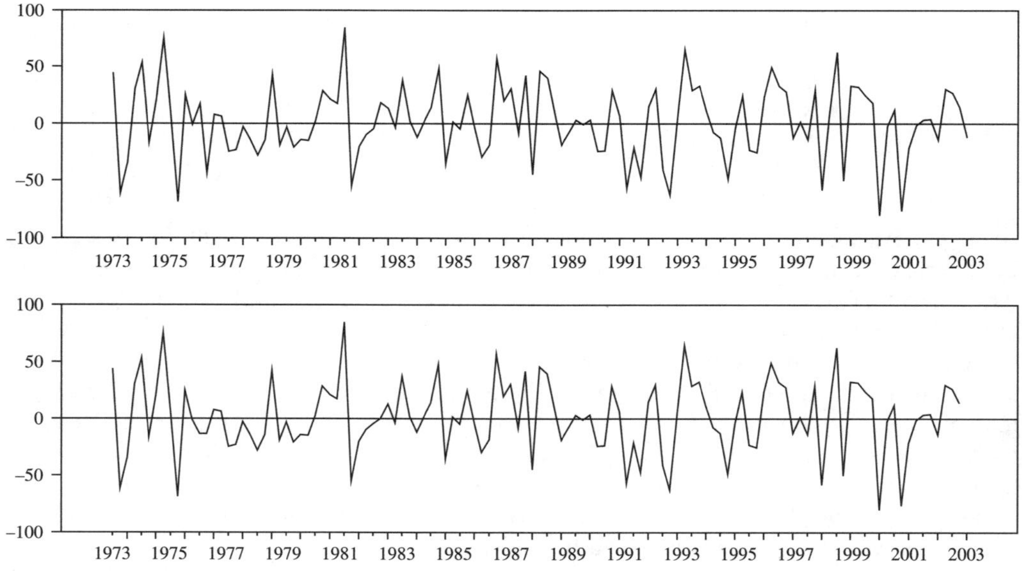

Fig 17.1 The first polynomially cointegrating relation.

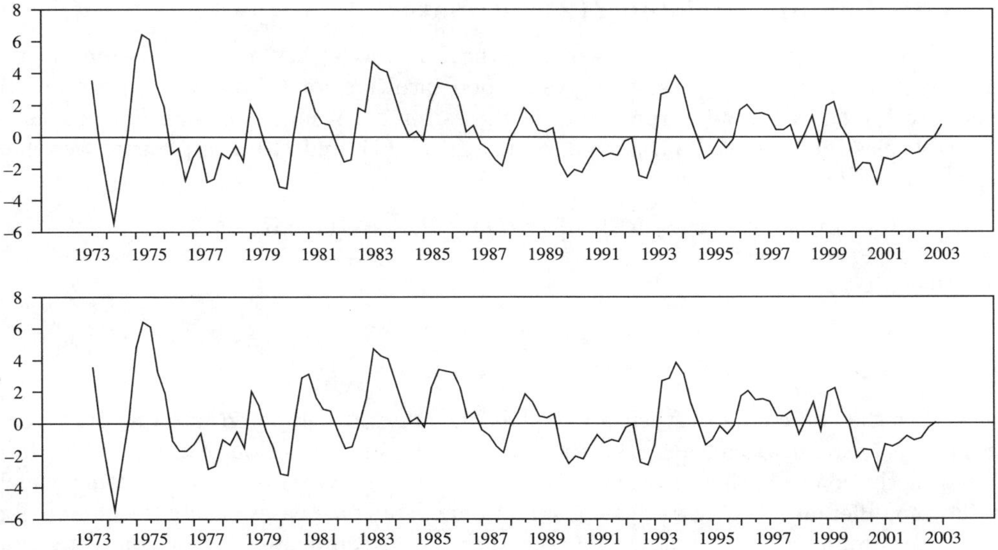

Fig 17.2 The second polynomially cointegrating relation.

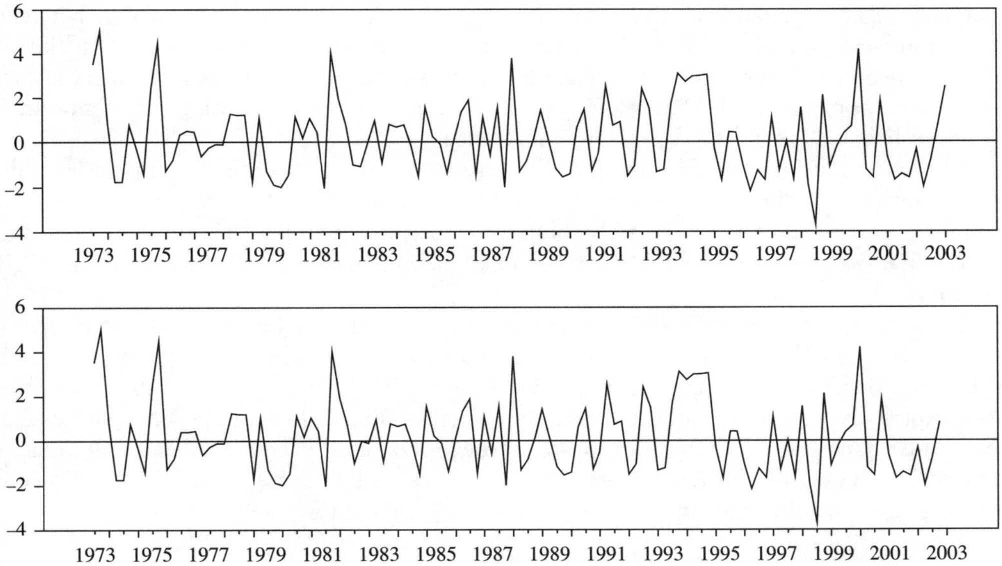

Fig 17.3 The third polynomially cointegrating relation.

largest unrestricted eigenvalue root for $r = 3$ is 0.90 which suggests that one of the common stochastic trends contains an additional (near) unit root. Thus, all the information seems to support $(r = 3, s_1 = 1, s_2 = 1)$ and we shall continue with this choice.

17.4.2 The unrestricted $I(2)$ estimates

As demonstrated in the previous sections, the $I(2)$ model has a rich and complicated structure and it is no easy task to give a good intuition for its many components. To facilitate the subsequent interpretation of the estimated results, we shall first discuss a plausible classification of the Danish data into $I(2)$, $I(1)$, and $I(0)$ components. We shall here assume that:

$$m_t \sim I(2),\ p_t \sim I(2),\ y_t^r \sim I(1),^4\ R_{m,t} \sim I(1),\ R_{b,t} \sim I(1)$$

and that:

$$\underbrace{r = 3}_{r_0=2, r_1=1} \text{ and } \underbrace{p - r}_{s_1=1, s_2=1} = 2.$$

Note that the two common stochastic trends have been decomposed into one $I(1)$ trend and one $I(2)$ trend. Because $r > s_2$, the three cointegration relations can be divided into two directly cointegrating relations and one polynomially cointegrated relation which needs the differenced process to become stationary. In some cases such a decomposition can make economic sense but, in general, there is no compelling reason for restricting the differenced process to enter exclusively in s_2 of the r relations.

The left-hand side of Table 17.3 illustrates the decomposition of $\mathbf{x}_t$ into $\boldsymbol{\tau} = (\boldsymbol{\beta}, \boldsymbol{\beta}_{\perp 1})$ and $\boldsymbol{\tau}_\perp = \boldsymbol{\beta}_{\perp 2}$. This decomposition defines three stationary polynomially cointegrating relations, $\boldsymbol{\beta}_i'\mathbf{x}_t + \boldsymbol{\delta}_i'\Delta\mathbf{x}_t$, $i = 1, \ldots, 3$ and four stationary cointegration relations between the differenced variables, $\boldsymbol{\tau}'\Delta\mathbf{x}_t$. The difference between $\boldsymbol{\beta}'\mathbf{x}_t$ and $\boldsymbol{\beta}_{\perp 1}'\mathbf{x}_t$ is that the latter can only become stationary by differencing, whereas the former can become stationary by polynomial cointegration. Finally, $\boldsymbol{\beta}_{\perp 2}'\mathbf{x}_t \sim I(2)$, is a non-cointegrating relation, which can only become stationary by differencing twice.

The right-hand side of Table 17.3 illustrates the corresponding decomposition into the $\boldsymbol{\alpha}$ and the $\boldsymbol{\alpha}_\perp$ directions, where $\boldsymbol{\alpha}_i$, $i = 1, \ldots, 3$, measure the short-run adjustment coefficients associated with the polynomially cointegrating relations, whereas $\boldsymbol{\alpha}_{\perp 1}$ and $\boldsymbol{\alpha}_{\perp 2}$ define the first and second order stochastic trends as a linear function of the VAR residuals.

Table 17.4 reports the ML estimates of the $I(2)$ components. To obtain standard errors of the estimated $\boldsymbol{\beta}$ coefficients we have imposed two just-identifying restrictions on each of the polynomially cointegrating relations reported in the first part of Table 17.4. The asymptotic distribution of an identified $\hat{\boldsymbol{\beta}}$ is given in Johansen (1997). When discussing the adjustment dynamics with respect to the polynomially cointegrating relations it is useful to interpret the adjustment coefficients $\boldsymbol{\alpha}$ and $\boldsymbol{\delta}$ as two levels of equilibrium correction. As an illustration, consider the following model for the variable $x_{i,t}$:

$$\Delta^2 x_{i,t} = + \cdots + \sum_{j=1}^{r} \alpha_{ij}(\boldsymbol{\delta}_j'\Delta\mathbf{x}_{t-1} + \boldsymbol{\beta}_j'\mathbf{x}_{t-1}) + \cdots \tag{17.23}$$

If $\alpha_{ij}\delta_{ij} < 0$ then the acceleration rates, $\Delta^2 x_{i,t}$, is equilibrium correcting to the changes, $\Delta x_{i,t}$, and if $\delta_{ij}\beta_{ij} > 0$, then the changes, $\Delta x_{i,t}$, are equilibrium correcting to the levels,

[4]The subsequent results will demonstrate that the assumption $y_t^r \sim I(1)$ has to be modified to some extent.

Table 17.3 Decomposing the data vector using the $I(2)$ model.

	The $\boldsymbol{\beta}, \boldsymbol{\beta}_\perp$ decomposition of $\mathbf{x}_t$	The $\boldsymbol{\alpha}, \boldsymbol{\alpha}_\perp$ decomposition
$r = 3$	$[\underbrace{\boldsymbol{\beta}_1'\mathbf{x}_t}_{I(1)} + \underbrace{\boldsymbol{\delta}_1'\Delta\mathbf{x}_t}_{I(1)}] \sim I(0)$	$\boldsymbol{\alpha}_1$: short-run adjustment coefficients
	$[\underbrace{\boldsymbol{\beta}_2'\mathbf{x}_t}_{I(1)} + \underbrace{\boldsymbol{\delta}_2'\Delta\mathbf{x}_t}_{I(1)}] \sim I(0)$	$\boldsymbol{\alpha}_2$: short-run adjustment coefficients
	$[\underbrace{\boldsymbol{\beta}_3'\mathbf{x}_t}_{I(1)} + \underbrace{\boldsymbol{\delta}_3'\Delta\mathbf{x}_t}_{I(1)}] \sim I(0)$	$\boldsymbol{\alpha}_3$: short-run adjustment coefficients
$s_1 = 1$	$\boldsymbol{\beta}_{\perp 1}'\mathbf{x}_t \sim I(1)$	$\boldsymbol{\alpha}_{\perp 1}' \sum_{i=1}^{t} \varepsilon_i$: $I(1)$ stochastic trend
$p - s_2 = 4$	$\boldsymbol{\tau}'\Delta\mathbf{x}_t = (\boldsymbol{\beta}, \boldsymbol{\beta}_{\perp 1})'\Delta\mathbf{x}_t \sim I(0)$	
$s_2 = 1$	$\boldsymbol{\beta}_{\perp 2}'\mathbf{x}_t = \boldsymbol{\tau}_\perp'\mathbf{x}_t \sim I(2)$	$\boldsymbol{\alpha}_{\perp 2}' \sum_{j=1}^{t} \sum_{i=1}^{j} \varepsilon_j$: $I(2)$ stochastic trend

$x_{i,t-1}$. In the interpretation below we shall pay special attention to whether a variable is equilibrium correcting or not as defined above, as this is in general a very important feature of the data.

The first relation has been identified by imposing the real money restriction $(1, -1)$ on nominal money and prices and a $(1, -1)$ restriction on *trend* and *trend83*. The latter restriction implies that money velocity is allowed to have a trend before 1983 and no trend after that date. The estimates of $\boldsymbol{\delta}_1$ suggest that Δm^n and Δy^r are equilibrium correcting to money velocity but, interestingly, not Δp. The estimates of $\boldsymbol{\alpha}_1$ shows that the acceleration rates, $\Delta^2 m^n$, $\Delta^2 p$ and $\Delta^2 y^r$, are all equilibrium correcting. Finally, note that the estimates of $\boldsymbol{\beta}_1$ are broadly consistent with the hypothesis $\mathcal{H}_{13}$ in Chapter 10, describing a stationary money velocity with a mean shift.

The second relation has been identified by imposing a zero restriction on money stock and a $(1, 1)$ restriction on prices and real income ($p + y^r = y^n$). The estimated coefficients suggest that nominal income corrected for a broken linear trend has been negatively related to the nominal bond rate. The estimate of $\boldsymbol{\delta}_2$ suggests equilibrium correction in Δy^r, but again not in Δp. The estimate of $\boldsymbol{\alpha}_2$ shows that real income and the bond rate are equilibrium correcting to this relation.

The third relation imposes two just-identifying zero restrictions on the interest rates and leave the remaining coefficients unrestricted. The estimated coefficients of $\boldsymbol{\beta}_3$ suggest that the price level corrected for a broken linear trend has been negatively related to real income and positively to nominal money. The estimates of $\boldsymbol{\delta}_3$ suggest that Δp is now equilibrium correcting, but not Δm^n and Δy^r. The estimates of $\boldsymbol{\alpha}_3$ indicate that both $\Delta^2 p$ and $\Delta^2 m^n$ are equilibrium correcting.

The $\widehat{\boldsymbol{\beta}}_{\perp 1}'\mathbf{x}_t$ relation is a $CI(2,1)$ cointegrating relation which only can become stationary by differencing. The estimated coefficients suggest that in the medium run, nominal money growth has been negatively related to real income growth and positively

Table 17.4 The $I(0)$, $I(1)$, and $I(2)$ directions of $\boldsymbol{\alpha}$ and $\boldsymbol{\beta}$.

	m^n	p	y^r	R_m	R_b	*trend*	*trend83*	*const.*	*Ds831*
The cointegrating relations $\boldsymbol{\beta}$									
β'_1	**1.0**	**−1.0**	**−1.05**	−21.38	14.97	0.00	−0.00	–	–
			[−7.76]	[−0.51]	[0.54]	[0.02]	[−0.02]		
δ'_1	4.86	3.86	−4.25	0.22	−0.06	–	–	1.05	−0.04
β'_2	0.0	**1.0**	**1.0**	6.33	**17.04**	**−0.03**	**0.03**	–	–
				[1.15]	[5.73]	[−19.74]	[11.40]		
δ'_2	−0.43	−0.43	0.34	−0.02	−0.00	–	–	−5.93	0.21
β'_3	**−0.24**	**1.0**	**0.63**	0.0	0.0	**−0.02**	**0.01**	–	–
	[−2.22]		[9.61]			[−5.20]	[4.63]		
δ'_3	1.05	0.80	−0.93	0.05	−0.01	–	–	−1.88	-0.01
The adjustment coefficients $\boldsymbol{\alpha}$									
$\alpha'_{.1}$	−0.19	−0.02	0.05	−0.00	−0.00				
	[−7.00]	[−1.86]	[2.65]	[−2.67]	[−2.76]				
$\alpha'_{.2}$	−0.23	0.02	−0.15	−0.01	−0.02				
	[−4.25]	[1.02]	[−4.06]	[−3.26]	[−5.11]				
$\alpha'_{.3}$	0.36	−0.26	−0.00	0.01	0.01				
	[3.21]	[−5.85]	[−0.01]	[2.22]	[1.18]				
The orthogonal relations $\boldsymbol{\beta}_\perp$									
$\beta'_{\perp 1}$	1.00	−0.31	0.86	0.00	−0.03	–	–	−0.02	0.00
$\tilde{\beta}'_{\perp 2}$	1.50	1.18	−1.31	0.07	−0.02	–	–	–	–
The common trends $\boldsymbol{\alpha}_\perp$									
$\alpha'_{\perp 1}$	0.00	0.00	**0.00**	−0.00	**−0.05**				
	[1.60]	[0.65]	[1.85]	[−0.54]	[−4.14]				
$\alpha'_{\perp 2}$	−0.02	0.02	−0.01	1.00	−0.07				
	[−1.50]	[0.83]	[−0.67]	[*NA*]	[−0.46]				
$\hat{\sigma}_\varepsilon$	0.0198	0.0076	0.0129	0.0010	0.0013				

to inflation rate:

$$\Delta m_t^n = -0.86\Delta y_t^r + 0.31\Delta p_t + \cdots$$

The interpretation of this relation is not straightforward, but by rewriting it in the equivalent form

$$\Delta m_t^n - \Delta p_t = -0.86\Delta y_t^r - 0.69\Delta p_t + \cdots \tag{17.24}$$

we can reproduce some of the previously found results showing that the growth in real money stock has been countercyclical to the real income growth and the inflation rate. Even though the negative inflation coefficient can be interpreted as a money demand effect, the negative income effect is more puzzling and we conclude, as in the previous chapters, that a structural interpretation is not warranted in this case. We conclude that

$\widehat{\boldsymbol{\beta}}'_{\perp 1}\Delta\mathbf{x}_t$ may be interpreted as a partially specified medium-run steady-state relation which does not make much sense given the present information set.

The estimates of $\tilde{\boldsymbol{\beta}}_{\perp 2}$ give the weights with which the $I(2)$ trend, $\boldsymbol{\alpha}'_{\perp 2}\sum\sum\hat{\varepsilon}_i$, have influenced the variables $\mathbf{x}_t$. Under the assumption that nominal money and prices are $I(2)$ and real income and the interest rates are $I(1)$, we would expect the first two coefficients to be large and significant whereas the remaining three coefficients should be small and not significantly different from zero. Under the additional assumption of long-run price homogeneity we would expect the first two coefficients to be equal with the same sign. In Chapter 16 we already found that price homogeneity in $\boldsymbol{\beta}$ was rejected, so finding the first two coefficients to be (1.5, 1.2) is not surprising. But the finding that real aggregate income has a large and negative coefficient is a puzzling result which needs to be explained.

By re-estimating the model for $\mathbf{x}'_t = [m^n_t, p, y^n_t, R_{m,t}, R_{b,t}]$ which is just a linear transformation of $\mathbf{x}'_t = [m^n_t, p, y^r_t, R_{m,t}, R_{b,t}]$ and, therefore, equivalent from a likelihood point of view we can obtain some interesting results. With nominal income we obtained an estimated value of $\tilde{\boldsymbol{\beta}}'_{\perp,2} = [1.00, 0.91, 0.05, 0.07, 0.00, 0.00]$ suggesting that $\tilde{m}^n_t \sim I(2)$, $\tilde{p} \sim I(2)$ but $\tilde{y}^n_t \sim$I(1), where $\tilde{x}$ stands for 'corrected for a broken linear trend'. Thus, $\tilde{y}^r_t = \tilde{y}^n_t - \tilde{p} \sim I(2)$, because $\tilde{p} \sim I(2)$ dominates $\tilde{y}^n_t \sim I(1)$ in $\tilde{y}^r_t$. From a practical point of view this is a puzzling result. One possibility is that the deterministic broken linear trend in y^n_t allows for too much curve fitting. Another possibility is that the measurements of nominal and real GNE are problematic in some unknown way.

The estimated $\boldsymbol{\alpha}_{\perp 2}$ suggest that it is primarily the twice cumulated empirical shocks to the short-term interest rate which have generated the $I(2)$ stochastic trend in prices, however with a *positive* coefficient. In addition, there seem to be some small *negative* effects from the twice cumulated empirical shocks to nominal money. The estimated coefficients of $\widehat{\boldsymbol{\alpha}}_{\perp 1}$ shows that the cumulated shocks to the bond rate are highly significant and enter the $I(1)$ trend with a negative weight, whereas shocks to the real income are borderline significant but with a positive weight. Thus, the $I(1)$ trend might be interpreted as capturing permanent shocks to the *IS* curve. Since the estimated coefficients are based on the non-standardized VAR residuals their standard deviations are reported in the last row of Table 17.4. We note that the residuals to nominal money, prices and real income are much larger than those to the interest rates.

17.5 Concluding discussion

Altogether the results indicate that the long-run stochastic trend in nominal prices does not derive from shocks to nominal money stock as *a priori* was assumed based on the nominal scenario analysis in Chapter 2. Instead, the nominal $I(2)$ trend seems to derive from unanticipated shocks to the short-term nominal interest rates. The effect of an interest rate shock on the price trend is, however, not consistent with the conventional hypothesis that central banks can bring inflation down by increasing the short-term interest rate. Similar findings have frequently been reported in the literature, the so-called 'price puzzle'.

It is of some interest to compare the estimated common trends from the $I(2)$ model with the estimated common trends from the $I(1)$ model discussed in Chapter 14. First we note that the estimated stochastic trends in Chapter 14 were derived from a VAR model based on an assumption of (a) long-run price homogeneity between nominal money and prices, and (b) long-run exclusion of any broken linear trend in the cointegration relations. Provided that these assumptions had been correct, then the differenced $I(2)$ trend, $\boldsymbol{\alpha}'_{\perp 2}\sum\boldsymbol{\varepsilon}_i = \sum \mathbf{u}_{1,i}$, and the $I(1)$ trend, $\boldsymbol{\alpha}'_{\perp 1}\sum\boldsymbol{\varepsilon}_i = \sum \mathbf{u}_{1i}$, of this chapter would have been roughly the same as the two stochastic $I(1)$ trends of Chapter 14. Even though the results in Table 17.4 are similar to the ones in Table 14.1, the latter seemed to suggest that the nominal stochastic trend is primarily associated with permanent shocks to the long-term interest rate and to some extent to the short-term interest rate, whereas the real trend seemed related to permanent shocks to the real income. The results in Table 17.4 clearly suggest that it is the shocks to the short-term interest rate which are important for the long-run stochastic $I(2)$ trend in prices, whereas the shocks to the bond rate and the real income are important for the $I(1)$ trend. Also the coefficient to the short-term interest rate shocks was large but imprecisely estimated in Table 14.1, whereas in Table 17.4 the shocks to the short-term interest rate seem highly significant. One possible explanation to the statistical imprecision in the $I(1)$ model is that neither long-run price homogeneity, nor long-run exclusion of the broken linear trend turned out to be an acceptable assumption. In the last part of this book we shall argue that the reason for this is related to a regime shift in the Danish economy as a result of deregulating capital movements, which fundamentally changed the functioning of the labour market.

18

Testing hypotheses in the $I(2)$ model

The test procedures to be discussed in this chapter are based on Johansen (2006). They are all based on the ML principle and are similar to the ones discussed in Chapter 10 for the $I(1)$ model. There are, however, some important differences due to the fact that the cointegration relations are now defined by $\boldsymbol{\tau}'\mathbf{x}_t = [\boldsymbol{\beta}, \boldsymbol{\beta}_{\perp 1}]'\mathbf{x}_t$, rather than just by $\boldsymbol{\beta}'\mathbf{x}_t$. A major difficulty is that different distributional results apply for $\boldsymbol{\beta}$ and for $\boldsymbol{\beta}_{\perp 1}$ (Johansen 2006a). This is why it is not possible to derive ML procedures for testing identifying restrictions directly on $\boldsymbol{\tau}'\mathbf{x}_t$, whereas this is possible if we exclusively test $\boldsymbol{\beta}'\mathbf{x}_t$. There are, however, two types of test (none of them identifying) that can be performed on $\boldsymbol{\tau}$: the test of the same restriction on all $\boldsymbol{\tau}$ and the test of a known vector in $\boldsymbol{\tau}$. Tests of restrictions on $\boldsymbol{\delta}$ in the polynomially cointegrating relations are not available in any of these cases. Thus, even though many interesting hypotheses can now be formally tested within the $I(2)$ model, there are still some questions which cannot. The applications in this chapter will illustrate how far we can go within the present framework.

Section 18.1 tests long-run price homogeneity as a restriction on all $CI(2,1)$ relations and discusses additionally medium-run price homogeneity as a restriction on the nominal growth rates. Section 18.2 discusses a variety of hypotheses which were implicitly and/or explicitly assumed to be valid in the previously estimated $I(1)$ model, such as long-run exclusion of the deterministic trend components as well as the hypothesis that $y^r \sim I(1)$. It also investigates the sensitivity of long-run price homogeneity to the specification of deterministic trends in the model. Finally, we illustrate two types of over-identifying restrictions on $\boldsymbol{\beta}$, one which corresponds to the identified structure found in the $I(1)$ analysis and another which allows for deterministic trends in $\boldsymbol{\beta}$. Section 18.3 summarizes the results of the Danish money market model in terms of a data consistent empirical scenario.

18.1 Testing price homogeneity

Long-run price homogeneity plays an important role for the economic interpretation of the results and is one of the fundamental assumptions underlying monetary macroeconomics. Because the nominal to real transformation requires long-run price homogeneity to be valid, it is also econometrically important. Jørgensen (2000), Kongsted (2005) and Kongsted and Nielsen (2004) discuss the case when the nominal-to-real transformation is applied even though long-run price homogeneity is not satisfied and show, among others, that it is likely to seriously distort the trace test and the properties of the $I(1)$ model. Thus, price homogeneity is a crucial concept and rejecting it can have important implications both for the economic and the econometric interpretation of the results.

In this section we shall take a closer look at price homogeneity in the long-run and in the medium-run and discuss how to examine it empirically within the $I(2)$ model.

18.1.1 Long-run price homogeneity

In the $I(2)$ model, long-run price homogeneity can be defined as a zero sum restriction on $\boldsymbol{\tau} = (\boldsymbol{\beta}, \boldsymbol{\beta}_{\perp 1})$. Under the assumption that the $I(2)$ trend is not affecting the real income and the interest rates, long-run price homogeneity for the Danish data can be expressed as:

$$\boldsymbol{\tau} = \begin{bmatrix} \boldsymbol{\beta}_1' \\ \boldsymbol{\beta}_2' \\ \boldsymbol{\beta}_3' \\ \boldsymbol{\beta}_{\perp 1}' \end{bmatrix} = \begin{bmatrix} a_i, -a_i, *, *, *, *, * \\ b_i, -b_i, *, *, *, *, * \\ c_i, -c_i, *, *, *, *, * \\ d_i, -d_i, *, *, *, *, * \end{bmatrix} \tag{18.1}$$

or equivalently as:

$$\boldsymbol{\tau}_{\perp}' = [e, e, 0, 0, 0, 0, 0]. \tag{18.2}$$

Thus, long-run price homogeneity can be tested either as a linear hypothesis on $\boldsymbol{\tau}$ expressed as $\mathbf{R}'\boldsymbol{\tau}_i = 0$, $i = 1, 2, \ldots, p - s_2$, where, for the Danish data, $\mathbf{R}' = [1, 1, 0, 0, 0, 0, 0]$, or as $\boldsymbol{\tau} = \mathbf{H}\boldsymbol{\varphi}$, where $\boldsymbol{\varphi}$ is a $(p1 - s_2) \times p1$ matrix of free coefficients and

$$\mathbf{H} = \begin{bmatrix} 1 & 0 & 0 & 0 & 0 & 0 \\ -1 & 0 & 0 & 0 & 0 & 0 \\ 0 & 1 & 0 & 0 & 0 & 0 \\ 0 & 0 & 1 & 0 & 0 & 0 \\ 0 & 0 & 0 & 1 & 0 & 0 \\ 0 & 0 & 0 & 0 & 1 & 0 \\ 0 & 0 & 0 & 0 & 0 & 1 \end{bmatrix}.$$

The condition for price homogeneity between nominal money and prices in $\boldsymbol{\beta}'\mathbf{x}_t$, described by the first three rows of (18.1), can easily be tested within the standard $I(1)$ procedure. If homogeneity is rejected in $\boldsymbol{\beta}'\mathbf{x}_t$ then it will also be rejected in $\boldsymbol{\tau}'\mathbf{x}_t$. But, even if it is accepted in $\boldsymbol{\beta}'\mathbf{x}_t$, it can, nevertheless, be rejected in $\boldsymbol{\beta}'_{\perp 1}\mathbf{x}_t$. Thus, violation of long-run price homogeneity can be inferred from the $I(1)$ procedure, but accepting it is only possible within the $I(2)$ procedure.

The test of price homogeneity was strongly rejected based on a LR test statistic of 20.44, asymptotically distributed as $\chi^2(4)$. This outcome is just a confirmation of the results in Chapter 16, where price homogeneity of $\boldsymbol{\beta}'\mathbf{x}_t$ was already rejected. Note, however, that applying a Bartlett correction to the test statistic is likely to substantially decrease the test value and, thus, increase the p-value. But even though we might then be able to accept price homogeneity on the 5% level, say, the test sends a signal that price homogeneity is probably not fully satisfied at least in some of the $\boldsymbol{\tau}$ components. Because of its economic and econometric importance we shall try to understand the reason why long-run homogeneity does not seem to obtain empirical support.

A first step of such an assessment is to find out which of the $\boldsymbol{\tau}'\mathbf{x}_t$ relations exhibits the strongest violation of homogeneity. As already discussed in Chapter 16, when $r > 1$ it is in general meaningless to examine the individual $\boldsymbol{\beta}$ vectors for price-homogeneity without taking account of the $\boldsymbol{\alpha}$ coefficients. Because the rows of the $\boldsymbol{\Pi}$ matrix give the $\boldsymbol{\beta}$ relations weighted by the $\boldsymbol{\alpha}$ coefficients, it is useful to begin the analysis of long-run price homogeneity with an examination of the estimated $\boldsymbol{\Pi}$ matrix reported in the upper part of Table 18.1.

As already noted in Chapter 16 the coefficients to money and prices in the first row are almost equal with opposite signs, indicating that nominal money has followed prices one to one, whereas the coefficients in the second row suggest that prices have followed nominal money one to 0.2. Note, however, that this result would be logically inconsistent unless another variable, here real trend-adjusted income (cf. the discussion in Chapter 17), would be empirically $I(2)$. If nominal money and prices had been the only $I(2)$ variables and $s_2 = 1$, then the relationship between money and prices would have been identical in all equations.

The third row shows that nominal trend-adjusted income is negatively related to nominal interest rates. As nominal interest rates are clearly $I(1)$, this is consistent with the previously found result that trend-adjusted nominal income is approximately $I(1)$. The fourth and the fifth row essentially tells us that the short-term, as well as the long-term, interest rate has been negatively related to the level of excess liquidity in the economy.

Thus, the violation of long-run price homogeneity between nominal money and prices seem to be associated with the behaviour of money, prices, and income in the price and the income equation.

18.1.2 Medium-run price homogeneity

The representation in Table 17.3 in the previous chapter differed from the $I(1)$ results by the explicit inclusion of growth rates in the long-run relations. As nominal variables are usually found to be $I(2)$, it is the growth rates of these variables, being $I(1)$, which are of particular interest. Therefore, we also need to understand the relations between the growth rates that can be found in the $\boldsymbol{\Gamma}$ matrix.

Section 17.3.3 demonstrated that the levels component, $\boldsymbol{\Pi}\mathbf{x}_{t-1}$, and the differences component, $\boldsymbol{\Gamma}\Delta\mathbf{x}_{t-1}$, are closely tied together by polynomial cointegration. In addition, $\boldsymbol{\Gamma}\Delta\mathbf{x}_{t-1}$ may contain information about the medium-run relations between growth rates,

Table 18.1 The estimates of the $\mathbf{\Pi}$ and the $\mathbf{\Gamma}$ matrices.

The estimated $\mathbf{\Pi}$ matrix

eq.\var.	m^n	p	y^r	R_m	R_b	*trend83*	*trend*
$\Delta^2 m^n$	**−0.27** [−5.48]	**0.32** [2.85]	**0.20** [2.62]	**2.55** [5.27]	**−6.65** [−5.65]	−0.00 [−1.48]	0.00 [0.53]
$\Delta^2 p_y$	**0.04** [2.18]	**−0.22** [−5.07]	**−0.12** [−4.10]	**0.56** [2.98]	0.07 [0.15]	**−0.00** [−4.81]	**0.00** [5.64]
$\Delta^2 y^r$	0.05 [1.43]	**−0.19** [−2.62]	**−0.20** [−3.96]	**−1.98** [−6.08]	**−1.78** [−2.24]	**−0.00** [−4.58]	**0.01** [4.04]
$\Delta^2 R_m$	**−0.01** [−2.71]	0.01 [1.37]	0.00 [0.83]	0.02 [0.94]	**−0.21** [−3.46]	−0.00 [−1.35]	0.00 [0.65]
$\Delta^2 R_b$	**−0.01** [−2.19]	−0.00 [−0.55]	−0.01 [−1.44]	−0.01 [−0.30]	**−0.37** [−4.91]	**−0.00** [−4.45]	**0.00** [3.62]

The estimated $\mathbf{\Gamma} = -(\mathbf{I} - \mathbf{\Gamma}_1)$ matrix

eq.\var.	Δm^n	Δp	Δy^r	ΔR_m	ΔR_b
$\Delta^2 m^n$	**−1.00** [−12.5]	−0.18 [−0.83]	**−0.31** [−2.33]	−1.94 [−1.21]	0.08 [0.06]
$\Delta^2 p_y$	−0.04 [−1.35]	**−0.81** [−10.1]	−0.03 [−0.55]	−0.71 [−1.17]	**1.15** [2.30]
$\Delta^2 y^r$	−0.05 [−0.86]	−0.12 [−0.84]	**−0.90** [−10.0]	0.55 [0.51]	**−1.52** [−1.72]
$\Delta^2 R_m$	**−0.01** [−2.06]	**0.05** [4.70]	−0.00 [−0.70]	**−0.96** [−12.0]	**0.40** [6.02]
$\Delta^2 R_b$	**−0.02** [−3.74]	0.02 [1.15]	**0.02** [2.36]	0.14 [1.40]	**−0.61** [7.62]

$\boldsymbol{\beta}'\Delta\mathbf{x}_{t-1}$ and $\boldsymbol{\beta}'_{\perp 1}\Delta\mathbf{x}_{t-1}$. Thus, medium-run price homogeneity defined as homogeneity between nominal growth rates, is also a relevant concept to be investigated within the $I(2)$ model.

Under long-run price homogeneity and assuming that the nominal-to-real transformed variables are $I(1)$, $\boldsymbol{\tau}'\Delta\mathbf{x}_t$ describes a medium-run homogeneous effect in nominal growth rates. For example, if $(m-p) \sim I(1)$ and $(y-p) \sim I(1)$, then $(\Delta m - \Delta p) \sim I(0)$ and $(\Delta y - \Delta p) \sim I(0)$. In this case there would be medium-run price homogeneity in the sense of nominal growth rates being pair-wise cointegrated $(1, -1)$.

An obvious question is whether long-run price homogeneity in the $\mathbf{\Pi}$ matrix implies medium-run homogeneity in the $\mathbf{\Gamma}$ matrix. To examine this, we use the results from Section 17.3.3 that $\mathbf{\Gamma}\Delta\mathbf{x}_{t-1}$ is the sum of the three components:

$$\mathbf{\Gamma}\Delta\mathbf{x}_{t-1} = (\mathbf{\Gamma}\overline{\boldsymbol{\beta}})\boldsymbol{\beta}'\Delta\mathbf{x}_{t-1} + (\boldsymbol{\alpha}\overline{\boldsymbol{\alpha}}'\mathbf{\Gamma}\overline{\boldsymbol{\beta}}_{\perp 1} + \boldsymbol{\alpha}_{\perp 1})\,\boldsymbol{\beta}'_{\perp 1}\Delta\mathbf{x}_{t-1} + (\boldsymbol{\alpha}\overline{\boldsymbol{\alpha}}'\mathbf{\Gamma}\overline{\boldsymbol{\beta}}_{\perp 2})\,\boldsymbol{\beta}'_{\perp 2}\Delta\mathbf{x}_{t-1},$$

of which the first two will exhibit medium-run price homogeneity given long-run price homogeneity. The third component, on the other hand, is proportional to $\boldsymbol{\beta}_{\perp 2}$, which is orthogonal to $(\boldsymbol{\beta}', \boldsymbol{\beta}'_{\perp 1})$. Hence, $\mathbf{R}'\boldsymbol{\beta} = \mathbf{0}$ implies $\mathbf{R}'\boldsymbol{\beta}_{\perp 2} \neq \mathbf{0}$ and one will not, in general, find medium-run price homogeneity in the rows of the $\mathbf{\Gamma}$ matrix. This is also evident from the estimates of $\mathbf{\Gamma}$ in the lower part of Table 18.1, which shows that medium-run price homogeneity between Δm and Δp is completely absent in all equations except for the last one. Even in the money equation, medium-run homogeneity seems totally absent.

The intuition is as follows: Given long-run price homogeneity and nominal-to-real transformed variables being $I(1)$, a non-homogeneous reaction in nominal growth rates is generally needed to achieve an adjustment towards a stationary long-run equilibrium position. For example, $m - p \sim I(1)$ and $(\Delta m - \Delta p) \sim I(0)$ cannot be cointegrated as they are of different order of integration, whereas $m - p$ and Δm (alternatively Δp) are of the same order of integration and, therefore, can be cointegrated. Therefore, medium-run price homogeneity interpreted as a zero sum restriction on all rows of $\mathbf{\Gamma}$ is in general inconsistent with overall long-run price homogeneity.

18.2 Assessing the $I(1)$ results within the $I(2)$ model

The $I(1)$ model was estimated subject to three implicit and one explicit assumptions:

1. The nominal-to-real transformation is empirically valid:

$$\begin{bmatrix} m^n \sim I(2) \\ p \sim I(2) \end{bmatrix} \rightarrow \begin{bmatrix} (m^n - p) \sim I(1) \\ \Delta p \sim I(1) \end{bmatrix}.$$

2. m^n and p are cobreaking with respect to a possible broken linear trend, i.e. $(m^n - p) \sim I(1)$ with a linear trend but without a break.
3. y^n and p are cobreaking with respect to a possible broken linear trend, i.e. $(y^n - p) \sim I(1)$ with a linear trend but without a break.
4. The linear trend in m^r and y^r cancels in the cointegration relations, i.e. the linear trend is long-run excludable (this was tested and accepted in the $I(1)$ model).

The previous section showed that long-run price homogeneity, necessary for the nominal-to-real transformation to be empirically valid, was strongly rejected. In this section we shall further test whether *trend* and *trend83* can be jointly excluded from $\boldsymbol{\tau}'\mathbf{x}_t$, whether *trend83* is excludable (only a linear trend is needed in $\boldsymbol{\tau}'\mathbf{x}_t$), whether *trend* is excludable (a linear trend is only needed in the period after 1983), or whether the restriction *trend-trend83* can be imposed on all $\boldsymbol{\tau}'\mathbf{x}_t$ (a linear trend is needed in the period from 1973–1982, but not in 1983–2003). Note that these tests are now correctly formulated on $\boldsymbol{\tau}$ rather than on $\boldsymbol{\beta}$ as in Chapter 16. Because the test of long-run homogeneity is likely to be very sensitive to the specification of the deterministic trend components in the model, we shall also test whether the former can be accepted conditional on restricting the broken linear trend to zero.

18.2.1 Testing the restrictions of the $I(1)$ model

The results of testing the above hypotheses are reported in Table 18.2. Even though all hypotheses are rejected, there are a number of interesting findings. First, long-run price homogeneity would have been accepted[1] conditional on excluding any deterministic trends in the cointegration relations. In this sense the results support the nominal-to-real

[1]The difference between test values of hypothesis 1 and 5 is roughly 6 and the difference in degrees of freedom is 4. Thus, the additional homogeneity restriction would not be statistically significant.

Table 18.2 Testing the restrictions implied by the previous $I(1)$ model.

	$\mathcal{H}1$: no broken trend	$\mathcal{H}2$: no *trend83*	$\mathcal{H}3$: no *trend*	$\mathcal{H}4$: *trend* = *trend83*	$\mathcal{H}5$. price homog. and no trends
$\chi^2(v)$	63.99	29.70	24.32	18.61	69.90
v	8	4	4	4	12
p-value	0.00	0.00	0.00	0.00	0.00

transformation implicitly assumed to hold in the $I(1)$ model. Second, the results suggest that restricting the trend to be exclusively present in the first period seems to be less strongly rejected. Altogether, the results point to the sensitivity and to the importance of the deterministic terms for the $I(2)$ results.

Thus, whether one includes a broken linear trend or not in the $I(2)$ model can change the conclusions in one direction or the other, and such a decision should, therefore, be carefully motivated.

Because $\mathcal{H}5$ contains the main assumptions of the $I(1)$ model, it is of some interest to report the $I(2)$ estimates subject to the $\mathcal{H}5$ restrictions, i.e. long-run price homogeneity and no broken trends in the $\boldsymbol{\tau}'\mathbf{x}_t$ relations. In this restricted $I(2)$ model, the estimates of $\boldsymbol{\beta}'\mathbf{x}_t + \boldsymbol{\delta}'\Delta\mathbf{x}_t$ should essentially correspond to the unrestricted estimates of $\boldsymbol{\beta}'\mathbf{x}_t$ in the $I(1)$ model. Table 18.3 reports the estimates. We note that the first cointegration relation looks like the interest rate relation, that the second relation closely replicates the money demand relation, but that the third relation is not directly interpretable in terms of the $I(1)$ results. This is because we have not yet imposed identifying restrictions, so that linear combinations of the three polynomially cointegrated relations may very well produce the 'inflation–real income' relation of the $I(1)$ model. Identifying restrictions will be discussed below.

We note also that bond rate does not seem to be significantly adjusting to any of the $\boldsymbol{\beta}$ relations and the same is almost true for real income, which is precisely what we found in the $I(1)$ analysis. Nonetheless, while the estimated $\boldsymbol{\alpha}_{\perp 1}$ is consistent with the weak exogeneity of the bond rate, the estimated coefficients of $\boldsymbol{\alpha}_{\perp 2}$ seem to suggest that it is the shocks to the short-term interest rate that has generated the stochastic $I(2)$ trend. Thus, given long-run price homogeneity and no broken trend, the $I(2)$ analysis confirms the previous finding that the shocks to the bond rate have generated one of the stochastic trends, whereas the second trend is not found to be generated by shocks to real income but, instead, by shocks to the short-term interest rate. In this sense, the $I(2)$ analysis provides additional evidence on the driving forces of the system. As a matter of fact, the short-term interest rate was found to be borderline weakly exogenous in the $I(1)$ model and the choice of the bond rate and the real income to be jointly exogenous rather than the bond rate and the short rate was only slightly more supported by the tests.

An additional advantage of the $I(2)$ model is that we can get an estimate of the medium-run relation between growth rates, $\boldsymbol{\beta}'_{\perp 1}\Delta\mathbf{x}_t$. In practice, the estimates are often economically difficult to interpret. This is amply exemplified by the estimated $\boldsymbol{\beta}'_{\perp 1}\Delta\mathbf{x}_t$ relation in Table 18.3 showing that real money growth has been negatively related to real income growth. This might be due to technological progress in the banking sector, or it might be the case that agents have been able to economize on money holdings as the

Table 18.3 The estimates of the $I(2)$ model subject to long-run price homogeneity and exclusion of trend.

	m^n	p	y^r	R_m	R_b	*trend*	*trend83*	*const.*	*Ds831*
The cointegrating relations $\boldsymbol{\beta}$									
$\boldsymbol{\beta}_1'$	−0.01	0.01	−0.01	1.00	−0.49	0.00	0.00	–	–
$\boldsymbol{\delta}_1'$	0.01	0.01	0.00	0.00	0.00	–	–	−0.14	−0.01
$\boldsymbol{\beta}_2'$	1.00	−1.00	−1.18	−15.26	12.17	0.00	0.00	–	–
$\boldsymbol{\delta}_2'$	−0.27	−0.27	0.00	0.00	0.00	–	–	2.12	−0.17
$\boldsymbol{\beta}_3'$	0.11	−0.11	−0.02	−0.44	1.00	0.00	0.00	–	–
$\boldsymbol{\delta}_3'$	1.22	1.22	0.00	0.00	0.00	–	–	−0.57	0.01
The adjustment coefficients $\boldsymbol{\alpha}$									
$\boldsymbol{\alpha}_{.1}'$	−0.84	0.02	−1.46	−0.10	0.12				
	[−1.01]	[0.06]	[−2.50]	[−2.38]	[2.04]				
$\boldsymbol{\alpha}_{.2}'$	−0.17	0.03	0.07	−0.00	0.00				
	[−4.63]	[1.92]	[2.76]	[−0.49]	[0.39]				
$\boldsymbol{\alpha}_{.3}'$	−0.54	−0.42	−0.06	0.02	0.00				
	[−5.25]	[−10.30]	[−0.85]	[3.23]	[0.43]				
The orthogonal relations $\boldsymbol{\beta}_\perp$									
$\boldsymbol{\beta}_{\perp 1}'$	1.00	−1.00	1.01	−0.17	−0.27	0.00	0.00		
$\tilde{\boldsymbol{\beta}}_{\perp 2}'$	1.00	1.00	0.00	0.00	0.00				
The common trends $\boldsymbol{\alpha}_\perp$									
$\boldsymbol{\alpha}_{\perp 1}'$	−0.00	0.00	−0.00	−0.02	−0.06				
	[−1.16]	[0.52]	[−1.12]	[−2.00]	[−6.44]				
$\boldsymbol{\alpha}_{\perp 2}'$	−0.02	0.08	−0.07	1.00	−0.26				
	[−1.30]	[2.38]	[−1.70]	[*NA*]	[−1.79]				
$\hat{\sigma}_\varepsilon$	0.0198	0.0076	0.0129	0.0010	0.0013				

level of prosperity has increased in the economy. This, for example, could be the case if the precautionary demand for money has become less important as the financial system has become more developed.

As mentioned above, it is hard to compare the $\boldsymbol{\beta}'\mathbf{x}_t$ relations with the previously found results without imposing identifying restrictions. We have, therefore, imposed the $\mathcal{H}_{S.4}$ restrictions discussed in Chapter 12 on the $I(2)$ model and the estimates are reported in Table 18.4. Because the distributional results for calculating standard errors of estimates of an identified $\boldsymbol{\beta}$ structure are not applicable to $\boldsymbol{\beta}_{\perp 1}$, the latter is unrestricted in Table 18.4. The first $\boldsymbol{\beta}$ relation imposes the restrictions of the money demand relation, the second of the interest rate relation, and the third of the 'real income-inflation' restrictions with the inflation rate being part of $\boldsymbol{\delta}\Delta\mathbf{x}_{t-1}$.

The 10 over-identifying restrictions were, as expected, rejected with a p-value of 0.00 and a test statistic of $\chi^2(10) = 69.90$. As a matter of fact, the latter is identical to the test of long-run price homogeneity and long-run exclusion of a broken trend in $\boldsymbol{\tau}'\mathbf{x}_t$, which

Table 18.4 The estimated $\boldsymbol{\beta}$ structure subject to the restrictions of the $I(1)$ model.

	m^n	p	y^r	R_m	R_b	*trend*	*trend83*	*const.*	*Ds831*
The cointegrating relations $\boldsymbol{\beta}$									
$\boldsymbol{\beta}_1'$	1.00	−1.00	−1.00	−10.93	10.93	0.00	0.00	–	–
	[*NA*]	[*NA*]	[*NA*]	[−6.59]	[6.59]	[*NA*]	[*NA*]		
$\boldsymbol{\delta}_1'$	0.09	0.11	0.00	0.00	0.00	–	–	0.88	−0.17
$\boldsymbol{\beta}_2'$	0.00	0.00	0.00	**1.00**	−0.48	0.00	0.00	–	–
	[*NA*]	[*NA*]	[*NA*]	[*NA*]	[−8.58]	[*NA*]	[*NA*]		
$\boldsymbol{\delta}_2'$	−0.41	−0.47	−0.00	−0.00	−0.01	–	–	0.02	−0.02
$\boldsymbol{\beta}_3'$	0.00	0.00	**1.00**	0.00	0.00	0.00	0.00	–	–
	[*NA*]	[*NA*]	[*NA*]	[*NA*]	[*NA*]	[*NA*]	[*NA*]		
$\boldsymbol{\delta}_3'$	−11.00	−11.00	0.00	0.00	0.00	–	–	−7.60	0.46
The adjustment coefficients $\boldsymbol{\alpha}$									
$\boldsymbol{\alpha}_{.1}'$	−0.25	−0.02	0.05	−0.00	0.00				
	[−6.13]	[−0.92]	[1.59]	[−0.13]	[0.62]				
$\boldsymbol{\alpha}_{.2}'$	−0.75	−0.40	−2.15	−0.09	0.10				
	[−0.81]	[−1.07]	[−3.29]	[−2.04]	[1.60]				
$\boldsymbol{\alpha}_{.3}'$	−0.05	−0.04	−0.06	−0.00	0.00				
	[−2.06]	[−3.99]	[−3.50]	[−0.99]	[1.37]				
The orthogonal relations $\boldsymbol{\beta}_\perp$									
$\boldsymbol{\beta}_{\perp 1}'$	1.00	−0.86	0.00	−0.16	−0.33	0.00	0.00		
$\tilde{\boldsymbol{\beta}}_{\perp 2}'$	0.87	1.00	0.00	0.01	0.02				
The common trends $\boldsymbol{\alpha}_\perp$									
$\boldsymbol{\alpha}_{\perp 1}'$	−0.00	0.01	−0.01	0.02	−0.13				
	[−1.06]	[1.23]	[−1.17]	[0.73]	[−5.61]				
$\boldsymbol{\alpha}_{\perp 2}'$	−0.01	0.06	−0.04	1.00	0.13				
	[−0.72]	[1.90]	[−1.09]	[*NA*]	[0.75]				
$\hat{\sigma}_\varepsilon$	0.0198	0.0076	0.0129	0.0010	0.0013				

suggests that the identifying restrictions are in fact acceptable subject to long-run price homogeneity and long-run exclusion of the broken linear trend. The estimated $\boldsymbol{\beta}$ and $\boldsymbol{\alpha}$ coefficients are similar to the ones in Table 12.3. Finally, the graphs of the polynomially cointegrating relations look completely stationary (though not reported here). Thus, we have essentially been able to replicate the results of the $I(1)$ analysis within the $I(2)$ model framework.

Based on the above, the rather puzzling result discussed in Chapter 17 that trend-adjusted nominal income was $I(1)$ is more understandable. To get some further insight into this question we can formally test whether nominal income and the price variable both corrected for a broken trend is in the span of $\boldsymbol{\beta}$. The former hypothesis was accepted with a p-value of 0.05 based on $\chi^2(2) = 5.85$, whereas the latter was rejected with a p-value of 0.00 based on $\chi^2(2) = 16.04$. Thus, trend-corrected $y^n \sim$I(1) cannot cointegrate with trend-corrected $p \sim I(2)$. This explains why $y^r \sim I(2)$.

It is also interesting to compare the estimated average linear growth rates of y^n and p over the sample period. For nominal income the estimated cointegration vector $(y^n - 0.024trend + 0.015trend83)$ indicates that the latter grew on average with approximately 10% per year in 1973–1982 and with 4% in 1983–2003. For prices the estimated cointegration vector $(y^n - 0.024trend + 0.019trend83)$ indicates that prices grew on average as much as nominal income in 1973–1982, but only with 2% per year in 1983–2003. In this sense prices and income have behaved differently over the two periods, confirming the previous finding of a non-constant relationship between the inflation rate and real income.

Finally, we tested the hypothesis, $\boldsymbol{\tau}^c = (\mathbf{b}, \boldsymbol{\varphi})$ with $\mathbf{b}' = [0,0,1,0,0,0,0]$, i.e. real income is $I(1)$ when restricting the broken linear trend to zero. It was rejected based on $\chi^2(3) = 14.31$, but the test value is not too far from acceptance. With some good will, we conclude that real income in the $I(1)$ analysis can be considered approximately $I(1)$ over this period.

18.2.2 A data consistent long-run structure

As a final exercise we shall present the results based on an over-identified long-run structure in which one of the $\boldsymbol{\beta}$ relations corresponds to the money demand relation from the $I(1)$ analysis, whereas the other two relations differ from the $I(1)$ model by allowing for a broken linear trend and by not imposing long-run price homogeneity. The over-identifying restrictions of the estimated $\boldsymbol{\beta}$ structure reported in Table 18.4 were accepted with a p-value of 0.25 based on a test value of $\chi^2(3) = 4.08$.

The first relation is very close the estimated demand-for-money relation of structure $\mathcal{H}_{S.4}$ in Table 12.3 of Chapter 12. The second $\boldsymbol{\beta}$ relation is essentially describing that nominal income corrected for a broken linear trend has been negatively related to the long-term bond rate. It resembles the fourth unrestricted $\boldsymbol{\beta}$ relation in Section 7.6 of the $I(1)$ model, which was interpreted as a partially specified IS relation between real income and the interest rates. It was not included among the r cointegration relations as it was found to be only very borderline stationary. By including the long-term bond rate in the present relation, the estimated annual trend coefficients have changed compared

Table 18.5 An acceptable long-run structure.

	m_t^n	p_t	y_t^r	$R_{m,t}$	$R_{b,t}$	$trend$	$trend83$	$const$	$Ds831$
$\boldsymbol{\beta}_1'\mathbf{x}_t$	**1.00** [NA]	**−1.00** [NA]	**−0.79** [−14.65]	**−12.20** [−9.53]	**12.20** [9.53]	0.00 [NA]	0.00 [NA]	–	–
$\boldsymbol{\delta}_1'\Delta\mathbf{x}_t$	**3.12**	**3.82**	**−4.02**	0.21	0.01	–	–	**−0.68**	**−0.07**
$\boldsymbol{\beta}_2'\mathbf{x}_t$	0.00 [NA]	**1.00** [NA]	**1.00** [NA]	0.00 [NA]	**17.81** [20.05]	**−0.034** [−56.30]	**0.029** [40.17]		
$\boldsymbol{\delta}_2'\Delta\mathbf{x}_t$	0.27	0.35	−0.52	0.03	−0.00	–	–	**−5.76**	**0.20**
$\boldsymbol{\beta}_3'\mathbf{x}_t$	**0.92** [15.94]	**1.00** [NA]	0.00 [NA]	**−31.40** [−12.77]	0.00 [NA]	**−0.034** [−5.52]	**0.014** [2.97]		
$\boldsymbol{\delta}_3'\Delta\mathbf{x}_t$	**10.74**	**13.16**	**−13.84**	0.74	0.03	–	–	**−2.49**	**−0.43**
$\boldsymbol{\beta}_{\perp 1}'\Delta\mathbf{x}_t$	1.00	−0.15	0.64	0.02	−0.03	−0.02			

to the estimates discussed above from 10% to 14% in 1973–1982 and from 4% to 2% in 1983–2003. Thus, nominal income in the first period would have grown with 14% per year, *ceteris paribus*, but only with 10% when accounting for the effect of the high and steadily increasing bond rate. In the second period, nominal income would have grown with only 2% per year, *ceteris paribus,* but with 4% when accounting for the effect of the declining bond rate. Thus, 2% of the actual 4% growth in nominal income was due to the declining level of the bond rate in the more recent period, whereas −4% of the growth had to be sacrificed in the first period.

The third $\boldsymbol{\beta}$ relation is essentially describing a positive relationship between the short-term interest rate, the average level of nominal money and prices and the average growth in prices, money and real income. It is interesting to note that $(\boldsymbol{\beta}_3'\mathbf{x}_t + \boldsymbol{\delta}_3'\Delta\mathbf{x}_t) - (\boldsymbol{\beta}_2'\mathbf{x}_t + \boldsymbol{\delta}_2'\Delta\mathbf{x}_t)$ will approximately recover the homogeneous relationship between inflation rate and the two interest rates of $\mathcal{H}_{S.4}$ in Table 12.3, with some small additional effects from trend-adjusted nominal money and real income.

18.3 An empirical scenario for nominal money and prices

The idea of the theoretical scenario of Chapter 2 was to explicitly specify *all* implications of a specific choice of integration and cointegration indices, so that they can be checked against the data. However, some of these implications have been shown to be strongly dependent on whether we exclude a deterministic trend in the cointegration relations or not. As this choice is at least to some extent subjective, the assessment of the theoretical scenario should preferably be made for both alternatives. To economize on space, we shall restrict ourselves to the more general specification of Table 18.5 when assessing the nominal scenario for the Danish money market.

The theory consistent nominal scenario of Chapter 2 can be specified as follows:

$$\begin{bmatrix} m^n \\ p \\ y^r \\ R_m \\ R_b \end{bmatrix} = \begin{bmatrix} c \\ c \\ 0 \\ 0 \\ 0 \end{bmatrix} \left[\sum_{j=1}^{t} \sum_{i=1}^{j} u_{2,i} \right] + \begin{bmatrix} e & d \\ e & 0 \\ 0 & d \\ c & 0 \\ c & 0 \end{bmatrix} \begin{bmatrix} \sum_{j=1}^{t} u_{2,j} \\ \sum_{j=1}^{t} u_{1,j} \end{bmatrix} + \begin{bmatrix} f \\ g \\ f-g \\ 0 \\ 0 \end{bmatrix} t$$
$$+ \text{ stationary components.}$$

based on the assumption that

1. only nominal money and prices are affected by the stochastic $I(2)$ trend, $\sum\sum u_{2,i}$, where $u_{2,t} = \boldsymbol{\alpha}_{\perp 2}'\hat{\boldsymbol{\varepsilon}}_i$;
2. $m^r = m^n - p \sim I(1)$ and m^r is exclusively affected by the real stochastic trend $\sum u_{1,i}$, where $u_{1,t} = \boldsymbol{\alpha}_{\perp 1}'\hat{\boldsymbol{\varepsilon}}_i$;
3. y^r is exclusively affected by the real stochastic trend;
4. money velocity is stationary, i.e. $m^r - y^r \sim I(0)$;

5. real interest rates and the interest rate spread are stationary, i.e. nominal interest rates are exclusively affected by the nominal stochastic trend with coefficients identically equal to the coefficient of the inflation rate.

In this scenario $r = 3$, $s_1 = 1$, and $s_2 = 1$, a result which was supported by the econometric tests. But, even though the basic structure seems to be theory consistent, the estimated coefficients reported below are less supportive.

$$\begin{bmatrix} m^n \\ p \\ y^r \\ R_m \\ R_b \end{bmatrix} = \begin{bmatrix} 0.82 \\ 1.00 \\ -1.05 \\ 0.06 \\ 0.00 \end{bmatrix} \begin{bmatrix} \sum_{j=1}^{t}\sum_{i=1}^{j} u_{2,i} \end{bmatrix} + \begin{bmatrix} c_{11} & c_{12} \\ c_{21} & c_{22} \\ c_{31} & c_{32} \\ c_{41} & c_{42} \\ c_{51} & c_{52} \end{bmatrix} \begin{bmatrix} \sum_{j=1}^{t} u_{2,j} \\ \sum_{j=1}^{t} u_{1,j} \end{bmatrix}$$
$$+ \begin{bmatrix} d_{11} & d_{12} \\ d_{21} & d_{22} \\ d_{31} & d_{32} \\ 0 & 0 \\ 0 & 0 \end{bmatrix} \begin{bmatrix} trend \\ trend83 \end{bmatrix}$$
$$+ \text{stationary components}$$

where $u_{1,t} = \boldsymbol{\alpha}'_{\perp,1}\boldsymbol{\varepsilon}_i$, $u_{2,t} = \boldsymbol{\alpha}'_{\perp,2}\boldsymbol{\varepsilon}_i$, and

	$\hat{\varepsilon}_t(m_t^n)$	$\hat{\varepsilon}_t(p_{y,t})$	$\hat{\varepsilon}_t(y_t^r)$	$\hat{\varepsilon}_t(R_{m,t})$	$\hat{\varepsilon}_t(R_{b,t})$
$\boldsymbol{\alpha}'_{\perp,1} =$	0.002 [1.28]	0.002 [1.58]	**0.004** [1.96]	0.011 [1.15]	**−0.057** [−4.03]
$\boldsymbol{\alpha}'_{\perp,2} =$	−0.028 [−1.77]	0.009 [0.40]	−0.027 [−0.96]	**1.00** [*NA*]	0.194 [1.00]

The theoretical scenario assumed that the autonomous nominal shock originated from shocks to money stock and that the real shock originated from shocks to productivity. This is in contrast to the empirical results suggesting that the two stochastic trends derive primarily from unanticipated shocks to the short-term interest rate and the bond rate. However, if shocks to the two interest rates are the main driving forces of this system, then the interest rates would not be cointegrated as in the third $\boldsymbol{\beta}$ relation of $\mathcal{H}_{S.3}$ in Table 12.3. Thus, the $I(2)$ analysis suggests that the homogeneous relation between inflation and the two interest rates of structure $\mathcal{H}_{S.4}$ is preferable to the interest rates relation of $\mathcal{H}_{S.3}$ in Table 12.3.

The loadings to the $I(2)$ trend show that the latter has affected nominal money less strongly than prices. The difference between 0.82 and 1.00 is statistically significant because overall long-run price homogeneity of $\boldsymbol{\tau}$ was rejected. The negative coefficient to real income was already commented on in the previous chapter.

As shown in Chapter 17, the $\mathbf{C}_1$ matrix is a complicated function of all parameters and cannot be decomposed similarly as the $\mathbf{C}_2$ matrix. Therefore, at this stage we are not able to report the estimated loadings to the $I(1)$ trends, but from the cointegration results we can conclude that none of the restrictions on the coefficients in the theoretical scenario seems to be empirically satisfied.

The pulling forces of the $I(2)$ system are described by the estimated equilibrium correction mechanisms of the $I(2)$ model. Contrary to the $I(1)$ model we need to distinguish between two different equilibrium adjustment mechanisms, one to the medium-run relations, $\boldsymbol{\tau}'\Delta\mathbf{x}_{t-1}$ described by the adjustment coefficients $\boldsymbol{\zeta}$ and the other to the long-run polynomially cointegrated relations described by the coefficients $\boldsymbol{\alpha}$. Most of the estimated coefficients in the $\boldsymbol{\zeta}$ matrix are highly significant which to some extent is due to the formulation of the VAR system in acceleration rates. In particular, if a variable $x_{i,t}$ is $I(1)$, then $\Delta^2 x_{i,t}$ is 'over-differenced'. The latter need to be 'corrected' by including $\Delta x_{i,t-1}$ as a regressor (cf. the discussion in Section 4.2.3), causing the diagonal element of $\mathbf{\Gamma} = \boldsymbol{\zeta\tau}' + \boldsymbol{\alpha\delta}'$ to be large by construction. Thus, some of the coefficients in $\boldsymbol{\zeta\tau}'$ may seem highly significant when tested against zero, even though one should rather test if they deviate significantly from one. In the discussion below we shall primarily focus on the long-run adjustment dynamics.

First, we note that nominal money stock has been equilibrium correcting to the money-demand relation and that excess liquidity has had some small positive effects

Table 18.6 A fully structured $I(2)$ model.

$$
\begin{bmatrix} \Delta^2 m_t^n \\ \Delta^2 p_t \\ \Delta^2 y_t^r \\ \Delta^2 R_{m,t} \\ \Delta^2 R_{b,t} \end{bmatrix}
=
\begin{bmatrix}
\underset{[0.76]}{0.07} & \underset{[-0.86]}{-0.05} & \underset{[1.12]}{0.06} & \underset{[-8.53]}{\mathbf{-0.85}} \\
\underset{[9.61]}{\mathbf{0.35}} & \underset{[-7.29]}{\mathbf{-0.17}} & \underset{[-5.41]}{\mathbf{-0.12}} & \underset{[1.12]}{0.04} \\
\underset{[2.72]}{\mathbf{0.17}} & \underset{[-5.76]}{\mathbf{-0.23}} & \underset{[-2.64]}{\mathbf{-0.10}} & \underset{[-5.50]}{\mathbf{-0.38}} \\
\underset{[-0.02]}{-0.00} & \underset{[7.03]}{\mathbf{0.02}} & \underset{[9.43]}{\mathbf{0.03}} & \underset{[-7.00]}{\mathbf{-0.04}} \\
\underset{[-4.80]}{\mathbf{-0.03}} & \underset{[-3.06]}{\mathbf{-0.01}} & \underset{[1.95]}{\mathbf{0.01}} & \underset{[0.82]}{0.01}
\end{bmatrix}
\begin{bmatrix} \hat{\boldsymbol{\beta}}_1' \Delta\mathbf{x}_{t-1} \\ \hat{\boldsymbol{\beta}}_2' \Delta\mathbf{x}_{t-1} \\ \hat{\boldsymbol{\beta}}_3' \Delta\mathbf{x}_{t-1} \\ \hat{\boldsymbol{\beta}}_{\perp 1}' \Delta\mathbf{x}_{t-1} \end{bmatrix}
$$

$$
+
\begin{bmatrix}
\underset{[-5.47]}{\mathbf{-0.39}} & \underset{[-2.01]}{\mathbf{-0.09}} & \underset{[3.98]}{\mathbf{0.09}} \\
\underset{[2.68]}{\mathbf{0.08}} & \underset{[-2.40]}{\mathbf{-0.04}} & \underset{[-5.51]}{\mathbf{-0.05}} \\
\underset{[0.50]}{0.02} & \underset{[-4.93]}{\mathbf{-0.16}} & \underset{[1.26]}{0.02} \\
\underset{[-2.64]}{\mathbf{-0.01}} & \underset{[-1.42]}{-0.00} & \underset{[2.66]}{\mathbf{0.00}} \\
\underset{[-1.66]}{-0.01} & \underset{[-5.31]}{\mathbf{-0.02}} & \underset{[1.59]}{0.00}
\end{bmatrix}
\begin{bmatrix} \hat{\boldsymbol{\beta}}_1' \mathbf{x}_{t-2} + \boldsymbol{\delta}_1' \Delta\mathbf{x}_{t-1} \\ \hat{\boldsymbol{\beta}}_2' \mathbf{x}_{t-2} + \boldsymbol{\delta}_2' \Delta\mathbf{x}_{t-1} \\ \hat{\boldsymbol{\beta}}_3' \mathbf{x}_{t-2} + \boldsymbol{\delta}_3' \Delta\mathbf{x}_{t-1} \end{bmatrix}
$$

$$
+
\begin{bmatrix}
\underset{[-1.35]}{-0.02} & \underset{[0.84]}{0.02} \\
\underset{[1.91]}{0.01} & \underset{[-0.68]}{-0.01} \\
\underset{[0.73]}{0.01} & \underset{[-1.64]}{-0.02} \\
\underset{[6.21]}{\mathbf{0.00}} & \underset{[0.30]}{0.00} \\
\underset{[0.14]}{0.00} & \underset{[-6.11]}{\mathbf{-0.01}}
\end{bmatrix}
\begin{bmatrix} D_{tr}764_t \\ D_p 831_t \end{bmatrix}
+
\begin{bmatrix} \varepsilon_{1,t} \\ \varepsilon_{2,t} \\ \varepsilon_{3,t} \\ \varepsilon_{4,t} \\ \varepsilon_{5,t} \end{bmatrix}
$$

on prices and negative effects on interest rates. These effects were already found in the $I(1)$ analysis. Real income and the bond rate have both been equilibrium correcting to the second $\boldsymbol{\beta}$ relation, 'the income-bond rate relation'. Prices have been equilibrium correcting and nominal money has been negatively affected by this relation. Prices and the short rate have both been equilibrium correcting to the third $\boldsymbol{\beta}$ relation, but not nominal money. Since the α coefficients of the second and third $\boldsymbol{\beta}$ relation enter money equation with coefficients which are almost equal with opposite signs, the effect of these two is equivalently described by $-0.09\left\{(\boldsymbol{\beta}_2'\mathbf{x}_t + \boldsymbol{\delta}_2'\Delta\mathbf{x}_t) - (\boldsymbol{\beta}_3'\mathbf{x}_t + \boldsymbol{\delta}_3'\Delta\mathbf{x}_t)\right\}$, i.e. by a negative effect on money stock when the opportunity cost of holding money is high.

One may ask whether we have learnt anything new and useful from identifying the above $\boldsymbol{\beta}$ structure in the $I(2)$ model. First, we have beyond any doubt been able to confirm the presence of a homogeneous long-run money demand relation with a significant opportunity cost of holding money relative to bonds. Second, we have recovered a positive relationship between the short-term interest rate and nominal money and prices corrected for a broken trend that seem consistent with the strong and robust finding that the twice cumulated shocks to the short-term interest rate have generated the $I(2)$ trend in nominal money and prices. Third, the negative relationship between the bond rate and nominal income corrected for a broken trend seem to be consistent with the strong and robust finding that the $I(1)$ trend consists primarily of cumulated shocks to the bond rate.

However, these results were based on the inclusion of a broken linear trend in the cointegration relations, which in some sense has to be considered a proxy for more fundamental changes in the macroeconomic mechanism of this period. But, to understand such changes in the economy the mechanisms need to be modelled rather than proxied. This will be the aim of the last part of this book.

18.4 Concluding discussion

The $I(2)$ analysis in this chapter revealed some problems with the nominal-to-real transformation needed for the $I(1)$ analysis to be valid. The problem seemed primarily to be related to the specification of the deterministic components in the long-run relations. When allowing for a broken linear trend in these relations, the nominal income and the implicit price index did not cointegrate and long-run price homogeneity was rejected. When restricting the broken linear trend to zero, long-run price homogeneity was accepted and almost all of the findings in the $I(1)$ analysis were recovered within the $I(2)$ analysis. Furthermore, the trends in nominal income and in prices behaved very differently between the two periods in terms of the absolute and the relative size of their slope coefficients. In general, the $I(2)$ analysis suggested that long-run price homogeneity between money and prices was strongly supported over the sample period, but that it was the non-homogeneous relationship between nominal income and prices that had generated the puzzling results. Thus, the $I(2)$ analysis confirmed the previous conclusion from the $I(1)$ analysis that we need to better understand the macroeconomic mechanisms having generated the long-run movements between real income and inflation in this period.

Furthermore, the $I(2)$ model allowed us to get much more reliable estimates of the shocks that have generated the stochastic $I(2)$ trend in nominal money and prices. In the present case we found that these shocks derived from unanticipated shocks to the short-term interest rate, possibly with some small negative effects from shocks to nominal money stock. In both cases the effect on the nominal variables was opposite to the expected: interest rate shocks had positive effects and money shocks had negative effects on price levels.

The $I(1)$ trend was found to be generated primarily from shocks to the long-term bond rate. Since the $I(2)$ analysis makes a sharp distinction between $I(1)$ and $I(2)$ trends, we believe this is a fairly reliable result.

Thus, the $I(2)$ analysis helped us to better understand the mechanisms behind nominal price levels, rather than the inflation rate in the $I(1)$ model and provided more reliable results regarding the pushing forces of the model. Nevertheless, the analysis of the $I(2)$ model is still in its infancy and the verdict whether it is empirically useful or not, must be assessed against future empirical work.

Part VI

A methodological approach

19

Specific-to-general and general-to-specific

Up to this point we have analysed just one set of variables representing a broadly formulated money market model. The unrestricted VAR model estimated at the first stage of the analysis was just a convenient reformulation of the covariances of the data, and bore little resemblance to the underlying economic model. By systematically imposing more and more, statistically acceptable, restrictions on the VAR, we were able to uncover economically meaningful structures in the data. Such a procedure is called general-to-specific modelling. However, some of the findings were consistent with our prior economic hypotheses, others seemed to need a further explanation. In general, we were not able to explain satisfactorily the determination of the inflation rate based on the money market model. Since most estimated VAR models contain only a few of the relevant variables, such puzzling results are the rule rather than the exception in practical work.

In this chapter we shall, therefore, address the question of how to extend the data set so that the determination of inflation can be investigated based on a broader information set. At the same time, we shall discuss some general principles for how to proceed when the analysis of the cointegrated VAR model has produced puzzling or less satisfactory results.

The organization of this chapter is as follows: Section 19.1 discusses the VAR model as an example of the general-to-specific principle in econometric modelling and contrasts it with the specific-to-general as a modelling device. Section 19.2 discusses advantages and disadvantages of the two principles in the choice of information set. Section 19.3 suggests a systematic procedure for gradually increasing the information set and Section 19.4 for combining several partial systems. Section 19.5 discusses an extension of the Danish data, with the purpose of improving our understanding of some of the puzzling results found in the previous chapters.

19.1 The general-to-specific and the VAR

The difference between the economists' and the statisticians' way of thinking can be recognized in two fundamentally different approaches to empirical modelling: (1) the specific to general and (2) the general to specific. The proponents of the first principle, usually preferred by people with a strong economic background, would start from a structural model based on precise economic hypotheses, derive the corresponding reduced form and ask questions about identification (Gilbert 1986). For this approach to be valid one needs an axiom of correct specification as pointed out by Hendry and Richard (1983). This is because all statistical inference would be invalid if the stochastic assumptions of the model were incorrect. In reality economists are, of course, seldom omnipotent and the structural model is usually re-specified in the light of empirical evidence until an approximate fit is achieved. The proponents of the second principle, usually preferred by people with a strong statistical background, begin with a statistically well-specified model and then impose *data consistent* restrictions given by prior economic hypotheses (Hendry 1995). The advantage of this approach, to which the cointegrated VAR belongs, is that a precise derivation of likelihood-based procedures for estimation and inference is usually straightforward.

Unfortunately, the generality of the VAR formulation comes at a cost: adding one variable to a p-dimensional VAR(k) system introduces $(2p + 1)k$ new autoregressive parameters. This can easily become prohibitive, in particular when the sample period is short, such as the typical 50–100 quarterly observations for a macroeconomic model. Whatever the case, the force of VAR modelling lies in the analysis of fairly small systems, with a limited number of cointegration relations, for example one or two economic relationships. However, for very low values of p, there can be a trade-off between the number of variables in the system and the number of lags needed to obtain uncorrelated residuals. Since one extra lag corresponds to p^2 additional parameters, one can in some cases reduce the total number of VAR parameters by adding a relevant variable to the model. For example, assume that uncorrelated residuals can be achieved in a VAR model with either $p = 2$ and $k = 5$ or $p = 3$ and $k = 2$. Adding a variable in this case would reduce the number of estimated coefficients by two (20–18).

Since the VAR model from the outset does not distinguish between endogenous and exogenous variables, but the information set is chosen with one or two 'endogenous' variables in mind, it is often the case that some, but not all, of the cointegration relations make economic sense. For example, the five variables in the Danish data set were sufficient to identify and estimate a plausible money demand relation but, since important variables explaining Danish export were missing, insufficient to identify an aggregate demand relation. Similarly, the data set was sufficient for the domestic, but not the open economy Fisher parity. Since Denmark is a small, open and deregulated economy, it seems obvious that an empirical analysis exclusively focusing on domestic variables, will inevitably yield only partial answers to the macroeconomic questions at hand. This point is important to keep in mind when assessing the overall results of the Danish monetary analysis.

19.2 The specific-to-general in the choice of variables

While we were able to estimate an interpretable money-demand function with remarkably constant parameters, and a reasonably constant interest rate relation, other results were less satisfactory. First, the monetary model of Danish inflation did not obtain much empirical support. Second, the cointegration relation between inflation and real aggregate income, to which inflation rate was exclusively adjusting, exhibited lack of constancy and was economically implausible. All this suggests that we need to expand the VAR analysis in order to get a more satisfactory explanation of what has caused inflation in this period.

There are at least two obvious candidates for an alternative explanation of the Danish price inflation in this period: (1) the labour market and the role of wage inflation, and (2) the foreign transmission effects and the role of imported price inflation. Consistent with this, Chapter 20 will empirically analyse wage, price and unemployment dynamics in the Danish labour market and Chapter 21 the joint determination of the purchasing power parity and the uncovered interest rate parity between Denmark and Germany. Based on the extended analyses, we shall demonstrate that most of the puzzling/surprising results from the money market analysis can be given a plausible explanation. However, as we extend the information set new questions will appear prompting further empirical investigations. In this sense, an empirical analysis is never complete.

Extending the set of variables means increasing the dimensionality of the VAR and, thus, increasing the number of potentially important economic relationships. The five-dimensional VAR model analysed in the preceding chapters was already quite demanding. Increasing the variable set with two variables, say, the real exchange rate and foreign aggregate demand, would significantly increase the complexity of the system. In such a system searching for a formally, empirically and economically identified long-run structure with plausible equilibrium correction coefficients is almost like looking for a needle in a haystack, unless one has a systematic way of handling the large amount of information inherent in each step of estimation and testing.

We shall here discuss two possible procedures to overcome the dimensionality problem. Common to both is that they build on the invariance of the cointegration property to extensions of the information set. This means that if cointegration is found between a set of variables, this cointegration result will remain valid even if more variables are added to the analysis. They differ in the way they exploit the duality between cointegration and common trends. The first one can be recommended when the sample period is long enough for a large-dimensional system to be estimated. The second one is more useful when the sample is relatively short.

19.3 Gradually increasing the information set

The idea behind the first procedure, which we shall refer to as the specific-to-general in the choice of variables, is to expand the information set gradually, at each step building upon previously found cointegration results. For a practical example, see Juselius and MacDonald (2004, 2006). Such a gradual approach greatly facilitates the identification of cointegration relations between sets of variables and, additionally, contains useful information about driving stochastic trends and how they influence the variables.

As an illustration we shall here assume that the five variables of the Danish monetary data are extended with two variables, the German inflation rate and German long-term bond rate.

Adding two variables to the previous information set implies three possible cases regarding the cointegration rank (remembering that the rank was previously set to 3):

- $r = 3$, $p - r = 4$. The rank is unchanged and the number of autonomous stochastic trends have increased to four. This would imply that the two German variables are neither cointegrated between themselves nor with the Danish variables. Hence, the two new variables would not add any useful long-run information to the Danish monetary model. *A priori* not a very plausible outcome.
- $r = 4$, $p - r = 3$. Adding the two German variables have produced one new cointegration relation and introduced one new stochastic trend. The new cointegration relation can either be a relation exclusively between German inflation rate and the German bond rate, or between the German and the Danish variables. By restricting three of the cointegration relations at the previously identified structure, while leaving the fourth relation unrestricted it is often easy to see what additional information the new variables bring to the system.
- $r = 5$, $p - r = 2$. There are two new cointegration relations and no additional common stochastic trend. For example, there might be one cointegration relation between the German bond rate and the German inflation rate, and another one between the German bond rate and the Danish bond rate. The extended system is driven by the same common stochastic trends as the smaller money market model.

In this way, the determination of cointegration rank in the extended system is very important as it contains valuable information about the common stochastic trends in the new variables and how the former are related to the previously found stochastic trends. This procedure will be followed in Chapter 20 where we gradually extend the variables of a labor market model and in Chapter 21 where we first analyse a smaller model consisting of Danish and German inflation rates, long-term interest rates, and the real exchange rate and then add two short-term interest rates.

There is, however, even more information to be gained by gradually extending the system with one variable at the time as exemplified with the wage, price, and unemployment dynamics in Chapter 20. In addition to checking the cointegration rank, it is useful at each step to exploit the information provided by the information in the automated CATS test procedures:

1. The tests of *long-run exclusion*. Is the new variable long-run excludable? Does the new variable add any relevant information to the structure of long-run relations?
2. The tests of *a unit vector in* β (possibly conditional on any deterministic components). Is the new variable stationary? Has the increase in cointegration rank changed the previous classification into stationary–non stationary variables?
3. The tests of *a zero row in* α, i.e. of long-run weak exogeneity. Is the new variable weakly exogenous? Has the previous classification into endogenous and weakly exogenous variables changed?
4. The tests of *a unit vector in* α. Is the new variable purely adjusting? Has the previous classification into purely adjusting/pushing variables changed?

As already discussed in Chapters 10 and 11, these tests depend crucially on a correct choice of rank and we should base the latter on all relevant information as discussed in

Chapter 8. Moreover, the tests are strongly interrelated and many of them ask the same question from different angles. For example, if the new variable is found to be long-run excludable, then the cointegration rank should not change. If the new variable is found to be weakly exogenous, then the test for a unit vector in α for this variable should reject.

In practice, the picture is often much more blurred and inconclusive. For example, a new variable might seem to improve the long-run specification even though the trace test does not suggest an additional cointegration relation. Such outcomes are often due to small sample properties, to low power, or in some cases to a badly specified model. The empirical analyses in the subsequent two chapters will illustrate some of these problems.

The automated test procedures in CATS are calculated for $r = 1, 2, \ldots p - 1$ and, therefore, provide a lot of information. To illustrate how one can gain more and more information by gradually increasing the information set we shall discuss a few examples below.

Assume that our previous model was based on $r = 3$ and the trace test suggests the same rank when we add one new variable. If the tests of long-run exclusion of the new variable are significant for any $r \leq 3$, then the new variable has probably, nonetheless, improved the specification of the previously estimated long-run relations. If the rank increases to four with the new variable, and the tests for long-run exclusion are insignificant for $r \leq 3$, but significant for $r = 4$, then the fourth cointegration relation (and the corresponding $\boldsymbol{\alpha}$ vector) contain all information about the value added of the new variable.

If the new variable is long-run excludable and the rank is unchanged, then the new variable has not added any useful information to the long-run structure. In this case, the new variable contains at least one stochastic trend not shared with the old variables. This, however, does not imply that the variable should be thrown out, as it may very well become highly significant when combined with the next new variable. For example, adding the German inflation rate to the Danish variables might not improve the long-run structure, whereas adding German inflation rate and the German bond rate together might very well make both variables appear significant in the long-run structure. In this case we would expect the number of cointegration relations to increase by one and the number of common stochastic trends to increase by one.

In general, we expect the cointegration rank to increase if a highly significant variable is added to the cointegration space. Again, practise is often much more ambiguous. For example, assume that the German inflation rate was included in the VAR model, that the tests reject long-run exclusion, that the trace test borderline supports one additional cointegration relation, and that the fourth relation is essentially a unit vector in the German interest rate. In this case, the new cointegration vector would not add much information about long-run comovements between our variables. Whether we should add the German inflation rate to our system or not, could, for example, depend on the significance of the $\boldsymbol{\alpha}$ coefficients. If, for example, the new vector were only significant in the German inflation equation our Danish analysis would not gain a lot by including it.

The above example is closely related to the third question, whether the increase in the number of cointegration relations change the classification of stationary and non-stationary variables. This can be examined by checking the tests of a unit vector in $\boldsymbol{\beta}$ conditional on any deterministic components in the model. As already discussed in Chapter 10 the outcome of this test is strongly dependent on the choice of rank: a liberal choice will make it easier to accept the unit vector hypothesis of a variable, a conservative choice will make it more difficult. Therefore, to call the unit vector hypothesis a test of the stationarity of a variable may sometimes convey the wrong connotation. This is particularly so when any of the variables defining the cointegration relations contain a small $I(2)$ component. In this case the interpretation of stationarity becomes even more problematic, as it is in general easier to accept a unit vector hypothesis when one of the directions of the process is close to $I(2)$. If the new variable is a 'near $I(2)$ variable' a similar problem is likely to occur. In this case the tests of stationarity defined as a unit vector in the cointegration space, are not necessarily comparable based on the old and the new data vector. The next two chapters will illustrate this problem.

The last two automated tests are formulated as hypotheses on $\boldsymbol{\alpha}$. As neither of them are invariant to changes in the information set, they are of particular interest in this context. For example, assume that the previous finding of weak exogeneity of the Danish bond rate is rejected when adding the German bond rate. This would suggest that the cumulated shocks to the Danish bond rate, defined as one of the underlying driving trends in the monetary model, have originated from shocks to the German interest rate. Assume, additionally, that the Danish bond rate had exclusively adjusted to the German bond rate in this period. In this case the test of weak exogeneity of the Danish bond rate would be rejected and the test of a unit vector in $\boldsymbol{\alpha}$ for the Danish bond rate would be accepted. Thus, whether previous findings of weak exogeneity/unit vector in $\boldsymbol{\alpha}$ changes or not when adding a new variable is a valuable piece of information about the underlying pulling and pushing forces of the system.

Exploiting this information makes it possible to learn about the influence of the new variable on the pulling and pushing forces of the system. When applied systematically, it is an indispensable tool in the construction of an empirically coherent scenario for the economic problem (cf. the discussion in Chapter 2). Without doing so, it is close to impossible to successfully construct such a scenario. An additional advantage of the gradual expansion of the information set is that the robustness of the conclusions from a small model regarding the '*ceteris paribus*' assumption can be empirically assessed in a systematic way.

19.4 Combining partial systems

The idea of the second approach is to use cointegration analysis of smaller blocks of variables as a means to restructure and simplify the empirical problem. The full set of relevant variables are divided into (often overlapping) subsets of variables defining some of the economic relationships we are interested in. Each submodel is first analysed separately, then the cointegration results from the partial systems are combined into a full model extending some basic ideas in Juselius (1992). See also de Brouwer and Ericsson (1998) and Pesaran and Smith (1998).

The deviation from the long-run equilibrium position, given by an identified cointegration relation between a set of variables, is assumed to represent an overall measure of the relative importance of these variables on the economic system. For example, if real wages are exactly on the long-run sustainable level we should not expect any wage effects on price inflation and/or employment. Thus, a key hypothesis is that the variables of interest, defining our economic model, are primarily affected by the relative magnitude of these long-run equilibrium errors estimated from each subsystem. If a sector of the economy is on its long-run equilibrium path, there should be no pressure arising from that sector. Conversely, the larger the imbalance the greater the pressure.

Figure 19.1 illustrates the approach by extending the Danish money market data with two new data sets, describing the wage, price, and unemployment dynamics in the Danish labour market and the foreign transmission effects on the Danish economy exemplified by Germany. A similar procedure was used in Juselius (1992), in which the estimated cointegration relations, i.e. equilibrium errors, from three partial models were the main determinants in a single equation model of the Danish price inflation. Juselius (2005) applied the procedure to Finnish data, where he examined how the estimated cointegration relations affected a variety of key variables. Here we shall follow the latter approach, and estimate a dynamic adjustment model for price inflation, real productivity growth, unemployment rate, real exchange rate, short- and long-term interest rates, and real money stock, using as main determinants, the estimated cointegration relations from three partial systems. Tuxen (2006) has applied the same approach to Eurowide data, extending the partial models to include the government sector.

The scheme in Figure 19.1 defines an information set $I_i, (i = W, M, F)$ for each subsystem containing the most important variables in that sector. I_W contains real wages $(w - p_c)$, productivity (c), the wedge between consumer and producer prices $(p_c - p_y)$, unemployment rate (u), and price inflation (Δp_c). I_M contains real money stock $(m-p_y)$, real aggregate income (y^r), the bank deposit rate (R_m), the bond rate, (R_b), and price inflation (Δp_y). To illustrate the idea of gradually increasing the information set, $I_{W,a}$ adds the long-term bond rate (R_b) and the real exchange rate (q) to I_W. I_F contains

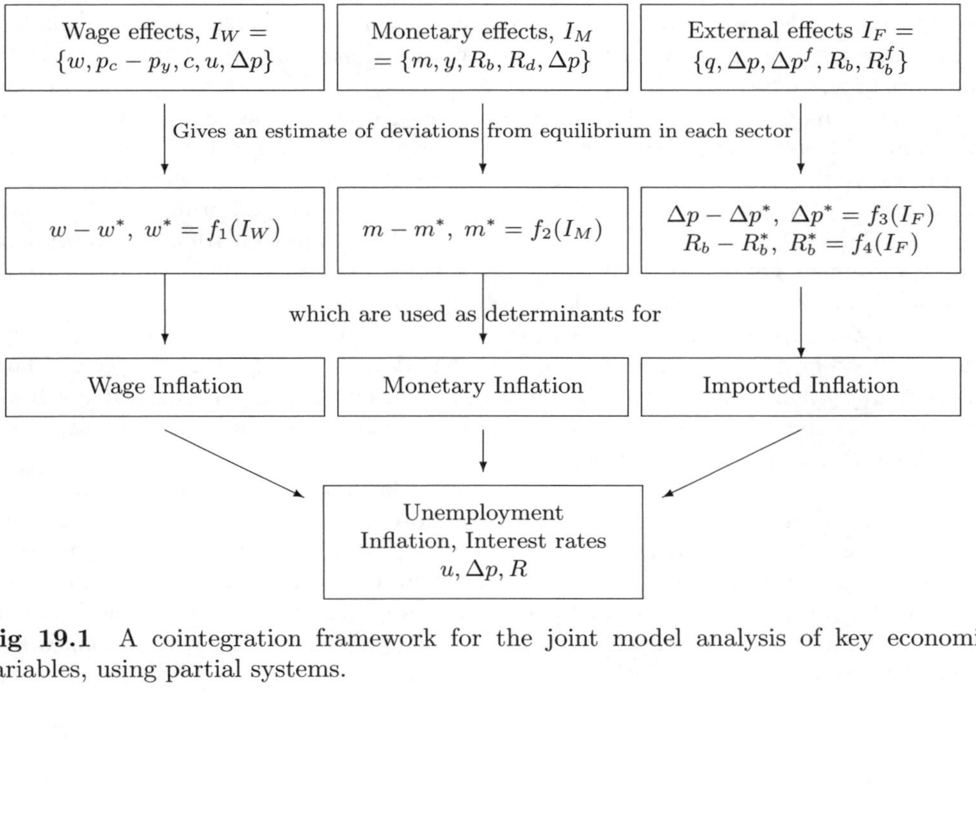

Fig 19.1 A cointegration framework for the joint model analysis of key economic variables, using partial systems.

the real exchange rate vis-à-vis to Germany ($q = s + p_c^f - p_c$), the Danish and German inflation rates ($\Delta p_c, \Delta p_c^f$), the Danish and German long-term bond rate (R_b, R_b^f). $I_{F,a}$ adds the Danish and German short-term interest rates to I_F.

The imbalance in each sector is measured as the deviations from long-run equilibrium states, given by the identified cointegration relations, $Mecm(i)$, $i = 1, \ldots, r_1$, $Wecm(i)$, $i = 1, \ldots, r_2$, $Fecm(i)$, $i = 1, \ldots, r_3$, where M, W, and F stand for a cointegration relation from each submodel respectively. For example, $Mecm(1)$ could be a measure of money stock in excess of long-run money demand, $Wecm(1)$ could be a cointegration relation measuring the deviation of real wages from its long-run benchmark value, $Fecm(1)$ could be a measure of how far away the Danish inflation was from its steady-state value compared to Germany. This can in fact be thought of as analogous to a general *AS–AD* equilibrium model in macroeconomics, defined by imposing equilibrium conditions on three markets (labour, goods and money/financial) when determining the economic endogenous variables.

19.5 Introducing the new data

In the money market analysis we found evidence of a structural change around 1983 in the money demand relation and in the interest rate spread relation. As the analysis suggested that the break was essentially in the equilibrium mean it was modelled by the shift dummy, $D_s83.1$. However, there was also evidence of non-constancy in the third relation between real income and inflation which seemed to be of more fundamental nature. Thus, when extending the information set, it is likely that we shall have to address the issue of possibly changing macroeconomic mechanisms. The 1970s and the first part of the 1980s was distinctly different in many ways compared to the remaining part of the sample period. To illustrate the distinctly different macroeconomic behaviour that some of the key macroeconomic variables have exhibited in the 1970s as compared to the rest of the sample, Figures 19.2–19.4 report graphs of their development over the last decades. In all graphs, a vertical line divides the sample period into 1971:1–1983:1 and 1983:1–2003:1. The division coincides with a general deregulation of international capital movements and with a turnover of the political government from a long period of social democratic rule to a long period of conservative rule.

Figure 19.2, upper panel, illustrates the fairly high inflation rates in the first period and the steadily declining rates in the second period. Figure 19.2, lower panel, shows that unemployment rate was steadily growing in the seventies up to 1983 and essentially continued to grow until 1994 with the exception of a few years between 1983 and 1986. After 1994 it finally started to decline.

Figure 19.3, upper panel, illustrates the high volatility of the real growth rates, particularly in the first period as a result of two major oil price shocks. The growth rates were fairly high in 1983–1986, much lower in 1987–1994 and quite reasonable since then. Figure 19.4, lower panel, demonstrates the very high levels of the nominal bond rate and the steadily increasing real rates in the first period, the significant drop at 1983 and the subsequent declining nominal rates, but fairly high levels of the real bond rate until 1994 when they finally started to decline.

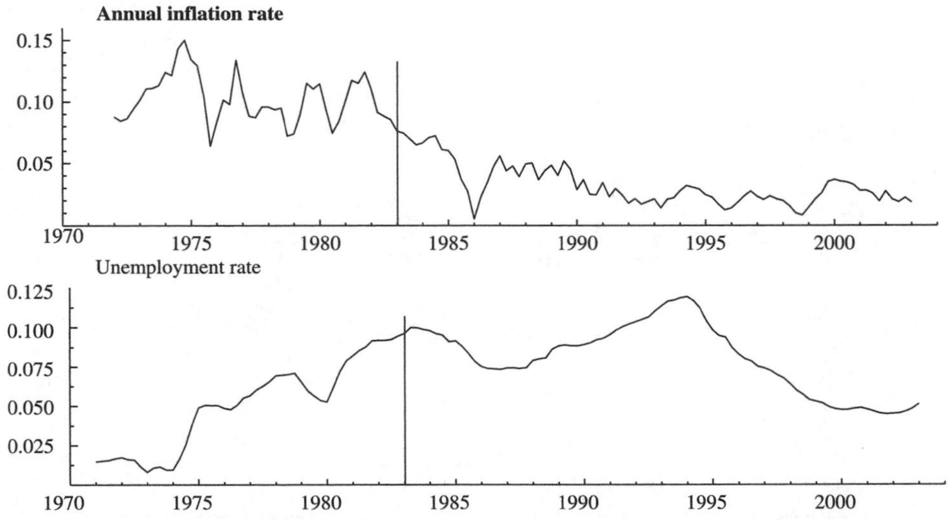

Fig 19.2 The annual CPI inflation rate (upper panel) and the unemployment rate (lower panel) in 1971–2003.

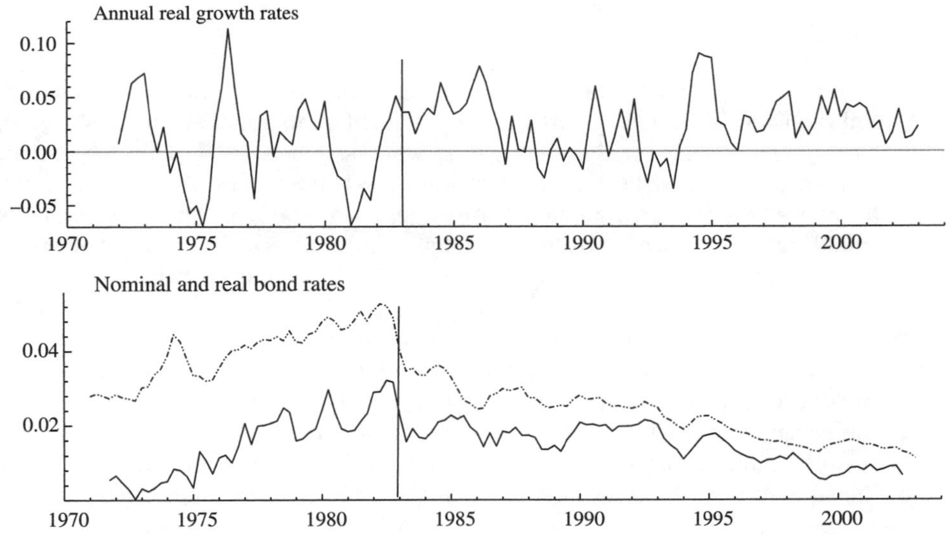

Fig 19.3 The Danish real growth rates (upper panel) and the nominal and real bond rate (lower panel) 1970–2003.

Figure 19.4, upper panel, illustrates that nominal exchange rates have been more volatile than the price differential, particularly so in the first period due to many small devaluations and realignments. Figure 19.4, lower panel, shows the big cyclical swings in the real exchange rates over this period.

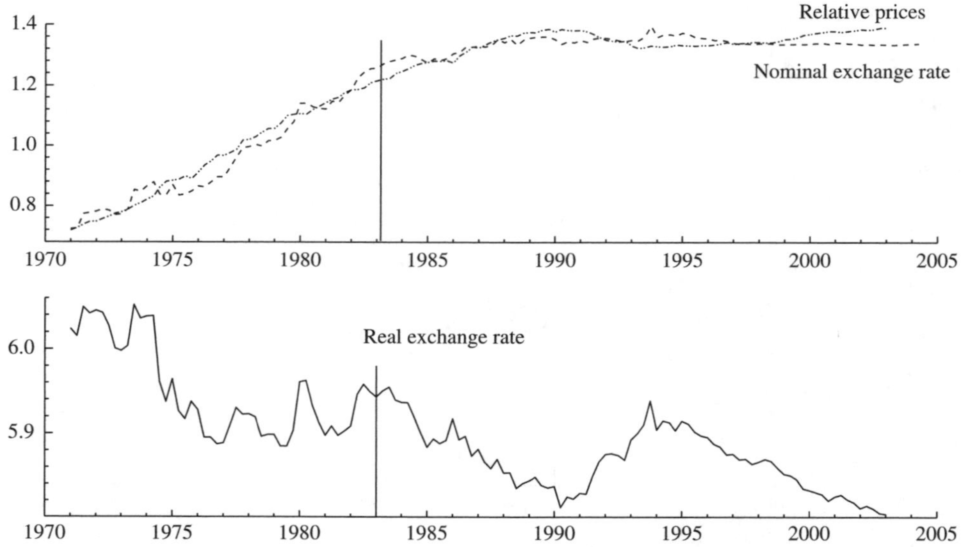

Fig 19.4 Relative consumer prices between Denmark and Germany together with the nominal exchange rate in Dkr/Dmk (upper panel) and the real exchange rate (lower panel) in 1970–2003.

Thus, the first period was characterized by high inflation and increasing unemployment (stagflation), volatile real growth rates, frequent realignments and devaluations, low but steadily increasing real interest rates, whereas the second period by steadily decreasing inflation rates, a short growth cycle in 1984–1986, a long recession in 1987–1994 with generally high unemployment rates, modest real growth rates, and fairly stable nominal exchange rates (no devaluations), and high real interest rates followed by a gradual improvement of real growth rates, declining unemployment rates and real interest rates.

There are several institutional differences between the two periods that potentially can explain these differences: The first period was characterized by a relatively free trade within the European Common Market and by restrictions on capital movements, whereas the second period by increasingly free capital movements and essentially no restrictions on intra-european trade. Denmark was part of the exchange rate regime 'the snake in the tunnel' until 1979 when she joined the EMS with a commitment to peg its currency to the narrow bands (±2.25%) of the ERM. However, the previously frequent devaluations/realignments continued until 1983 when the commitment to the 'hard' EMS put a stopper to them.

The purpose of the empirical analyses of the next chapters is to improve our empirical understanding of how these fundamental changes influenced the working of the economy. The results will demonstrate that the largest impact by any means was associated with the way the labour market was forced to adjust in the new regime. Indeed, we shall demonstrate that the non-constancy of the 'income–inflation' relation to a large extent can be explained by the changing role of labour unions in the more globalized economy of the last two decades, and by the way this has influenced the determination of wages, unemployment, productivity, and inflation. Due to its importance, the information set $I_W + I_{Wa}$ from the labour market will be subject to a more detailed analysis in Chapter 20 than $I_F + I_{Fa}$ describing the PPP/UIP analysis in Chapter 21.

As the purpose of the next chapters is to illustrate methodological aspects of the specific-to-general approach in the choice of information set, the econometric results of the next three chapters will be reported with less detail than in the first part of this book. Instead, the interested reader can find all tests and estimation results under the link http://www.econ.ku.dk/okokj/book.htm.

20

Wage, price, and unemployment dynamics

The main purpose of this chapter is partly to illustrate the stepwise procedure to gradually identify a long-run structure discussed in Chapter 19, partly to learn about the relative importance of the labour market for the determination of nominal prices, real income, and interest rates. The data to be analysed consist of wages, consumer and output prices, productivity, unemployment, inflation rate, the long-term bond rate and the real exchange rate. We begin with a VAR analysis of the first five variables and extend the model first adding the bond rate and then the real exchange rate. At each step we identify a long-run structure and interpret the results in terms of the pulling and pushing forces. A step-wise identification procedure is shown to facilitate the final specification of a long-run structure. Because the determination of wages and prices was found to be fundamentally different between the first post-Bretton–Woods period and the more recent EMS–EMU period, the VAR analysis is done separately for the two regimes. Since the more recent period is longer, more interesting, and gives a convincing demonstration of the 'specific-to-general' principle in the choice of information, the focus of the discussion will be on this period.

Section 20.1 provides a brief theoretical background. Section 20.2 reports the empirical analysis of the EMS–EMU period and Section 20.3 of the post-Bretton–Woods regime. Section 20.3 concludes.

20.1 Economic background

In the following capital letters will denote variables in levels, lower case letters will denote logarithmic values, X_t^e generally stands for agents' expectation at time t of a future value of X, and $v_{i,t}$ stands for the residual in equation i.

We first introduce the basic economic relationships in a completely general manner. Agents are supposed to receive utility from consumption $C_t = C(C_{Y,t}, C_{F,t})$, where C_Y is consumption of domestic goods and C_F of foreign goods, and from leisure L_E. They maximize utility by allocating their available time, L_T, between leisure, L_E, and work,

L, subject to the budget constraint:

$$P_tC_t + K_t = W_tL_t + (1 + R_{t-1})K_{t-1} \tag{20.1}$$

where $P_t = P(P_{Y,t}, P_{F,t})$ is the consumer price as a function of the price of domestically produced goods, P_Y, and imported goods P_F, W_t is wages, K_t is capital stock, and R_t is the interest rate. This gives the demand curve:

$$Y_t^d = Y^d(P, R) \tag{20.2}$$

and the labour supply curve

$$L_t^s = L(W/P, Z) \tag{20.3}$$

where Z depends on the structure of the labour market, for example union strength, unemployment, etc.

The level of output, Y_t, that can be produced by the firm is given by the production function:

$$Y_t = \tau_t Y(L, K)$$

where τ_t is total factor productivity. Minimizing costs gives the demand for capital and labour. The latter is specified as:

$$L_t^d = L^d(P_y, W, \tau, H) \tag{20.4}$$

where H can include capital market variables to allow for a sufficiently general form of the production function. For given cost minimizing factor quantities, firms maximize profits which gives the supply curve

$$Y_t^s = Y^s(P_y, \pi) \tag{20.5}$$

where π is the mark-up over costs.

In the following we shall primarily focus on the determination of price inflation when wages are determined by (20.3) and (20.4) and prices by (20.2) and (20.5) and the equilibrium conditions $L_t^d = L_t^s$ and $Y_t^s = Y_t^d$. While the general theory model does not allow for any involuntary unemployment in the long run, unemployment can deviate from a constant natural rate in the short run. This can be due to search costs, imperfect knowledge, different kinds of menu costs, etc. However, as the graphs in Figures 20.3 and 20.4 below illustrate, the Danish unemployment rate has not just exhibited short-run deviations from a constant rate, but pronounced persistence suggesting non-stationarity instead of stationarity. This property of the data prompts for theoretical models that can allow for persistent deviations in the unemployment rate from the natural rate. Strong labour unions, centralized wage formation, high search costs, low mobility, and generous social security have often been offered as possible explanations of the observed persistence in unemployment. The next subsections will discuss modifications and additions to the above framework and will suggest a number of relationships that can be empirically tested using cointegration techniques.

20.1.1 Centralized wage bargaining and an aggregate wage relation

In most of the investigated period Danish wages have been set by centralized wage bargaining, albeit recent years have seen a strong increase in decentralized bargaining. Within all major employment sectors of the economy centralized wage negotiations have generally taken place every second or third year. In addition to these high level negotiations local bargaining at the level of the firm has resulted in additional 'wage drifts'. In some years the latter has amounted to as much as 60–70% of the total wage increase. Thus, even though the centralized part of the wage increase can be assumed given for prolonged periods of time, the wage drift is likely to have reacted more endogenously to the economic determinates of the system. Nevertheless, Danish wages are to a large extent collectively determined and the factors H and Z in (20.3) and (20.4) need to be specified to account for this feature.

The bargaining power of the unions is strongly related to the unemployment rate. A proposed pay rise by the labour union reflects generally a trade-off between a higher consumption wage against a lower employment as a result of an increase in the real product wage increase (Flanagan, Moene, and Wallerstein 1993). Whether the pay rise is accepted or not by the employers' organizations is likely to depend on a trade-off between future profits and firm competitiveness against the increased risk of a union strike.

In accordance with our inductive/deductive approach we shall not choose a specific theory model for wage bargaining, nor from the outset hinge the analyses on a few detailed hypotheses. Instead, the subsequent interpretation of the empirical results will be based on a few broadly defined relationships, some of which represent reduced form relations consistent with several theoretical hypotheses. As the main purpose is to illustrate an econometric methodology we shall interpret the results in terms of the dynamics of the pulling and pushing forces and how these are reflected in the institutional changes over this period. In the following all testable hypotheses will be reported as log linearized relations.

The centralized part of the wage formation is assumed to be a struggle over the mark-up, where expectations of future outcomes of key variables play a significant role (Layard and Nickell 1992). This implies that unions strive to maximize their share of the productivity increase where productivity is defined as output per employment, $pr_t = y_t - l_t$. The employers' unions attempt to maximize the mark-up on unit costs,[1] defined here as the negative of $(w_t - p_{y,t} - pr_t)$, at the same time accounting for the anticipated effect of the increase in the real product wage on competitiveness. The mark-up is assumed to be a function of the expected real exchange rate, $q_t^e = (s + p^f - p_y)_t^e$, where s is nominal exchange rate, p^f is the foreign price level, and of expected real interests, $R_t^{r^e}$, i.e.

$$(w_t - p_{y,t} - pr_t) = f(q_t^e, R_t^{r^e}) + v_{1,t} \tag{20.6}$$

where $f_{q^e} < 0$ implies a lower mark-up as a result of a real appreciation (see Phelps 1994) and $f_{R^{r^e}} > 0$ as a result of a rise in the real interest rate.

[1] Note that the Danish government, which is the largest employer in Denmark, is not a profit maximizer.

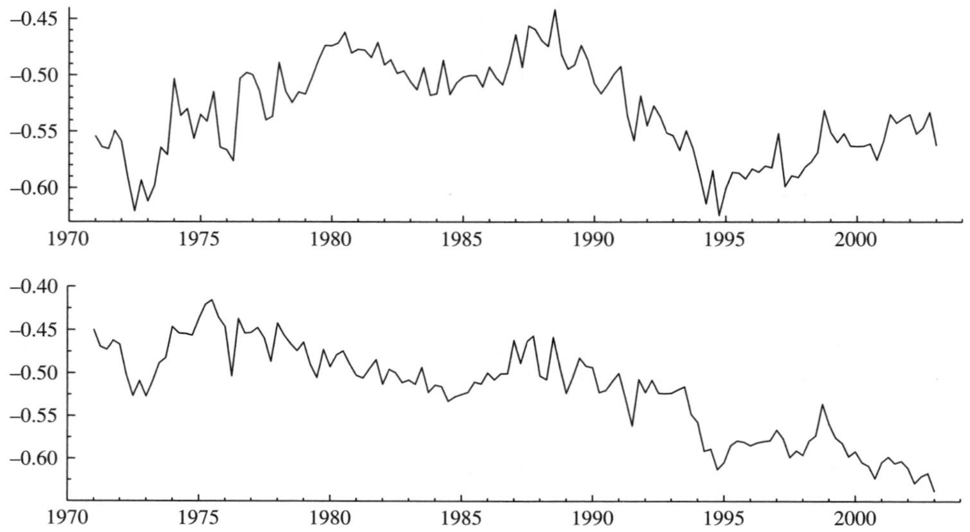

Fig 20.1 The graph of $w_t - p_{y,t} - c_t$ in the upper panel, and of $w_t - p_{c,t} - c_t$ in the lower panel.

The labour unions attempt to maximize the purchasing power for their members by increasing the real consumption wage, $(w_t - p_{c,t})$ conditional on the level of productivity, pr_t, and accounting for the expected effect on the unemployment rate, U_t^e, and expected inflation rate, i.e.

$$(w_t - p_{c,t} - pr_t) = g(U_t^e, \Delta p_t^e,) + v_{2,t} \tag{20.7}$$

where $g_{U^e} < 0$, and $g_{\Delta p^e} > 0$.

Figure 20.1 shows the development of the wage share of output in producer prices in the upper panel and in consumer prices in the lower panel. Both series exhibit typical non-stationary behaviour implying that the testing of (20.6) and (20.7) can be based on cointegration analyses. Whether the non-stationarity in the wages shares can be accounted for by the hypothetical indicator variables will be tested in Section 20.3.

The bargaining power of the labour unions is assumed to be approximated by a fraction ω, where $0 \leq \omega \leq 1$, so that the outcome of the negotiations can be formulated as a weighted average of the real consumption wage (20.7) and the real product wage (20.6) corrected for productivity:

$$\begin{aligned}\omega(w_t - p_{c,t} - pr_t) + (1-\omega)(w_t - p_{y,t} - pr_t) \\ = \omega g(U_t^e, \Delta p_t^e) + (1-\omega) f(q_t^e, R_t^{r^e}) + v_{3,t}\end{aligned}$$

An aggregate wage relation for the real product wage can now be formulated as:

$$w_t - p_{y,t} = a_0 - \omega(p_{y,t} - p_{c,t}) + pr_t + h(U_t^e, \Delta p_t^e, q_t^e, R_t^{r^e}) + v_{3,t} \tag{20.8}$$

or, equivalently, for the real consumption wage:

$$w_t - p_{c,t} = a_0 - (1-\omega)(p_{c,t} - p_{y,t}) + pr_t + h(U_t^e, \Delta p_t^e, q_t^e, R_t^{r^e}) + v_{3,t} \qquad (20.9)$$

Under log linearity and assuming that expected values only deviate from actual values with a stationary error (see Chapter 2, p. 31) (20.9) can be formulated as a cointegration relation:

$$w_t - p_{c,t} = a_0 + a_1(p_{c,t} - p_{y,t}) + pr_t + a_2 U_t + a_3 \Delta p_t + a_4 q_t + a_5 R_t^r + v_{3,t} \qquad (20.10)$$

where expected values have been replaced with actual observations, $a_1 = (1-\omega)$, $a_2 \leq 0$, $a_3 \geq 0$, $a_4 \geq 0$ and $a_5 \geq 0$. It seems plausible that the coefficient a_1 will change if the bargaining power of the unions change. This will partly be taken account of by splitting the sample period into the strong and weak labour union regimes.

20.1.2 The price wedge, productivity and unemployment

The price wedge $(p_{c,t} - p_{y,t})$ has often been found highly relevant in empirical wage relations and, therefore, needs some further clarification. Different bargaining structures imply different terms of trade between a rise in the real consumption wage and the real product wage (Flanagan, Moene, and Wallerstein 1993). For example under mark-up pricing, if wages increase in one employment sector, but not in the others, then output price will increase but the impact on the consumer price will be smaller. Thus, the increase in real consumption wage will be higher than the increase in real product wage. If, on the other hand, bargaining is highly centralized so that wages increase in most of the economy, then the increase in real product wage will be similar to the increase in real consumption wage.

However, the extent of product market competition is even more important for the price wedge. If an industry is exposed to a high degree of foreign competition, product prices cannot be raised by much even though the domestic wages rise. But, because the consumption basket also contains imported goods and services, foreign trade and the domestic service sector will also influence the price of real consumption wage. Therefore, a nationwide wage rise can increase real consumption wage more than the real product wage if import prices remain unchanged or decrease. This leads to the important question of where in the system the adjustment takes place after a wage rise (Boeri, Jimeno, Marimon, and Pissarides 2001).

Assume that a nationwide wage rise hits a highly exposed industry, the output prices of which are already on (or above) the competitive foreign trade level. In this case the industry has the possibility to (1) reduce employment until the marginal cost equals the competitive price, (2) increase labour productivity, or (3) close down the industry. This scenario seems to be very relevant in particular for the second part of the sample period, where the increased European integration, the deregulation of capital movements, and the almost fixed exchange rates put a strong pressure on the Danish prices to be on a competitive level. We shall argue below that output prices in this period did not fully reflect the increase in wages and that competitiveness was achieved by improvement in labour productivity.

Furthermore, as argued in Juselius (1993), we need to distinguish between a rise in labour productivity due to technological progress and to elimination of previous slack in the work process. The latter includes measures such as increasing the work pace, eliminating coffee breaks, and generally making employees run faster. Such an increase in productivity implies that the same output can be produced with less labour and, therefore, might be accompanied by layoffs and/or no new hirings. While the assumption that some workers are more productive than others is at odds with the homogeneous labour assumption of the theory model of Section 20.1, not surprisingly, the empirical evidence seems to require a heterogeneous labour force.

We assume here that the long-run growth in technology can be approximated with a linear trend, whereas the productivity increase due to elimination of slack can be approximated with a stochastic trend. Recalling that $pr_t = y_t - l_t$ we note that productivity can increase either as a result of an increase in aggregate output with constant employment or as a result of a decrease in employment with constant GDP. Thus, if we find that $(pr_t - b_1 t)$ is empirically $I(1)$ and cointegrates with unemployment (similarly as in Juselius 2002) we shall assume that improvements in labour productivity have been achieved by laying off a fraction of the work force and/or not hiring new people. In this case, output prices are not likely to increase as much as wages, so that real consumption wages will increase less than real product wages corrected for productivity and $(p_{c,t} - p_{y,t})$ will increase.

Therefore, an increase in trend-adjusted productivity is assumed to be associated with the increase in unemployment rate and an increase in the consumer-output price wedge. This leads to the following relation:

$$(pr_t - b_1 t) = a_6 + a_7 U_t + a_8(p_{c,t} - p_{y,t}) + v_{4,t}, \tag{20.11}$$

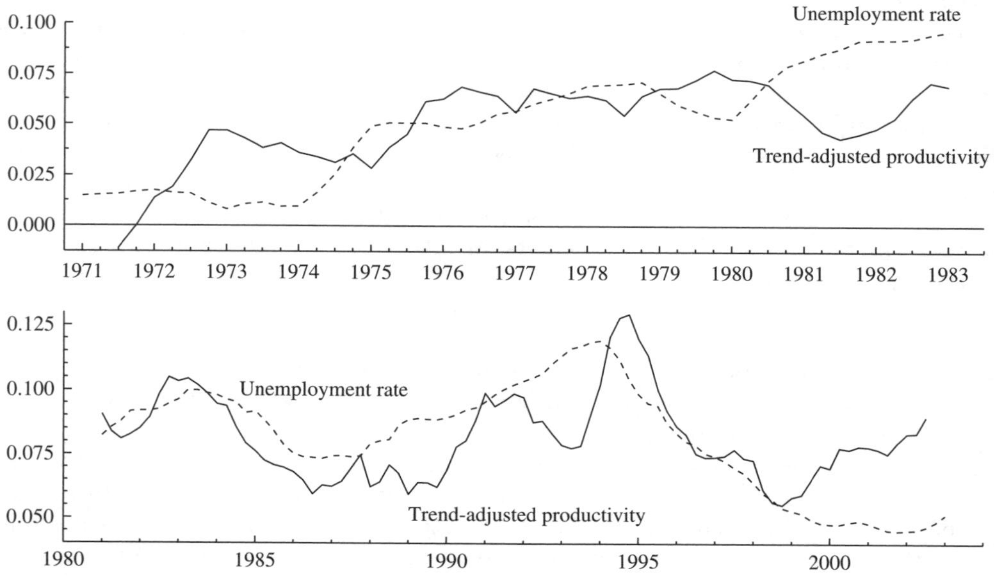

Fig 20.2 The graphs of unemployment and trend-adjusted productivity 1971–1983 (upper panel), and 1983–2003 (lower panel).

where $a_7 \geq 0$, $a_8 \geq 0$. Note, however that (20.11) is assumed to capture labour market behaviour in a transition period, for example from a more closed (regulated) economy to a deregulated economy exposed to foreign competition. Obviously, this kind of improvement in labour productivity is only possible up to the point where there is no slack left to eliminate and where increased work stress becomes counterproductive.

Figure 20.2 illustrates the comovements between unemployment rate and trend-adjusted productivity in the periods 1971:1–1983:1 (upper panel) and 1983:1–2003:1 (lower panel). The difference between the two periods is quite notable: The movements are essentially countercyclical in the first period characterized by less competitive pressure and more regulation, whereas procyclical in the second period characterized by high trade competition and deregulation. This difference will also show up in the subsequent cointegration results.

20.1.3 Phillips-curve type relations

While the general theory model is completely silent on the order of integration of different variables, this is a strong feature of the data that has serious implications for which type of empirical relationships we can possibly find in the data. We will show below that inflation rate being empirically $I(1)$ and, hence, the price level $I(2)$, has strong implications for how to empirically specify many important economic relations.

The representation of the VAR model for $I(2)$ data discussed in Part V showed that polynomial cointegration should be expected between $CI(2,1)$ relations of nominal variables and $I(1)$ nominal growth rates, but also that directly stationary combinations between the variables in levels would be possible when $r > s_2$. Thus, the two mark-up

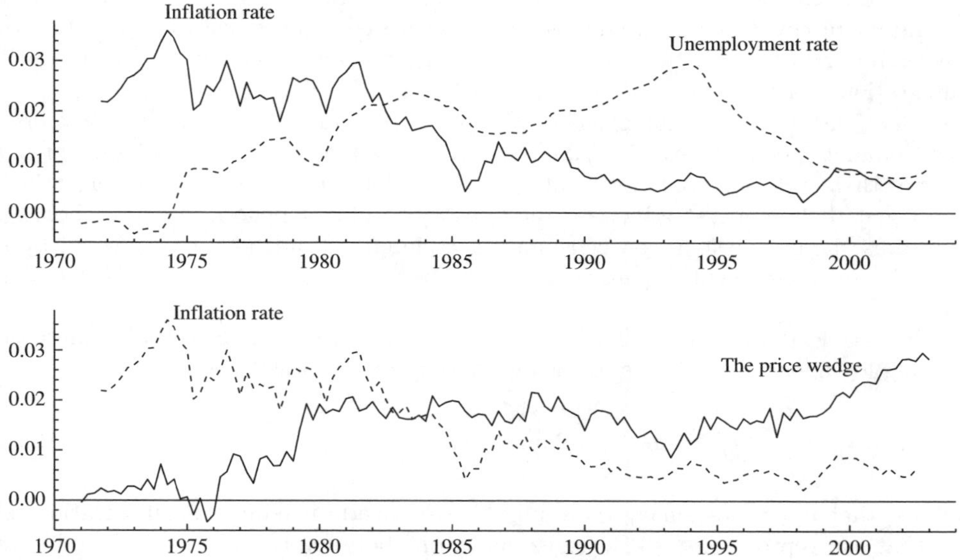

Fig 20.3 The graphs of unemployment rate and CPI inflation rate (upper panel) and of CPI inflation rate and the price wedge CPI and output prices (lower panel).

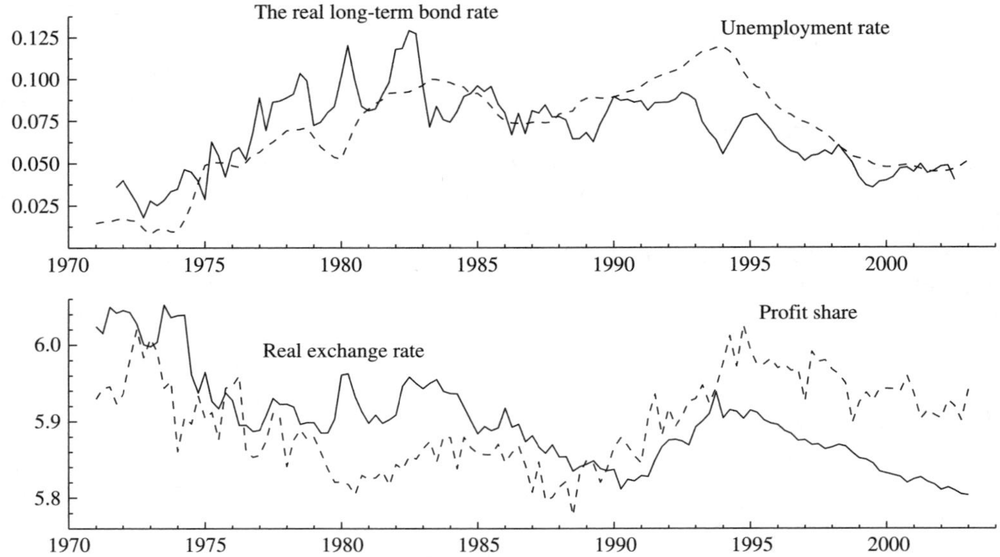

Fig 20.4 The graphs of unemployment and the real long-term bond rate (upper panel) and of the mark-up and the real exchange rate (lower panel).

relationships, (20.6) and (20.7), may very well be consistent with a polynomially cointegrated relation between the inflation rate and the profit share and a directly stationary relation between the profit share and the unemployment rate. In such a case inflation rate and unemployment rate would also be cointegrated. This is just an illustration that an economic relation can be (and often is) a linear combination of several irreducible cointegration relations.

Under long-run price homogeneity Chapters 16 and 17 showed that any of the three nominal growth rates, $\Delta w_t, \Delta p_{y,t}$, or $\Delta p_{c,t}$, can be used as a measure of nominal growth in the polynomially cointegrated relations, but that the interpretation of the estimated dynamic steady-state relations will differ depending on the choice. As the purpose here is to focus on consumer price inflation and how it is affected by the wage-price-unemployment dynamics, $\Delta p_{c,t}$ will be our preferred measure of the nominal growth.

Subtracting (20.7) from (20.6), replacing expectations with actual values, and assuming log linearity, gives the following relation for the price wedge:

$$p_{c,t} - p_{y,t} = a_9 + a_{10}\Delta p_{ct} + a_{11}U_t + a_{12}R_t^r + a_{13}q_t + v_{5,t}. \tag{20.12}$$

Provided that $v_{5,t}$ is stationary there might exist several irreducible cointegration relations that can reproduce (20.12), for example, one between $(p_{y,t} - p_{c,t})$, R_t^r and q_t and another between U_t and Δp_t. In this case, the five variables would share three common stochastic trends. If there are fewer common stochastic trends then there would be correspondingly more cointegration. Of particular interest here is whether U_t and $\Delta p_{c,t}$ are

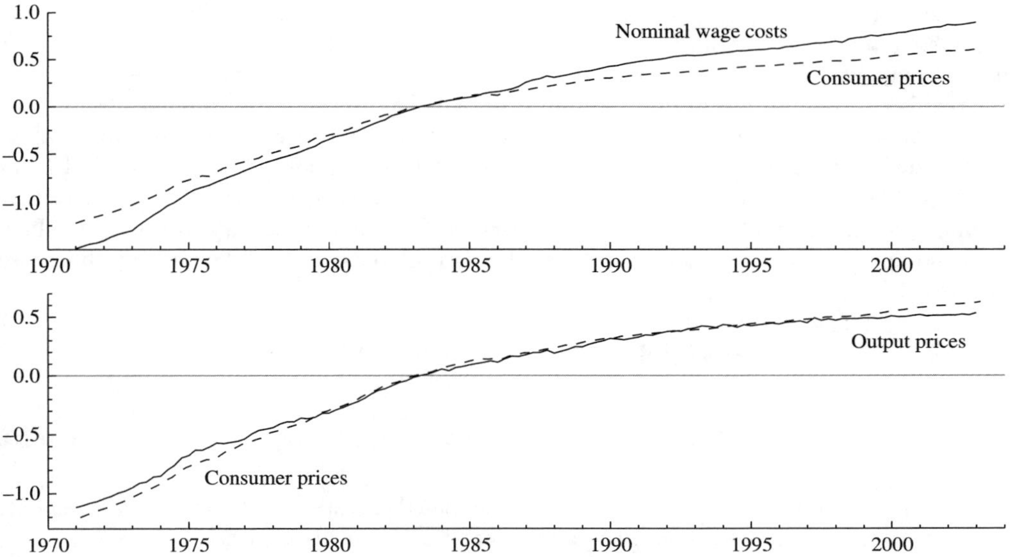

Fig 20.5 Nominal wages and prices.

cointegrated as a Phillips curve relation with a constant natural rate:[2]

$$\Delta p_{ct} = a_{14} + a_{15} U_t + v_{6,t} \tag{20.13}$$

where $a_{15} \leq 0$. A stationary Phillips curve relation with a constant natural rate would be consistent with most theories explaining the determination of wages and prices with monetary factors. On the other hand, if $v_{6,t} \sim I(1)$ then (20.13) needs to be combined with (any one of) the other variables in (20.12). Clearly, there can be several economically relevant cointegration relations among the subsets of stationary relations consistent with (20.12). For example, the hypothesis that inflation rate is dynamically adjusting to the domestic and the foreign price wedge can be specified as:

$$\Delta p_{ct} = a_{16} + a_{17}(p_c - p_y)_{t-1} + a_{18} q_{t-1} + v_{7,t} \tag{20.14}$$

where $a_{17} \leq 0$ and $a_{18} \geq 0$ implies equilibrium correction given that $v_{7,t} \sim I(0)$.

Figure 20.3, upper panel, illustrates dominantly countercyclical movements in inflation and unemployment strongly suggesting some elements of a Phillips curve relationship in the data. Similarly, the countercyclical movements between the inflation rate and the price wedge in the lower panel suggest that inflation has adjusted to the price wedge. Whether the three variables share one or two common stochastic trends cannot be judged from the graphs alone, but needs to be based on formal testing.

The cointegration analysis of the next chapter will show that the Phillips curve relation is not stationary by itself but needs to be combined with the real bond rate to become so. This is interesting as it corresponds to one of the major hypotheses proposed

[2]Note that the Phillips curve is defined here to be a relation between non-stationary variables.

by Phelps (1994) in his book *Structural Slumps: The Modern Equilibrium Theory of Unemployment, Interest, and Assets.* The main purpose of his 'structuralist' approach to unemployment was to endogenize the natural rate of unemployment in order to explain the persistent long swings in European unemployment typical of the whole post-Bretton–Woods period. The idea was to treat unemployment as 'the outcome of the configuration of real demands and supplies, the "structure" of the economy in some sense' (Phelps 1994, p. 157). One of the crucial predictions from this theory is that the natural rate of unemployment should be positively related to the real interest rate through its effect on production and investment. This can be formulated as the following modification of (20.12):

$$\begin{aligned}\Delta p_{c,t} &= a_{19} + a_{20}U_t + a_{21}(R_b - \Delta p)_t + v_{8t}\\ &= a_{20}(U_t - \bar{U}_t) + v_{5t}\\ \bar{U}_t &= -\frac{1}{a_{20}}\left[a_{19} + a_{21}(R_b - \Delta p)_t\right] + v_{8t}\end{aligned} \tag{20.15}$$

where $a_{20} \leq 0$ and $a_{21} \geq 0$. Figure 20.4, upper panel, illustrates the close comovements between unemployment rate and the real interest rate over this period.

Another important hypothesis from Phelps' theoretical model is that the mark-up should be negatively related to the real exchange rate. This can be formulates as a subhypothesis of (20.6):

$$w_t - p_{y,t} - pr_t = a_{22} + a_{23}q_t + v_{9,t} \tag{20.16}$$

where $a_{23} \leq 0$ is consistent with Phelps' theoretical model.

20.2 The data and the models

The data consist of seasonally adjusted variables from the database MONA of the National Bank of Denmark. The following variables will be analysed:

$w_c^r = w - p_c$	=	real consumption wage, where
w	=	the log of wage costs, and
p_c	=	the log consumer price index.
$pp = p_c - p_y$	=	the internal price wedge, where
p_y	=	the log of the GDP deflator.
$pr = y^r - e$	=	the log of labour productivity, where
y^r	=	the log of real GDP, and
e	=	the log of total employment.
$\Delta p_c = p_{c,t} - p_{c,t-1}$	=	consumer price inflation.
$U = U^T/L$	=	the unemployment rate, where
U^T	=	the total number of unemployed, and
L	=	the labour force.

$R_b = R_b^a/400$ = the quarterly nominal long-term bond rate, where
R_b^a = the annual rate in %.
$q = s - p_c + p_c^{ge}$ = the real exchange rate, where
p_c^{ge} = the log of German consumer price index, and
s = the log of the nominal exchange rate in Dkr/Dmk.

Graphs of the inflation rate, the unemployment rate, the price wedge, nominal and real bond rate and the real exchange rate were already shown in Chapter 19 and in Section 20.1. Here we shall take a closer look at the nominal variables with the purpose of illustrating long-run price homogeneity, or rather the lack of it. The upper panel of Figure 20.5 illustrates the development of nominal wages compared to consumer prices and the lower panel consumer prices compared to output prices. As a result of the productivity growth, nominal wages have grown more than consumer prices. Although output prices and consumer prices have followed each other quite closely, output prices seem to have grown relatively more in the first period but relatively less in the second period. This is an interesting empirical observation which will be further discussed in the next sections.

The upper panel of Figure 20.6 shows the development of nominal wage growth and the lower panel of consumer price inflation. Both series exhibit a steadily declining growth over the whole period. Even though the growth rates are on a higher level in the first part of the sample period, there is not much evidence of a deterministic drop from one level to the next at around 1983 which would be the case if the inflation rate had been stationary with a shift in the mean around 1983. Thus, the graphs suggest that nominal price levels are approximately $I(2)$ and growth rates $I(1)$. Formal $I(2)$ tests, not reported here, support this conclusion.

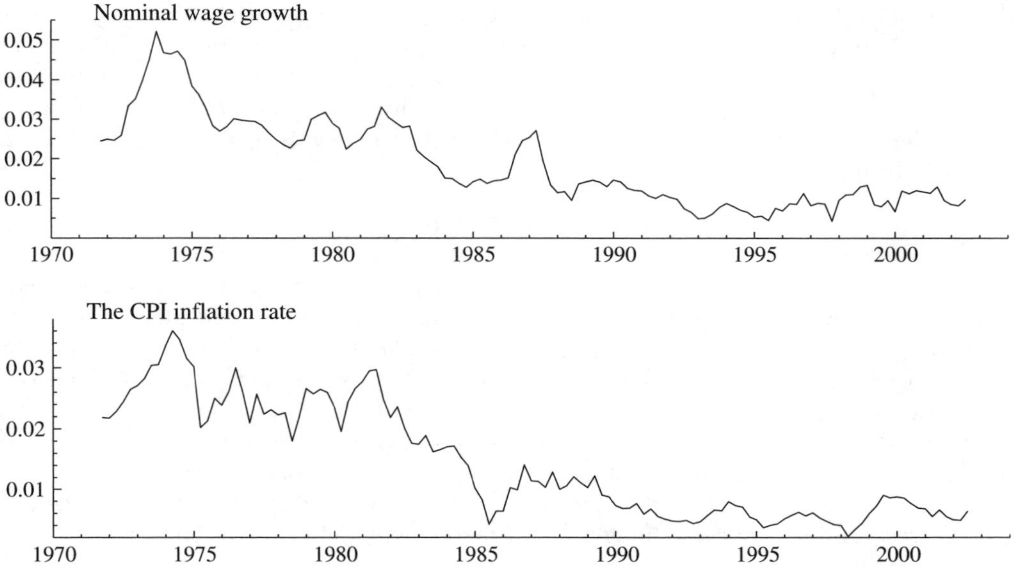

Fig 20.6 Graphs of the nominal wage growth and CPI inflation rate.

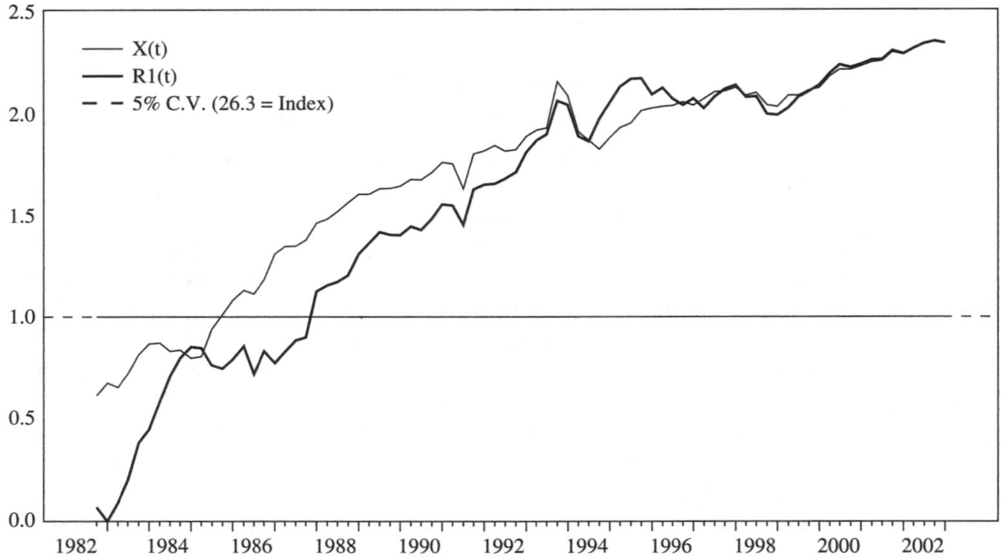

Fig 20.7 The graphs of the recursively calculated test statistic for constant β scaled with the 5% test value. Values > 1.0 reject constancy.

Furthermore, Chapters 16 and 17 demonstrated that long-run price homogeneity is needed for the nominal-to-real transformation to produce $I(1)$ variables. Therefore, if $\{w_t, p_{y,t}, p_{c,t}\} \sim I(2)$ and long-run price homogeneity is satisfied, then $(w_t - p_{c,t}) \sim I(1)$, $(p_{c,t} - p_{y,t}) \sim I(1)$, and Δw_t, $\Delta p_{c,t}$, and $\Delta p_{y,t}$ are pair-wise cointegrating. In this case, the nominal $I(1)$ trend can be described by any of the three growth rates.

Also, Chapter 16 demonstrated that under long-run price homogeneity the nominal system $[w, p_y, p_c, pr, U, R_b, q]$ can be transformed into a real variable system $[w - p_c, p_c - p_y, pr, \Delta p_c, U, R_b, q]$ without loss of information. The hypothesis of long-run homogeneity among the $\boldsymbol{\tau}'\mathbf{x}_t$ relations[3] is formulated as $\mathbf{R}'\boldsymbol{\tau} = 0$, where $\boldsymbol{\tau}$ is $p_1 \times (r + s_1)$ and $\mathbf{R}'$ is $(1 \times p_1)$ given by:

$$\mathbf{R}' = [1, 1, 1, 0, 0, 0, 0]\,.$$

Because price homogeneity might need a fairly long period to be properly established, it was first tested based on the full sample period ignoring any evidence of parameter non-constancy. It was rejected in the full period, but with estimates quite close to the homogeneity hypothesis. It was also rejected for both subperiods, strongly so for the first period and less strongly for the more recent period. Price homogeneity between the variables w, p_y, p_c and p_c^f was additionally tested in a model where the real exchange restriction had been relaxed, but homogeneity was rejected, nonetheless.

Thus, the results are similar to the money market data where long-run price homogeneity was also rejected even though the estimates were quite close to homogeneity. It is

[3]As discussed in Chapter 17 long-run homogeneity among the $\boldsymbol{\beta}$ relations is a necessary, but not sufficient condition for overall homogeneity.

a strong signal that there are some features in the data and in the determination of nominal magnitudes which are not yet fully understood. These would need to be examined more formally in the $I(2)$ model.

As the deviation from price homogeneity was fairly small in absolute value we have chosen to continue the analysis based on the nominal-to-real transformed models, albeit noting that the real wages and the price wedge are likely to contain a small $I(2)$ component. Kongsted (2005) showed that an invalid nominal-to-real transformation is likely to influence the properties of the trace test as well as various tests on $\boldsymbol{\beta}$. Some caution in the subsequent interpretation of the results is, therefore, needed. The subsequent results in Section 20.4 will demonstrate that this is indeed a problem for the first period in which homogeneity was strongly rejected.

The following VAR(2) model was chosen as our baseline model:

$$\Delta \mathbf{x}_t = \boldsymbol{\Gamma}_1 \Delta \mathbf{x}_{t-1} + \boldsymbol{\alpha}\boldsymbol{\beta}'\mathbf{x}_{t-1} + \boldsymbol{\alpha}\boldsymbol{\beta}_1 t + \boldsymbol{\mu}_0 + \boldsymbol{\varepsilon}_t \tag{20.17}$$

where $\mathbf{x}_t$ is assumed $I(1)$, $\boldsymbol{\mu}_0 = \boldsymbol{\alpha}\boldsymbol{\beta}_0 + \boldsymbol{\alpha}_\perp \boldsymbol{\gamma}_0$ is unrestricted, so $\boldsymbol{\beta}_0$ is an intercept in the cointegrating relations, $\boldsymbol{\gamma}_0$ measures the slope of linear trends in the data, and $\boldsymbol{\beta}_1$ is the slope of a linear time trend restricted to be in the cointegration relations.

Parameter constancy was checked using the recursive test procedures discussed in Chapter 9. Generally, the tests indicated non-constancy of parameters around 1983 which coincides with the beginning of the hard EMS. The graphs in Figure 20.7 based on the recursively calculated test of constant $\boldsymbol{\beta}$ in Hansen and Johansen (1999) provide ample evidence of non-constancy. For example, the hypothesis that $\tilde{\boldsymbol{\beta}} \in \text{sp}(\boldsymbol{\beta}_{(t_1)}), t_1 =$ 1982:4, ... , 2003:1, where $\tilde{\boldsymbol{\beta}}$ is the estimate of $\boldsymbol{\beta}$ based on the sample period 1971:1–1983:1, was rejected for essentially all recursive sample periods. The sample was, therefore, divided in the following subperiods: 1971:2–1983:1 and 1983:1–2003:1.

The empirical analyses of the two subperiods are done for three different models, illustrating the methodological approach of Chapter 19. A more profound discussion of how this can be used to bridge empirical evidence and underlying theory models can be found in Møller (2006). Model 1 contains the following five basic variables:

$$\mathbf{x}_t' = [w - p_c, p_c - p_y, pr, \Delta p_c, U]_t.$$

Model 2 adds the long-term bond rate, R_b, to the data vector, partly motivated by Phelps' structuralist hypothesis (20.15), partly by the previous finding of the long-term bond rate to be weakly exogenous in Chapter 11. Thus, by including the bond rate in the labour market analysis we are able to test whether the weak exogeneity result still holds within this data set. Model 3 adds the Dkr/Dmk real exchange rate to model 2, allowing us to test the second of Phelps' hypothesis of a positive relationship between the mark-up and the real exchange rate as given by (20.16).

20.3 Empirical analysis: the EMS regime

20.3.1 Specification testing

Table 20.1 reports p-values of the trace test with and without a Bartlett correction, the eigenvalues of the trace test, the modulus of the largest unrestricted characteristic roots

Table 20.1 Determination of rank.

r	0	1	2	3	4	5	6	7
Model 1								
$p-r$	5	4	3	2	1	0		
p-value	0.00	0.01	**0.18**	0.58	0.89	–		
p^*-value	0.00	0.04	**0.39**	0.76	0.90	–		
λ_i	0.42	0.37	**0.24**	0.14	0.03	–		
$\rho_{\max}$	–	0.68	**0.76**	0.82	0.91	0.92		
$t_{\max}$	–	5.9	**3.4**	4.1	3.3	1.5		
Model 2								
$p-r$	6	5	4	3	2	1	0	
p-value	0.00	0.01	**0.14**	**0.32**	0.55	0.90	–	
p^*-value	0.00	0.10	**0.44**	**0.62**	0.73	0.91	–	
λ_i	0.50	0.39	0.27	**0.20**	0.15	0.03	–	
$\rho_{\max}$	–	0.71	0.77	**0.78**	0.79	0.90	0.91	
$t_{\max}$	–	4.0	3.4	**4.2**	3.6	1.3	1.3	
Model 3								
$p-r$	7	6	5	4	3	2	1	0
p-value	0.00	0.00	0.00	0.01	**0.03**	0.15	0.31	–
p^*-value	0.00	0.01	**0.11**	**0.18**	**0.17**	0.51	0.38	–
λ_i	0.55	0.49	0.32	0.27	**0.25**	0.17	0.09	–
$\rho_{\max}$	–	0.72	0.75	0.83	**0.84**	0.91	0.93	0.97
$t_{\max}$	–	6.7	4.3	4.7	**2.9**	2.7	2.8	2.3

for a given value of r, and the largest t value in each of $\boldsymbol{\alpha}_i$, $i = 1, \ldots p$. Regarding the latter, we note that the ordering of the λ_i (and, hence, the stationarity of the unrestricted cointegration relations) is a weighted average of the significance of all adjustment coefficients (recalling that $\lambda_i = \boldsymbol{\alpha}_i'\mathbf{S}_{00}\boldsymbol{\alpha}_i$), so the largest t value is not informative about the total number of significant coefficients in $\boldsymbol{\alpha}_i$. Thus, checking the largest t value can be seen as a safeguard against including a completely irrelevant cointegration relation in the stationary part of the model.[4]

Chapter 8 discussed the difficulty of choosing the cointegration rank when the sample size is moderate and the distinction between small and large eigenvalues is diffuse. The results in Table 20.1 give ample evidence of this problem: Almost any choice of rank can be argued for, depending on whether one is more concerned about type 1 or type 2 errors. In model 1 both the asymptotic trace test and the Bartlett corrected test suggests $r = 2$, whereas a t value of 4.7 in the third cointegration might suggest $r = 3$. The largest unrestricted root is 0.76 for $r = 2$ and 0.82 for $r = 3$. In a situation like this, sensitivity analyses can be useful: What do we gain/lose by choosing more/less cointegration? After having carefully checked the consequences of the two alternatives,

[4]Note, however, that multicollinearity between estimated $\boldsymbol{\beta}$ relations might result in small t values for $\boldsymbol{\alpha}$, even though the $\boldsymbol{\beta}$ relation in question is stationary.

$r = 2$ was our preferable choice. This is roughly in line with the choice of $r = 3$ in model 2 and $r = 4$ in model 3, so that there are three common stochastic trends in all models. Thus, if the number of cointegration relations increase by the same number as the number of new variables added to the system, then the stochastic trends remain unchanged. Thus, extending the information set with the bond rate and the real exchange rate may not have added any new autonomous shocks to the system. This, of course, is correct to the extent as our choice of cointegration rank is correct.

20.3.2 The overall tests

Chapter 19 argued that the tests of long-run exclusion can be informative about whether adding a new variable is likely to improve the specification of a previously estimated structure. To economize on space, Table 20.2 reports the tests of long-run exclusion for $r = 3, 4$ and only for model 3. The results suggest that real wages and unemployment rate are long-run excludable, the former even with a high p-value. This seems to be contradicted by the quite high t values of the real wage and the unemployment rate in the $\mathbf{\Pi}$ matrix reported in Table 20.4.[5] For this reason, and since the two variables are key economic variables in our model, we keep them in the model.

The tests of stationarity (a unit vector in $\boldsymbol{\beta}$) were all rejected and only the results for model 3 with $r = 4$ is reported in the lower part of Table 20.2. However, when allowing for a linear trend in $\boldsymbol{\beta}$, the test of trend-stationarity (not reported here) was accepted for the inflation rate. Since a linear trend in the inflation rate does not make economic sense, except possibly as a local approximation, such a result essentially signals that the stochastic trend in inflation rate can be approximated by a deterministic linear trend over the period of examination.

Chapter 19 discussed how changes in long-run weak exogeneity, after having added new variables to the system, contain valuable information about the pulling and pushing forces of the system. Table 20.3 reports tests of weak exogeneity for each variable in each of the three models. The results strongly suggest that shocks to real consumption wages and the price wedge have been pushing the system in this period. In addition, the unemployment rate is borderline weakly exogenous in model 3. It is quite interesting

Table 20.2 Testing long-run exclusion and stationarity in Model 3.

r		$w - p_c$	$p_c - p_y$	c	Δp_c	U	R_b	q	*trend*
Testing a zero row in $\boldsymbol{\beta}$ (long-run exclusion)									
3	$\chi^2(3)$	**2.02**	10.60	25.15	36.35	**3.60**	14.28	9.56	19.75
	[*pval*]	[0.57]	[0.01]	[0.00]	[0.00]	[0.31]	[0.00]	[0.02]	[0.00]
4	$\chi^2(4)$	**2.90**	11.02	27.25	37.07	**5.90**	15.32	12.25	21.69
	[*pval*]	[0.57]	[0.03]	[0.00]	[0.00]	[0.21]	[0.00]	[0.02]	[0.00]
Testing a unit vector in $\boldsymbol{\beta}$ (stationarity)									
4	$\chi^2(4)$	21.37	22.95	22.92	16.00	18.00	21.85	17.61	
	[*pval*]	[0.00]	[0.00]	[0.00]	[0.00]	[0.00]	[0.00]	[0.00]	

[5] Multicollinearity among variables can sometimes lead to acceptance of long-run exclusion even though the variable is in fact significant in the long-run relations.

Table 20.3 Testing a zero row and a unit vector in α in the three models.

		$w-p_c$	p_c-p_y	pr	Δp_c	U	R_b	q
Testing a zero row in α (weak exogeneity)								
Model 1	$\chi^2(2)$	**0.21**	**0.45**	9.38	18.08	6.50	–	–
	[*pval*]	[0.90]	[0.80]	[0.01]	[0.00]	[0.04]		
Model 2	$\chi^2(3)$	**3.94**	**2.92**	12.01	19.25	12.33	10.32	–
	[*pval*]	[0.27]	[0.40]	[0.01]	[0.00]	[0.01]	[0.02]	
Model 3	$\chi^2(4)$	**2.84**	**3.40**	10.27	24.87	**8.48**	14.27	11.21
	[*pval*]	[0.59]	[0.49]	[0.04]	[0.00]	[0.08]	[0.01]	[0.02]
Testing a unit vector in α (pure adjustment)								
Model 1	$\chi^2(3)$	25.28	21.18	9.12	**0.79**	10.17	–	–
	[*pval*]	[0.00]	[0.00]	[0.03]	[0.85]	[0.02]		
Model 2	$\chi^2(3)$	15.18	9.57	**6.20**	**1.29**	**3.98**	**6.70**	–
	[*pval*]	[0.00]	[0.02]	[0.10]	[0.73]	[0.26]	[0.08]	
Model 3	$\chi^2(3)$	8.43	9.62	**3.24**	**1.13**	**4.38**	**5.52**	**4.10**
	[*pval*]	[0.04]	[0.02]	[0.36]	[0.77]	[0.22]	[0.14]	[0.25]

to note that the long-term bond rate is no longer weakly exogenous in this system, suggesting that it has been influenced by excess real wages and unemployment or other imbalances in the Danish labour market.

The joint test of $(w-p_c)$ and (p_c-p_y) being weakly exogenous was accepted with a p-value of 0.96 in model 1, 0.38 in model 2, and 0.72 in model 3. The joint weak exogeneity of $(w-p_c)$, (p_c-p_y) and U was accepted with a p-value of 0.11 in model 1, 0.05 in model 2, and 0.14 in model 3.

As weak exogeneity is not invariant to changes in the information set, it was quite interesting to find that the weak exogeneity results were essentially unchanged when adding the new variables. There is no reason *a priori* why this would be the case. For example, assume that the wage relation would need either the long-term interest rate, the real exchange rate, or both to become stationary and that real wages and the price wedge are equilibrium correcting to this relation. In this case the real wage and the price wedge would no longer be weakly exogenous when adding the bond rate and the real exchange rate to the system.[6]

Treating the consumption wages, the internal price wedge and the unemployment rate as jointly weakly exogenous would give us a nice separation between the pulling and pushing variables. However, the joint exogeneity of the three variables was only borderline acceptable and the subsequent analysis seems to suggest that the third variable, the unemployment rate, has in fact adjusted to some of the long-run relations. Thus, the unemployment rate is a borderline case and will not be treated as a weakly exogenous variable in the subsequent analysis.

The test of a unit vector in α is essentially a mirror image of the test of weak exogeneity. If we find that $p-r$ of the variables are weakly exogenous, then the remaining r variables will have a unit vector in α and the p-value of the joint test will be identical in both cases. The individual unit vector tests reported in Table 20.3 provide information

[6]Adding a different set of new variables might, of course, have changed the weak exogeneity results.

about which variables (i.e. the shocks of which) have only had transitory effects on the system. It is interesting to note that the inflation rate has the highest p-value in all models suggesting that *inflationary shocks have not been pushing the labour market* in this period. A similar result was found in Chapter 11 for the monetary analysis. We shall argue at the end of this chapter that this has to do with increased European economic integration and trade competition, or with globalization in general.

The unit vector hypothesis is also accepted for productivity and unemployment rate in model 1 though with quite low p-values. It is similarly accepted for the unemployment rate, the bond rate, and productivity in model 2, but for the last two variables with low p-values. Finally, in model 3, the p-values are fairly large for all variables except real wages and the price wedge. An interesting result is that the unit vector hypothesis for unemployment rate has a fairly high p-value in all three models, which seems to contradict the weak exogeneity test results. To understand why this can happen it is useful to consider the following representation:

$$\begin{bmatrix} \vdots \\ \Delta U_t \\ \vdots \end{bmatrix} = + \cdots + \begin{bmatrix} & & \mathbf{0} & \\ 0 & 0 & * & 0 \\ & & \mathbf{0} & \end{bmatrix} \begin{bmatrix} \boldsymbol{\beta}_1'\mathbf{x}_{t-1} \\ \boldsymbol{\beta}_2'\mathbf{x}_{t-1} \\ \boldsymbol{\beta}_3'\mathbf{x}_{t-1} \\ \boldsymbol{\beta}_4'\mathbf{x}_{t-1} \end{bmatrix} + \cdots \qquad (20.18)$$

In (20.18) the unemployment rate is only adjusting to one cointegration relation, so the condition for a unit vector in $\boldsymbol{\alpha}$ is satisfied and the test should accept. However, the joint test of four zero coefficients in the $\boldsymbol{\alpha}$ row, of which only one is different from zero, might also be accepted if the significance of the non-zero adjustment coefficient is not very high. Thus, in a case like this, the power of the weak exogeneity test is likely to be low.

20.3.3 Exploiting the information in the Π matrix

The purpose of this subsection is to discuss an identification strategy for the $\boldsymbol{\beta}$ relations and how it is facilitated by gradually increasing the information set. In general, there exists several long-run structures, $\boldsymbol{\alpha\beta}'$, that can reproduce the $\boldsymbol{\Pi}$ matrix. Therefore, it is often useful to first exploit the information in the $\boldsymbol{\Pi}$ matrix, recalling that each row defines a stationary relation. Table 20.4 reports the estimated rows of the $\boldsymbol{\Pi}$ matrix for each of the three models. Significant coefficients are given in bold face.

Table 20.3 showed that the *real consumption wages* and the *price wedge* were weakly exogenous in all three models with fairly high p-values. Thus, we should not expect to find evidence of any long-run relations in the first two blocks of equations. This is more or less the case: Among the wage equations the t values are quite small in model 1 and 2 but, with the inclusion of real exchange rates, t values become much more significant in model 3. This suggests some, albeit not very strong, comovements between real wages, unemployment rate (though 'wrongly' signed for a wage relation to be) and the real exchange rates. The fact that the relationship was not statistically significant implies that real wage shocks have been pushing this system. However, it can also be a sign that important variables are still omitted. For example, the reservation wage, the level of unemployment benefits, taxes, etc. might be needed to achieve a stationary real wage relation. In the price wedge equations there is no evidence of equilibrium correction and only weak evidence of some effects from real wages and the unemployment rate.

Table 20.4 Comparing the rows of the Π matrices.

	$(w-p_c)$	(p_c-p_y)	pr	Δp_c	U	R_b	q	$trend$
Wage equation $\Delta(w-p_c)$								
Mod. 1	0.03 [0.47]	0.02 [0.47]	−0.04 [−0.49]	−0.05 [−0.15]	0.03 [0.33]	–	–	0.01 [0.45]
Mod. 2	−0.15 [−1.83]	0.06 [1.38]	−0.12 [−1.23]	−0.28 [−0.74]	0.20 [1.90]	−0.06 [−0.14]	–	0.00 [1.87]
Mod. 3	**−0.17** [−2.64]	−0.01 [−0.23]	−0.08 [−0.74]	0.14 [0.36]	**0.27** [2.66]	−0.05 [−0.11]	**−0.12** [−2.17]	0.11 [1.67]
Wedge equation $\Delta(p_c-p_y)$								
Mod. 1	−0.01 [−0.10]	−0.01 [−0.09]	0.02 [0.15]	0.29 [0.73]	0.02 [0.22]	–	–	−0.00 [−0.04]
Mod. 2	**0.18** [2.00]	−0.04 [−0.76]	0.08 [0.63]	0.46 [1.03]	−0.16 [−1.35]	0.24 [0.52]	–	−0.00 [−1.35]
Mod. 3	**0.20** [2.64]	0.00 [0.00]	0.03 [0.21]	0.31 [0.67]	**−0.26** [−2.14]	0.62 [1.02]	0.09 [1.31]	−0.07 [−0.95]
Productivity equation Δpr								
Mod. 1	**0.35** [4.33]	**0.32** [4.32]	**−0.59** [−4.34]	0.38 [0.74]	**0.45** [3.87]	–	–	**0.20** [4.30]
Mod. 2	−0.06 [−0.48]	**0.28** [4.44]	**−0.69** [−4.42]	−0.30 [−0.50]	**0.62** [3.90]	**1.70** [2.79]	–	**0.00** [4.47]
Mod. 3	−0.06 [−0.62]	**0.38** [4.18]	**−0.71** [−4.32]	−0.89 [−1.47]	**0.54** [3.39]	0.91 [1.13]	0.14 [1.65]	**0.44** [4.32]
Inflation equation $\Delta^2 p_c$								
Mod. 1	−0.02 [−0.75]	−0.02 [−0.82]	0.02 [0.41]	**−0.96** [−5.40]	**−0.11** [−2.82]	–	–	−0.02 [−1.13]
Mod. 2	−0.02 [−0.49]	−0.04 [−1.88]	0.06 [1.18]	**−1.01** [−4.93]	**−0.17** [−3.07]	0.24 [1.11]	–	−0.00 [−1.09]
Mod. 3	**0.09** [2.93]	**0.08** [2.70]	−0.01 [−0.26]	**−1.27** [−6.76]	**−0.18** [−3.51]	0.06 [0.24]	**0.14** [−5.04]	−0.04 [−1.23]
Unemployment equation ΔU								
Mod. 1	**0.03** [3.71]	**0.03** [3.70]	**−0.06** [−3.79]	−0.02 [−0.36]	**0.04** [2.91]	–	–	**0.02** [3.62]
Mod. 2	**0.06** [4.65]	0.01 [1.88]	**−0.04** [−2.60]	−0.03 [−0.55]	−0.02 [−1.01]	**0.32** [5.22]	–	0.00 [0.77]
Mod. 3	**0.03** [2.59]	0.00 [0.03]	**−0.03** [−1.87]	−0.04 [−0.69]	−0.02 [−1.33]	**0.41** [4.86]	−0.01 [0.63]	0.02 [1.52]
Bond rate equation ΔR_b								
Mod. 2	−0.00 [−0.53]	**−0.01** [−2.99]	**0.04** [3.35]	**0.08** [2.04]	−0.02 [−1.59]	**−0.14** [−3.49]	–	**−0.00** [−3.02]
Mod. 3	−0.01 [−1.03]	**−0.01** [−1.84]	**0.04** [3.79]	0.05 [1.24]	−0.01 [−1.27]	**−0.24** [−4.64]	0.00 [0.52]	**−0.02** [−3.81]
Real exchange rate equation Δq								
Mod. 3	**−0.23** [−3.92]	**−0.26** [−4.83]	**0.35** [3.56]	0.00 [0.01]	0.03 [0.31]	−0.56 [−1.17]	**−0.27** [−5.21]	**−0.13** [−2.04]

The *productivity* equations give strong support to (20.11) by the positive relationship between trend-adjusted productivity, unemployment and the price wedge. We note that the significant relationship between productivity and real wages in model 1 disappears when adding the bond rate, which again disappears when adding the real exchange rates. Altogether, the results tentatively suggest that productivity, rather than wages, has adjusted and that the productivity improvement has been achieved by a parallel increase in the unemployment rate.

The *inflation rate* equation in models 1 and 2 provide strong support for the standard Phillips curve relation (20.13), whereas model 3 suggests a natural rate which is increasing with real wages and real exchange rates. The sign of the coefficients suggests equilibrium correction with respect to real wages, $w - p_c$, and the real exchange rate consistent with (20.14). Thus, there seem to be two mechanisms driving inflation in this period: a Phillips curve effect, $\Delta p_{c,t} = -0.17U_t$, and an inflation adjustment effect $\Delta p_{c,t} = 0.3(w-p_c)_t-0.45(p_c-p_c^*-s)_t$. This suggests that inflation rate equation in model 3 should be considered a weighted average of $-\{(\Delta p_{c,t}+0.17U_t)+0.27[\Delta p_{c,t}-0.3(w-p_c)_t+0.45q_t]\}$.

None of the three *unemployment* equations exhibit significant equilibrium correction. In model 1, unemployment has a positive coefficient suggesting overshooting, consistent with the empirically strong feature of persistence in this series. Furthermore, the results show that the unemployment rate has been comoving with the bond rate and with real wages in excess of productivity. Thus, there is some evidence supporting (20.15).

The *bond rate* equation in model 1 and model 2 suggests that the bond rate has been significantly equilibrium correcting to the determinants in the domestic labour market. Model 2 contains an (almost homogeneous) relation between the bond rate, the inflation rate, trend-adjusted productivity and the price wedge. Adding the real exchange rate to model 3 makes the picture more diffuse.

Finally, the *real exchange rate* equation provides strong support for (20.16), i.e. for a positive relationship between the real exchange rate and the mark-up.

The inspection of the $\mathbf{\Pi}$ matrix illustrated that each row contains some tentative information about the long-run relations and their adjustment dynamics. Comparing the three models provided some insight into the importance of the new variables and, thus, of the role of the *ceteris paribus* assumption in 'small' models. Furthermore, the inspection of the wage and unemployment equations suggested that additional variables are possibly needed to improve their long-run specification.

20.3.4 Identifying the long-run structure

The purpose of this section is to illustrate the step-wise, 'specific-to-general' identification of the long-run structure. It roughly runs as follows: First we identify a 'small' $\boldsymbol{\alpha\beta}'$ structure preferably describing some of the basic relations introduced in Section 20.1, then we add a new variable, run the automated test procedures to find out how the new variable has affected the system, and, if the rank has increased, estimate the new cointegration relation by keeping the previously estimated structure fixed. If some of the estimated relations in a previous step were less satisfactory from an interpretational point of view, we check whether the new variable can improve the specification. Thus, by gradually enlarging the information set we might also learn to modify, improve, and adjust our intuition as a result of relaxing the *ceteris paribus* clause of the underlying theory model.

Table 20.5 Identified β structures in the three models.

	$(w-p_c)$	(p_c-p_y)	pr	Δp_c	U	R_b	q	$trend$[1]
Model 1: $\chi^2(2) = 0.58(0.75)$								
$\hat{\beta}_1^c$	**−0.56** [−3.93]	**−0.54** [−4.50]	**1.00** [0.00]	–	**−0.72** [−4.63]	–	–	**−0.35** [−6.05]
$\hat{\alpha}_1^c$	∗	∗	−0.59 [−4.36]	∗	−0.06 [−3.78]	–	–	–
$\hat{\beta}_2^c$	**0.04** [7.18]	–	–	**1.00** [0.00]	**0.07** [3.21]	–	–	–
$\hat{\boldsymbol{\alpha}}_2^c$	∗	∗	∗	−0.95 [−5.11]	∗	–	–	
Model 2: $\chi^2(5) = 4.46(0.49)$								
$\hat{\beta}_1^c$	–	**−0.40** [4.44]	**1.00** [0.00]	–	**−0.93** [−6.89]	–	–	**−0.57** [−59.76]
$\hat{\boldsymbol{\alpha}}_1^c$	∗	∗	−0.75 [−4.85]	∗	−0.04 [−2.44]	0.03 [2.82]	–	–
$\hat{\beta}_2^c$	–	–	–	**1.00** [0.00]	**0.11** [4.94]	**−0.62** [−8.46]	–	–
$\hat{\boldsymbol{\alpha}}_2^c$	∗	∗	∗	−1.05 [−5.32]	∗	0.07 [1.97]	–	–
$\hat{\beta}_3^c$	**−0.93** [−6.04]	–	–	–	**1.00** [0.00]	**−14.3** [−7.04]	–	–
$\hat{\boldsymbol{\alpha}}_3^c$	∗	∗	∗	0.04 [2.03]	−0.02 [−3.33]	0.01 [3.38]	–	
Model 3: $\chi^2(7) = 3.33(0.85)$								
$\hat{\beta}_1^c$	–	**−0.39** [−4.58]	**1.00** [0.00]	–	**−0.93** [−7.90]	–	–	**−0.57** [−63.32]
$\hat{\boldsymbol{\alpha}}_1^c$	−0.21 [−2.00]	∗	−0.65 [−4.14]	0.12 [2.28]	−0.05 [−2.61]	0.03 [3.38]	∗	–
$\hat{\beta}_2^c$	–	–	–	**1.00** [0.00]	**0.08** [4.53]	**−0.53** [−8.44]	–	–
$\hat{\boldsymbol{\alpha}}_2^c$	∗	∗	∗	−1.27 [−6.94]	∗	∗	∗	–
$\hat{\beta}_3^c$	**−0.55** [6.24]	–	–	∗	**1.00** [0.00]	**−9.51** [−8.26]	–	–
$\hat{\boldsymbol{\alpha}}_3^c$	∗	∗	∗	0.07 [2.55]	−0.04 [−3.72]	0.02 [4.26]	∗	–
$\hat{\beta}_4^c$	**1.00** [0.00]	**1.00** [0.00]	**−1.00** [0.00]	–	–	–	**0.99** [9.52]	**0.20** [12.53]
$\hat{\boldsymbol{\alpha}}_4^c$	−0.16 [−2.80]	∗	0.14 [1.62]	0.14 [5.10]	∗	∗	−0.27 [4.91]	–

[1]The trend has been scaled by a factor of 100.

While an inspection of the $\boldsymbol{\Pi}$ matrix is indispensable as a first step, it is seldom a substitute for a structural formulation of $\boldsymbol{\beta}$. But the choice of an identified structure is inherently more ambiguous because there may exist many different representations of the long-run structure that will reproduce the $\boldsymbol{\Pi}$ matrix. Thus, different researchers are likely to identify different structures. The question is whether it is possible to tell two (or several) radically different stories based on the same $\boldsymbol{\Pi}$ matrix. Though a theoretical possibility, we find it unlikely in practise, provided that (1) the identified $\boldsymbol{\beta}$ relations satisfy the conditions for formal, empirical, and economic identification and (2) the estimated adjustment dynamics, $\boldsymbol{\alpha}$, make sense. The latter is in particular worth stressing as published results often focus on $\boldsymbol{\beta}$ without paying due attention to $\boldsymbol{\alpha}$. A credible structure should describe both a plausible equilibrium correction behaviour and interpretable long-run relations. The chance of identifying two such structures describing radically different economic behaviour does not seem overly large.

Table 20.5 reports an identified structure for each of the three models. The $\boldsymbol{\beta}$ estimates are in bold face to distinguish them from the $\boldsymbol{\alpha}$ coefficients. A * means an $\boldsymbol{\alpha}$ coefficient with an absolute t value < 2.0. When discussing the results we shall pay special attention to whether an equation is equilibrium correcting or not with respect to an identified long-run relation. To facilitate the investigation of this important feature of the model, we have reported $\boldsymbol{\beta}_i$ and $\boldsymbol{\alpha}_i$ in pairs.

The first $\boldsymbol{\beta}$ relation in model 1 describes that trend-adjusted productivity is positively related to the unemployment rate and to the real product wage. It resembles relation (20.11), but might also be interpreted in terms of the real product wage relation (20.8). The reason why we interpret it as a productivity relation rather than a real wage relation is because $\hat{\boldsymbol{\alpha}}_1$ suggests that productivity rather than real wage has been equilibrium correcting to this relation. An interesting result is that the unemployment rate has been significantly influenced by this relation, but not in an equilibrium-correcting manner. Thus, unemployment has been pushed by, rather than adjusted to, labour productivity in this period.

The second relation resembles the standard Phillips curve relation (20.13) augmented with a negative effect from real wages. It might also be interpreted as evidence of the real consumption wage relation (20.9) with a negative effect from the unemployment rate. However, real wages have not been significantly equilibrium correcting to this relation, whereas the inflation rate has. This suggests a Phillips curve interpretation.

Model 2 adds the bond rate to the system. It is now possible to replace the previous Phillips curve relation with a more plausible version, where the natural rate is a positive function of the real bond rate consistent with Phelps' structuralist hypothesis (20.15). To see this, we rewrite the relation as $\hat{\boldsymbol{\beta}}_2^{c\prime}\mathbf{x}_t = 0.38\Delta p_{c,t} + 0.11U_t - 0.62(R_{b,t} - \Delta p_{c,t})$. The inflation rate, but not the unemployment rate, is equilibrium correcting to this relation. The first cointegration relation describes a similar productivity relation as in model 1, except that the real wage can now be omitted (without changing the adjustment coefficients).[7] Instead, real consumption wage enters the third cointegration relation together with the unemployment rate and the bond rate, both of which are equilibrium correcting to this relation.

Thus, the effect of including the bond rate to the system is essentially that we were able to replace a puzzling 'Phillips curve' relation with a more credible one, and obtained a third relation describing that the unemployment rate and the long-term bond rate have been comoving with the real consumption wage over this period. The insignificant equilibrium correction coefficient in the unemployment row of the $\boldsymbol{\Pi}$ matrix can be explained by the overshooting, property of $\boldsymbol{\beta}_1'\mathbf{x}_{t-1}$ combined with the equilibrium correcting property of $\boldsymbol{\beta}_3'\mathbf{x}_{t-1}$.

[7]Stationarity was rejected when the real wage was omitted from the first relation in model 1. This might seem contradictory, but can easily happen as the two-dimensional space of $\boldsymbol{\beta}$ in model 1 is not the same as the three-dimensional space of $\boldsymbol{\beta}$ in model 2.

Finally, model 3 adds the real exchange rate to model 2. We note that the first three $\boldsymbol{\beta}$ relations and their adjustment coefficients are essentially unchanged compared to model 2. The fourth relation is consistent with the Phelps' hypothesis (20.16) showing that the real exchange rate and the mark-up have been co-moving. We note that both the mark-up and the real exchange rate are equilibrium correcting, whereas the inflation rate is affected by this relation though not in an equilibrium correcting manner. Altogether the results provide quite strong empirical support for two of Phelps' structuralist hypotheses.

To conclude: The effect of adding the bond rate and the real exchange rate to the system is that we have been able to specify a fully identified long-run structure where all relations can be interpretable as meaningful economic relations. In particular, the results tentatively provide empirical support for two of Phelps' structuralist hypotheses.

20.4 Empirical analysis: The post-Bretton–Woods regime

Econometrically, this period is more problematic than the EMS period: The sample (1971:1–1983:1) is fairly small, and the test of long-run price homogeneity of the nominal variables was quite strongly rejected, but imposed nevertheless. The reader may rightly ask whether it makes sense to continue with real variables in this case. There are three reasons why we think it is worthwhile: First, the absolute deviations from price homogeneity were relatively small, though significant. Second, since many empirical papers are based on real variables without a prior testing homogeneity, it may be useful to point out potential consequences of using real variables when homogeneity is in fact violated. No doubt, this will render inference and, hence, conclusions less reliable, so the results have to be interpreted with some caution. Third, in spite of these econometric problems the results contain some interesting differences in the wage, price, and unemployment dynamics between the two periods.

The VAR analysis was also here done for three models of which models 1 and 2 were similarly defined as in the EMS period, whereas model 3 contained the real exchange rate, but not the bond rate. This was because the bond rate was only marginally needed in model 3 after the real exchange rate was included. Because the previous section already illustrated the methodological approach in great detail, the empirical results will be given a more cursory treatment. Even though we shall mention some results from models 1 and 2, only the analysis of model 3, defined by the data vector $\mathbf{x}_t' = [w - p_c, p_c - p_y, pr, \Delta^2 p_c, U, q]$, will be properly reported.

20.4.1 Specification tests

The p-values of the trace test, the eigenvalues, the largest characteristic roots and the largest t value for each $\boldsymbol{\alpha}_i$ reported in Table 20.6 provide (again) ample evidence of the difficulty of discriminating between stationary and non-stationary processes. In a short sample like the present one, one would expect the type 2 error to be large when the size of the test is small (cf. the discussion in Section 8.5). To illustrate, the Bartlett corrected test in Table 20.6 based on a 5% test would suggest no cointegration at all in this model, whereas the largest t value of $\boldsymbol{\alpha}_i$ suggests approximately three cointegration relations.

Table 20.6 Determination of cointegration rank.

Model 3							
$p-r$	6	5	4	**3**	2	1	
p-value	0.00	0.01	0.14	**0.49**	0.47	0.55	
p^*-value	0.15	0.18	0.42	**0.70**	0.76	0.72	
λ_i	0.59	0.57	0.45	**0.26**	0.21	0.11	
$\rho_{\max}$		0.63	0.81	**0.79**	0.86	0.89	0.91
$t_{\max}$		5.8	4.4	**4.9**	2.4	2.1	2.1

Table 20.7 Testing long-run exclusion, stationarity, weak exogeneity, and pure adjustment.

r		$w-p_c$	p_c-p_y	pr	Δp_c	U	q	*trend*
Testing a zero row in β (long-run exclusion)								
3	$\chi^2(3)$	12.09	15.66	18.84	15.53	21.80	19.07	26.38
	[*pval*]	[0.01]	[0.00]	[0.00]	[0.00]	[0.00]	[0.00]	[0.00]
Testing a unit vector in β (stationarity)								
3	$\chi^2(4)$	20.92	19.29	20.88	**2.27**	26.60	18.37	
	[*pval*]	[0.00]	[0.00]	[0.00]	[0.69]	[0.00]	[0.00]	
Testing a zero row in α (weak exogeneity)								
3	$\chi^2(3)$	17.50	**0.71**	18.74	11.13	13.75	11.62	
	[*pval*]	[0.00]	[0.87]	[0.00]	[0.01]	[0.00]	[0.01]	
Testing a unit vector in α (pure adjustment)								
3	$\chi^2(3)$	9.85	16.66	15.07	11.10	11.86	13.93	
	[*pval*]	[0.02]	[0.00]	[0.00]	[0.01]	[0.01]	[0.00]	

In the present case, the underlying lack of price homogeneity is likely to make the trace tests less reliable (Kongsted 2005) and, therefore, the choice of rank even more difficult. After some sensitivity analysis, we found ($r = 3$, $p - r = 3$) to be reasonable choice. A similar choice was also made in the EMS period for model 2, also based on six variables. Thus, a common feature of the models discussed in this chapter is that they are all based on the assumption of three common stochastic trends.

Table 20.7 reports the four automated specification tests for $r = 3$ in model 3. The tests of long-run exclusion showed that none of the variables were excludable and the tests of stationarity found the inflation rate to be stationary. The latter might seem surprising as the 1970s are generally considered to describe a high inflation period. There are two possible explanations to this: First, the unit root property is about the persistency of shocks, but not necessarily the magnitude of shocks. Even though the inflation rates were quite high and volatile in this period they, nevertheless, seemed to fluctuate around a fairly constant level. Second, imposing (incorrectly) long-run price homogeneity on the nominal variables is likely to leave a small $I(2)$ component in the real variables, which is likely to affect the tests of stationarity (Kongsted 2005).

The tests of weak exogeneity in Table 20.7 suggest that the price wedge is weakly exogenous. This is similar to the EMS period, where the price wedge (as well as real wages) was also weakly exogenous. The tests of a unit vector in $\boldsymbol{\alpha}$ found none of the variables to be purely adjusting, in contrast to the EMS period where productivity, inflation rate, real exchange rate and the bond rate had this property.

Altogether, the above results shows that the information about the pushing and the pulling forces is more diffuse in this period.

20.4.2 Investigating the Π matrix

Table 20.8 reports the estimates of $\boldsymbol{\Pi} = \boldsymbol{\alpha\beta}'$ based on $r = 3$ in model 3 with significant coefficients in bold face. When discussing the results we shall mostly focus on similarities and differences between the estimates of this period and the EMS period.

All coefficients in the *real consumer wage* equation are significant suggesting that the first row describes more than one irreducible long-run relation. Real consumption wages seem to have been equilibrium correcting to a long-run wage relation with a negative effect from the unemployment rate and a positive effect from the inflation rate and the real exchange rate. Thus, the results suggest that the high inflation rates and the frequent devaluations (real depreciations) of the Danish krona have exerted strong cost-push pressure on real wages. However, the negative effect of trend-adjusted productivity

Table 20.8 Comparing the Π matrices.

	$(w - p_c)$	$(p_c - p_y)$	pr	Δp_c	U	q	$trend^1$
The real wage equation							
$\Delta(w - p_c)$:	**−0.26** [−3.92]	**−0.42** [−4.67]	**−0.32** [−2.88]	**0.52** [2.04]	**−0.96** [−3.52]	**−0.19** [−3.73]	**0.58** [3.93]
The price wedge equation							
$\Delta(p_c - p_y)$:	0.04 [0.43]	0.11 [0.83]	0.14 [0.91]	0.17 [0.46]	0.33 [0.85]	0.04 [0.57]	−0.19 [−0.89]
The productivity equation							
Δpr:	**−0.34** [−3.77]	**−0.56** [−4.47]	**−0.84** [−5.55]	**−1.39** [−3.97]	**−1.64** [−4.35]	**−0.32** [−4.62]	**1.08** [5.28]
The inflation rate equation							
$\Delta^2 p$:	**0.13** [2.55]	0.04 [0.58]	−0.11 [−1.32]	**−0.72** [−3.74]	−0.17 [−0.83]	**0.07** [1.72]	0.03 [0.28]
Unemployment equation							
ΔU:	**0.04** [2.72]	**−0.04** [−1.58]	−0.02 [−0.65]	0.10 [1.55]	**−0.17** [−2.41]	**0.03** [2.53]	0.03 [0.88]
The real exchange rate equation							
Δq:	**−0.54** [−4.64]	**−0.35** [−2.19]	−0.31 [−1.60]	0.14 [0.32]	−0.40 [−0.82]	**−0.39** [−4.39]	**0.57** [2.17]

[1] The trend has been scaled by a factor of 100.

together with the price wedge is more puzzling and needs to be addressed in a more structural setting. Altogether the estimated results differ substantially from the EMS period where real wages were essentially weakly exogenous.

There are no significant effects in the *price wedge* equations consistent with the weak exogeneity result. This is similar to the EMS period.

The *productivity* variable is equilibrium correcting with significantly negative effects from all included variables. Thus, the movements in productivity seem to have been countercyclical to the unemployment rate, the inflation rate, the price wedge, and the real exchange rate. This might suggest that real business cycles in the 1970s were negatively affected by the above variables. This is strikingly different compared to the EMS period where trend-adjusted productivity was found to be positively related to the unemployment rate, the price wedge, and the real exchange rate.

The *inflation rate* equation shows fairly strong evidence of the inflation rate having adjusted to real consumer wages and the real exchange rate (the purchasing power parity) consistent with (20.14). This is similar to the EMS period, where inflation was equilibrium correcting to the real exchange rate and the real product wage. However, the evidence of a Phillips curve effect is weaker than in the EMS period.

The *unemployment rate* equation exhibits significant equilibrium correction and provides evidence of a positive relationship between the unemployment rate and the real product wage, i.e. the demand for labour has decreased when real product wages have increased. Even though the unemployment rate seems positively related to the real exchange rate, this effect became insignificant when the bond rate was included in the VAR system. Thus, the positive relationship between unemployment rate and the bond rate strongly present in the EMS period can also be found in the 1970s. However, trend-adjusted productivity is insignificant in this period, contrary to the strong positive effects in the EMS period.

The *real exchange rate* and the real product wage have moved in a countercyclical manner over this period. The results are similar to the EMS period, except that in the EMS period real exchange rates were associated with real product wages corrected for productivity, i.e. with the mark-up.

20.4.3 An identified long-run structure

Table 20.9 reports an identified long-run structure for model 3. The first relation seems to describe elements of the real wage relation (20.9) with $(1-\omega) = 0.41$, productivity proxied by a linear trend and with real exchange rate as the major determinant. The estimated $\boldsymbol{\alpha}$ shows that the real consumption wage is overshooting to this relation while productivity and the unemployment rate are positively affected. This seems to provide empirical evidence for the hypothetical consequences of a nationwide wage increase in excess of the competitive level as discussed in Section 20.1.2.

The second relation describes a Phillips curve relationship between inflation and unemployment, which is negatively related to trend-adjusted productivity and real exchange rate. This means that the movements in unemployment rate and inflation rate have been countercyclical to productivity and real exchange rate. The unemployment rate and productivity have been equilibrium correcting, while real consumption wage has been negatively affected, i.e. has decreased with unemployment rate above its steady-state value.

Table 20.9 An identified $\boldsymbol{\beta}$ structure in model 3.

Model 3: $\chi^2(3) = 1.77(0.62)$

	$w - p_c$	$p_c - p_y$	pr	Δp_c	U	q	$trend^1$
First relation:							
$\hat{\boldsymbol{\beta}}_1^c$	**1.00** [0.00]	**0.41** [4.77]	–	–	–	**0.59** [8.06]	**−0.53** [−12.04]
$\hat{\boldsymbol{\alpha}}_1^c$	0.25 [1.86]	*	0.42 [2.20]	*	0.14 [4.07]	*	
Second relation:							
$\hat{\boldsymbol{\beta}}_2^c$	–	–	**1.05** [13.14]	**5.06** [7.04]	**1.00** [0.00]	**0.33** [10.07]	**−0.74** [−21.51]
$\hat{\boldsymbol{\alpha}}_2^c$	−1.00 [3.68]	*	−1.72 [−4.53]	*	−0.14 [−2.09]	*	
Third relation:							
$\hat{\boldsymbol{\beta}}_3^c$	**1.00** [0.00]	**1.00** [0.00]	**−1.38** [−11.35]	**−9.93** [−6.73]	–	–	–
$\hat{\boldsymbol{\alpha}}_3^c$	−0.55 [−4.17]	*	−0.73 [−3.92]	*	−0.09 [−2.52]	*	

[1] The trend has been scaled by a factor of 100.

Thus, the overshooting in real wages (evidence of the fact that real wage claims often exceeded the productivity increase in this period) resulted in increasing unemployment and wage claims were gradually moderated. That is, the overshooting in real wages (a positive α coefficient) was off-set by the increased unemployment so that real wages were, nonetheless, indirectly subject to the equilibrating forces of the labour market system. This is an empirical illustration of the theoretical example at the end of Chapter 5 Section 5.5. Note that unless the wage effects had been offset by the unemployment effects, there would have been an explosive root in the model. However, all estimated roots were either inside or on the unit circle.

Taken together, the first $\boldsymbol{\alpha}$ and $\boldsymbol{\beta}$ relations can be interpreted as strong evidence of labour unions that in the 1970s were able to enforce excessive wage claims, but not to avoid the consequence of reduction in employment due to layoffs and improvement in labour intensity.

The third relation describes a negative relationship between the mark-up and the inflation rate supporting Banerjee and Russell (2005). Real consumption wage is equilibrium correcting and productivity is overshooting, while the unemployment rate is negatively affected by this relation.

Finally, it is notable that neither the inflation rate nor the real exchange rate exhibit any significant t values in their adjustment coefficients. This is contrary to the information in the $\boldsymbol{\Pi}$ matrix which suggests strongly significant equilibrium correction in both equations. Such seemingly contradictory results are far from uncommon and can be explained by multicollinearity between the identified $\boldsymbol{\beta}$ relations.

20.5 Concluding discussion

To summarize the main results is far from easy, partly because no single theory model was tested, but the empirical regularities in the data were interpreted at the background of several broadly defined relations describing economic behaviour in the labour market, partly because there is no obvious way to distinguish between robust and less robust results. Nonetheless, the following is an attempt to point out some of the major conclusions from the above analysis.

In both periods, shocks to the price wedge were strongly pushing. As discussed in Section 20.1.2 the wedge can potentially measure various labour market effects, but we prefer to interpret the weak exogeneity result as evidence of the strong international competition in the product market due to the increased globalization over this period. But, in the 1970s it might also reflect the importance of collective wage bargaining and the relative strength between the labour and employers unions. In this period, real wages were first overshooting, after which unemployment increased and wage claims were then moderated. Increases of the real exchange rate (a real depreciation) generally seemed to improve competitiveness, the mark-up and employment. This can be interpreted as a result of competitive devaluations which were frequent in this period.

In the more recent period, productivity, rather than wages, seemed to have adjusted. This is likely to be the consequence of the commitment to keep the Danish currency within the narrow bands of the ERM regime (realignments were no longer acceptable) and of the increased European competition. Because competitive devaluations were no longer possible, the improvement in productivity as a result of excessive real wage demands seemed to have resulted in a parallel increase in the unemployment rate but not in increases in product prices. At the same time, the unemployment rate and the bond rate were cointegrated (together with real wages), both of them were equilibrium correcting. This seems to suggest that the financing of unemployment benefits had exerted an upward pressure on the government bond rates.

Thus, at the same time as high unemployment rates increased the long-term interest rate, the increased product market competition exerted a downward pressure on the inflation rate. As the level of unemployment rate decreased at the end of the period, the bond rate started to decline. Thus, the previous finding in Chapter 10 that inflation rate was not cointegrated with the nominal interest rates can now be better understood. Increases in productivity have been achieved by improvement of labour intensity, which has increased unemployment. Increased unemployment has decreased real wage pressure and inflation has declined. But high unemployment has also increased the bond rate. Therefore, the bond rate and the inflation rate have not been comoving into a stationary real interest rate as the Fisher parity would assume.

The most distinct difference between the two periods was in the way productivity was related to the other variables of the system. In particular, productivity in the 1970s was negatively associated with inflation, unemployment, real product wages and the real exchange rate, whereas in the EMS period productivity was positively associated with unemployment and the price wedge. Since productivity is defined as real GDP per employed, this might in fact explain the negative, but non-constant, relationship between real income and inflation rate previously found in the monetary analysis.

Thus, the first regime seems to be a story about strong labour unions, rigid institutions, productivity adjustment, devaluations and realignments, not as a cure but as a means to hide the symptoms of the illness. In the second regime the story is about increasingly weak labour unions, large-scale labour layoffs, and productivity adjustment. Excessive real wage claims seemed to have caused both price inflation and unemployment in the first period, but foremost unemployment in the second period. Competitiveness was largely achieved by producing the same output with less labour, evidenced by unemployment and trend-adjusted productivity moving together in the data. This seems to explain both the slow-down in real growth and the high level of unemployment rates of this period.

21

Foreign transmission effects: Denmark versus Germany

Denmark, as a small open economy, is strongly dependent on its trade with Europe, in particular with her influential neighbour Germany. As a result, Denmark has over the whole sample period tied its currency to the German mark, first by participating in the 'snake-in-the-tunnel' float against the US dollar, and then since 1979 in the EMS exchange rate regime with the narrow bands of the ERM ($\pm 2.25\%$). Even though Denmark did not join the EMU in 1999, the Danish krona has tightly followed the euro. In the period of the snake and the first years of the EMS, the Danish krona was frequently subject to realignments and minor devaluations. Only after the commitment in 1983 to stop the realignments the narrow bands of the ERM became binding also in practice. From 1995 onwards the Danish krona became almost fixed, first to the German Dmk and later to the euro.

The aim of this chapter is to examine the international transmission mechanisms between Denmark and Germany through an empirical analysis of the basic international parity conditions linking the Danish inflation and interest rates with the German ones. An important empirical question of this chapter is whether the Danish inflation has been primarily imported from Germany. At the same time the chapter offers another methodological illustration of the principle 'specific-to-general' in the choice of information set.

The organization of the chapter is as follows: Section 1 discusses the international parity conditions and provides a detailed graphical analysis of the main determinants. Section 2 defines the two empirical models to be analysed; a small model based on the Danish/German inflation, long-term interest, and real exchange rates and a larger model extending the variable set with the short-term interest rates. Section 3 discusses two identified long-run structures: one for the small model and the other for the extended model. The common stochastic trends representation for the extended model is also discussed.

21.1 International parity conditions

Purchasing power parity (PPP) is one of the cornerstones in international finance relating the prices in one country to another measured in the same currency. Since at an aggregate level, prices are only available as a price index, only relative but not absolute purchasing power parity can be inferred from such data without additional information. We define relative PPP as:

$$p_t = p_t^* + s_t + v_t. \tag{21.1}$$

where p_t is the log of the domestic price level, p_t^* is the log of the foreign price level, and s_t denotes the log of the spot exchange rate (home currency price of a unit of foreign currency). The deviation from equilibrium state at time t is denoted $ppp_t = p_t - p_t^* - s_t$.[1] For PPP to hold empirically, ppp_t needs to be stationary, but most empirical papers do not find this to be the case (Rogoff 1996). This has spurred a large number of papers trying to explain why.

It is frequently found that $p_t \sim I(2)$, $p_t^* \sim I(2)$, and $s_t \sim I(1)$, so one would expect $(p_t - p_t^*) \sim I(1)$ and $(p_t - p_t^* - s_t) \sim I(0)$ as the movements in nominal exchange rate should reflect movements in price differential in the absence of trade barriers. The graphs of relative log prices and log exchange rate in the upper panel of Figure 21.1 seem to

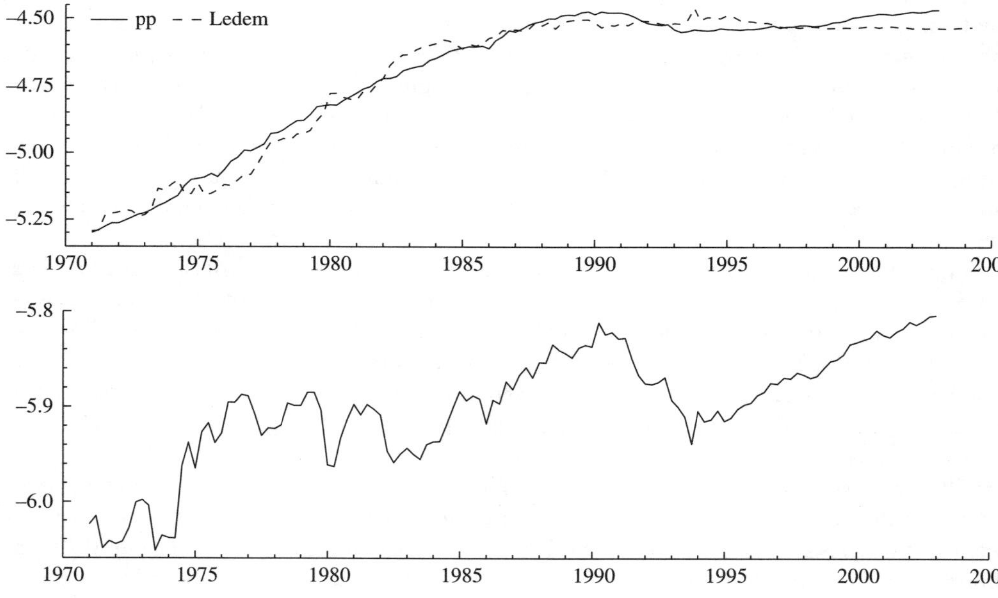

Fig 21.1 The graphs of the price differential and the nominal exchange rate (upper panel) and the *ppp* term (lower panel).

[1] Note that the *ppp* term is also the (logarithm) of the real exchange rate. We prefer to use the label *ppp* in this chapter because we are adopting a parity perspective and also because we do not model the real exchange rate in terms of real fundamentals.

suggest that the two have, indeed, moved fairly closely together. Nevertheless, the graph of the *ppp* term in the lower panel clearly exhibits persistent movements away from a stationary equilibrium state and the stationarity of the *ppp* was rejected with a p-value of 0.0005.[2]

Through the balance of payments constraint we know that any current account imbalance generated by such persistent movements away from equilibrium has to be financed through the capital account. The implication of this is that the PPP condition is likely to be strongly related to another parity condition, namely uncovered interest rate parity (UIP) (see Johansen and Juselius 1992; Juselius 1991a, 1995; MacDonald and Marsh 1997, 1999; Juselius and MacDonald 2004, 2006). By combining the two parity conditions we hope to be able to pick up the influence from the financial markets on the PPP.

The UIP is defined by:

$$E_t^e(\Delta_m s_{t+m})/m - (i_t^m + i_t^{m*}) = 0, \tag{21.2}$$

where i_t^m denotes the yield of a bond with maturity m at time t and E_t^e an economic expectation on the basis of time t information. Similar to the PPP, the empirical support for the UIP condition has generally been very weak (Frydman and Goldberg 2001). In the

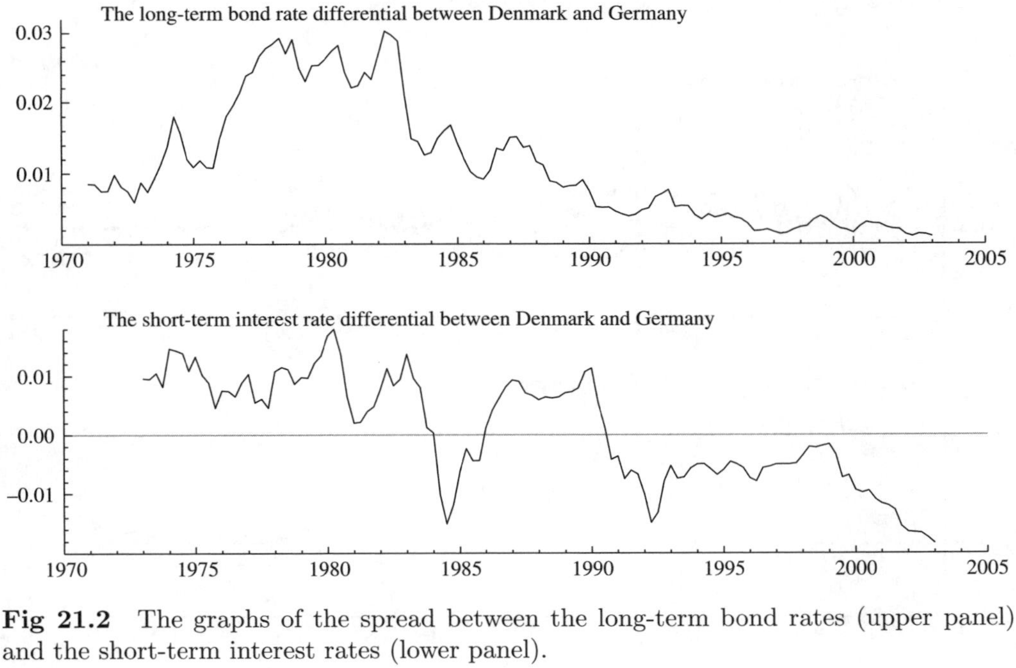

Fig 21.2 The graphs of the spread between the long-term bond rates (upper panel) and the short-term interest rates (lower panel).

[2]The stationarity hypotheses referred to in this section are testing a unit vector in β allowing for a constant and based on the extended model in Section 21.3.

literature, this is often interpreted as evidence of a risk premium to be added to (21.2):

$$E_t^e(\Delta_m s_{t+m})/m - (i_t^m + i_t^{m*}) = v_t. \tag{21.3}$$

By combining (21.2) and (21.1) we get:

$$\begin{aligned}(i_t^l - i_t^{l*}) &= E_t(\Delta_l s_{t+l})/l + v_t \\ &= E_t(\Delta_l p_{t+l} - \Delta_l p_{t+l}^*)/l + v_t\end{aligned} \tag{21.4}$$

which shows that if the spread between expected domestic and foreign inflation over the period of maturity l is non-stationarity, then the domestic and foreign yield gap would also have to be non-stationary.

The question whether $(i_t^l - i_t^{l*})$ (the forward premium) is stationary or not is of considerable interest and needs to be discussed further. From (21.4) it appears that a non-stationary spread can be due to a non-stationary risk premium or a non-stationary expected depreciation rate. However, the fact that the latter is not observable complicates the empirical testing of how to choose between the two. Because expectations play a prominent role in all the remaining parity conditions discussed here, this is a problem that cannot be ignored. But, as already discussed in Chapter 2, replacing expectations with actual values will yield valid cointegration results under two fairly weak assumptions on the expectations formation: (1) the difference between $E_t(x_{t+l})$ and x_{t+l} is stationary or, preferably, white noise (i.e. agents do not make systematic forecast errors) and (2) the differenced process $(x_{t+l} - x_t)/l$ is stationary.

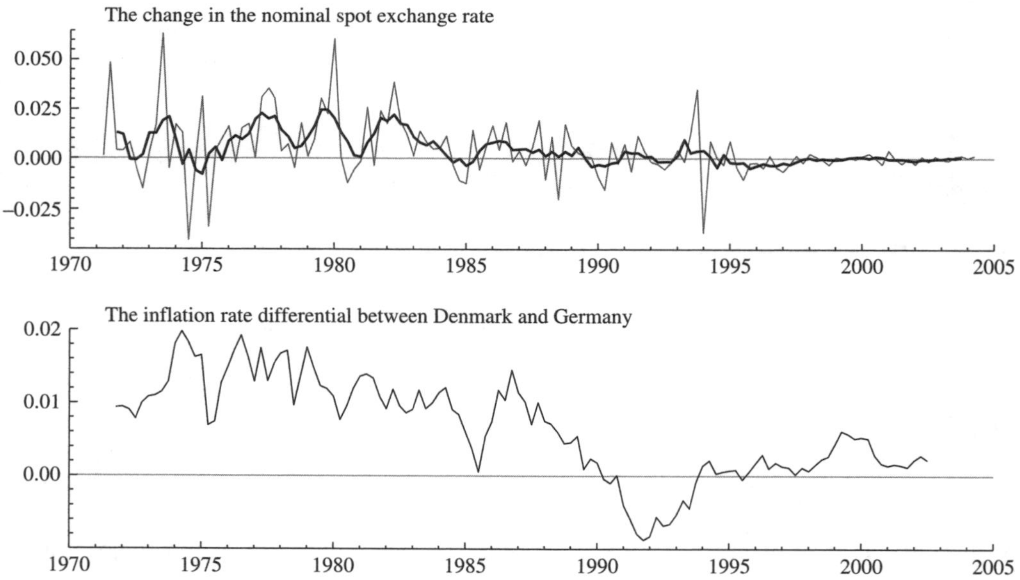

Fig 21.3 The graphs of the exchange rate of the Dkr versus Dmk (dotted line) and a four-quarter moving average (solid line) in the upper panel and inflation rate differential in the lower panel.

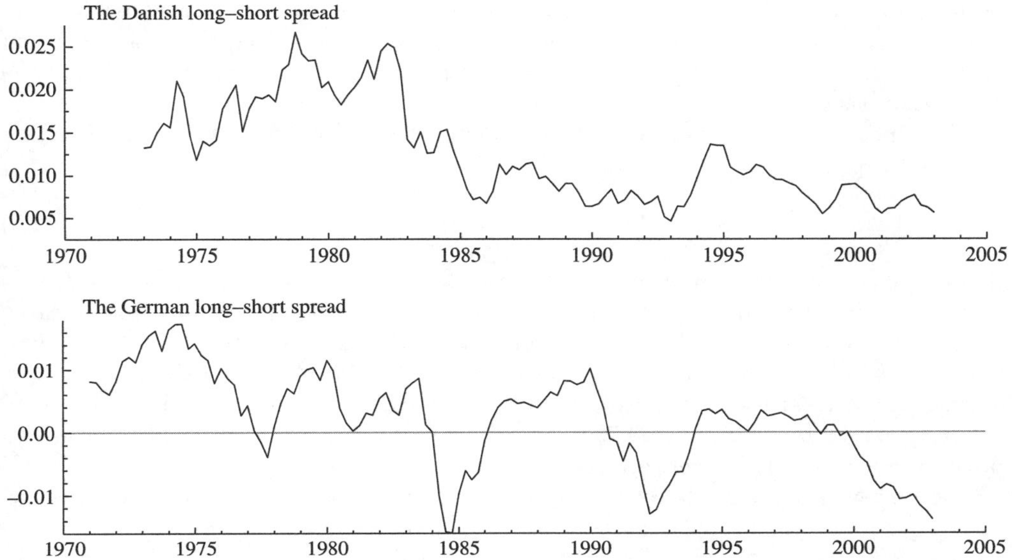

Fig 21.4 The graphs of the long–short interest rate spread in Denmark (upper panel) and Germany (lower panel).

From (21.3) it appears that if Δs_t is stationary, i.e. $s_t \sim I(1)$ as is usually assumed, then the interest rate spread should also be stationary unless the risk premium is non-stationary. Figure 21.2 illustrates the time-series graphs of the long-term and the short-term interest rate spread and Figure 21.3 the change in the spot exchange rate and the inflation rate differential. All series seem to exhibit pronounced persistent behaviour, possibly with the exception of the exchange rate for which the persistence is less dominant but where the variance instead seems to have become much smaller after 1995.

The persistence in the inflation spread in Figure 21.3 suggests that the assumption of $(p_t - p_t^*) \sim I(1)$ may not be adequate. However, if the assumption that $(p_t - p_t^* - s_t) \sim I(1)$ and $(p_t - p_t^*) \sim I(2)$ is correct, then s_t has to be $I(2)$. As a matter of fact, the four-quarter moving average of Δs_t graphed in Figure 21.3 exhibits a fair degree of persistence hidden in the highly volatile short-run exchange rate changes.[3] The test of stationarity of the interest rate spreads were rejected with a p-value of 0.0005 (long spread) and 0.002 (short spread) and the inflation spread with 0.0007. Finally, the stationarity of Δs_t was rejected with a p-value of 0.000.

A modified version of (21.3), where $E_t^e(\Delta_m s_{t+m})/m$ has been replaced with Δs_t and the coefficient to the bond rate spread is unrestricted, resulted in the estimated relation $\{\Delta s_t - 0.57(R_b^{dk} - R_b^{ge})\}$, which was accepted as stationary with a p-value of 0.39. A similar relation for the short rates was estimated as $\{\Delta s_t - 0.73(R_s^{dk} - R_s^{ge})\}$, and was only borderline accepted as stationary with a p-value of 0.07. Thus, it seems likely that

[3] Similar results were also found between German and US data (Juselius and MacDonald 2006) and Japan and US data (Juselius and MacDonald 2004).

the non-stationarity in the long-term forward premium is a result of a non-stationary expected depreciation rate. This is an interesting result suggesting that the persistent movement in Δs_t is more closely related to the persistent movements in the long-term spread than the short-term.

The expectations hypothesis links nominal interest rates of different maturity together in the term spread:

$$i_t^s - i_t^l = v_t \tag{21.5}$$

where v_t is assumed stationary provided that $(E_t^e(\Delta_l p_{t+l})/l - E_t^e(\Delta_s p_{t+s})/s) \sim I(0)$, a condition which depending on the distance between l and s may or may not be satisfied. Figure 21.4 shows the long–short spread for Denmark and Germany. At the first sight both series look non-stationary. However, for the Danish spread there is a strong indication of a mean shift in 1983 and when allowing for this the spread was found to be stationary with a p-value of 0.79. The shift dummy was not significant for German spread and it was only borderline accepted as stationary with a p-value of 0.07.

The Fisher parity, already discussed in Chapter 2, defines nominal interest rates as:

$$i_t^m = r_t^m + E_t^e(\Delta_m p_{t+m})/m, \tag{21.6}$$

where r_t^m denotes the real interest rate of maturity m and $E_t^e(\Delta_m p_{t+m})/m$ is the expected inflation m periods ahead. Figures 21.5 and 21.6 show the graphs of the long-term/short-term real interest rates for Denmark and Germany where expected inflation has been replaced by actual inflation using the arguments above. Because the volatile short-run changes in the real interest rates makes it hard to see the persistent movements in the

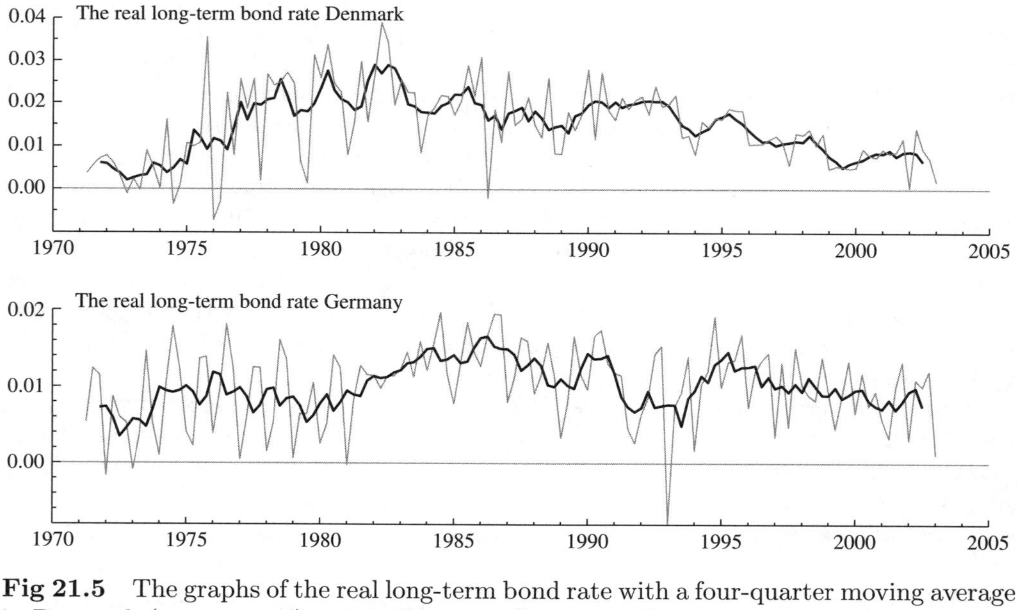

Fig 21.5 The graphs of the real long-term bond rate with a four-quarter moving average in Denmark (upper panel) and in Germany (lower panel).

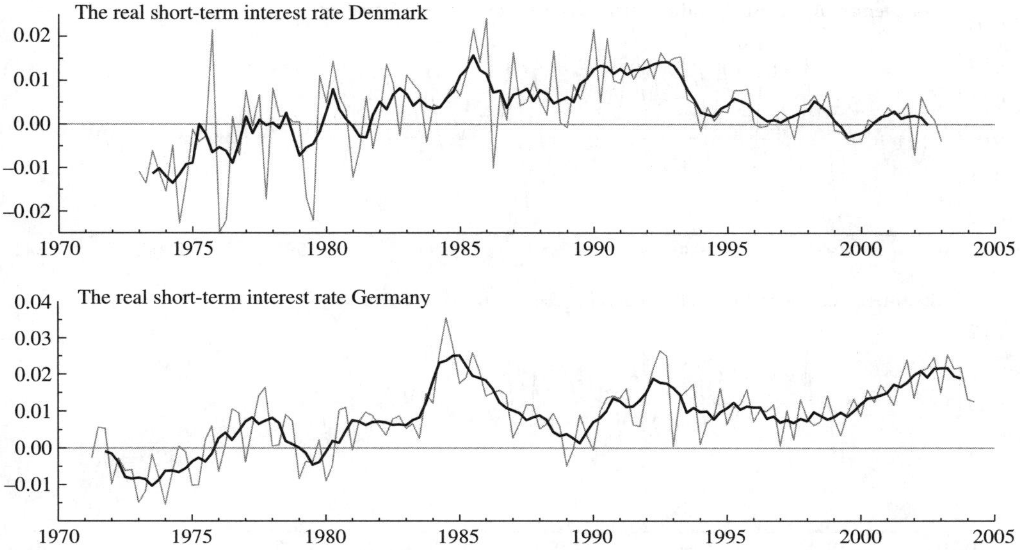

Fig 21.6 The graphs of the Danish real short-term interest rate with a four-quarter moving average (upper panel) and the corresponding German rate (lower panel).

latter we have added a four-quarter moving average to the picture. The smoothed series clearly suggests that real interest rates have exhibited pronounced persistence over this period. Stationarity was clearly rejected for the Danish real interest rates, whereas it was borderline accepted for the German rates with p-value 0.09 (long rate) and 0.11 (short rate).

The final parity condition to consider here is the real interest rate parity (RIP) defined as:

$$(i_t^m - E_t\Delta_m p_t/m) = (i_t^{m*} - E_t\Delta_m p_t^*/m) + v_t \tag{21.7}$$

where m is the maturity of the underlying asset. Even though $v_t = 0$ is the theoretical requirement for the parity condition to hold, we shall relax the condition and interpret $v_t \sim I(0)$ to mean empirical support. Even though the Danish and the German real interest rates are non-stationary by themselves, it is still possible that the parity condition between the two countries holds as a stationary relation. Figure 21.7 shows the graphs of the long-term and the short-term real interest rate spread. They seem to suggest that the Danish real interest rates have persistently deviated from the German ones over extended periods of time. The stationarity tests of the conditions were rejected with a p-value of 0.004 (long rates) and 0.03 (short rates).

Thus, both the graphical analysis and the stationarity tests have revealed a fair amount of persistence in the parity conditions, a feature of the data that does not go well with standard theory. However, the theoretical models developed by Frydman and Goldberg (2002, 2006a) suggest that this kind of persistence in the data can arise as a result of risk averse and myopic agents that make forecasts based on imperfect knowledge. In particular, they show that it is the speculative behaviour in the foreign exchange

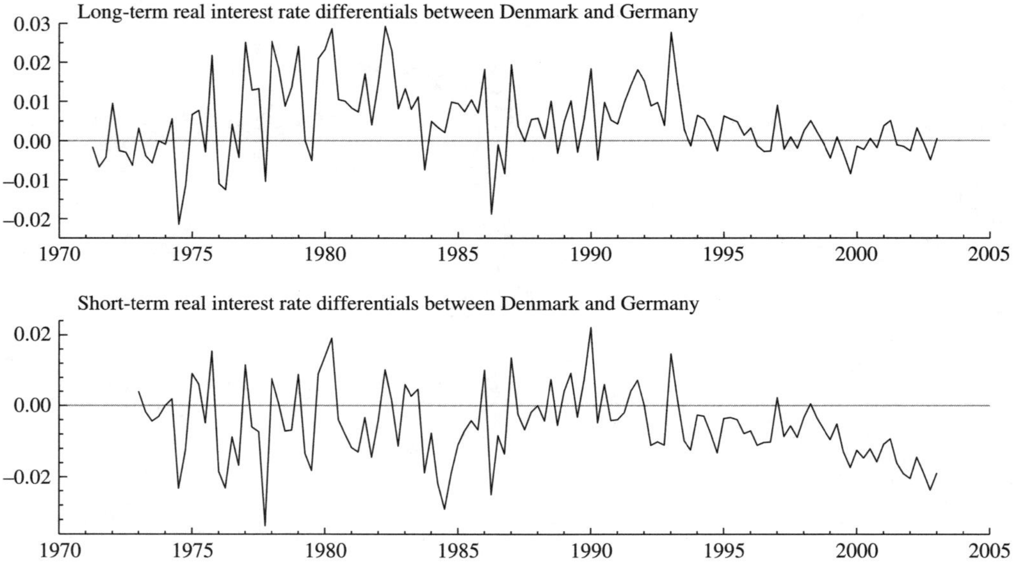

Fig 21.7 The graphs of the real long-term interest rate differential between Denmark and Germany (upper panel) and the corresponding graph for the short-term interest rates (lower graph).

market that drives the real exchange rate away from its historical benchmark values for persistent periods of time. The implication of this is that the PPP and the UIP cannot be analysed independently of each other.

To arrive at a testable expression for a combined PPP and UIP relation, we make the plausible assumption that the expected depreciation rate is a linear function of the observed inflation rate differential and the deviation from the long-run PPP benchmark levels as measured by the *ppp* term:

$$E_t^e \Delta_m s_{t+m} = \omega_{m1}\Delta(p_t - p_t^*) + \omega_{m2} ppp_t + v_t. \tag{21.8}$$

From (21.2) we know that $E_t^e \Delta_m s_{t+m} = (i^m - i_t^{m*})$. This leads to the following testable relationship for the long maturity PPP/UIP relation:

$$(i_t^l - i_t^{l*}) = \omega_{l1}\Delta(p_t - p_t^*) + \omega_{l2} ppp_t + v_t. \tag{21.9}$$

and the short maturity relation:

$$(i_t^s - i_t^{s*}) = \omega_{s1}\Delta(p_t - p_t^*) + \omega_{s2} ppp_t + v_t. \tag{21.10}$$

Subtracting (21.10) from (21.9) gives a testable relation for the short-term and the long-term spreads:

$$(i_t^l - i_t^{l*}) - (i_t^s - i_t^{s*}) = (\omega_{l1} - \omega_{s1})\Delta(p_t - p_t^*) + (\omega_{l2} - \omega_{s2}) ppp_t + v_t. \tag{21.11}$$

We note that (21.9)–(21.11) contain all the parity conditions as special cases. For example, (21.9) becomes the real long-term interest parity relationship for $\omega_{l1} = 1$ and

$\omega_{l2} = 0$. Based on the joint UIP and PPP relationships we can test the stationarity of the two Fisher conditions, the international real interest rate parity condition, the *ppp* condition, and the term structure condition as special cases of the more general specification.

21.2 The data and the models

The data are quarterly observations 1973:1–2003:1 from the database Mona of the National Bank of Denmark and consists of the following variables:

$$
\begin{aligned}
\Delta p^{dk} &= \text{the log of Danish consumer price index} \\
\Delta p^{ge} &= \text{the log of German consumer price index} \\
R_b^{dk} &= \text{the Danish long-term government bond rate} \\
R_b^{ge} &= \text{the German long-term government bond rate} \\
R_s^{dk} &= \text{the Danish short-term interest rate} \\
R_s^{ge} &= \text{the German short-term interest rate} \\
ppp &= p^{dk} - p^{ge} - s, \text{the real exchange rate between Denmark and Germany,} \\
\text{where } s &= \text{the log of spot exchange rate in Dkr/Dmk.}
\end{aligned}
$$

All annual interest rates (in %) have been divided by 400 to achieve comparability between the quarterly inflation rates in log differences. Graphs of the data were already shown in the previous section.

Two models are estimated: One based on all the variables and the other without the short-term interest rates. To illustrate the 'specific-to-general' principle we report the estimates of the small model first and then discuss how our estimates and conclusions change when we extend the information set. In both models we need to include a shift dummy at 1983:1 in the cointegration relations to account for a shift in the equilibrium mean of the interest rates, interpreted as a change in the risk premium, as a result of the Danish financial deregulation in 1983:1. In addition, we need to include the value added dummy $D_{tr}754_t$ already discussed in Chapter 6 and the permanent blip dummy, D_p931_t, to account for a large excise tax in Germany to finance the reunification of East and West Germany. In the extended model we include the permanent blip dummy, D_p764_t, to account for a big increase of the Danish short-term interest rate in 1976:4, and D_p842_t to account for a big increase in the German short-term interest rate in 1984:2.

With these dummies, the model specification seems quite satisfactory, albeit showing some signs of excess kurtosis in the financial variables and ARCH effect in the Danish bond rate. None of these are likely to have much effect on the model estimates. Recursive testing revealed some evidence of a structural break in the mid-1980s, but its impact on the long-run structure seemed generally moderate. Estimating the extended model based on the full sample period and the subperiod 1983:1–2003:1 produced essentially the same identified long-run structure. But, while the magnitude of the estimated long-run coefficients varied to some extent, the signs were unchanged. Also, the coefficients were generally more significant in the full sample version due to the longer sample and to more variability in the data. Since the full sample estimates would generally be less significant if there had been a serious regime shift, we take this as evidence that the coefficients are sufficiently stable to justify a full sample analysis.

21.2.1 Rank determination

Table 21.1 reports the p-values of the trace test with a Bartlett correction and simulated with a shift dummy in the cointegration relations. We can clearly reject five and four unit roots, and possibly even three unit roots in both models, which implies rank of 2, possibly 3. The table also reports the largest characteristic root for $r = 1, 2, \ldots, p$, as well as the largest t value of $\boldsymbol{\alpha}_i$, $i = 1, \ldots, p$. For $r = 2$ the largest root is 0.54 whereas for $r = 3$ it is 0.80. As the largest t value in $\boldsymbol{\alpha}_3$ is 2.8, $\boldsymbol{\beta}_3'\mathbf{x}_t$, if stationary, is likely to describe a slowly adjusting cointegration relation. However, the estimated coefficients are difficult to interpret in terms of any sensible long-run relation. Hence, our preferred choice is $r = 2$.

In the extended model the trace test seems to reject seven, six, and five unit roots, whereas four are borderline acceptable and three quite safely acceptable. We note that the largest unrestricted root is 0.62 for $r = 3$, 0.84 for $r = 4$ and 0.86 for $r = 5$. Thus, by choosing $r = 4$ or 5 we shall include a cointegration relation with a fairly slow, but nevertheless significant, adjustment coefficient, as the largest t value of the α coefficients is 3.6 to $\boldsymbol{\beta}_4'\mathbf{x}_t$ and 3.9 to $\boldsymbol{\beta}_5'\mathbf{x}_t$. A closer examination reveals that it is the Danish bond rate (t value 3.6) and the German short-term interest rate (t value 3.1) that are adjusting to $\boldsymbol{\beta}_4'\mathbf{x}_t$. The latter seems to contain relevant information about the comovements of the short-term spread relative to the bond rates. Since $\boldsymbol{\beta}_5'\mathbf{x}_t$ is not easy to interpret and only significant in the German bond rate equation our preferred choice is $r = 4$.

The choice of $r = 2$ in the small model and $r = 4$ in the extended model implies that we have the same number of common trends in both models. Hence, the introduction

Table 21.1 Determination of rank.

Model 1

r	0	1	**2**	**3**	4	5
$p - r$	5	4	**3**	**2**	1	0
λ_i	0.59	0.45	**0.14**	**0.10**	0.06	–
p^*-value	0.00	0.00	**0.04**	**0.07**	0.13	–
p^*_{shift}-value	0.00	0.00	0.22	**0.31**	0.36	–
$\rho_{\max}$	–	0.52	**0.53**	0.90	0.90	0.92
$t_{\max}$	–	11.0	**8.9**	2.8	3.4	2.4

Model 2

r	0	1	2	3	4	5	6	7
$p - r$	7	6	5	4	**3**	**2**	1	0
λ_i	0.60	0.46	0.21	0.18	**0.15**	**0.09**	0.05	
p^*-value	0.00	0.00	0.02	0.03	**0.08**	**0.19**	0.26	
p^*_{shift}-value	0.00	0.00	0.12	0.17	**0.31**	**0.50**	0.55	
$\rho_{\max}$		0.57	0.57	0.62	**0.84**	**0.86**	0.90	0.92
$t_{\max}$		11.0	8.5	3.0	**3.6**	**3.9**	2.6	1.9

of the short-term interest rates have not added any new common stochastic trends. We conclude that the long-term and the short-term interest rates seem to contain the same underlying shocks.[4]

Finally, we note that the third and fourth relation in the extended model correspond to rather small λ values, although significantly different from zero. This is because a sample of 121 observations is long enough for the trace test to have quite good power to distinguish between unit roots and near unit roots. For example, in the extended model the hypothesis that $\lambda = 0.18$ corresponds to a unit root obtains only a small p-value. This is in contrast to the split sample analysis of the labour market in Chapter 20, where the unit root hypothesis based on a much higher λ could not be rejected using conventional p-values. This serves as an illustration of the general difficulties in determining the rank and the number of common trends exclusively based on the trace test.

21.2.2 Tests of a unit vector in $\boldsymbol{\beta}$ and zero row and a unit vector in $\boldsymbol{\alpha}$

Chapter 19 discussed the so-called automated test procedures and how they provide useful information about the driving forces in the system when extending the information set. Table 21.2 reports the tests of a unit vector in $\boldsymbol{\beta}$ (stationarity of a variable) a zero row in $\boldsymbol{\alpha}$ (weak exogeneity of a variable) and a unit vector in $\boldsymbol{\alpha}$ (a purely adjusting variable) but does not report the tests of a zero row in $\boldsymbol{\beta}$ as none of the variables were excludable. The tests of stationarity, which are conditional on a mean shift at 1983, show that none of the variables can be considered a unit vector in the two-dimensional $\boldsymbol{\beta}$ vector space of the small model. However, in the extended model the hypothesis can be accepted for German short-term interest rate with a fairly high p-value and borderline for the Danish bond rate and inflation rate. The latter seems to contradict the result both in the small model and in Chapter 10 where the stationarity of both the Danish inflation and bond rate conditional on a mean shift in 1983 was rejected. However, the space spanned by the three cointegration vectors in Chapter 10 is not identical to the space spanned by the four cointegration vectors in the present model, two of which correspond to fairly small λ values. Because the choice of a higher value of r is likely to influence the properties of the test in the direction of making it easier to accept a stationarity hypothesis, there is not necessarily any contradiction involved. This is just another illustration of the fact that stationarity/non-stationarity is not, in general, a structural property but, instead, is a statistical approximation that only makes sense in a given model, data, and sample period (cf. Chapter 2).

The tests of a zero row in $\boldsymbol{\alpha}$ provide information about the purely pushing behaviour in the system and how it changes when adding the new variables. In the small model the real exchange rate and the German bond rate are found to be weakly exogenous with high p-values and the Danish bond rate with a slightly lower p-value. The joint weak exogeneity of the first two was accepted based on $\chi^2(4) = 4.33\,[0.36]$ and all three based on $\chi^2(6) = 7.23\,[0.30]$. A similar result was found in Juselius and MacDonald (2006). Thus, the analysis suggests that it is the shocks to the two long-term bond rates and the real exchange rate that have been driving this system.

[4] A different result was found in Juselius and MacDonald (2006) where, in a similar analysis based on German and US data, adding the short-term interest rates produced an additional common stochastic trend.

Table 21.2 Automated tests on $\boldsymbol{\beta}$ and $\boldsymbol{\alpha}$.

	r	ν	$\chi^2_{.95}(\nu)$	Δp^{dk}	Δp^{ge}	R_b^{dk}	R_b^{ge}	ppp	R_s^{dk}	R_s^{ge}
Tests of a unit vector in $\boldsymbol{\beta}$										
Model S	2	3	7.81	11.81 [0.01]	42.83 [0.00]	56.48 [0.00]	61.70 [0.00]	58.75 [0.00]	–	–
Model B	4	3	7.81	6.80 [0.08]	9.24 [0.03]	6.48 [0.09]	14.91 [0.00]	11.61 [0.01]	12.29 [0.01]	**2.99** [0.39]
Tests of a zero row in α										
Model 1	2	2	5.99	47.91 [0.00]	74.85 [0.00]	**1.39** [0.50]	**2.06** [0.36]	**0.93** [0.63]	–	–
Model 2	4	4	9.49	45.08 [0.00]	70.23 [0.00]	**5.56** [0.23]	**2.56** [0.63]	**0.88** [0.93]	**7.71** [0.10]	17.74 [0.00]
Tests of a unit vector in α										
Model 1	2	3	7.81	**1.72** [0.63]	**3.18** [0.37]	51.38 [0.00]	57.59 [0.00]	50.96 [0.00]	–	–
Model 2	4	3	7.81	**1.58** [0.66]	**2.31** [0.51]	**1.22** [0.75]	6.98 [0.07]	11.29 [0.01]	10.39 [0.02]	**4.18** [0.24]

The test results in the extended model are similar: The German bond rate and the real exchange rate are weakly exogenous with a very high p-value, and the Danish bond rate with a somewhat lower p-value. The joint weak exogeneity test of the real exchange rate and the German bond rate was accepted based on $\chi^2(8) = 3.91\,[0.87]$. When all three were tested jointly we obtained $\chi^2(12) = 15.99\,[0.19]$. The large increase in the test value suggests that the Danish bond rate should probably not be considered weakly exogenous. A joint test of the first two variables together with the Danish short rate (which was weakly exogenous in the single test with a p-value of 0.10) produced a more acceptable result with $\chi^2(12) = 11.56\,[0.48]$. Thus, we find essentially the same indeterminacy regarding the causality link between the two Danish interest rates already discussed in Chapter 11. Since there cannot be more than three weakly exogenous variables with $r = 4$, it seems safe to conclude that shocks to the real exchange rate, the German bond rate and some combination of the two Danish interest rates have been pushing the inflation rates.

The test of a unit vector in $\boldsymbol{\alpha}$ is complementary to the test of a zero row in $\boldsymbol{\alpha}$ in the sense that acceptance of the former implies purely adjusting behaviour, whereas acceptance of the latter implies purely pushing behaviour. It is notable that the two inflation rates seem purely adjusting in both model, implying that inflationary shocks have not had any permanent effect on the variables of this system. The joint test was accepted with a p-value of 0.68. A similar result was found for Danish inflation in the money market analysis and in the more recent period of the labour market analysis, whereas not in the 'strong labour union' regime of the 1970s.

In the extended model, the German short-term interest rate, in addition to the inflation rates, seems purely adjusting and, more surprisingly, also the Danish bond rate. The result that the Danish bond rate was individually both weakly exogenous and purely adjusting seems contradictory. To understand why this may happen, we refer to Section 20.3.2 where a similar result was discussed.

Altogether, the results suggest that the weak exogeneity status of the Danish bond rate has changed when the short-term interest rates are included in the analysis, whereas the finding that the real exchange rate and the German bond rate are jointly weakly exogenous and the two inflation rates are purely adjusting is robust.

21.3 Analysing the long-run structure

Given the above results that only the two inflation rates were equilibrium correcting in the small model, it seems likely that the identifying restrictions on the two cointegration relations should describe some kind of long-run relation for each of the two inflation rates. In the extended model we should be able to find the same two cointegration relations (due to the invariance of cointegration to extensions of the information set) and two additional relations, one towards which the German short-term interest rate is equilibrium correcting and the other the Danish bond rate. One possibility is to impose the two (four) unit vectors in the small (big) model and consider the corresponding $\boldsymbol{\beta}$ vectors to be the identified long-run relations. The latter are identical to the rows of the purely adjusting variables in the $\boldsymbol{\Pi}$ matrix. However, by allowing the latter to be able to react on several $\boldsymbol{\beta}$ relations one can often identify more interpretable long-run relations. Below we shall choose the latter procedure.

21.3.1 Identifying the long-run relations

The data makes a fairly clear distinction between the pulling and the pushing forces in this case, so the two inflation rows of the $\boldsymbol{\Pi}$ matrix are essentially describing the $\boldsymbol{\beta}$ relations. To economize on space we have, therefore not reported the estimates of the $\boldsymbol{\Pi}$ matrix. Table 21.3 reports an identified $\boldsymbol{\beta}$ structure for the small model together with the significant $\boldsymbol{\alpha}$ coefficients. The two over-identifying restrictions were accepted based on $\chi^2(2) = 1.23\,[0.54]$. The first relation describes that the Danish inflation rate is equilibrium correcting to the *ppp* term and is positively related to the Danish bond rate.[5] It is strongly significant in the Danish inflation equation, but somewhat surprisingly, also in the German inflation equation.

Table 21.3 An identified $\boldsymbol{\beta}$ structure in the small model. Test of over-identifying restrictions $\chi^2(2) = 0.45\,[0.80]$.

	Δp^{dk}	Δp^{ge}	R_b^{dk}	R_b^{ge}	ppp	$Ds831$	$const.$
$\hat{\beta}_1^c$	**1.00** [0.00]	–	**−0.18** [−3.41]	–	**0.04** [2.75]	**0.01** [6.22]	**0.19** [2.55]
$\hat{\alpha}_1^c$	**−1.06** [−8.62]	**−0.31** [−3.84]	*	*	*	–	–
$\hat{\beta}_2^c$	**−0.28** [−7.30]	**1.00** [0.00]	**0.28** [7.30]	**−1.00** [0.00]	**−0.02** [−3.23]	**0.00** [6.51]	**−0.13** [−3.15]
$\hat{\alpha}_2^c$	*	**−1.25** [−11.24]	*	*	*	–	–

[5] A similar cointegration relation was found in Juselius and MacDonald (2006) for the German inflation rate in an analysis between Germany and the USA.

Table 21.4 An identified $\boldsymbol{\beta}$ structure in the extended model. Test of over-identifying restrictions $\chi^2(5) = 1.20[0.94]$.

	Δp^{dk}	Δp^{ge}	R_b^{dk}	R_b^{ge}	R_s^{dk}	R_s^{ge}	ppp	$Ds831$	$const.$
$\hat{\boldsymbol{\beta}}_1^c$	0.00 [NA]	0.00 [NA]	**1.00** [NA]	0.00 [NA]	**−0.96** [−11.79]	0.00 [NA]	0.00 [NA]	**0.01** [8.71]	**−0.02** [−10.40]
$\hat{\boldsymbol{\alpha}}_1^c$	*	*	−0.10 [−1.81]	*	0.11 [2.61]	0.27 [3.57]	*	–	
$\hat{\boldsymbol{\beta}}_2^c$	0.00 [NA]	0.00 [NA]	**−1.00** [NA]	**1.00** [NA]	**0.74** [6.21]	**−0.74** [−6.21]	**0.09** [4.26]	**−0.02** [−4.81]	**0.58** [4.40]
$\hat{\boldsymbol{\alpha}}_1^c$	*	−0.14 [−1.75]	*	*	0.04 [1.99]	0.21 [5.31]	*	–	–
$\hat{\boldsymbol{\beta}}_3^c$	**−0.33** [−8.94]	**1.00** [NA]	**0.33** [8.94]	**−1.00** [NA]	0.00 [NA]	0.00 [NA]	**−0.03** [−3.87]	**0.01** [6.72]	**−0.18** [−3.82]
$\hat{\boldsymbol{\alpha}}_1^c$	*	−1.29 [−11.11]	*	*	*	0.22 [3.99]	*	–	–
$\hat{\boldsymbol{\beta}}_4^c$	**1.00** [NA]	0.00 [NA]	**−0.25** [−3.30]	0.00 [NA]	0.00 [NA]	0.00 [NA]	**0.04** [2.85]	**0.01** [4.97]	**0.20** [2.68]
$\hat{\boldsymbol{\alpha}}_1^c$	−1.05 [−8.16]	−0.36 [−4.28]	*	*	*	*	*	–	–

The second relation describes a modified real interest rate parity relation between Denmark and Germany. The Danish real long-term interest rate is only one third of the German and the relation needs the *ppp* term to become stationary. Combining interest and inflation spreads as in (21.9) led to rejection of stationarity. This may not be so surprising, considering that all interest rates were weakly exogenous in this system and that (21.9)–(21.11) were assumed to describe interest rate parity relations. The German, but not the Danish, inflation rate is strongly equilibrium correcting to the second relation.

Table 21.4 reports an identified $\boldsymbol{\beta}$ structure for the extended model together with significant $\boldsymbol{\alpha}$ coefficients. The five over-identifying restrictions were accepted based on $\chi^2(5) = 1.20\,[0.94]$. The first new relation is the spread relation (21.5) between the two Danish interest rates already estimated in Chapter 10 with a somewhat lower coefficient. The Danish short-term and long-term interest rates are both equilibrium correcting to this relation and, more surprisingly, the German short-term interest rate. The second new relation corresponds to (21.11), describing a relationship between the long-term and the short-term interest rate spread as a function of the real exchange rate. The German (but not the Danish) short-term interest rate is equilibrium correcting to this relation. The third and the fourth relation correspond to the two relations in the small model with similar adjustment coefficients.

The result that the German variables exhibited more equilibrium correction than the Danish variables may seem puzzling, considering the size of the two economies. However, in a globalized world economy, any inflation rate and interest rate is likely to contain a large international component. When German variables equilibrium correct to the Danish variables, they probably do so to the international component in the Danish rates.

To conclude, we have found strong support for the importance of combining PPP and UIP to obtain acceptable empirical results. In all cointegration relations describing international parity relations the *ppp* term was needed to achieve stationarity. Thus, the

Table 21.5 The estimated common stochastic trends and their loadings. The long-run impact matrix $\boldsymbol{C}$.

	$\varepsilon_{\Delta p^{dk}}$	$\varepsilon_{\Delta p^{ge}}$	$\varepsilon_{R_b^{dk}}$	$\varepsilon_{R_b^{ge}}$ $\hat{\boldsymbol{\beta}}_{\perp,1}$	$\varepsilon_{R_s^{dk}}$ $\hat{\boldsymbol{\beta}}_{\perp,2}$	$\varepsilon_{R_s^{ge}}$	ε_{ppp} $\hat{\boldsymbol{\beta}}_{\perp,3}$
Δp^{dk}	0.00 [0.00]	0.00 [0.00]	−0.00 [−0.00]	**0.30** [2.23]	**0.26** [2.06]	0.00 [0.00]	**−0.03** [−3.59]
Δp^{ge}	0.00 [0.00]	−0.00 [−0.00]	0.00 [0.00]	**1.40** [4.79]	−0.41 [−1.50]	0.00 [0.00]	0.03 [1.48]
R_b^{dk}	0.00 [0.00]	0.00 [0.00]	−0.00 [−0.00]	**0.73** [2.42]	**1.13** [4.04]	0.00 [0.00]	−0.02 [−1.21]
R_b^{ge}	0.00 [0.00]	−0.00 [−0.00]	0.00 [0.00]	**1.53** [5.51]	−0.13 [−0.49]	0.00 [0.00]	0.00 [0.12]
R_s^{dk}	0.00 [0.00]	0.00 [0.00]	−0.00 [−0.00]	**0.82** [2.41]	**1.40** [4.41]	0.00 [0.00]	−0.00 [−0.17]
R_s^{ge}	0.00 [0.00]	−0.00 [−0.00]	0.00 [0.00]	**1.88** [3.35]	−0.54 [−1.03]	0.00 [0.00]	**0.13** [3.32]
ppp	−0.00 [−0.00]	0.00 [0.00]	−0.00 [−0.00]	−2.86 [−0.95]	1.09 [0.39]	0.00 [0.00]	**1.00** [4.83]

international parity conditions in their conventional form can only be recovered provided that the real exchange rate becomes a stationary variable.

21.3.2 The common driving trends

Because the weak exogeneity results were very similar in the small and the big model, the estimates reported in Table 21.5 are only for the extended model. They have been calculated subject to the three weak exogeneity restrictions discussed above. In this case the three non-zero columns of the **C** matrix correspond to $\boldsymbol{\beta}_{\perp}$ (*cf.* Chapter 14). The results show that shocks to the Danish short-term interest rate have exclusively influenced the Danish variables in the long-run, whereas shocks to the German bond rate have had a positive long-run impact on all variables except the *ppp* term. A positive shock to the *ppp* term (a depreciation of the Dmk) has tended to increase the German short-term interest rate by a factor of 0.13 in the long run. However, real exchange rate shocks do not seem to have had any significant long-run impact on the Danish interest rates, only a negative impact on the Danish inflation rate. That is, an appreciation/depreciation of the Dkr has made the Danish inflation decrease/increase in the long run. The German bond rate and the *ppp* term seem to be strongly exogenous (cf. Chapter 11), as both of them approximately correspond to a unit vector row in the $\boldsymbol{C}$ matrix.

21.4 Concluding remarks

The results of this chapter showed a surprisingly small direct effect on the Danish variables from the German ones. The Danish inflation was found to be equilibrium correcting to the *ppp* term, which was found to be strongly exogenous in both systems. This might indicate that nominal exchange rates are essentially determined in the speculative market for foreign exchange without being much affected by fundamentals in goods market.

However, the finding in the previous chapter that the real exchange rate was cointegrated with movements in the mark-up contradicts such a conclusion. The Danish bond rate was found to be weakly exogenous in the small system, but seemed to be equilibrium correcting to the domestic spread in the big system, though not very significantly so. The short-term interest was also modestly adjusting to the domestic spread and, possibly, to the German-Danish long–short interest rate spread.

Altogether, the most significant result seem to be the strong pushing effects from the real exchange rate, the German short-term interest rate and the Danish long-term bond rate. Altogether, it seems quite safe to conclude that the level of the Danish exchange rate and interest rates is to a large extent determined by the international level.

22

Collecting the threads

The first 18 chapters provided a detailed analysis of the pushing and the pulling forces underlying the monetary model based on the $I(1)$ model. The analysis showed that inflation rate, real money stock and the short-term interest rate were exclusively adjusting, whereas permanent shocks to the long-term interest rate and the real income were primarily pushing. The inflation rate was found to be adjusting negatively to real income, a puzzling result that seemed to reflect the fact that over the sample period inflation has steadily decreased whereas real income has increased. However, no effect on inflation from excess money was detected. The $I(2)$ analysis, allowing us to investigate hypothetical long-run relationships between nominal money and prices, showed strong evidence that prices were causing money but not the other way around. Thus, the empirical regularities in the data were difficult to reconcile with the logic of the monetary model. The question what has caused inflation over the last three decades was still waiting for an answer.

To improve our understanding of the underlying mechanisms driving price inflation and some of the empirical puzzles/implausible coefficients in the money market analysis we then continued the VAR analysis based on two new data sets: one describing the wage, price, and unemployment dynamics in the Danish labour market and the other describing the foreign transmission effects on Danish inflation rate, interest rates, and real exchange rate.

It is now time to bring all the results together into a large model, illustrating the methodological approach described in Section 19.4 and, at the same time, investigating the robustness of our previous conclusions to the *ceteris paribus* assumption.

Section 22.1 reports the joint determination of real money, inflation, short- and long-term interests, real wages, productivity, unemployment, and real exchange rate. The previously estimated equilibrium correction mechanisms of the three VAR models are the main determinants together with lagged changes of the variables. In addition, the price wedge and the German variables are treated as exogenous to the system. Section 22.2 discusses the main findings and their implications for the determination of price inflation in this period. Section 22.3 ends the book with a methodological discussion.

22.1 The full model estimates

The equation system is estimated for the following eight variables:

$$[\Delta m_t^r, \Delta^2 p_t, \Delta R_{m,t}, \Delta R_{b,t}, \Delta w_t^r, \Delta pr_t, \Delta U_t, \Delta q_t]. \tag{22.1}$$

The real GDP is not directly represented, but is, nevertheless, indirectly represented by the productivity variable. The following three variables are assumed to be exogenous to the system:

$$[\Delta pp73_t, \Delta pp83_t, \Delta^2 p_t^{ge}, \Delta R_{b,t}^{ge}] \tag{22.2}$$

where $pp73_t$ is the price wedge, $p_{c,t} - p_{y,t}$, for t = 1973:1,... ,1984:4, 0 otherwise, and $pp83_t$ is the price wedge for t = 1983:1,... ,2003:1, 0 otherwise. Thus, the price wedge, assumed to be a proxy for globalization, has been allowed to have different effects on the system in the first and the second regime. In addition, lagged values of all system variables were included as explanatory variables in the original system. Among them, $\Delta R_{m,t-1}, \Delta w_{t-1}^r, \Delta pr_{t-1}$ were found insignificant based on the F-test and, therefore, omitted from the system. The lagged equilibrium errors from the three sectorial models, supposed to provide the bulk of explanatory power, are reproduced in Table 22.2. To distinguish between them, M stands for the monetary model, W for the labour market model, and F the foreign transmission model. Among the lagged equilibrium errors, $Mecm2$, describing the puzzling negative relationship between real income and inflation, was insignificant based on the F-test (p-value 0.42) and was, therefore, left out. In addition, $Fecm1$ was removed because it was almost identical to $Mecm3$, and $Fecm2$ because it was only important for the German variables (cf. Chapter 21). The two equilibrium errors, $Fecm3$ and $Fecm4$, were only borderline significant based on the F-test, but were retained, nevertheless, because they seemed to be important in some of the equations. The weak significance of the $Fecm$'s in the model might be the consequence of having conditioned on $\Delta^2 p_t^{ge}$ and $\Delta R_{b,t}^{ge}$ in the model. Similarly, $W83ecm3$ was not highly significant judged by the F-test, but seemed to be relevant in some of the equations and was, therefore, retained in the model. Finally, the three intervention dummies were all found to be highly significant in the model.

With this choice of variables we have defined a system of eight equations with eight cointegration relations (two from the money market, four from the labour market, two from the external market) and three conditioning variables (the price wedge and the two German rates). Given this specification, the main driving force to the Danish domestic economy is globalization and foreign competition, measured by the price wedge, the German inflation rate and the German long-term bond rate. This, of course, is correct only to the extent that the included ecm's define a full rank matrix. Also, if we had decided to omit any of the borderline significant cointegration relations $W83ecm3$, $Fecm3$ and $Fecm4$ from the model, the number of common driving trends would have increased correspondingly.

Following a similar procedure as in Chapter 13, the system was sequentially simplified by testing and setting insignificant coefficients to zero. The final model reported in

Table 22.1 Combining the labour, monetary and foreign analysis in one model. Test of overidentifying restrictions $\chi^2(118) = 120.9[0.41]$.

	Δm^r_t	$\Delta^2 p_{c,t}$	$\Delta R_{m,t}$	$\Delta R_{b,t}$	Δw^r_t	Δc_t	ΔU_t	Δq_t
$\Delta pp73_t$	–	0.33 [6.8]	–	–	−0.51 [−6.7]	–	–	−0.24 [2.3]
$\Delta pp83_t$	–	0.16 [3.7]	–	–	−0.21 [−2.8]	0.30 [2.5]	–	–
$\Delta^2 p^{ge}_t$	–	–	–	−0.04 [−2.0]	–	–	–	0.67 [−3.3]
$\Delta R^{ge}_{b,t}$	–	–	–	0.68 [6.8]	–	–	–	–
$\Delta R_{b,t-1}$	−2.76 [−2.4]	–	0.27 [5.6]	0.22 [3.3]	–	−1.26 [−1.5]	0.22 [2.1]	–
Δm^r_{t-1}	–	–	−0.01 [−3.6]	−0.01 [−3.5]	–	–	–	−0.08 [2.1]
$\Delta^2 p_{c,t-1}$	–	−0.20 [−3.5]	–	–	–	0.54 [3.2]	–	–
ΔU_{t-1}	–	–	–	−0.10 [−2.7]	–	–	0.67 [10.5]	−0.83 [2.1]
Δq_{t-1}	–	–	0.01 [−1.9]	0.02 [−2.2]	–	–	–	–
$Mecm1_{t-1}$ [Mon. demand]	−0.27 [−6.3]	0.02 [2.0]	–	–	–	–	–	–
$Mecm3_{t-1}$ [Short-long spread]	–	–	−0.14 [−3.4]	0.23 [4.2]	–	−1.53 [−2.4]	–	1.19 [−2.3]
$W73ecm1_{t-1}$ [Wage-ppp relation]	−0.61 [−2.5]	0.22 [7.8]	0.03 [−3.4]	–	–	0.38 [5.0]	0.04 [3.2]	0.51 [7.4]
$W73ecm2_{t-1}$ [Phillips curve]	1.04 [2.4]	−0.13 [−6.9]	−0.09 [−4.6]	–	−0.36 [−3.9]	−0.54 [−5.3]	–	–
$W73ecm3_{t-1}$ [Wage share/infl]	0.57 [2.5]	–	−0.05 [−5.0]	–	−0.21 [−4.5]	–	−0.007 [−2.2]	–
$W83ecm1_{t-1}$ [Globalization]	−0.53 [−3.2]	–	–	0.02 [3.0]	−0.16 [−2.5]	−0.84 [−7.6]	–	–
$W83ecm2_{t-1}$ [Phillips curve]	–	−0.84 [−7.1]	–	–	–	−3.03 [−4.9]	–	0.57 [−2.1]
$W83ecm3_{t-1}$ [unempl.- bond rt.]	0.24 [2.4]	–	–	0.02 [3.6]	–	–	−0.03 [−2.7]	–
$W83ecm4_{t-1}$ [prod.wages- ppp]	–	0.07 [4.3]	−0.007 [−2.7]	–	−0.11 [−3.6]	–	0.02 [3.2]	0.30 [7.4]
$Fecm3_{t-1}$ [R int.rts. r.ex. rel]	–	–	–	0.07 [−2.4]	–	–	–	−1.06 [4.1]
$Fecm4_{t-1}$ [DK inflation]	–	–	–	–	–	2.06 [4.0]	–	–
$D75.4_t$	–	−0.02 [−4.8]	–	−0.003 [−3.1]	–	–	–	–
$D76.4_t$	–	–	0.005 [5.6]	–	–	–	–	–
$Dp83.1_t$	–	–	–	−0.007 [−6.8]	–	–	–	–

Table 22.2 Defining the equilibrium errors of Table 22.1.

$Mecm1$	$= m^r - y^r - 13.27(R_m - R_b) - 0.15D_s83$
$Mecm3$	$= R_m - 0.81R_b - 0.10D_s83$
$W73ecm1$	$= w - p_c + 0.41(p_c - p_y) - 0.59q - 0.01t$
$W73ecm2$	$= U + 5.06\Delta p_c - 0.33q + 1.05(pr - 0.01t)$
$W73ecm3$	$= w - p_y - 1.38pr - 9.93\Delta p_c$
$W83ecm1$	$= (pr - 0.01t) - 0.39(p_c - p_y) - 0.93q$
$W83ecm2$	$= \Delta p_c - 0.53R_b + 0.08U$
$W83ecm3$	$= U - 9.51R_b - 0.55(w - p_c)$
$W83ecm4$	$= (w - p_y - pr) - 0.99q$
$Fecm3$	$= (R_b^{ge} - \Delta p_c^{ge}) - 0.33(R_b^{dk} - \Delta p_c^{dk}) + 0.03q$
$Fecm4$	$= \Delta p_c - 0.25R_b - 0.04q$

Table 22.1 is estimated subject to 118 overidentifying restrictions which were accepted with a p-value of 0.41.

This is a very large model and it is far from easy to present the main results and the most important conclusions without becoming lost in the numerous details. We shall first present some very broad results regarding the full system, then discuss some major findings related to the individual equations and, finally, discuss some major differences between the two regimes.

22.1.1 Some general results

The estimated system seems to convey the following broad picture:

1. The *ecm*'s provide the bulk of explanatory power of the model, signifying the importance of long-run equilibrium correction in macroeconomic behaviour.
2. Among the *ecm*'s, the ones from the labour market model are by far the most important.
3. The international parity conditions ($Fecm3$ and $Fecm4$) have surprisingly small effects on the system.
4. Among the transitory effects, the lagged bond rate seems most important.

Table 22.3 reports the standardized residual covariance matrix, with residual standard errors on the diagonal. Only a few of the correlations are larger than 0.3 in absolute value, suggesting that current effects between the system variables, conditional on the three exogenous variables, are not very important in this model. Most of the larger correlation coefficients are associated with the real exchange rate equation, suggesting either that the real exchange rate has reacted swiftly on shocks to the domestic economy, or the domestic economy has done so to exchange rate shocks. Also, shocks to the two interest rates are quite strongly correlated as they already were in the monetary model. This, of course, is because interest rates shocks are transmitted through the term structure in the course of a few days, so with quarterly data it is hard to uncover causality links between current changes. Finally, shocks to the real wage and the inflation rate are quite strongly correlated with a negative coefficient. The latter might seem somewhat surprising, but

Table 22.3 The standardized residual covariance matrix. Residual standard errors on the diagonal (in italics).

	Δm_t^r	$\Delta^2 p$	ΔR_m	ΔR_b	Δw_c^r	Δpr	ΔU	Δq
Δm_t^r	*0.0225*	−0.22	−0.18	−0.06	0.02	0.12	−0.15	0.00
$\Delta^2 p$	−0.22	*0.0054*	0.04	0.05	**−0.49**	0.00	−0.02	**−0.32**
ΔR_m	−0.18	0.04	*0.0010*	**0.42**	0.14	**−0.30**	0.02	0.19
ΔR_b	−0.06	0.05	**0.42**	*0.0012*	0.15	0.13	−0.08	**0.27**
Δw_c^r	0.02	**−0.49**	0.14	0.15	*0.0091*	0.14	−0.07	**0.36**
Δpr	0.12	0.00	**−0.30**	0.13	0.14	*0.0150*	−0.10	0.17
ΔU	−0.15	−0.02	0.02	−0.08	−0.07	−0.10	*0.0021*	**0.22**
Δq	0.00	**−0.32**	0.19	**0.27**	**0.36**	0.17	**0.22**	*0.0132*

can be explained by the increased product market competition and its effect on prices and wages.

22.1.2 A more detailed analysis

In the following we shall take a closer look at each equation and discuss whether the results confirm or change previously found results.

Real money stock is equilibrium correcting to the estimated money demand relation with a similar adjustment coefficient as in the money market model. However, we can now see additional effects from the equilibrium errors in the labour market and a negative effect from the lagged change in the bond rate. However, most of these effects are only borderline significant and the main conclusion from the earlier analysis, that real money stock has essentially been purely adjusting to the long-run money demand, seems still valid.

The *inflation rate*, which was exclusively adjusting to real income in the monetary analysis, is now found to be strongly affected by equilibrium errors in the labour market. In addition, excess money is now found to have a tiny, but only borderline significant, effect on price inflation in this period. A somewhat surprising result is that $Fecm4$, strongly significant in Table 21.4, dropped out completely as an explanatory variable. This suggest that the necessary price adjustment due to foreign competition has taken place in the Danish labour market as described in Chapter 20.

The *short-term interest* rate is equilibrium correcting to the long-term bond rate with an adjustment coefficient almost identical to the one in Chapter 11. In addition, it is quite strongly influenced by imbalances in the labour market. This is particularly so in the first period where short-term interest rate has gone up when real wages have been above their steady-state value ($W73ecm1$), has gone down when unemployment has been above its steady-state value ($W73ecm2$), and up when inflation has been above its steady-state value ($W73ecm3$). These are plausible monetary policy reaction effects. In the second period characterized by a steadily declining inflation rate, these effects seem to have been more or less absent.

The *long-term bond rate*, which was found to be weakly exogenous in the money market analysis, is now significantly equilibrium correcting to the short-term interest rate ($Mecm3$), to the 'unemployment-real wage' relation ($W83ecm3$) and to the 'real interest rates-real exchange rate' relation ($Fecm3$). It has also increased with the 'globalization' relation ($W83ecm1$). Among the short-run effects, changes in German bond rate has had a strong (0.68) and highly significant effect on the Danish bond rate. Finally, excess liquidity exhibits a small negative effect. It is notable that the Danish bond rate was not influenced by the labour market in the 1970s, but quite strongly so in the more recent period characterized by deregulation and increased market power.

The *price inflation, real wages, productivity and unemployment* are primarily determined by the determinants from the labour market and the results are similar to the ones of Chapter 20, though with some changes. Real wages in the 1970s were not equilibrium correcting to the estimated wage relation ($W73ecm1$), whereas the inflation rate, productivity and the unemployment rate were positively affected by it. Moreover, the real exchange rate was appreciating as the Danish inflation was increasing and productivity had to increase to compensate for lost competitiveness. When unemployment rate increased above its 'natural rate' level (measured by $W73ecm2$) both the real wage and inflation pressure decreased. But also productivity went down (a recession). Finally, the mark-up was equilibrium correcting to inflation ($W73ecm3$) describing the Banerjee–Russel effect, but the inflation rate and the unemployment rate remained unaffected. In the 1980s, when increased competitiveness due to globalization ($W83ecm1$) exerted a downward pressure on output prices, real wages were no longer increasing in excess of productivity. This period is characterized by strong Phillips curve effects, measured by the Phelps' relation ($W83ecm2$) with the inflation rate strongly equilibrium correcting. The unemployment rate, on the other hand, was strongly equilibrium correcting to the demand for labour relation ($W83ecm3$). Real wages were strongly equilibrium correcting to the 'markup-real exchange rate' relation ($W83ecm4$), and the inflation rate and the real exchange rate were responding. Productivity was strongly equilibrium correcting to the 'globalization' relation ($W83ecm1$) describing the pressure on productivity as a result of the steadily increasing competition since the 1980s.

The real exchange rate was weakly exogenous in the PPP/UIP analysis of Chapter 21 and was only equilibrium correcting to $W83ecm4$ in the labour market analysis of Chapter 20. Given the increased information set of this chapter, we can now find many more significant effects. In the 1970s the real exchange rate was equilibrium correcting to $W73ecm1$, the real wage relation, and in the 1980s (as before) to $W83ecm4$, the mark-up relation. In addition, the real exchange rate has depreciated with increasing short-long interest rate spread ($Mecm3$) and depreciated when the unemployment rate has been above its 'natural rate' level ($W83ecm1$). Contrary to the PPP/UIP analysis in Chapter 21, the real exchange rate is now found to be equilibrium correcting to the real interest rate parity relation.

22.1.3 Comparing the two periods

To be able to discuss the overall effect of the various *ecm*'s on the variables of the system, Table 22.3 reports the combined effects (essentially the $\mathbf{\Pi}$ matrix of the extended model) separating between the two periods. The equilibrium correction effects (in bold face) show that all system variables are either equilibrium correcting or do not correct at all. None of them exhibit overshooting behaviour.

Table 22.4 The long-run combined effects based on the estimates in Table 22.1.

	m^r	y^r	Δp_c	R_m	R_b	w_c^r	pp	pr	U	q	Δp^{ge}	R^{ge}
$\Delta m^r I$	**−0.27**	0.27	−0.40	3.6	−3.6	−0.04	0.32	0.31	1.04	−0.02		–
$\Delta m^r II$	**−0.27**	0.27	–	3.6	−5.9	−0.13	0.30	−0.53	0.73		–	–
$\Delta^2 pI$	0.02	−0.02	**−0.66**	−0.21	0.21	0.22	0.09	−0.14	−0.13	0.09	–	–
$\Delta^2 pII$	0.02	−0.02	**−0.84**	−0.21	0.66	0.07	0.07	−0.07	−0.07	0.07	–	–
$\Delta R_m I$	–	–	0.06	**−0.14**	0.11	−0.02	−0.04	−0.02	−0.09	−0.01	–	–
$\Delta R_m II$	–	–	–	**−0.14**	0.11	−0.01	−0.01	0.01	–	−0.01	–	–
$\Delta R_b I$	–	–	0.02	0.23	**−0.21**	–	–	–	–	–	−0.07	0.07
$\Delta R_b II$	–	–	0.02	0.23	**−0.36**	−0.01	−0.01	0.01	–	–	−0.07	0.07
$\Delta w_c^r I$	–	–	0.26	–	–	**−0.21**	−0.21	−0.09	−0.36	−0.12		–
$\Delta w_c^r II$	–	–	–	–	−0.15	**−0.01**	−0.01	0.02			–	–
$\Delta pr I$	–	–	−0.67	−1.5	0.72	0.38	0.15	**−0.57**	−0.54	−0.04	–	–
$\Delta pr II$	–	–	−0.97	−1.5	2.33	0.00	0.33	**−0.84**	0.54	−0.08		–
ΔUI	–	–	0.07	–	–	0.03	0.01	0.01	**0.00**	0.02	–	–
ΔUII	–	–	–	–	0.25	0.04	0.02	−0.02	**−0.03**	−0.02		
ΔqI	–	–	0.35	−1.19	0.61	0.51	0.21	–	–	**−0.27**	−1.07	1.07
ΔqII	–	–	−0.33	−1.19	0.92	0.30	0.30	−0.30	−0.05	**−0.27**	−1.07	1.07

We shall now focus on the most interesting differences between the two periods. The money market analysis demonstrated fairly strong evidence of parameter non-constancy in the relationship between inflation rate and real income, but suggested a reasonably constant money demand relation as well as an interest rate relation when allowing for an equilibrium mean shift at 1983. We can now examine the equations for real money, inflation, and the interest rates using the extended information set to find out whether our previous conclusions still hold.

The combined effect for the real money equation shows that most of the money demand parameters have been constant over the two periods. The bond rate effect has increased somewhat and the negative (and probably insignificant) inflation effect in the first period is not present in the next. It is, however, interesting to note that an increase in productivity has increased real money stock in the first period, but decreased it in the second period. This is likely to be related to the non-constant inflation–income relationship discussed above.

The results for the inflation rate show that the real wage effects on inflation have been much smaller in the EMS period than in the 1970s, and that the productivity effect was more negative in the 1970s than in the EMS period. Again, this confirms the negative, non-constant 'reduced form' relationship between inflation and real income previously found.

Regarding the short-term interest rate and the bond rate, the results are quite similar between the two periods. However, the negative effect between the short rate and the unemployment rate and the positive effect between short rate and inflation in the first period, though not in the second, suggests that the central bank was more inclined to react on movements in unemployment and inflation in the first period.

The most dominant changes seem, not surprisingly, to be associated with the determination of real wages, productivity and unemployment rate. In the EMS period real consumer wages have not been significantly equilibrium correcting (only weak evidence of the mark-up adjusting to the cost of capital measured by R_b). In the 1970s, real wages were affected by most determinants (except for the money market *ecm*'s). Productivity was negatively associated with unemployment rate in the 1970s, but positively in the EMS period. This is fairly strong evidence of productivity improvements through increased labour intensity (by producing the same output with less labour). The reason why this effect is strong in the productivity equation, but not in the unemployment equation, is that this type of productivity improvement occurs after a reduction in employment. The fairly strong effect of the bond rate on unemployment rate in the EMS period (while not very strong in the 1970s) is quite interesting as it suggests that employment was primarily demand determined in the EMS period.

The real exchange rate equations are quite similar over the two periods, except for the productivity and unemployment effects present in the EMS period, but absent in the 1970s.

Altogether, the comparative analysis seems to strengthen our previous conclusion that the non-constant and negative relationship between real income and inflation rate is related to the changing mechanisms in the labour market.

22.2 What have we learnt about inflationary mechanisms?

The purpose of this book was to demonstrate how to apply the cointegrated VAR model in a systematic way to answer questions of economic relevance. As an illustration of this approach we first attempted to answer the question 'Is inflation always and everywhere a monetary problem?' and then the related one 'If not, what then?' Chapter 2 demonstrated that many important aspects of the monetary model for inflation could be translated into a set of testable hypotheses, all of which had to be accepted for the theory model to have empirical validity. The hypothetical scenario showed that the validity of the monetary model was based on the Fisher parity and the expectations' hypothesis of the term structure as auxiliary hypotheses.

22.2.1 Main findings

The VAR analysis of the first 16 chapters provided strong evidence that the Fisher parity as a stationary relation was not satisfied in the data, that money velocity and the interest rate spread might be accepted as stationary relations when allowing for a mean shift in 1983:1. However, this was contradicted by the common trends representation in Chapter 14 which clearly suggested that money velocity needed the bond rate to become truly stationary and that the bond rate and the short rate had been affected by the common stochastic trends with different coefficients. Furthermore, the finding in Chapter 11 that the effects of empirical shocks to excess money, inflation, and the short-term interest rate were exclusively transitory in the system strongly suggested that *the Danish inflation cannot be adequately explained by monetary factors* in this period. Thus, the logic of the monetary model was in several ways inconsistent with the logic of the econometric analysis and the answer to the first question seemed to be negative. The question 'if not monetary inflation, what then?' prompted us to investigate the possibility that the Danish price inflation had its origin in wage inflation and/or imported inflation.

By extending the data set to include new variables relevant for the wage, price, unemployment dynamics and for the international transmission mechanisms with respect to Germany, the idea was partly to gain a better understanding of the mechanisms that have generated inflation in this period, partly to be able to explain the puzzling results that the money market analysis had revealed. We shall first summarize the main results from the extended model with the purpose of answering the 'what then' question. At the same time we shall discuss whether some of the previously reached conclusions have changed as a result of modelling the three markets jointly. This can be seen as a discussion of the robustness of the previous conclusions to the *ceteris paribus* assumption. The extended model analysis seems to be consistent with the following main results:

- Money stock was almost exclusively adjusting to the estimated long-run money demand relation, with the caveat that there was some, though not very strong, evidence that imbalances in the labour market have affected money stock. The latter were interpretable as plausible central bank reaction effects.
- Inflation was to a large extent determined by the determinants of the labour market in the 1970s and by globalization, proxied by the price wedge, the mark-up, and the real exchange rate in both periods. The high levels of inflation rate in the 1970s and the low and decreasing levels since the mid-1980s was explained by the estimated changes in the wage, price, productivity, and unemployment dynamics, where an important difference was the almost absent Phillips curve effect in the 1970s compared to its very significant effect since then. Finally, tiny and only borderline significant effects from excess money was detected.
- The short-term interest rate was previously found to adjust to the long-term bond rate. This is still the case in the extended model, but in addition there were quite significant effects from imbalances in the labour market, interpretable as plausible central bank policy reaction effects. However, theses effects were primarily observable in the 1970s, likely to reflect a greater inflationary concern by the central bank. Based on the combined effects in Table 22.4, there is some evidence that inflation rate and the short-term interest rate were negatively related, suggesting that the above policy reactions had been effective in reducing inflationary pressure, at least in the short and the medium run. The result from the $I(2)$ analysis, that the twice cumulated shocks to the short rate had a positive effect on the price level, might suggest that after the central bank had raised the interest rate in anticipation of increasing inflation, the inflation rate (and the price level) actually increased.

- The exogeneity of the Danish bond rate, in the money market analysis, was rejected in the labour market analysis. However, the effects on the bond rate from imbalances in the labour market were generally tiny. When the current change in the German bond rate was included as an exogenous variable, the Danish bond rate was strongly reacting to it with a coefficient of 0.68. Thus, it seems safe to conclude that the Danish long-term interest rate has primarily been determined in the international market, but with some effects from the domestic economy, probably reflecting changes in the perceived risk premium or simply changes in the demand and supply of government bonds.
- Real wages were found to exclusively react on the determinants of the labour market with strong negative effects from the exogenous price wedge, suggesting that real wages have declined with globalization (interpreting the price wedge as a proxy for this development). Otherwise the effects were similar to the wage, price, and unemployment analysis.
- Productivity was strongly adjusting in both periods, but with opposite signs to its main determinants. Most importantly, trend-adjusted productivity and unemployment were countercyclical in the first period, but procyclical in the second. This gives strong support to productivity improvement being achieved primarily by producing the same output with less labour in a period characterized by increasing globalization and product market competition.
- The comovements between the unemployment rate and the production factor costs in the second period suggest that employment in this period has foremost adjusted to the demand for labour. Contrary to productivity, unemployment has not adjusted to the globalization relation ($W83ecm1$) and the Phillips curve relation ($W83ecm2$). This suggests that labour reductions preceded productivity improvements, consistent with the discussion in Section 20.1.2.
- The real exchange rate, while accepted as weakly exogenous in Chapter 21, was found to be equilibrium correcting to the modified real interest rate spread relation ($Fecm3$), to the real wage relation ($W73ecm1$) and to the mark-up relation ($W83ecm4$). Furthermore, it was reacting on the domestic interest rate spread ($Mecm3$) and quite strongly on the current change in the German inflation rate. Thus, the real exchange rate has indeed adjusted to the fundamentals in the labour market, but the effects became statistically visible only after including sufficiently many explanatory variables in the model. Whether the adjustment has been primarily in nominal exchange rate or in domestic prices is difficult to say based on the present analysis.

22.2.2 Do we now understand previous puzzles better?

We shall now ask whether, with the background of what we have learnt from the extended model, we can better understand the mechanisms that have generated the non-stationarity of money velocity, the Fisher parity and the interest rate spreads. For this reason it is useful to reproduce the common trends representation of Chapter 14, describing how the variables of the system have been affected by the cumulated empirical shocks to real income and the bond rate.

$$\begin{bmatrix} m_t^r \\ y_t^r \\ \Delta p_t \\ R_{m,t} \\ R_{b,t} \end{bmatrix} = \begin{bmatrix} \underset{[4.2]}{\mathbf{1.02}} & \underset{[-3.7]}{\mathbf{-10.1}} \\ \underset{[5.2]}{\mathbf{1.14}} & \underset{[-2.2]}{\mathbf{-5.4}} \\ \underset{[-5.2]}{\mathbf{-0.03}} & \underset{[2.2]}{\mathbf{0.16}} \\ \underset{[1.3]}{0.02} & \underset{[4.7]}{\mathbf{1.00}} \\ \underset{[1.3]}{0.03} & \underset{[4.7]}{\mathbf{1.35}} \end{bmatrix} \begin{bmatrix} \sum_{i=1}^{t} \varepsilon_{y,i} \\ \sum_{i=1}^{t} \varepsilon_{Rb,i} \end{bmatrix} + \begin{bmatrix} 0.0031 \\ 0.0029 \\ 0.0001 \\ 0.0000 \\ 0.0001 \end{bmatrix} t + \cdots \quad (22.3)$$

First, the loadings to the two trends in real money and real income suggests that money demand has been more interest elastic than investment demand. This can explain the non-stationarity of money velocity. Second, the non-stationarity of the interest rate spread can be explained by the bond rate being more strongly affected by the stochastic trends than the short-term interest rate. In both cases, the non-stationarity has become less pronounced as the interest rates have been declining over the last decade.[1]

Third, the non-stationarity of the Fisher parity can be explained by the negative effect on inflation rate from the cumulative real income shocks, as opposed to the positive effects on the interest rates. That $\sum \varepsilon_y$ loaded negatively into the inflation rate and positively into the bond rate seems to be explained by the downward pressure on prices due to increased competition in the product market, forcing enterprises to improve productivity (increase in labour intensity combined with new technology), leading to a parallel increase in unemployment (as a result of workers being laid off, of fewer hirings, and of outsourcing), but with hardly any increase in price inflation. Thus, in the more recent period productivity and the inflation rate were moving in opposite directions, whereas productivity and the unemployment rate were moving together, similarly as unemployment and the long-term bond rate. The latter is likely to be explained by the need to supply government bonds to finance unemployment compensations.

The strong rejection of the Fisher parity is because the stochastic trend(s) in inflation rate and the nominal interest rates seem to move in opposite directions. It seems likely that the underlying shocks were triggered off as a consequence of removing trade barriers and deregulating international capital movements, rather than being generated from shocks to inflationary expectations or from central bank policy actions.

Altogether, it seems likely that many of the surprising results in the monetary model are related to institutional changes in this period. In particular, the creation of the European Community and more generally the deregulation of international capital markets seem to have influenced macroeconomic mechanisms in a very fundamental manner. To summarize:

1. The increased competition in the product market significantly weakened the labour unions and put a downward pressure on nominal wage claims and, thus, on price inflation.

2. The increased internationalization of the capital market moved the determination of the Danish bond rate away from the domestic to the international capital markets

[1] Based on a sample from 1973–1993, the stationarity of money velocity and interest rate spreads were much more strongly rejected.

and, thus, caused a large part of the Danish bond rate to be exogenously determined in the more recent model.

22.2.3 Which theories seem empirically relevant?

Up to this point we have presented and discussed a large number of empirical findings describing macroeconomic transmission mechanisms in the Danish economy over a transition period from a more regulated to an almost fully deregulated economy. The VAR approach discussed in this book is data-based in the sense that we look at the data structured by the statistical model through different glasses of a variety of economic theories or hypotheses. This means that we usually end up obtaining partial support for several theories. We shall now give our own assessment of which theoretical models seem to have been best in explaining the variation in the data. Without claiming decisive evidence, some tentative conclusions can be drawn:

1. A number of Phelps' structuralist hypotheses related to the wage, price, and unemployment dynamics (Phelps 1994) found fairly strong empirical support as stationary cointegration relations.
2. 'Pricing-to-market' as a theory for price and exchange rate determination in a global product market (Krugman 1993) seemed more consistent with the empirical results than 'mark-up pricing'. This is particularly so in the more recent period.
3. 'Imperfect knowledge expectations and forecasting' as a theory for exchange rate (and interest rate) determination in the speculative market for foreign exchange (Frydman and Goldberg 2006a) seem to be able to explain the empirical finding of a non-stationary real exchange rate, whereas most other theories would presume a stationary rate.

The theories mentioned above should, however, be considered theoretical pieces in the large jigsaw puzzle describing the dynamics of the Danish macroeconomy. To claim theoretical consistency, many missing pieces would have to be added. In particular, the following issues seem to prompt for more research, empirical as well as theoretical:

1. The role of productivity adjustment in periods of increased product market competition, distinguishing between productivity increases as a result of technological progress and improvement in labour intensity. Most theoretical work addressing the persistence in European (in particular) unemployment over the last decades do not distinguish between these two components of productivity, but assume technology shocks to be purely pushing. See, for example, Blanchard (1998, 2000a, 2000b, 2000c).
2. The role of the price wedge between consumer and producer prices as a proxy for competition in the tradeable sector compared to the non-tradable sector. The price wedge clearly played an important role as an exogenous driving force in our model and has frequently been found to be one of the most important determinants in estimated wage, price and unemployment dynamics. See for example, Juselius (2003), Juselius and Ordóñez (2005), Tuxen (2006), Koch (2006). This is likely to be closely related to the Balassa–Samuelson effect (Balassa 1964; Samuelson

1964) mostly used to explain the movements of real exchange rates in catching-up economies. However, we believe that this effect has a generality that goes beyond the catching-up economies.

22.2.4 About the VAR analysis and the theory model

A major difference between the 'specific-to-general' and the 'general-to-specific' approach to empirical macromodelling is that, in the former case, we focus on just a few empirical aspects of a specific theory model, in the latter case we try to extract as much information as possible from the data. In this view, empirical regularities in the data are interpreted with the background of broadly defined relations describing economic behaviour, whereas no specific theory model is tested. Structured by a stringent statistical model analysis, these regularities are translated into a set of 'stylized facts' which are much richer than the more conventional graphs, mean values, and correlation coefficients, of which the latter are inappropriate when data are non-stationary.

For example, Phelps (1994) was an impressive attempt to tell a large, overriding theoretical story that was consistent with (and probably strongly influenced by) broad 'stylized facts' about European unemployment in the 1980s and the 1990s. Nonetheless, it seems likely that several elements of that story would need to be modified to satisfactorily describe the 'more sophisticated facts' generated by a well-structured cointegrated VAR analysis.

One may ask whether the Danish results discussed at length in this book has any generality outside the context of a very small open European economy. As a matter of fact, similar results have been found in a variety of empirical studies based on other countries data.[2] In particular, Tuxen (2006) finds surprisingly similar results in a comprehensive study of inflationary mechanisms in the Eurowide area. This seems to be a strong signal that a careful VAR analysis might be a progressive way to better understand the dynamics of domestic macroeconomic mechanisms in a dynamic and fast changing world. We believe there is a large unexploited potential for analysing data from various economies that are different in certain aspects, for example the institutional set-up, and similar in others. By comparing the results with respect to similarities and differences one might be able to achieve something similar to a designed experiment in economics. We also believe there is a large unexploited potential for econometricians and theoretical economists to work closely together with the econometrician producing sophisticated stylized facts and the theorist generating empirically relevant theory models.

In this book, we have illustrated how empirical puzzles detected in one VAR model often generate new hypotheses which prompts for an extension of the data set of the current VAR model or leads to a new VAR analysis based on a different data set. In the ideal case the empirical analysis suggests new directions for modifying the theoretical model. Alternatively, it might suggest how to modify the empirical model (for example by adding more data) to make it more consistent with the theory. In either case the analysis points forward, which is why we believe the VAR methodology has the potential of being a progressive research paradigm.

[2] In a series of summer schools in the 'Cointegrated VAR model' organized in Copenhagen, 2003–2005, approximately 100 participants from all over the world have analysed similar models based on their own country's data and obtained very similar conclusions.

22.3 Concluding discussion

The VAR approach takes the properties of the data as seriously as possible by starting from a well-specified statistical model which is just a convenient summary of the covariances of the data (see Chapter 3). Within this framework we are able to test not just a restricted number of hypotheses relevant for one economic model, but as many as seem relevant given the basic features of the DGP. Provided that further reductions (simplifications) of the VAR model satisfy the rules for valid statistical inference, the final results should, therefore, essentially reflect the relevant information in the data.

The purpose of this book was to illustrate how to extract information from the data based on the cointegrated VAR model and its decomposition into pulling and pushing forces. Methodologically the approach combines deduction and induction. The deductive part of the analysis is based on a theory model, the testable implications of which have been translated into a set of hypotheses on the parameters of the VAR model describing long-run relations, adjustment dynamics, driving trends, and their effects on the variables of the system. Since the theory model (by necessity) is based on numerous simplifying assumptions, the VAR analysis usually detects discrepancies between empirical and theoretical behaviour. The inductive part of the analysis treats such discrepancies as a useful piece of information helping us to adjust our intuition of how the economic and the empirical model work together, sometimes leading to modifications of a too narrowly specified theoretical model, in other cases to the generation of new hypotheses.

Thus, by embedding the theory model in a broader empirical framework, the analysis of the statistically based model often provides evidence of possible pitfalls in macroeconomic reasoning. It also generates a set of relevant 'stylized facts', such as the number of autonomous shocks and how they affect the variables of the system. Finally, it provides a check on how sensitive theory based conclusions are to the *ceteris paribus* assumption.

The empirical application of a model for monetary inflation demonstrated that many aspects of the theory model can be translated into a set of testable hypotheses, all of which should be accepted for the theory model to have full empirical validity. This is in contrast to many empirical investigations, where inference is based on test procedures that only make sense in isolation, but not in the full context of the empirical model.

As demonstrated above empirical puzzles detected in the VAR analysis often suggest how to proceed to make empirical evidence and theory fit together more closely.

To end this discussion we cite a passage from Hoover (2006) discussing the difference between Walrasian and Marshallian economics, which in many ways pinpoints the fundamental scientific difference between the specific-to-general and the general-to-specific approach to empirical economics:

> The Walrasian approach is totalizing. Theory comes first. Empirical reality must be theoretically articulated before it can be empirically observed. There is a sense that the Walrasian attitude is that to know anything, one must know everything.
>
> ...There is a fundamental problem: How do we come to our *a priori* knowledge? Most macroeconomists expect empirical evidence to be relevant to our understanding of the world. But if that evidence only can be viewed through totalizing *a priori* theory, then it cannot be used to revise the theory.
>
> ...The Marshallian approach is archaeological. We have some clues that a systematic structure lies behind the complexities of economic reality. The problem is how to lay this structure

bare. To dig down to find the foundations, modifying and adapting our theoretical understanding as new facts accumulate, becoming ever more confident in our grasp of the super structure, but never quite sure that we have reached the lowest level of the structure.

The cointegrated VAR approach discussed in this book is clearly more consistent with the Marshallian approach to macroeconomics than with the Walrasian. For example, the significant finding of the negative comovements between inflation and real aggregate income in the money market model is an example of an important piece of information in the data signalling the need to dig deeper in order to understand more. By taking this piece of information in the data seriously, instead of just ignoring it, we were able to uncover more structure improving our understanding. Needless to say, the need to dig deeper does not stop here.

Thus, a careful analysis of the empirical results might at an early stage suggest how to modify either the empirical or the economic model. This is one way of translating the notion of a design of experiment and the link between theory and empirical evidence when the latter is based on data collected by passive observation suggested in Haavelmo:

In the second case we can only try to adjust our theories to reality as it appears before us. And what is the meaning of a design of experiment in this case. It is this: We try to choose a theory and a design of experiments to go with it, in such a way that the resulting data would be those which we get by passive observation of reality. And to the extent that we succeed in doing so, we become masters of reality – by passive agreement.

The alternative, which is to force the chosen economic model on the data, thereby squeezing an exuberant reality into 'all-too-small-size clothes', is a frustrating experience that often makes the desperate researcher choose solutions that are not scientifically justified.

For those readers who have got an appetite for writing a paper based on the cointegrated VAR methodology, a road map for the major steps in the analysis is given in the Appendix.

APPENDIX A

The asymptotic tables for cointegration rank

Case 1: no deterministics

$p-r$	0.50	0.75	0.80	0.85	0.90	0.95	0.975	0.99
1	0.61	1.55	1.88	2.32	2.95	4.07	5.22	6.77
2	5.49	7.85	8.53	9.36	10.47	12.28	14.00	16.17
3	14.51	18.10	19.07	20.25	21.79	24.21	26.45	29.21
4	27.52	32.31	33.57	35.08	37.05	40.10	42.86	46.23
5	44.53	50.49	52.05	53.90	56.29	59.96	63.27	67.26
6	65.54	72.68	74.52	76.71	79.53	83.82	87.67	92.28
7	90.54	98.86	100.99	103.52	106.76	111.68	116.06	121.30
8	119.55	129.03	131.46	134.32	137.98	143.53	148.46	154.33
9	152.55	163.20	165.92	169.12	173.21	179.38	184.85	191.35
10	189.55	201.38	204.38	207.92	212.43	219.23	225.25	232.38
11	230.55	243.55	246.84	250.72	255.65	263.09	269.64	277.41
12	275.55	289.72	293.30	297.52	302.88	310.94	318.04	326.43

Case 2: restricted constant

$p-r$	0.50	0.75	0.80	0.85	0.90	0.95	0.975	0.99
1	3.52	5.41	5.97	6.66	7.60	9.14	10.63	12.53
2	11.53	14.69	15.56	16.60	17.98	20.16	22.18	24.69
3	23.50	27.88	29.04	30.43	32.25	35.07	37.64	40.78
4	39.52	45.08	46.53	48.26	50.50	53.94	57.05	60.81
5	59.53	66.27	68.01	70.08	72.74	76.81	80.46	84.84
6	83.54	91.45	93.49	95.90	98.98	103.68	107.87	112.88
7	111.56	120.64	122.96	125.71	129.22	134.54	139.27	144.91
8	143.57	153.82	156.43	159.52	163.45	169.41	174.68	180.95
9	179.58	191.00	193.91	197.33	201.69	208.27	214.09	220.99
10	219.59	232.18	235.38	239.14	243.92	251.13	257.49	265.03
11	263.60	277.36	280.85	284.94	290.15	297.99	304.90	313.06
12	311.61	326.54	330.32	334.75	340.38	348.85	356.30	365.10

Case 3: unrestricted constant

$p-r$	0.50	0.75	0.80	0.85	0.90	0.95	0.975	0.99
1	0.45	1.32	1.64	2.07	2.71	3.84	5.02	6.63
2	7.75	10.48	11.24	12.18	13.42	15.41	17.28	19.62
3	19.05	23.08	24.16	25.46	27.16	29.80	32.23	35.21
4	34.12	39.33	40.70	42.33	44.45	47.71	50.66	54.23
5	53.18	59.57	61.22	63.19	65.73	69.61	73.10	77.29
6	76.23	83.79	85.74	88.05	91.01	95.51	99.54	104.36
7	103.29	112.02	114.26	116.90	120.28	125.42	129.98	135.43
8	134.34	144.24	146.77	149.75	153.56	159.32	164.43	170.50
9	169.39	180.46	183.28	186.60	190.83	197.22	202.87	209.58
10	208.44	220.69	223.79	227.45	232.10	239.12	245.32	252.66
11	251.49	264.91	268.30	272.30	277.38	285.02	291.77	299.74
12	298.54	313.13	316.81	321.14	326.65	334.92	342.21	350.81

Case 4: restricted linear trend and unrestricted constant

$p-r$	0.50	0.75	0.80	0.85	0.90	0.95	0.975	0.99
1	5.77	8.11	8.77	9.59	10.68	12.45	14.12	16.22
2	16.01	19.63	20.61	21.78	23.32	25.73	27.95	30.67
3	30.14	34.97	36.24	37.76	39.73	42.77	45.53	48.87
4	48.19	54.19	55.75	57.61	60.00	63.66	66.95	70.91
5	70.25	77.42	79.26	81.46	84.27	88.55	92.38	96.97
6	96.30	104.64	106.78	109.30	112.54	117.45	121.82	127.04
7	126.35	135.86	138.28	141.15	144.81	150.35	155.26	161.11
8	160.40	171.08	173.79	177.00	181.08	187.25	192.71	199.18
9	198.45	210.30	213.30	216.84	221.35	228.15	234.15	241.26
10	240.50	253.52	256.81	260.69	265.62	273.04	279.59	287.34
11	286.55	300.73	304.32	308.53	313.89	321.94	329.04	337.41
12	336.60	351.95	355.83	360.38	366.16	374.84	382.48	391.49

Case 5: unrestricted linear trend and constant

$p-r$	0.50	0.75	0.80	0.85	0.90	0.95	0.975	0.99
1	0.45	1.32	1.64	2.07	2.71	3.84	5.02	6.63
2	9.88	12.92	13.76	14.79	16.14	18.30	20.30	22.81
3	23.23	27.69	28.87	30.29	32.15	35.03	37.65	40.87
4	40.47	46.11	47.58	49.33	51.60	55.08	58.22	62.01
5	61.66	68.46	70.22	72.31	75.00	79.10	82.77	87.17
6	86.80	94.78	96.83	99.25	102.36	107.09	111.30	116.33
7	115.92	125.07	127.41	130.17	133.70	139.05	143.81	149.47
8	149.02	159.34	161.97	165.07	169.03	175.00	180.30	186.59
9	186.10	197.59	200.51	203.95	208.33	214.94	220.78	227.70
10	227.17	239.83	243.04	246.82	251.62	258.86	265.25	272.80
11	272.23	286.06	289.56	293.68	298.91	306.77	313.70	321.89
12	321.28	336.28	340.07	344.52	350.18	358.67	366.15	374.97

APPENDIX B

A roadmap for writing an empirical paper

A cointegrated VAR paper should roughly include the following parts:

1. A motivational background for the paper. What is the purpose of the empirical investigation? Which question(s) do you want to answer? Are there other studies in the field that are closely related?
2. A theoretical part. Introduce the theoretical steady-state relations you expect to find in your data and the expected sign of the coefficients. How many common trends would the theory suggest? Specify a plausible scenario for how these common stochastic trends (defined as the cumulated sum of the underlying autonomous shocks) are supposed to affect your variables.
3. A descriptive part. Define the variables and present the graphs of the data in levels and differences. In addition, it is often useful to illustrate specific properties of the data, for example by cross-plots or other graphs relating two or more series to each other. (The 'Graphics' option of GiveWin is recommended.) If your subsequent analysis contain empirical 'surprises' it is a good idea to prepare the reader for them from the outset. It is much easier to make the reader interested in any novel aspects of your results if your graphs demonstrate that previously held beliefs are inconsistent with the data. For example, if the cointegration analysis suggests that liquidity ratio needs a trend, then you should present a graph showing that the liquidity ratio is indeed trending. If there are outlier observations in the data, then you should demonstrate it graphically to the reader.
4. The statistical model. Define the VAR model and the system variables. Specify the deterministic components, and indicate whether the latter are restricted to the cointegration relations or not.
5. Estimation of the baseline VAR model. Report misspecification tests for residual normality, independence and homoscedasticity. Check the parameter constancy of your model by recursive tests. If parameter constancy is rejected discuss how to reformulate your model. Motivate your choice of lag length.

6. Cointegration rank. Determine the cointegration rank r by the trace test. Discuss the appropriateness of the asymptotic tables for your model. If you have included dummy variables in your model discuss how they influence the tables. As a sensitivity analysis calculate the roots for alternative values of r. Check the t values of the rth (± 1) cointegrating relation as well as the corresponding graphs. Is your choice of r consistent with this information and with the number of hypothetical common trends in the scenario?
7. Tests of model specific data properties. Perform tests of long-run exclusion, stationarity and weak exogeneity and of a unit vector in alpha and summarize the main conclusions.
8. Hypotheses testing. After you have found a well-specified model, test the stationarity of your hypothetical steady-state relations. Discuss whether the results suggest possible modifications of the theory model you started with.
9. Long-run identification. Impose just-identifying restrictions on your cointegration relations. Are they empirically identified? If possible, impose over-identifying restrictions. Is the structure economically identified?
10. Common driving trends. Calculate the C-matrix in the moving average representation and interpret the results. Perform a structural MA (VAR) analysis.
11. Identification of a short-run dynamic adjustment structure. Impose over-identifying restrictions on the short-run adjustment parameters. PcGive is easy to use for this purpose.
12. Nominal to real transformations. If your data contain nominal variables, check whether there is any indication of $I(2)$'ness in your model. If feasible, test the hypothesis of long-run price homogeneity. Discuss the statistical adequacy of the nominal-to-real transformation. If there are alternative measurements available for your nominal variables (for example CPI, implicit price deflator, etc.) it is a good idea to investigate whether the choice of measurements matters or not for your cointegration analyses. This can be done by finding out whether the (price) differential is stationary or not.
13. Summarize the results and conclude!

Bibliography

Anderson, T. W. (2003). *An Introduction to Multivariate Statistical Analysis* (3rd edn.). John Wiley: New York.

Anderson, T. W. (1991). Trygve Haavelmo and simultaneous equation models. *Scandinavian Journal of Statistics*, **18**, 1–19.

Baba, Y., D. F. Hendry, and R. M. Starr (1992). The demand for M1 in the USA, 1960–1988. *Review of Economic Studies*, **59**(1), 25–61.

Backhouse, R. and A. Salanti (Eds.) (2000a). *Macroeconomics and the Real World, Volume 1: Econometric Techniques and Macroeconomics.* Oxford University Press: Oxford.

Backhouse, R. and A. Salanti (Eds.) (2000b). *Macroeconomics and the Real World, Volume 2: Keynesian Economics, Unemployment and Policy.* Oxford University Press: Oxford.

Balassa, B. (1964). The purchasing-power parity doctrine: A reappraisal. *Journal of Political Economy*, **72**(6), 584–596.

Banerjee, A. and B. Russell (2005). Inflation and measures of the markup. *Journal of Macroeconomics*, **27**, 289–306.

Barnett, W. A., D. F. Hendry, S. Hylleberg, T. Teräsvirta, D. Tjøstheim, and A. Würtz (Eds.) (2006). *Nonlinear Econometric Modeling in Time Series.* Cambridge University Press: Cambridge.

Baumol, W. (1952). The transaction demand for cash: An inventory theoretic approach. *Quarterly Journal of Economics*, **66**(4), 545–556.

Bec, F. and A. Rahbek (2004). Vector equilibrium correction models with non-linear discontinuous adjustments. *Econometrics Journal*, **7**, 628–651.

Bec, F., M. B. Salem, and M. Carrasco (2004). Tests for unit-root versus threshold specification with an application to the purchasing power parity relationship. *Journal of Business and Economic Statistics*, **22**(4), 382–395.

Beyer, A., J.A. Doornik, and D.F. Hendry (2001). Constructing historical Euro-Zone data. *Economic Journal*, **111**, 308–327.

Blanchard, O. J. and D. Quah (1989). The dynamic effects of aggregate demand and supply disturbances. *American Economic Review*, **79**(4), 665–673.

Blanchard, O. (1998). European unemployment. Shocks and institutions. Technical report, MIT. Paper prepared for the Baffi lecture, Rome.

Blanchard, O. (2000a). Shocks, factor prices, and unemployment. Lionel Robbins Lectures Lecture 1, LSE.

Blanchard, O. (2000b). Rents, product and labor market regulation and unemployment. Lionel Robbins Lectures Lecture 2, LSE.

Blanchard, O. (2000c). Employment, protection, sclerosis, and the effect of shocks on unemployment. Lionel Robbins Lectures Lecture 3, LSE.

Boeri, T., J. F. Jimeno, R. Marimon, and C. Pissarides (2001). EU welfare systems and labor markets: Diverse in the past, integrated in the future? In G. Bertola, T. Boeri, and G. Nicoletti (Eds.), *Welfare and Employment in a United Europe.* MIT Press: Cambridge, Mass.

Bowdler, C. and H. B. Nielsen (2006). Inflation adjustment in the open economy: An $I(2)$ analysis of UK prices. *Empirical Economics*. Online issue.

Campbell, J. Y. and P. Perron (1991). Pitfalls and opportunities: What macroeconomists should know about unit roots. In O. Blanchard and S. Fischer (Eds.), *NBER Macroeconomic Annual 6*, pp. 141–201. The MIT Press: Cambridge, Mass.

Campbell, J. Y. and R. J. Shiller (1987). Cointegration and tests of present value models. *Journal of Political Economy*, **95**(5), 1062–1088.

Campbell, J. Y. and R. J. Shiller (1991). Yield spreads and interest rate movements: A bird's eye view. *Review of Economic Studies*, **58**(3), 495–514.

Campos, J., N. R. Ericsson, and D. F. Hendry (1990). An analogue model of phase-averaging procedures. *Journal of Econometrics*, **43**(3), 275–292.

Campos, J., N. R. Ericsson, and D. F. Hendry (1996). Cointegration tests in the presence of structural breaks. *Journal of Econometrics*, **70**(1), 187–220.

Caselli, F. and S. Tenreyro (2005). Is Poland the next Spain? CEP Discussion Paper No 668, Centre for Economic Performance, London School of Economics.

Cheung, Y.-W. and K. S. Lai (1993). Long-run purchasing power parity during the recent float. *Journal of International Economics*, **34**, 181–192.

Christensen, A. M. and H. B. Nielsen (2005). US monetary police 1988-2004: An empirical analysis. Finance Research Unit working paper 0501, Department of Economics, University of Copenhagen.

Clarida, R., J. Gali, and M. Gertler (1999). The science of monetary policy: A New Keynesian perspective. *Journal of Economic Literature*, **37**, 1661–1707.

Clements, M. P. and D. F. Hendry (1999a). *Forecasting Non-stationary Economic Time Series.* MIT Press: Cambridge, Mass.

Clements, M. P. and D. F. Hendry (1999b). *Nonlinear Econometric Modeling in Time Series.* MIT Press: Cambridge, Mass.

Coenen, G. and J. L. Vega (1999). The demand for M3 in the Euro area. Working Paper Series 6, European Central Bank.

Colander, D. (1991). *Why Aren't Economists As Important As Garbagemen?* M. E. Sharpe.

Colander, D. (Ed.) (1996). *Beyond Micro Foundations: Post Walrasian Macroeconomics.* Cambridge University Press: Cambridge, Mass.

Colander, D. (1999). New millenium economics: How did it get this way, and what way is it? *Journal of Economic Perspectives*, **14**(1), 121–132.

Colander, D. (2000a). The death of Neoclassical economics. *Journal of the History of Economic Thought*, **22**(2), 127–143.

Colander, D. (2000b). Teaching macroeconomic principles: Telling better stories in introductory macro. *Journal of Economic Perspectives*, **90**(2).

Colander, D. (2001). *The Lost Art of Economics.* Edward Elgar: Cheltenham.

Colander, D. (2006). Some historical threads of post Walrasian macro. In D. Colander (Ed.), *Post Walrasian Macroeconomics: Beyond the Dynamic Stochastic General Equilibrium Model*, Chapter 2. Cambridge University Press: Cambridge.

Cumby, R. and M. Obstfeld (1981). Exchange rate expectations and nominal interest rates: A test of the Fisher hypothesis. *Journal of Finance*, **36**, 697–703.

Cuthbertson, K. (1996). The expectations hypothesis of the term structure: the UK interbank market. *Economic Journal*, **106**(436), 578–592.

Davidson, J. (1998). Structural relations, cointegration and identification: Some simple results and their application. *Journal of Econometrics*, **87**(1), 87–113.

Dennis, J. G., H. Hansen, S. Johansen, and K. Juselius (2006). *CATS in RATS. Cointegration Analysis of Time Series, Version 2.* Estima: Evanston, Illinois, USA.

de Brouwer, G. and N. Ericsson (1998). Modeling inflation in Australia. *Journal of Business and Economic Statistics*, **16**(4), 433–449.

Doornik, J. A. (1998). Approximations to the asymptotic distribution of cointegration tests. *Journal of Economic Surveys*, **12**(5), 573–593.

Doornik, J. A., D. F. Hendry, and B. Nielsen (1998). Inference in cointegrating models: UK M1 revisited. *Journal of Economic Surveys*, **12**, 533–572.

Doornik, J. A. and D. F. Hendry (2001a). *Empirical Econometric Modelling Using PcGive. Volumes I, II and III.* Timberlake Consultants Press: London.

Doornik, J. A. and D. F. Hendry (2001b). *GiveWin. An Interface to Empirical Modelling* (3rd edn.). Timberlake Consultants Press: London.

Dornbusch, R. (1976). Expectations and exchange rate dynamics. *Journal of Political Economy*, 1161–1176.

Engle, R. F. and C. W. J. Granger (1987). Cointegration and error correction: Representation, estimation, and testing. *Econometrica*, **55**(2), 251–276.

Feige, E. L. (1967). Expectations and adjustments in the monetary sector. *American Economic Review, Papers and Proceedings*, **5**, 462–473.

Flanagan, R., K. O. Moene, and M. Wallerstein (1993). *Trade Union Behaviour, Pay-Bargaining, and Economic Performance.* Clarendon Press: Oxford.

Fountas, S. and J-L. Wu (1998). Tests for interest rate convergence and structural breaks in the EMS. *Applied Financial Economics*, **8**(2), 127–132.

Franses, P. H. and N. Haldrup (1994). The effects of additive outliers on tests for unit roots and cointegration. *Journal of Business and Economic Statistics*, **12**(4), 471–478.

Friedman, M. (1970). The counterrevolution in monetary theory. Occasional paper, No. 33, Institute of Economic Affairs.

Froot, K. and K. Rogoff (1995). Perspectives on PPP and long-run real exchange rates. In E. Grossman and K. Rogoff (Eds.), *Handbook of International Economics*, Volume 3. North Holland: Amsterdam.

Frydman, R. and M. D. Goldberg (1996). Imperfect knowledge and behavior in the foreign exchange market. *Economic Journal*, **106**, 869–893.

Frydman, R. and M. D. Goldberg (2001). Macroeconomic fundamentals and the DM/USD exchange rate: Temporal instability and the monetary model. *International Journal of Finance and Economics*, **6**(4), 421–435.

Frydman, R. and M. D. Goldberg (2002). Imperfect knowledge and exchange rate dynamics. In P. Aghion, R. Frydman, J. Stiglitz, and M. Woodford (Eds.), *Knowledge, Information and Expectations in Modern Economics: In Honor of Edmund S. Phelps.* MIT Press: Cambridge, Mass.

Frydman, R. and M. D. Goldberg (2004). Limiting exchange rate swings in a world of imperfect knowledge. In P. B. Sørenson (Ed.), *Monetary Union in Europe, Historical Perspectives and Prospects for the Future: Essays in Honor of Nils Thygesen,* Chapter 1, pp. 35–49. DJØF Publishing: Copenhagen, Denmark.

Frydman, R. and M. D. Goldberg (2006a). *Imperfect Knowledge Economics: Exchange Rates and Risk.* Princeton University Press: Princeton, New Jersey, Under contract.

Frydman, R. and M. D. Goldberg (2006b). Imperfect knowledge expectations, uncertainty premia and exchange rate dynamics. In A. Morales-Zumaquero (Ed.), *International Macroeconomics: Recent Developments.* Nova Science Publishers. forthcoming.

Garrat, A., K. Lee, M. H. Pesaran, and Y. Shin (2000). A structural cointegrating VAR approach to macroeconomic modelling. In S. Holly and M. Weale (Eds.), *Econometric Modelling: Techniques and Applications.* Cambridge University Press: Cambridge, Mass.

Gilbert, C. L. (1986). Professor Hendry's econometric methodology. *Oxford Bulletin of Economics and Statistics*, **48**(3), 283–307.

Godfrey, L. G. (1988). *Misspecification Tests in Econometrics.* Cambridge University Press: Cambridge.

Granger, C. W. J. (1981). Some properties of time series data and their use in econometric model specification. *Journal of Econometrics*, **16**, 121–130.

Granger, C. (1986). Developments in the study of cointegrated economic variables. *Oxford Bulletin of Economics and Statistics*, **48**, 213–228.

Granger, C. W. J. and T. Teräsvirta (1993). *Modelling Nonlinear Economic Relationships.* Oxford University Press: Oxford.

Gregory, A. W. and B. E. Hansen (1996). Tests for cointegration in models with regime and trend shifts. *Oxford Bulletin of Economics and Statistics*, **58**(3), 555–560.

Haavelmo, T. (1944). The probability approach in econometrics. *Econometrica*, **12** (Supplement), 1–118.

Hamilton, H. (1994). *Time Series Analysis.* Princeton University Press: Princeton, New Jersey.

Hansen, H. and J. A. Doornik (1994). An omnibus test for univariate and multivariate normality. Discussion paper, Nuffield College, Oxford University.

Hansen, H. and S. Johansen (1999). Some tests for parameter constancy in cointegrated VAR-models. *The Econometrics Journal*, **2**(2), 306–333.

Hansen, H. and A. Rahbek (2002). Approximate conditional unit root inference. *Journal of Time Series Analysis*, **23**(1), 1–28.

Hansen, H. and A. Warne (2001). The cause of Danish unemployment: Demand or supply shocks? *Empirical Economics*, **26**(3), 461–486.

Hansen, P. R. and S. Johansen (1998). *Workbook on Cointegration.* Oxford University Press: Oxford.

Harbo, I., S. Johansen, B. Nielsen, and A. Rahbek (1998). Asymptotic inference on cointegrating rank in partial systems. *Journal of Business and Economic Statistics*, **16**(4), 388–399.

Hendry, D. F. (1980). Predictive failure and econometric modelling in macroeconomics: The transactions demand for money. In *Economic Modelling*. Heinemann Education Books: London.

Hendry, D. F. (1987). Econometric methodology: A personal perspective. In T. F. Bewley (Ed.), *Advances in Econometrics*. Cambridge University Press: Cambridge, Mass.

Hendry, D. F. (1995). *Dynamic Econometrics*. Oxford University Press: Oxford.

Hendry, D. F. and N. R. Ericsson (1991a). An econometric analysis of UK money demand. In *Monetary trends in the United States and United Kingdom* by Milton Friedman and Anna J. Schwartz. *American Economic Review*, **81**(1), 8–38.

Hendry, D. F. and N. R. Ericsson (1991b). Modeling the demand for narrow money in the United Kingdom and the United States. *European Economic Review*, **35**(4), 833–886.

Hendry, D. F. and K. Juselius (2000). Explaining cointegration analysis: Part I. *Energy Journal*, **21**(1), 1–42.

Hendry, D. F. and K. Juselius (2001). Explaining cointegration analysis: Part II. *Energy Journal*, **22**(1), 75–120.

Hendry, D. F. and H.-M. Krolzig (2001). *Automatic Econometric Model Selection*. Timberlake Consultants Press: London.

Hendry, D. F. and H.-M. Krolzig (2002). New developments in automatic general-to-specific modelling. In B. P. Stigum (Ed.), *Econometrics and the Philosophy of Economics*, 379–419. Princeton University Press: Princeton.

Hendry, D. F. and G. E. Mizon (1993). Evaluating econometric models by encompassing the VAR. In P. C. B. Phillips (Ed.), *Models, Methods and Applications of Econometrics: Essays in Honor of A.R. Bergström*. MIT Press: Cambridge, Mass.

Hendry, D. F. and J. F. Richard (1983). The econometric analysis of economic time series (with discussion). *International Statistical Review*, **51**, 111–163.

Hendry, D. F., A. Spanos, and N. R. Ericsson (1989). The contributions to econometrics in Trygve Haavelmo's 'The probability approach in econometrics'. *Socialøkonomen*, **43**(11), 12–17.

Holden, S. and R. Nymoen (2002). Measuring structural unemployment: NAWRU estimates in the Nordic Countries. *Scandinavian Journal of Economics*, **104**, 87–104.

Hoover, K. (1988). *The New Classical Macroeconomics: A Sceptical Inquiry*. Basil Blackwell: Oxford.

Hoover, K. (2001a). *Causality in Macroeconomics*. Cambridge University Press: Cambridge, Mass.

Hoover, K. (2001b). *The Methodology of Empirical Macroeconomics*. Cambridge University Press: Cambridge, Mass.

Hoover, K. (2003). Searching for the causal structure of a vector autoregression. *Oxford Bulletin of Economics and Statistics*, 65 (supplement), 745–767.

Hoover, K. (2005). Automatic inference of the contemporaneous causal order of a system of equations. *Econometric Theory*, **21**, 69–77.

Hoover, K. (2006). The past as the future: The Marshallian approach to Post-Walrasian macro. In D. Colander (Ed.), *Post Walrasian Macroeconomics: Beyond the Dynamic Stochastic General Equilibrium Model*, Chapter 12. Cambridge University Press: Cambridge, Mass.

Hoover, K. and S. Perez (1999). Data mining reconsidered: encompassing and the general-to-specific approach to specification search. *Econometrics Journal*, **2**(2), 167–191.

Hosking, J. R. M. (1980). The multivariate portmanteau statistic. *Journal of the American Statistical Association*, **75**, 602–608.

Jensen, S. T. and A. Rahbek (2004a). Asymptotic normality for non-stationary, explosive GARCH. *Econometric Theory*, **20**(6), 1203–1226.

Jensen, S. T. and A. Rahbek (2004b). Asymptotic normality of the QMLE estimator of ARCH in the nonstationary case. *Econometrica*, **72**, 641–646.

Johansen, S. (1988). Statistical analysis of cointegration vectors. *Journal of Economic Dynamics and Control*, **12**(213), 231–254.

Johansen, S. (1991). Estimation and hypothesis of cointegration vectors in Gaussian vector autoregressive models. *Econometrica*, **59**(6), 1551–1580.

Johansen, S. (1992a). Cointegration in partial systems and the efficiency of single equation analysis. *Journal of Econometrics*, **52**(3), 389–402.

Johansen, S. (1992b). Determination of cointegration rank in the presence of a linear trend. *Oxford Bulletin of Economics and Statistics*, **54**, 383–397.

Johansen, S. (1992c). A representation of vector autoregressive processes integrated of order 2. *Econometric Theory*, **8**(2), 188–202.

Johansen, S. (1994). The role of the constant and linear terms in cointegration analysis of non-stationary variables. *Econometric Reviews*, **13**, 205–229.

Johansen, S. (1995a). Identifying restrictions of linear equations. With applications to simultaneous equations and cointegration. *Journal of Econometrics*, **69**(1), 111–132.

Johansen, S. (1995b). A statistical analysis of cointegration for $I(2)$ variables. *Econometric Theory*, **11**(1), 25–59.

Johansen, S. (1996). *Likelihood-Based Inference in Cointegrated Vector Autoregressive Models, 2.edn.* Advanced Texts in Econometrics, Oxford University Press: Oxford.

Johansen, S. (1997). Likelihood analysis of the $I(2)$ model. *Scandinavian Journal of Statistics*, **24**(4), 433–462.

Johansen, S. (2000). A Bartlett correction factor for tests on the cointegrating relations. *Econometric Theory*, **16**(5), 740–778.

Johansen, S. (2002a). A small sample correction for tests of hypotheses on the cointegrating vectors. *Journal of Econometrics*, **111**(2), 195–221.

Johansen, S. (2002b). A small sample correction of the test for cointegrating rank in the vector autoregressive model. *Econometrica*, **70**, 1929–1961.

Johansen, S. (2003). The asymptotic variance of the estimated roots in a cointegrated vector autoregressive model. *Journal of Time Series Analysis*, **24**, 663–678.

Johansen, S. (2004). A small sample correction of the Dickey-Fuller test. In A. Welfe (Ed.), *New Directions in Macromodelling*, Chapter 3, 49–68. Elsevier.

Johansen, S. (2005a). The interpretation of cointegrating coefficients in the cointegrated vector autoregressive model. *Oxford Bulletin of Economics and Statistics*, **67**, 93–104.

Johansen, S. (2005b). Representation of cointegrated autoregressive processes with application to fractional processes. Preprint 7, University of Copenhagen.

Johansen, S. (2005c). Testing weak exogeneity and the order of cointegration in the UK money demand data. *Journal of Policy Modeling*, **14**, 313–334. Reprinted in (eds. N. R. Ericsson and J. S. Irons) *Testing Weak Exogeneity*, 121–143. Oxford University Press. (1994): Oxford.

Johansen, S. (2006a). Statistical analysis of hypotheses on the cointegrating relations in the $I(2)$ model. *Journal of Econometrics*, **132**, 81–115.

Johansen, S. (2006b). Confronting the economic model with the data. In D. Colander (Ed.), *Post Walrasian Macroeconomics: Beyond the Dynamic Stochastic General Equilibrium Model*, Chapter 15. Cambridge University Press.

Johansen, S. and K. Juselius (1990). Maximum likelihood estimation and inference on cointegration with application to the demand of money. *Oxford Bulletin of Economics and Statistics*, **52**(2), 169–210.

Johansen, S. and K. Juselius (1992). Testing structural hypotheses in a multivariate cointegration analysis of the PPP and the UIP for UK. *Journal of Econometrics* **53**, 211–244.

Johansen, S. and K. Juselius (1994). Identification of the long-run and short-run structure: an application to the ISLM model. *Journal of Econometrics*, **63**, 7–36.

Johansen, S. and K. Juselius (2001). Controlling inflation in a cointegrated vector autoregressive model with an application to US data. Working Paper 01-03, European University Institute, Florence.

Johansen, S. and K. Juselius (2006). Extracting information from the data: A European view on empirical macro. In D. Colander (Ed.), *Post Walrasian Macroeconomics: Beyond the Dynamic Stochastic General Equilibrium Model*, Chapter 16. Cambridge University Press: Cambridge, Mass.

Johansen, S., R. Mosconi, and B. Nielsen (2000). Cointegration analysis in the presence of structural breaks in the deterministic trend. *Econometrics Journal*, **3**, 216–249.

Johansen, S. and B. G. Nielsen (1993). Asymptotics for cointegration rank tests in the presence of intervention dummies. Manual for the simulation program Disco. Working paper, University of Copenhagen.

Johansen, S. and A. R. Swensen (1999). Testing rational expectations in vector autoregressive models. *Journal of Econometrics*, **93**, 73–91.

Johansen, S. and A. R. Swensen (2004). More on testing exact rational expectations in vector autoregressive models: Restricted drift term. *The Econometric Journal*, **7**.

Jørgensen, C. (2000). A simulation study of tests in the cointegrated VAR model. Ph.D Dissertations 66, Department of Economics, University of Copenhagen.

Juselius, K. (1991a). Long-run relations in a well defined statistical model for the data generating process: Cointegration analysis of the PPP and UIP relations between Denmark and Germany. In G. J. (Ed.), *Econometric Decision Models: New Methods of Modeling and Applications.* Springer Verlag: New York, NY.

Juselius, K. (1991b). On the design of experiments when data are collected by passive observation. In K. Juselius, K. Nordström, J. Palmgren, and G. Rosenqvist (Eds.), *A Spectrum of Statistical Thought: Essays in Statistical Theory, Economics and Population Genetics in Honour of Johan Fellman.* Svenska Handelshögskolan: Helsinki.

Juselius, K. (1992). Domestic and foreign effects on prices in an open economy: The case of Denmark. *Journal of Policy Modelling*, **14**(4), 401–428. Reprinted in N. R. Ericsson and J. S. Irons (Eds.), *Testing Weak Exogeneity.* Oxford University Press. (1994): Oxford.

Juselius, K. (1993). VAR modelling and Haavelmo's probability approach to macroeconomic modelling. *Empirical Economics*, **18**(4), 595–622.

Juselius, K. (1994). On the duality between long-run relations and common trends in the $I(1)$ and $I(2)$ case. An application to aggregate money holdings. *Econometric Reviews*, **13**(2), 151–179.

Juselius, K. (1995). Do purchasing power parity and uncovered interest rate parity hold in the long run? An example of likelihood inference in a multivariate time-series model. *Journal of Econometrics*, **69**, 211–240.

Juselius, K. (1996). An empirical analysis of the changing role of the German Bundesbank after 1983. *Oxford Bulletin of Economics and Statistics*, **58**(4), 791–819.

Juselius, K. (1998a). Changing monetary transmission mechanisms within the EU. *Empirical Economics*, **23**(3), 455–481.

Juselius, K. (1998b). A structured VAR for Denmark under changing monetary regimes. *Journal of Business and Economic Statistics*, **16**(4), 400–411.

Juselius, K. (1999a). Models and relations in economics and econometrics. *Journal of Economic Methodology*, **6**(2), 259–290.

Juselius, K. (1999b). Price convergence in the long run and the medium run. An $I(2)$ analysis of six price indices. In R. Engle and H. White (Eds.), *Cointegration, Causality, and Forecasting? Festschrift in Honour of Clive W.J. Granger*. Oxford University Press: Oxford.

Juselius, K. (2001). European integration and monetary transmission mechanisms: The case of Italy. *Journal of Applied Econometrics*, **16**(3), 341–358.

Juselius, K. (2003). Wage, price, and unemployment dynamics and the convergence to purchasing power parity in the Euro area. Working Paper 0301, Department of Economics, University of Copenhagen.

Juselius, M. (2005). Estimating the determinants of inflation: Evidence from Finland. Working Paper 479, Swedish School of Economics and Business Administration.

Juselius, K. and R. MacDonald (2004). International parity relationships between the USA and Japan. *Japan and the World Economy*, **16**(1), 17–34.

Juselius, K. and R. MacDonald (2006). Imperfect knowledge expectations, uncertainty premia and exchange rate dynamics. In A. Morales-Zumaquero (Ed.), *International Macroeconomics: Recent Developments*. Nova Science Publishers. forthcoming.

Juselius, K. and J. Ordóñez (2005). The Balassa-Samuelson effect and the wage, price and unemployment dynamics in Spain. Working Paper 0529, Department of Economics, University of Copenhagen.

Juselius, K. and J. Toro (2005). Monetary transmission mechanisms in Spain: The effect of monetization, financial deregulation, and the EMS. *Journal of International Money and Finance*, **24**(3), 509–531.

King, R. G., C. I. Plosser, J. H. Stock, and M. W. Watson (1991). Stochastic trends and economic fluctuations. *American Economic Review*, **81**(4), 819–840.

Kongsted, H. C. (2005). Testing the nominal-to-real transformation. *Journal of Econometrics*, **124**, 202–225.

Kongsted, H. C. and H. B. Nielsen (2004). Analyzing $I(2)$ systems by transformed vector autoregressions. *Oxford Bulletin of Economics and Statistics*, **66**(3), 379–397.

Krugman, P. (1993). *Exchange-Rate Instability*. The MIT Press: Cambridge, Mass.

Layard, R. and S. J. Nickell (1992). An analogue model of phase-averaging procedures. Discussion Papers 081, Centre for Economic Performance, LSE.

Layard, R., S. Nickell, and R. Jackman (1991). *Unemployment. Macroeconomic Performance and the labour market*. Oxford University Press: Oxford.

Leijonhufvud, A. (2006). Stories from the haunted vault: Notes on a century of macroeconomics. In D. Colander (Ed.), *Post Walrasian Macroeconomics: Beyond the Dynamic Stochastic General Equilibrium Model*, Chapter 1. Cambridge University Press: Cambridge, Mass.

Levtchenkova, S., A. R. Pagan, and J. C. Robertson (1998). Shocking stories. *Journal of Economic Surveys*, **12**(5), 507–532.

Ljung, G. and G. Box (1978). On a measure of lack of fit in time series models. *Biometrika*, **66**, 67–72.

Lucas, R. E. (1972). Expectations and the neutrality of money. *Journal of Economic Theory*, **4**(2), 103–124.

Lütkepohl, H. (2005). *New Introduction to Multiple Time Series Analysis* (2nd edn.). Springer-Verlag: Berlin.

MacDonald, R. (1995). Long-run exchange rate modelling: A survey of the recent evidence. International Monetary Fund Staff Papers 42.

MacDonald, R. and I. W. Marsh (1997). On fundamentals and exchange rates: A Casselian perspective. *Review of Economics and Statistics*, **78**, 655–664.

MacDonald, R. and I. W. Marsh (1999). *Exchange Rate Modelling.* Kluwer Academic Publishers: Dordrecht.

MacDonald, R. and M. P. Taylor (1992). A stable US money demand function, 1874–1975. *Economic Letters*, **39**, 191–198.

MacDonald, R. and M. P. Taylor (1991). Exchange rates, policy convergence, and the European Monetary System. *Review of Economics and Statistics*, **73**(3), 553–558.

MacDonald, R. (1988). *Floating Exchange Rates: Theories and Evidence.* Allen and Unwin: London.

Mellander, E., A. Vredin, and A. Warne (1992). Stochastic trends and economic fluctuations in a small open economy. *Journal of Applied Econometrics*, **7**(4), 369–394.

Milbourne, R. (1988). Disequilibrium buffer stock models: A survey. *Journal of Economic Surveys*, **2**(3), 187–208.

Miller, M. and D. Orr (1966). A model of the demand for money by firms. *Quarterly Journal of Economics*, **109**, 68–72.

Mosconi, R. and A. Rahbek (1999). The role of stationary regressors in the cointegration test. *Econometrics Journal*, **2**, 76–91.

Møller, N.F. (2006). Analyzing Danish Unemployment Persistence in the Cointegrated Vector Autoregressive Model. M.Sc. thesis at the Economics Department, University of Copenhagen.

Nielsen, B. (2001). The asymptotic distribution of unit root tests of unstable autoregressive processes. *Econometrics Journal*, **69**, 211–219.

Nielsen, B. and H. B. Nielsen (2006). The asymptotic distribution of the estimated characteristic roots in a second order autoregression. Preprint, Economics Dept., University of Copenhagen.

Nielsen, B. and A. Rahbek (2000). Similarity issues in cointegration analysis. *Oxford Bulletin of Economics and Statistics*, **62**(1), 5–22.

Nielsen, H. B. (2004a). Cointegration analysis in the presence of outliers. *The Econometrics Journal*, **7**(1), 249–271.

Nielsen, H. B. (2004b). UK money demand 1973-2001: A cointegrated VAR analysis with additive data corrections. Working Paper 0401, Department of Economics, University of Copenhagen.

Nielsen, H. B. and A. Rahbek (2004). The likelihood ratio test for cointegration ranks in $I(2)$ VAR models. *Working Paper Series, Department of Economics, University of Copenhagen*, **03-42**, 1–25. Forthcoming in *Econometric Theory.*

Nielsen, H. B. (2002). An $I(2)$ cointegration analysis of price and quantity formation in Danish manufactured exports. *Oxford Bulletin of Economics and Statistics*, **64**(5), 449–472.

Nyblom, J. (1989). Testing for the constancy of parameters over time. *Journal of The American Statistical Association*, **84**, 223–230.

Padoa-Schioppa, T. (1995) The influence of Bretton Woods on European monetary integration. *Economic Bulletin* (10).

Pagan, A. R. (1987). Three econometric methodologies: A critical appraisal. *Journal of Economic Surveys*, **1**(1), 3–24.

Paruolo, P. (1996). On the determination of integration indices in $I(2)$ systems. *Journal of Econometrics*, **72**(1-2), 313–356.

Paruolo, P. (1997). Asymptotic inference on the moving average impact matrix in cointegrated $I(1)$ VAR systems. *Econometric Theory*, **13**, 79–118.

Paruolo, P. and A. Rahbek (1999). Weak exogeneity in $I(2)$ VAR systems. *Journal of Econometrics*, **93**, 281–308.

Pesaran, M. H. and R. P. Smith (1998). Structural analysis of cointegrating VARs. *Journal of Economic Surveys*, **12**(5), 471–505.

Pesaran, M. H. and Y. Shin (1997). Generalized impulse response analysis in linear multivariate models. *Economic Letters*, **58**(1), 17–29.

Phelps, E. S. (1994). *Structural Slumps: The Modern Equilibrium Theory of Unemployment, Interest, and Assets.* Harvard University Press: Cambridge, Mass.

Phillips, P. C. B. (2001). Optimal inference in cointegrated systems. *Econometrica*, **59**(2), 283–306.

Rahbek, A. (2003). Stochastic properties of multivariate time series equations with emphasis on ARCH. Technical Report ISC-225, 13th IFAC Symposium on System Identification.

Rahbek, A., E. Hansen, and J. G. Dennis (2002). ARCH innovations and their impact on cointegration rank testing. Preprint no. 12, 1998, Department of Theoretical Statistics. Working paper no. 22, Centre for Analytical Finance.

Rahbek, A., H. C. Kongsted, and C. Jørgensen (1999). Trend-stationarity in the $I(2)$ cointegration model. *Journal of Econometrics*, **90**(2), 265–289.

Rao, C. R. (1973). *Linear Statistical Inference and Its Applications* (2nd edn.). John Wiley: New York.

Rogoff, K. (1996). The purchasing power parity puzzle. *Journal of Economic Literature*, **34**(2), 647–668.

Romer, D. (1996). *Advanced Macroeconomics*. McGraw Hill: New York.

Rubin, J. (1998). On the permanent-transitory decomposition in the cointegrated VAR. In *Econometric Studies of a European Economic and Monetary Union*. Ph.D. thesis, no. 45, Department of Economics, University of Copenhagen.

Samuelson, P. (1964). Theoretical notes on trade problems. *Review of Economics and Statistics*, **46**(2), 145–154.

Shenton, L. R. and K. O. Bowman (1977). A bivariate model for the distribution of $\sqrt{b_1}$ and b_2. *Journal of American Statistical Association*, **72**(357), 206–211.

Sims, C. A. (1980). Macroeconomics and reality. *Econometrica*, **48**(1), 1–48.

Sims, C. A. (1992). Interpreting the macroeconomic time series facts: The effects of monetary policy. *European Economic Review*, **36**(5), 975–1000.

Summers, L. H. (1991). The scientific illusion in empirical macroeconomics. *Scandinavian Journal of Economics*, **93**(2), 129–148.

Tuxen, C. (2006). An empirically relevant model of inflation in the Euro area. M.Sc. thesis at the Economics Department, University of Copenhagen.

Walsh, C. E. (1998). *Monetary Theory and Policy*. The MIT Press: Cambridge, Mass.

Warmendinger, T. (2004). Import prices and pricing-to-market effects in the Euro area. Working paper, no. 299, European Central Bank.

Index